ALL ■ IN ■ ONE

DB2
Administration
EXAM GUIDE

Roger E. Sanders

McGraw-Hill / Osborne

New York • Chicago • San Francisco • Lisbon
London • Madrid • Mexico City • Milan • New Delhi
San Juan • Seoul • Singapore • Sydney • Toronto

McGraw-Hill/Osborne
2600 Tenth Street
Berkeley, California 94710
U.S.A.

To arrange bulk purchase discounts for sales promotions, premiums, or fund-raisers, please contact **McGraw-Hill**/Osborne at the above address. For information on translations or book distributors outside the U.S.A., please see the International Contact Information page immediately following the index of this book.

DB2 Administration All-in-One Exam Guide

1234567890 DOC DOC 0198765432

Book p/n 0-07-213374-0 and CD p/n 0-07-213373-2
parts of

ISBN 0-07-213375-9

Publisher	**Acquisitions Coordinator**
Brandon A. Nordin	Alex Corona
Vice President & Associate Publisher	**Technical Editor**
Scott Rogers	IBM Education
Editorial Director	**Compositor and Indexer**
Gareth Hancock	MacAllister Publishing Services, LLC
Acquisitions Editor	**Cover Design**
Michael Sprague	Greg Scott
Project Manager	
Jenn Tust	

FOREWORD

In my job as the DB2 Certification Program Manager, I am often asked about the value of becoming certified. To me, certification is a tool to help you increase your knowledge and skills. Certification gives you a clear goal and roadmap for learning. The goal is to pass the exam. The roadmap is to study and learn about parts of the product that you may never have learned otherwise. There are some functions that you may never need in your job, but by learning about them, you have the power to know what product features are available to help you become more effective and efficient in your job.

This is an excellent book to help you learn about DB2 Universal Database in your job as either a DB2 User or a DB2 UDB Database Administrator and will significantly enhance your ability to pass the DB2 Universal Database Certification Exams. Beyond becoming certified, this book is also an excellent source of reference information that you'll continue to use for years to come.

This book was written in a straightforward manner to take you through the certification process step-by-step. It also outlines the different levels of certification, making it simple to determine the right path for you. It helps to prepare you for the tests by providing all the information you will need and includes sample tests to ensure you are understanding the material.

Roger has done an amazing job at covering all you need to know about DB2 Universal Database, giving you hints and tips to sharpen your technical edge. I'm sure you'll find this book both a joy to read as well as helpful in your quest to improve your skills.

—Susan Visser, IBM DB2 Certification Program Manager

Today's computing environment is fast paced, competitive, and dynamic. As a computer professional, one of the most effective ways to stay ahead of the technology curve and validate your skills is through certification. Certification increases your credibility and expertise in the workplace and it represents a direct path to knowledge of the hottest technology in the market today: IBM DB2 Universal Database.

More than 20 years ago, relational database technology was invented in IBM Research, which delivered the first commercially available database in the early 1980s. This invention created the unique ability to represent data in a simple tabular form, access it through the powerful SQL query language, and make it readily available to the business community. Today, tens of thousands of business all over the world rely on DB2 databases to store their key corporate data assets and run their business both traditionally and over the Web.

The twenty-first century promises to be one of the fastest moving and challenging decades in computing history. As a computer professional, you have to keep ahead of the technology demands of tomorrow's companies who are building applications, services, and portals for e-commerce, customer relationship management, business-to-business (B2B), supply chain management, and business intelligence solutions. With the growing demand for skilled data management professionals, there is no better time to obtain your DB2 UDB certification. I wish you much success with your studies.

—Judith Escott, WW Executive, Data Management Skills Development, IBM

DEDICATION

To my long time friend, William "Bill" Lohmeyer

ABOUT THE AUTHOR

Roger Sanders is a Database Performance Engineer with Network Appliance, Inc. He has been designing and programming software applications for IBM PCs for more than 15 years, and he was worked with DB2 Universal Database and its predecessors for the past 10 years. He has written several computer magazine articles, presented at two International DB2 User's Group (IDUG) conferences, and is the author of *The Developer's Handbook to DB2 for Common Servers, ODBC 3.5 Developer's Guide, DB2 Universal Database CLI Developer's Guide, DB2 Universal Database API Developers Guide,* and *DB2 Universal Database SQL Developer's Guide.* His background in database application design and development is extensive, and he holds the following professional certifications: IBM Certified Advanced Technical Expert—DB2 for Clusters; IBM Certified Solutions Expert—DB2 UDB V7.1 Database Administration for UNIX, Windows, and OS/2; IBM Certified Solutions Expert—DB2 UDB V6.1 Application Development for UNIX, Windows, and OS/2; and IBM Certified Specialist—DB2 UDB V6/V7 User.

ACKNOWLEDGMENTS

A project of this magnitude requires both a great deal of time and the support of many different people. I would like to express my gratitude to the following people for their contributions:

Susan Visser—DB2 UDB Certification Program Manager

Susan's help was invaluable—without her, this book would not have been written with the level of focus it has on providing you with the information you need to pass the certification exams covered. Susan provided me with sample test questions, detailed test objectives, and paraphrased certification exam questions for each objective covered by the 512 and 513 exams. More importantly, Susan reviewed each chapter as it was written, compared the material against the actual certification exam questions, and provided me with feedback I could use to ensure that I covered all of the concepts needed in a clear and concise manner.

Paul Rivot—IBM

Paul provided me with DB2 Universal Database, Version 7.1 software and introduced me to several key contacts at the DB2 development lab in Toronto, Canada.

Sheila Richardson—IBM Toronto

Sheila was my key contact at IBM Toronto. She was instrumental in getting me in touch with Susan Visser.

I would also like to thank my wife Beth for all of her help and encouragement, and for once again overlooking the things that did not get done while I worked on yet another book.

CONTENTS

INTRODUCTION

In the world of relational database management systems (RDBMSs), DB2 Universal Database is a well-established veteran. It began as DATABASE 2 in 1983 and at that time, it was only available for IBM mainframes running MVS. Then in 1989, a version called Database Manager was bundled with IBM's newest operating system for the PC —OS/2—to produce a product called OS/2 Extended Edition and for the first time, DB2 could be run on something besides a mainframe. Several years (and several name changes) later, DB2 Universal Database made its debut. Today, DB2 runs on a wide range of platforms and operating systems and has become one of the most powerful database products available.

DB2 certification, on the other hand, is relatively new. A few years ago, certifications like Microsoft Certified System Engineer and Certified Software Quality Engineer became the rage among network managers and systems administrators. Now it seems like every major hardware and software vendor offers some sort of certification program. But what can certification do for you? Many people believe that certification by a creditable source (such as IBM) provides individuals with credentials that validate their professional competency. Others believe that skills and on-the-job experience count the most. However, research has shown that possessing certification does have its benefits. For IT professionals who lack experience with a particular tool or technology, certification can give them an advantage over equally inexperienced individuals. For IT professionals who already have experience with a particular tool or technology, certification can help advance their careers or open doors to new opportunities.

If you've bought this book (or are thinking about buying this book), chances are you have already decided that you want to acquire the IBM Certified Solutions Expert—DB2 UDB V7.1 Database Administration for UNIX, Windows, and OS/2 certification. As an IT professional who has acquired four DB2 certifications from IBM, let me share my experience with you. The exams you must pass in order to become a certified professional are not easy. IBM prides itself on designing comprehensive certification exams that are relevant to the work environment that an individual holding a particular certification would be exposed to. To accomplish this, their certification exams are designed with the following in mind:

- What are the critical tasks that must be performed by an individual in this position?
- What skills are needed in order to perform each critical task?
- What is the frequency with which each critical task needs to be performed?

You will find that in order to pass a DB2 certification exam, it is essential that you have a solid understanding of DB2 Universal Database and all of its nuances. (Having some hands-on experience is helpful too.) I can't provide you with the hands-on experience, but I can help you understand how DB2 Universal Database works and teach you the things you need to know in order to obtain the IBM Certified Solutions Expert —DB2 UDB V7.1 Database Administration for UNIX, Windows, and OS/2 certification.

Audience

This book was written for anyone who is interested in obtaining one or both of the following professional certifications:

- IBM Certified Specialist—DB2 UDB V6/V7 User Professional Certification
- IBM Certified Solutions Expert—DB2 UDB V7.1 Database Administration for UNIX, Windows, and OS/2

The book is written primarily for database administrators (DBAs) who have experience working with DB2 Universal Database and want to obtain professional certification from IBM. However, any IT professional who is familiar with a relational database management system (such as Oracle, SQL Server, or Sybase) and wants to learn how to use DB2 Universal Database will also benefit from the material covered in this book.

How This Book Is Organized

Knowing how this book is organized may help you work through the material covered more efficiently. Knowing the layout will also enable you to jump directly to the sections you are interested in most. This book is divided into the following three major parts:

Part I—DB2 Certification

This section contains one chapter (Chapter 1) that is designed to introduce you to the various paths that can be taken to obtain DB2 certification from IBM. In this chapter, you will learn about the three levels of certification that are offered by the Professional Certification Program from IBM; the levels of DB2 Universal Database professional certification available; and what's involved in the certification process. This chapter also discusses some of the benefits that professional certification provides.

Part II—DB2 UDB Fundamentals (Tests 509 and 512)

This section contains six chapters (Chapters 2 through 7) that are designed to teach you the concepts you need to know in order to pass the DB2 UDB 7.1 Family Fundamentals exam:

Chapter 2 is designed to introduce you to the various products that make up the DB2 Family and present the set of tools that come with DB2 Universal Database, Version 7.x. In this chapter, you will learn about the functionality that each edition of DB2 Universal Database provides; the functionality that each DB2 client component provides; and the purpose of each product that makes up the DB2 Family. You will also see what each component of the DB2 Administration Tools looks like (on the Windows NT operating system) and you will learn what action or actions each tool is designed to perform.

Chapter 3 is designed to introduce you to the concept of instances and provide an in-depth look at the various authorization levels and privileges that are provided by DB2 Universal Database, Version 7.x. In this chapter, you will learn what an instance is, how instances are typically used, and what purpose the DB2 Administration Server (DAS) instance serves. You will also learn how and where users are authenticated; how authorization levels and privileges determine what a user can and cannot do; and how authorization levels and privileges are given to and taken away from an individual or a group of users.

Chapter 4 is designed to provide you with everything you need to know about creating and managing DB2 Universal Database databases. This chapter is also designed to introduce you to most of the objects that are available with DB2 Universal Database and provide you with information on how each of these objects can be created and destroyed. In this chapter, you will learn what a DB2 Universal Database database is, what its underlying structure looks like, and how that structure is physically stored. You will also learn how to create and destroy a DB2 Universal Database database; how to catalog and uncatalog a DB2 Universal Database database; what kinds of objects can exist with in a DB2 Universal Database database; what those objects are used for; and how to create and destroy most of the objects available using the various tools that are provided with DB2 Universal Database.

Chapter 5 is designed to provide you with everything you need to know about creating a table object and defining its characteristics. In this chapter, you will learn which built-in data types are available with DB2 Universal Database; how user-defined data types, DataLinks, and extenders can be incorporated into a table's definition; and how to create a table object with the CREATE TABLE SQL statement. You will also learn what constraints are; what constraints are available with DB2 Universal Database; and how constraints can be used to ensure that data adheres to business rules.

Chapter 6 is designed to introduce you to the SQL statements that are commonly used to work with DB2 Universal Database objects and user data. In this chapter, you will learn what SQL is and how SQL statements are grouped, according to their functionality. You will also learn which SQL statements make up the Data Definition Language (DDL) and the Data Manipulation Language (DML) and how those statements are used to create database objects, and store, manipulate, and retrieve data in those objects.

Chapter 7 is designed to introduce you to the concept of data consistency and the various mechanisms that are used by DB2 Universal Database to maintain database consistency in both single- and multiuser environments. In this chapter, you will learn what data consistency is; what transactions are and how they are initiated and terminated; and how transactions are isolated from each other in a multiuser environment. You will also learn how DB2 Universal Database provides concurrency control through the use of locks; what types of locks are available; and how locks are acquired.

Part III—DB2 UDB Administration (Test 513)

This section contains seven chapters (Chapters 8 through 14) that are designed to teach you the concepts you need to know in order to pass the DB2 UDB 7.1 for UNIX, Windows, and OS/2 Database Administration exam.

Chapter 8 is designed to introduce you to the concept of instances, provide you with information about configuring communications for client and server workstations, and provide a second in-depth look at the various authorization levels and privileges that are provided by DB2 Universal Database, Version 7.x. In this chapter, you will learn what an instance is and how instances are used; how distributed connections enable clients to communicate with servers; how to configure communications for a client and a server workstation; and what DB2 Discovery is and how it is used. You will also review information on how (and where) users are authenticated; how authorization levels and privileges determine what a user can and cannot do; and how authorization levels and privileges are given to (granted) and taken away from (revoked) an individual or a group of users.

Chapter 9 is designed to provide you with everything you need to know about how data in a database is stored and accessed. In this chapter, you will learn what buffer pools are, how buffer pools are created, and how they are used; what table spaces are, how table spaces are created, and how they are used; and the differences between system managed space (SMS) and database managed space (DMS) table spaces. You will also learn how a table space's page size, extent size, and prefetch size affect a database's performance as well as how to obtain information about existing table spaces without querying the system catalog tables.

Chapter 10 is designed to enforce and enhance your knowledge of views, indexes, and constraints and provide in-depth coverage of the tools that are available for viewing the contents of tables and views, performing repetitive operations against database objects, and reverse-engineering a database to produce DDL script files. In this chapter, you will learn how to use views to control what data a user can and cannot access; what types of indexes are available and how to choose the right type for a given situation; and what referential integrity constraints are and how they can be used to maintain data consistency between two tables. You will also learn what the system catalog tables and views are used for; what the purpose of the Script Center is; how to examine the contents of tables and views without using queries; and how to use the DB2LOOK tool.

Chapter 11 is designed to introduce you to the tools that are available for monitoring events that take place in a database system and the tool that enables you to analyze SQL operations to locate weaknesses in applications or database design that results in poor performance. In this chapter, you will learn how to capture and analyze snapshots; how to create and manipulate event monitors; how to analyze event monitor output; and how to capture and analyze Explain information. You will also learn how to obtain and modify configuration information for a specific database or for the DB2 Database Manager.

Chapter 12 is designed to introduce you to the data movement and data management utilities that are provided by DB2 Universal Database, Version 7.x. In this chapter, you will learn what file formats are recognized by DB2 Universal Database's data movement utilities; how to use the Export utility to extract specific portions of data from a database and externalize it to a file; and how to use the Import utility to make data stored in external files available to a database. You will also learn how to use the Load utility to bulk load a table using data stored in external files; how to use the DB2MOVE utility to copy a database from one platform to another; how to optimize the physical distribution of all data stored in a table; and how to update the information stored in the system catalog tables so that the DB2 Optimizer can choose the best data access path available when resolving a query.

Chapter 13 is designed to introduce you to the concept of transaction logging and provide an in-depth look at the various tools that are used to return an inconsistent database to a consistent state and a corrupted database to the state it was in at a specific point in time. In this chapter, you will learn what transaction logging is and how it is performed; how to return a database that has been placed in an inconsistent state to a consistent state; and how to create a backup image of a database. You will also learn how to return a database to the state it was in when a backup image was made; how to reapply (or roll-forward) some or all changes made to a database since the last backup image was made; and which database configuration parameters affect logging and data recovery.

Chapter 14 is designed to introduce you to the common types of errors than can be encountered when using DB2 Universal Database and introduce you to some of the tools that are available to help identify the source of problems and provide resolutions for them when they occur. In this chapter, you will learn about some of the common types of problems and errors that can be encountered when using DB2 Universal Database and what error codes are, how they are categorized, and how they are interpreted. You will also learn how First Failure Data Capture (FFDC) information is collected, where that information is stored, and how that information is interpreted.

Syntax Conventions Used in This Book

You will find information that describes the basic syntax to use when executing a DB2 Universal Database command or a Structured Query Language (SQL) statement throughout this book. The following conventions are used wherever a command or SQL statement syntax is presented:

[*Parameter*]	Parameters that are shown inside of brackets are required parameters and must be specified.
<*Parameter*>	Parameters that are shown inside of angle brackets are optional parameters and do not have to be specified.
Parameter | *Parameter*	Parameters or other items that are separated by vertical bars indicate that you must select one item from the list of items presented.
Parameter, . . .	Parameters that are followed by a comma and three periods (ellipsis) indicate that multiple instances of the parameter can be included in the statement.

The following examples illustrate these syntax conventions:

Example 1

```
CONNECT TO [ServerName] <ConnectionMode> <USER [AuthorizationID]
USING [Password]
```

In this example, both *ConnectionMode* and USER [*AuthorizationID*] USING [*Password*] are optional parameters, as indicated by the angle brackets (< >). The *ServerName*, *AuthorizationID*, and *Password* parameters are required, as indicated by the brackets ([ ]). However, *AuthorizationID* and *Password* are only required parameters if the USER [*AuthorizationID*] USING [*Password*] option is specified.

Example 2

```
RELEASE [ServerName | CURRENT | ALL <SQL>]
```

In this example, *ServerName*, CURRENT, or ALL <SQL> can be specified, as indicated by the vertical bar (|). One of these items must be specified, as indicated by the brackets ([ ]). If ALL is selected, the keyword SQL can be added (ALL SQL); however, it is not required, as indicated by the angle brackets (< >).

Example 3

```
CREATE <UNIQUE> INDEX [IndexName] ON [TableName] ([ColumnName
<ASC | DESC>], . . . )
```

In this example, *IndexName*, *TableName*, and at least one *ColumnName* must be specified, as indicated by the brackets ([ ]). UNIQUE, ASC, and DESC are options, as indicated by the angle brackets (< >). Either ASC or DESC can be specified as an option, but not both as indicated by the vertical bar (|). More than one *ColumnName* <ASC | DESC> option can be specified, as indicated by the comma-ellipsis (, . . .) characters that follow the [*ColumnName* <ASC | DESC>] parameter. (The list of column parameters is enclosed in parenthesis.)

PART I

DB2 Certification

■ **Chapter 1** DB2 Universal Database Professional Certification

DB2 Universal Database Professional Certification

In this chapter, you will learn

- The levels of certification offered by the Professional Certification Program from IBM
- The levels of DB2 Universal Database professional certification available
- The certification process
- The benefits of professional certification

One of the biggest challenges that computer professionals face today is keeping up with the constant changes in technology. When this industry was in its infancy, it was possible to become an expert across all areas, because the scope of the field was relatively small and changes did not happen very quickly.

Things are different now; our industry is both broad and fast paced, and the skills needed to master a single area can be quite complex. Because of this complexity, many application/software vendors have initiated certification programs to test and validate an individual's skills in a specific area. Businesses benefit because professional certification gives them confidence that an individual has the expertise needed to perform the job. Computer professionals benefit because professional certification allows us to deliver higher levels of service and technical expertise than noncertified employees, and it can lead to new opportunities within the computer industry. Professional certification puts our careers in our control. This chapter introduces you to the various paths (and there are several) you can take to obtain DB2 Universal Database professional certification from IBM.

The Professional Certification Program from IBM

IBM offers three levels of certification with its Professional Certification Program. A different level of competency characterizes each level, and role names within each level emphasize competency with a particular skill. Within each level, one or more role names may be possible, depending on the discipline being certified. All levels and possible role names of the Professional Certification Program from IBM are shown in Table 1-1.

A certification role consists of one of the standard role names shown in Table 1-1, followed by the product name or skill area to which the certification applies. Examples include

- IBM Certified Specialist—MQSeries
- IBM Certified Solutions Expert—Business Intelligence
- IBM Certified Developer—Object-Oriented VisualAge for C++

Table 1-1   Levels and Roles in the Professional Certification Program from IBM

Level 1	
Role	**Certifies the Candidate**
IBM Certified Specialist	Performs basic operational services such as basic planning, configuration, installation, support, management, and maintenance of a product with limited assistance
	Performs administration of a product, with limited assistance
IBM Certified Developer Associate	Has working product and environment knowledge and can code to design
Level 2	
Role	**Certifies the Candidate**
IBM Certified Solutions/ Systems Expert	Demonstrates breadth of basic operational services skills in two or more environments
	Demonstrates depth of advanced operational services skills such as customizing, integrating, migrating, and tuning, in a single environment
IBM Certified Developer	Demonstrates the capability to plan and design an application requirements specification and build a working prototype

Level 2	
Role	**Certifies the Candidate**
IBM Certified Instructor	Demonstrates training skills and has been certified in a Level 1 or Level 2 certification role
IBM Certified for e-business	Demonstrates a broad working knowledge of the IBM Application Framework for e-business and can apply its methodologies, best practices, and use of open standards to sell, advise, design, and/or consult on e-business solutions

Level 3	
Role	**Certifies the Candidate**
IBM Certified Advanced Technical Expert	Demonstrates multiple skills, such as expert advice and leadership in understanding and use of IBM solutions without assistance, and with references
	Has demonstrable skill, or experience, on the job
	Demonstrates depth and breadth of advanced operational services skills in more than one environment

Currently, more than 100 certification roles exist in the Professional Certification Program from IBM.

DB2 Universal Database Certification Roles

Under the Professional Certification Program from IBM, each certification category does not necessarily have the same set of certification roles. Instead, many categories have certification roles only at the levels that are appropriate. The DB2 Universal Database certification category is such a category. Each certification role (and its respective level) that is available under the DB2 Universal Database certification category is shown in Table 1-2.

As you might expect, each of the certification roles shown in Table 1-2 implies that an individual has demonstrated some level of expertise by meeting all of the requirements of that role. Thus, to better understand a particular certification role, we need to examine that role's prerequisites and requirements.

Table 1-2   IBM DB2 Universal Database Certification Roles

Certification Role	Level
IBM Certified Specialist—DB2 UDB V6/V7 User	1
IBM Certified Solutions Expert—Business Intelligence	2
IBM Certified Solutions Expert—DB2 UDB V7.1 Database Administration for UNIX, Windows, and OS/2	2
IBM Certified Solutions Expert—DB2 UDB V7.1 Family Application Development	2
IBM Certified Solutions Expert—DB2 UDB V7.1 Database Administration for OS/390	2
IBM Certified Solutions Expert—DB2 UDB V6.1 Database Administration for UNIX, Windows, and OS/2	2
IBM Certified Solutions Expert—DB2 UDB V6.1 Application Development for UNIX, Windows, and OS/2	2
IBM Certified Advanced Technical Expert —DB2 for Clusters	3
IBM Certified Advanced Technical Expert—DB2—DRDA	3
IBM Certified Advanced Technical Expert—DB2 Data Replication	3

IBM Certified Specialist— DB2 UDB V6/V7 User

The IBM Certified Specialist—DB2 UDB V6/V7 User certification role is designed for individuals who are knowledgeable about the fundamental concepts of DB2 Universal Database. This certification role is applicable to users who have an in-depth knowledge of basic Structured Query Language (SQL); understand how DB2 Universal Database is packaged and installed; understand how to create databases and database objects; and have a basic knowledge of database security and transaction isolation. Individuals seeking this certification should have a good understanding of DB2 Universal Database and significant experience using one of the DB2 Universal Database editions available. The roadmap for acquiring the IBM Certified Specialist—DB2 UDB V6/V7 User certification role is outlined in Figure 1-1.

As Figure 1-1 illustrates, to acquire the IBM Certified Specialist—DB2 UDB V6/V7 User certification, candidates must pass the DB2 Family Fundamentals test. This test is a software-based test that is neither platform nor product specific.

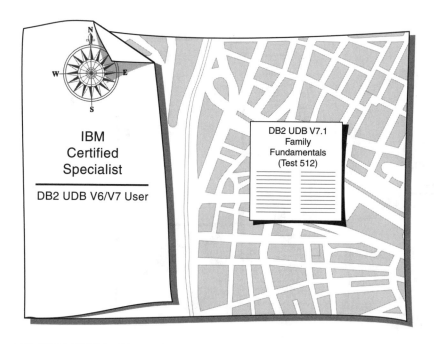

IBM
Certified
Specialist

DB2 UDB V6/V7 User

DB2 UDB V7.1
Family
Fundamentals
(Test 512)

Figure 1-1   IBM Certified Specialist—DB2 UDB V6/V7 User certification roadmap

IBM Certified Solutions Expert—Business Intelligence

The IBM Certified Solutions Expert—Business Intelligence certification role is designed for individuals who

- Are knowledgeable about IBM's Business Intelligence solutions

- Are knowledgeable about the fundamental concepts of DB2 Universal Database

- Can perform the intermediate and advanced skills required to design, develop, and support Business Intelligence applications

This certification role is applicable to experts who evaluate Business Intelligence opportunities, identify the business and technical requirements of Business Intelligence solutions, and consult, architect, and manage the implementation of Business Intelligence solutions. Individuals seeking this certification should have a good understanding of DB2 Universal Database and significant experience using and/or implementing IBM's Business Intelligence solutions. The roadmap for acquiring the IBM Certified Solutions Expert—Business Intelligence certification role is outlined in Figure 1-2.

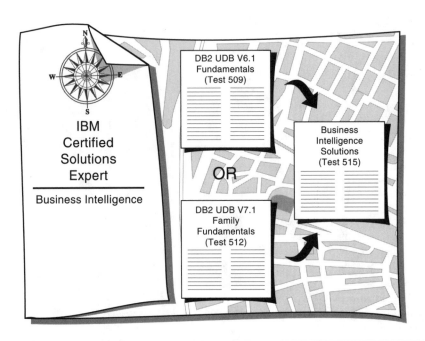

Figure 1-2   IBM Certified Solutions Expert—Business Intelligence certification roadmap

As Figure 1-2 illustrates, to acquire the IBM Certified Solutions Expert—Business Intelligence certification, candidates must pass two tests. Both tests are software-based tests and neither is platform/product specific.

IBM Certified Solutions Expert—DB2 UDB V7.1 Database Administration for UNIX, Windows, and OS/2

The IBM Certified Solutions Expert—DB2 UDB V7.1 Database Administration for UNIX, Windows, and OS/2 certification role is designed for individuals who

- Are knowledgeable about the fundamental concepts of DB2 Universal Database, Version 7.1

- Can perform both the intermediate and the advanced skills required to perform the day-to-day administration of DB2 instances and databases in the UNIX, Windows, and/or OS/2 environment

Individuals seeking this certification should have a good understanding of DB2 Universal Database, Version 7.1 and significant experience as a DB2 Universal Database

Administrator on the UNIX, Windows, or OS/2 platform. The roadmap for acquiring the IBM Certified Solutions Expert—DB2 UDB V7.1 Database Administration for UNIX, Windows, and OS/2 certification role is outlined in Figure 1-3.

As Figure 1-3 illustrates, to acquire the IBM Certified Solutions Expert—DB2 UDB V7.1 Database Administration for UNIX, Windows, and OS/2 certification, candidates must pass two tests. Both tests are software-based tests; the second is platform/product specific.

NOTE Although the test numbers are different, the roadmap for the IBM Certified Solutions Expert—DB2 UDB V6.1 Database Administration for UNIX, Windows, and OS/2 certification role is similar to the roadmap shown in Figure 1-3. This certification role is not discussed in detail because the IBM Certified Solutions Expert—DB2 UDB V7.1 Database Administration for UNIX, Windows, and OS/2 certification is the latest certification available in this area of expertise. If you already have the IBM Certified Solutions Expert—DB2 UDB V6.1 Database Administration for UNIX, Windows, and OS/2 certification or the IBM Certified Solutions Expert—DB2 UDB V5 Database Administration certification, you can obtain the IBM Certified Solutions Expert—DB2 UDB V7.1 Database Administration for UNIX, Windows, and OS/2 certification by taking (and passing) Test 513.

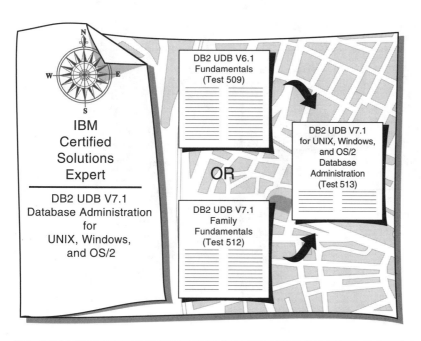

Figure I-3   IBM Certified Solutions Expert—DB2 UDB V7.1 Database Administration for UNIX, Windows, and OS/2 certification roadmap

IBM Certified Solutions Expert—DB2 UDB V7.1 Family Application Development

The IBM Certified Solutions Expert—DB2 UDB V7.1 Family Application Development certification role is designed for individuals who

- Are knowledgeable about the fundamental concepts of DB2 Universal Database, Version 7.1

- Can perform the intermediate/advanced skills required to design and develop applications that interact with one or more DB2 Universal Database, Version 7.1 databases

Individuals seeking this certification should have a good understanding of DB2 Universal Database, Version 7.1 (for the UNIX, Windows, OS/2, and/or OS/390 platforms) and significant experience as a DB2 Universal Database Application Developer. The roadmap for acquiring the IBM Certified Solutions Expert—DB2 UDB V7.1 Family Application Development certification role is outlined in Figure 1-4.

Figure 1-4 IBM Certified Solutions Expert—DB2 UDB V7.1 Family Application Development certification roadmap

As Figure 1-4 illustrates, to acquire the IBM Certified Solutions Expert—DB2 UDB V7.1 Family Application Development certification, candidates must pass two tests. Both tests are software-based tests and neither is platform/product specific.

> **NOTE** Although the test numbers are different, the roadmap for the IBM Certified Solutions Expert—DB2 UDB V6.1 Application Development for UNIX, Windows, and OS/2 certification role is similar to the roadmap shown in Figure 1-4. This certification role is not discussed in detail because the IBM Certified Solutions Expert—DB2 UDB V7.1 Family Application Development certification is the latest certification available in this area of expertise. If you already have the IBM Certified Solutions Expert—DB2 UDB V6.1 Application Development for UNIX, Windows, and OS/2 certification or the IBM Certified Solutions Expert—DB2 UDB V5 Application Development certification, you can obtain the IBM Certified Solutions Expert—DB2 UDB V7.1 Family Application Development certification by taking (and passing) Test 514.

IBM Certified Solutions Expert—DB2 UDB V7.1 Database Administration for OS/390

The IBM Certified Solutions Expert—DB2 UDB V7.1 Database Administration for OS/390 certification role is designed for individuals who

- Are knowledgeable about the fundamental concepts of DB2 Universal Database, Version 7.1

- Can perform both the intermediate and the advanced skills required for the day-to-day administration of DB2 instances and databases in the OS/390 environment

Individuals seeking this certification should have a good understanding of DB2 Universal Database, Version 7.1 and significant experience as a DB2 Universal Database Administrator on the OS/390 platform. The roadmap for acquiring the IBM Certified Solutions Expert—DB2 UDB V7.1 Database Administration for OS/390 certification role is outlined in Figure 1-5.

As Figure 1-5 illustrates, to acquire the IBM Certified Solutions Expert—DB2 UDB V7.1 Database Administration for OS/390 certification, candidates must pass two tests. Both tests are software-based tests; the second is platform/product specific.

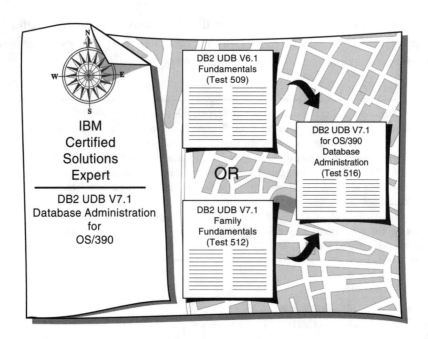

Figure 1-5 IBM Certified Solutions Expert—DB2 UDB V7.1 Database Administration for OS/390 certification roadmap

IBM Certified Advanced Technical Expert—DB2 for Clusters

The IBM Certified Advanced Technical Expert—DB2 for Clusters certification role is designed for individuals who

- Are knowledgeable about the fundamental concepts of DB2 Universal Database

- Can perform both the intermediate and the advanced skills required to perform the day-to-day administration of DB2 instances and databases or can perform the intermediate/advanced skills required to design and develop applications that interact with one or more DB2 Universal Database databases

- Are in the business of providing applications and/or services that, using DB2 Universal Database and its related products, provide homogeneous access to and/or retrieve enterprise data stored across a number of different data sources

Individuals seeking this certification should have extensive experience using DB2 Universal Database, Version 5.x, 6.1, or 7.1; significant experience with DB2 Universal Database Enterprise—Extended Edition; and experience as a DB2 Universal Database

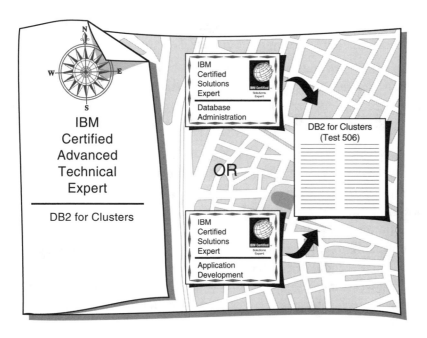

Figure I-6   IBM Certified Advanced Technical Expert—DB2 for Clusters certification roadmap

Administrator. The roadmap for acquiring the IBM Certified Advanced Technical Expert —DB2 for Clusters certification role is outlined in Figure 1-6.

As Figure 1-6 illustrates, to acquire the IBM Certified Advanced Technical Expert— DB2 for Clusters certification, candidates must hold one of the Level 2 Database Administration or Application Development certifications shown in Table 1-2 and pass a comprehensive test. This test is a software-based test that is neither platform nor product specific.

IBM Certified Advanced Technical Expert—DB2—DRDA

The IBM Certified Advanced Technical Expert—DB2—DRDA certification role is designed for individuals who

- Are knowledgeable about the fundamental concepts of DB2 Universal Database
- Can perform both the intermediate and the advanced skills required to perform the day-to-day administration of DB2 instances and databases or can perform the

intermediate/advanced skills required to design and develop applications that interact with one or more DB2 Universal Database databases

- Are in the business of providing applications and/or services that, using DB2 Universal Database and its related products (particularly DB2 Connect), provide homogeneous access to enterprise data that is stored on one or more servers that use Distributed Relational Database Architecture (DRDA)

Individuals seeking this certification should have extensive experience using DB2 Universal Database, Version 5.x, 6.1, or 7.1; significant experience with DB2 Connect and DRDA servers; and experience as a DB2 Universal Database Administrator. The roadmap for acquiring the IBM Certified Advanced Technical Expert—DB2—DRDA certification role is outlined in Figure 1-7.

As Figure 1-7 illustrates, to acquire the IBM Certified Advanced Technical Expert—DB2—DRDA certification, candidates must hold one of the Level 2 Database Administration or Application Development certifications shown in Table 1-2 and pass a comprehensive test. This test is a software-based test that is neither platform nor product specific.

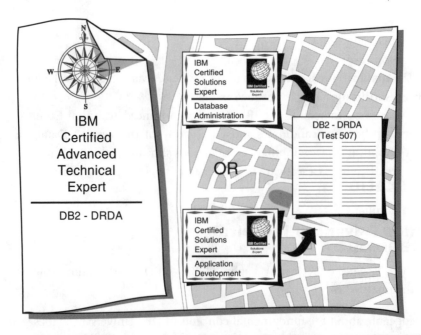

Figure 1-7 IBM Certified Advanced Technical Expert—DB2 - DRDA certification roadmap

IBM Certified Advanced Technical Expert—DB2 Data Replication

The IBM Certified Advanced Technical Expert—DB2 Data Replication certification role is designed for individuals who

- Are knowledgeable about the fundamental concepts of DB2 Universal Database

- Can perform both the intermediate and the advanced skills required to perform the day-to-day administration of DB2 instances and databases or can perform the intermediate/advanced skills required to design and develop applications that interact with one or more DB2 Universal Database databases

- Are in the business of providing applications and/or services that, using DB2 Universal Database and its related products (particularly DB2 DataPropagator), capture changes to data and asynchronously replicate those changes across a number of different data sources

Individuals seeking this certification should have extensive experience using DB2 Universal Database, Version 5.x, 6.1, or 7.1; significant experience with DB2 DataPropagator; and experience as a DB2 Universal Database Administrator. The roadmap for acquiring the IBM Certified Advanced Technical Expert—DB2 Data Replication certification role is outlined in Figure 1-8.

As Figure 1-8 illustrates, to acquire the IBM Certified Advanced Technical Expert—DB2 Data Replication certification, candidates must hold one of the Level 2 Database Administration or Application Development certifications shown in Table 1-2 and pass a comprehensive test. This test is a software-based test that is neither platform nor product specific.

The Certification Process

Now that you are familiar with the certification roles that are available for DB2 Universal Database, you are probably wondering, "How do I obtain one or more of these certifications?" The following steps show you how to proceed:

1. Choose the certification role you wish to pursue, and make sure you meet its prerequisites.

2. Determine which tests you need to take by examining the roadmap for the certification role you have chosen.

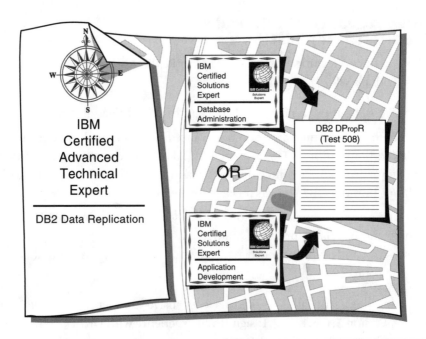

Figure 1-8 IBM Certified Advanced Technical Expert—DB2 Data Replication certification roadmap

3. Prepare for the tests you need to take by:

- Attending one or more of the DB2 training courses provided by IBM

- Reviewing books such as this one and the DB2 Universal Database manuals

- Obtaining experience using DB2 Universal Database on the job

- Taking the sample tests found on the CD provided with this book and on the IBM Certification Program Web site (refer to the next section in this chapter "Preparing for the Tests," for more information on sample tests)

4. Make arrangements to take the tests (refer to the "Testing Procedure" section later in this chapter for specific information on scheduling tests).

5. Take (and pass) the appropriate tests.

Once you have successfully completed all of the requirements outlined for a particular certification role, you qualify for certification. At that time, you will be sent a copy of the IBM Certification Agreement and a welcome package that includes a certificate suitable for framing, a wallet-sized certificate, a lapel pin, and camera-ready artwork of the IBM certification logo. Upon acceptance of the terms of the IBM Certification Agreement, you will become certified and you can begin using the IBM Professional Certification title and trademark.

Preparing for the Tests

If you have already taken some training for, have experience with, or are currently using DB2 Universal Database, you may be ready to take the tests for a particular certification role right away. But to help guarantee your success in obtaining the certification you desire, you may want to take advantage of one or more of the following resources:

Education and Publications   IBM Learning Services and some independent training companies offer courses to help prepare you for certification. You can find a listing of some of the courses that are recommended for each certification test by using the Certification Navigator tool provided at the Professional Certification Program from the IBM Web site (**http://www.ibm.com/certify**). For more information on course schedules, locations, and pricing, contact IBM Learning Services (or the appropriate training vendor) or visit their Web site.

Self-study books (such as this one) and computer-based training (CBT) programs are also available for some certification roles. Both are designed to help you prepare for certification at your own pace.

Other reference materials (that is, IBM reference manuals, product manuals, and so on) are also available to help you prepare for certification. You can find a listing of possible reference materials for each certification test by using the Certification Navigator tool provided at the Professional Certification Program from IBM Web site (**http://www.ibm.com/certify**). Ordering information is often included in the listing.

Test Objectives   Test objectives describe the topics that are most likely to be covered on a particular certification test. Test objectives for each certification test can also be found by using the Certification Navigator tool provided at the Professional Certification Program from IBM Web site (**http://www.ibm.com/certify**).

Sample Tests   Sample tests will acquaint you with the format of the certification tests, and they can help you determine whether you are ready to take a particular test. You can find sample tests for each certification test by using the Certification Navigator tool provided at the Professional Certification Program from IBM Web site (**http://www.ibm.com/certify**).

The Testing Procedure

Once you've decided to take a test for a particular certification role, the next step is to contact the testing vendor and make arrangements to take the test. The following steps show you how to schedule and take any of the certification tests available:

1. *Locate a test center that is convenient to you.* IBM Certification Program tests are administered worldwide by Prometric, Inc. Before you contact them to schedule a test, you should visit their Web site (**http://www.2test.com**) and use their Test Center Locator tool to find the testing center that is closest to you.

2. *Contact the testing vendor and make arrangements to take the test.* In the United States and Canada, Prometric, Inc. can be reached at (800) 959-3926. The number to call for other countries can be found at their Web site (**http://www.2test.com**). You may call to schedule a test anytime up to the day before the date you want to take it.

NOTE   If you need to reschedule or cancel a test, you must do so at least 24 hours before your scheduled test time.

When you call, be ready to provide the following information:

- Your name (exactly as you want it to appear on your certification certificate)
- An identification number (usually your Social Security/Social Insurance number)
- Your telephone number
- Your fax number
- Your mailing address (where you want your certification welcome package sent)
- A billing address (if different from your mailing address)
- The test number of the test you wish to take
- The method of payment (credit card or check) you are using
- Your company's name (if applicable)
- The testing center where you would like to take the test
- The date that you would like to take the test

When you call, you should also have a pencil/pen and paper ready to record the test applicant identification number they assign you. You will need this number when you arrive at the testing center. (If time permits, you will be sent a letter of confirmation with instructions about the test date, time, and location; if you register within 48 hours of the test date, you will not receive a letter.)

TIP   If you have taken a certification test in the past, you should tell the testing vendor to assign you the same applicant identification number that was used before. This will help the people at IBM to quickly recognize when you have met all of the requirements for a particular certification role. If you are assigned different applicant identification numbers each time you take a test, you will probably have to contact IBM before you will receive your certification welcome package.

---

3. *Schedule to take the test (if you paid by check)*. Scheduling procedures vary according to how you pay for the test. If you pay by credit card, you can schedule your test immediately. If you pay by check, you will have to wait until it has been received and payment has been confirmed before you can schedule to take the test. Prometric, Inc. recommends that if you pay by check, you write your registration ID on the front of the check and call them seven business days after you mail it to them. At that time, they should have received and confirmed your payment, and you should be able to schedule to take the test.

4. *Arrive at the testing location early and sign in*. You should arrive at least 15 minutes before the scheduled time to sign in. Be ready to provide two forms of identification and the ID number you were assigned when you made arrangements to take the test. One form of identification must have a recent photograph, and the other must have a signature. Examples include a driver's license (photograph) and a credit card (signature).

5. *Take the test*. All of the DB2 certification tests are knowledge-based, multiple-choice tests (closed book) that are administered on a personal computer. Each test generally contains between 50 and 70 questions and must be completed within a specified time frame. (Test 515: *Business Intelligence Solutions* must be completed within 60 minutes; all other tests must be completed within 75 minutes—tests can be completed before their designated time limit has expired.)

6. *Review the results*. As soon as you complete the test, you will receive a full score report and a section analysis. When you pass a test, you automatically receive credit toward certification. If you fail a test, you must repeat steps one through six (including paying for the test again) in order to retake it. There are no restrictions on how many times you can take a particular test; however, you are only allowed to take the same test twice within a 30-day period.

TIP If you plan on retaking a test you have failed, pay close attention to the section analysis on your score report and brush up on the areas where you scored the lowest.

After a test has been taken, your demographic data (that is, name, address, phone number, and so on) and test results are automatically sent from the testing vendor to IBM for processing within five working days. If the test you took (and passed) completes all of the requirements of a particular certification role, IBM will send you an IBM Certification Agreement and welcome package four to six weeks after they receive the test results.

Benefits Professional Certification Provides

Certification is a tool that is designed to help objectively measure the performance of a professional on a given job at a defined skill level. Therefore, certification is beneficial both for individuals who wish to validate their own skills and performance levels and for employers who want to validate the skills and performance levels of current and/or potential employees. In addition to assessing job skills and performance levels, professional certification may also offer the following benefits:

For employees,

- Helping to create advantages in interviews
- Assisting in gaining salary increases and/or corporate advancement
- Increasing self-esteem
- Providing you with credentials that you can use to obtain industry recognition
- Providing you with ongoing technical vitality (IBM Certified professionals receive special mailings from the Professional Certification Program from IBM)

For employers,

- Helping to measure the effectiveness of training
- Reducing training course redundancy and unnecessary expenses
- Providing objective benchmarks for validating skills
- Making long-range planning easier
- Helping to manage professional development

- Aiding as a hiring tool

- Contributing to competitive advantage

- Increasing productivity

For business partners and consultants,

- Providing independent validation of technical skills

- Creating competitive advantage and business opportunities

- Enhancing prestige of the team

- Contributing to IBM's requirements for various business partner programs

 NOTE   In a study of the "Return on Investment" for IBM Certification that was conducted across approximately 200 businesses in July 1999, the majority of respondents indicated that certification has a positive effect on sales volumes, profitability, and ability to close a sale; that certification reduces the time it takes to perform various tasks; and that certification has a positive effect on customer satisfaction. Details of this study can be found on the Internet at http://www-1.ibm.com/certify/program/roistudy.shtml.

Summary

The goal of this chapter was to provide you with an overview of the Professional Certification Program from IBM and to introduce you to the certification roles that are available for DB2 Universal Database. The Professional Certification Program from IBM offers three levels of certification; a different level of competency characterizes each. Each level contains one or more standard role names, and a certification role consists of one of these standard role names, followed by the product name or skill area to which the certification applies. Currently, over 100 certification roles exist.

The DB2 Universal Database certification category of the Professional Certification Program from IBM contains one Level 1 certification role, eight Level 2 certification roles, and three Level 3 certification roles. The Level 1 certification role can be attained by receiving a passing grade on a test that focuses on DB2 Universal Database Fundamentals. All Level 2 certification roles can be attained by receiving a passing grade on two knowledge-based tests. The first of these tests focuses on DB2 Universal Database Fundamentals; the second focuses on Business Solutions, DB2 Database Administration, or DB2 Application Development. All Level 3 certification roles can be attained by obtaining one of the Level 2 Database Administration or Application Development certifications and receiving a passing grade on one advanced knowledge-based test.

To obtain one or more certifications:

1. Choose the certification role you wish to pursue.

2. Determine which tests you need to take by examining the roadmap for the certification role you have chosen.

3. Prepare for the tests you need to take by

   - Attending one or more of the DB2 training courses

   - Reviewing books and manuals

   - Obtaining experience using DB2 Universal Database

   - Taking sample tests

4. Locate a test center that is convenient to you.

5. Contact the testing vendor and arrange to take the necessary tests.

6. Arrive at the testing location and sign in.

7. Take (and pass) the required tests.

Upon successful completion of the requirements outlined for a particular certification role, you will receive a copy of the IBM Certification Agreement and a welcome package that includes a certificate, a wallet-sized certificate, a lapel pin, and camera-ready artwork of the IBM certification logo. Upon acceptance of the terms of the IBM Certification Agreement, you will become certified and you may begin using the IBM Professional Certification title and trademark.

PART II

DB2 UDB Fundamentals
(Tests 509 and 512)

Installation and Planning

In this chapter, you will learn

- The functionality that each edition of DB2 Universal Database provides
- The functionality that each DB2 client component provides
- The purpose of each product that makes up the DB2 Family
- What each component of the DB2 administration tools look like (on the Windows NT operating system) and what action or actions each tool is designed to perform

The first objective of the DB2 Universal Database Family Fundamentals exam is to evaluate your ability to install the products that make up the DB2 Family and to test your knowledge of the various tools that are provided with DB2 Universal Database. From a certification viewpoint, knowing how to install a particular product is not as important as knowing what products you need to install in order to create a desired environment/configuration. Likewise, knowing the intricate details about how each tool works is not as important as knowing what tools are available and which tool to use to perform a specific task.

This chapter is designed to introduce you to the various products that make up the DB2 Family and to the set of tools that come with DB2 Universal Database, Version 7.x.

 TIP Eleven percent of the DB2 Universal Database Family Fundamentals exam is designed to test your knowledge of DB2 installation and planning.

The DB2 Universal Database Family

DB2 Universal Database, Version 7.x is the latest version of IBM's object-relational database that was first introduced on mainframe computers in 1983. Over the years, this product has grown and now DB2 Universal Database runs on the mainframe (OS/390 and AS/400) as well as on the Windows, OS/2, UNIX, AIX, HP-UX, Linux, Solaris, and NUMA-Q operating environments. Scaled down versions that have smaller footprints are also available for hand-held device operating systems such as Windows CE and the Palm Computing platform. In addition to providing a scalable database client/server solution for many different operating environments and hardware configurations, IBM also offers a suite of products that provide additional storage and connectivity capabilities to the base DB2 Universal Database system. The different flavors of DB2 Universal Database that are currently available and this suite of add-on products are collectively known as the DB2 Family.

DB2 Universal Database Products

The core of the DB2 Family consists of six object-relational database management system editions that support increasingly complex database/user environments and two developer's editions that provide tools for building applications that interact with DB2 Universal Database databases in one or more of these environments. Figure 2-1 outlines the database management editions that are available; Figure 2-2 outlines the developer editions that are available.

All of these editions contain the same database management engine, recognize ANSI SQL, and provide graphical user interfaces for constructing and submitting queries and for performing database administration operations. With the exception of DB2 Everyplace, DB2 Universal Database Satellite Edition, DB2 Universal Database Personal Edition, and DB2 Personal Developer's Edition, all are multi-user relational database management systems that can be accessed from one or more remote client workstations through software known as Client Application Enablers (CAEs).

DB2 Everyplace (Personal Edition and Enterprise Edition)

DB2 Everyplace is a full-function version of the DB2 Universal Database that has a footprint of approximately 150K. It is designed for low-cost, low-power, small form-factor devices such as personal digital assistants (PDAs), hand-held personal computers (HPCs), and embedded devices. DB2 Everyplace provides a local data store on a mobile or embedded device that can be used to store relational data obtained from other data

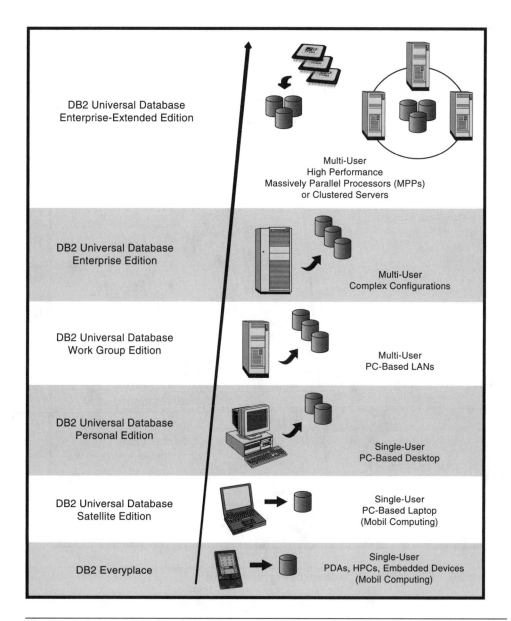

Figure 2-1 DB2 Universal Database object-relational database management system editions

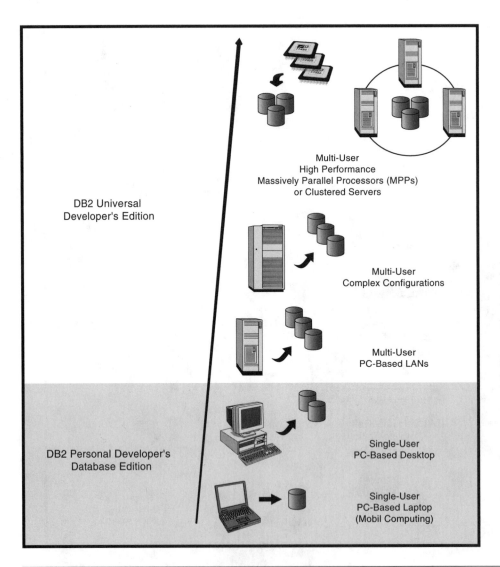

Multi-User
High Performance
Massively Parallel Processors (MPPs)
or Clustered Servers

DB2 Universal
Developer's Edition

Multi-User
Complex Configurations

Multi-User
PC-Based LANs

DB2 Personal Developer's
Database Edition

Single-User
PC-Based Desktop

Single-User
PC-Based Laptop
(Mobil Computing)

Figure 2-2   DB2 Universal Database developer editions

sources such as DB2 Universal Database for UNIX, OS/2, and Windows NT, DB2 for OS/390, and DB2 for AS/400. In addition, because DB2 Everyplace implements a subset of the SQL 99 standard and supports a subset of the DB2 Call Level Interface, Open Database Connectivity (ODBC), and Java Database Connectivity (JDBC), application developers can deliver easy-to-use mobile database applications with familiar technologies.

DB2 Everyplace runs on Palm OS devices, Symbian EPOC devices, QNX Neutrino devices, embedded Linux devices, Windows CE devices, and Pocket PC devices. DB2 Everyplace also recognizes Type II Compact Flash storage devices such as the IBM Microdrive so it can take advantage of higher capacity storage that might be available on mobile devices.

DB2 Universal Database Satellite Edition

DB2 Universal Database Satellite Edition is a full-function, high-performance version of DB2 Universal Database that has a lightweight footprint that enables it to execute on laptop computers running the Windows NT, Windows 98, or Windows 95 operating system. It is designed to simplify large-scale deployments of remote mobile-computing applications that rely heavily on enterprise data. With DB2 Universal Database Satellite Edition installed, systems can operate disconnected from remote servers the majority of the time, yet immediately gain access to and/or modify enterprise data whenever a connection to a remote system is established. (Advanced replication capabilities found in DB2 Universal Database Satellite Edition keep data stored on satellite systems in sync with data stored on enterprise servers.) Figure 2-3 shows the components of a satellite

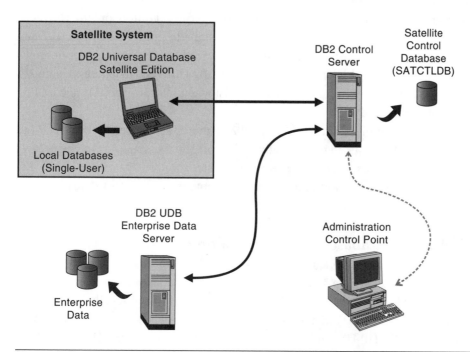

Figure 2-3   DB2 Universal Database Satellite Edition environment

environment and illustrates how enterprise data moves to and from a satellite system when a connection to a remote system is established.

With DB2 Universal Database Satellite Edition, the end user does not have to manage the local databases being used by the satellite system. In fact, the end user does not even need to know that a local database exists. Instead, database administrators (DBAs) and/or system administrators can perform administrative activities for satellite systems through the Satellite Administration Center (which is part of the DB2 Universal Database Control Center, which we will look at a little later).

DB2 Universal Database Personal Edition

DB2 Universal Database Personal Edition provides a single-user object-relational database management system for PC-based desktop computers that are running the Windows NT, Windows 2000, Windows XP, Windows 98, Windows 95, OS/2, or Linux operating system. As the name suggests, DB2 Universal Database Personal Edition is designed so that only one user is allowed to create and administer databases, and those databases can only be created on the workstation in which the DB2 product has been installed. Remote clients cannot access databases that reside on a workstation in which DB2 Universal Database Personal Edition has been installed; however, such a workstation can be used as a remote client to access any other server where DB2 Universal Database Workgroup Edition, DB2 Universal Database Enterprise Edition, or DB2 Universal Database Enterprise-Extended Edition has been installed. Thus, DB2 Universal Database Personal Edition is appropriate for users who need to access one or more stand-alone databases and possibly one or more remote DB2 Universal databases. Figure 2-4 shows the two types of environments that can exist when DB2 Universal Database Personal Edition is installed.

In the first environment shown in Figure 2-4, the end user can only access and administer local databases that physically reside on the workstation. In the second environment, the end user can access and administer local databases that physically reside on the workstation, and access remote databases (via a LAN) that physically reside on another DB2 server.

DB2 Universal Database Workgroup Edition

DB2 Universal Database Workgroup Edition provides a multi-user object-relational database management system for applications and data that are shared in a workgroup or small business/department setting. This edition is designed specifically for PC-based Local Area Networks (LANs) that are running the Windows NT, Windows 2000, Windows XP, OS/2, AIX, HP-UX, Linux, or Solaris operating system. DB2 Universal Database Workgroup Edition contains all of the functionality that is provided with DB2

Stand-Alone Database Server Environment

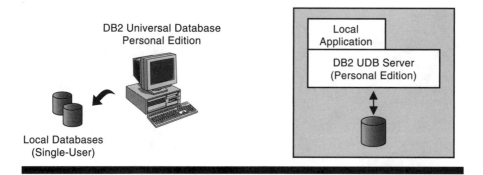

DB2 Universal Database
Personal Edition

Local
Application

DB2 UDB Server
(Personal Edition)

Local Databases
(Single-User)

Remote Client Environment

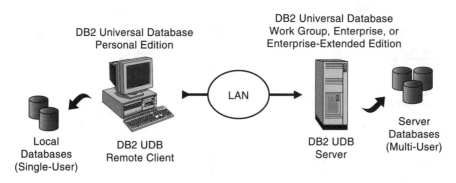

DB2 Universal Database
Personal Edition

DB2 Universal Database
Work Group, Enterprise, or
Enterprise-Extended Edition

LAN

Local
Databases
(Single-User)

DB2 UDB
Remote Client

DB2 UDB
Server

Server
Databases
(Multi-User)

Figure 2-4   DB2 Universal Database Personal Edition environments

Universal Database Personal Edition, plus it can receive and process requests from other DB2 Universal Database remote client workstations (this edition also provides server functionality). Figure 2-5 shows a basic client/server environment that can be created with DB2 Universal Database Workgroup Edition.

DB2 remote clients communicate with a DB2 Universal Database Workgroup Edition server using a recognized client/server protocol. Depending upon the remote client and server operating systems involved, the following communication protocols are supported:

- Transmission Control Protocol/Internet Protocol (TCP/IP)
- NetBIOS
- Internet Packet Exchange/Sequence Packet Exchange (IPX/SPX)

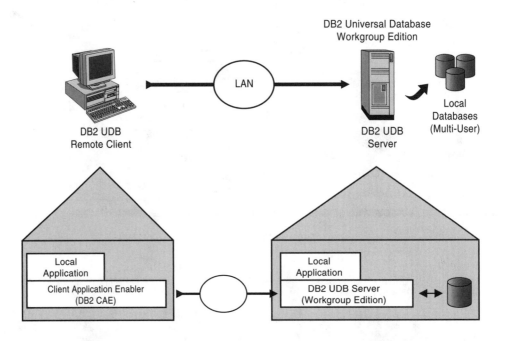

Figure 2-5   Basic DB2 Universal Database Workgroup Edition environment

- Advanced Program-to-Program Communication (APPC)
- Named Pipes

DB2 Universal Database Enterprise Edition (EE)

DB2 Universal Database Enterprise Edition provides a multi-user, object-relational database management system for complex configurations (such as symmetric multiprocessor platforms) and large database needs. This edition is ideal for midsize to large businesses and departments, particularly where Internet and/or enterprise connectivity is important. In addition to providing all of the functionality that DB2 Universal Database Workgroup Edition provides, DB2 Universal Database Enterprise Edition supports a greater number of concurrent users and can participate in heterogeneous networks using a protocol that is known as Distributed Relational Database Architecture (DRDA).

NOTE   In actuality, DRDA is made up of two distinct protocols: an Application Requestor (AR) protocol and an Application Server (AS) protocol. Any client that implements the AR protocol can connect to any server that implements the AS protocol and any server that implements the AS protocol can be accessed by any client that implements the AR protocol.

Using DRDA, DB2 Universal Database Enterprise Edition can communicate with DB2 databases that reside on host systems such as DB2 for OS/390 and DB2 for AS/400 (and vice versa). Figure 2-6 shows a basic client/server environment that can be created with DB2 Universal Database Enterprise Edition.

DB2 Universal Database Enterprise Edition is designed specifically for large servers that are running the Windows NT, Windows 2000, Windows XP, OS/2, AIX, HP-UX, Linux, or Solaris operating system.

DB2 Universal Database Enterprise-Extended Edition (EEE)

DB2 Universal Database Enterprise-Extended Edition contains all of the features and functionality found in DB2 Universal Database Enterprise Edition, but it also has the capability to divide (or partition) a single database into two or more sections that are physically stored on one or more workstations that are running the same operating

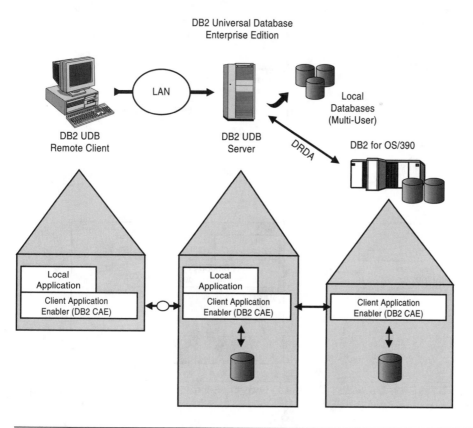

Figure 2-6   Basic DB2 Universal Database Enterprise Edition environment

system. This feature offers greater scalability in Massively Parallel Processor (MPP) or clustered server environments. Although DB2 Universal Database Workgroup Edition and DB2 Universal Database Enterprise Edition both support large databases, DB2 Universal Database Enterprise-Extended Edition is specifically designed for situations in which a database is simply too large for a single computer to manage efficiently. By partitioning large databases, SQL operations can execute in parallel on each individual partition, thereby increasing the overall performance of all interaction with that particular database. Figure 2-7 illustrates how a basic client/clustered server environment created with DB2 Universal Database Enterprise-Extended Edition might look.

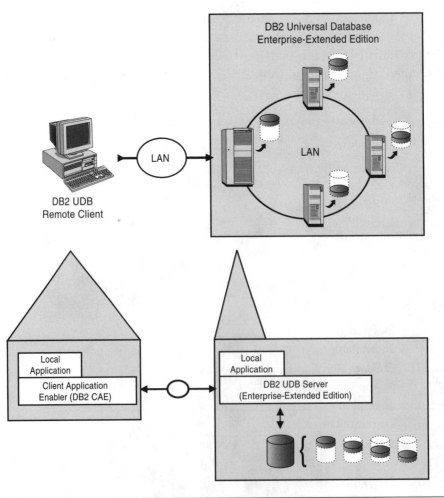

Figure 2-7 DB2 Universal Database Enterprise-Extended Edition clustered server environment

DB2 Universal Database Enterprise-Extended Edition is ideal for applications and data that are used for data warehousing, data mining, and large-scale Online Transaction Processing (OLTP) applications. This edition is available for servers that are running the Windows NT, AIX, HP-UX, Solaris, or NUMA-Q operating system.

DB2 Personal Developer's Edition

DB2 Personal Developer's Edition contains both an object-relational database management system and a complete set of tools for developing desktop applications that are designed to work with single-user DB2 Universal Database databases. The set of tools provided with this edition enables a developer to construct software programs that communicate with DB2 databases using any of the following methods:

- Embedded SQL (static and/or dynamic)
- IBM's Call Level Interface (CLI), which is compatible with Microsoft's Open Database Connectivity (ODBC) interface
- DB2's set of administrative Application Programming Interfaces (APIs)
- Java Database Connectivity (JDBC) (Java applets and/or Java applications)
- SQLJ (Java applets and/or Java applications)

The programming environment provided by DB2 Personal Developer's Edition includes the programming libraries, header files, and SQL precompilers that are needed for each programming language that is supported by DB2 and the operating system that DB2 has been installed on. These programming languages include COBOL, FORTRAN, C, C++, Java, and REXX.

The same object-relational database management system that is packaged as DB2 Universal Database Personal Edition is also included in DB2 Personal Developer's Edition (thus, the rules that govern the use of that edition also apply). DB2 Personal Developer's Edition is available for PC-based desktop computers that are running the Windows NT, Windows 2000, Windows XP, Windows 98, Windows 95, OS/2, or Linux operating system. Applications that are developed with the tools provided by DB2 Personal Developer's Edition can be run directly on the server, or they can be run on any client that (1) has remote access to the server, and (2) is running the same operating system as the server.

DB2 Universal Developer's Edition

In addition to providing the same rich set of development tools found in DB2 Personal Developer's Edition, DB2 Universal Developer's Edition gives developers the ability to construct and execute client/server applications on any platform that any edition of DB2 Universal Database supports (as opposed to a single platform). To facilitate the testing of these applications, DB2 Universal Developer's Edition contains fully functional versions of DB2 Universal Database Satellite Edition, DB2 Universal Database Personal Edition, DB2 Universal Database Workgroup Edition, and DB2 Universal Database Enterprise Edition that can be run on any of the following platforms: Windows NT, Windows 2000, Windows XP, Windows 98, Windows 95, OS/2, AIX, HP-UX, Linux, Solaris, NUMA-Q, and Silicon Graphics IRIX (DB2 Run-Time Client only). Applications that are developed with the tools provided by DB2 Universal Developer's Edition can be run directly on the server, or they can be run on any client that has remote access to the server. Furthermore, the operating system used by the client does not have to match that used by the server.

DB2 Universal Database Clients

In addition to providing a robust object-relational database server, five of the six database management editions that make up the core of the DB2 Family contain the following common client components:

- DB2 Run-Time Client
- DB2 Administration Client
- DB2 Application Development Client

Examples of how these client components communicate with the different database servers available can be seen in Figures 2-4 through 2-7. Any of these client components can be installed on any number of workstations; however, the client component you choose to install should be based upon the requirements for a particular workstation as well as the operating system used on that workstation. For example, if you need to be able to execute a database application that has already been written and if you do not need to perform administration operations on the database the application is running against, the DB2 Run-Time Client that is appropriate for the operating system found on the client workstation should be installed.

DB2 Run-Time Client

The DB2 Run-Time Client provides workstations that are running a variety of operating systems (such as Windows NT, Windows 2000, Windows XP, Windows 98, Windows 95, OS/2, AIX, HP-UX, Linux, Solaris, NUMA-Q, and Silicon Graphics IRIX) with the capability to access DB2 Universal Database databases. In addition to providing a way for client applications to communicate with remote database servers, the DB2 Run-Time Client provides a way for users to

- Issue interactive SQL statements on client workstations that access data on remote DB2 servers.
- Access data on remote DB2 servers with applications that were developed using Microsoft's Open Database Connectivity (ODBC).

DB2 Administration Client

The DB2 Administration Client provides workstations that are running a variety of operating systems with the capability to access and perform administrative operations on DB2 Universal Database databases that reside on remote servers. The DB2 Administration Client contains all of the features and functionality found in the DB2 Run-Time Client, plus it contains the DB2 administration tools, the documentation for those tools, and support for Thin Clients. The DB2 Administration Client also includes the client components for DB2 Query Patroller, another product in the DB2 Family (DB2 Query Patroller is a sophisticated query management and workload distribution tool that will be covered in greater detail later in this chapter). The DB2 Administration Client can be run on any of the following platforms: Windows NT, Windows 2000, Windows XP, Windows 98, Windows 95, OS/2, AIX, HP-UX, Linux, and Solaris.

DB2 Application Development Client

The DB2 Application Development Client (known as the DB2 Software Development Kit, or SDK in earlier versions) provides the tools and environment needed to build and run applications that access both DB2 Universal Database databases that reside on remote servers and application servers that implement DRDA. The DB2 Application Development Client contains all of the features and functionality found in the DB2 Administration Client, plus it contains many of the programming libraries, header files, and SQL precompilers that are available with DB2 Personal Developer's Edition and DB2 Universal Developer's Edition. The DB2 Application Development Client can be run on any of the following platforms: Windows NT, Windows 2000, Windows XP, Windows 98, Windows 95, OS/2, AIX, HP-UX, Linux, Solaris, NUMA-Q, and Silicon Graphics IRIX.

Other DB2 Universal Database Products

It was mentioned earlier that six object-relational database management system editions and two developer's editions make up the core of the DB2 Family. Several other products that expand the capabilities and functionality of DB2 Universal Database make up the remainder of the DB2 Family. These products include the following:

- DB2 Connect Personal Edition
- DB2 Connect Enterprise Edition
- DB2 Image, Audio, and Video Extenders
- DB2 Text Extender
- DB2 XML Extender
- DB2 Spatial Extender
- DB2 Net Search Extender
- DB2 Warehouse Manager
- Query Patroller
- DB2 OLAP Server Starter Kit
- Net.Data

DB2 Connect Personal Edition

DB2 Connect Personal Edition provides a way for one PC-based desktop computer that is running the Windows NT, Windows 2000, Windows 98, Windows 95, OS/2, or Linux operating system to connect to mainframe and midrange databases that are stored on servers that use DRDA protocol. This includes database servers such as DB2 for OS/390, DB2 for MVS/ESA, DB2 for VSE/VM, or DB2 for OS/400. DB2 Connect Personal Edition is designed for two-tier environments, where each client connects directly to one or more host databases without going through a gateway server. Often, this kind of transparent connection is a very convenient and desirable configuration. Figure 2-8 illustrates how an environment where a client workstation accessing data stored in a DB2 for OS/390 database using DB2 Connect Personal Edition might look.

It is important to note that, unlike DB2 Universal Database EE, which implements both an Application Requestor and an Application Server protocol, DB2 Connect Personal Edition only implements an Application Requestor protocol. Thus, DB2 Connect Personal Edition does not accept inbound client requests for data.

DB2 Connect Enterprise Edition (EE)

DB2 Connect Enterprise Edition (EE) is essentially a connectivity server that concentrates and manages connections between multiple clients and/or Web applications and mainframe/midrange databases that are stored on servers that use DRDA protocol. Again, this includes database servers such as DB2 for OS/390, DB2 for MVS/ESA, DB2

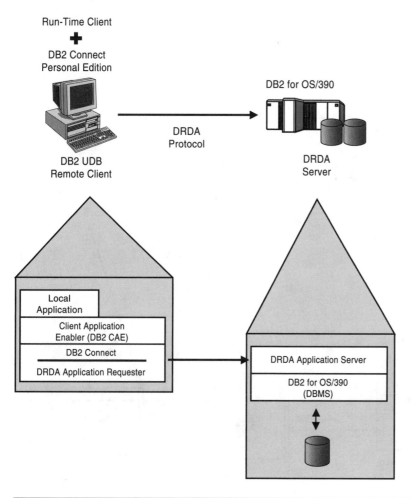

Figure 2-8 DB2 Connect Personal Edition environment

for VSE/VM, or DB2 for OS/400. DB2 Connect Enterprise Edition is designed specifically for three-tier environments that have at least one gateway server that is running the Windows NT, Windows 2000, Windows 98, Windows 95, OS/2, AIX, HP-UX, Linux, Solaris, or NUMA-Q operating system. Figure 2-9 illustrates how an environment where two client workstations accessing data stored in a DB2 for OS/390 database using DB2 Connect Enterprise Edition might look.

Because DB2 Connect Enterprise Edition implements both an Application Requestor and an Application Server, it can accept inbound client requests for data as well as send outbound client requests to DRDA servers.

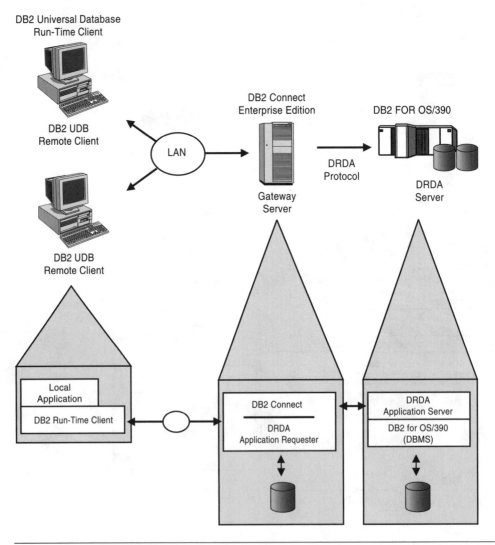

Figure 2-9   DB2 Connect Enterprise Edition environment

DB2 Extenders

Data is stored in most relational databases according to its data type. For example, character data is typically stored as an array of consecutive single byte blocks (one block for each character used) and numeric data whose values fall in the range of $-32,768$ to $32,767$ are typically stored in a single two- or four-byte block. In order to store a wide variety of data, DB2 Universal Database contains a rich set of built-in data types, along with a set of functions that are designed to manipulate those data types. DB2 Universal Database also provides a way to create user-defined data types and supporting user-defined functions to better handle data that does not map directly to one of the built-in types. Using this capability, IBM went one step farther and created several different sets of user-defined data types and functions to manage particular kinds of data that have begun to emerge over the last few years. Collectively, these sets of data types and functions are referred to as *extenders* (because, when installed, they extend the basic functionality and capabilities of all DB2 Universal Database editions). Currently, five different extender products are available for DB2 Universal Database, Version 7.x; each is named for the particular type of data they support.

DB2 Image, Audio, and Video Extenders   The DB2 Image, Audio, and Video Extenders product provides a set of data types and functions that enable a DB2 Universal Database to store and manipulate image, audio, and video objects. This extender exploits DB2 Universal Database's support for binary large objects (up to 2 gigabytes in size) and it provides image, audio, and video objects with the same security, integrity, and recovery protections that are available for traditional data.

The data types and functions that are provided by the DB2 Image, Audio, and Video Extenders can be used just like any of the built-in data types and functions in SQL. In addition, because SQL can be used to construct multi-data-type queries, this extender product provides a lot of flexibility when searching for information. For example, a query could be written in such a way that when executed, it locates a particular audio clip by searching for its description, the date it was recorded, or its total playing time. In addition, the Query By Image Content (QBIC) capability provided with this extender can be used to locate images that have a particular color combination, or that have colors and/or textures that are similar to those of a master image.

DB2 Text Extender   The DB2 Text Extender provides a powerful way to search for and extract key information from complex text documents that are stored both in DB2 Universal Database databases and in file systems that are outside the control of DB2. This extender's strength comes from IBM's powerful linguistic search and text-mining technology that enables users to construct queries that quickly search through thousands of large text documents, looking for either specific items or for word variations and synonyms. The DB2 Text Extender can access any kind of text document, including most word processing documents, in their original native format and it offers a rich set of capabilities including the

- Capability to search for a specific word
- Capability to search for a specific phrase

- Capability to search for a particular word sequence

- Capability to search for word variations (such as plural forms of a word or the word in a different tense)

- Capability to search for synonyms of a word

- Capability to search for words that have a similar sound

- Capability to search for words that have a similar spelling

- Capability to perform wildcard searches (for example, search for all words that begin with the characters "net")

DB2 XML Extender   The DB2 XML Extender provides a set of data types that enable extensible markup language (XML) documents to be stored in DB2 Universal Database databases. This extender also provides a set of functions that assist in working with these structured documents. With the DB2 XML Extender, entire XML documents can be stored as character data in a database table, or they can reside in a file system and still be managed by DB2. This extender can extract and store XML elements and attributes in multiple columns and tables and, using existing character and numerical data (or extracted XML data), it can compose new XML documents. In addition, because the same powerful search functions that are found in the DB2 Text Extender are available with the DB2 XML Extender, specific items can be quickly located within a set of XML documents.

DB2 Spatial Extender   In the past, geospatial data has been managed by specialized Geographic Information Systems (GISs) that, because of their design, have been unable to integrate their spatial data with business data stored in other relational database management systems and/or sources. This changed with the introduction of user-defined data types and user-defined functions. Shortly after DB2 Universal Database, Version 5.0 was released, IBM, together with the Environmental Systems Research Institute (ESRI), a leading manufacturer of spatial database systems, created a set of data types for describing spatial data (for example, points, lines, and polygons) and a set of functions to query spatial objects (for example, to find area, endpoints, intersects, and so on). This set of data types and functions makes up the DB2 Spatial Extender product.

In addition to providing a way to integrate business data and spatial data in a single database system, the DB2 Spatial Extender can exploit the features of the DB2 Data-Joiner product to apply spatial intelligence to data that is stored in a variety of data sources. Thus, the DB2 Spatial Extender can be used to address geospatial business-intelligence requirements that need access to data stored in both IBM and non-IBM data sources without having to physically move any data from its original location.

DB2 Net Search Extender   The Net Search Extender provides application developers using Net.Data, Java, or DB2's Call Level Interface (CLI) a way to incorporate fast, powerful search functionality (similar to the search functionality provided by the DB2 Text Extender) in their applications. Because the DB2 Net Search Extender is similar to, but provides a higher search speed than the DB2 Text Extender, it can be particularly advantageous when used with Internet applications, where search performance on large indexes and scalability based on concurrent queries are important factors. Some of the key features of the DB2 Net Search Extender include the

- Capability to create multiple indexes on a single column (indexing proceeds without acquiring row-level locks)
- Capability to create indexes across multiple processors
- Capability to search for a particular word or phrase
- Capability to search for words that have a similar spelling
- Capability to perform wildcard searches (for example, search for all words that begin with the characters "net")
- Capability to control how search results are sorted
- Capability to limit the number of search results returned
- Capability to search for tags or sections (with or without using Boolean operations)

Unlike other extenders that provide their functionality through user-defined data types and user-defined functions, the DB2 Net Search Extender provides its functionality through a set of stored procedures.

DB2 Warehouse Manager

Being able to analyze data before making a business decision can often provide a company with a big competitive advantage. However, in order to use existing data for business intelligence and customer relationship management (CRM), you must have the right tools, and more importantly, the data must exist in a format that is suitable for analysis. Often, this means that data must be extracted from the system it is stored in, cleansed and/or transformed, and stored in data warehouses (or data marts), which must be updated on a regular basis and managed themselves. With DB2 Warehouse Manager, you can build high-performance data warehouses that can grow and change with your business needs and that can leverage more of your information resources. Once you have a data warehouse in place, DB2 Warehouse Manager's set of flexible tools makes it easy to manage the data warehouse and to govern and track its usage.

One of the options provided with the DB2 Control Center (the main administrative tool for DB2 Universal Database) is the Data Warehouse Center. The Data Warehouse Center is the command console for data warehouse management; it provides easy access to DB2, Oracle, Sybase, Informix, Microsoft, flat file, ODBC, and OLE DB data sources. Also, because the Data Warehouse Center is integrated tightly with the DB2 Control Center, database administrators (DBAs) can perform the following tasks, all from a single common user environment:

- Access multiple data sources.
- Build and test data warehouse extraction and transformation processes.
- Analyze and tune extractions and queries.
- Automate and monitor processes.
- Authorize users.
- Put data warehouses into production.

In addition to basic SQL-related data warehouse transformations, DB2 Warehouse Manager provides special transformers (in the form of user-defined functions (UDFs) and stored procedures) that are designed to cleanse data and generate keys, pivot tables, and so on. A unique graphical environment in the Data Warehouse Center makes it easy for warehouse designers to specify any of these built-in transformations (over 150 exist) and to visualize the flow of the data warehouse build process. If a needed transformation is not part of the built-in transformations set, warehouse designers can add their own custom transformations, using the DB2 Stored Procedure Builder or another development tool of their choice.

Query Patroller

As the number of end users interacting with a data warehouse increases, the response time associated with each individual query tends to decline due to resource contention. Because of this, one of the challenges of any large-scale data warehouse system is to provide quick response time to an ever-increasing number of end users. One way to facilitate this is to store such data warehouses on powerful Symmetric Multiprocessing Processor (SMP) and Massively Parallel Processor (MPP) servers. However, with this approach, if multiple queries reach the data warehouse at the same time, the core database's load management capability could end up spending excessive amounts of resources just handling query switching, which would increase, rather than decrease overall response time. A better solution is to have queries prioritized and scheduled in such a way that query switching overhead is minimized while resource utilization is maximized.

DB2 Query Patroller provides a way for database administrators (DBAs) to govern the execution of queries and manage the resources required by those queries so that hundreds of users can safely submit queries on multiterabyte class systems and receive results within an acceptable time frame. DB2 Query Patroller also enables administrators to set individual user and group priorities, as well as user query cost threshold limits. This allows a data warehouse to deliver query results to its most important users first. DB2 Query Patroller also has the capability to limit usage of system resources by stopping runaway queries before they can start. In addition, it captures information such as the requesting user's ID, input/output (I/O) cost, result data set/table size, and elapsed query run time each time a query is processed. This information makes it easy to charge end-user departments for their use of the data warehouse.

Because DB2 Query Patroller is closely integrated with the DB2 optimizer, it performs cost analysis on queries as they are submitted, and then schedules and dispatches those queries so that the load is balanced across database partitions (in a DB2 Universal Database Enterprise-Extended Edition environment). It accomplishes this by performing an Explain plan operation to check the cost of dynamic SQL queries. If the value returned exceeds the query cost threshold assigned to the user (or the user's group), DB2 Query Patroller places the query on hold and runs it at a later time. This does not negatively impact the end user because as soon as a query is submitted, DB2 Query Patroller frees up his or her desktop so he or she can perform other work (including submitting other queries) while waiting for the original query results to be returned.

DB2 OLAP Server Starter Kit

Today's diverse end-user community has a wide array of needs. With the explosive growth in e-business driving industry segments such as e-commerce and customer relationship management (CRM), successful businesses rely more and more on powerful tools that can help them make sense of the vast amount of data they acquire. Whether it's account status, financial data, or information that is shared with new business partners, businesses are being inundated with more data than ever before. Today's analysts need to formulate queries using a three-dimensional model; such *cubes* depict the intersection of three axes, which is known specifically as a *fact*. Some businesses store facts in proprietary formats called multidimensional databases (MDAs). Others store them, using a star-schema model, in a relational database or cube. In either case, online retrieval and analysis tools are then used to analyze and reveal business trends and statistics that are not always directly visible.

The DB2 OLAP Server Starter Kit contains an online analytical processing (OLAP) product that can be used to create a wide range of multidimensional planning, analysis, and reporting applications. DB2 OLAP Server is based on the OLAP technology that was developed by Hyperion Solutions Corporation (which is marketed as Hyperion Essbase). In addition to providing all the functionality of Hyperion Essbase, DB2 OLAP Server provides the capability of storing multidimensional databases as sets of relational database tables. Regardless of which storage management option you choose, with the DB2 OLAP Server you can use the Essbase Application Manager and Essbase commands to create an Essbase application and its associated databases. Because DB2 OLAP Server fully supports the widely adopted Hyperion Essbase Application Programming Interface (API), it is accessible by a broad range of front-end analysis tools and business applications, as well as by standard SQL query tools. (A large and growing number of third-party vendors—more than 70 at last count—provide analytical tools and applications that work with the Hyperion Essbase API.) In addition to supporting the Hyperion Essbase API, DB2 OLAP Server also contains over 100 built-in functions, including financial, statistical, and mathematical functions.

With DB2 OLAP Server, end users don't need to understand relational database concepts or SQL, so they can quickly become productive. The Application Manager, an intuitive administration and development tool, helps you build custom OLAP applications to meet even the most complex analytical needs. To tune your applications, you can either use precalculated data for the fastest query response times or you can use dynamic computation at query run time to optimize database size. Because DB2 OLAP Server supports a large number of concurrent users while preserving cell-level security, it's safe to grant broad access privileges to those applications.

Net.Data

Just as the explosive growth in e-business has forced businesses to rely on powerful tools that can help them make sense of the data they acquire, it has also forced businesses to investigate ways to deliver portions of that data to end users via the Internet. One of the best ways to make DB2 Universal Database data available over the Internet is with IBM's Net.Data product. Net.Data is a fast common gateway interface (FastCGI) application that runs in conjunction with a Web server to deliver data through the World Wide Web. Along with a FastCGI application, Net.Data supports a full-featured, easy-to-learn scripting language that can be used to construct Web macros that dynamically retrieve data from a data source whenever a Web browser requests a page from a Web server.

This is how it works. When a page containing one or more Web macros is requested, the Web server calls Net.Data, which in turn expands and executes the macros to produce dynamic content for the page. Typically, each Web macro contains one or more SQL statements that are submitted to a DB2 Universal Database server for processing. Using the dynamic content produced by each macro, Net.Data generates any necessary HTML (that is needed to display the content) and returns it to the Web server, which in turn passes it to the Web browser.

In addition to accessing data stored in DB2 Universal Databases databases, Net.Data Web macros can also be used to access data stored in other popular data sources (such as Oracle, DRDA-enabled data sources, ODBC data sources, as well as flat file and Web registry data). Net.Data for OS/2, Windows NT, and UNIX, Version 7.1, also provides XML output, XHTML compatibility, file upload capability, and SQL statement nesting support.

DB2 Universal Database Packages

Now that you are familiar with the products that make up the DB2 Family, it's a good idea to become familiar with how those products are packaged. Table 2-1 shows the various DB2 Universal Database packages that are available and identifies the set of products that are found in each.

Table 2-1   DB2 Universal Database Packages and Their Products

Package	Products
DB2 Everyplace Personal Edition	DB2 Everyplace DB2 Everyplace Personal Application Builder
DB2 Everyplace Enterprise Edition	DB2 Everyplace DB2 Everyplace Sync Server DB2 Everyplace Personal Application Builder
DB2 Universal Database Satellite Edition	DB2 Universal Database Satellite Edition (Single User) DB2 Image, Audio, and Video Extenders DB2 Text Extender Run-Time Client
DB2 Universal Database Personal Edition	DB2 Universal Database Personal Edition (Single User) DB2 Image, Audio, and Video Extenders (Windows, OS/2) DB2 Text Extender (Windows, OS/2) DB2 XML Extender (Windows) DB2 OLAP Starter Kit (Windows) Application Development Client Administration Client Run-Time Client

(continued)

Table 2-1   DB2 Universal Database Packages and Their Products *(continued)*

Package	Products
DB2 Universal Database Workgroup Edition	DB2 Universal Database Workgroup Edition DB2 Image, Audio, and Video Extenders DB2 Text Extender DB2 XML Extender DB2 OLAP Starter Kit Application Development Client Administration Client Run-Time Client Net.Data Websphere Application Server, Standard Edition Query Management Facility (QMF)
DB2 Universal Database Enterprise Edition	DB2 Universal Database Enterprise Edition DB2 Image, Audio, and Video Extenders DB2 Text Extender DB2 XML Extender DB2 OLAP Starter Kit Application Development Client Administration Client Run-Time Client Net.Data Websphere Application Server, Standard Edition Query Management Facility (QMF)
DB2 Universal Database Enterprise-Extended Edition	DB2 Universal Database Enterprise-Extented Edition DB2 Image, Audio, and Video Extenders DB2 Text Extender DB2 XML Extender DB2 OLAP Starter Kit Application Development Client Administration Client Run-Time Client Net.Data Websphere Application Server, Standard Edition Query Management Facility (QMF)
DB2 Personal Developer's Edition	DB2 Universal Database Personal Edition (Single User) DB2 Connect Personal Edition DB2 Image, Audio, and Video Extenders (Windows, OS/2) DB2 Text Extender (Windows, OS/2) DB2 XML Extender (Windows) DB2 OLAP Starter Kit (Windows) Application Development Client Administration Client Run-Time Client VisualAge for Java, Entry Edition

Package	Products
DB2 Universal Developer's Edition	DB2 Universal Database Satellite Edition (Single User)
	DB2 Universal Database Personal Edition (Single User)
	DB2 Universal Database Workgroup Edition
	DB2 Universal Database Enterprise Edition
	DB2 Connect Personal Edition
	DB2 Connect Enterprise Edition
	DB2 Image, Audio, and Video Extenders (Windows, OS/2)
	DB2 Text Extender (Windows, OS/2)
	DB2 XML Extender (Windows)
	DB2 OLAP Starter Kit (Windows)
	Application Development Client
	Administration Client
	Run-Time Client
	Net.Data
	VisualAge for Java, Professional Edition (Windows, OS/2)
	Websphere Studio
	Websphere Application Server, Standard Edition
	Query Management Facility (QMF)

DB2's Administration Tools

In addition to providing a rich object-relational database management system, each edition of DB2 Universal Database, with the exception of DB2 Everywhere, contains a comprehensive set of tools that enable you to administer and access data stored in DB2 Universal Database databases. This tool set consists of the

- Control Center
- Command Center
  - SQL Assist
  - Visual Explain
- Script Center
- Alert Center
- Journal
- Command Line Processor (CLP)
- Performance Monitor
- Client Configuration Assistant

In addition to this set of tools, each edition also includes a series of wizards that provide step-by-step guidance for performing many of the database administration functions available. Not only do these wizards provide help for performing most administrative tasks, some of them also make calculations and recommendations using information they collect as they are executed. For example, the Index wizard can be used to analyze and suggest the optimal index configuration for a particular database table.

The Control Center

The Control Center is the central point for managing systems and performing common administration tasks for DB2 instances, databases, database objects (such as tables, views, and indexes), and users/user groups. The Control Center presents a clear, concise view of an entire system, enables users to administer databases remotely, and provides step-by-step assistance to help conduct some of the more complex tasks. From the Control Center, users can perform operations such as

- Creating and/or dropping (deleting) databases
- Creating, altering, and/or dropping table spaces, tables, views, indexes, triggers, and schemas
- Loading, importing, or exporting data
- Backing up and/or restoring databases or table spaces
- Reorganizing data and collecting table statistics
- Replicating data between systems
- Managing database connections
- Monitoring resources and events that take place on a server
- Configuring and fine-tuning instances and databases

Figure 2-10 shows how the Control Center looks on a Windows NT server. Because of operating system differences, the Control Center shown in this figure may be different from the Control Center found on other systems. (This is true for all of the screen shots shown in this book.)

The Control Center can also be used to launch most of the other administration tools that are provided with DB2 Universal Database, Version 7.x. Figure 2-11 identifies the administration tools that can be invoked directly from the Control Center's main toolbar.

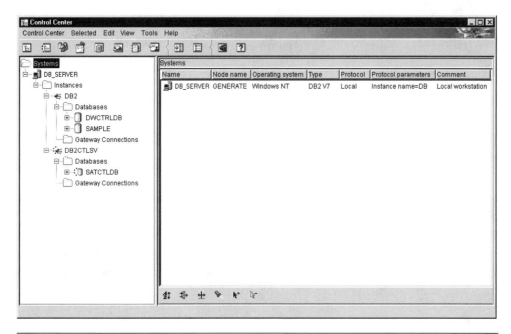

Figure 2-10 The Control Center

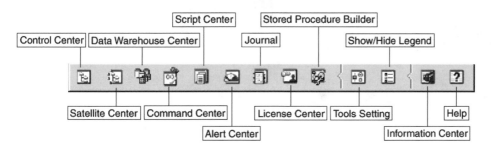

Figure 2-11 The Control Center's main toolbar

The Command Center

The Command Center is an interactive window application that enables users to

- Run SQL statements, DB2 commands, and operating system commands.

- View the results of the execution of SQL statements and DB2 commands.

- Save the results of the execution of SQL statements and DB2 commands to an external file.

- Save a sequence of SQL statements and DB2 commands to a script file.

- Use the SQL Assist tool to build complex queries.

- Examine the execution plan and statistics associated with a SQL statement before it is executed.

Figure 2-12 shows how the Command Center looks on a Windows NT server.

With the Command Center, many commands and SQL statements can be composed and run at once, whereas with the Command Line Processor, each statement/command must be typed and run individually.

SQL Assist

SQL Assist is an interactive notebook application that enables users to visually construct complex queries and examine their results. Once a query has been constructed, the SQL associated with the query can be written to the Command Center where it can then be executed immediately or saved to a script file.

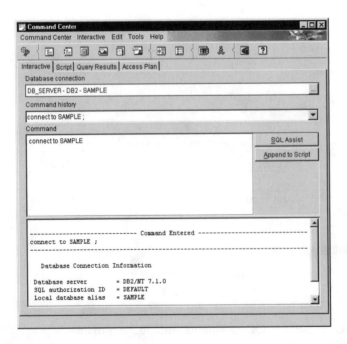

Figure 2-12   The Command Center

At the most basic level, SQL Assist can construct a query in just four simple steps:

1. Once a connection to a database has been established, the table(s) to be queried should be selected on the Tables page of the SQL Assist notebook. Figure 2-13 shows how the Tables page of SQL Assist looks on a Windows NT server.

2. After the appropriate tables have been selected, the Columns page of the SQL Assist notebook should be selected and all column(s) that are to be queried should be identified. Figure 2-14 shows how the Columns page of SQL Assist looks on a Windows NT server.

3. Complex queries can be created by selecting any of the remaining pages in the SQL Assist notebook and providing the information asked for on those pages. Once all appropriate information has been provided, the SQL for the query that was just constructed can be seen by selecting the Review page of the SQL Assist notebook. Figure 2-15 shows how the Review page of SQL Assist looks on a Windows NT server.

4. After the query has been constructed, it can be tested by selecting the Run push button shown on the Review page of the SQL Assist notebook. This action will

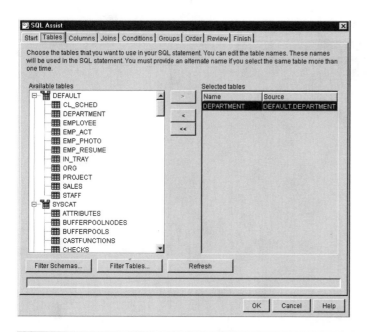

Figure 2-13   The Tables page of SQL Assist

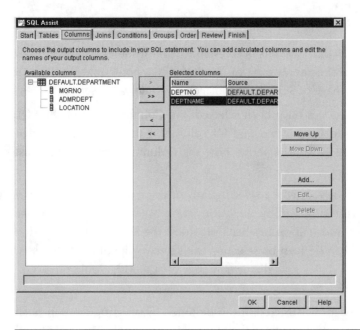

Figure 2-14   The Columns page of SQL Assist

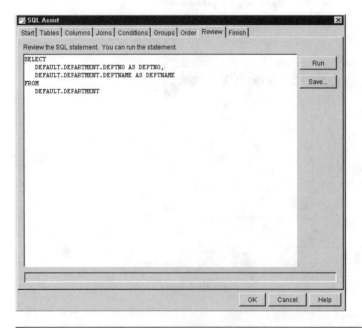

Figure 2-15   The Review page of SQL Assist

cause the query to be executed and the results to be displayed in a separate pop-up window. Figure 2-16 shows how the Results pop-up window might look on a Windows NT server.

Visual Explain

Visual Explain is a part of the Command Center that enables database administrators and application developers to

- View all the details of the access plan (including the statistics in the system catalogs) chosen by the DB2 Optimizer for a given SQL statement.

- Decide whether or not an index should be created for a particular table.

- Identify how to fine-tune SQL statements for optimum performance.

- Design application programs and databases for optimum performance.

Figure 2-17 shows how Visual Explain's output looks on a Windows NT server.

 NOTE Before Visual Explain can be used, the Explain tables must be added to the appropriate database and the *Automatically generate access plan* Command Center option must be turned on. A DB2 Command Line Processor script that creates the Explain tables (**EXPLAIN.DDL**) can be found in the *misc* subdirectory of the *sqllib* directory where DB2 Universal Database was installed. Refer to the header portion of this file for information on how to use it.

	DEPTNO	DEPTNAME
1	A00	SPIFFY COMPUTER SERVICE DIV.
2	B01	PLANNING
3	C01	INFORMATION CENTER
4	D01	DEVELOPMENT CENTER
5	D11	MANUFACTURING SYSTEMS
6	D21	ADMINISTRATION SYSTEMS
7	E01	SUPPORT SERVICES
8	E11	OPERATIONS
9	E21	SOFTWARE SUPPORT

Copy to clipboard   Save...   OK

Figure 2-16 The Results pop-up window

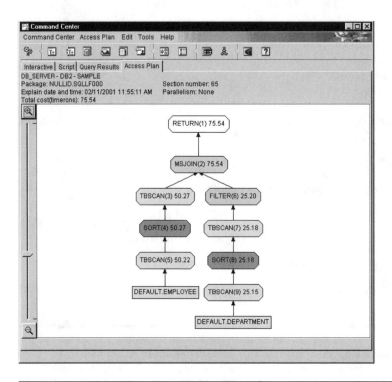

Figure 2-17 Sample output from Visual Explain (as shown on the Access Plan page of the Command Center)

The Script Center

The Script Center is a tool that enables users to create scripts consisting of DB2 commands, system commands, and SQL statements. With the Script Center, users can also

- View information about all command scripts that are known to the system.
- Run a saved command script immediately.
- Schedule a script to run unattended at a later date or at a regular interval.
- Import a script that was created outside the Script Center or that was saved in the Command Center.
- Edit a saved command script. (When a saved script is modified, all jobs dependent on the saved script inherit the new modified behavior.)
- Copy a command script.
- Delete a saved command script.

- Access the Journal to see the results that were logged when a particular script was run and to see the status of all scheduled jobs.

Figure 2-18 shows how the Script Center looks on a Windows NT server.

The Alert Center

The Alert Center is a tool that monitors a database system and warns the user about potential problems as they occur. The Alert Center can be set to automatically open to display any monitored objects that have exceeded their threshold values and therefore are in a state of alarm or warning. Threshold values for monitored objects are set from the Performance Monitor, which is invoked from the Control Center.

Figure 2-19 shows how the Alert Center looks on a Windows NT server. In this example, an event has placed the SAMPLE database in an alarm state.

The Journal

The Journal is a notebook that provides a way for users to monitor jobs and review various information that has been generated, either by jobs that have completed execution or by other administrative tools. The Journal notebook consists of the

- Jobs page
- Recovery page

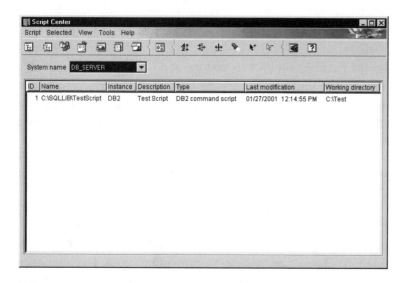

Figure 2-18   The Script Center

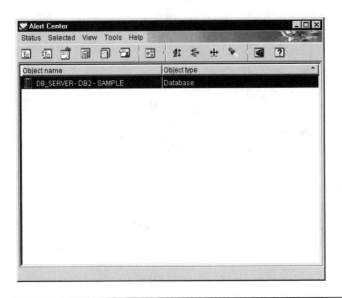

Figure 2-19 The Alert Center

- Alerts page
- Messages page

The Jobs page is used to monitor pending jobs, running jobs, and job histories. This page is also used to perform actions on a pending job (for example, to reschedule it), show the scripts associated with a job, or run a pending job immediately. The Recovery page is used to display the details from backup, restore, and load operations (i.e., the contents of the recovery history file) and to restore a database's recovery history. The Alerts page shows any alert messages that have been generated by the Performance Monitor and the Messages page shows a running history of messages that have been generated by the other DB2 administration tools.

Figure 2-20 shows how the Messages page of the Journal looks on a Windows NT server.

The Command Line Processor (CLP)

The Command Line Processor (CLP) is a text-oriented interface that enables users to access and manipulate databases from a system command prompt. Like the Script Center, the CLP enables users to issue DB2 commands, system commands, and SQL

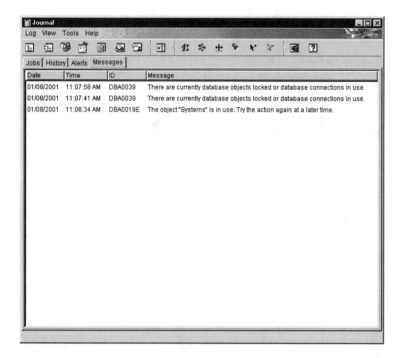

Figure 2-20   The Messages Page of the Journal

statements and view their output. Unlike the Script Center, the CLP can be run in three different modes:

- Command mode
- Interactive input mode
- Batch mode

When the CLP is run in command mode, every command entered must be preceded by the characters "db2" (for example, **db2 list database directory**). If the command contains characters that have special meaning on the operating system being used, it must be entered in quotation marks to ensure that it will be run properly (for example, **db2 "select *from employee"**). To enter long commands that do not fit on a single line, a space followed by the line continuation character (\) must be placed at the end of the line that is to be continued, and the rest of the command must begin on a new line.

When the CLP is run in interactive input mode, the required db2 prefix is pre-entered for you (as characterized by the **db2 =>** input prompt). Aside from that, the rules that apply to using the command mode of the CLP also apply to using the interactive input mode.

When the CLP is run in batch mode, it is assumed that the commands to be executed have been stored in an ASCII text file. Therefore, in batch mode, the initial command passed to the CLP must be in the format **"db2 -f** *xxxxxxxx.xxx"* where *xxxxxxxx.xxx* is the name of the file that contains the set of commands that are to be executed.

Figure 2-21 shows how the CLP looks on a Windows NT server when it is run in interactive input mode.

The Performance Monitor

The Performance Monitor is a tool that, when activated, gathers comprehensive information about the state of a DB2 Universal Database system. The information collected can then be used to analyze, fine-tune, and manage a database's overall performance.

With the DB2 Performance Monitor, users can

- Identify and analyze performance problems with the Database Manager.
- Identify and analyze performance problems in database applications.
- Use the early warning system to detect potential problems in database applications or with the Database Manager.
- Automate the actions that need to take place to correct problems that are discovered.
- Define the set of statistics to be monitored, in addition to using the default set that is provided.

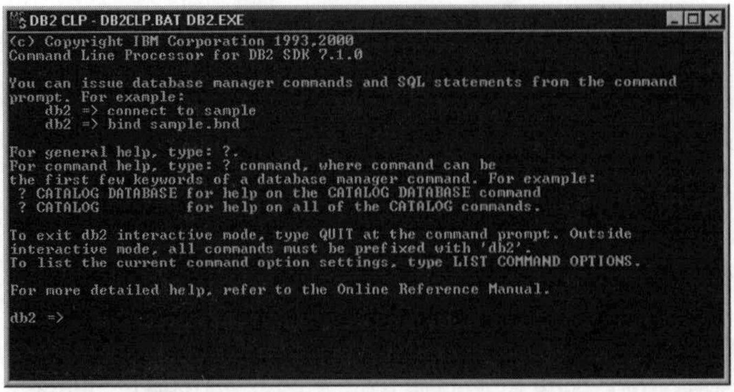

Figure 2-21   The Command Line Processor (in interactive input mode)

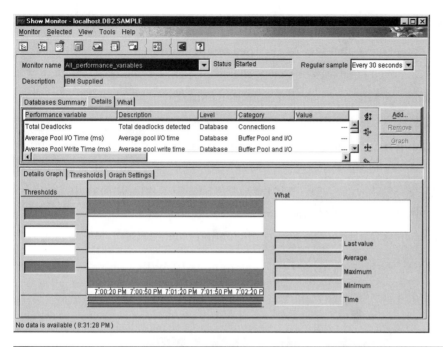

Figure 2-22 The Performance Monitor

Figure 2-22 shows how the Performance Monitor looks on a Windows NT server.

NOTE When DB2 Universal Database is installed on the Windows NT or Windows 2000 platform, the Windows Performance Monitor can be used to monitor both database and system performance.

The Client Configuration Assistant (CCA)

The Client Configuration Assistant (CCA) is primarily a tool that contains several wizards that are designed to help you set up clients that access local or remote DB2 servers. It can also be used to help configure DB2 Connect servers. The CCA enables you to maintain a list of databases your applications can connect to and with it, you can quickly catalog nodes and databases without having to know the inherent complexities of performing these tasks.

With the CCA, you can

- Catalog databases so that they can be used by applications.
- Remove cataloged databases or change the properties of a cataloged database.
- Add, modify, and delete database connection entries.
- Configure CLI/ODBC settings.
- Export and import client profiles that contain database and configuration information for a given client.
- Test connections to local or remote databases identified on your system.
- Bind applications to a cataloged database.
- Fine-tune client Database Manager configuration parameters.

Figure 2-23 shows how the Client Configuration Assistant looks on a Windows NT server.

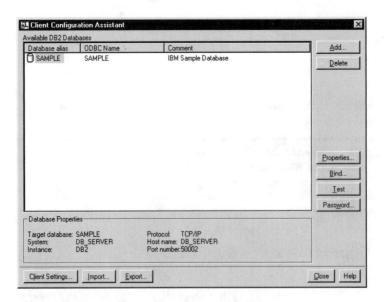

Figure 2-23   The Client Configuration Assistant

Summary

The goal of this chapter was to introduce you to the different flavors of DB2 Universal Database that are available and to the suite of add-on products that collectively make up the DB2 Family. The core of the DB2 Family consists of six object-relational database management system editions that support increasingly complex database/user environments and two developer's editions that provide tools for building DB2 database applications. These editions are

- DB2 Everyplace (Personal Edition and Enterprise Edition)
- DB2 Universal Database Satellite Edition
- DB2 Universal Database Personal Edition
- DB2 Universal Database Workgroup Edition
- DB2 Universal Database Enterprise Edition
- DB2 Universal Database Enterprise-Extended Edition
- DB2 Personal Developer's Edition
- DB2 Universal Developer's Edition

All of these editions contain the same database management engine, recognize ANSI SQL, and provide graphical user interfaces for constructing and submitting queries and for performing database administration operations. With the exception of DB2 Everyplace, DB2 Universal Database Satellite Edition, DB2 Universal Database Personal Edition, and DB2 Personal Developer's Edition, all are multi-user relational database management systems that can be accessed from one or more remote client workstations through software known as Client Application Enablers (CAEs).

In addition to providing a robust object-relational database server, five of the six database management editions that make up the core of the DB2 Family contain the following common client components:

- DB2 Run-Time Client
- DB2 Administration Client
- DB2 Application Development Client

Any one of these client components can be installed on any number of workstations; however, the client component you choose to install should be dependant upon 1) the requirements of a particular workstation, and 2) the operating system used on that workstation.

In addition to the eight editions that make up the core of the DB2 Family, IBM provides several other products that expand the capabilities and functionality of DB2 Universal Database. These products, which make up the remainder of the DB2 Family, include

- DB2 Connect Personal Edition
- DB2 Connect Enterprise Edition
- DB2 Image, Audio, and Video Extenders
- DB2 Text Extender
- DB2 XML Extender
- DB2 Spatial Extender
- DB2 Net Search Extender
- DB2 Warehouse Manager
- Query Patroller
- DB2 OLAP Server Starter Kit
- Net.Data

With the exception of DB2 Everyplace, each edition of DB2 Universal Database also contains a rich set of tools that enable you to administer and access data stored in DB2 databases. This tool set consists of the

- Control Center
- Command Center
  - SQL Assist
  - Visual Explain
- Script Center
- Alert Center
- Journal
- Command Line Processor (CLP)
- Performance Monitor
- Client Configuration Assistant

Along with this set of tools, each edition also includes a series of wizards that provide step-by-step guidance for performing many of the database administration functions available. Not only do these wizards provide help for performing most administrative tasks, but some of them can also make calculations and recommendations using information they collect as they are executed.

Questions

1. Which of the following products is allowed to access other DB2 servers, but cannot accept requests from other remote clients?
   a. DB2 Universal Database Personal Edition
   b. DB2 Universal Database Workgroup Edition
   c. DB2 Universal Database Enterprise Edition
   d. DB2 Universal Database Enterprise-Extended Edition

2. Which of the following products must be installed in order to build an application on AIX that will access a DB2 for OS/390 database?
   a. DB2 Universal Database Enterprise Edition
   b. DB2 Personal Developer's Edition
   c. DB2 Universal Developer's Edition
   d. DB2 Universal Database Enterprise Edition and DB2 Connect Enterprise Edition

3. Which of the following products contains both a DB2 server and a set of tools for creating applications that interact with DB2 databases?
   a. DB2 Universal Database Workgroup Edition
   b. DB2 Personal Developer's Edition
   c. DB2 Universal Database Enterprise Edition
   d. DB2 Universal Developer's Edition

4. A client application on OS/390 must access a DB2 server on Windows, UNIX, or OS/2. At a minimum, which of the following must be installed on the DB2 server workstation?
   a. DB2 Connect Enterprise Edition
   b. DB2 Universal Database Enterprise Edition
   c. DB2 Universal Database Workgroup Edition and DB2 Connect Enterprise Edition
   d. DB2 Universal Database Enterprise Edition and DB2 Connect Enterprise Edition

5. What is the main function of DB2 Connect?
   a. APPC Gateway
   b. DRDA Application Requestor
   c. TCP/IP Gateway
   d. DRDA Application Server

6. Which of the following tools can be used to catalog a database?
   a. Visual Explain
   b. Alert Center
   c. Journal
   d. Client Configuration Assistant

7. Which of the following processes does DB2 Warehouse Manager NOT perform?
   a. Query
   b. Loading
   c. Extraction
   d. Transformation

8. Which of the following DB2 components provides resource contention management for large-scale data warehouses?
   a. Warehouse Manager
   b. Spatial Extender
   c. Query Patroller
   d. OLAP Server

9. Which of the following tools enables the entering and execution of an SQL statement, and then checking to see how it was optimized?
   a. Control Center
   b. Script Center
   c. Visual Explain
   d. Command Center

10. In which of the following tools is the threshold value for an alert situation defined?
    a. Performance Monitor
    b. Control Center
    c. Alert Center
    d. Journal

Answers

1. **A**. DB2 Universal Database Personal Edition can be used as a remote client to other DB2 servers; however, it can only accept requests from local applications.

2. **C**. DB2 Universal Developer's Edition contains both the tools to build an application and a DRDA Application Requestor. DB2 Personal Developer's Edition does not provide a DRDA Application Requestor.

3. **D**. The key word here is *server*. Because DB2 Universal Database Personal Edition (which is packaged with DB2 Personal Developer's Edition) does not accept requests from remote clients, only the DB2 Universal Developer's Edition contains both a DB2 server and the tools that can be used to build applications.

4. **B**. DB2 Universal Database Enterprise Edition contains both a DRDA Application Requestor and a DRDA Application Server. Client applications on OS/390 only communicate with DB2 servers on Windows, UNIX, or OS/2 via a DRDA Application Server.

5. **B**. Both DB2 Connect Personal Edition and DB2 Connect Enterprise Edition provide DRDA Application Requestor support. They do not provide DRDA Application Server support.

6. **D**. One of the primary uses of the Client Configuration Assistant is to catalog remote server databases on client workstations so they can be accessed by applications.

7. **A**. DB2 Warehouse Manager can be used to load data into a data warehouse, cleanse/transform data stored in a data warehouse, and extract data from a data warehouse. It cannot be used to construct queries against a data warehouse.

8. **C**. Query Patroller provides a way for database administrators (DBAs) to manage the resources required by queries so that hundreds of users can safely submit queries on multiterabyte class systems and receive results within an acceptable time frame.

9. **D**. Because Visual Explain is actually part of the Command Center, the Command Center is the tool that provides a way to both enter and execute a query, and examine the access plan generated by that query.

10. **A**. Threshold values for monitored items are set in the Performance Monitor. This is also where you indicate whether or not a message is to be sent to the Alert Center whenever one or more of the threshold values are exceeded.

Instances and Security

3

In this chapter, you will learn

- What an instance is and how instances are typically used
- The purpose of the DB2 Administration Server (DAS) instance
- How (and where) users are authenticated
- How authorization levels and privileges determine what a user can and cannot do
- How authorization levels and privileges are given to (granted) and taken away from (revoked) an individual or a group of users

The second objective of the DB2 Universal Database Family Fundamentals exam is to evaluate your understanding of instances—particularly the DB2 Administration Server (DAS) instance—and to test your knowledge about the authorization levels and privileges that are used by DB2 Universal Database to protect data and database objects against unauthorized access and modification. Knowing what authorization levels and privileges are available is just as important as knowing how to give a user the right combination of authorizations and privileges to control exactly what he or she can and cannot do while working with an instance or database. This chapter is designed to introduce you to the concept of instances and to provide an in-depth look at the various authorization levels and privileges that are provided by DB2 Universal Database, Version 7.x.

TIP Nine percent of the DB2 Universal Database Family Fundamentals exam is designed to test your knowledge of DB2 instances and security.

Instances

DB2 Universal Database sees the world as a hierarchy of several different types of objects. Workstations on which any edition of DB2 Universal Database has been installed are known as system objects and they occupy the highest level of this hierarchy. Systems objects can represent systems that are accessible to other DB2 clients or servers within a network, or they can represent stand-alone systems that neither have access to nor can be accessed from other DB2 clients or servers.

When any edition of DB2 Universal Database is installed on a particular workstation (system), program files for the DB2 Database Manager are physically copied to a specific location on that workstation and one instance of the DB2 Database Manager is created and assigned to the system as part of the installation process. (Instances comprise the next level in the object hierarchy.) If needed, additional instances of the DB2 Database Manager can be created for a particular system. Each time a new instance is created, it references the DB2 Database Manager program files that were stored on that workstation during the installation process; thus, each instance behaves like a separate installation of DB2 Universal Database, even though all instances within a particular system share the same binary code. Although all instances share the same physical code, they can be run concurrently and each has its own environment (which can be modified by altering the contents of its configuration file).

You may be wondering why you would want to create multiple instances of the DB2 Database Manager on the same physical machine. Reasons for creating multiple instances are to

- Separate your development environment from your production environment
- Obtain optimum performance for each application that is to be run against a particular system. (For example, you may wish to create an instance for each application and then fine-tune each instance specifically for the application it will service.)
- Protect sensitive data from database administrators. For example, you could have your payroll database stored on its own instance so that owners of other instances (on the same server) cannot see payroll data.

The default instance for a particular system is defined by the *DB2INSTANCE* environment variable and this is the instance that is used for most operations. However, you can attach to any other instance available (including instances that exist on other systems). Once attached, you can perform maintenance and utility tasks that can only be done at the instance level (for example, create a database, force applications off a database, monitor database activity, or change the contents of the DB2 Database Manager configuration file that is associated with that particular instance).

Each instance controls access to one or more databases. (Databases make up the third level in the object hierarchy.) Every database within an instance is assigned a unique name, has its own set of system catalog tables (which are used to keep track of objects that are created within the database), and has its own configuration file. Each database also has its own set of grantable authorities and privileges that govern how users interact with the data and database objects stored in it. Figure 3-1 shows the hierarchic relationship among systems, instances, and databases; Figure 3-2 shows how this hierarchy is presented in the Control Center.

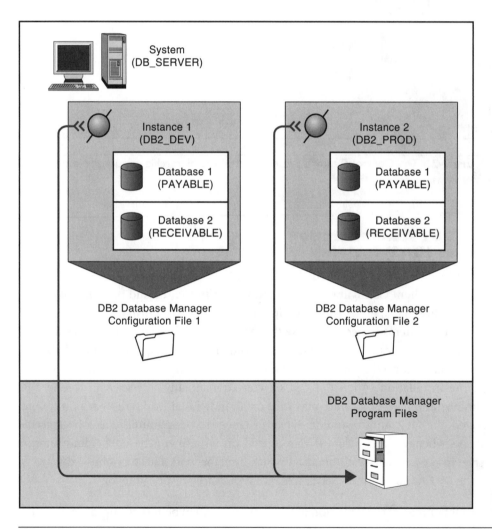

Figure 3-1 Hierarchic relationship among DB2 systems, instances, and databases

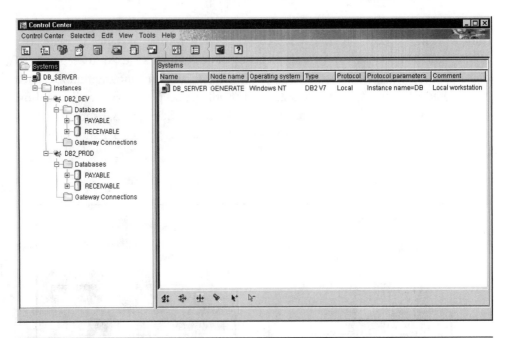

Figure 3-2 The Control Center's presentation of the hierarchic relationship among DB2 systems, instances, and databases

The DB2 Administration Server (DAS) Instance

Most of the tools that are provided with DB2 Universal Database (such as the Control Center, the Client Configuration Assistant, the Script Center, and so on) require their own instance that operates concurrently with all other instances that have been defined for a single system. To accommodate this need, a special instance, known as the DB2 Administration Server (DAS) instance, is automatically created as part of the DB2 Universal Database installation process. If for some reason this instance is not created during the installation process, it can be created manually; however, only one DB2 Administration Server instance may exist on an individual workstation at a time. Once created, the DB2 Administration Server instance runs continuously as a background process whenever the system it was created on is online. (The DB2 Administration Server instance is started automatically each time the workstation is rebooted.)

The DB2 Administration Server instance is primarily responsible for

- Obtaining the configuration of the operating system being used by the workstation that DB2 Universal Database is installed on

- Obtaining user and group authentication information

- Starting and stopping instances (other than the DAS instance)

- Setting up communications for DB2 Universal Database servers

- Enabling remote administration of DB2 Universal Database servers

- Attaching to instances (other than the DAS instance)

- Providing a mechanism for returning specific information about the DB2 Universal Database server to remote clients

- Collecting information (and displaying the results) for the DB2 Discovery tool that is provided as part of the Client Configuration Assistant

- Providing a facility for managing, scheduling, and executing user-defined DB2 and operating system command scripts

Managing the DB2 Administration Server Instance

Because the DB2 Administration Server instance is created and started automatically, you rarely have to interact directly with it (or for that matter, even concern yourself with its existence). However, in the event you need to work directly with the DB2 Administration Server instance, the following are some of the commands that are available:

- **db2admin start**   Starts the DB2 Administration Server instance

- **db2admin stop**   Stops the DB2 Administration Server instance

- **db2admin create**   Creates the DB2 Administration Server instance (Windows and OS/2)

- **dasicrt**   Creates the DB2 Administration Server instance (UNIX)

- **db2admin drop**   Removes the DB2 Administration Server instance (Windows and OS/2)

- **dasidrop**   Removes the DB2 Administration Server instance (UNIX)

- **db2admin setid**   Modifies the user account that is associated with the DB2 Administration Server instance

- **db2 get admin cfg**   Displays the contents of the DB2 Database Manager configuration file that is associated with the DB2 Administration Server instance

- **db2 update admin cfg**   Enables you to update one or more parameter values in the DB2 Database Manager configuration file that is associated with the DB2 Administration Server instance

- **db2 reset admin cfg**   Enables you to set all of the parameters in the DB2 Database Manager configuration file that is associated with the DAS instance to their recommended default values

---

 NOTE When you update or reset the contents of the DB2 Database Manager configuration file that is associated with the DB2 Administration Server instance, you must stop and restart the DB2 Administration Server instance before any changes made will take effect.

Controlling Database Access

Protecting data against unauthorized access and modification is an essential task that every database management system must perform. DB2 Universal Database uses a combination of external security services and internal access control measures to perform this essential task. In most cases, three levels of security are used to control access to data stored in a DB2 Universal Database database. The first level controls access to the instance that the database was created under (using a process known as authentication); the second level controls access to the database itself; and the third level controls access to data and/or the data objects that reside within the database (the second and third levels are performed by checking authorities and privileges).

Authentication

The first step in managing database security is to verify that the user really is who he or she says they are. This step is called authentication. Authentication is performed by an external security facility that is not provided as part of DB2 Universal Database. This security facility may be part of the operating system (which is the case with UNIX, Windows NT, and many others), a separate product (such as Distributed Computing Environment [DCE] Security Services), or it may not exist at all (which, by default, is the case with Windows 95 and Windows 98). Most security facilities require two items in order to authenticate a user: a unique user ID and a corresponding password. The user ID identifies the user to the security facility; the password, which is information that is only known by both the user and the security facility, is used to verify the user during the authentication process.

How and where authentication takes place is determined by the authentication type being used by an instance. The authentication type is stored at the server (and sometimes at the client as well) in DB2 Database Manager configuration files that are associated with each instance. (The actual value is stored in the *authentication* configuration parameter.) The following authentication types are available:

- **SERVER**   Authentication occurs on the server using the security facility that is provided by the server's operating system. When a user ID and password are specified during an attempt to attach to an instance or connect to a database, they are checked at the server to determine whether or not the user is permitted to access the instance. By default, this is the authentication type used when an instance is first created.

- **SERVER_ENCRYPT**   This is similar to SERVER in the sense that authentication occurs on the server using the security facility that is provided by the server's operating system. However, with this authentication type, all passwords are encrypted at the client before they are sent to the server.

- **CLIENT**   Authentication typically occurs on the client workstation or database partition where a client application is invoked using the security facility that is provided by the client's operating system. When a user ID and password are specified during an attempt to attach to an instance or connect to a database, they are checked at the client/node to determine whether or not the user is permitted to access the instance. If the server indicates that CLIENT authentication will be used, two other parameters (which we will look at shortly) are used to determine the final authentication type.

- **DCS**   Primarily used to catalog a database that is accessed using DB2 Connect, this authentication type is similar to SERVER in the sense that authentication occurs on the server using the security facility that is provided by the server's operating system—unless the server is being accessed via Distributed Relational Database Architecture (DRDA) Application Server (AS) architecture using the Advanced Program-to-Program Communications (APPC) protocol. In this case, the DCS authentication type indicates that authentication will occur at the server, but only in the APPC layer.

- **DCS_ENCRYPT**   This is similar to DCS; however, with this authentication type, all passwords are encrypted at the client before they are sent to the server.

- **DCE**   Authentication occurs on the server using the security facility that is provided by the Distributed Computing Environment (DCE) Security Services.

- **DCE_SERVER_ENCRYPT**   This is similar to DCE; however, with this authentication type, all passwords are encrypted at the client before they are sent to the server.

- **KERBEROS**   This can be used when both the client and the server are using the Windows 2000 operating system, which supports the Kerberos security protocol. The Kerberos security protocol performs authentication as a third-party authentication service by using conventional cryptography to create a shared secret key. This key becomes a user's credential and is used to verify the identity of users during all occasions when local or network services are requested; the key eliminates the need to pass the user ID and password across the network as text.

- **KRB_SERVER_ENCRYPT**   The server recognizes and accepts either the KERBEROS or the SERVER_ENCRYPT authentication scheme. If the client's authentication type is KERBEROS, authentication is performed using the Kerberos security system. If the client's authentication type is not KERBEROS, the server's acts as if the SERVER_ENCRYPT authentication type was specified.

 NOTE   The authentication type used by the default instance for a particular system (which is defined by the **DB2INSTANCE** environment variable) determines how access to the database server and to all databases under its control will be authenticated.

Trusted vs. Untrusted Clients

We saw earlier that if a client uses the CLIENT authentication type, authentication occurs on the client workstation or database partition where a client application is invoked by using the security facility that is provided by the client's operating system. However, if a server uses the CLIENT authentication type, additional information must be provided so the DB2 Database Manager will know which clients are responsible for validating users and which clients depend on the server for user authentication. To help make this determination, clients are placed into one of two groups:

- **Trusted clients**   Clients that use an operating system that provides an integrated security facility (for example, Windows NT, Windows 2000, OS/2, all supported versions of UNIX, MVS, OS/390, VM, VSE, and AS/400)

- **Untrusted clients**   Clients that use an operating system that does not provide an integrated security facility (for example, Windows 95, and Windows 98)

How and where authentication for both trusted clients and untrusted clients takes place is also specified in the DB2 Database Manager configuration files that are associated with each instance. (The actual values are stored in the *trust_allclnts* and *trust_* *clntauth* configuration parameters.) If the *trust_allclnts* configuration parameter is set to YES (which is the default), the DB2 Database Manager for that instance assumes that all clients that will access the server are trusted clients. This implies that all clients can validate the user on behalf of the server. However, if this configuration parameter is set to NO, the DB2 Database Manager assumes that one or more untrusted clients will access the server; therefore, all users must be authenticated at the server. (If this configuration parameter is set to DRDAONLY, only MVS, OS/390, VM, VSE, and OS/400 clients will be treated as trusted clients.)

In some cases, it may be desirable to perform authentication at the server, even for trusted clients. For this reason, the *trust_clntauth* configuration parameter is used to indicate where trusted clients are to be validated. By accepting the default value for this parameter (which is CLIENT), all users of trusted clients are validated at the client workstation. By setting this configuration parameter to SERVER, all users of trusted clients will be authenticated at the server.

Authorities

Once a user has been authenticated, the DB2 Database Manager must determine whether or not the user has the authority needed to perform the task requested. This determination is made by evaluating the set of authorities and privileges that have either been assigned to an individual or that have been assigned to a group that an individual is a member of. Authorities convey rights that are required in order to perform certain kinds of administrative and maintenance operations. Privileges convey rights that are required in order to perform certain actions on a specific database or database object.

With DB2 Universal Database, five authorization levels are used to control which administrative and maintenance operations a user can perform. Three of these authorization levels apply to the DB2 Database Manager instance (and all databases that are managed by that instance), whereas the remaining two only apply to a specific database. The five levels of authority that are recognized by DB2 Universal Database are

- System Administrator authority (SYSADM)

- System Control authority (SYSCTRL)

- System Maintenance authority (SYSMAINT)

- Database Administrator authority (DBADM)

- Load authority (LOAD)

Figure 3-3 shows the relationship among these five authorities, as well as their span of control (that is, instance versus database).

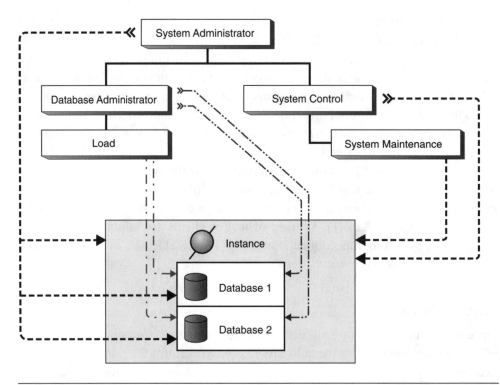

Figure 3-3   Hierarchy and relationship of DB2 Universal Database authorities

Each of the instance-level authorities can only be given to a group of users (rather than to one or more individuals) and the names of the groups that have been given these authorities are recorded in the DB2 Database Manager configuration files that are associated with each instance. On the other hand, the two database-level authorities can be held by a group of users and/or by one or more individuals. Groups and individuals that have been given these authorities are recorded in the system catalog table SYSCAT.DBAUTH, which is part of the database that the authority applies to.

> **TIP**   The names of the groups that have been given instance-level authorities can be seen by executing the **GET DATABASE MANAGER CONFIGURATION** command and examining the values shown for the *sysadmn_group, sysctrl_ group,* and *sysmaint_group* parameters. The names of the users and groups that have been given database-level authorities can be seen by running a query against the appropriate **SYSCAT.DBAUTH** system catalog table.

System Administrator Authority

The System Administrator authority is the highest level of administrative authority recognized by DB2 Universal Database. Users who belong to the group that has this authority have the ability to run any DB2 Universal Database utility, execute any DB2 command, SQL statement, or API function call, and may access any database or database object that is being managed by a specific DB2 Database Manager instance. Additionally, users with System Administrator authority may perform the following tasks:

- Migrate a database.
- Modify the values stored in the DB2 Database Manager configuration file that is associated with the instance. (This includes specifying the groups that have System Control and/or System Maintenance authority.)
- Give (grant) an individual or a group of users Database Administrator authority.

Users with System Administrator authority may also perform the same functions that users with System Control authority, System Maintenance authority, and Database Administration authority may perform.

NOTE When a user with System Administrator authority creates a database, he or she is automatically given Database Manager authority on that database. If the user is removed from the System Administrator group, he or she can still access any database that he or she created, as a Database Administrator, unless that authority is explicitly removed (revoked).

System Control Authority

The System Control authority is the highest level of instance control authority recognized by DB2 Universal Database. Users who belong to the group that has this authority have the ability to perform maintenance and utility operations against a specific DB2 Database Manager instance and against any databases that fall under that instance's control. However, users with System Control authority are not automatically given the right to access or modify data stored in any database that is controlled by the instance. System Control authority is designed to enable special users to administer an instance that contains sensitive data that they most likely do not have access to.

Users with System Control authority or higher may perform the following tasks:

- Update entries in a database, node, or distributed connection services (DCS) directory.
- Force users off the system.

- Create or destroy (drop) a database.

- Create, alter, or drop a table space.

- Create a new database from an existing database backup image.

Users with System Control authority may also perform the same functions that users with System Maintenance authority may perform. In addition, users with System Control authority are automatically given the CONNECT privilege for every database that is being managed by the instance.

 NOTE When a user with System Control authority creates a database, he or she is automatically given Database Manager authority on that database. If the user is removed from the System Control group, he or she can still access any database he or she created, as a Database Administrator, unless that authority is explicitly revoked.

System Maintenance Authority

The System Maintenance authority is the second highest level of instance control authority recognized by DB2 Universal Database. Users who belong to the group that has this authority have the ability to perform maintenance and utility operations against a specific DB2 Database Manager instance and against any databases that fall under that instance's control. However, users with System Maintenance authority are not allowed to create new databases and/or drop existing databases, and are not automatically given the right to access or modify data stored in any of the databases that already exist. Like System Control authority, System Maintenance authority is designed to enable special users to administer an instance that contains sensitive data that they most likely do not have access to.

Users with System Maintenance authority or higher may perform the following tasks:

- Modify the values stored in database configuration files.

- Make a backup image of a database or a table space.

- Restore a database using a backup image (the database must already exist).

- Restore a table space using a backup image.

- Perform a roll-forward recovery operation.

- Start or stop a DB2 Database Manager instance.

- Run a trace.

- Take database system monitor snapshots of a DB2 Database Manager instance or its databases.
- Query the state of a table space.
- Update log history files.
- Quiesce (restrict access to) a table space.
- Reorganize a table.
- Collect catalog statistics using the RUNSTATS utility.

In addition, users with System Maintenance authority are automatically given the CONNECT privilege for every database that is being managed by a particular instance.

Database Administrator Authority

The Database Administrator authority is the second highest level of administrative authority recognized by DB2 Universal Database. Users who have this authority have the ability to run most DB2 Universal Database utilities, issue database-specific DB2 commands, and access data and/or database objects that are stored in a specific database. However, they can only perform these functions on the database for which Database Administrator authority is held.

Users with Database Administrator authority or higher may perform the following tasks:

- Query the state of a table space.
- Update log history files.
- Quiesce (restrict access to) a table space.
- Reorganize a table.
- Collect catalog statistics using the RUNSTATS utility.

Users with Database Administrator authority or System Administrator may also

- Read database log files.
- Create, activate, and drop event monitors.

In addition, users with Database Administrator authority may perform the same functions that users who hold all of the database privileges available may perform. (In fact, when a user is given Database Administrator authority, he or she receives all but one of the database privileges available as well.)

NOTE When a user creates a new database, he or she is automatically given Database Manager authority (along with the appropriate privileges) on that database.

Load Authority

The Load authority is a special level of database authority that is used to determine whether a user holds the right to bulk load data into an existing table, using either the AutoLoader utility or the LOAD command/API. In previous releases, the Load authority was only available with DB2 Universal Database for OS/390; now it is available for the entire DB2 Universal Database family. Load authority is designed to allow users to perform bulk load operations without having to have System Administrator or Database Administrator authority. This enables users to perform more DB2 functions, while giving Database Administrators more granular control over the administration of their database.

In addition to being able to bulk load data, users with Load authority or higher may

- Query the state of a table space.
- Quiesce (restrict access to) a table space.
- Collect catalog statistics using the RUNSTATS utility.

In addition to holding Load authority, users wishing to perform bulk load operations must also hold the following:

- INSERT privilege on the table data is to be loaded into when the load utility is invoked in INSERT mode, TERMINATE mode (to terminate a previous load insert operation), or RESTART mode (to restart a previous load insert operation).
- INSERT and DELETE privilege on the table data is to be loaded into when the load utility is invoked in REPLACE mode, TERMINATE mode (to terminate a previous load replace operation), or RESTART mode (to restart a previous load replace operation).
- INSERT privilege on the exception table used, if such a table is used as part of the load operation.

Privileges

As mentioned earlier, privileges are used to convey the right to perform certain actions on a specific object (for example, a table, a view, an index, and so on) within a database to an individual or a group of users. With DB2 Universal Database, two types of privileges exist: database and object privileges.

Database Privileges

Database privileges apply to a database as a whole, rather than to a specific object within a database. Figure 3-4 shows the different types of database privileges available.
  As you can see in Figure 3-4, six different database privileges exist:

- **CONNECT**   Conveys the right to establish a connection to (and access) a database.

- **CREATETAB**   Conveys the right to create new tables in a database.

- **BINDADD**   Conveys the right to create packages in a database when precompiling and/or binding application program files to that database.

- **CREATE_NOT_FENCED**   Conveys the right to create user-defined functions (UDFs) that are considered safe enough to run in the DB2 Database Manager operating environment's process or address space. If a function is registered as FENCED, the DB2 Database Manager insulates its internal resources (for example, data buffers and control blocks) so that they cannot be accessed by that function. Most functions will have the option of running as FENCED or NOT FENCED.

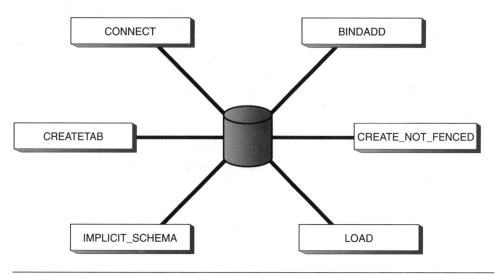

Figure 3-4   Database privileges

- **IMPLICIT_SCHEMA**   Conveys the right to implicitly create a new schema by creating an object with a schema name that is different from the schema names that already exist in a database.

- **LOAD**   Conveys the right to load data into existing tables.

 NOTE   When a user is given Database Administrator authority, he or she automatically receives **CONNECT, CREATETAB, BINDADD, CREATE_NOT_FENCED,** and **IMPLICIT_SCHEMA** privileges.

Object Privileges

Unlike database privileges, which apply to a database as a whole, object privileges apply only to a specific object within a database. The object privileges that are available with DB2 Universal Database are categorized as follows:

- **Ownership or CONTROL privileges**   Usually, when an individual creates a database object, he or she receives full control of that object. Control of an object is given to a user through a special ownership privilege, known as the CONTROL privilege. The CONTROL privilege is like a master privilege that includes all privileges that are applicable to a given object. The CONTROL privilege also conveys the right to remove (drop) the object from the database and the right to grant or revoke any applicable privilege for that particular object (other than CONTROL privilege) to/from other users and groups. In most cases, the creator of a database object automatically receives CONTROL privilege for that object. This rule has one exception: the creator of a view will only receive CONTROL privilege for that view if he or she also has CONTROL privilege for each base table that is referenced by the view.

- **Individual privileges**   Individual privileges convey the right to perform a specific operation on a specific object.

- **Implicit privileges**   Implicit privileges are privileges that are automatically given to a user when a higher level privilege is explicitly given to a user (refer to the section on the Database Administrator privilege for an example). It is important to remember that implicit privileges are not automatically revoked when the higher level privilege that caused them to be granted is revoked.

- **Indirect privileges**   Indirect privileges are typically associated with packages. When a user executes a package that requires additional privileges (for example, a package that deletes a row of data from a table requires DELETE privilege on that table), the user is indirectly given those privileges while he or she is executing the package. Indirect privileges are temporary and do not exist outside the scope in which they are granted.

Figure 3-5 shows the ownership and individual object privileges that are available.

As you can see in Figure 3-5, individual privileges vary among database objects. The following sections describe the individual privileges that are available for a particular object.

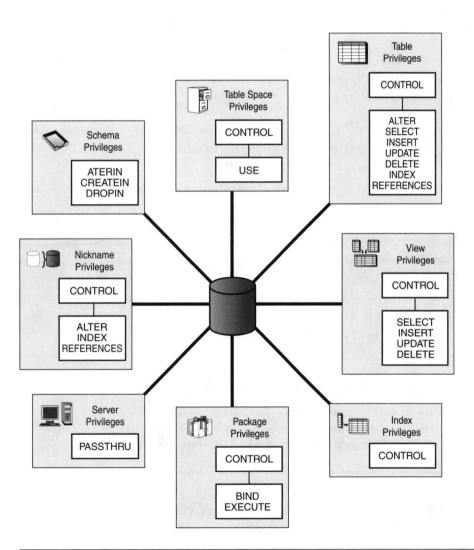

Figure 3-5   Object privileges (ownership and individual)

Schema Privileges   Schema privileges are designed to control what users can (and cannot) do with a particular schema. The following schema privileges are available:

- **CREATEIN**   Conveys the right to create objects within a schema
- **ALTERIN**   Conveys the right to change the comment associated with any database object in a schema or to alter any table within a schema
- **DROPIN**   Conveys the right to remove (drop) any database object stored in a schema

The owner of a schema (typically the creator) is implicitly given these privileges along with the ability to grant any combination of these privileges to other users and groups. The database objects that are manipulated within a schema include tables, views, indexes, packages, user-defined data types, user-defined functions, triggers, stored procedures, and aliases.

Table Space Privileges   Table space privileges are designed to control what users can (and cannot) do with a particular table space. In addition to the CONTROL privilege, the following table space privilege is available:

- **USE**   Conveys the right to create tables within a table space

In previous releases, the USE table space privilege was only available with DB2 Universal Database for OS/390; now it is available for the entire DB2 Universal Database family. The USE privilege prevents users from creating tables in table spaces that they have not been given access to. It also provides administrators with more control over a database. The owner of a table space (typically the creator who must have System Administrator or System Control authority) is implicitly given both the CONTROL privilege and the USE privilege along with the ability to grant the USE privilege to other users and groups.

NOTE   The USE privilege cannot be used to convey the right to create tables within the SYSCATSPACE table space or within any system temporary table space. By default, when a database is created, the USE privilege for table space USERSPACE1 is given to the group PUBLIC; however, this privilege can be revoked.

Table Privileges   Table privileges are designed to control what users can (and cannot) do with a particular database table. In addition to the CONTROL privilege, the following table privileges are available:

- **ALTER**   Conveys the right to add columns to a table, add or change comments associated with a table and/or any of its columns, create a primary key for a table, create a unique constraint for a table, and create or drop a check constraint for a table. Users who have been given this privilege also have the right to create triggers for the table (however, additional object privileges may be required).

- **SELECT**   Conveys the right to retrieve data from a table, to create a view that references the table, and to run the Export utility.

- **INSERT**   Conveys the right to add data to a table and to run the Import utility.

- **UPDATE**   Conveys the right to modify data in a table. This privilege can be granted for the entire table, or it can be restricted to one or more specific columns within the table.

- **DELETE**   Conveys the right to remove rows of data from a table.

- **INDEX**   Conveys the right to create an index for a table.

- **REFERENCES**   Conveys the right to create and drop foreign key constraints that reference a table in a parent relationship. This privilege can be granted for the entire table, or it can be restricted to one or more specific columns within the table.

The owner of a table (typically the creator) is implicitly given these privileges, along with the CONTROL privilege, and the ability to grant any combination of these privileges (excluding the CONTROL privilege) to other users and groups.

NOTE   A user must have **CONNECT** privilege on the database before he or she can use any of the table privileges available.

View Privileges   View privileges are designed to control what users can (and cannot) do with a particular view. In addition to the CONTROL privilege, the following view privileges are available:

- **SELECT**   Conveys the right to retrieve data from a view, create a view that references the view, and run the Export utility.

- **INSERT**   Conveys the right to add data to an updateable table and run the Import utility.

- **UPDATE**   Conveys the right to modify data in an updateable view. This privilege can be granted for the entire view, or it can be restricted to one or more specific columns within the view.

- **DELETE**   Conveys the right to remove rows of data from an updateable view.

The owner of a view (typically the creator) is implicitly given these privileges, the CONTROL privilege for the view if he or she holds CONTROL privilege on every table that the view references, and the ability to grant any combination of these privileges (excluding the CONTROL privilege) to other users and groups.

 NOTE   A user must have **CONNECT** privilege on the database before he or she can use any of the view privileges available.

Index Privileges   Only one index privilege is available. That privilege is the CONTROL privilege, which in this case conveys the right to remove (drop) an index from the database. The owner of an index (typically the creator) is implicitly given the CONTROL privilege. However, the owner is not given the ability to grant that privilege to other users and groups unless he or she holds System Administrator or Database Administrator authority.

Package Privileges   A package is a database object that contains the information needed by the DB2 Database Manager to access data in the most efficient way possible in order to meet the needs of a specific application program. Package privileges are designed to control what users can (and cannot) do with a particular package. In addition to the CONTROL privilege (which in this case provides the user with the ability to rebind, drop, or execute a package as well as the ability to grant those privileges to others), the following package privileges are available:

- **BIND**   Conveys the right to rebind a package that has already been bound to a database. However, in order to rebind a package, a user must have, in addition to the BIND privilege for that package, the privileges that are needed to execute each SQL statement stored in the package.

- **EXECUTE**   Conveys the right to execute a package. A user that has EXECUTE privilege for a particular package can execute that package, even if he or she does not have the privileges that are needed to execute the SQL statements stored in the package. That's because any privileges needed to execute the SQL statements are implicitly granted to the package user. It is important to note that in order for privileges to be implicitly granted, the creator of the package must hold privileges as an individual user or as a member of the group PUBLIC—not as a member of a named group.

The owner of a package (typically the creator) is implicitly given these privileges, along with the CONTROL privilege, and the ability to grant any combination of these privileges (excluding the CONTROL privilege) to other users and groups.

NOTE A user must have **CONNECT** privilege on the database before he or she can use any of the package privileges available.

Users who have the authority to execute a package containing nicknames do not need additional authorities or privileges for the nicknames within the package; however, they must be able to pass any authentication checks performed at the data source(s) in which the objects that are referenced by the nicknames are stored. Additionally, users must hold the appropriate authorizations and privileges for all referenced objects at the data source itself.

Server Privileges   A DB2 federated system is a distributed computing system that consists of a DB2 server, known as a *federated server* (in a DB2 installation, any number of DB2 instances can be configured to function as federated servers) and one or more data sources to which the federated server sends queries. Each data source consists of an instance of a relational database management system plus the database or databases that the instance supports. The data sources in a DB2 federated system can include Oracle instances as well as instances of any member of the DB2 family.

Server privileges are designed to control what users can (and cannot) do with a particular federated server. Only one server privilege is available. That privilege is the PASSTHRU privilege, which conveys the right to issue Data Definition Language (DDL) and Data Manipulation Language (DML) SQL statements directly to a data source (as pass-through operations).

Nickname Privileges   When a client application submits a distributed request to a federated database server, the server sends the request to the appropriate data source for processing. Such a request does not identify the data source itself; instead, it references tables and views within the data source by using nicknames that map to specific table and view names at the data source. Nicknames are not alternate names for tables and views in the same way that aliases are; instead, they are pointers by which a federated server references these objects.

Nickname privileges are designed to control what users can (and cannot) do with a particular nickname. Nickname privileges do not affect any privileges that might exist for the data source objects that are referenced by a nickname. In addition to the CONTROL privilege, the following nickname privileges are available:

- **ALTER** Conveys the right to change column names in a nickname, add or change the DB2 data type that a nickname column's data type maps to, and specify column options for a particular nickname column.

- **INDEX** Conveys the right to create an index specification on a nickname.

- **REFERENCES** Conveys the right to create and drop a foreign key that specifies a nickname as the parent in a relationship. This privilege can be granted for the entire nickname, or it can be restricted to one or more specific columns within the nickname.

The owner of a nickname (typically the creator) is implicitly given these privileges, along with the CONTROL privilege, and the ability to grant any combination of these privileges (excluding the CONTROL privilege) to other users and groups.

 NOTE A user must have **CONNECT** privilege on the database before he or she can use any of the nickname privileges available.

Granting and Revoking Authorities and Privileges

During the DB2 Universal Database installation process, System Administrator (SYSADM) authority is granted to the following users, by default (according to the operating system being used):

- **Windows 95/98**   Any Windows 95 or Windows 98 user

- **Windows NT/2000**   A valid DB2 username that belongs to the Administrators group

- **OS/2**   A valid DB2 user ID that belongs to the User Profile Management (UPM) Administrator or Local Administrator group

- **UNIX**   A valid DB2 username that belongs to the primary group of the instance owner's user ID

Once DB2 Universal Database is successfully installed, the individual who will act as the system administrator should create new usernames, group names, and passwords before creating the instances where the databases will reside. This action serves two purposes:

1. As mentioned earlier, the instance-level authorities (such as System Administrator, System Control, and System Maintenance authority) can only be given to a group of users. By creating new groups and storing the names of those groups in the DB2 Database Manager configuration file, the system administrator can control who gets instance-level authority.

2. By creating new usernames, group names, and passwords, the risk of a user other than the system administrator learning of the defaults and using them in an improper fashion is minimized.

Database-level authorities, database privileges, and object privileges can be given to (or taken from) an individual user or a group of users by any user who has the authority to do so. Database-level authorities, database privileges, and object privileges can be given to (granted) and taken away from (revoked) a user or a group of users by selecting *Authorities* or *Privileges* from the database and object menus found in the Control Center. Figure 3-6 shows how the Table Privileges dialog, which is used to grant and revoke table privileges might look after it has been activated by the Control Center.

Authorities and privileges can also be given to a user or a group of users by executing the appropriate form of the GRANT SQL statement. Authorities and privileges can be taken away from a user or group of users by executing the appropriate form of the REVOKE SQL statement. The syntax for these two statements are:

```
GRANT [Authority | Privilege, . . . ] ON [DATABASE | Object
[ObjectName] ] TO [Recipient, . . . ] <WITH GRANT OPTION>

REVOKE [Authority | Privilege, . . . ] ON [DATABASE | Object
[ObjectName] ] FROM [Forfeiter, . . . ]
```

where:

Authority   Identifies the authority(ies) to be given to or taken from a specific user, a specific group of users, or all users.

Privilege   Identifies the privilege(s) to be given to or taken from a specific user, a specific group of users, or all users.

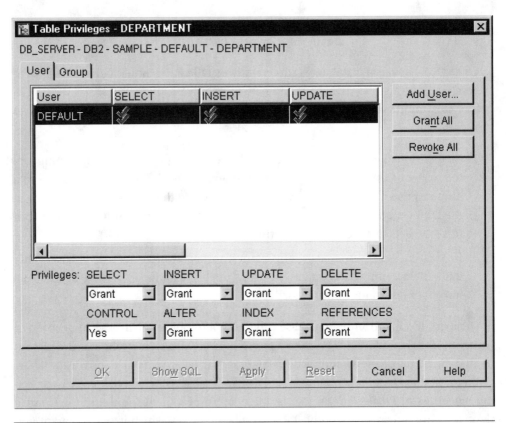

Figure 3-6   Control center tool for granting and revoking table privileges

Object	Identifies the type of object that the privilege(s) specified are associated with.
ObjectName	Identifies the specific object (by name) that the privilege(s) specified are associated with.
Recipient - Forfeiter	Identifies the user(s) and/or group(s) that are to receive/lose the privileges specified. This can be any of the following values:

- USER [*UserName*]
  Identifies a specific user that the specified authority(ies) and/or privilege(s) are to be given to.

- GROUP [*GroupName*]
  Identifies a specific group of users that the specified authority(ies) and/or privilege(s) are to be given to.

■ PUBLIC

Indicates that the specified authority(ies) and/or privilege(s) are to be given to the group PUBLIC (all users).

(If the `WITH GRANT OPTION` option is specified, the *Recipient* will be able to grant the schema, table, view, or nickname privilege(s) received to other users or groups of users).

For example, the following GRANT statement would give USER_1 the ability to retrieve rows of data from a table named EMPLOYEE, along with the ability to give this privilege to other users:

```
GRANT SELECT ON TABLE EMPLOYEE TO USER_1 WITH GRANT OPTION
```

On the other hand, the following REVOKE statement would take this ability away:

```
REVOKE SELECT ON TABLE EMPLOYEE FROM USER_1
```

Not only do authorization levels and privileges control what a user can and cannot do, they also control what authorities and privileges a user can grant and revoke to/from other users and groups. Table 3-1 shows the authorization requirements for granting and revoking database-level authorities, database privileges, and object privileges.

Table 3-1 Authorization Requirements for Granting and Revoking Authorities and Privileges

If a User Holds . . .	He or She Can Grant . . .	He or She Can Revoke . . .
System Administrator (SYSADM) authority	Database Administrator (DBADM) authority	Database Administrator (DBADM) authority
	Load (LOAD) authority Any database privilege	Load (LOAD) authority Any database privilege
	Any CONTROL privilege Any object privilege	Any CONTROL privilege Any object privilege
System Control (SYSCTRL) authority	Table space privileges	Table space privileges
System Maintenance (SYSMAINT) authority		
Database Administrator (DBADM) authority	Any database privilege	Any database privilege
	Any CONTROL privilege	Any CONTROL privilege
	Any object privilege	Any object privilege

Table 3-1 Authorization Requirements for Granting and Revoking Authorities and Privileges *(Continued)*

If a User Holds . . .	He or She Can Grant . . .	He or She Can Revoke . . .
CONTROL privilege on an object	Any object privilege associated with the object the user holds CONTROL privilege for	Any table, view, nickname, or package privilege associated with the table, view, nickname, or package the user holds CONTROL privilege for
An object privilege that was assigned with WITH GRANT OPTION specified	The object privilege that was assigned with WITH GRANT OPTION specified	

Summary

The goal of this chapter was to introduce you to instances (in particular, the DB2 Administration Server instance) and to the levels of security that are used to control access to data stored in a DB2 Universal Database database. When any edition of DB2 Universal Database is installed on a particular workstation, program files for the DB2 Database Manager are physically copied to a specific location on that workstation and one instance of the DB2 Database Manager is created and assigned to the system as part of the installation process. More than one instance can exist and each instance behaves like a separate installation of DB2 Universal Database, even though all instances within a particular system share the same binary code.

Most of the tools that are provided with DB2 Universal Database (such as the Control Center, the Client Configuration Assistant, the Script Center, and so on) require their own private instance that can operate concurrently with all other instances on a system. To accommodate this need, a special instance, known as the DB2 Administration Server (DAS) instance, is automatically created as part of the DB2 Universal Database installation process.

The DB2 Administration Server instance is primarily responsible for

- Obtaining the configuration of the operating system being used by the workstation that DB2 Universal Database is installed on
- Obtaining user and group authentication information
- Starting and stopping instances (other than the DAS instance)
- Setting up communications for DB2 Universal Database servers
- Enabling remote administration of DB2 Universal Database servers
- Attaching to instances (other than the DAS instance)

- Providing a mechanism for returning specific information about the DB2 Universal Database server to remote clients

- Collecting information (and displaying the results) for the Discovery tool that is provided as part of the Client Configuration Assistant

- Providing a facility for managing, scheduling, and executing user-defined DB2 and operating system command scripts

Because the DB2 Administration Server instance is created and started automatically, you rarely have to interact directly with it (or for that matter, even concern yourself with its existence).

DB2 Universal Database uses a combination of external security services and internal access control measures to protect data against unauthorized access and modification. The first step in managing database security is to verify that the user really is who he or she says they are. This step is called authentication. Authentication is performed by an external security facility that is not provided as part of DB2 Universal Database. This security facility may be part of the operating system (which is the case with UNIX, Windows NT, and many others), a separate product (such as Distributed Computing Environment [DCE] Security Services), or it may not exist at all (which, by default, is the case with Windows 95 and Windows 98). Most security facilities require two items in order to authenticate a user: a unique user ID and a corresponding password. The user ID identifies the user to the security facility; the password, which is information that is only known by both the user and the security facility, is used to verify the user during the authentication process. How and where authentication takes place is determined by the authentication type being used by an instance.

Once a user has been authenticated, the DB2 Database Manager must determine whether or not the user has the authority needed to perform the task requested. This determination is made by evaluating the set of authorities and privileges that have either been assigned to an individual or that have been assigned to a group that an individual is a member of. Authorities convey rights that are required in order to perform certain kinds of administrative and maintenance operations. Privileges convey rights that are required in order to perform certain actions on a specific database or database object.

The five levels of authority that are recognized by DB2 Universal Database are

- System Administrator authority (SYSADM)

- System Control authority (SYSCTRL)

- System Maintenance authority (SYSMAINT)

- Database Administrator authority (DBADM)

- Load authority (LOAD)

Six different database privileges exist:

- CONNECT
- CREATETAB
- BINDADD
- CREATE_NOT_FENCED
- IMPLICIT_SCHEMA
- LOAD

Fifteen different object privileges exist:

- ALTER (Table, Nickname)
- ALTERIN (Schema)
- BIND (Package)
- CONTROL (Table Space, Table, View, Index, Package, Nickname)
- CREATEIN (Schema)
- DELETE (Table, View)
- DROPIN (Schema)
- EXECUTE (Package)
- INDEX (Table, Nickname)
- INSERT (Table, View)
- PASSTHRU (Server)
- REFERENCES (Table, Nickname)
- SELECT (Table, View)
- UPDATE (Table, View)
- USE (Table Space)

Database-level authorities, database privileges, and object privileges can be given to (or taken from) an individual user or a group of users by any user who has the authority to do so. These authorities and privileges are given (granted) to a user or a group of users by executing the appropriate form of the GRANT SQL statement. These authorities and privileges are taken away (revoked) from a user or group of users by executing the appropriate form of the REVOKE SQL statement.

Questions

1. When do changes to the configuration file that is associated with the DB2 Administration Server instance take effect?
    a. Immediately
    b. After a new database connection is established
    c. After the DAS instance is restarted
    d. When all active database connections have been terminated

2. Which of the following is NOT a method of authentication that is supported by DB2 Universal Database?
    a. CLIENT
    b. CLIENT_ENCRYPT
    c. SERVER
    d. SERVER_ENCRYPT

3. Which of the following is NOT a function of the DB2 Administration Server (DAS) instance?
    a. Performing user authentication
    b. Starting and stopping instances
    c. Enabling remote clients to use the Control Center against an instance
    d. Providing communications for DB2 Universal Database servers

4. Which authority or privilege is granted by the DB2 Database Manager configuration file?
    a. CONNECT
    b. CONTROL
    c. SYSMAINT
    d. EXECUTE

5. Which two of the following authorities enable a user to create a new database?
    a. SYSADMN
    b. SYSCTRL
    c. SYSMAINT
    d. DBADM
    e. DBCTRL

6. Which of the following database privileges is required in order to add a new package?
   a. CREATETAB
   b. CREATEPKG
   c. BINDADD
   d. PACKAGEADD

7. Which of the following statements would explicitly give USER1 the ability to remove an index from a table?
   a. `GRANT DELETE ON TABLE Table1 TO User1`
   b. `GRANT CONTROL ON INDEX Index1 TO User1`
   c. `GRANT INDEX ON TABLE Table1 TO User1`
   d. `GRANT CONTROL ON TABLE Table1 TO User1`

8. The purpose of the USE privilege is to
   a. Give a user temporary access to a table.
   b. Give a user temporary access to a table space.
   c. Create table spaces within a database.
   d. Create tables within a table space.

9. In which of the following cases is the object creator NOT always given CONTROL privilege?
   a. When a table is created
   b. When a view is created
   c. When an index is created
   d. When a package is created

10. Which of the following two privileges is required in order to use a package?
    a. BINDADD
    b. BIND
    c. CONNECT
    d. EXECUTE
    e. USE

11. Given the following table:

EMPLOYEE

EMPNO	LNAME	FNAME	SSN	SALARY
1	Bogart	Humphrey	555-12-1234	$45,000.00
2	Bacall	Lauren	555-24-4567	$48,000.00

What is the best way to prevent users who are not in the Payroll department from viewing salary information?

   a. Only grant SELECT privileges for each column in the table that a specific user is allowed to see.

   b. Create a separate table that has only employee numbers and salary information in it; remove the salary information from the original table; grant SELECT privilege on this table and the original table to members of the Payroll department; grant SELECT privilege on the original table to other users; and use a join when a user needs to see the data in both tables.

   c. Create a group called PAYROLL; assign all members of the Payroll department to the PAYROLL group; grant SELECT privilege for this table to the group PAYROLL; create a view for this table that does not include the SALARY column; and grant SELECT privilege for this view to all other users.

   d. Create a separate table that has only employee numbers and salary information in it; remove the salary information from the original table; create a view that combines both tables; grant SELECT privilege on the view to members of the Payroll department; and grant SELECT privilege on the original table to other users.

Answers

  1. **C.** When you make changes to the DB2 Database Manager configuration file that is associated with the DB2 Administration Server instance, you must stop and restart the DB2 Administration Server instance before those changes will take effect.

  2. **B.** When user authentication takes place at the client, the user ID and password information do not need to be encrypted; therefore, CLIENT_ENCRYPT is not a valid method of authentication.

  3. **A.** Authentication is performed by an external security facility that is not provided as part of DB2 Universal Database therefore the DAS is not responsible for performing user authentication.

  4. **C.** Each of the instance-level authorities (SYSADM, SYSCTRL, and SYSMAINT) can only be given to a group of users and the names of the groups that have been given these authorities are recorded in the DB2 Database Manager configuration files that are associated with each instance.

5. **A and B.** Only users with System Administrator (SYSADM) authority or System Control (SYSCTRL) authority are allowed to create a new database.

6. **C.** The BINDADD privilege conveys the right to create packages in a database when precompiling and/or binding application program files to that database.

7. **B.** The CONTROL privilege for an index conveys the right to remove that index. INDEX privilege conveys the right to create an index on a table. When an index is created, the creator is implicitly given CONTROL privilege on that index; therefore, they can delete it. CONTROL privilege must be explicitly given to a user before he or she can delete an index he or she did not create.

8. **C.** The USE privilege conveys the right to create tables within a table space.

9. **B.** The owner of a view (typically the creator) is only given the CONTROL privilege for the view if he or she holds CONTROL privilege on every table that the view references.

10. **C and D.** A user must be able to connect to a database before he or she can use a package and the user needs to be able to execute the package once he or she is connected. Therefore, both CONNECT and EXECUTE privileges are required if the user does not have SYSADM authority.

11. **C.** The best way to handle security for a group of users is to create a group; add the appropriate users to the group; and then assign authorities and privileges to that group. With this approach, if a new employee joins the Payroll department, the employee can be given all the authorities and privileges he or she needs just by being added to the PAYROLL group. The rest of the answer shows an efficient way to use a view, along with group privileges, to accomplish the desired result.

Creating and Accessing DB2 Databases and DB2 Database Objects

In this chapter, you will learn

- What a DB2 Universal Database database is, what its underlying structure looks like, and how that structure is physically stored
- How to create and destroy a DB2 Universal Database database
- How to catalog and uncatalog a DB2 Universal Database database
- What kinds of objects can exist within a DB2 Universal Database database and what those objects are used for
- How to create and destroy most of the objects available using the various tools that are provided with DB2 Universal Database

The third objective of the DB2 Universal Database Family Fundamentals exam is to evaluate your ability to create, catalog, access, and remove DB2 Universal Database databases. This section of the exam also tests your knowledge of how the various tools that come with DB2 Universal Database can be used to construct objects within those databases. Knowing how to create a database is only the beginning. To ward off potential problems, it is also important to understand how a database is structured, as well as how that structure is translated to physical storage on a workstation. Likewise, knowing what objects are available and what those objects are used for is just as important as knowing how to create them.

This chapter is designed to provide you with everything you need to know about creating and managing DB2 Universal Database databases. This chapter is also designed to introduce you to most of the objects that are available with DB2 Universal Database and to provide you with information on how each of these objects can be created and destroyed.

 TIP Thirteen percent of the DB2 Universal Database Family Fundamentals exam is designed to test your knowledge of creating and accessing DB2 Universal Database databases and database objects.

The Relational Database Model

In order to understand how DB2 Universal Database databases and their associated objects are constructed, it helps to understand the basic concepts that most relational database management systems are built upon. A relational database management system is a database management system that is designed around a set of powerful mathematical concepts known as Relational Algebra. The first relational database model was introduced in the early 1970s by Mr. E. F. Codd at the IBM San Jose Research Center. This model is based on the following operations that are identified in Relational Algebra:

- **SELECTION** This operation selects a record or group of records from a table based on some specified condition.

- **PROJECTION** This operation returns a column or group of columns from a table based on some specified condition.

- **JOIN** This operation enables users to paste two or more tables together. However, each table must have a common column before a JOIN can work.

- **UNION** This operation combines two similar tables to produce a set that contains all records found in both tables. Every column in each table must be compatible before a UNION can work. In other words, the data type used for each column (field) in the first table must match the data type used for each column (field) in the second table. Essentially, the UNION of two tables is the same as the mathematical addition of two tables.

- **DIFFERENCE** This operation tells users what records are unique to one particular table when two tables are compared. Again, every column in each table must be compatible before a DIFFERENCE can work. Essentially, the DIFFERENCE of two tables is the same as the mathematical subtraction of two tables.

- **INTERSECTION**   This operation tells users what records are found in every table when to two or more tables are compared. This operation actually involves performing the UNION and DIFFERENCE operations twice.

- **PRODUCT**   This operation combines two dissimilar tables to produce a set that contains all records found in both tables. Essentially, the PRODUCT of two tables is the same as the mathematical multiplication of two tables. Unfortunately, the PRODUCT operation often produces unwanted side effects that require use of the PROJECTION operation to clean up.

As you can see, in a relational database, data is perceived to exist in one or more two-dimensional tables. These tables are made up of rows and columns, where each record (row) is divided into fields (columns) that contain individual pieces of information. Although data is not actually stored this way, visualizing data as a collection of two-dimensional tables makes it easier to illustrate how each of the Relational Algebra operations just described are performed.

What Is a DB2 Universal Database Database?

In its simplest form, a DB2 Universal Database database is a set of related database objects. In fact, when you create a DB2 Universal Database database, you are establishing an administrative relational database entity that provides an underlying structure for an eventual collection of database objects (such as tables, views, indexes, and so on). This underlying structure consists of a set of system catalog tables (along with a set of corresponding views), a set of table spaces in which both the system catalog tables and the eventual collection of database objects will reside, and a set of files that will be used to handle database recovery and other bookkeeping details. Figure 4-1 illustrates the underlying structure of a simple DB2 Universal Database database.

Although Figure 4-1 shows you how the underlying structure of a DB2 Universal Database database looks, it does not show you where and how this structure is physically stored. Typically, a DB2 Universal Database database is stored as a collection of files that physically reside within the file space of a server workstation. The root directory for this collection of files is specified, along with other information as part of the database creation process. (If a root directory is not specified during the database creation process, the root directory name stored in the *dftdbpath* parameter of the DB2 Database Manager configuration file is used as the default.) This root directory will

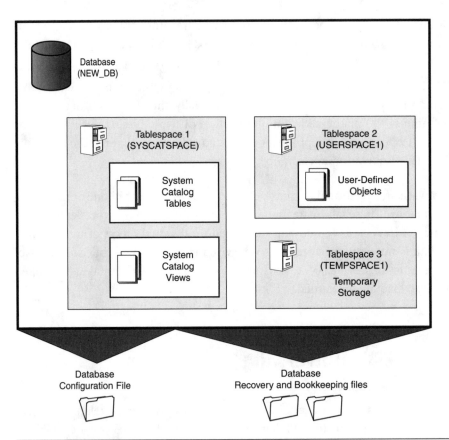

Figure 4-1   A simple DB2 Universal Database database

contain a subdirectory that has the same name as the instance that the database is associated with. This instance directory will contain another subdirectory whose name corresponds to the node number that has been assigned to the server. (If a database is partitioned across several workstations, each workstation partition is assigned a unique node number. If the database is a nonpartitioned database, this directory will be named NODE0000.) The node directory will in turn contain one subdirectory for each database that has been created (under this node and instance). The first database created will be stored in a subdirectory named SQL0001, the second in a subdirectory named SQL0002, and so on.

Each database is made up of at least three table spaces, which in turn are made up of containers. Table spaces are not stored explicitly in this directory hierarchy since they do not map directly to directories or files. However, because each container associated with a system managed (SMS) table space is a physical directory and because, by default, three SMS table spaces are created along with a new database, each database directory usually contains three additional subdirectories that map to the containers associated with these table spaces. Each directory that corresponds to an SMS table space container will contain one or more files that hold the data that belongs to a given table or index. For example, data that belongs to a specific table might be stored in a file named SQL00001.DAT. Figure 4-2 illustrates how this directory hierarchy would look for a server that contains three nonpartitioned databases that use the default SMS table spaces provided.

NOTE   You should never tamper with this directory structure or with any of the files found in this structure—such actions could destroy one or all databases stored on a workstation.

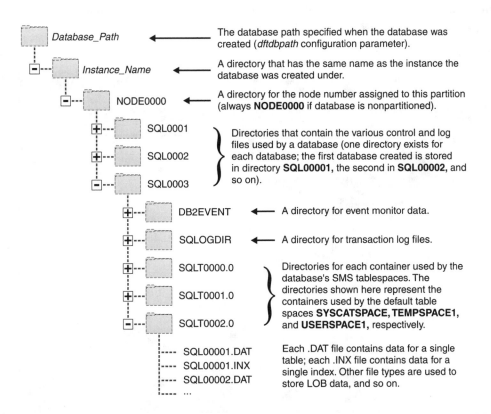

Figure 4-2   Physical organization of a nonpartitioned database using default SMS table spaces

Creating a DB2 Universal Database Database

Now that you have a basic understanding of what a DB2 Universal Database database is and how its data and data objects are stored, let's look at how a database is created. The easiest way to create a DB2 Universal Database database is by using the Create Database Wizard, which is invoked from the Control Center. Figure 4-3 shows the Control Center menu items that must be selected in order to activate the Create Database Wizard.

If you have had the opportunity to use one in the past, you are probably already aware that a wizard is a sequenced set of dialogs that are designed to guide a user through the steps needed to perform a complex task. The dialogs (often referred to as pages) that make up a wizard are normally accessed in the order that they have been sequenced; thus, they orchestrate a step one, step two, step three, . . . input scenario. The seven dialogs/pages that make up the Create Database Wizard are designed to capture specific information about the characteristics of the database that is to be created. Figure 4-4 shows the first page of this wizard.

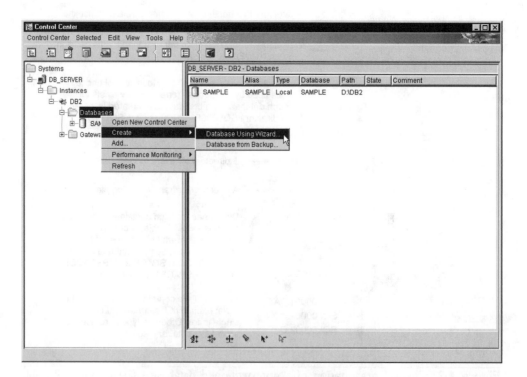

Figure 4-3 Invoking the Create Database Wizard from the Control Center

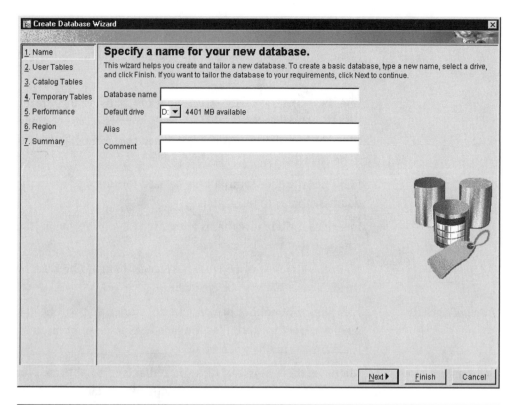

Figure 4-4   The first page of the Create Database Wizard

A database can also be created by executing the CREATE DATABASE command, either from the Command Center or from the Command Line Processor (CLP). The syntax for this command is

```
CREATE [DATABASE | DB] [DatabaseName] <AT NODE>
```

or

```
CREATE [DATABASE | DB] [DatabaseName] <ON [Path]> <ALIAS [Alias]>
<USING CODESET [CodeSet] TERRITORY [Territory]> <COLLATE USING
[CollateType]> <NUMSEGS [NumSegments]> <DFT_EXTENT_SZ
[ExtentSize]> <CATALOG TABLESPACE [TableSpaceDefinition]> <USER
TABLESPACE [TableSpaceDefinition]> <TEMPORARY TABLESPACE
[TableSpaceDefinition]> <WITH [Description]>
```

where:

DatabaseName   Identifies the name that is to be assigned to the database that is to be created.

Path   Identifies the drive and/or the directory where the database that is to be created is to be physically stored.

Alias   Identifies the alias that is to be assigned to the database that is to be created.

CodeSet   Identifies the code set that is to be used for storing data in the database that is to be created.

Territory   Identifies the territory that is to be used for storing data in the database that is to be created.

CollateType   Identifies the type of collating sequence that is to be used by the database that is to be created.

NumSegments   Identifies the number of segment directories that will be created and used to store files for each SMS table space used by the database that is to be created.

ExtentSize   Identifies the amount of disk space that is to be allocated for every container that is associated with an SMS table space that is used by the database that is to be created.

TableSpaceDefinition   Specifies the definition of the table spaces that will be used to hold the system catalog tables (SYSCATSPACE), user-defined objects (USERSPACE1), and/or temporary objects (TEMP-SPACE1) that will be associated with the database that is to be created. The syntax used to define a database managed (DMS) table space is

```
MANAGED BY DATABASE USING ( [FILE | DEVICE] Container
NumberOfPages , . . .   ) <EXTENTSIZE [NumberOfExtentPages]>
<PREFETCHSIZE [NumberOfPrefetchPages]> <OVERHEAD [OverheadTime]>
<TRANSFERRATE [TransferRateTime]>
```

The syntax used to define a system managed (SMS) table space is

```
MANAGED BY SYSTEM USING ( Container, . . .   )
<EXTENTSIZE [NumberOfPages]> <PREFETCHSIZE [NumberOfPages]>
<OVERHEAD [OverheadTime]> <TRANSFERRATE [TransferRateTime]>
```

where:

Container	Identifies one or more containers that will belong to the specified table space (and that will be used to physically store the table space's data). For FILE DMS containers or SMS containers, the container definition must identify a valid directory or file. For DEVICE DMS containers, the container definition must identify a specific device that already exists.
NumberOfPages	Specifies the number of 4K or 8K pages that are to be used by the table space container.
NumberOfExtentPages	Specifies the number of 4K or 8K pages of data that will be written to a single table space container before another table space container will be used.
NumberOfPrefetchPages	Specifies the number of 4K or 8K pages of data that will be read from the specified table space when data prefetching is performed. Prefetching enables data that is needed by a query to be read before it is referenced, so that the query does not have to wait as long for I/O to be performed.
OverheadTime	Identifies the I/O controller overhead and disk-seek latency, time in number of milliseconds, that is associated with the containers that belong to a specified table space.
TransferRate	Identifies the time, in number of milliseconds, that it takes to read one 4K or 8K page of data from a table space container and store it in memory.
Description	A comment that is used to describe the database entry that will be made in the database directory for the database that is to be created.

For example, when executed, the command

```
CREATE DATABASE SAMPLEDB ON D: ALIAS MY_DB USING CODESET 1252
TERRITORY US COLLATE USING SYSTEM USER TABLESPACE MANAGED BY
DATABASE (FILE 'D:\TS\USERSPACE.DAT', 121)
```

would create a database that

- Is physically located on drive D:
- Has been assigned the name SAMPLEDB

- Has been assigned the alias MY_DB

- Recognizes the United States/Canada code set

- Will use a collating sequence that is based on the territory used (which in this case is United States/Canada)

- Will store all user data in a DMS table space that has a size limit of 121 pages

Regardless of how the process is initiated, whenever a new database is created, the DB2 Database Manager performs the following set of tasks (in the order shown):

1. It creates the physical directories needed in the appropriate location.

2. It creates files that are needed for database recovery and other bookkeeping tasks.

3. It creates three table spaces and assigns them the names SYSCATSPACE, USER-SPACE1, and TEMPSPACE1. The first of these table spaces is used to store the system catalog tables and views, the second is used to store user data, and the third is used for temporary storage. The characteristics of these table spaces can be specified as part of the input for the Create Database Wizard or the CREATE DATA-BASE command; however, if no characteristics are provided, all three will be created as system managed (SMS) table spaces.

4. It creates all the system catalog tables and views in the catalog table space and populates the tables as appropriate. Initially, this set of tables and views will occupy about 3.5 megabytes of disk space.

5. It initializes the database configuration file for the new database. Some of the parameters in this file will be set using values that were specified as input for the Create Database Wizard or CREATE DATABASE command; others will be assigned system default values.

6. It binds a set of utility programs to the new database so that the packages that are required before those programs can be executed will be created.

7. It grants Database Administrator (DBADM) authority to the user who created the database.

8. It grants CONNECT, CREATETAB, and BINDADD privileges to the group PUBLIC. This step enables all users to connect to the new database, create tables in the new database, and bind application programs to the new database. Once the database has been created, these privileges can be explicitly revoked.

Destroying a DB2 Universal Database Database

The easiest way to destroy (or drop) an existing DB2 Universal Database database is by selecting the *Drop Database* action from the Control Center menu. Figure 4-5 shows the Control Center menu items that must be selected in order to drop an existing database.

A database can also be destroyed by executing the DROP DATABASE command, either from the Command Center or from the Command Line Processor. The syntax for this command is

```
DROP [DATABASE | DB] [DatabaseName] <AT NODE>
```

where:

    DatabaseName   Identifies the name that has been assigned to the database that is to be destroyed.

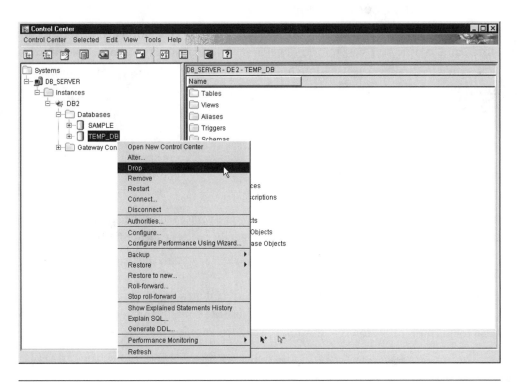

Figure 4-5   Dropping a database from the Control Center

For example, the following DROP DATABASE command would destroy a database named SAMPLEDB:

```
DROP DATABASE SAMPLEDB
```

It is important to remember that only users with System Administrator (SYSADM) authority or System Control (SYSCTRL) authority are allowed to drop a database.

 NOTE   A database cannot be destroyed as long as one or more users/applications are connected to it. If a database must be destroyed before all users/applications can gracefully terminate their connections to it, those connections can be forcefully terminated by executing the FORCE APPLICATION command either from the Command Center or the Command Line Processor. This command can also be invoked by selecting the *Force Applications* action from the Control Center menu.

The DB2 Universal Database Directory Files

DB2 Universal Database uses a set of special files to keep track of where databases are stored and to provide access to both local and remote databases. Because the information stored in these files is used much like the information in an office-building directory is used, they are referred to as directory files. The following types of directory files exist:

- Local database directory files
- System database directory files
- Node directory files

Local database directory and system database directory files are automatically created the first time a database is created on a specific workstation or path.

The Local Database Directory File

A local database directory file exists on each path (called a drive on many operating systems) in which a database has been created. This file contains one entry for each database that is physically stored at that location. Each entry contains

- The database name
- The database alias (which is the same as the database name, if an alias has not been specified)

- A comment that describes the database (if one has been provided)
- The name of the root directory for the database
- The product name and release number associated with the database
- Other system information including the code page the database was created under and entry type (which is always **Home**)

The contents of this file can be viewed by issuing the following command from either the Command Center or the Command Line Processor:

```
LIST DATABASE DIRECTORY ON [Location]
```

where:

Location   Identifies the path/drive where one or more databases have been created.

The System Database Directory File

A system database directory file exists for each DB2 Database Manager instance. This file resides on the logical disk drive where the DB2 Universal Database product software is installed and it contains one entry for each database that has been cataloged for a particular instance. Each entry contains

- The database name provided when the database was created or cataloged
- The database alias (which is the same as the database name, if an alias has not been specified)
- A comment that describes the database (if one has been provided)
- The location of the local database directory file that contains information about the database
- The logical disk drive that the database resides on if the database is local
- The node name that the database resides on if the database is remote
- The database entry type, which tells whether or not, the database is indirect (which means that it resides on the same workstation as the system database directory file)
- The product name and release number associated with the database
- Other system information including the code page the database was created under

The contents of this file can be viewed by issuing the LIST DATABASE DIRECTORY command without specifying a location.

The Node Directory File

A node directory file is created on each client workstation when the first database partition is cataloged. Like the system database directory file, the node directory file also resides on the logical disk drive where the DB2 Universal Database product software is installed. Entries in the node directory are used in conjunction with entries in the system database directory for making connections and instance attachments to remote DB2 database servers. Each entry in this file contains information about the type of communication protocol that the client should use to communicate to the remote database partition.

The contents of the node directory file can be viewed by issuing the following command from either the Command Center or the Command Line Processor:

```
LIST NODE DIRECTORY
```

Uncataloging a DB2 Universal Database Database

Before the DB2 Database Manager can access a database, it must be cataloged (listed) in the system database directory file. By default, databases are implicitly cataloged in both the system database directory file and in a local database directory file immediately after they are created. However, sometimes it is appropriate to remove the catalog entry for a database from the system database directory. For example, you might want to uncatalog a database before removing one version of DB2 Universal Database to install another version. Once the new version has been installed, the database can then be recataloged (and migrated if necessary) so that it can be accessed by other users once again. Or if you want to change the authentication type that is used by a particular database when communicating with a down-level server, you can do so by first uncataloging the database, and then cataloging it again with a different authentication type specified.

Cataloged databases can be uncataloged by selecting the *Remove Database* action from the Control Center menu. Figure 4-6 shows the Control Center menu items that must be selected in order to uncatalog a database.

A database can also be uncataloged by executing the UNCATALOG DATABASE command, either from the Command Center or from the Command Line Processor. The syntax for this command is

```
UNCATALOG [DATABASE | DB] [DatabaseName]
```

where:

DatabaseName   Identifies the name that has been assigned to the database that is to be uncataloged.

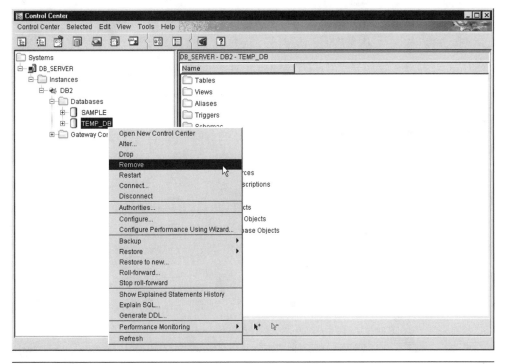

Figure 4-6   Uncataloging a database from the Control Center

For example, the following UNCATALOG DATABASE command would uncatalog a
database named SAMPLEDB:

```
UNCATALOG DATABASE SAMPLEDB
```

NOTE   Only entries in the system database directory are removed when a database is uncataloged. Entries in a local database directory can only be removed
by dropping a database.

Cataloging a DB2 Universal Database Database

Uncataloged databases can be explicitly cataloged by selecting the *Add Database* action
from the Control Center menu (to catalog local databases) or by running the Client
Configuration Assistant (to catalog remote databases). Figure 4-7 shows the Control
Center menu items that must be selected in order to catalog a local database.

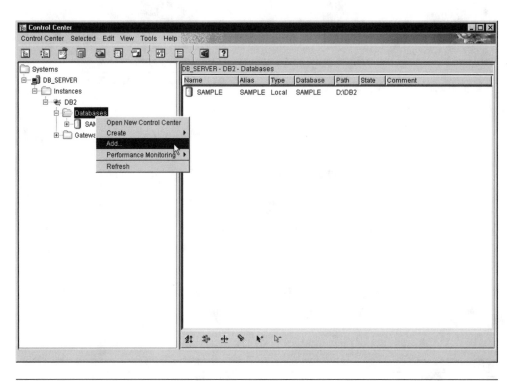

Figure 4-7 Cataloging a local database from the Control Center

A database can also be cataloged by executing the CATALOG DATABASE command, either from the Command Center or from the Command Line Processor. The syntax for this command is

```
CATALOG [DATABASE | DB] [DatabaseName] <AS [AliasName]>
<ON [Path] | AT NODE [NodeName]>
<AUTHENTICATION [AuthenticationType]> <WITH [Description]>
```

where:

DatabaseName	Identifies the name that has been assigned to the database that is to be cataloged.
Alias	Identifies the alias that is to be assigned to the database that is to be cataloged.
Path	Identifies the drive and/or the directory where the database that is to be cataloged is physically stored.

NodeName   Identifies the node where the database that is to be cataloged resides. The node name specified should match an entry in the node directory file.

AuthenticationType   Identifies where and how authentication is to take place when a user attempts to access the database. (Refer to Chapter 3 for more information about the authentication types available.)

Description   A comment that is used to describe the database entry that will be made in the database directory for the database that is to be cataloged.

For example, the following CATALOG DATABASE command would catalog a database named SAMPLEDB that physically resides on drive C:, assign it the alias MY_DB, and tell the DB2 Database Manager that all users who attempt to access it are to be authenticated at the server:

```
CATALOG DATABASE SAMPLEDB AS MY_DB ON C: AUTHENTICATION SERVER
```

Understanding Objects

It was mentioned earlier that a DB2 Universal Database database is an organized collection of related components known as objects. Four types of objects exist:

- System objects
- Recovery objects
- Storage objects
- Database (or data) objects

System Objects

System objects consist of DB2 Database Manager configuration files and individual database configuration files. A DB2 Database Manager configuration file is created whenever a DB2 instance is created. The values assigned to its parameters affect system resources at the instance level, and are independent of any one database that is part of that instance. Values for many of the parameters in the DB2 Database Manager configuration file can be changed from the system default values to improve performance or increase capacity, depending upon a workstation's configuration.

A database configuration file is created whenever a database is created, and it resides where that database physically resides. One configuration file exists per database. The values assigned to its parameters specify, among other things, the amount of resources that are to be allocated to that database. Values for many of the parameters in a database configuration file can be changed to improve performance or increase capacity, depending upon the type of activity a specific database sees.

Recovery Objects

Recovery objects consist of recovery log files and recovery history files. One recovery history file and one or more recovery log files are automatically created when a database is created. Recovery log files are used in combination with database backup images to recover from application, user, and/or system errors. The recovery history file contains information about every backup image that has been made. This information can be used to restore the consistency of a database right up to a given point in time in which an error occurred.

You cannot directly modify a recovery log file or the recovery history file; however, you will find that their contents are important should you need to use a database backup image to replace data that has been lost or damaged.

Storage Objects

Storage objects let you define how data will be stored on your system, and how data access performance can be improved. The following storage objects are available:

- Buffer pools
- Containers
- Table spaces

Buffer Pools

A buffer pool is an area of main memory that has been allocated to the DB2 Database Manager for the purpose of caching table and index data pages as they are read from disk or modified. Using a set of heuristic algorithms, the DB2 Manager Database prefetches pages of data that it thinks a user is about to need into one or more buffer pools and it moves pages of data that it thinks are no longer needed back to disk. This approach improves overall system performance because data can be accessed much faster from memory than from disk. (The fewer times the DB2 Database Manager needs to perform disk I/O, the better the performance.)

Creating, Dropping, and Modifying a Buffer Pool   By default, DB2 Universal Database creates one buffer pool (named IBMDEFAULTBP) of an appropriate size for the platform used whenever a database is created. Additional buffer pools can be created, dropped, and modified by selecting the appropriate action from the *Buffer Pools* menu found in the Control Center. Figure 4-8 shows the Control Center menu items that must be selected in order to create a new buffer pool. Figure 4-9 shows how the Create Buffer Pool dialog (which is activated by the Control Center) might look after its input fields have been populated.

Buffer pools can also be created, dropped, and modified by executing the SQL statements CREATE BUFFERPOOL, DROP BUFFERPOOL, and ALTER BUFFERPOOL, either from the Command Center, the Command Line Processor, or an application program. The syntax for these statements will be covered in more detail in Chapter 6.

NOTE Although several buffer pools can be created, for most situations only one buffer pool is needed.

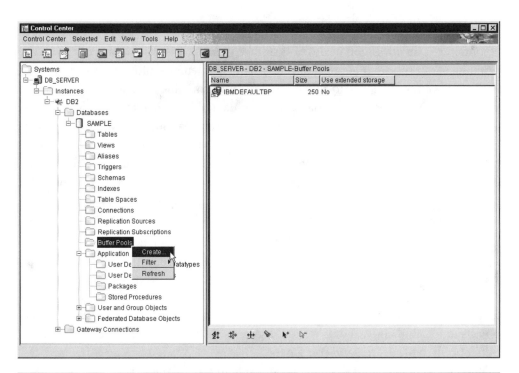

Figure 4-8   Creating a buffer pool from the Control Center

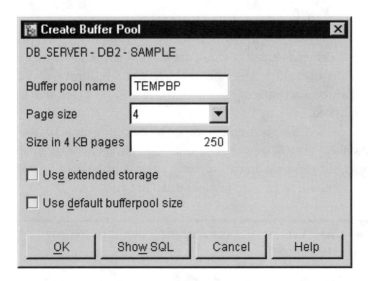

Figure 4-9   Sample Create Buffer Pool dialog

Containers

A container is an allocation of physical storage the DB2 Database Manager can access. Containers can be identified by a directory name, a filename, or by the name of a particular device (such as a hard disk). One or more containers are assigned to a table space, which in turn is used to logically group data objects such as tables and indexes and large object (LOB) data. A single table space can span many containers, but each container can only belong to one table space. When a table space spans multiple containers, data associated with that table space is stored on all of its respective containers in a round-robin fashion; the extent size used when the container was assigned to the table space determines how many pages of data the DB2 Database Manager will write to that container before moving to another one. This helps balance the data across all containers that belong to a given table space.

Table Spaces

Table spaces are used to specify where data in a database is physically stored on a system and to provide a layer of indirection between the database and the container objects in which the actual data resides. Figure 4-10 illustrates the relationship among buffer pools, table spaces, and containers.

Because every table in a database must reside in a table space, table spaces give you the ability to create a physical database design that fits your particular environment. For

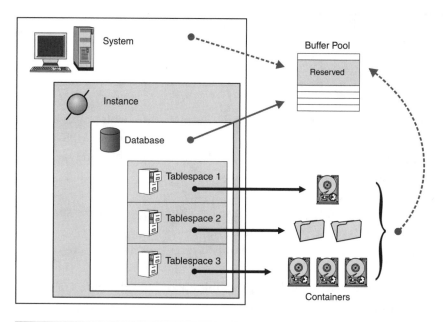

Figure 4-10   Relationship among buffer pools, table spaces, and containers

example, frequently accessed data can be stored on faster devices whereas legacy data can reside on older, slower devices.

A table space can be either a system managed space (SMS) or a database managed space (DMS). For an SMS table space, each container used is a directory that resides within the file space of the operating system, and the operating system's file manager is responsible for controlling the storage space. For a DMS table space, each container used is either a fixed-size, pre-allocated file or a physical raw device such as a disk, and the DB2 Database Manager is responsible for controlling the storage space.

Regardless of how they are managed, three types of table spaces can exist: regular, temporary, and long. Tables that contain user data can reside in regular DMS table spaces. Indexes can also be stored in regular DMS table spaces. Tables that contain long field data or large object (LOB) data, such as multimedia objects, can reside in long DMS table spaces. Temporary table spaces are classified as either system or user; system temporary table spaces are used to store internal temporary data that is required during SQL operations such as sorting, reorganizing tables, index creation, and table joins. User temporary table spaces are used to store declared global temporary tables that, in turn, are used to store application specific temporary data.

TIP Although you can create any number of system temporary table spaces, it is recommended that you create only one and assign it the page size that the majority of your tables will use.

As mentioned earlier, each time a database is first created, three table spaces are also created (and assigned the names SYSCATSPACE, USERSPACE1, and TEMPSPACE1). The first of these table spaces is used to store the system catalog tables and views, the second is used to store user data, and the third is used for temporary storage. Unless otherwise specified, all three of these table spaces will be SMS table spaces; TEMPSPACE1 will be a system temporary table space. User temporary table spaces are *not* created by default at database creation time.

Additional table spaces can be created, dropped, and modified by selecting the appropriate action from the *Table Spaces* menu found in the Control Center. The easiest way to create a table space is by using the Create Table Space Wizard. Figure 4-11 shows the Control Center menu items that must be selected in order to activate the Create

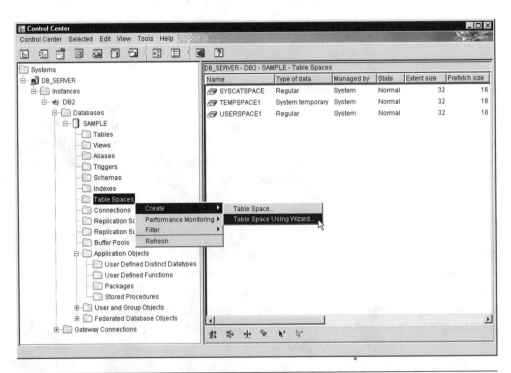

Figure 4-11   Invoking the Create Table Space Wizard from the Control Center

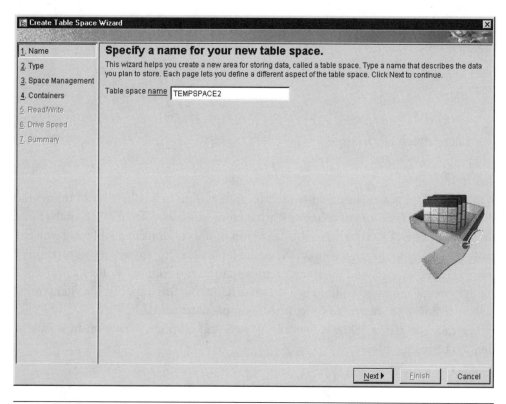

Figure 4-12   The first page of the Create Table Wizard

Table Space Wizard. Figure 4-12 shows how the first page of this wizard might look after its input fields have been populated.

Table spaces can also be created, dropped, and modified by executing the SQL statements CREATE TABLESPACE, DROP TABLESPACE, and ALTER TABLESPACE, either from the Command Center, the Command Line Processor, or an application program. The syntax for these statements will be covered in more detail in Chapter 6.

Database (or Data) Objects

Database objects, otherwise known as data objects, are the components that are used to store and manipulate data and control how all user data (and some system data) is organized. Data objects include

- Tables
- Views

- Aliases
- Indexes
- Schemas
- Triggers
- User-defined data types
- User-defined functions

Tables

A table is a logical structure that is used to present data as a collection of unordered rows with a fixed number of columns. Each column contains a set of values of the same data type or one of its subtypes—the definition of the columns in a table make up the table structure and the rows contain the actual table data. The storage representation of a row is called a *record,* and the storage representation of a column is called a *field.* Each intersection of a row and column in a database table contains a specific data item called a *value.* Figure 4-13 shows the structure of a simple database table.

Typically, data in a table is logically related and additional relationships can be defined between tables.

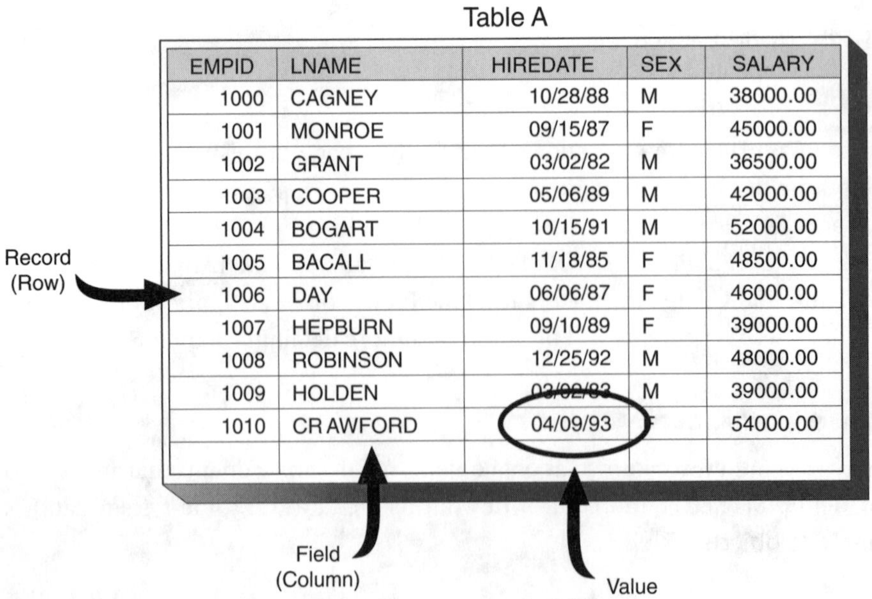

Table A

EMPID	LNAME	HIREDATE	SEX	SALARY
1000	CAGNEY	10/28/88	M	38000.00
1001	MONROE	09/15/87	F	45000.00
1002	GRANT	03/02/82	M	36500.00
1003	COOPER	05/06/89	M	42000.00
1004	BOGART	10/15/91	M	52000.00
1005	BACALL	11/18/85	F	48500.00
1006	DAY	06/06/87	F	46000.00
1007	HEPBURN	09/10/89	F	39000.00
1008	ROBINSON	12/25/92	M	48000.00
1009	HOLDEN	03/02/83	M	39000.00
1010	CRAWFORD	04/09/93	F	54000.00

Record (Row)

Field (Column)

Value

Figure 4-13   A simple database table

Five types of tables can exist in a DB2 Universal Database database:

- **Base tables**   Tables that are created by the user in order to store persistent user data.

- **Result tables**   Temporary tables that are created (and deleted) by the DB2 Database Manager from one or more base tables in order to satisfy the results of a query.

- **Summary tables**   Tables that are defined by the results of a query. Summary tables can often be used to improve the performance of a query. For example, if the DB2 Database Manager determines that a portion of a query could be resolved by using a summary table, that query may be rewritten by the DB2 Database Manager to use the summary table.

- **Declared temporary tables**   Tables that are created with the SQL statement DECLARE GLOBAL TEMPORARY TABLE that are used to hold temporary data on behalf of a single application. Declared temporary tables are implicitly dropped when the application that declared them disconnects from the database.

- **Typed tables**   A table whose columns are based on the attributes of a user-defined structured data type. Because a user-defined structured data type can be part of a type hierarchy (a subtype is said to inherit attributes from its supertype), a typed table can be part of a table hierarchy. Thus, a subtable is said to inherit columns from its supertable. Note that the term *subtype* applies to a user-defined structured type and all user-defined structured types that are below it in the type hierarchy. Similarly, the term *subtable* applies to a typed table and all typed tables that are below it in the table hierarchy.

Tables can be created, dropped, and modified by selecting the appropriate action from the *Tables* menu found in the Control Center. The easiest way to create a table is by using the Create Table Wizard. Figure 4-14 shows the Control Center menu items that must be selected in order to activate the Create Table Wizard. Figure 4-15 shows how the first page of this wizard might look after its input fields have been populated.

Tables can also be created, dropped, and modified by executing the SQL statements CREATE TABLE, DROP TABLE, and ALTER TABLE, either from the Command Center, the Command Line Processor, or an application program. The syntax for the CREATE TABLE statement will be covered in more detail in Chapter 5. The syntax for the DROP TABLE and ALTER TABLE statements will be covered in more detail in Chapter 6.

Although every table in a database must reside in a table space, when a table is created, you can decide whether to have certain objects such as indexes and large object (LOB) data kept separate from or stored in the same table space as the table data (but

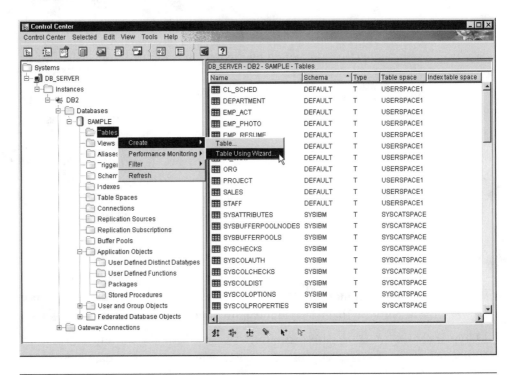

Figure 4-14   Invoking the Create Table Wizard from the Control Center

only if DMS table spaces are used). Up to three DMS table spaces can be utilized by every table; typically, the first one is used for table data (by default), the second one is used for indexes, and the third one is used for large object (LOB) data fields.

Views

A view provides an alternative way of working with data that exists in one or more base tables. Essentially, a view is a named specification of a result table that is produced whenever the view is referenced in an SQL statement. For this reason, a view can be thought of as having columns and rows, just like a base table, and in most cases, data can be retrieved from a view just as it can be retrieved from a base table. However, whether or not a view can be used to add, update, or delete data depends on how it was defined.

Although a view looks like a base table, it does not exist as a table in physical storage therefore it does not contain data. Instead, a view refers to data stored in other base

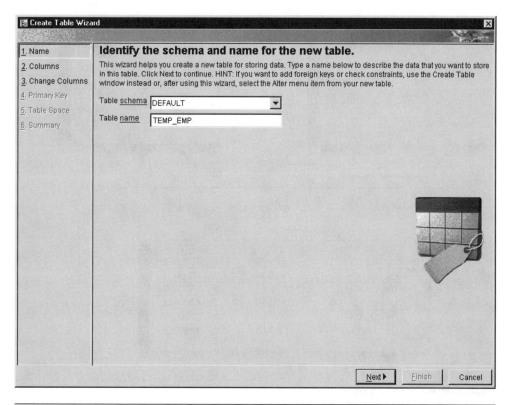

Figure 4-15   The first page of the Create Table Wizard

tables (a view may refer to another view, but ultimately the reference will be resolved to data stored in one or more base tables). A view can include any or all of the columns or rows contained in the table(s) on which it is based. A view can also include any number of columns from other views, and a view can include a combination of columns from both tables and other views. Figure 4-16 illustrates the basic relationship between base tables and views.

In this figure, a view is created from two separate base tables. Because the EMPID column is common in both tables, that column is used to join the tables to create a single view that contains all columns.

When a column of a view is derived from a column of a base table, that column inherits any constraints that apply to the column of the base table. For example, if a view includes a column that is a unique key for its base table, operations performed

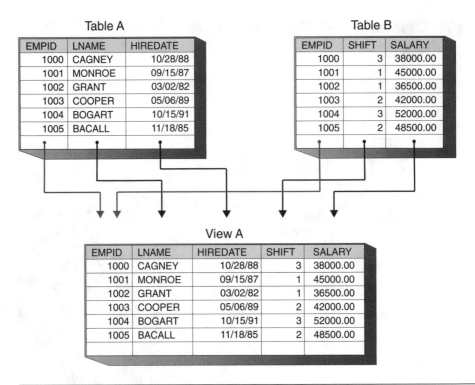

Table A

EMPID	LNAME	HIREDATE
1000	CAGNEY	10/28/88
1001	MONROE	09/15/87
1002	GRANT	03/02/82
1003	COOPER	05/06/89
1004	BOGART	10/15/91
1005	BACALL	11/18/85

Table B

EMPID	SHIFT	SALARY
1000	3	38000.00
1001	1	45000.00
1002	1	36500.00
1003	2	42000.00
1004	3	52000.00
1005	2	48500.00

View A

EMPID	LNAME	HIREDATE	SHIFT	SALARY
1000	CAGNEY	10/28/88	3	38000.00
1001	MONROE	09/15/87	1	45000.00
1002	GRANT	03/02/82	1	36500.00
1003	COOPER	05/06/89	2	42000.00
1004	BOGART	10/15/91	3	52000.00
1005	BACALL	11/18/85	2	48500.00

Figure 4-16   A simple view

against that view are subject to the same constraints as operations performed against the base table the view was derived from.

The data type of each column in a view can be derived from the base table the view is built upon, or the data type for each column can be based upon the attributes of a user-defined structured data type. In this case, the view is known as a typed view. Similar to a typed table, a typed view can be part of a view hierarchy. (A subview is said to inherit columns from its superview—the term *subview* applies to a typed view and all typed views that are below it in the view hierarchy.)

Views can be created, dropped, and modified by selecting the appropriate action from the *Views* menu found in the Control Center. Figure 4-17 shows the Control Center menu items that must be selected in order to create a new view. Figure 4-18 shows how the Create View dialog (which is activated by the Control Center) might look after its input fields have been populated.

Views can also be created, dropped, and modified by executing the SQL statements CREATE VIEW, DROP VIEW, and ALTER VIEW, either from the Command Center, the

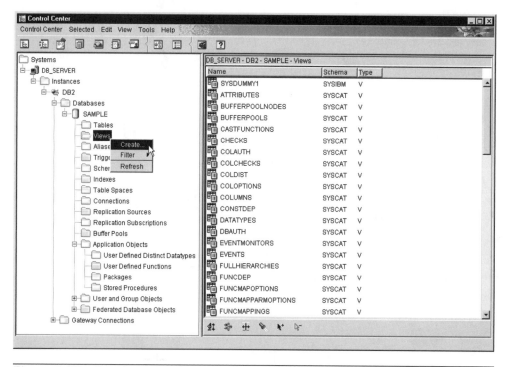

Figure 4-17   Creating a view from the Control Center

Command Line Processor, or an application program. The syntax for these statements will be covered in more detail in Chapter 6.

Aliases

An alias is an alternate name for a table, view, or nickname. Once created, aliases can be referenced in the same way any table, view, or nickname can be referenced. However, an alias cannot be used in every context that a table, view, or nickname can be used in. For example, an alias cannot be used in the check condition of a check constraint and it cannot reference a user-defined temporary table.

Like tables and views, aliases can be created, dropped, and have comments associated with them. Unlike tables and views, aliases can also refer to other aliases. The process of aliases referring to each other is known as alias chaining. Because aliases are publicly referenced names, no special authority or privilege is required to use them (unlike tables and views). However, appropriate authorization may still be required before a table or view that an alias refers to can be used.

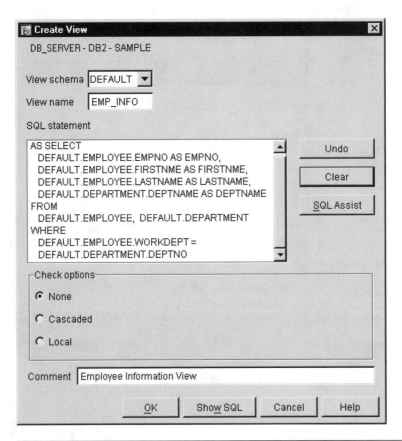

Figure 4-18   Sample Create View dialog

Aliases can be created and dropped by selecting the appropriate action from the *Aliases* menu found in the Control Center. Figure 4-19 shows the Control Center menu items that must be selected in order to create a new alias. Figure 4-20 shows how the Create Alias dialog (which is activated by the Control Center) might look after its input fields have been populated.

Aliases can also be created and dropped by executing the SQL statements CREATE ALIAS and DROP ALIAS, either from the Command Center, the Command Line Processor, or an application program. The syntax for these statements will be covered in more detail in Chapter 6.

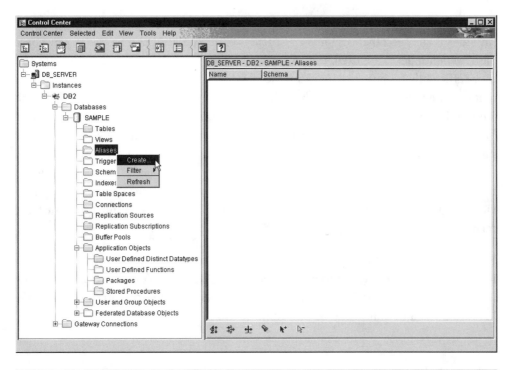

Figure 4-19 Creating an alias from the Control Center

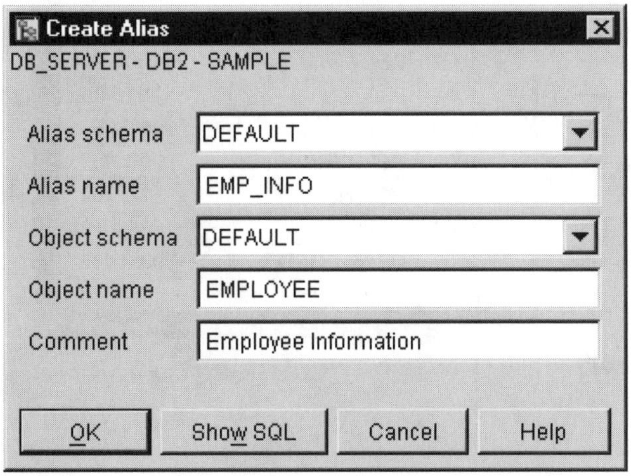

Figure 4-20 Sample Create Alias dialog

Indexes

An index is an object that contains an ordered set of pointers that refer to a key in a base table. When indexes are used, the DB2 Database Manager can access data directly and more efficiently because the index provides a direct path to the data through pointers that have been ordered based on the values of the columns that the index(es) is associated with. (When an index is created, the DB2 Database Manager uses a balanced binary tree [a hierarchical data structure in which each element may have at most one predecessor but may have many successors] to order the values of the key columns in the base table that the index refers to.) More than one index may be defined for a given table, and because indexes are stored separately from their associated table, they provide a way to define keys outside of the table definition. Figure 4-21 illustrates the basic relationship between an index and a base table.

Keys   A key is a column (or set of columns) in a table or index that can be used to identify or access a particular row (or rows) of data. Keys are normally identified in the description of a table, an index, or a referential constraint. Any column can be part of a key and the same column can be part of more than one key.

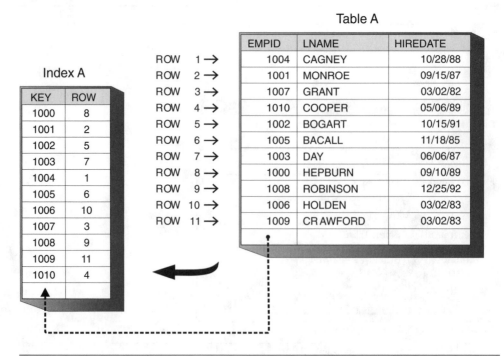

Figure 4-21   A simple index

A key that is composed of more than one column is called a composite key. In a table that has a composite key, the ordering of the columns within the key does not have to match the ordering of the columns in the table. A key that is defined in such a way that it identifies a single row of data within a table is called a unique key. Unique keys help maintain data integrity by ensuring that multiple rows of data in a table do not have identical key values. Thus, the columns of a unique key cannot contain null (missing) values. A unique key that is part of the definition of a table is called a primary key. A table can have only one primary key, and because the primary key is a unique key, its columns cannot contain null values. In Figure 4-21, the EMPID column is the primary key for Table A. A key in one table that references (or points to) a primary key in another table is called a foreign key. A foreign key establishes a referential link to a primary key, and the columns defined in each key must be identical. A partitioning key is a key that is part of the definition of a table that resides in a partitioned database. The partitioning key is used to determine the partition on which a particular row of data is stored. If a partitioning key is defined, unique keys and primary keys must include the same columns as the partitioning key (they may have additional columns). A table can only have one partitioning key.

The primary use of indexes is to help the DB2 Database Manager locate rows (records) in a table quickly. If an index is created for frequently used columns in a table, performance can often be greatly improved for data access and update operations. In addition, indexes provide greater concurrency when more than one transaction is accessing the same table—because row retrieval is faster, locks do not have to be held as long. However, these benefits do not come without a price. Indexes increase the amount of disk space required to store a database and they cause a slight decrease in performance whenever an indexed table's data is updated (because all indexes defined for the table must also be updated).

Indexes can be created and dropped by selecting the appropriate action from the *Indexes* menu found in the Control Center. Figure 4-22 shows the Control Center menu items that must be selected in order to create a new index. Figure 4-23 shows how the Create Index dialog (which is activated by the Control Center) might look after its input fields have been populated.

The Create Index Wizard is a special tool that can also be invoked from the *Indexes* menu found in the Control Center. This wizard enables you to enter a set of SQL statements that are frequently executed. Then, after analyzing those statements, the Create Index Wizard will recommend indexes that, if created, should improve the performance of the database. Figure 4-24 shows how the second page of the Create Index Wizard might look after its input fields have been populated (the first page of this wizard provides an overview of how the Create Index Wizard works).

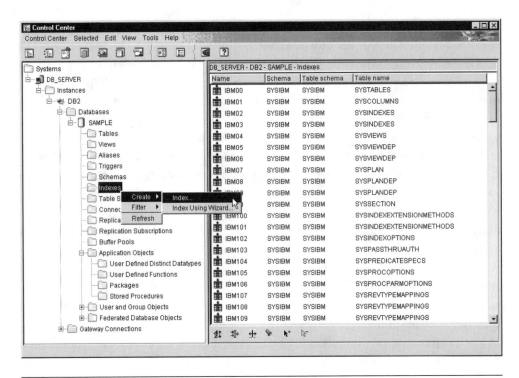

Figure 4-22   Creating an index from the Control Center

Indexes can also be created and dropped by executing the SQL statements CREATE INDEX and DROP INDEX, either from the Command Center, the Command Line Processor, or an application program. The syntax for these statements will be covered in more detail in Chapter 6.

Schemas

A schema is an identifier that helps provide a logical grouping or classification of objects in a database. A schema is also an object itself therefore an individual can own it and can control access to both the data and the objects that reside within it.

Most objects in a database are assigned a unique name that consists of two parts. The first (leftmost) part is called the qualifier or schema, and the second (rightmost) part is called the simple (or unqualified) name. Syntactically, these two parts are concatenated as a single string of characters separated by a period. When any object that can be qualified by a schema name (such as a table, index, view, user-defined data type, user-defined function, nickname, package, or trigger) is first created, it is assigned to a

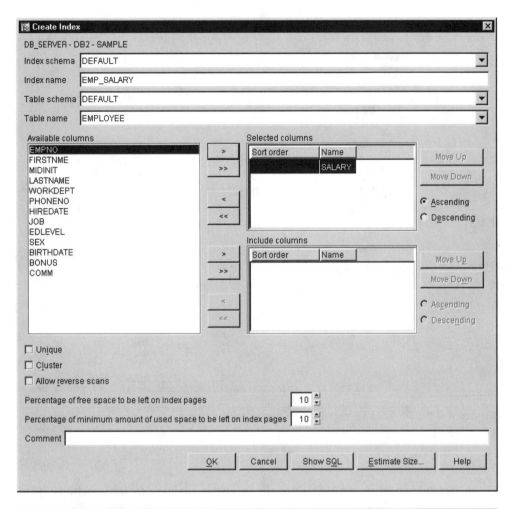

Figure 4-23 Sample Create Index dialog

particular schema based on the qualifier in its name. Figure 4-25 illustrates how a table is assigned to a particular schema during the table creation process.

NOTE If a schema/qualifier is not specified as part of the name of the object to be created, that object is assigned to the default schema, which is usually the user ID of the individual who created the object.

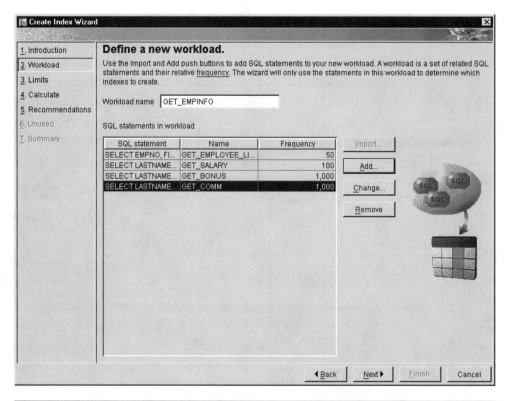

Figure 4-24 The second page of the Create Index Wizard

Often, schemas are implicitly created the first time a data object in the schema is created, provided the user creating the object holds the IMPLICIT_SCHEMA privilege. Schemas can also be explicitly created (and dropped) by selecting the appropriate action from the *Schemas* menu found in the Control Center. Figure 4-26 shows the Control Center menu items that must be selected in order to create a schema. Figure 4-27 shows how the Create Schema dialog (which is activated by the Control Center) might look after its input fields have been populated.

Schemas can also be explicitly created and dropped by executing the SQL statements CREATE SCHEMA and DROP SCHEMA, either from the Command Center, the Command Line Processor, or an application program. The syntax for these statements will be covered in more detail in Chapter 6.

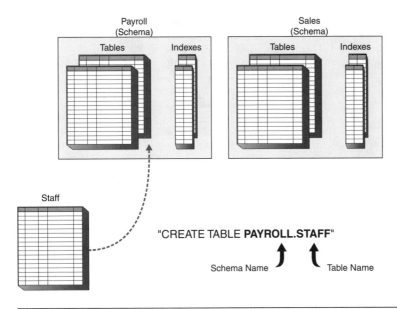

Figure 4-25 How a table object is assigned to a schema

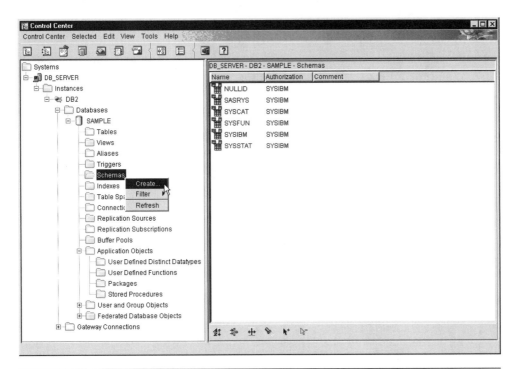

Figure 4-26 Creating a schema from the Control Center

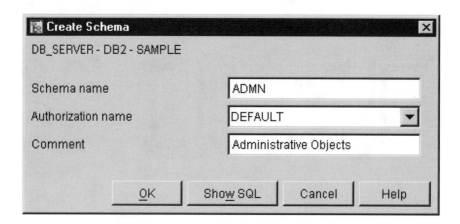

Figure 4-27 Sample Create Schema dialog

Triggers

Triggers are a group of actions that are automatically executed (or triggered) whenever an insert, update, or delete operation is performed on a specified table. (When such an operation takes place, the trigger is said to be activated.) Triggers are often used along with foreign keys (referential constraints) and check constraints to enforce data integrity rules. Triggers can also be used to apply updates to other tables in the database, to automatically generate and/or transform values for inserted or updated rows, to keep audit trails, and to detect exceptional conditions. By using triggers, the logic needed to enforce business rules can be placed in the database; applications using the database are relieved from having to enforce them. Additionally, having business rules enforced at the database means easier maintenance because no application program changes are required when the business rules change.

In order to create a trigger, the following criteria must be defined:

- **Subject table**   The table that the trigger expects the Trigger Event to interact with.

- **Trigger event**   A specific SQL operation that interacts with the Subject Table. This operation can be an insert, update, or delete operation.

- **Activation time**   Indicates when the trigger is to be activated. A *before* trigger will be activated before the Trigger Event is executed. (Thus, before triggers are able to see new data values before they are inserted into the Subject Table.) An *after* trigger will be activated after the Trigger Event has successfully completed execution. (Thus, after triggers can only see new data values after they have been inserted into the Subject Table.)

- **Set of affected rows** The rows of the Subject Table that are affected by the insert, update, or delete operation being performed.

- **Trigger granularity** Indicates whether the triggered actions are to be performed once for the complete operation, or once for each row in the Set of Affected Rows.

- **Triggered action** An optional search condition and the set of SQL statements that are to be executed whenever the trigger is activated. The triggered action is only executed if the search condition evaluates to TRUE.

At times, Triggered Actions may need to refer to the original values in the Set of Affected Rows. This reference is made possible through the use of transition variables and/or transition tables. Transition variables are temporary storage variables that use the names of the columns in the subject table, preceded by a qualifier that identifies whether the reference is to the old value (the value before the SQL operation is performed) or the new value (the value after the SQL operation is performed). Transition tables also use the names of the columns of the subject table, but they enable the complete set of affected rows to be treated as a single read-only table. As with transition variables, transition tables can be defined for both the old the new values.

NOTE Transition tables can only be used in after triggers.

Multiple triggers can be specified for a single table; when multiple triggers exist, they are activated in the order in which they were created. Therefore, the most recently created trigger will always be the last trigger that is activated. The activation of one trigger that executes SQL statements may cause the activation of other triggers (or even the reactivation of the same trigger). This event is known as trigger cascading. When trigger cascading occurs, the enforcement of referential integrity rules and the activation of multiple triggers can cause significant change to occur to the database as a result of a single SQL operation. Therefore, whenever a trigger is created, the effects its activation will have on referential integrity constraints and on other triggers should be thoroughly examined.

Triggers can be created and dropped by selecting the appropriate action from the *Triggers* menu found in the Control Center. Figure 4-28 shows the Control Center menu

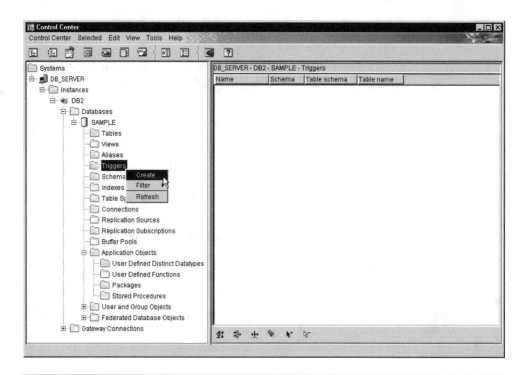

Figure 4-28   Creating a trigger from the Control Center

items that must be selected in order to create a new trigger. Figure 4-29 shows how the first tab of the Create Trigger dialog (which is activated by the Control Center) might look after its input fields have been populated.

Triggers can also be created and dropped by executing the SQL statements CREATE TRIGGER and DROP TRIGGER, either from the Command Center, the Command Line Processor, or an application program. The syntax for these statements will be covered in more detail in Chapter 6.

User-Defined Data Types

User-defined data types (UDTs) are named data types that are created by the user. A user-defined data type can be a distinct data type that shares a common representation with a built-in data type that is provided with DB2 Universal Database, or it can be a structured type that consists of a sequence of named attributes, each of which have their own data type. A structured data type can also be created as a subtype of another structured type (called a supertype) to make a type hierarchy.

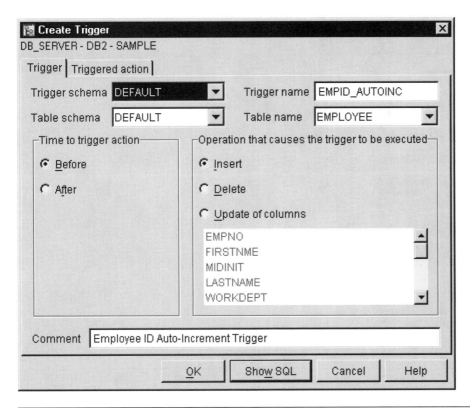

Figure 4-29 Sample Create Trigger dialog

User-defined data types support strong typing, which means that even though they may share the same representation as other built-in or user-defined data types, values of one UDT are only compatible with values of the same UDT or of other UDTs within the same data type hierarchy.

NOTE A user-defined data type cannot be used as an argument for most system-provided or built-in functions. Special user-defined functions must be provided to enable these and other operations.

User-defined distinct data types can be created and dropped by selecting the appropriate action from the *User-Defined Distinct Datatypes* menu found in the Control Cen-

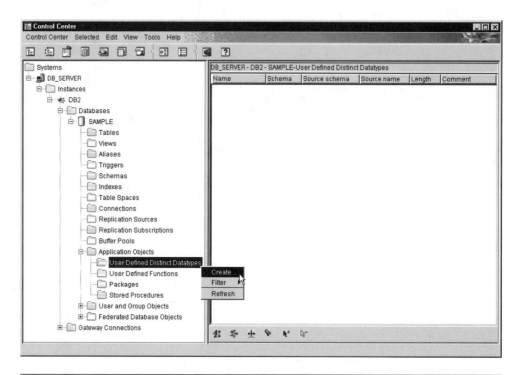

Figure 4-30   Creating a user-defined distinct data type from the Control Center

ter. Figure 4-30 shows the Control Center menu items that must be selected in order to create a new user-defined distinct data type. Figure 4-31 shows how the Create Distinct Type dialog (which is activated by the Control Center) might look after its input fields have been populated.

User-defined distinct data types can also be created, dropped, and modified by executing the SQL statements CREATE DISTINCT TYPE and DROP DISTINCT TYPE, either from the Command Center, the Command Line Processor, or an application program. User-defined reference and structured data types can be created and dropped by executing the SQL statements CREATE TYPE and DROP TYPE, either from the Command Center, the Command Line Processor, or an application program. The syntax for these statements will be covered in more detail in Chapter 6.

User-Defined Functions

User-defined functions (UDFs) are named functions that are created by the user. User-defined functions extend and/or enhance the support that is provided by the built-in

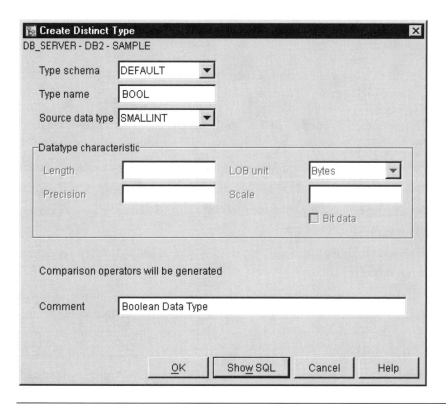

Figure 4-31   Sample Create Distinct Type dialog

functions that are provided with DB2 Universal Database, and can be used wherever a built-in function can be used.

All functions, including user-defined functions, fall under one of the following categories:

- **Scalar**   Scalar functions return a single answer each time they are called. For example, the built-in function SUBSTR() is a scalar function.

- **Column**   Column functions (sometimes called aggregating functions) return a single value from a set of like values (such as from a column). For example, the built-in function AVG() is a column function.

- **Table**   Table functions return a table to the SELECT SQL statement that references it in the FROM clause. For example, the built-in function SQLCACHE_SNAPSHOT is a table function. Table functions can be used to convert data that is not DB2 data into a format that resembles a DB2 table. This data can then be joined with other tables in the database.

To ensure that all functions fall in one of these three categories, DB2 Universal Database supports the following types of user-defined functions:

- **Source**   A user-defined function that is implemented by invoking another function (either built-in or user-defined) that is already registered in the database.

- **SQL scalar**   A user-defined function, written in SQL and defined when registered, that returns a scalar value.

- **SQL table**   A user-defined function, written in SQL and defined when registered, that returns a complete table of data.

- **SQL row**   A user-defined function, written in SQL and defined when registered, that returns a single row of data.

- **External scalar**   A user-defined function, written in a programming language such as C, that returns a scalar value. The external executable that contains this function must be registered in the database along with the function's attributes before it can be used.

- **External table**   A user-defined function, written in a programming language such as C, that returns a complete table of data. The external executable that contains this function must be registered in the database along with the function's attributes before it can be used.

- **OLE DB external table**   A user-defined OLE DB function that returns a complete table of data from an OLE DB provider.

- **Template**   A partial function that defines what types of values are to be returned, but that does not contain executable code. Function templates are mapped to a data source within a federated system so that a corresponding function within that data source can be invoked from DB2 Universal Database.

Built-in and user-defined functions can be displayed by selecting the *User-Defined Functions* object in the Control Center. Figure 4-32 shows the Control Center menu items that must be selected in order to display the functions that are recognized by a database.

User-defined functions can be created and dropped by executing the SQL statements CREATE FUNCTION and DROP FUNCTION, either from the Command Center, the Command Line Processor, or an application program. The syntax for these statements will be covered in more detail in Chapter 6.

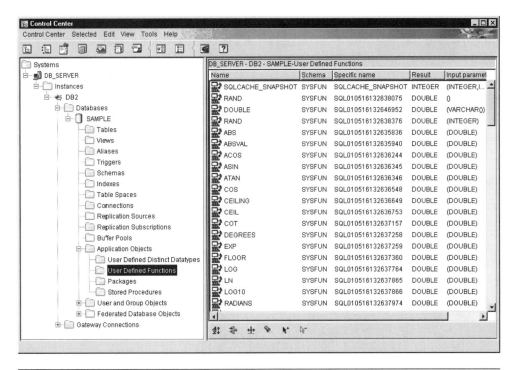

Figure 4-32   Displaying the built-in and user-defined functions available from the Control Center

Summary

The primary goal of this chapter was to provide you with an understanding of how a DB2 Universal Database database is constructed and to introduce you to the types of objects that can reside in a database once it has been created. The second goal of this chapter was to show you the various ways that both DB2 Universal Database databases and the objects within those databases can be created and, if necessary, destroyed.

In its simplest form, a DB2 Universal Database database is a set of related database objects. In fact, when you create a DB2 Universal Database database, you are establishing an administrative relational database entity that provides an underlying structure for an eventual collection of database objects (such as tables, views, indexes, and so on). This underlying structure consists of a set of system catalog tables (along with a set of corresponding views), a set of table spaces in which both the system catalog tables and the eventual collection of database objects will reside, and a set of files that will be used to handle database recovery and other bookkeeping details.

The easiest way to create a DB2 Universal Database database is by using the Create Database Wizard, which is invoked from the Control Center. A database can also be created by executing the CREATE DATABASE command, either from the Command Center or from the Command Line Processor. Regardless of how the process is initiated, whenever a new database is created the DB2 Database Manager performs the following set of tasks (in the order shown):

1. It creates the physical directories needed in the appropriate location.

2. It creates files that are needed for database recovery and other bookkeeping tasks.

3. It creates three table spaces and assigns them the names SYSCATSPACE, USERSPACE1, and TEMPSPACE1. The first of these table spaces is used to store the system catalog tables and views, the second is used to store user data, and the third is used for temporary storage. The characteristics of these table spaces can be specified as part of the input for the Create Database Wizard or the CREATE DATABASE command; however, if no characteristics are provided, all three will be created as system managed (SMS) table spaces.

4. It creates all the system catalog tables and views in the catalog table space and populates the tables as appropriate. Initially, this set of tables and views will occupy about 3.5 megabytes of disk space.

5. It initializes the database configuration file for the new database. Some of the parameters in this file will be set using values that were specified as input for the Create Database Wizard or CREATE DATABASE command; others will be assigned system default values.

6. It binds a set of utility programs to the new database so that the packages that are required before those programs can be executed will be created.

7. It grants Database Administrator (DBADM) authority to the user who created the database.

8. It grants CONNECT, CREATETAB, and BINDADD privileges to the group PUBLIC. This step enables all users to connect to the new database, create tables in the new database, and bind application programs to the new database. Once the database has been created, these privileges can be explicitly revoked.

The easiest way to destroy (or drop) an existing DB2 Universal Database database is by selecting the *Drop Database* action from the Control Center menu. A database can also be destroyed by executing the DROP DATABASE command, either from the Command Center or from the Command Line Processor. A database cannot be destroyed as long as one or more users/applications are connected to it. However, if a database must be destroyed before all users/applications can gracefully terminate their connections to it, those connections can be forcefully terminated by executing the FORCE APPLICA-TION command either from the Command Center or the Command Line Processor. This command can also be invoked by selecting the *Force Applications* action from the Control Center menu.

DB2 Universal Database uses a set of special files to keep track of where databases are stored and to allow access to both local and remote databases. Because the information stored in these files is used much like the information in an office-building directory is used, they are referred to as directory files. The following types of directory files exist:

- Local database directory files
- System database directory files
- Node directory files

A local database directory file exists on each path (called a drive on many operating systems) in which a database has been created. This file contains one entry for each database that is physically stored at that location. A system database directory file exists for each DB2 Database Manager instance. This file resides on the logical disk drive where the DB2 Universal Database product software is installed and it contains one entry for each database that has been cataloged for a particular instance. A node direc-tory file is created on each client workstation when the first database partition is cata-loged. Like the system database directory file, the node directory file also resides on the logical disk drive where the DB2 Universal Database product software is installed. Entries in the node directory are used in conjunction with entries in the system data-base directory for making connections and instance attachments to remote DB2 database servers. Local database directory and system database directory files are auto-matically created the first time a database is created on a specific workstation or path.

Before the DB2 Database Manager can access a database, it must be cataloged (listed) in the system database directory file. By default, databases are implicitly cataloged in both the system database directory file and in a local database directory file immedi-ately after they are created. Cataloged databases can be uncataloged by selecting the *Remove Database* action from the Control Center menu or by executing the UNCATA-LOG DATABASE command, either from the Command Center or from the Command Line Processor. Uncataloged databases can be explicitly cataloged by selecting the *Add Database* action from the Control Center menu (to catalog local databases), by running the Client Configuration Assistant (to catalog remote databases), or by executing the CATALOG DATABASE command, either from the Command Center or from the Com-mand Line Processor.

Four types of objects make up a DB2 Universal Database database:

- System objects
- Recovery objects
- Storage objects
- Database (or data) objects

System objects consist of DB2 Database Manager configuration files and individual database configuration files. Recovery objects consist of recovery log files and recovery history files. Recovery log files are used in combination with database backup images to recover from application, user, and/or system errors. The recovery history file contains information about every backup image that has been made.

Storage objects let you define how data will be stored on your system, and how data access performance can be improved. The following storage objects are available:

- Buffer pools
- Containers
- Table spaces

A buffer pool is an area of main memory that has been allocated to the DB2 Database Manager for the purpose of caching table and index data pages as they are read from disk, or modified. A container is an allocation of physical storage the DB2 Database Manager can access. Table spaces are used to specify where data in a database is physically stored on a system and to provide a layer of indirection between the database and the container objects in which the actual data resides.

A table space can be either a system managed space (SMS) or a database managed space (DMS). For an SMS table space, each container used is a directory that resides within the file space of the operating system, and the operating system's file manager is responsible for controlling the storage space. For a DMS table space, each container used is either a fixed-size, pre-allocated file or a physical raw device such as a disk, and the DB2 Database Manager is responsible for controlling the storage space.

When a database is first created, three table spaces are also created (and assigned the names SYSCATSPACE, USERSPACE1, and TEMPSPACE1). The first of these table spaces is used to store the system catalog tables and views, the second is used to store user data, and the third is used for temporary storage. Unless otherwise specified, all three of these table spaces will be SMS table spaces.

Database objects, otherwise known as data objects, are the components that are used to store and manipulate data and to control how all user data (and some system data) is organized. Data objects include

- Tables

- Views

- Aliases

- Indexes

- Schemas

- Triggers

- User-defined data types

- User-defined functions

A table is a logical structure that is used to present data as a collection of unordered rows with a fixed number of columns. Each column contains a set of values of the same data type or one of its subtypes—the definition of the columns in a table make up the table structure and the rows contain the actual table data. The storage representation of a row is called a record, and the storage representation of a column is called a field. Each intersection of a row and column in a database table has a specific data item called a value. Five types of tables can exist in a DB2 Universal Database database:

- Base tables

- Result tables

- Summary tables

- Declared temporary tables

- Typed tables

A view provides an alternative way of working with data that exists in one or more base tables. Essentially, a view is a named specification of a result table that is produced whenever the view is referenced in an SQL statement. For this reason, a view can be thought of as having columns and rows, just like a base table, and in most cases, data can be retrieved from a view just as it can be retrieved from a base table. Although a view looks like a base table, it does not exist as a table in physical storage therefore it does not contain data.

An alias is an alternate name for a table, view, or nickname. Once created, aliases can be referenced in the same way any table, view, or nickname can be referenced. However, an alias cannot be used in every context that a table, view, or nickname can be used in. For example, an alias cannot be used in the check condition of a check constraint and cannot reference a user-defined temporary table.

An index is an object that contains an ordered set of pointers that refer to a key in a base table. When indexes are used, the DB2 Database Manager can access data directly and more efficiently because the index provides a direct path to the data through pointers that have been ordered based on the values of the columns that the index(es) is associated with. More than one index may be defined for a given table, and because indexes are stored separately from their associated table, they provide a way to define keys outside of the table definition.

A schema is an identifier that helps provide a logical grouping or classification of objects in a database. A schema is also an object itself; therefore, an individual can own it and can control access to both the data and the objects that reside within it.

Triggers are a group of actions that are automatically executed (or triggered) whenever an insert, update, or delete operation is performed on a specified table (when such an operation takes place, the trigger is said to be activated). Triggers are often used along with foreign keys (referential constraints) and check constraints to enforce data integrity rules. Triggers can also be used to apply updates to other tables in the database, to automatically generate and/or transform values for inserted or updated rows, to keep audit trails, and to detect exceptional conditions.

User-defined data types (UDTs) are named data types that are created by the user. A user-defined data type can be a distinct data type that shares a common representation with a built-in data type that is provided with DB2 Universal Database, or it can be a structured type that consists of a sequence of named attributes, each of which have their own data type.

User-defined functions (UDFs) are named functions that are created by the user. User-defined functions extend and/or enhance the support that is provided by the built-in functions that are provided with DB2 Universal Database, and can be used wherever a built-in function can be used.

Most system objects and database (data) objects can be created, dropped, and in some cases modified by selecting the appropriate action from the one of the object menus found in the Control Center or by executing the appropriate Data Definition Language (DDL) SQL statements, either from the Command Center, the Command Line Processor, or an application program.

Questions

1. If the command

```
"db2 CREATE DATABASE SAMPLEDB ALIAS MY_DB DFT_EXTENT_SZ 6
CATALOG TABLESPACE MANAGED BY DATABASE USING
(DEVICE '/dev/dskdrive1' 2000)"
```

is executed, how many system managed space (SMS) table spaces will be created?

   a. 0
   b. 1
   c. 2
   d. 3
   e. 4

2. Which of the following statements will catalog the database MYDB on the node MYNODE with an alias of MYNEWDB?
   a. `CATALOG DATABASE MYNEWDB AT NODE MYNODE`
   b. `CATALOG DATABASE MYNEWDB AS MYDB AT NODE MYNODE`
   c. `CATALOG DATABASE MYDB AT NODE MYNODE`
   d. `CATALOG DATABASE MYDB AS MYNEWDB AT NODE MYNODE`

3. Which of the following is the best way to change the information stored in the local database directory for the database DB1 without affecting its data?
   a. Backup the database, drop the database, and provide the new information while creating a new database from the backup image.
   b. Uncatalog the database and then catalog the database using the new information.
   c. Export the data, drop the database, create the database using the new information, and import the exported data.
   d. Uncatalog the database, change the information with the UPDATE DATABASE DIRECTORY command, and catalog the database.

4. Which of the following tools cannot be used to catalog a database?
   a. Control Center
   b. SQL Assist
   c. Client Configuration Assistant
   d. Command Line Processor

5. Cataloging a remote database is
   a. Performed on a PC or UNIX machine to identify the server the DB2 Database Manager instance for the database is on.
   b. Never performed—as only one database per node is allowed, cataloging a node automatically catalogs the database at that node.
   c. Performed on a PC or UNIX machine to identify the database to users and applications.
   d. Performed on a PC or UNIX machine to open the catalogs in the DB2 database and present a user with a list of all accessible tables within that database.

6. Which two of the following cannot be created using the Control Center?
   a. A user-defined function
   b. A table space
   c. A database
   d. A stored procedure
   e. A buffer pool

7. Database Managed Space (DMS) table space TS1 has been created. Which of the following statements is accurate?
   a. Buffer pools can now be associated with table space TS1.
   b. Containers used by TS1 cannot be used by other table spaces.
   c. Space for all containers associated with TS1 is not pre-allocated.
   d. Tables may be split across TS1, as well as other table spaces.

8. A declared temporary table is used for which of the following purposes?
   a. Backup purposes
   b. Storing intermediate results
   c. Staging area for load operations
   d. Sharing result data sets between applications

9. Given the following table:

EMPLOYEE

EMPNO	LNAME	FNAME	SSN	SALARY
1	Bogart	Humphrey	555-12-1234	$45,000.00
2	Bacall	Lauren	555-24-4567	$48,000.00

If the view V1 is created in such a way that it contains information from every column in the EMPLOYEE table except the SALARY column, which of the following is NOT accurate?
   a. View V1 can be used in the same context as the EMPLOYEE table for all data retrieval operations that do not acquire SALARY information.
   b. View V1 can be used as a data source for other views.
   c. View V1 does not have to reside in the same schema as the EMPLOYEE table.
   d. All data except SALARY data that is stored in the EMPLOYEE table is copied to the physical location associated with view V1.

PART II

10. Which of the following events do NOT have the potential of causing a trigger to be activated?

   a. An insert operation

   b. A delete operation

   c. Enforcement of a check constraint

   d. Enforcement of a referential integrity constraint

   e. The activation of a trigger

Answers

1. C. By default, when a DB2 Universal Database database is created, three system managed space (SMS) table spaces are created. However, when this form of the CREATE DATABASE command is executed, one of the default SMS table spaces will be replaced with a database managed space (DMS) table space, so only two SMS table spaces will be created.

2. D. The correct syntax for the CATALOG DATABASE command is

```
CATALOG [DATABASE | DB] [DatabaseName] <AS [AliasName]>
<ON [Path] | AT NODE [NodeName]>
<AUTHENTICATION [AuthenticationType]> <WITH [Description]>
```

3. A. The only way to change the entry for a database in the local database directory file is to drop the database and create a new one. Obviously, backing up and restoring the database is easier than exporting and importing the data stored in every table.

4. B. The Control Center and the Client Configuration Assistant provide visual tools for cataloging databases and the CATALOG DATABASE command can be executed from the Command Line Processor. However, because the CATALOG DATABASE command is a command and not an SQL statement, it cannot be issued from the SQL Assist tool.

5. C. The purpose for cataloging a remote database is to make the database available to users and applications.

6. A and E. User-defined functions and stored procedures can be viewed from the Control Center, but they cannot be created from the Control Center.

7. C. Containers for database managed space (DMS) table spaces must be pre-allocated. Storage space for system managed space (SMS) table spaces is allocated by the system as it is needed.

8. **B.** Declared temporary tables are used to hold temporary data on behalf of a single application and are automatically destroyed when the application that declared them disconnects from the database.

9. **D.** Although a view looks like a base table, it does not exist as a table in physical storage; therefore, it does not contain data. Instead, a view refers to data that is stored in other base tables.

10. **C.** Insert, update, and delete operations; the enforcement of referential constraints that cause cascaded update or delete operations to occur; and the activation of triggers that cause insert, update, or delete operations to occur can cause a trigger to be activated.

Creating Table Objects

In this chapter, you will learn

- What built-in data types are available with DB2 Universal Database
- How user-defined data types, DataLinks, and extenders can be incorporated into a table's definition
- What constraints are and what constraints are available with DB2 Universal Database
- How constraints can be used to ensure that data adheres to business rules
- How to create a table object with the CREATE TABLE SQL statement
- How to identify the characteristics of a table by examining the SQL statement that was used to create it

The fourth objective of the DB2 Universal Database Family Fundamentals exam is to evaluate your ability to create table objects and to test your knowledge of the different data types that can be used to create a table's underlying structure. It was mentioned earlier that tables are made up of rows and columns, where each record (row) is divided into fields (columns) that contain individual pieces of information. Knowing which data type to use to hold these pieces of information is a large part of the table creation process. However, to incorporate one or more business rules into a database's design, it is also important to understand what constraints are and how constraints can be used in a table's definition to ensure data validity and enforce data integrity. This chapter is designed to provide you with everything you need to know about creating a table object and defining its characteristics.

TIP Eighteen percent of the DB2 Universal Database Family Fundamentals exam is designed to test your knowledge of creating table objects and your ability to identify a table's characteristics.

Understanding Data Types

All data is classified, to some extent, according to its type (for example, some data might be numerical, whereas other data might be textual). Because a table is comprised of one or more columns that are designed to hold data values, each column must be assigned a specific data type. This data type determines the internal representation that will be used to store the data, what the ranges of the data's values are, and what set of operators and functions can be used to manipulate that data once it has been stored. Data types are specified for a column as part of the table creation process.

DB2 Universal Database supports 19 different built-in data types (along with an infinite number of user-defined data types that are based on the built-in data types). However, the code page being used by a particular database determines the actual set of data types that can be used. (In a DB2 database, each single-byte character is represented internally as a unique number between 0 and 255. This number is referred to as the code point of the character; assignments of code points to every character in a particular character set are collectively called the code page. The code page determines how bit patterns are used to represent characters.) In a single-byte code page such as 850 (the English language in the United States of America), each character is represented by 1 byte; in a double-byte code page such as 932 (Japanese), some characters are represented by 1 byte, whereas others are represented by 2 bytes. A database that uses a single-byte code page can use any of the following data types:

- Small integer
- Integer
- Big integer
- Decimal
- Single-precision floating point
- Double-precision floating point
- Fixed-length character string
- Varying-length character string

- Varying-length long character string
- Date
- Time
- Timestamp
- Binary large object
- Character large object
- DataLink

In addition to these data types, a database that uses a double-byte code page can also take advantage of the following data types:

- Fixed-length double-byte character string
- Varying-length double-byte character string
- Varying-length double-byte long character string
- Double-byte character large object

Small Integer

The small integer data type is used to store binary integer values that have a precision of 15 bits. The range for a small integer value is −32,768 to +32,767. The small integer data type uses the smallest amount of storage space possible to store numerical values (2 bytes of space is required for each value stored). The term SMALLINT is used to declare a small integer column in a table definition.

Integer

The integer data type is used to store binary integer values that have a precision of 31 bits. Although the integer data type requires twice as much storage space as the small integer data type (4 bytes of space is required for each value stored), its range of values is much greater. The range for an integer value is −2,147,483,648 to +2,147,483,647. The terms INTEGER and INT can be used to declare an integer column in a table definition.

Big Integer

The big integer data type is used to store binary integer values that have a precision of 63 bits on platforms that provide native support for 64 bit integers (for example, Solaris). On such systems, processing large numbers that are stored as big integers is more efficient than processing similar numbers that have been stored as decimal values. In addition, calculations performed with big integer values are more precise than calculations performed with real or double values.

The big integer data type requires four times as much storage space as the small integer data type (8 bytes of space is required for each value stored). The range for a big integer is $-9,223,372,036,854,775,808$ to $+9,223,372,036,854,775,807$. The term BIGINT is used to declare a big integer column in a table definition.

Decimal

The decimal data type is used to store numbers that contain both whole and fractional parts; the parts are combined and stored in what is known as packed decimal format. A precision (the total number of digits) and a scale (the number of digits to use for the fractional part of the number) must be specified whenever a decimal data type is declared. The range for the precision of a decimal is 1 to 31. The amount of storage space needed to store a decimal value can be calculated by using the following equation: *precision$\div$2 (truncated) + 1 = bytes of space required.* For example, a DECIMAL(8,2) value would require 5 bytes of storage space ($8\div2 = 4$; $4 + 1 = 5$), whereas a DECIMAL(7,2) value would require 4 bytes of storage space ($7\div2 = 3.5$ (truncated to 3); $3 + 1 = 4$).

The terms DECIMAL, DEC, NUMERIC, and NUM can all be used to declare a decimal column in a table definition.

NOTE If the precision and scale values are not provided for a decimal column definition, by default, a precision value of 5 and a scale value of 0 are used (therefore, 3 bytes of storage space is needed).

Single-Precision Floating Point

The single-precision floating-point data type is used to store a 32-bit approximation of a real number. Although the single-precision floating-point data type and the integer data type require the same amount of storage space (4 bytes of space is required for each value stored), the range for a single-precision floating-point number is much greater: $10E^{-38}$ to $10E^{+38}$.

The terms REAL and FLOAT can be used to declare a single-precision floating-point column in a table definition. However, if the term FLOAT is used, the length specified for the column must be between 1 and 24—the term FLOAT can be used to represent both single- and double-precision floating-point data types; the length specified determines which actual data type is to be used.

Double-Precision Floating Point

The double-precision floating-point data type is used to store a 64-bit approximation of a real number. Although the double-precision floating-point data type requires the same amount of storage space as the big integer data type (8 bytes of space is required for each value stored), the range for a double-precision floating-point number is the largest possible: $-1.79769E^{+308}$ to $-2.225E^{-307}$, 0, and $2.225E^{-307}$ to $-1.79769E^{+308}$

The terms DOUBLE and FLOAT can be used to declare a double-precision floating-point column in a table definition. However, if the term FLOAT is used, the length specified for the column must be between 25 and 53—the term FLOAT can be used to represent both single- and double-precision floating-point data types; the length specified determines which actual data type is to be used.

Fixed-Length Character String

The fixed-length character string data type is used to store character and character string data that has a specific length that does not exceed 254 characters. The terms CHARACTER and CHAR can be used to declare a fixed-length character string column in a table definition; the length of the character string data to be stored must be specified whenever a fixed-length character string data type is declared. The amount of storage space needed to store a fixed-length character string value can be determined by using the following equation: *fixed length*$\times 1$ = *bytes of space required*. For example, a CHAR(8) value would require 8 bytes of storage space.

 NOTE When fixed-length character string data types are used, storage space can be wasted if the actual length of the data is significantly smaller than the length specified when the column was defined (for example, if the values YES and NO were to be stored in a column that was defined as CHAR(20)). Therefore, the fixed length specified for a fixed-length character string column should be as close as possible to the actual length of the data that will be stored in the column.

Varying-Length Character String

The varying-length character string data type is used to store character string data that varies in length. In earlier versions of DB2, varying-length character string data could be up to 4,000 characters long. In Version 7.1, varying-length character string data can be up to 32,672 characters long; however, the actual length allowed is governed by one restriction: the data must fit on a single table space page. This means that for a table that resides in a table space that uses 4K pages, varying-length character string data cannot be more than 4,092 characters long; for a table that resides in a table space that uses 8K pages, varying-length character string data cannot be more than 8,188 characters long, and so on, up to 32K. Because table spaces are created with 4K pages by default, you must explicitly create a table space with a larger page size if you want to use a varying-length character string data type to store strings that contain more than 4,092 characters. (You must also have sufficient space in the table row to accommodate the character string data. In other words, the storage requirements for other columns in the table must be added to the storage requirements of the character string data and the total amount of storage space needed must not exceed the size of the table space's page.)

 NOTE When a varying-length character string data value is updated and the new value is larger than the original value, the record containing the value will be moved to another page in the table. Such records are known as tombstone records or pointer records. Too many tombstone records can cause a significant decrease in performance because multiple pages must be retrieved in order to process a single data record.

The terms CHARACTER VARYING, CHAR VARYING, and VARCHAR can be used to declare a varying-length character string column in a table definition. When a varying-length character string column is defined, the maximum number of characters that are expected to be stored in that column must be specified as part of the declaration. Subsequent character string data values that are stored in the column can be shorter than or equal to the maximum length specified; if they are longer, they will not be stored and an error will be generated.

The amount of storage space needed to store a varying-length character string value can be determined by using the following equation: (*string length* $\times 1$) $+ 4 =$ *bytes of space required*. Thus, if a character string containing 30 characters were stored using a VARCHAR(30) data type, that particular value would require 34 bytes of storage space. (All character strings using this data type would have to be less than or equal to 30 characters in length.)

Varying-Length Long Character String

The varying-length long character string data type is also used to store character string data that varies in length. In earlier versions of DB2, varying-length long character string data types were used whenever character string data was too large to fit in a varying-length character string data type (that is, whenever character string data was more than 4,000 characters long). In Version 7.1 and later, the varying-length long character string data type is used to store character string data that is less than or equal to 32,700 characters long in a table that resides in a table space that uses 4K pages. In other words, when the varying-length long character string data type is used, the page size/character string data length restrictions that apply to varying-length character string data are not applicable.

The term LONG VARCHAR is used to declare a varying-length long character string column in a table definition. The amount of storage space needed to store a varying-length long character string value can be determined by using the following equation: ($string\ length \times 1$) $+\ 24\ =$ *bytes of space required*. Thus, if a character string containing 8,200 characters were stored using a LONG VARCHAR data type, that particular value would require 8,224 bytes of storage space. The amount of storage space needed to store a varying-length long character string value in a base record is 24 bytes, regardless of how long the character string data is. The character string data is physically stored on separate pages and references to those pages are stored in the record. So in the previous example, 24 bytes would be stored in the row itself, and 8,200 bytes would be stored in another location. Unfortunately, with this storage model more time to process varying-length long character string data requests is required because the DB2 Database Manager must load at least two pages into the buffer pool in order to get to the data.

 NOTE   The FOR BIT DATA clause can be used with any character string data type when declaring a column in a table definition. If this clause is used, code page conversions will not be performed during data exchange operations and the data itself will be treated and compared as binary (bit) data.

Fixed-Length Double-Byte Character String

The fixed-length double-byte character string data type is used to store double-byte character set (DBCS) characters and character string data that has a specific length that does not exceed 127 characters. The term GRAPHIC is used to declare a fixed-length double-byte character string column in a table definition; the length of the DBCS character string data to be stored must be specified whenever a fixed-length double-byte character string data type is declared. The amount of storage space needed to store a fixed-length double-byte character string value can be determined by using the following equation: *fixed length* $\times 2\ =$ *bytes of space required*. For example, a GRAPHIC(8) value would require 16 bytes of storage space.

Varying-Length Double-Byte Character String

The varying-length double-byte character string data type is used to store double-byte character set (DBCS) character string data that varies in length. In earlier versions of DB2, varying-length double-byte character string data could be up to 2,000 characters long. In Version 7.1, varying-length double-byte character string data can be up to 16,336 characters long; however, the actual length allowed is governed by the same restriction that governs the length of varying-length character string data—the data must fit on a single table space page. (Refer to the varying-length character string data type for more information.)

The term VARGRAPHIC is used to declare a varying-length double-byte character string column in a table definition. When a varying-length double-byte character string column is defined, the maximum number of characters that are expected to be stored in that column must be specified as part of the declaration. Subsequent character string data values that are stored in the column can be shorter than or equal to the maximum length specified; if they are longer, they will not be stored and an error will be generated.

The amount of storage space needed to store a varying-length double-byte character string value can be determined by using the following equation: *(string length* $\times 2$ *)* $+ 4$ $= bytes\ of\ space\ required$. Thus, if a character string containing 22 characters were stored using a VARGRAPHIC(22) data type, that particular value would require 48 bytes of storage space.

Varying-Length Double-Byte Long Character String

The varying-length double-byte long character string data type is also used to store double-byte character set (DBCS) character string data that varies in length. In earlier versions of DB2, varying-length double-byte long character string data types were used whenever double-byte character string data was too large to fit in a varying-length double-byte character string data type (that is, whenever DBCS character string data was more than 2,000 characters long). In Version 7.1 and later, the varying-length double-byte long character string data type is used to store DBCS character string data that is less than or equal to 16,350 characters long in a table that resides in a table space that uses 4K pages.

The term LONG VARGRAPHIC is used to declare a varying-length double-byte long character string column in a table definition. The amount of storage space needed to store a varying-length double-byte long character string value can be determined by using the following equation: *(string length* $\times 2$ *)* $+ 24 = bytes\ of\ space\ required$. Thus, if a character string containing 5,100 characters were stored using a LONG VARGRAPHIC data type, that particular value would require 10,224 bytes of storage space. The amount of storage space needed to store a varying-length double-byte long character string value in a base record is 24 bytes, regardless of how long the double-byte character string data is. The character string data is physically stored on separate pages and references to those pages are stored in the record. So in the previous example, 24 bytes would be stored in the row itself, and 8,200 bytes would be stored in another location.

Date

The date data type is used to store a three-part value (year, month, and day) that designates a valid calendar date. The range for the year part is 0001 to 9999; the range for the month part is 1 to 12; and the range for the day part is 1 to n (28, 29, 30, or 31) where n is dependent upon the month part and whether the year part corresponds to a leap year. Externally, the date data type appears to be a fixed-length character string data type that has a length of 10. However, internally, the date data type requires much less storage space—4 bytes of space is required for each value stored. That's because date values are stored as packed strings. The term DATE is used to declare a date column in a table definition.

Because the representation of dates varies in different parts of the world, the format of a date value is determined by the country code associated with the database being used. Table 5-1 shows the date formats that are available with DB2 Universal Database, along with an example of their string representation.

Time

The time data type is used to store a three-part value (hours, minutes, and seconds) that designates a valid time of day under a 24-hour clock. The range for the hours part is 0 to 24; the range for the minutes part is 0 to 59; and the range for the seconds part is also 0 to 59. (If the hours part is set to 24, the minutes and seconds parts must be set to 0.) Externally, the time data type appears to be a fixed-length character string data type that has a length of 8. However, like date values, time values are stored as packed strings —in this case, 3 bytes of space is required for each time value stored. The term TIME is used to declare a time column in a table definition.

Like dates, the representation of time varies in different parts of the world. Thus, the format of a time value is also determined by the country code associated with the

Table 5-1 DB2 Date Formats (YYYY = Year, MM = Month, DD = Day)

Format Name	Abbreviation	Date String Format
International Standards Organization	ISO	YYYY-MM-DD
IBM USA Standard	USA	MM/DD/YYYY
IBM European Standard	EUR	DD.MM.YYYY
Japanese Industrial Standard	JIS	YYYY-MM-DD
Site specific	LOC	Based on database's country code

Table 5-2 DB2 Time Formats (HH = Hours, MM = Minutes, SS = Seconds)

Format Name	Abbreviation	Time String Format
International Standards Organization	ISO	HH.MM.SS
IBM USA Standard	USA	HH:MM AM or PM
IBM European Standard	EUR	HH.MM.SS
Japanese Industrial Standard	JIS	HH.MM:SS
Site specific	LOC	Based on database's country code

database being used. Table 5-2 shows the time formats that are available with DB2 Universal Database, along with an example of their string representation.

Timestamp

The timestamp data type is used to store a seven-part value (year, month, day, hours, minutes, seconds, and microseconds) that designates a valid calendar date and time of day under a 24-hour clock. Like the date and time data types, the range for the year part is 0001 to 9999; the range for the month part is 1 to 12; the range for the day part is 1 to n (28, 29, 30, or 31) where n is dependent upon the month part and whether the year part corresponds to a leap year; the range for the hours part is 0 to 24; the range for the minutes part is 0 to 59; and the range for the seconds part is also 0 to 59. The range for the microseconds part is 0 to 999,999. Externally, the time data type appears to be a fixed-length character string data type that has a length of 26. However, like date and time values, timestamp values are stored as packed strings—in this case, 10 bytes of space is required for each timestamp value stored. The term TIMESTAMP is used to declare a timestamp column in a table definition.

Unlike date and time values whose format is determined by the country code associated with the database being used, the format of a timestamp value never changes. Its string representation is always YYYY-MM-DD-HH.MM.SS.NNNNNN (Year-Month-Day-Hour.Minute.Second.Microsecond).

NOTE Although timestamp data types require the most storage, they contain the most accurate time information (because they include microseconds).

Binary Large Object

The binary large object data type is used to store binary string data that varies in length. It is frequently used to store nontraditional data such as documents, graphic images, pictures, audio, and video.

The term BLOB is used to declare a binary large object column in a table definition. When a binary large object column is defined, the maximum number of bytes that are expected to be stored in that column must be specified as part of the declaration. However, because binary large object data types are used to store data of varying lengths, the amount of storage space that is allocated for a single binary large object value is determined by the size of the object, not by the maximum size specified in the table definition. Binary large object values can be up to 2 gigabytes in size (2 billion bytes) provided that modifications to that object are not to be recorded in the database log file (if modifications are to be recorded, the object cannot exceed 1 gigabyte in size). Each binary large object value has a corresponding LOB descriptor in the base record that points to the location of the actual data. The size of the LOB descriptor varies according to the maximum data size specified in the table definition. Table 5-3 shows the most common LOB descriptor sizes used.

NOTE   Binary large object data cannot be manipulated by SQL the same way that other data can. For example, binary large object values cannot be sorted.

Table 5-3   Common LOB Descriptor Sizes

Maximum LOB Length Specified	LOB Descriptor Size
1,024	72
8,192	96
65,536	120
524,000	144
4,190,000	168
134,000,000	200
536,000,000	224
1,070,000,000	256
1,470,000,000	280
2,147,483,647	316

Character Large Object

The character large object data type is used to store single-byte character set (SBCS) or multibyte character set (MBCS) character string data that is too large to fit in a varying-length long character string data type. The character large object data type is essentially a binary large object data type that enables you to manipulate textual data that is greater than 32,700 characters in length. Like binary large object values, character large object values can be up to 2 gigabytes in size (2 billion bytes) provided that modifications to that object are not to be recorded in the database log file (if modifications are to be recorded, the object cannot exceed 1 gigabyte in size).

The term CLOB is used to declare a character large object column in a table definition. When a character large object column is defined, the maximum number of bytes that are expected to be stored in that column must be specified as part of the declaration. Like binary large object values, each character large object value has a corresponding LOB descriptor in the base record that points to the location of the actual data. Again, the size of the LOB descriptor varies according to the maximum data size specified in the table definition.

Double-Byte Character Large Object

The double-byte character large object data type is used to store double-byte character-set (DBCS) character string data that is too large to fit in a varying-length double-byte long character string data type. The double-byte character large object data type is essentially a character large object data type that uses 2 bytes to store each character as opposed to 1. Double-byte character large object values can be up to 1,073,741,823 characters long.

The term DBCLOB is used to declare a double-byte character large object column in a table definition. When a double-byte character large object column is defined, the maximum number of bytes that are expected to be stored in that column must be specified as part of the declaration. Like binary large object values, each double-byte character large object value has a corresponding LOB descriptor in the base record that points to the location of the actual data. Again, the size of the LOB descriptor varies according to the maximum data size specified in the table definition.

DataLink

The DataLink data type is used to store an encapsulated value that contains a logical reference to a file that is stored in a file system controlled by a DB2 DataLink Server (which resides outside of the database). DataLink values serve as encapsulated anchor values that provide reference information that enables the database to establish and maintain a link to external data. The attributes of this encapsulated value are as follows:

- **Link type**   Identifies how the data is to be linked. Currently, the only link type supported is Uniform Resource Locator (URL).

- **Scheme**   For URLs, this is the value **HTTP** or **FILE**.

- **File server name**   The complete address of the file server.

- **File path**   The identity of the file and its location within the file server.

- **Access control token**   When appropriate, an access token is embedded within the file path.

- **Comment**   Up to 254 characters of descriptive information.

The first four of these values are collectively known as the linkage attributes. Without linkage attribute values, a file cannot be linked to a DataLink column. Because a DataLink value is an encapsulated value, it is created and accessed via a set of built-in scalar functions. Specifically, the function DLVALUE() is used to create a new DataLink value and the functions DLCOMMENT(), DLLINKTYPE(), DLURLCOMPLETE(), DLURLPATH(), DLURLPATHONLY(), DLURLSCHEME(), and DLURLSERVER() are used to extract specific information from a DataLink encapsulated value.

The term DATALINK, along with a set of options, is used to declare a DataLink column in a table definition. The amount of storage space needed to store a DataLink is 254 bytes.

User-Defined Data Types (UDTs)

As mentioned earlier, user-defined data types (UDTs) are named data types that are explicitly created by the user. A user-defined data type can be a distinct data type that shares a common representation with a built-in data type, or it can be a structured type that consists of a sequence of named attributes, each of which have their own data type. For example, a user could create a distinct data type called AUDIO that uses the binary large object data type as its source data type. The term AUDIO could then be used to declare an audio column in a table definition. Behind the scenes, audio data values would be stored as binary large objects; however, they would not be treated as binary large objects.

User-defined data types support strong typing, which means that even though they may share the same representation as other built-in or user-defined data types, they are considered to be separate, incompatible data types for most SQL operations. Because of this, user-defined data types do not automatically acquire the functions and operators of their source types (one or more of these functions and/or operators may no longer be meaningful). However, user-defined functions and operators can be created and applied to distinct user-defined data types to replace this lost functionality.

Extenders

The extender products that are available for DB2 Universal Database provide an additional set of user-defined data types and functions that can be used as part of a table definition. For example, the DB2 Image Extender data type is a user-defined data type that has been assigned the name DB2IMAGE. Because most of the data types provided by the DB2 Extenders are based on the binary large object data type, the size limits and storage requirements of an extender data type is usually the same as those of a binary large object data type, provided that the extender data is to be stored in the database. The DB2 Extenders provide the added flexibility of allowing large object data to be stored in an external file whose location is pointed to from the database. When this functionality is used, the storage requirements for an extender data type can be drastically reduced.

Understanding Constraints

Within most businesses, data often must adhere to certain restrictions or rules. Such restrictions may apply to single pieces of information, such as the format and sequence to use for purchase order numbers; or they may apply to several pieces of information, such as which employees are members of which departments and which employees manage those departments. Constraints are DB2 Universal Database's way of enforcing such rules within the confines of the database system. Essentially, constraints are rules that govern or influence the way in which data values can be added and/or modified. The following types of constraints are available with DB2 Universal Database:

- NOT NULL constraints
- Column default constraints
- Unique constraints
- Referential integrity constraints
- Check constraints

Constraints are only associated with base table objects; they are enforced by the DB2 Database Manager whenever insert or update operations occur. Constraints can be defined as part of the table creation process, and in some cases, they can be added after a table has been created. However, once a constraint has been created, no special way is available to change its definition if your business rules change. In these situations, the old constraint must be dropped and a new constraint that reflects the new business rules must be created (with the ALTER TABLE statement). In most cases, existing constraints can be dropped at any time; this action will not affect the table's structure or the data stored in it.

The NOT NULL Constraint

The null value is used in a DB2 Universal Database to represent an unknown state. By default, all of the built-in data types provided with DB2 Universal Database support the presence of null values. However, some business rules may dictate that a value must always be provided (for example, every employee is required to provide emergency contact information). The NOT NULL constraint is used to ensure that a given column of a base table is never assigned the null value. Once a NOT NULL constraint has been defined for a particular column, any insert or update operation that attempts to place a null value in that column will fail. Figure 5-1 illustrates how the NOT NULL constraint prevents null data.

Because constraints only apply to a particular base table, they are usually defined, along with a table's attributes, during the table creation process. (The table creation

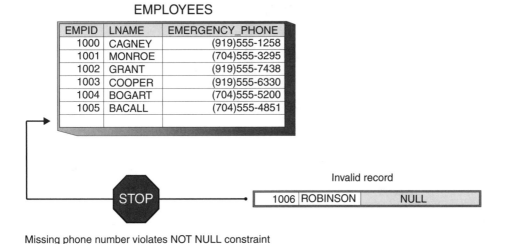

Figure 5-1   NOT NULL constraints prevent null data.

process will be discussed a little later in this chapter.) The following CREATE TABLE SQL statement shows how the NOT NULL constraint would be defined for a particular column:

```
CREATE TABLE EMPLOYEES    ( . . .
                          EMERGENCY_PHONE     CHAR(14)   NOT NULL,
                          . . .
                          ) ;
```

The Column Default Constraint

Just as some business rules may dictate that a value must always be provided, other business rules may dictate what that value is to be (for example, unless otherwise noted, each employee that is assigned a company car does not have any outstanding citations). The column default constraint is used to ensure that a given column of a base table is always assigned a predefined value whenever a row that does not have a specific value for that column is added to the table. Figure 5-2 illustrates how the column default constraint is used to ensure that a column is always assigned a value.

The default value provided for a column can be null, a constant value that is compatible with the data type of the column, or a value that is provided by the DB2 Database Manager. Table 5-4 shows the default values that are provided by the DB2

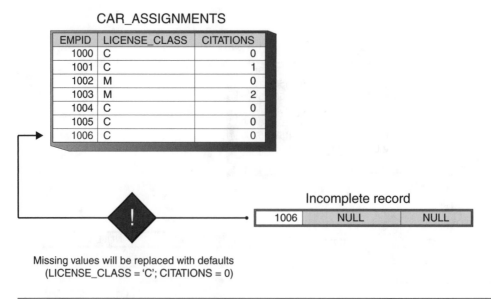

Figure 5-2   Column default constraints provide values when data is missing.

Table 5-4   Default Values Provided by DB2 Universal Database

Data Type	Default Value
Small integer Integer Decimal Single-precision floating point Double-precision floating point	0
Fixed-length character string Fixed-length double-byte character string	Blanks
Varying-length character string Varying-length long character string Varying-length double-byte character string Varying-length double-byte long character string Binary large object Character large object Double-byte character large object	Zero-length string
Date	The system date at the time the row is inserted. (When a date column is added to an existing table, existing rows are assigned the date January, 01, 0001.)
Time	The system time at the time the row is inserted. (When a time column is added to an existing table, existing rows are assigned the time 00:00:00.)
Timestamp	The system date/time timestamp at the time the row is inserted. (When a timestamp column is added to an existing table, existing rows are assigned a timestamp that contains the date January, 01, 0001 and the time 00:00:00.)
Distinct user-defined data type	The system-defined default value for the base data type of the distinct user-defined data type (cast to the distinct user-defined data type).

Database Manager if a column default constraint is used and no default value is specified.

Like the NOT NULL constraint, column default constraints are usually defined along with a table's attributes during the table creation process. The following CREATE TABLE

SQL statement shows how the column default constraint could be defined for two columns:

```
CREATE TABLE CAR_ASSIGNMENTS  (. . .
                              LICENSE_CLASS  CHAR(1) WITH DEFAULT 'C',
                              CITATIONS      SMALLINT WITH DEFAULT,
                              . . .
                              );
```

In this example, the LICENSE_CLASS column would be assigned the value "C" and the CITATIONS column would be assigned the value 0 whenever rows that did not contain values for those columns were added to the table.

NOTE When a new column that has a column default constraint associated with it is added to an existing table (with the ALTER TABLE SQL statement), existing rows in that table are automatically assigned the default value for that column.

Unique Constraints

A unique constraint (or primary key constraint) is used to ensure that a given column of a base table will always receive a unique value (that is, data values for a given column will never be duplicated). For example, a unique constraint could be used to ensure that each employee in a company is assigned an identification number that no other employee in the company has. As you might imagine, columns that are assigned the unique constraint must also be assigned the NOT NULL constraint. Once a unique constraint has been defined for a particular column, any insert or update operation that attempts to place a duplicate value in that column will fail. Figure 5-3 illustrates how the unique constraint is used to ensure that a column is always assigned a unique value.

Unique constraints can be defined with the CREATE TABLE or ALTER TABLE SQL statement by using the PRIMARY KEY or the UNIQUE clause. The following CREATE TABLE SQL statement shows how a unique constraint would be defined for a particular column:

```
CREATE TABLE EMPLOYEES  (EMPID    INTEGER NOT NULL,
                        . . .
                        PRIMARY KEY (EMPID));
```

When a unique constraint is defined as part of the table creation process, the DB2 Database Manager automatically creates a unique index for the appropriate columns and designates it a primary or unique system-required index. This index is then used to

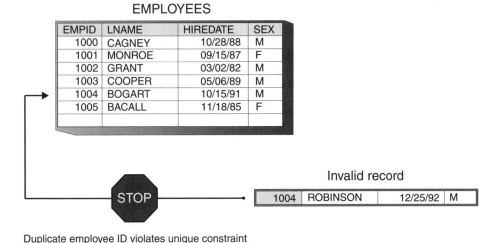

EMPLOYEES

EMPID	LNAME	HIREDATE	SEX
1000	CAGNEY	10/28/88	M
1001	MONROE	09/15/87	F
1002	GRANT	03/02/82	M
1003	COOPER	05/06/89	M
1004	BOGART	10/15/91	M
1005	BACALL	11/18/85	F

Invalid record

STOP

| 1004 | ROBINSON | 12/25/92 | M |

Duplicate employee ID violates unique constraint

Figure 5-3   Unique constraints prevent duplicate data values.

enforce the unique constraint. When a unique constraint is defined for a table that already exists, the DB2 Database Manager looks for an index that already exists for the columns specified. If an index exists, that index is designated as unique and system required; if such an index does not exist, the DB2 Database Manager automatically creates a unique index and designates it a primary or unique system-required index.

NOTE   A distinction can be made between defining a unique constraint and creating a unique index. Although both enforce uniqueness, a unique index allows nullable columns and generally cannot be referenced by the foreign key of a referential constraint.

A table can have an arbitrary number of unique constraints, with, at most, one unique constraint defined as a primary key. However, a table cannot have more than one unique constraint defined on the same set of columns. Because unique constraints are enforced by indexes, all the limitations of index keys apply to unique constraints as well. For example, no more than 16 columns (with a combined length of 255 bytes) can be used in a unique constraint; none of the columns in a unique constraint can have a large object or long character string (single- or double-byte) data type, and so on.

Referential Constraints

A referential constraint (also known as a foreign key constraint) is used to define a required relationship between and within base tables. For example, a referential constraint could be used to ensure that every record stored in the EMPLOYEE table of a company's database reflects that the employee is a member of a department that exists in the DEPARTMENT table of that database. The relationship between these two tables is based on matching values between the set of columns that make up the primary key or unique key in the DEPARTMENT table (also known as the parent key), and a set of columns in the EMPLOYEE table known as the foreign key. So to establish the relationship just described, you would define a primary key constraint for the department number column in the DEPARTMENT table and you would create a foreign key using the department number column in the EMPLOYEE table. Figure 5-4 illustrates how a referential constraint is used to define a relationship between two tables.

As you can see, several special terms are used to describe the different components that make up a referential constraint. Table 5-5 provides the complete set of terminology used.

Referential constraints can be defined with the CREATE TABLE or ALTER TABLE SQL statement by using the CONSTRAINT or FOREIGN KEY clause. The following CREATE TABLE SQL statement shows how a referential constraint would be defined for a particular column:

```
CREATE TABLE EMPLOYEES    (. . .
                          DEPT_ID    CHAR(3) NOT NULL,
                          . . .
                          CONSTRAINT DEPT_FK FOREIGN KEY (DEPT_ID)
                          REFERENCES DEPARTMENTS (DEPT_ID));
```

In this example, the DEPT_ID column would be the foreign key, the EMPLOYEES table would be the child table, and the DEPT_ID column in the DEPARTMENTS table (the parent table) would be the parent key of the referential constraint.

NOTE Once defined, referential constraints can be turned on or off with the **SET INTEGRITY** SQL statement. Most of the time, referential constraints should be left on. However, when performing operations such as loads and imports, it is usually a good idea to temporarily suspend referential constraint checking until the operation is completed.

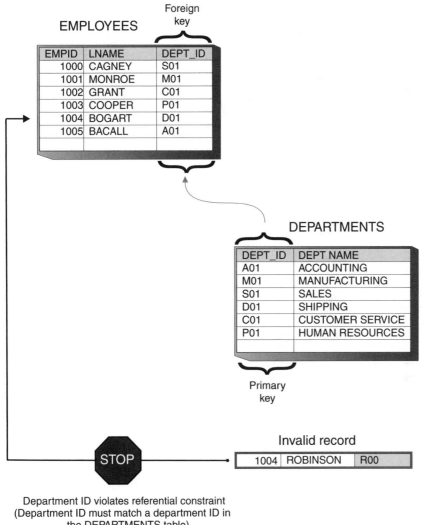

Figure 5-4   Referential constraints define data relationships.

Rules Used to Enforce Referential Integrity

The purpose of a referential constraint is to guarantee that table relationships are maintained and that data entry rules are followed. This means that as long as a referential constraint is in effect, the DB2 Database Manager guarantees that for each row in

Table 5-5 Referential Constraint Terminology

Term	Default Value
Unique key	A column or set of columns in which every row of values is unique (different from the values of all other rows).
Primary key	A special unique key. Only one primary can be defined for a given table.
Foreign key	A column or set of columns in a table whose values are required to match those of at least one unique key or primary key of a parent table. A foreign key is used to establish a relationship with a unique key or primary key.
Parent key	A primary key or unique key in a parent table that is referenced by a foreign key.
Parent table	A table that contains a parent key of a referential constraint. A table can be a parent in any number of referential constraints. A parent table can also be the dependent table of any number of referential constraints.
Parent row	A row in a parent table that has at least one matching dependent row.
Dependent or child table	A table that contains at least one foreign key of a referential constraint. A table can be a dependent in any number of referential constraints. A dependent table can also be the parent table of any number of referential constraints.
Dependent or child row	A row in a dependent table that has at least one matching parent row.
Descendant table	A dependent table or a descendant of a dependent table.
Descendant row	A dependent row or a descendant of a dependent row.
Referential cycle	A set of referential constraints that are defined in such a way that each table in the set is a descendant of itself.
Self-referencing table	A table that is both a parent and a dependent in the same referential constraint. The constraint is called a self-referencing constraint.
Self-referencing row	A row that is a parent of itself.
Referential integrity	The state a database is in when all values of all foreign keys in the database are valid.

a child table that has a non-null value in its foreign key columns, a row exists in a corresponding parent table that has a matching value in its parent key. So what happens when an SQL operation attempts to change data in such a way that referential integrity will be compromised? In order to answer this question, it helps to understand the ways a referential constraint could be violated:

- An insert operation could attempt to add a row of data to a child table that has a value in its foreign key columns that does not match a value in the corresponding parent table's parent key.

- An update operation could attempt to change the value in a child table's foreign key columns to a value that has no matching value in the corresponding parent table's parent key.

- An update operation could attempt to change the value in a parent table's parent key to a value that does not have a matching value in a child table's foreign key columns.

- A delete operation could attempt to remove a record from a parent table that has a matching value in a child table's foreign key columns.

The DB2 Database Manager handles these types of situations by enforcing a set of rules that are associated with each referential constraint. This set of rules consists of

- An insert rule

- An update rule

- A delete rule

The Insert Rule

The insert rule of a referential constraint ensures that non-null values are only inserted into the columns that make up a foreign key in a child table if a parent key containing the same values exists in the parent table. If a null value is inserted into any of the columns that make up a foreign key in a child table, the value of the foreign key for that record is null. Any attempt to insert values into a child table that violate the insert rule will result in an error. On the other hand, non-null values can be inserted into the columns that make up the parent key of a parent table at any time; no checking will be performed on the child table.

The insert rule is implicitly created when a referential constraint is created and it is enforced by the DB2 Database Manager whenever an insert operation is performed on the child table of the constraint.

The Update Rule

The update rule of a referential constraint controls how referential integrity checks are to be performed when the values of the columns that make up a foreign key in a child table or the values of the columns that make up a parent key in a parent table are changed. How the update rule of a referential constraint was specified when the constraint was defined determines how referential integrity violation checking is conducted when an update operation is performed on either table. The update rule for a referential constraint can be specified in one of two ways:

- **ON UPDATE NO ACTION**   This specification ensures that, when an update operation is performed, every row in the child table that contains non-null values in the columns that make up its foreign key will have *some* matching value in the parent key of the associated parent table, but not necessarily the same matching value that it had before the update operation occurred. If this condition is not met, the update operation will fail and all changes made will be rolled back.

- **ON UPDATE RESTRICT**   This specification ensures that, when an update operation is performed, every row in the child table that contains non-null values in the columns that make up its foreign key will have the same matching value in the parent key of the associated parent table that it had before the update operation occurred. If this condition is not met, the update operation will fail and all changes made will be rolled back.

By default, the ON UPDATE NO ACTION specification is enforced when a value in a column of a foreign key or a parent key is updated. If the ON UPDATE RESTRICT specification is used, it is only enforced when a value in a column of a parent key is updated. When a value in a column of a foreign key is updated, the ON UPDATE NO ACTION specification is enforced. As you can see, the ON UPDATE RESTRICT specification is more restrictive than the ON UPDATE NO ACTION specification. For example, an update operation that is designed to exchange the parent key values of two rows in a parent table could violate an ON UPDATE RESTRICT specification, but not an ON UPDATE NO ACTION specification.

The update rule is implicitly created with the ON UPDATE NO ACTION specification when a referential constraint is created. Like the insert rule, this rule is also enforced by the DB2 Database Manager.

The Delete Rule

The delete rule of a referential constraint controls how referential integrity checks are to be performed and, in some cases, how integrity violations are to be resolved when a row is deleted from a parent table. More precisely, the delete rule controls what happens when a row of the parent table is the object of a delete or propagated delete operation (defined in the following section) and that row has dependents in the dependent table of the referential constraint. Again, how the delete rule of a referential constraint was specified when the constraint was defined determines how referential integrity violation checking/resolution is conducted when a delete operation is performed on a parent table. The delete rule for a referential constraint can be specified in one of four ways:

- **ON DELETE CASCADE** This specification ensures that, when a parent row is deleted from a parent table, every row in the child table that contains matching values in the columns that make up its foreign key will also be deleted. (If the deletion of a parent row causes the deletion of a dependent row, the delete operation on the parent table is said to be *propagated* to the child table. If the child table is also a parent table, the delete operation may also be propagated to another child table. Therefore, any table that may be involved in a delete operation on a parent table is said to be *delete-connected* to that parent table. Thus, a table is delete-connected to a parent table if it is a dependent of that parent table or if it is a dependent of a table to which delete operations from the parent table cascade.)

- **ON DELETE SET NULL** This specification ensures that, when a parent row is deleted from a parent table, every nullable column in every row in the child table that contains matching values in the columns that make up its foreign key will be set to null. (Of course, in order for this specification to work, at least one of the columns in the foreign key must be nullable.)

- **ON DELETE NO ACTION** This specification ensures that when a delete operation is performed, every row in the child table that contains non-null values in the columns that make up its foreign key will have *some* matching value in the parent key of the associated parent table, but not necessarily the same matching value that it had before the delete operation occurred. If this condition is not met, the delete operation will fail and all changes made will be rolled back.

- **ON DELETE RESTRICT** This specification ensures that, when a delete operation is performed, every row in the child table that contains non-null values in the columns that make up its foreign key will have the same matching value in the parent key of the associated parent table that it had before the delete operation occurred. If this condition is not met, the delete operation will fail and all changes made will be rolled back.

By default, the ON DELETE NO ACTION specification is enforced when a row in a parent table is deleted. When a delete operation is performed on a parent table, the DB2 Database Manager looks for rows in the corresponding child table whose values in the columns that make up its foreign key are the same as the values in the parent key of the row that is about to be deleted.

Each referential constraint in which a table is a parent has its own delete rule, and all applicable delete rules are used to determine the end result of a delete operation. Thus, a row cannot be deleted if it has dependents in a referential constraint with a delete rule specification of ON DELETE RESTRICT or ON DELETE NO ACTION, or if the deletion cascades to any of its descendants that are dependents in a referential constraint with the delete rule specification of ON DELETE RESTRICT or ON DELETE NO ACTION.

Check Constraints

A check constraint (also known as a table check constraint) is used to set restrictions that control what values will be accepted by one or more columns of a base table. For example, a check constraint could be used to ensure that the annual salary for an employee is never less than $20,000.00 and never exceeds $140,000.00. Check constraints are made up of one or more predicates (which are connected by the keywords AND or OR) that collectively are known as the *check condition*. Each check condition must be some test that can be evaluated to "TRUE", "FALSE", OR "Unknown" by examining a single row of data in the table that the check constraint is attached to. In other words, a check constraint is like a WHERE clause in a SELECT SQL statement that does not contain subqueries or references to special registers and that only refers to the columns of a single table.

Once a check constraint has been defined for a particular table, each time an insert or update operation occurs against that table, the test defined by the check condition of that check constraint is performed against the affected row. If the test evaluates to FALSE or unknown, the insert or update operation fails and all changes made by that operation are rolled back. (However, when an insert or update operation is rolled back because it violates a check constraint, the current transaction remains in progress and other SQL operations within that transaction are not affected.) Figure 5-5 illustrates how the check constraint is used to control what values will be accepted by a column in a base table.

Check constraints can be defined with the CREATE TABLE or ALTER TABLE SQL statement by using the CONSTRAINT or CHECK clause. The following CREATE TABLE SQL statement shows how a check constraint would be defined for a particular column:

```
CREATE TABLE EMPLOYEES    (. . .
                          SALARY      DECIMAL(10,2) NOT NULL,
                          . . .
                          CONSTRAINT SAL_RANGE
                             CHECK (SALARY >= 20000.00 AND
                                    SALARY <= 140000.00));
```

By default, when a check constraint is defined for a table that already exists (by using the ALTER TABLE SQL statement), the test defined by the check condition of that check

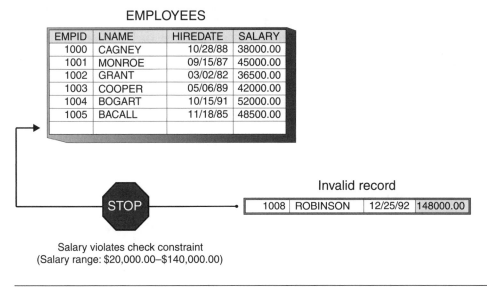

EMPLOYEES

EMPID	LNAME	HIREDATE	SALARY
1000	CAGNEY	10/28/88	38000.00
1001	MONROE	09/15/87	45000.00
1002	GRANT	03/02/82	36500.00
1003	COOPER	05/06/89	42000.00
1004	BOGART	10/15/91	52000.00
1005	BACALL	11/18/85	48500.00

STOP

Invalid record

1008	ROBINSON	12/25/92	148000.00

Salary violates check constraint
(Salary range: $20,000.00–$140,000.00)

Figure 5-5   Check constraints control what data values are accepted.

constraint is performed against every row of data in that table. If any row of data in the table fails the test, the new check constraint is not created. This behavior can be overridden by placing the table in the check pending state (with the SET INTEGRITY SQL statement) before defining the check constraint, and removing the table from the check pending state (again, with the SET INTEGRITY SQL statement) immediately after the check constraint is created. With this approach, when the table is taken out of the check pending state, any existing rows that fail to pass the new check constraint's test are moved to an exception table. Records that are moved to an exception table can then be copied back to the original table once the data values that caused the failure to occur have been changed.

The CREATE TABLE SQL Statement

The CREATE TABLE SQL statement is used to define and create new database tables. Typically, a database table is created by specifying the names, data types, and attributes of one or more columns in what is known as a table definition. In addition to column declarations, a table definition can also include other information such as the definition of primary keys, unique constraints, referential constraints, and check constraints.

NOTE Tables can also be created, dropped, and modified by selecting the appropriate action from the *Tables* menu found in the Control Center. Refer to Chapter 4 for more information about creating tables from the Control Center.

Three types of tables can be created by the CREATE TABLE statement:

- **Normal** Used to organize and store most types of data
- **Typed** Used to store data that can be accessed via a structured data type
- **Summary** Used to gather summary information from one or more Normal tables or views

Because the CREATE TABLE statement can be used to create three different types of tables (each of which have their own set of CREATE TABLE statement options), the statement itself is quite complex. From a certification viewpoint, knowing how to create Typed and Summary tables as well as knowing all the CREATE TABLE statement options available is not important. Instead, emphasis is placed on knowing how to create Normal tables that contain columns that use built-in data types and that have one or more constraints defined. With these objectives in mind, the following is the basic syntax for the CREATE TABLE SQL statement:

```
CREATE TABLE [TableName] ( [Element] ,...) <IN [TableSpaceName]>
<INDEX IN [TableSpaceName]> <LONG IN [TableSpaceName]>
```

where:

TableName Identifies the name that is to be assigned to the table that is to be created.

Element Identifies one or more elements (such as columns, unique/primary key constraints, referential constraints, and check constraints) that are to be included in the table definition. The following section shows the syntax used for adding each of these elements:

The syntax used to add a column element is

```
[ColumnName] [DataType] <NOT NULL> <WITH DEFAULT <DefaultValue>>
<DataLinkOptions> <UniqueConstraint | ReferentialConstraint |
CheckConstraint>
```

where:

ColumnName   Specifies the name that is to be assigned to the column that is
                    to be created.

DataType   Identifies the type of data that is to be stored in the column
                    that is to be created.

DefaultValue   Specifies a default value that is to be provided for the column
                    (in a row of data) in the event that a value is not supplied by an
                    INSERT or UPDATE operation.

DataLinkOptions   Specifies the options that are associated with a DATALINK col-
                    umn data type.

UniqueConstraint   Identifies how the column is to be part of a unique or primary
                    key constraint. The syntax used for defining a unique or pri-
                    mary key constraint as part of a column definition is as
                    follows:

```
<CONSTRAINT [ConstraintName]> UNIQUE | PRIMARY KEY
```

where:

ConstraintName   Specifies the name that is to be assigned to the unique or pri-
                    mary key constraint that is to be created for the column.

ReferentialConstraint Identifies how the column is to be part of a referential con-
                    straint. The syntax used for defining a referential constraint
                    for a column as part of the column definition is as follows:

```
<CONSTRAINT [ConstraintName]> REFERENCES [PKTableName]
<( [PKColumnName] ,...)> <ON DELETE [DeleteAction]>
<ON UPDATE [UpdateAction]>
```

where:

ConstraintName   Specifies the name that is to be assigned to the referential
                    constraint that is to be created for the column.

PKTableName   Identifies the parent table of the referential constraint.

PKColumnName   Identifies one or more columns that make up the parent key
                    that has been defined for the table being referenced (the
                    table referred to by the *TableName* parameter).

DeleteAction   Specifies the action that is to be taken on dependent tables
                    whenever a delete operation is performed.

UpdateAction   Specifies the action that is to be taken on dependent tables whenever an update operation is performed.

CheckConstraint   Identifies how the column is to be part of a check constraint. The syntax used for defining a check constraint for a column as part of the column definition is as follows:

```
<CONSTRAINT [ConstraintName] > CHECK ( [CheckCondition] )
```

where:

ConstraintName   Specifies the name that is to be assigned to the check constraint that is to be created for the column.

CheckCondition   Identifies a condition that must evaluate to TRUE before data can be added to or changed in the table.

The syntax to add a unique/primary key constraint element is

```
<CONSTRAINT [ConstraintName] > UNIQUE | PRIMARY KEY
(ColumnName ,...)
```

where:

ConstraintName   Specifies the name that is to be assigned to the unique or primary key constraint that is to be created.

ColumnName   Identifies one or more columns that are to be part of the unique or primary key constraint.

The syntax to add the referential constraint element is

```
<CONSTRAINT [ConstraintName]> FOREIGN KEY (ColumnName ,...)
REFERENCES [PKTableName] <( [PKColumnName] ,...)>
<ON DELETE [DeleteAction]> <ON UPDATE [UpdateAction]>
```

where:

ConstraintName   Specifies the name that is to be assigned to the referential constraint that is to be created.

ColumnName   Identifies one or more columns that are to be part of the foreign key that makes up the referential constraint.

PKTableName   Identifies the parent table of the referential constraint.

PKColumnName   Identifies one or more columns that make up the parent key that has been defined for the table being referenced (the table referred to by the PK *TableName* parameter).

DeleteAction   Specifies the action that is to be taken on dependent tables whenever a delete operation is performed.

UpdateAction   Specifies the action that is to be taken on dependent tables whenever an update operation is performed.

The syntax to add a check constraint element is

```
<CONSTRAINT [ConstraintName]> CHECK ( [CheckCondition] )
```

where:

ConstraintName   Specifies the name that is to be assigned to the check constraint that is to be created.

CheckCondition   Identifies a condition that must evaluate to TRUE before data can be added to the table.

TableSpaceName   Identifies the table space that the table, the table's indexes, and/or the table's long data/large object data is to be stored in.

As you can see from the syntax, unique constraints, referential constraints, and check constraints can be defined as part of a column definition, or they can be defined as a completely separate element in the table definition.

NOTE   The maximum number of columns that can be specified for a table is dependent upon the page size being used by the table space in which the table is to be stored and the byte count for a single row of data (which is determined by adding the byte counts of every data type used in the table definition and 1 additional byte for every column that is nullable). Tables stored in table spaces that use 4K pages can have up to 500 columns provided that the byte count for a single row does not exceed 4,005 bytes. Tables stored in table spaces that use 8K, 16K, or 32K pages can have up to 1,012 columns provided that the byte count for a single row does not exceed 8,101 bytes, 16,293 bytes, and 32,677 bytes, respectively.

CREATE TABLE SQL Statement Examples and Resulting Table Characteristics

Now that we've seen the basic syntax for the CREATE TABLE statement, let's take a look at two examples. In addition to examining the CREATE TABLE statement's syntax, we will also examine the characteristics of the table that would be created if the CREATE TABLE statements shown were executed.

Example I

If the following CREATE TABLE SQL statement were executed

```
CREATE TABLE DEPARTMENT
        (DEPT_NO     CHAR(3) NOT NULL,
        DEPT_NAME    VARCHAR(40) NOT NULL,
        MGR_ID       SMALLINT WITH DEFAULT,
        BUDGET       DECIMAL(8,2),
        PRIMARY KEY (DEPT_NO))
        IN MY_SPACE
```

the following table would be created in the table space MY_SPACE:

DEPARTMENT

DEPT_NO	DEPT_NAME	MGR_ID	BUDGET

This table would have the following attributes:

- The DEPT_NO column will accept fixed-length character string data that is usually three characters in length (for example, E01, S02, and so on).

- The DEPT_NAME column will accept variable length character string data that can be up to 40 characters in length (for example, Executive/Management, Sales & Marketing, and so on).

- The MGR_ID column will accept numeric values that are in the range of $-32{,}768$ to $+32{,}767$.

- The BUDGET column will accept numbers that contain both whole and fractional parts. Up to eight numbers can be specified—six for the whole number part and two for the fractional part (for example, 8000.00, 10500.50, and so on).

- A value must always be provided for both the DEPT_NO column and the DEPT_NAME column because the NOT NULL constraint was defined for both of these columns.

- If no value is provided for the MGR_ID column, the value 0 will be written to the column by default.

- Every value entered in the DEPT_NO column must be unique.

- An index will automatically be created for the DEPT_NO primary key, and as data is added to the table, the values provided for the DEPT_NO column will be sorted in ascending order (in the index).

- The table will reside in the MY_SPACE table space.

- The amount of space required to store a single row of data (the byte count for this table) is calculated as follows:

DEPT_NO	3
DEPT_NAME	44
MGR_ID	3 (2 + 1 because column is nullable)
BUDGET	6 (5 + 1 because column is nullable)
Total:	56 bytes

Example 2

If the following CREATE TABLE SQL statement were executed

```
CREATE TABLE EMPLOYEE
 (EMP_ID       SMALLINT NOT NULL PRIMARY KEY,
  NAME         VARCHAR(40),
  DEPT_ID      CHAR(3) NOT NULL,
  TITLE        CHAR(5) CHECK (JOBTITLE IN ('Sales','Mgr.','Clerk')),
  HIREDATE     DATE WITH DEFAULT,
  SALARY       DECIMAL(7,2),
  BONUS        DECIMAL(7,2),
  CONSTRAINT FK_DEPT FOREIGN KEY (DEPT_ID)
       REFERENCES DEPARTMENT (DEPT_NO) ON DELETE CASCADE)
```

the following table would be created in the table space USERSPACE1 (the default table space used for user-defined data objects):

EMPLOYEE

EMP_ID NAME	DEPT_ID	TITLE	HIREDATE	SALARY	BONUS

This table would have the following attributes:

- The EMP_ID column will accept numeric values that are in the range of −32,768 to +32,767.

- The NAME column will accept variable length character string data that can be up to 40 characters in length (for example, Bogart, Humphrey; Bacall, Lauren; and so on).

- The DEPT_ID column will accept fixed-length character string data that is usually three characters in length (for example, E01, S02, and so on).

- The TITLE column will accept fixed-length character string data that is usually five characters in length (for example, Sales, Clerk, and so on).

- The HIREDATE column will accept date values.

- The SALARY column will accept numbers that contain both whole and fractional parts. Up to seven numbers can be specified—five for the whole number part and two for the fractional part (for example, 8000.00, 10500.50, and so on).

- The BONUS column will accept numbers that contain both whole and fractional parts. Up to seven numbers can be specified—five for the whole number part and two for the fractional part (for example, 1000.00, 10500.50, and so on).

- A value must always be provided for both the EMP_ID column and the DEPT_ID column because the NOT NULL constraint was defined for both of these columns.

- The TITLE column will only accept the values Sales, Mgr., and Clerk because a check constraint that only accepts these three values has been defined for the TITLE column.

- If no value is provided for the HIREDATE column, the system date at the time a row is inserted into this table will be written to the column by default.

- Every value entered in the EMP_ID column must be unique.

- Every value entered in the DEPT_ID column must have a matching value in the DEPT_NO column of the DEPARTMENT table created in Example 1 (because a referential constraint in which the DEPT_NO column of the DEPARTMENT table is the parent key and the DEPT_ID column of this table is the foreign key has been created). In addition, whenever a row is deleted from the DEPARTMENT table, all rows in this table that have a DEPT_ID value that matches the primary key of the row being deleted in the DEPARTMENT table will also be deleted.

- An index will automatically be created for the EMP_ID primary key, and as data is added to the table, the values provided for the EMP_ID column will be sorted in ascending order (in the index).

- The table will reside in the USERSPACE1 table space.

- The amount of space required to store a single row of data (the byte count for this table) is calculated as follows:

EMP_ID	2	
NAME	45	(44 + 1 because column is nullable)
DEPT_ID	3	
TITLE	6	(5 + 1 because column is nullable)
HIREDATE	5	(4 + 1 because column is nullable)
SALARY	5	(4 + 1 because column is nullable)
BONUS	5	(4 + 1 because column is nullable)
Total:	71	bytes

System Catalog Tables

When a database is created, a special set of tables, known as the *system catalog tables*, is constructed and initialized as part of the creation process. The DB2 Database Manager uses the system catalog tables to keep track of the following information:

- Table/index definitions
- Column data types
- Defined constraints
- Object dependencies
- Object privileges

A set of system catalog views is created along with the system catalog tables and these views are typically used to access the data stored in the system catalog tables. The system catalog views are designed to use more consistent naming conventions than their underlying system catalog tables. Table 5-6 shows the system catalog views that are available with DB2 Universal Database, Version 7.1.

Table 5-6   System Catalog Views

System Catalog View Name	Contents
SYSCAT.ATTRIBUTES	Attributes of structured data types
SYSCAT.BUFFERPOOLS	Buffer pool configuration for a nodegroup
SYSCAT.BUFFERPOOLNODES	Buffer pool size information for a node

(continued)

Table 5-6   System Catalog Views *(continued)*

System Catalog View Name	Contents
SYSCAT.CHECKS	Check constraints
SYSCAT.COLAUTH	Column privileges
SYSSTAT.COLDIST	Detailed column statistics
SYSCAT.COLUMNS SYSSTAT.COLUMNS	Columns
SYSCAT.COLCHECKS	Columns referenced by check constraints
SYSCAT.COLOPTIONS	Detailed column options
SYSCAT.COLDIST	Detailed column statistics
SYSCAT.CONSTDEP	Constraint dependencies
SYSCAT.DATATYPES	Data types
SYSCAT.DBAUTH	Authorities on a database
SYSCAT.EVENTMONITORS	Event monitor definitions
SYSCAT.EVENTS	Events currently being monitored
SYSCAT.FULLHIERARCHIES	Types, tables, and views hierarchies
SYSCAT.FUNCDEP	Function dependencies
SYSCAT.FUNCMAPPINGS	Function mapping
SYSCAT.FUNCMAPOPTIONS	Function mapping options
SYSCAT.FUNCMAPPARMOPTIONS	Function mapping parameter options
SYSCAT.FUNCPARMS	Function parameters
SYSCAT.FUNCTIONS SYSSTAT.FUNCTIONS	User-defined functions
SYSCAT.HIERARCHIES	Types, tables, and views hierarchies
SYSCAT.INDEXAUTH	Index privileges
SYSCAT.INDEXCOLUSE	Index columns
SYSCAT.INDEXDEP	Index dependencies
SYSCAT.INDEXES SYSSTAT.INDEXES	Indexes
SYSCAT.INDEXOPTIONS	Index options
SYSCAT.KEYCOLUSE	Columns used in keys

System Catalog View Name	Contents
SYSCAT.NODEGROUPS	Nodegroup definitions
SYSCAT.NODEGROUPDEF	Nodegroup partitions
SYSCAT.NAMEMAPPINGS	Object mapping
SYSCAT.PACKAGEDEP	Package dependencies
SYSCAT.PACKAGEAUTH	Package privileges
SYSCAT.PACKAGES	Packages
SYSCAT.PARTITIONMAPS	Partitioning maps
SYSCAT.PASSTHRUAUTH	Pass-through privileges
SYSCAT.PROCEDURES	Stored procedures
SYSCAT.PROCOPTIONS	Procedure options
SYSCAT.PROCPARMOPTIONS	Procedure parameter options
SYSCAT.PROCPARMS	Procedure parameters
SYSCAT.REFERENCES	Referential constraints
SYSCAT.REVTYPEMAPPINGS	Reverse data type mapping
SYSCAT.SCHEMAAUTH	Schema privileges
SYSCAT.SCHEMATA	Schemas
SYSCAT.SERVEROPTIONS	Server options
SYSCAT.SERVERS	System servers
SYSCAT.STATEMENTS	Statements in packages
SYSCAT.SYSCASTFUNCTIONS	Cast functions
SYSIBM.SYSDUMMY1	Used for DB2 Universal Database for OS/390 compatibility
SYSCAT.TABAUTH	Table privileges
SYSCAT.TABCONST	Table constraints
SYSCAT.TABLES SYSSTAT.TABLES	Tables
SYSCAT.TABLESPACES	Table spaces
SYSCAT.TABOPTIONS	Remote table options
SYSCAT.TBSPACEAUTH	Table space use privileges

(continued)

Table 5-6 System Catalog Views *(continued)*

System Catalog View Name	Contents
SYSCAT.TRIGDEP	Trigger dependencies
SYSCAT.TRIGGERS	Triggers
SYSCAT.TYPEMAPPINGS	Type mapping information
SYSCAT.USEROPTIONS	Server options values
SYSCAT.VIEWDEP	View dependencies
SYSCAT.VIEWS	Views
SYSCAT.WRAPOPTIONS	Wrapper options
SYSCAT.WRAPPERS	Wrappers

The system catalog views that are stored in the SYSCAT schema are read-only tables; the views stored in the SYSSTAT schema are not. Thus, insert, update, and delete operations cannot be performed against the majority of the system catalog views. Instead, the contents of one or more system catalog tables that the system catalog views reference are modified by the DB2 Database Manager each time

- A new object (such as a table or index) is created.
- Authorizations/privileges are granted or revoked.
- Statistical information is collected for a table.
- Packages are bound to the database.

So whenever a base table is created, at the very minimum, the system catalog tables that SYSCAT.TABLES and SYSCAT.COLUMNS refer to will be modified. In addition, if the table contains constraint definitions, several other system catalog tables will also be affected.

Summary

The goal of this chapter was to introduce you to the components that make up a table definition and to show you how the CREATE TABLE SQL statement can be used to turn a table definition into a table object.

All data is classified, to some extent, according to its type (for example, some data might be numerical, whereas other data might be textual). Because a table is comprised of one or more columns that are designed to hold data values, each column must be assigned a specific data type. This data type determines the internal representation that will be used to store the data, what the ranges of the data's values are, and what set of operators and functions can be used to manipulate that data once it has been stored.

Table 5-7   DB2 Universal Database's Built-In Data Types

Data Type	Description	Term Used
Small integer	Binary integer values that have a precision of 15 bits	SMALLINT
Integer	Binary integer values that have a precision of 31 bits	INTEGER or INT
Big integer	Binary integer values that have a precision of 63 bits	BIGINT
Decimal	Numerical values that contain both whole and fractional parts	DECIMAL, DEC, NUMERIC, and NUM
Single-precision floating point	A 32-bit approximation of a real number	REAL and FLOAT(<25)
Double-precision floating point	A 64-bit approximation of a real number	DOUBLE and FLOAT(>25)
Fixed-length character string	Character and character string data that has a specific length (up to 254 characters)	CHARACTER and CHAR
Varying-length character string	Character string data that varies in length (stored on the same memory page as other table data)	CHARACTER VARYING, CHAR VARYING, and VARCHAR
Varying-length long character string	Character string data that varies in length (stored on a memory page away from other table data)	LONG VARCHAR
Fixed-length double-byte character string	DBCS character and character string data that has a specific length (up to 127 characters)	GRAPHIC

(continued)

Table 5-7 DB2 Universal Database's Built-In Data Types *(continued)*

Data Type	Description	Term Used
Varying-length double-byte character string	DBCS character string data that varies in length (stored on the same memory page as other table data)	VARGRAPHIC
Varying-length double-byte long character string	DBCS character string data that varies in length (stored on a memory page away from other table data)	LONG VARGRAPHIC
Date	Three-part value (year, month, and day) that designates a valid calendar date	DATE
Time	Three-part value (hours, minutes, and seconds) that designates a valid time of day under a 24-hour clock	TIME
Timestamp	Seven-part value (year, month, day, hours, minutes, seconds and microseconds) that designates a valid calendar date and time of day under a 24-hour clock	TIMESTAMP
Binary large object	Large binary string that varies in length	BLOB
Character large object	single-byte character set (SBCS) or multibyte character set (MBCS) character string data that is too large to fit in a varying-length long character string data type	CLOB
Double-byte Character large object	double-byte character set (DBCS) character string data that is too large to fit in a varying-length double-byte long character string data type	DBCLOB

DB2 Universal Database supports 19 different built-in data types (along with an infinite number of user-defined data types that are based on the built-in data types). Table 5-7 shows the complete set of built-in data types that are available.

In addition to these built-in data types, other special data types are available. They are

- DataLink data types
- User-defined data types
- Extender data types

The DataLink data type is used to store an encapsulated value that contains a logical reference to a file that is stored in a file system controlled by a DB2 DataLink Server (which resides outside of the database). DataLink values serve as anchor values that provide reference information that allows the database to establish and maintain a link to external data.

User-defined data types (UDT) are named data types that are explicitly created by the user. A user-defined data type can be a distinct data type that shares a common representation with a built-in data type, or it can be a structured type that consists of a sequence of named attributes, each of which have their own data type.

The extender products that are available for DB2 Universal Database provide an additional set of user-defined data types and functions that can be used as part of a table definition. Most of the data types provided by the DB2 Extenders are based on the binary large object data type. However, DB2 Extenders provide the added flexibility of allowing large object data to be stored in an external file whose location is pointed to from the database.

Within most businesses, data often must adhere to certain restrictions or rules. Such restrictions may apply to single pieces of information such as the format and sequence to use for purchase order numbers; or they may apply to several pieces of information such as which employees are members of which departments and which employees manage those departments. Constraints are DB2 Universal Database's way of enforcing such rules within the confines of the database system. Essentially, constraints are rules that govern or influence the way in which data values can be added and/or modified. The following types of constraints are available with DB2 Universal Database:

- NOT NULL constraints
- Column default constraints
- Unique constraints
- Referential integrity constraints
- Check constraints

The NOT NULL constraint is used to ensure that a given column of a base table is never assigned the null value. The column default constraint is used to ensure that a given column of a base table is always assigned a predefined value whenever a row that does not have a specific value for that column is added to the table. A unique constraint (or primary key constraint) is used to ensure that a given column of a base table will always receive a unique value (that is, data values for a given column will never be duplicated). A referential constraint (also known as a foreign key constraint) is used to define a required relationship between and within base tables—a referential constraint guarantees that table relationships are maintained and that data entry rules are always followed. A check constraint is used to set restrictions that control what values will be accepted by one or more columns of a base table.

A set of rules that are used to maintain referential integrity is associated with every referential constraint defined. This set of rules consists of the following:

- An insert rule
- An update rule
- A delete rule

The insert rule of a referential constraint ensures that non-null values are only inserted into the columns that make up a foreign key in a child table if a parent key containing the same values exists in the parent table. The update rule of a referential constraint controls how referential integrity checks are to be performed when the values of the columns that make up a foreign key in a child table or the values of the columns that make up a parent key in a parent table are changed. The delete rule of a referential constraint controls how referential integrity checks are to be performed and, in some cases, how integrity violations are to be resolved when a row is deleted from a parent table. More precisely, the delete rule controls what happens when a row of the parent table is the object of a delete or propagated delete operation and that row has dependents in the dependent table of the referential constraint.

The CREATE TABLE SQL statement is used to define and create a new database table. Typically, a database table is created by specifying the names, data types, and attributes of one or more columns in what is known as a table definition. In addition to column declarations, a table definition can also include other information such as the definition of primary keys, unique constraints, referential constraints, or check constraints.

When a database is created, a special set of tables, known as the system catalog tables, is constructed and initialized as part of the creation process. The DB2 Database Manager uses the system catalog tables to keep track of the following information:

- Table/index definitions
- Column data types
- Defined constraints
- Object dependencies
- Object privileges

The contents of one or more system catalog tables are modified by the DB2 Database Manager each time a new object (such as a table or index) is created, authorizations/

privileges are granted or revoked, statistical information is collected, or packages are bound to the database.

Questions

1. Given the requirements to store employee names, employee numbers, and when employees were hired, which of the following built-in data types cannot be used to store the day an employee was hired?

   a. Character large object

   b. Time

   c. Varying-length character string

   d. Timestamp

2. Given the requirements to store customer names, billing addresses, and telephone numbers, which of the following would be the best way to define the telephone number column if all customers were located in the same country?

   a. PHONE CHAR(15)

   b. PHONE VARCHAR(15)

   c. PHONE LONG VARCHAR

   d. PHONE CLOB(1K)

3. If the SQL statement

   ```
   CREATE TABLE TABLE1(COL1 CHAR(4) NOT NULL)
   ```

   is executed, which of the following values can be inserted into the table that is created?

   a. 4

   b. NULL

   c. abc

   d. abcde

4. If the SQL statement

   ```
   CREATE TABLE TABLE1(COL1 INTEGER NOT NULL, COL2 INTEGER, FOREIGN
   KEY (COL2) REFERENCES (TABLE2))
   ```

   is executed, how many unique indexes would be defined for the table that is created?

   a. 0

     b. 1

     c. 2

     d. 3

5. Which of the following can prevent a user from inserting a row containing a large commission into a column that holds sales commission information?

     a. Defining a primary key constraint on the column

     b. Defining a user-defined scalar function

     c. Defining a user-defined data type

     d. Defining a referential constraint

     e. Defining a check constraint

6. Which of the following statements will create a table where employee ID numbers are unique?

     a. `CREATE TABLE T1 (EMPID INTEGER)`

     b. `CREATE TABLE T1 (EMPID UNIQUE INTEGER)`

     c. `CREATE TABLE T1 (EMPID INTEGER NOT NULL)`

     d. `CREATE TABLE T1 (EMPID INTEGER, PRIMARY KEY (EMPID))`

7. Which of the following delete rules will not allow a row to be deleted from the parent table if a row with a corresponding key value still exists in the child table?

     a. DELETE

     b. RESTRICT

     c. CASCADE

     d. SET NULL

8. In order to create a table that looks like the following

		T1	
EMPID	**NAME**	**SSN**	**SALARY**
1	Bogart, Humphrey	555-12-1234	45000.00
2	Bacall, Lauren	—	48000.00

which of these statements would have to be executed?

     a. `CREATE TABLE T1 (EMPID SMALLINT, NAME CHAR(14),`
        `SSN CHAR(11), SALARY FLOAT(24))`

     b. `CREATE TABLE T1 (EMPID SMALLINT, NAME VARCHAR(20),`
        `SSN VARCHAR(10), SALARY FLOAT(26))`

     c. `CREATE TABLE T1 (EMPID SMALLINT, NAME VARCHAR(20),`

```
                SSN CHAR(11), SALARY DEC(7,2))
```

   d. `CREATE TABLE T1 (EMPID SMALLINT, NAME VARCHAR(40),`
```
                SSN CHAR(11) NOT NULL, SALARY DEC(7,2))
```

9. If a table is defined with a check constraint for one or more columns, which of the following will perform data validation after the table is populated by the load utility?

   a. Check

   b. Runstats

   c. Runcheck

   d. Set Integrity

10. Which of the following statements will NOT create a table where invoice numbers must always be unique?

   a. `CREATE TABLE T1 (INVOICENUM INTEGER NOT NULL`
```
            CONSTRAINT P_K PRIMARY KEY)
```

   b. `CREATE TABLE T1 (INVOICENUM INTEGER UNIQUE)`

   c. `CREATE TABLE T1 (INVOICENUM INTEGER NOT NULL UNIQUE)`

   d. `CREATE TABLE T1 (INVOICENUM INTEGER NOT NULL,`
```
            PRIMARY KEY (INVOICENUM))
```

11. Which of the following update rules will allow a row to be changed in the parent table provided that a row with a corresponding key value in the child table can find a matching row in the parent once the update operation is completed?

   a. NO ACTION

   b. RESTRICT

   c. CASCADE

   d. UPDATE

12. If the SQL statement

```
CREATE TABLE TABLE1(COL1 INTEGER NOT NULL PRIMARY KEY, COL2
INTEGER WITH DEFAULT, FOREIGN KEY (COL2) REFERENCES (TABLE2))
```

   is executed, how many constraints will be defined for the table that is created?

   a. 1

   b. 2

   c. 3

   d. 4

   e. 5

13. Which of the following constraints cannot be added to a column in an existing table?

   a. Unique constraint

   b. NOT NULL constraint

   c. Check constraint

   d. Referential constraint

14. If the SQL statement

```
CREATE TABLE TEMPTABLE(COL1 CHAR(1) NOT NULL, PRIMARY KEY(COL1))
```

is executed, which two of the following system catalog views' results are changed?

   a. SYSCAT.INDEXES

   b. SYSCAT.PRIMKEYS

   c. SYSCAT.TABLES

   d. SYSCAT.NOTNULL

   e. SYSCAT.CONSTRAINTS

15. Given the following tables:

PC

SERIAL_NUM	MODEL	OWNER	SALARY

USER

USERID	NAME

which of the following actions will ensure that no row can be inserted into the PC table unless the OWNER value matches the USERID value in the USER table?

   a. Add a referential constraint to the USER table.

   b. Add a referential constraint to the PC table.

   c. Add a check constraint to the PC table.

   d. Add a unique constraint to the OWNER column.

Answers

1. **B**. A date value can be stored using a date, timestamp, or character string data type. The time data type, on the other hand, can only be used to store a time value.

2. **A**. Although each data type specified is valid, the CHAR(15) data type will only require 16 bytes of storage, whereas the VARCHAR(15) data type will need 20 bytes of storage, the LONG VARCHAR data type will need 40 bytes, and the CLOB(1K) data type will require over 1,024 bytes!

3. **C**. The value "abc" is the only character string value shown that will fit in the column. The value 4 is numeric, the value NULL violates the NOT NULL constraint, and the value "abcde" is too large to fit in the column.

4. **A**. Because no unique or primary constraints were included in the table definition, no unique indexes will be created.

5. **E**. A check constraint is the only item in the list provided that can be used to check sales commission values and ensure that no value exceeds a predefined limit.

6. **D**. This CREATE TABLE statement is the only one that contains the PRIMARY KEY clause, which is used to define a unique constraint.

7. **B**. The ON DELETE RESTRICT delete rule ensures that, when a delete operation is performed, every row in the child table that contains non-null values in the columns that make up its foreign key will have the same matching value in the parent key of the associated parent table that it had before the delete operation occurred. If this condition is not met, the delete operation will fail and all changes made will be rolled back.

8. **C**. This CREATE TABLE statement has a data type that is large enough to hold the employee names shown, allows null values to be stored in the Social Security Number column, and uses the best data type for salary information.

9. **D**. The SET INTEGRITY SQL statement is used to enable and disable constraint checking for tables. When a check constraint is enabled after data has been added to a table, that check constraint will then be performed against all loaded data (violations will be moved to an exception table).

10. **B**. In order for a column to have a unique constraint assigned to it, it must also have the NOT NULL constraint assigned to it.

11. **A**. The ON UPDATE NO ACTION update rule ensures that when an update operation is performed, every row in the child table that contains non-null values in the columns that make up its foreign key will have *some* matching value in the parent key of the associated parent table, but not necessarily the same matching value that it had before the update operation occurred.

12. **D**. The following constraints will be defined for this table: a NOT NULL constraint, a unique constraint, a default value constraint, and a referential constraint.

13. **B**. The NOT NULL constraint can only be defined when a table is created. All other constraints can be added to an existing table with the ALTER TABLE SQL statement.

14. **A and C**. When a table containing a unique constraint is created, information about the table will be recorded in the system catalog table that the SYSCAT. TABLES system catalog view refers to and, because an index is also created for the unique constraint, information about the associated index will be recorded in the system catalog table that the SYSCAT.INDEXES system catalog view refers to.

15. **B**. By adding a referential constraint that references the USER table to the PC table, only rows whose OWNER values match USERID values in the USER table can be added to the PC table. (Referential constraints must be defined in the child table of the constraint.)

Basic SQL

In this chapter, you will learn

- What SQL is and how SQL statements are grouped, according to their functionality
- What SQL statements make up the Data Definition Language (DDL) and how those statements are used to create database objects
- What SQL statements make up the Data Manipulation Language (DML) and how those statements are used to store, manipulate, and retrieve data

The fifth objective of the DB2 Universal Database Family Fundamentals exam is to evaluate your knowledge of the Structured Query Language (SQL) statements that are commonly used with DB2 Universal Database. From a certification viewpoint, knowing how to use every SQL statement available is not critical. Instead, it is important to know how to use the SQL statements that fulfill most data processing needs. Specifically, you should be able to examine a given SQL statement (that is commonly used) and correctly identify what the outcome would be if that statement were executed.

This chapter is designed to introduce you to the SQL statements that are commonly used to work with DB2 Universal Database objects and user data.

TIP   Thirty-eight percent of the DB2 Universal Database Family Fundamentals exam is designed to test your knowledge of basic SQL, test your ability to examine a given SQL statement, and identify its results.

Structured Query Language (SQL)

Structured Query Language (SQL) is a standardized language that is used to define database objects and to store, manipulate, and retrieve data in a relational database management system. One of the strengths of SQL is that it can be used in a variety of ways. SQL statements can be executed interactively via the Command Center, the Script Center, and/or the Command Line Processor or they can be embedded in one or more high-level programming language source code files that make up a database application. (Because SQL is nonprocedural by design, it is not an actual programming language; therefore, most database applications are built by combining the decision and sequence control of a high-level programming language with the data storage, manipulation, and retrieval capabilities of SQL statements.)

The majority of SQL statements available can be divided into the following categories:

- **Embedded SQL Application Construct statements**   Used to facilitate embedded SQL application development

- **Data Control Language (DCL) statements**   Used to grant and revoke authorizations and privileges

- **Data Definition Language (DDL) statements**   Used to create, modify, and destroy database objects

- **Data Manipulation Language (DML) statements**   Used to retrieve and/or modify the data stored in a database

- **Database Connection and Transaction Control statements**   Used to establish and terminate database connections and transactions

From a certification viewpoint, knowing how to use the Embedded SQL Application Construct statements is only important if you are planning on obtaining the IBM Certified Solutions Expert—DB2 UDB V7.1 Family Application Development certification. Because the Data Control Language statements (GRANT and REVOKE) were covered in Chapter 3 and the Database Connection and Transaction Control statements will be covered in Chapter 7, they will not be addressed in this chapter. Therefore, this chapter will focus on the DDL statements and the DML statements that are available with DB2 Universal Database.

Data Definition Language (DDL) Statements

As mentioned earlier, when a database is first created, all system catalog tables that are needed by that database are created and space is allocated for the recovery log files used. At this point, the database cannot be used to store data because no data objects have been defined. This is where the DDL statements come in. Most DDL statements are used to define and create the objects in the database that will be used to store user data and to improve data access performance. Other DDL statements are used to alter or remove objects that have already been created. Table 6-1 lists the group of SQL statements that make up the DDL.

Table 6-1 Data Definition Language Statements

SQL Statement	Description
CREATE NODEGROUP	Defines and creates a new nodegroup
CREATE BUFFERPOOL	Defines and creates a new buffer pool
CREATE TABLESPACE	Defines and creates a new table space
CREATE TABLE	Defines and creates a new table
CREATE VIEW	Defines and creates a new view
CREATE INDEX	Defines and creates a new index
CREATE SCHEMA	Defines and creates a new schema (and alternately, one or more objects in the schema)
CREATE ALIAS	Defines and creates a new alias for a table, view, or another alias
COMMENT ON	Adds or replaces the comment stored in the system catalog that is used to describe a particular object
ALTER NODEGROUP	Adds partitions to or removes partitions from an existing nodegroup
ALTER BUFFERPOOL	Modifies the size of an existing buffer pool, turns the use of extended memory on or off, or adds an existing buffer pool to a new nodegroup
ALTER TABLESPACE	Changes the definition of an existing table space
ALTER TABLE	Changes the definition of an existing table
RENAME TABLE	Changes the name of an existing table
DROP	Deletes an object and removes its definition from the system catalog

Just as a hierarchic relationship exists among systems, instances, and databases, a hierarchic relationship also exists among most database objects. Because of this, database objects often have to be created in a specific order. For example, buffer pools need to be created before table spaces, table spaces need to be created before tables, and so on. Figure 6-1 shows the hierarchic relationship among objects.

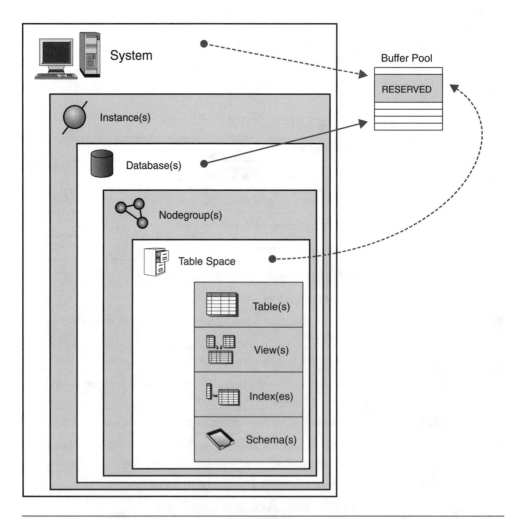

Figure 6-1   Hierarchic relationship among DB2 Universal Database objects

Creating Nodegroups—The CREATE NODEGROUP Statement

Since Version 5.0, DB2 Universal Database has allowed the DB2 Database Manager to operate in a parallel, multinode (workstation) environment. This means that instead of having to be physically stored in one single location, databases can be broken into several parts (known as database partitions) and each part can be stored in a different physical location. In a multinode environment, a single database partition usually exists on each physical node (workstation) used and the DB2 Database Manager uses the processors found at each node to manage that partition's portion of the database. This arrangement enables DB2 Universal Database to utilize the power of multiple processors to satisfy large data manipulation requests—data retrieval and update requests are divided into subrequests that are executed in parallel among all applicable partitions. The fact that the database is split across multiple partitions is transparent to the user.

A single-partition database is a database that has only one partition and all of the database's associated files and data are stored in that partition. A partitioned database is a database that has been divided into two or more partitions. In a partitioned database, tables and data can reside in one, several, or all of the partitions available. Each database partition contains its own indexes, configuration files, and transaction log files, and every database partition that is part of a larger database system must be defined in the partition configuration file named db2nodes.cfg. When a partitioned database is first created, database partitions are created for all nodes that have been identified in this file.

Database partitions are often referred to as nodes and one or more of the nodes (partitions) that make up a partitioned database can be stored in a subset known as a nodegroup. Each nodegroup that contains more than one database partition is known as a multipartition nodegroup and each database partition referenced in a multipartition nodegroup must belong to the same DB2 Database Manager instance. When a nodegroup is first created, a partitioning map is created and associated with it. Each entry in the partitioning map is used, in conjunction with a partitioning key and a hashing algorithm, by the DB2 Database Manager to determine which partition in the nodegroup is to be used to store a given row of data. In a single-partition database, a nodegroup is present; however, it does not provide any additional capability (and no partitioning key or partitioning map is required).

By default, the following nodegroups are defined whenever a database is created:

- IBMCATGROUP (for the SYSCATSPACE table space)
- IBMDEFAULTGROUP (for the USERSPACE1 table space)
- IBMTEMPGROUP (for the TEMPSPACE1 table space)

Additional nodegroups can be created by executing the CREATE NODEGROUP SQL statement. The syntax for this statement is

```
CREATE NODEGROUP [NodegroupName] ON [NODE | NODES] ( [NodeNumber]
, ...)
```

or

```
CREATE NODEGROUP [NodegroupName] ON NODES ( [StartingNodeNumber]
TO [EndingNodeNumber] )
```

or

```
CREATE NODEGROUP [NodegroupName] ON ALL NODES
```

where:

NodegroupName	Identifies the name that is to be assigned to the nodegroup that is to be created.
NodeNumber	Identifies one or more specific partitions (nodes) that are to be included in the new nodegroup definition. (Partitions are numbered from 0 to 999.)
StartingNodeNumber	A partition number that identifies the beginning of a range of partitions (nodes) that are to be included in the new node-group definition.
EndingNodeNumber	A partition number that identifies the end of a range of partitions (nodes) that are to be included in the new nodegroup definition.

For example, when executed, the SQL statement

```
CREATE NODEGROUP MAXGROUP ON ALL NODES
```

would create a nodegroup that

- Has been assigned the name MAXGROUP
- Consists of every available partition (that is, every partition listed in the partition configuration file db2nodes.cfg)

Creating Buffer Pools—The CREATE BUFFERPOOL Statement

A buffer pool is an area of main memory that has been allocated to the DB2 Database Manager for the purpose of caching table and index data pages as they are read from disk or modified. The purpose of buffer pools is to improve overall database performance by reducing disk input/output (I/O)—data can be accessed much faster from memory than from disk. In fact, how buffer pools are created and used is the single most important area where database performance can be improved.

So just how are buffer pools used? When a row of data in a table is first accessed, the DB2 Database Manager places the page that contains that data into a buffer pool before passing it on to the application or user that requested it. From that moment on, every available buffer pool is searched each time data is requested. If the requested data is found on a page that has been stored in a buffer pool, it is immediately passed to the appropriate application or user. If the requested data does not exist in a buffer pool, the DB2 Database Manager retrieves it from the disk and copies it to a buffer pool before passing it on. Once a page has been copied to a buffer pool, that page stays in the buffer pool until the database is shut down, or until the space that is occupied by that page is needed to store another page. In the latter case, the page that is to be removed from the buffer pool in order to make room for the new page is selected by examining the following:

- When the page was last referenced

- The likelihood that the page will be referenced again

- The page type

- Whether or not the page in memory has been changed but has not yet been written to disk (When changed pages are written to disk, they are not removed from memory unless the space they occupy is needed to store other pages.)

By default, DB2 Universal Database creates one buffer pool (named IBMDE-FAULTBP) of an appropriate size for the platform used whenever a database is created. Additional buffer pools can be created by selecting the appropriate action from the *Buffer Pools* menu found in the Control Center or by executing the CREATE BUFFER-POOL SQL statement. The syntax for this statement is

```
CREATE BUFFERPOOL [BufferPoolName] <NODEGROUP
[NodegroupName , . . . ]> SIZE [Size] <EXCEPT ON [NODE | NODES]
( [NodeNumber] SIZE [Size] , . . . )> <PAGESIZE [PageSize] <K>>
<NOT EXTENDED STORAGE | EXTENDED STORAGE>
```

or

```
CREATE BUFFERPOOL [BufferPoolName] <ALL NODES> SIZE [Size] <EXCEPT
ON [NODE | NODES] ( [NodeNumber] SIZE [Size] , . . . )> <PAGESIZE
[PageSize] <K>> <NOT EXTENDED STORAGE | EXTENDED STORAGE>
```

or

```
CREATE BUFFERPOOL [BufferPoolName] <NODEGROUP
[NodegroupName , . . . ]> SIZE [Size] <EXCEPT ON [NODE | NODES]
( [StartingNodeNumber] TO [EndingNodeNumber]
SIZE [Size] , . . . )> <PAGESIZE [PageSize] <K>>
<NOT EXTENDED STORAGE | EXTENDED STORAGE>
```

or

```
CREATE BUFFERPOOL [BufferPoolName] <ALL NODES> SIZE [Size]
<EXCEPT ON [NODE | NODES] ( [StartingNodeNumber]
TO [EndingNodeNumber] SIZE [Size] , . . . )> <PAGESIZE [PageSize]
<K>> <NOT EXTENDED STORAGE | EXTENDED STORAGE>
```

where:

BufferPoolName	Identifies the name that is to be assigned to the buffer pool that is to be created.
NodegroupName	Identifies the name of one or more nodegroups that identify the partitions that the new buffer pool is to be created on.
Size	Identifies the size, in *PageSize* pages, that the buffer pool is to be. In a partitioned database system, this will be the size that is used to create the buffer pool on all partitions specified.
NodeNumber	Identifies one or more specific partition (node) numbers that are not to be associated with the buffer pool being created.
StartingNodeNumber	A partition number that identifies the beginning of a range of partitions (nodes) that are not to be associated with the buffer pool being created.
EndingNodeNumber	A partition number that identifies the end of a range of partitions (nodes) that are not to be associated with the buffer pool being created.
PageSize	Specifies the size that each page used by the buffer pool should be (4,096, 8,192, 16,384, or 32,768 bytes). If the suffix K (kilobytes) is specified, this parameter must be set to 4, 8, 16, or 32. (Unless otherwise specified, each page used by a buffer pool is 4K in size.)

For example, when executed, the SQL statement

```
CREATE BUFFERPOOL BUFFPOOL1 SIZE 50 PAGESIZE 8K
```

would create a buffer pool that

- Has been assigned the name BUFFPOOL1
- Uses pages that are 8,192 bytes (8K) in size
- Can store up to 50 pages of data that are 8,192 bytes (8K) in size

Creating Table Spaces—The CREATE TABLESPACE Statement

Table spaces are used to specify where data in a database is physically stored and to provide a layer of indirection between the database and the specific directories, devices, or files (known as containers) in which the actual data resides. Table spaces can improve database and application performance, provide a more flexible database configuration, and provide better data integrity.

As mentioned earlier, a table space can be either a System Managed Space (SMS) or a Database Managed Space (DMS). For an SMS table space, each container used is a directory that resides within the file space of the operating system, and the operating system's file manager is responsible for controlling the storage space. For a DMS table space, each container used is either a fixed-size, pre-allocated file or a physical raw device such as a disk, and the DB2 Database Manager is responsible for controlling the storage space.

By default, DB2 Universal Database creates three table spaces (named SYSCATSPACE, USERSPACE1, and TEMPSPACE1) whenever a database is created. The first of these table spaces is used to store the system catalog tables and views, the second is used to store user data, and the third is used for temporary storage. Unless otherwise specified, all three of these table spaces will be SMS table spaces. Additional table spaces can be created by selecting the appropriate action from the *Table Spaces* menu found in the Control Center or by executing the CREATE TABLESPACE SQL statement. The syntax for this statement is

```
CREATE [REGULAR | LONG | SYSTEM TEMPORARY | USER TEMPORARY]
TABLESPACE [TableSpaceName] <IN <NODEGROUP> [NodegroupName]>
<PAGESIZE [PageSize] <K>> MANAGED BY DATABASE
[DatabaseContainer , . . . ] <EXTENTSIZE [ExtentPages | ExtentSize
<K | M | G>]> <PREFETCHSIZE [PrefetchPages | PrefetchSize
<K | M | G>]> <BUFFERPOOL [BufferpoolName]>
<OVERHEAD [OverheadTime]> <TRANSFERRATE [TransferRateTime]>
<DROPPED TABLE RECOVERY ON | DROPPED TABLE RECOVERY OFF>
```

or

```
CREATE [REGULAR | LONG | SYSTEM TEMPORARY | USER TEMPORARY]
TABLESPACE [TableSpaceName] <IN <NODEGROUP> [NodegroupName]>
<PAGESIZE [PageSize] <K>> MANAGED BY SYSTEM
[SystemContainer , . . . ] <EXTENTSIZE [ExtentPages | ExtentSize
<K | M | G>]> <PREFETCHSIZE [PrefetchPages | PrefetchSize
<K | M | G>]> <BUFFERPOOL [BufferpoolName]>
<OVERHEAD [OverheadTime]> <TRANSFERRATE [TransferRateTime]>
<DROPPED TABLE RECOVERY ON | DROPPED TABLE RECOVERY OFF>
```

where:

TableSpaceName   Identifies the name that is to be assigned to the table space that is to be created.

NodegroupName   Identifies the name of the nodegroup, if any, that the table space is to be created for.

PageSize   Identifies the size that each page used by the table space should be (4,096, 8,192, 16,384, or 32,768 bytes). If the suffix K (kilobytes) is specified, this parameter must be set to 4, 8, 16, or 32.

DatabaseContainer   Identifies one or more containers that will belong to the DMS table space. The syntax used to define DMS table space containers is as follows:

```
USING ( FILE | DEVICE [ContainerDefinition] [NumberOfPages |
ContainerSize <K | M | G>] , . . . ) <ON [NODE | NODES]
( [NodeNumber] | [StartingNodeNumber] TO [EndingNodeNumber] ,
. . . ) >
```

where:

ContainerDefinition   Identifies one or more containers that will belong to the specified table space (and that will be used to physically store the table space's data). For FILE containers, the container definition must identify an absolute or relative filename (if the filename is not absolute, it is relative to the database directory). For DEVICE containers, the container definition must identify a specific device that already exists.

NumberOfPages   Specifies the number of *PageSize* pages that are to be used by the table space container.

ContainerSize   Specifies the amount of memory that is to be used by the table space container. The value specified in the *Container-*

PART II

Size parameter is treated as the total number of bytes, unless the letter K (kilobytes), M (megabytes), or G (gigabytes) is also specified. If the amount of memory to be used is specified (instead of the number of pages), that value is divided by the size of a single page to determine a number of pages value.

NodeNumber   Identifies one or more specific partitions (nodes) that the table space container is to be created on (in a partitioned database system).

StartingNodeNumber   A partition number that identifies the beginning of a range of partitions (nodes) that the table space container is to be created on (in a partitioned database system).

EndingNodeNumber   A partition number that identifies the end of a range of partitions (nodes) that the table space container is to be created on (in a partitioned database system).

SystemContainer   Identifies one or more containers that will belong to the SMS table space. The syntax used to define SMS table space containers is as follows:

```
USING ( [ContainerDefinition] ,... ) < ON [NODE | NODES]
( [NodeNumber] | [StartingNodeNumber] TO [EndingNodeNumber] ,
. . . ) >
```

where:

ContainerDefinition   Identifies one or more containers that will belong to the specified table space (and that will be used to physically store the table space's data). Each container definition must identify an absolute or relative filename (if the filename is not absolute, it is relative to the database directory).

NodeNumber   Identifies one or more specific partitions (nodes) that the table space container is to be created on (in a partitioned database system).

StartingNodeNumber   A partition number that identifies the beginning of a range of partitions (nodes) that the table space container is to be created on (in a partitioned database system).

EndingNodeNumber   A partition number that identifies the end of a range of partitions (nodes) that the table space container is to be created on (in a partitioned database system).

ExtentPages	Identifies the number of pages of data that will be written to a single table space container before another container will be used. (The DB2 Database Manager cycles repeatedly through each container, as data is stored.)
ExtentSize	Identifies the amount of data that will be written to a single table space container before another container will be used. The value specified in this parameter is treated as the total number of bytes, unless the letter K (kilobytes), M (megabytes), or G (gigabytes) is also specified. If this parameter is used instead of the *ExtentPages* parameter, the value specified is divided by the size of a single page to determine a number of pages value.
PrefetchPages	Identifies the number of pages of data that will be read from the specified table space when data prefetching is performed (prefetching allows data that is needed by a query to be read before it is referenced so that the query does not have to wait for I/O to be performed).
PrefetchSize	Identifies the amount of data that will be read from the specified table space when data prefetching is performed. The value specified for this parameter is treated as the total number of bytes, unless the letter K (kilobytes), M (megabytes), or G (gigabytes) is also specified. If this parameter is used instead of the *PrefetchPages* parameter, the value specified is divided by the size of a single page to determine a number of pages value.
BufferpoolName	Identifies the name of the buffer pool that is to be used by all tables that are created in the specified table space.
OverheadTime	Identifies the I/O controller overhead and disk-seek latency time, in milliseconds, that is associated with the containers that belong to a specified table space.
TransferRate	Identifies the time, in milliseconds, that it takes to read one 4K or 8K page of data from a table space container and store it in memory.

For example, when executed, the SQL statement

```
CREATE REGULAR TABLESPACE SMS_SPACE PAGESIZE 8K MANAGED BY SYSTEM
USING ('C:\SMS_TBSP.TSP') PREFETCHSIZE 32
```

would create a table space that

- Can be used to store all data except data that is associated with temporary tables
- Has been assigned the name SMS_SPACE
- Uses pages that are 8,192 bytes (8K) in size
- Is managed by the operating system (an SMS table space)
- Uses the file SMS_TBSP.TSP in the root directory of drive C: for storing data (as its container)
- Will retrieve 32,767 bytes (32K) of data at a time when prefetching is performed

Creating Tables—The CREATE TABLE Statement

As mentioned earlier, a table is a logical structure that is used to present data as a collection of unordered rows with a fixed number of columns. Each column contains a set of values of the same data type—the definitions of the columns in a table make up the table structure and the rows contain the actual table data.

Tables can be created by selecting the appropriate action from the *Tables* menu found in the Control Center or by executing the CREATE TABLE SQL statement. Because tables are the basic data objects used to store information in a DB2 Universal Database database, the CREATE TABLE statement is the most fundamental DDL statement available. The basic job of the CREATE TABLE statement is to assign a name to the table that is to be created and to identify the names, data types, and attributes of one or more of the table's columns in what is known as a table definition. Along with column declarations, a table definition can also include other information such as the definition of primary keys, unique constraints, referential constraints, and check constraints. In addition to creating a table that matches a specific definition, the CREATE TABLE statement can also control where the resulting table is placed in physical storage.

Because the CREATE TABLE statement, along with the components that make up a table, is discussed in great detail in Chapter 5, this statement is not addressed in this chapter.

Creating Views—The CREATE VIEW Statement

One of the nice things about a relational database is that even when users are sharing data, they do not have to see that data in the same way. Some users can work directly with base tables, whereas other users can work with views. A view is essentially a named specification of a result table that is produced by a query whenever the view is referenced in a DML statement. For this reason, a view can be thought of as having columns and rows, just like a base table, and in most cases, data can be retrieved directly from a view just as it can be retrieved from a base table. However, whether or not a view can be used to add, update, or delete data depends on how it is defined.

Although a view looks like a base table, it does not exist as a table in physical storage; therefore, it does not contain data. Instead, a view refers to data stored in other base tables and it can include any or all of the columns or rows contained in the table(s) on which it is based. A view can also include any number of columns from other views, and a view can include a combination of columns from both tables and other views.

Kinds of Views

Based on their definition, some views are classified as read-only, whereas others are classified as insertable, updatable, or deletable. Read-only views can only be queried, but insertable, updatable, and deletable views can be both queried and used in insert, update, and delete operations.

A view is considered deletable if all of the following conditions are true:

- Each FROM clause of the outer SELECT statement (that is, not a SELECT statement in a subquery) used to create the view identifies only one base table (with no OUTER clause), deletable view (with no OUTER clause), deletable nested table expression, or deletable common table expression.

- The outer SELECT statement used to create the view does not include a VALUES clause, a GROUP BY clause, or a HAVING clause.

- The outer SELECT statement used to create the view does not include column functions (such as MIN(), MAX(), and so on) in the select list.

- The outer SELECT statement used to create the view does not include any set operations (such as UNION, EXCEPT, or INTERSECT), other than the UNION ALL operation.

- The base tables specified in the operands of a UNION ALL operation are not the same and each operand is deletable.

- The select list of the outer SELECT statement used to create the view does not include the DISTINCT keyword.

A view is considered updatable if all of the following conditions are true:

- The view is deletable.

- Any column of the view resolves to a column of a base table.

- All the corresponding columns of the operands of a UNION ALL operation have data types that match exactly (including length, precision, and scale) and default values that match exactly, if the SELECT statement of the view includes a UNION ALL operation.

In general, a view is considered updatable if each row in the view can be uniquely mapped onto one row of a base table. (This makes it possible for the DB2 Database Manager to map insert, update, and delete operations that are performed on the view into matching operations that are performed on the underlying base table.) A view is considered insertable if every column of the view is updatable and if the SELECT statement of the view does not include a UNION ALL operation. Finally, a view is considered read-only if it is deletable.

When you perform insert, update, and/or delete operations on rows in a view, you should remember that you are really performing these operations on rows of the underlying base table(s) of the view. This means that when you delete a row from a view, all the information in the underlying base table row is deleted, including information in columns that are not visible in the view. Similarly, when you insert a row into a view, all the columns of the underlying base table that are not visible in the view receive predefined default values (if some of these columns do not have predefined default values, you will not be able to insert a row into the view).

Inoperative Views

When a view is first defined, the DB2 Database Manager checks the privileges the view definer has on that view's underlying objects (such as base tables and/or views) and grants appropriate privileges on the view to the definer. For example, if the view definer has SELECT and INSERT privileges on the table a view is based on, and if the view is not a read-only view, the definer will receive SELECT and INSERT privileges on the view as well. However, what happens to the view if the definer loses one or both of these privileges on the underlying table? Or what if the underlying table disappears? Because, in either case, the view can no longer be used, it might seem reasonable for its definition to be dropped automatically. In many cases, this would be acceptable; however, sometimes this approach would be more heavy-handed than necessary. For example, suppose that the definition of an alias is changed from one table to another. It seems unfortunate, and even dangerous, for this event to cause the DB2 Database Manager to delete the definitions of every view that reference the alias. Similarly, if a user's privilege(s) is accidentally or temporarily revoked and then later reinstated, it seems unreasonable for the DB2 Database Manager to delete every view that has been defined by the user, only to have them redefined as soon as the appropriate authorizations have been granted. For this reason, DB2 Universal Database has adopted a somewhat gentler policy for dealing with views that depend on some object or privilege that is no longer available; such a view is classified as inoperative. (The definition of an inoperative view is retained in the SYSCAT.VIEWS system catalog view, and an *X* in the VALID column indicates its inoperative status.)

In practical terms, an inoperative view is one in which the view definition has been unintentionally dropped. When a view is made inoperative, all views that are dependent on the inoperative view are also made inoperative and packages that are dependent on the inoperative view are no longer valid. Until an inoperative view is explicitly recreated or dropped, all SQL statements that reference the inoperative view cannot be precompiled (with the exception of the CREATE ALIAS, CREATE VIEW, DROP VIEW, and COMMENT ON TABLE statements), and its qualified name cannot be used to name another view, table, or alias.

A user can restore an inoperative view to normal status by retrieving its definition from the TEXT column of the SYSCAT.VIEWS system catalog view and using this definition to create a new view. However, because all authorization records on a view are deleted if the view is marked inoperative, when an inoperative view is recreated, any privileges that are required by that view must be explicitly granted to other users. It is not necessary to explicitly drop an inoperative view before recreating it; creating a view with the same name as that of an inoperative view will cause the inoperative view to be replaced.

Creating Views

Views can be created by selecting the appropriate action from the *Views* menu found in the Control Center or by executing the CREATE VIEW SQL statement. Just as the CREATE TABLE statement can create three different types of tables, the CREATE VIEW statement can create two different types of views:

- **Normal**   Used to access data stored in base tables or views
- **Typed**   Used to access data via a structured data type

From a certification viewpoint, knowing how to create Typed views as well as knowing all of the CREATE VIEW statement options available is not important. Instead, emphasis is placed on knowing how to create Normal views that reference data stored in base tables or other Normal views. With these objectives in mind, the following is the basic syntax for the CREATE VIEW SQL statement:

```
CREATE VIEW [ViewName] <( [ColumnName] ,... )> AS
<WITH [TableExpresion , . . . ]> [SelectStatement]
<WITH CASCADED CHECK OPTION | WITH LOCAL CHECK OPTION>
```

where:

ViewName	Identifies the name that is to be assigned to the view that is to be created.
ColumnName	Identifies one or more columns that are to be included in the view that is to be created.
TableExpression	Identifies a common table expression that is to be used to create a temporary table that, when populated by retrieving one or more rows of data from other base tables or views, will provide the appropriate values for one or more columns in the view.
SelectStatement	Specifies the SELECT SQL statement that is used to define the columns and rows of the view being created. (This SELECT statement cannot contain parameter markers or references to host variables.)

CREATE VIEW SQL Statement Examples and Resulting Veiw Characteristics

Now that we've seen the basic syntax for the CREATE VIEW statement, let's take a look at two examples. In addition to examining the CREATE VIEW statement's syntax, we will also examine the characteristics of the view that would be created if the CREATE VIEW statements shown were executed.

Example 1 If the following CREATE VIEW SQL statement were executed

```
CREATE VIEW MA_PROJ
AS SELECT *FROM PROJECT
WHERE SUBSTR(PROJNO, 1, 2) = 'MA'
```

and if a table named PROJECT looked like this

PROJECT

PROJNO	PROJNAME	DEPTNO	RESPEMP	PRSTDATE	PRENDATE
AD3100	Administration Services	D01	000010	1982-01-01	1983-02-01
AD3111	General Administration Systems	D21	000070	1982-01-01	1983-02-01
MA2100	Weld Line Automation	D11	000010	1982-01-01	1983-02-01
MA2110	Weld Line Programming	D11	000060	1982-01-01	1983-02-01

the following view would be created:

MA_PROJ

PROJNO	PROJNAME	DEPTNO	RESPEMP	PRSTDATE	PRENDATE
MA2100	Weld Line Automation	D11	000010	1982-01-01	1983-02-01
MA2110	Weld Line Programming	D11	000060	1982-01-01	1983-02-01

Example 2 If the following CREATE VIEW SQL statement were executed

```
CREATE VIEW PRJ_LEADER
(PROJNO, PROJNAME, DEPTNO, PROJMGR, TOTALPAY)
        AS SELECT PROJNO,
        PROJNAME,
        DEPTNO,
        RESPEMP,
        SALARY + BONUS AS TOTAL_PAY
FROM PROJECT P, EMPLOYEE E
WHERE P.RESPEMP = E.EMPNO
```

and if a table named PROJECT looked like this

PROJECT

PROJNO	PROJNAME	DEPTNO	RESPEMP	PRSTDATE	PRENDATE
AD3100	Administration Services	D01	000010	1982-01-01	1983-02-01
AD3111	General Administration Systems	D21	000020	1982-01-01	1983-02-01
MA2100	Weld Line Automation	D11	000030	1982-01-01	1983-02-01
MA2110	Weld Line Programming	D11	000040	1982-01-01	1983-02-01

and a table named EMPLOYEE looked like this

EMPLOYEE

EMPNO	NAME	DEPT	HIREDATE	SALARY	BONUS
000010	BOGART	D01	1980-11-01	52000.00	1800.00
000020	CAGNEY	D21	1980-12-01	38000.00	1200.00
000030	BACALL	D11	1981-01-15	48500.00	1450.00
000040	GRANT	D11	1981-02-01	36500.00	1000.00

the following view would be created:

PRJ_LEADER

PROJNO	PROJNAME	DEPTNO	PROJMGR	TOTALPAY
AD3100	Administration Services	D01	000010	53800.00
AD3111	General Administration Systems	D21	000020	39200.00
MA2100	Weld Line Automation	D11	000030	49950.00
MA2110	Weld Line Programming	D11	000040	37500.00

Creating Indexes—The CREATE INDEX Statement

As mentioned earlier, an index is an object that contains an ordered set of pointers that refer to a key in a base table. When indexes are used, the DB2 Database Manager can access data directly and more efficiently because the index provides a direct path to the data through pointers that have been ordered based on the values of the columns that the index(es) is associated with. If an index is created for an empty table, that index will not have any entries stored in it until the table is populated. However, if an index is created for a table that already contains data, index entries are made for the existing data as soon as the index creation process is complete.

Indexes can serve the following purposes:

- They provide a fast, efficient way to find rows of data (based on the values in the key columns). Indexes can greatly improve the performance of queries that search for a particular column value or a range of column values. In some cases, all the information needed by a query may be found in the index itself, making it unnecessary to access table data.

- They always provide a logical ordering of the rows of a table (again, based on the values in the key columns). Because the values of each column can be sorted in ascending or descending order, the ordering property of an index is useful in processing queries with ORDER BY and GROUP BY clauses, and in some kinds of join algorithms.

- They can optionally enforce the uniqueness of a table's key columns. In other words, if specified, no two rows of a table may have the same key column values.

- They can optionally provide a clustering property for a table, which causes the rows of the table to be physically arranged according to the ordering of their index keys. This property is useful to the optimizer when choosing a data access plan. Note that all indexes provide a logical ordering, but only a clustering index provides a physical ordering for the rows of a table.

Indexes can be created by selecting the appropriate action from the *Indexes* menu found in the Control Center or by executing the CREATE INDEX SQL statement. The basic syntax for this statement is

```
CREATE <UNIQUE> INDEX [IndexName] ON [TableName] ( [KeyColumnName]
<ASC | DESC> , . . .  ) <INCLUDE ( [ColumnName] <ASC | DESC> ,
. . .  ) > <CLUSTER> <PCTFREE 10 | PCTFREE [PercentFreeSpace] >
<MINPCTUSED [MinPercentUsedSpace] >
<DISALLOW REVERSE SCANS | ALLOW REVERSE SCANS>
```

where:

IndexName	Identifies the name that is to be assigned to the index that is to be created.
TableName	Identifies the name of table that the index is to be created for.
KeyColumnName	Identifies one or more columns that are to be part of the index key (to enforce uniqueness).
ColumnName	Identifies one or more columns that are to be appended to the set of index key columns specified in the *KeyColumnName* parameter, but that are not to be used to enforce uniqueness.
PercentFreeSpace	Specifies what percentage of each index page to leave as free space when building the index.
MinPercentUsedSpace	Specifies whether or not the index is to be reorganized online and if so, identifies the threshold for the minimum percentage of space that is to be used on an index leaf page. If, after a

key is deleted from an index leaf page, the percentage of space used on the page is at or below the percentage specified in this parameter, an attempt is made to merge the remaining keys on the page with those of a neighboring page. If sufficient space is available on one of the neighboring pages, the data is merged and one of the pages is deleted.

For example, when executed, the SQL statement

```
CREATE UNIQUE INDEX PROJ_NAME ON PROJECT (PROJNAME)
```

would create an index that

- Has been assigned the name PROJ_NAME
- Ensures that no two entries in the table named PROJECT have the same value in the column PROJNAME.
- Sorts project names in ascending order

Any number of indexes can be created for a table, using various combinations of columns as keys. However, each index does not come without a cost. Part of this cost is paid in storage space requirements; each index replicates its key values and this replication requires additional storage space. The rest of this cost is paid in a slight reduction in performance for insert, update, and delete operations because each modification to a table results in a similar modification to all indexes that are defined on the table. In fact, creating a large number of indexes for a table that is updated frequently can slow down, rather than improve, overall performance. Therefore, indexes should only be created when having them provides a clear advantage.

Finding the optimum set of indexes for a particular database is an art that can only be learned from experience. However, one situation exists where an index will almost always guarantee an increase in performance. Any time an application frequently processes rows in a table, based on a specific value (which is specified in a WHERE clause), an index based on that specific value can be used to access rows directly. This is important because the rows in a base table are not ordered. When rows are inserted into a base table, they are typically placed in the first storage location found that can accommodate the row. Therefore, when searching for specific rows in a table that is not indexed, the entire table must be scanned. Because the rows will be ordered by an index, the need to perform a lengthy sequential search in order to locate specific rows will be eliminated.

NOTE An index is never directly used by an application or a user. Instead, the decision of whether or not to use an index, and which index to use, is made by the DB2 optimizer when Data Manipulation SQL statements are processed. The DB2 Optimizer bases its decision on statistical information such as the number of rows in a table, the indexes that exist for a table, and the overall size of a table. Unfortunately, these statistics are not automatically kept up-to-date. This means that in order for the DB2 Optimizer to make the best decision, this statistical information needs to be updated whenever a new index is created. Statistical information about a table can be updated at any time by executing the RUNSTATS command. (Any packages stored in the database should be rebound whenever the statistical information for a table is updated).

Creating Schemas—The CREATE SCHEMA Statement

A schema is an identifier that helps provide a means of classifying or grouping objects that are stored in a database. A schema is also an object itself; therefore, an individual can own it and can control access to both the data and the objects that reside within it. Whenever a data object (for example, a table, view, or index) is created, it is always assigned, either implicitly or explicitly, to a schema.

Most objects in a database are assigned a unique name that consists of two parts. The first (leftmost) part is called the qualifier (or schema) and the second (rightmost) part is called the simple (or unqualified) name. Syntactically, these two parts are concatenated as a single string of characters separated by a period. When any object that can be qualified by a schema name is first created, it is assigned to a particular schema based on the qualifier in its name.

Schemas are implicitly created whenever a data object is created and assigned a qualifier name that does not match any existing schema in the database. (If a schema is not included in the name provided when an object is created, the authorization ID of the user creating the object is used as the schema, by default.) Schemas can be explicitly created by selecting the appropriate action from the *Schemas* menu found in the Control Center or by executing the CREATE SCHEMA SQL statement. The basic syntax for this statement is

```
CREATE SCHEMA [SchemaName] <SQLStatement ,...>
```

or

```
CREATE SCHEMA AUTHORIZATION [AuthorizationName]
<SQLStatement , . . . >
```

or

```
CREATE SCHEMA [SchemaName] AUTHORIZATION [AuthorizationName]
<SQLStatement , . . . >
```

where:

SchemaName	Identifies the name that is to be assigned to the schema that is to be created.
AuthorizationName	Identifies the owner of the schema that is to be created.
SQLStatement	Identifies the one or more SQL statements that are to be executed as part of the CREATE SCHEMA statement. Only the following SQL statements are valid: CREATE TABLE (Normal), CREATE VIEW (Normal), CREATE INDEX, COMMENT ON, and GRANT (Table, View, or Nickname privileges).

For example, when executed, the SQL statement

```
CREATE SCHEMA STOCK
CREATE TABLE PART (PARTNO      SMALLINT NOT NULL,
                   DESCR       VARCHAR(24),
                   QUANTITY    INTEGER)
CREATE INDEX PARTIND ON PART (PARTNO)
```

would create a schema that has

- Been assigned the name STOCK

- A table associated with it named PART

- An index associated with it named PARTIND that is based on the table named PART

Because a schema can be created implicitly by creating an object with a new schema name, you may be wondering why anyone would want to use the CREATE SCHEMA statement to explicitly create a schema. The reason has to do with controlling access to the schema, as well as any objects associated with that schema. An explicitly created schema has an owner, which is either the authorization ID of the user who executed the CREATE SCHEMA statement or the authorization ID that was specified in the AUTHORIZATION parameter of the CREATE SCHEMA statement. A schema owner has the authority to create, alter, and drop any object stored in the schema; to drop the schema itself; and to grant these privileges to other users.

Implicitly created schemas, on the other hand, are considered to be owned by the imaginary user "SYSIBM." Any user can create any object in an implicitly created schema, and each object in the schema is controlled by the user who created it. In addition, only users with System Administrator (SYSADM) or Database Administrator (DBADM) authority are allowed to drop implicitly created schemas. Therefore, in order to have complete control over a schema and all the objects stored in it, the schema should be created explicitly.

Creating Aliases—The CREATE ALIAS Statement

An alias is an alternate name for a table, view, or nickname. Once created, aliases can be referenced in the same way any table, view, or nickname can be referenced. However, an alias cannot be used in every context that a table, view, or nickname can be used in. For example, an alias cannot be used in the check condition of a check constraint and it cannot reference a user-defined temporary table.

Aliases allow SQL statements to be independent of the fully qualified names of base tables and views that they reference; whenever an alias is used in an SQL statement, it is equivalent to using the target of that alias. Because an alias can be easily changed from one target to another, programs that use aliases can easily be redirected from one table or view to another. When the target of an alias is changed, no additional changes need to be made to applications that use the alias. However, before those applications can be executed, they must be rebound, either explicitly, using the REBIND command/function, or implicitly, using the DB2 Database Manager. (Because the database knows that an application uses an alias (by the contents of the package associated with the application), when the target of that alias changes, the DB2 Database Manager will automatically rebind the application the next time it is used so that the alias will reference the new target.)

Consider the following scenario. Suppose that you need to develop an application that interacts with the ORDERS table of your company's inventory database. During the development process, you need to run the application against a test table without interfering with the production data in your real ORDERS table. Then, when the program is debugged and ready to go into production, you would like to make it operate against the real ORDERS table. Of course, you can always edit the application's source code and globally change all table references so that they refer to the real ORDERS table. However, this process is time-consuming and prone to error. If an alias is used instead of a base table name in all table references, you can solve the problem by changing the target of the alias when the program is ready to go into production.

The target of an alias may be a real table, a view, or another alias. In fact, an alias can be defined even if its target doesn't exist at all! However, when an alias is referenced in an SQL statement, the target must exist and must be appropriate in the context where it is used when that statement is actually executed.

Aliases can be created by selecting the appropriate action from the *Aliases* menu found in the Control Center or by executing the CREATE ALIAS SQL statement. The basic syntax for this statement is

```
CREATE [ALIAS | SYNONYM] [AliasName] FOR [TableName | ViewName |
ExistingAlias]
```

where:

AliasName   Identifies the name that is to be assigned to the alias that is to be created.

TableName   Identifies the table that the new alias is to be defined for.

ViewName   Identifies the view that the new alias is to be defined for.

ExistingAlias Identifies the existing alias that the new alias is to be defined for.

For example, when executed, the SQL statement

```
CREATE ALIAS DEPT FOR DEPARTMENT
```

would create an alias that

- Has been assigned the name DEPT
- Refers to a table named DEPARTMENT

Describing an Object—The COMMENT ON Statement

It was mentioned earlier that the system catalog tables that are created when a database is created are used to store descriptions of all objects that are defined for that particular database. However, the information stored in the system catalog tables only pertains to the definition of a specific object; it does not provide descriptive information about the object itself. To overcome this, many of the system catalog tables have a column named REMARKS in which a user can store a description or a comment (of up to 254 characters in length) that indicates what the object is used for. Descriptions/comments on various types of objects can be entered into the system catalog tables by the COMMENT ON SQL statement. The basic syntax for this statement is

```
COMMENT ON [ObjectType] [ObjectName] IS [CommentText]
```

or

```
COMMENT ON COLUMN [TableName | ViewName].[ColumnName] IS
[CommentText]
```

or

```
COMMENT ON [TableName | ViewName] ( [ColumnName] IS [CommentText]
, ...)
```

or

```
COMMENT ON CONSTRAINT [TableName].[ConstraintName] IS
[CommentText]
```

where:

ObjectType	Identifies the type of database object (for example, table, view, index, and so on) that the comment (description) is to be created or changed for.
ObjectName	Identifies the name of the database object (as it is described in the system catalog) that the comment (description) is to be associated with.
TableName	Identifies the name of a distinct database table that the comment (description) is to be associated with.
ViewName	Identifies the name of a distinct view that the comment (description) is to be associated with.
ColumnName	Identifies one or more columns in a table or view that the comment (description) is to be associated with.
ConstraintName	Identifies the name of a check constraint that the comment (description) is to be associated with.
CommentText	The comment (description) that is to be assigned to the database object.

For example, when executed, the SQL statement

```
COMMENT ON TABLE EMPLOYEE 'Company employees as of 2001-01-01'
```

would store the comment "Company employees as of 2001-01-01" in the system catalog tables for the EMPLOYEE table object.

As you can see, comments for a specific object can be provided by invoking the COMMENT ON statement and providing the name of the object and a specific comment for that particular object. However, when entering comments for columns in a table or view, a special form of the COMMENT ON statement can be used to provide comments for several columns at one time.

For example, when executed, the SQL statement

```
COMMENT ON EMPLOYEE
(WORKDEPT IS 'See DEPARTMENT table for names',
 EDLEVEL IS 'Highest grade level passed in school')
```

would

- Store the comment "See DEPARTMENT table for names" in the system catalog tables for the record associated with the WORKDEPT column of the EMPLOYEE table object.

- Store the comment "Highest grade level passed in school" in the system catalog tables for the record associated with the EDLEVEL column of the EMPLOYEE table object.

Dropping an Object—The DROP Statement

Just as it is important to be able to add objects to a database, it is important to be able to remove objects that are no longer needed. Objects can be removed from a database by selecting the appropriate action from the object menus found in the Control Center or by executing the DROP SQL statement. The basic syntax for this statement is

```
DROP [ObjectType] [ObjectName]
```

or

```
DROP TABLESPACE | TABLESPACES [TablespaceName ,...]
```

or

```
DROP SCHEMA [SchemaName] RESTRICT
```

where:

ObjectType	Identifies the type of database object that is to be deleted (dropped).
ObjectName	Identifies the name of the database object, as it is described in the system catalog, that is to be deleted (dropped).
TablespaceName	Identifies the name of one or more table spaces, as they are described in the system catalog, that are to be deleted (dropped).

SchemaName   Identifies the name of the schema, as it is described in the system catalog, that is to be deleted (dropped).

 NOTE Objects that are to be removed (or dropped) from a database must be referenced by their two-part name. If an explicit schema/qualifier name is not provided, the authorization ID of the current user is implicitly used to name the object.

For example, when executed, the SQL statement

```
DROP TABLE STOCK.PARTS
```

would remove the table named PARTS (which was stored in the STOCK schema) from the database.

When an object is dropped, its removal may affect other objects that depend on its existence. For example, if a table that is used in a view definition is dropped, that view definition will no longer be valid, or if an index that is being used by a package is dropped, that package must be rebound before it can be executed. In some cases, the DB2 Database Manager will automatically repair the dependent object (for example, a package that depends on a dropped index will automatically be rebound to use a different access plan). In other cases, when an object is dropped, all objects that are dependent upon that object are also dropped (for example, when a table is dropped, all indexes defined on that table are also dropped). And in some cases, an object cannot be dropped if other objects are dependant upon its existence (for example, a schema cannot be dropped, unless all objects in that schema have been dropped).

It goes with out saying that built-in objects such as the system catalog tables cannot be dropped.

Modifying Object Definitions

As a database matures, it often becomes necessary to make modifications to one or more existing objects. When the volume of data in an object such as a table is small or when an object has few or no dependencies, its relatively easy to save the associated data, drop the object, recreate the object with the appropriate modifications, reload the previously saved data, and redefine any dependencies. But how do you accomplish this task when the volume of data is large or when dependency relationships are numerous? If the object is a nodegroup, a buffer pool, a table space, or a table, a form of the ALTER DDL statement can be used to perform such a task.

Modifying Nodegroups—The ALTER NODEGROUP Statement

As partitioned database systems grow and older nodes are replaced, it is often necessary to make modifications to one or more nodegroups. One or more database partitions (nodes) can be added to or removed from an existing nodegroup by executing the ALTER NODEGROUP SQL statement. The syntax for this statement is

```
ALTER NODEGROUP [NodegroupName] ADD [NODE | NODES] ( [NodeNumber]
,... ) <LIKE NODE [LikeNodeNumber] | WITHOUT TABLESPACES>
```

or

```
ALTER NODEGROUP [NodegroupName] ADD [NODE | NODES]
( [StartingNodeNumber] TO [EndingNodeNumber] , . . . )
<LIKE NODE [LikeNodeNumber] | WITHOUT TABLESPACES>
```

or

```
ALTER NODEGROUP [NodegroupName] DROP [NODE | NODES]
( [NodeNumber] ,... )
```

or

```
ALTER NODEGROUP [NodegroupName] DROP [NODE | NODES] (
[StartingNodeNumber] TO [EndingNodeNumber] , . . . )
```

where:

NodegroupName	Identifies the name of an existing nodegroup that is to be altered.
NodeNumber	Identifies one or more specific partitions (nodes) that are to be added to or removed from the existing nodegroup definition. (Partitions are numbered from 0 to 999.)
LikeNodeNumber	Identifies an existing partition (in the nodegroup specified) whose table space container definitions are to be duplicated for each new partition being added.
StartingNodeNumber	A partition number that identifies the beginning of a range of partitions (nodes) that are to be added to or removed from the existing nodegroup definition.
EndingNodeNumber	A partition number that identifies the end of a range of partitions (nodes) that are to be added to or removed from the existing nodegroup definition.

For example, when executed, the SQL statement

```
ALTER NODEGROUP MAXGROUP ADD NODES (6, 7) LIKE 2
```

would add partitions number 6 and 7 to the nodegroup named MAXGROUP and assign them a set of table space containers like those of partition number 2.

Remember that before a partition can be added to a nodegroup, it must be defined in the partition configuration file db2nodes.cfg. (The DB2 Database Manager has to be stopped and restarted before changes to this file will take effect.)

Once one or more database partitions have been added to or removed from a nodegroup, data associated with that nodegroup must be redistributed across the new set of partitions. This task can be performed by executing the REDISTRIBUTE NODEGROUP command.

Modifying Buffer Pools—The ALTER BUFFERPOOL Statement

It was mentioned earlier that how buffer pools are created and used is the single most important area where database performance can be improved. From this statement, it is easy to see how it might be necessary to modify an existing buffer pool many times in order to obtain optimum database performance. The size of an existing buffer pool can be changed, an existing buffer pool's use of extended memory can be turned on or off, or an existing buffer pool can be added to a new nodegroup by executing the ALTER BUFFERPOOL SQL statement. The syntax for this statement is

```
ALTER BUFFERPOOL [BufferPoolName] <NODE [NodeNumber]> SIZE [Size]
```

or

```
ALTER BUFFERPOOL [BufferPoolName] [EXTENDED STORAGE | NOT EXTENDED
STORAGE]
```

or

```
ALTER BUFFERPOOL [BufferPoolName] ADD NODEGROUP [NodegroupName]
```

where:

BufferPoolName   Identifies the name of an existing buffer pool that is to be altered.

NodeNumber   Identifies a specific partition that the size of the existing buffer pool is to be modified on.

Size	The amount of memory, in pages, that is to be allocated for the buffer pool. (If this parameter is set to -1, the value of the *buff-page* database configuration parameter will be used to determine the buffer pool's size.)
NodeGroupName	Specifies a nodegroup that the buffer pool's definition is to be added to. (The buffer pool will be created on any partition in the nodegroup specified that does not already have the buffer pool defined.)

For example, when executed, the SQL statement

```
ALTER BUFFERPOOL BUFFPOOL1 SIZE 16
```

would change the number of pages used by the buffer pool named BUFFPOOL1 to 16. (The actual amount of space used by the buffer pool would be 16 times the page size used when the buffer pool was created. If the buffer pool's page size was 4,096 [the default], the buffer pool's new size will be $16 \times 4,096 = 65,536$ bytes.)

It is important to note that although changes made to a buffer pool by the ALTER BUFFERPOOL SQL statement will be reflected in the system catalog after all changes made are committed, no changes will be made to the buffer pool itself until the DB2 Database Manager is stopped and restarted. The original attributes of all altered buffer pools will persist until then; none of the buffer pools will be impacted during the interim. Tables created in table spaces of nodegroups that a buffer pool has been added to will use a default buffer pool until the DB2 Database Manager is stopped and restarted.

Modifying Table Spaces—The ALTER TABLESPACE Statement

Because SMS table spaces rely on the operating system to manage physical storage requirements, the only changes that might be necessary after an SMS table space has been created are changes to the properties of the table space itself (such as the buffer pool used, the size of the prefetch buffer used, and so on) that might impact performance. On the other hand, because DMS table spaces use either a fixed-size, pre-allocated file or a physical raw device such as a disk for storage, they have to be monitored closely to ensure that they are always large enough to meet the database's storage requirements. The size of a DMS table space can be increased by either increasing the size of one or more of its containers or by adding one or more new containers to it. New containers can be added to an existing DMS table space, an existing table space's properties can be changed, or a new SMS table space can be added to a database partition that currently does not have any containers defined for it by executing the ALTER TABLESPACE SQL statement. The syntax for this statement is

```
ALTER TABLESPACE [TableSpaceName] <ADD [DatabaseContainer ,... |
SystemContainer , . . . ]>
```

or

```
ALTER TABLESPACE [TableSpaceName] <[EXTEND | RESIZE]
[DatabaseContainer , . . . ]>
```

or

```
ALTER TABLESPACE [TableSpaceName] <[EXTEND | RESIZE] ( ALL
<CONTAINERS> [NumberOfPages | ContainerSize <K | M | G>]>
```

or

```
ALTER TABLESPACE [TableSpaceName] <PREFETCHSIZE [PrefetchPages |
PrefetchSize <K | M | G>]> <BUFFERPOOL [BufferpoolName]>
<OVERHEAD [OverheadTime]> <TRANSFERRATE [TransferRateTime]>
<DROPPED TABLE RECOVERY ON | DROPPED TABLE RECOVERY OFF>
<SWITCH ONLINE>
```

where:

TableSpaceName   Identifies the name of an existing table space that is to be altered.

DatabaseContainer   Identifies one or more containers that will belong to the DMS table space. The syntax used to define DMS table space containers is as follows:

```
USING ( FILE | DEVICE [ContainerDefinition] [NumberOfPages |
ContainerSize <K | M | G>] , . . . ) <ON [NODE | NODES]
( [NodeNumber] | [StartingNodeNumber] TO [EndingNodeNumber] ,
. . . ) >
```

where:

ContainerDefinition   Identifies one or more containers that will belong to the specified table space (and that will be used to physically store the table space's data). For FILE containers, the container definition must identify an absolute or relative file-name (if the filename is not absolute, it is relative to the database directory). For DEVICE containers, the container definition must identify a specific device that already exists.

NumberOfPages Specifies the number of 4K or 8K pages that are to be used by the table space container.

ContainerSize Specifies the amount of memory that is to be used by the table space container. The value specified in the *ContainerSize* parameter is treated as the total number of bytes, unless the letter K (kilobytes), M (megabytes), or G (gigabytes) is also specified. If the amount of memory to be used is specified (instead of the number of pages), that value is divided by the size of a single page to determine a number of pages value.

NodeNumber Identifies one or more specific partitions (nodes) that the table space container is to be created on (in a partitioned database system).

StartingNodeNumber A partition number that identifies the beginning of a range of partitions (nodes) that the table space container is to be created on (in a partitioned database system).

EndingNodeNumber A partition number that identifies the end of a range of partitions (nodes) that the table space container is to be created on (in a partitioned database system).

SystemContainer Identifies one or more containers that will belong to the SMS table space. The syntax used to define SMS table space containers is as follows:

```
USING ( [ContainerDefinition] ,... ) < ON [NODE | NODES]
( [NodeNumber] | [StartingNodeNumber] TO [EndingNodeNumber] ,
. . . ) >
```

where:

ContainerDefinition Identifies one or more containers that will belong to the specified table space (and that will be used to physically store the table space's data). Each container definition must identify an absolute or relative filename (if the filename is not absolute, it is relative to the database directory).

NodeNumber Identifies one or more specific partitions (nodes) that the table space container is to be created on (in a partitioned database system).

StartingNodeNumber	A partition number that identifies the beginning of a range of partitions (nodes) that the table space container is to be created on (in a partitioned database system).
EndingNodeNumber	A partition number that identifies the end of a range of partitions (nodes) that the table space container is to be created on (in a partitioned database system).
NumberOfPages	Specifies the number of 4K or 8K pages that are to be used by the table space container.
ContainerSize	Specifies the amount of memory that is to be used by the table space container. The value specified in the *ContainerSize* parameter is treated as the total number of bytes, unless the letter K (kilobytes), M (megabytes), or G (gigabytes) is also specified. If the amount of memory to be used is specified (instead of the number of pages), that value is divided by the size of a single page to determine a number of pages value.
PrefetchPages	Identifies the number of pages of data that will be read from the specified table space when data prefetching is performed (prefetching allows data that is needed by a query to be read before it is referenced so that the query does not have to wait for I/O to be performed).
PrefetchSize	Identifies the amount of data that will be read from the specified table space when data prefetching is performed. The value specified for this parameter is treated as the total number of bytes, unless the letter K (kilobytes), M (megabytes), or G (gigabytes) is also specified. If this parameter is used instead of the *PrefetchPages* parameter, the value specified is divided by the size of a single page to determine a number of pages value.
BufferpoolName	Identifies the name of the buffer pool that is to be used by all tables that are created in the specified table space.
OverheadTime	Identifies the I/O controller overhead and disk-seek latency time (in number of milliseconds) that is associated with the containers that belong to a specified table space.
TransferRate	Identifies the time, in milliseconds, that it takes to read one 4K or 8K page of data from a table space container and store it in memory.

For example, when executed, the SQL statement

```
ALTER TABLESPACE PAYROLL ADD (DEVICE '/dev/rhdisk9' 10000)
```

would add the raw device /dev/rhdisk9 to the DMS table space named PAYROLL and assign it a size of 10,000 bytes.

When new containers are added to a table space, the contents of that table space are automatically redistributed such that data is evenly distributed across all available containers. Access to the table space is not blocked during this redistribution process; however, for optimum performance, if two or more containers are to be added to a table space, they should be added at the same time.

Modifying Tables—The ALTER TABLE Statement

Over time, a table that started out with one definition may be required to hold additional data that did not exist or that was not thought of at the time the table was created. Character data that was thought to be one size may turn out to be another. Or changes in business rules may dictate that old constraints be replaced. Additional columns and constraints can be added to an existing table, the length of an existing varying-length character data type column can be increased, or existing constraints can be removed by executing the ALTER TABLE SQL statement. The ALTER TABLE statement can also be used to change certain properties of a table.

Like the CREATE TABLE statement, the ALTER TABLE statement can be quite complex. From a certification viewpoint, knowing how to alter Typed and Summary tables as well as knowing all the ALTER TABLE statement options available is not important. Instead, emphasis is placed on knowing how to add new columns and constraints to existing Normal tables. With these objectives in mind, the following is the basic syntax for the ALTER TABLE SQL statement:

```
ALTER TABLE [TableName] ADD [Element]
```

or

```
ALTER TABLE [TableName] ALTER <COLUMN> [VARCHARColumnName] SET
DATA TYPE [VARCHAR | CHARACTER VARYING | CHAR VARYING] (Length)
```

or

```
ALTER TABLE [TableName] DROP [PRIMARY KEY | FOREIGN KEY
[ConstraintName] | UNIQUE [ConstraintName] | CHECK
[ConstraintName] | CONSTRAINT [ConstraintName]]
```

where:

TableName   Identifies the name of an existing table that is to be altered.

Element   Identifies one or more elements (such as columns, unique/primary key constraints, referential constraints, and check constraints) that are to be added to the table definition. The syntax used for adding each of these elements is as follows:

The syntax for adding a column element is

```
<COLUMN> [ColumnName] [DataType] <NOT NULL WITH DEFAULT
<DefaultValue> | WITH DEFAULT <DefaultValue>> <DataLinkOptions>
<UniqueConstraint | ReferentialConstraint | CheckConstraint>
```

where:

ColumnName   Specifies the name that is to be assigned to the column that is to be added.

DataType   Identifies the type of data that is to be stored in the column that is to be added.

DefaultValue   Specifies a default value that is to be provided for the column (in a row of data) in the event a value is not supplied by an INSERT or UPDATE operation.

DataLinkOptions   Specifies the options that are associated with a DATALINK column data type.

UniqueConstraint Identifies how the column is to be part of a unique or primary key constraint. The syntax used for defining a unique or primary key constraint as part of a column definition is as follows:

```
<CONSTRAINT [ConstraintName]> UNIQUE | PRIMARY KEY
```

where:

ConstraintName   Specifies the name that is to be assigned to the unique or primary key constraint that is to be created for the column.

ReferentialConstraint Identifies how the column is to be part of a referential constraint. The syntax used for defining a referential constraint for a column as part of the column definition is as follows:

```
<CONSTRAINT [ConstraintName]> REFERENCES [PKTableName]
<( [PKColumnName] , . . . )> <ON DELETE [DeleteAction]>
<ON UPDATE [UpdateAction]>
```

where:

ConstraintName	Specifies the name that is to be assigned to the referential constraint that is to be created for the column.
PKTableName	Identifies the parent table of the referential constraint.
PKColumnName	Identifies one or more columns that make up the parent key that has been defined for the table being referenced (such as the table referred to by the *PKTableName* parameter).
DeleteAction	Specifies the action that is to be taken on dependent tables whenever a delete operation is performed.
UpdateAction	Specifies the action that is to be taken on dependent tables whenever an update operation is performed.
CheckConstraint	Identifies how the column is to be part of a check constraint. The syntax used for defining a check constraint for a column as part of the column definition is as follows:

```
<CONSTRAINT [ConstraintName] > CHECK ( [CheckCondition] )
```

where:

ConstraintName	Specifies the name that is to be assigned to the check constraint that is to be created for the column.
CheckCondition	Identifies a condition that must evaluate to TRUE before data can be added to or changed in the table.

The syntax for adding a unique/primary key constraint element is

```
<CONSTRAINT [ConstraintName] > UNIQUE | PRIMARY KEY
(ColumnName , . . . )
```

where:

ConstraintName	Specifies the name that is to be assigned to the unique or primary key constraint that is to be created.
ColumnName	Identifies one or more columns that are to be part of the unique or primary key constraint.

The syntax for adding a referential constraint element is

```
<CONSTRAINT [ConstraintName]> FOREIGN KEY (ColumnName ,...)
REFERENCES [PKTableName] <( [PKColumnName] , . . . )>
<ON DELETE [DeleteAction]> <ON UPDATE [UpdateAction]>
```

where:

ConstraintName	Specifies the name that is to be assigned to the referential constraint that is to be created.
ColumnName	Identifies one or more columns that are to be part of the foreign key that makes up the referential constraint.
PKTableName	Identifies the parent table of the referential constraint.
PKColumnName	Identifies one or more columns that make up the parent key that has been defined for the table being referenced (such as the table referred to by the *PKTableName* parameter).
DeleteAction	Specifies the action that is to be taken on dependent tables whenever a delete operation is performed.
UpdateAction	Specifies the action that is to be taken on dependent tables whenever an update operation is performed.

The syntax for adding a check constraint element is

```
<CONSTRAINT [ConstraintName]> CHECK ( [CheckCondition] )
```

where:

ConstraintName	Specifies the name that is to be assigned to the check constraint that is to be created.
CheckCondition	Identifies a condition that must evaluate to TRUE before data can be added to the table.
VARCHARColumnName	Identifies an existing varying-length character column in the table whose size is to be altered.
Length	Identifies the new length for a VARCHAR column. The new length specified must be larger than the current length of the column.
ConstraintName	Identifies an existing unique, foreign key, or check constraint that is to be removed from the table definition.

For example, when executed, the SQL statement

```
ALTER TABLE DEPARTMENT ADD RATING CHAR(1) WITH DEFAULT 'S'
```

would add a new column named RATING, which is one character long, to the table named DEPARTMENT, and every existing row of data in the table would be assigned the value S for its RATING.

When executed, the SQL statement

```
ALTER TABLE EMPLOYEE ADD CONSTRAINT REVENUE CHECK
(SALARY + COMM > 30000)
```

would add a new check constraint named REVENUE to the table named EMPLOYEE. This constraint would verify that the combined salary and commission for an employee does not exceed $30,000. (If an existing record in the table violated this new constraint, the ALTER TABLE statement would fail.)

 NOTE When a column is added to an existing table, only the table description is modified, so access to the table is not affected immediately. All existing rows in the table receive a default value for the new column(s) and the records themselves are not physically altered until they are modified by an update operation. Columns that are added to a table after it has been created cannot be defined as NOT NULL; instead, they must be defined as NOT NULL WITH DEFAULT or as being nullable.

Suspending Constraint Checking—The SET INTEGRITY Statement The enforcement of referential and check constraints is important for maintaining data integrity, but it also carries a certain amount of overhead that can impact performance whenever large volumes of data are modified. Because of this overhead, at times, it may be beneficial to temporarily suspend constraint checking for a table. For example, suppose you want to add a new constraint to a table with the ALTER TABLE statement. If the table contains one or more rows that will violate the new constraint, the ALTER TABLE statement will fail. However, if constraint checking is suspended just before the new constraint is added, the ALTER TABLE statement will succeed and when constraint checking is turned back on, each row that violates the new constraint can be located, moved to another location, and corrected.

When constraint checking is suspended, the table is placed in "Check Pending" state to indicate that it may contain data that has not been checked for constraint violations. While a table is in "Check Pending" state, it cannot be used in insert, update, or delete operations (or by utilities such as Import and REORG that perform these operations). Indexes cannot be created on a table while it is in the "Check Pending" state and the table can not be referenced in the FROM clause of a SELECT statement.

Constraint checking for a particular table can be temporarily suspended and resumed by executing the SET INTEGRITY SQL statement.

The syntax for this statement is

```
SET INTEGRITY FOR [TableName ,...] OFF
```

or

```
SET INTEGRITY FOR [[TableName] [IntegrityType] ,...] IMMEDIATE
UNCHECKED
```

or

```
SET INTEGRITY FOR [TableName ,...] IMMEDIATE CHECKED <FORCE
GENERATED> <INCREMENTAL> <FOR EXCEPTION [IN [CheckedTableName] USE
[ExceptionTableName] , . . . ]>
```

where:

TableName	Identifies the name of one or more tables that integrity checking is to be turned on or off for.
IntegrityType	Identifies the type of integrity (constraint) checking that is to be turned on. This parameter can be set to one or more of the following values: FOREIGN KEY, CHECK, DATALINK RECONCILE PENDING, SUMMARY, GENERATED COLUMN, and ALL.
CheckedTableName	Identifies the table where rows that violate integrity constraints are to be copied from. The table name specified must identify either a base table or an alias that refers to a base table.
ExceptionTableName	Identifies the table where rows that violate integrity constraints are to be copied to.

For example, when executed, the SQL statement

```
SET INTEGRITY FOR DEPARTMENT OFF
```

would temporarily suspend constraint checking for the table named DEPARTMENT. On the other hand, when executed, the SQL statement

```
SET INTEGRITY FOR DEPARTMENT IMMEDIATE CHECKED
```

would turn constraint checking back on for the table named DEPARTMENT and every row of data in the DEPARTMENT table would immediately be checked for constraint violations.

When constraint checking is turned on, data that was added to the table while constraint checking was turned off is checked to ensure that it conforms to all constraints that have been defined for the table. By default, if any row is found that violates these constraints, checking is stopped and the table is returned to "Check Pending" state. However, if an exception table is used, all offending rows that violate one or more constraints are moved from the table being checked to an exception table where they can be examined and processed later.

> **NOTE** The SET INTEGRITY statement also provides a way to force a table to be taken out of "Check Pending" state without having its data checked for constraint violations. However, this is a dangerous thing to do, and should only be done if you have some independent means of ensuring that the table contains no data that violates predefined constraints.

Renaming Tables—The RENAME TABLE Statement

When designing and developing a relational database, it is common practice to give tables names that help identify the kind of data stored in them. However, because the number of characters that can be used to name a table is limited, and because we all think differently, sometimes a name that makes perfect sense to one person makes absolutely no sense to another. Likewise, sometimes a table that started out with one definition has been modified so many times that its original name no longer makes sense. If either of these are the case, an existing table can be given a new name (within a schema—a renamed table keeps its original schema name) by executing the RENAME TABLE SQL statement. The syntax for this statement is

```
RENAME <TABLE> [OriginalTableName] TO [NewTableName]
```

where:

OriginalTableName   Identifies the name of the table that is to be renamed. The table name specified must identify either a base table or an alias that refers to a base table.

NewTableName   Identifies the new name that is to be assigned to (and later used to identify) the table.

For example, when executed, the SQL statement

```
RENAME TABLE DEPARTMENT TO HQ_DEPTS
```

would change the name of a table named DEPARTMENTS to HQ_DEPTS.

When a table is renamed, all indexes that have been defined for the table are retained, and any users who have been granted privileges on the table retain these privileges. However, packages that reference the original table name become invalid and will need to be updated to reflect the name change (this is where an alias could make life easier). A table cannot be renamed if the

- Table is a system catalog table.
- Table is a Typed table.
- Table is a summary table.
- Table is referenced by name in a view definition.
- Table has one or more check constraints defined.
- Table is either a parent table or a child table in a referential integrity relationship.
- Table has a trigger attached to it or is referenced by a trigger.

Data Manipulation Language (DML) Statements

Eventually, almost every database application and/or database user needs to retrieve specific pieces of information (data) from the database they are interacting with. The operation that is used to retrieve data from a database is called a query (because it searches the database, usually to find the answer to some question). The answer returned by a query is expressed in two forms: either as a single row of data values or as a set of rows, otherwise known as a result data set (or result set). A query can also return an empty result data set.

In addition to being able to retrieve data from a database, applications and users often need to be able to add new information to, change information already stored in, or remove information from one or more base tables. A group of SQL statements known as Data Manipulation Language (DML) statements are used to accomplish these tasks. Table 6-2 lists the group of SQL statements that make up the DML.

Retrieving Data—The SELECT Statement and Its Clauses

The SELECT SQL statement is the heart of all queries and it is used specifically for retrieving information. The power of the SELECT statement lies in its capability to be used to construct complex queries with an infinite number of variations (using a finite set of rules). The SELECT verb is recursive, meaning that the input of most DML statements can be the output of a successive number of nested SELECT statements (also known as subqueries).

Table 6-2   Data Manipulation Language Statements

SQL Statement	Description
SELECT	Retrieves one or more rows of data from one or more base tables and/or views
INSERT	Adds data to a base table or an updatable view
UPDATE	Modifies existing data in a base table or an updatable view
DELETE	Removes data from a base table or updatable view

Because the SELECT statement is the primary statement used to retrieve data, it can be the most complex and the most complicated DML statement used. Six different clauses can be used with a SELECT statement and each of these clauses has its own set of predicates. Although some commercial implementations of SQL may support other SELECT statement clauses, DB2 Universal Database recognizes the following SELECT statement clauses:

- FROM
- WHERE
- GROUP BY
- HAVING
- UNION
- ORDER BY

The FROM Clause

The FROM clause is used, in conjunction with one or more references, to tell the DB2 Database Manager where to retrieve data from. The syntax for the simplest form of a SELECT SQL statement, which, by design, must always contain a FROM clause, is

```
SELECT <ALL | DISTINCT> [Item ,...] FROM [Source ,...]
```

where:

Item   Identifies one or more column names (specified alone or with an alias), literals, expressions, and/or scalar functions whose values are to be retrieved.

Source   Identifies one or more table names, table names with correlation names (such as user-created aliases to be used as a shortcut qualifier to column names elsewhere in the query or in a subquery), view names, view names with correlation names, or outer join specifications that specify the table names and condition to use for an outer join, that values are to be retrieved from.

For example, when executed, the SQL statement

```
SELECT EMPNO FROM EMPLOYEE
```

would return the value of the EMPNO column for every row stored in the table named EMPLOYEE.

 NOTE An asterisk (*) can be used in the *Item* list to specify that the values for all columns in a table are to be retrieved.

By default, the basic form of the SELECT statement will return all rows that match the query specification, including duplicate rows. However, if the DISTINCT qualifier is used, only unique rows that match the query specification will be returned (that is, no duplicates will exist in the result data set produced).

Inner Joins   The capability to join two or more tables with a single SELECT statement is one of the more powerful features of a relational database management system. A join is an operation that creates an intermediate result table that consists of data that has been collected from two or more tables that have one specific column in common. The simplest type of join, an inner join, can be thought of as the cross product of two tables where every row in one table is combined with every row of the other, keeping only the rows where the join condition specified is TRUE. This means that the result table produced may be missing rows from either or both of the tables that were joined.

Outer Joins   Outer joins are used when an inner join is needed and any rows that would be normally be eliminated by the join operation need to be preserved. Three types of outer joins are available:

- **Left outer join**   Rows from the left table (the table listed first in the join operation) that would have been eliminated by the inner join operation are retained.

- **Right outer join**   Rows from the right table (the table listed last in the join operation) that would have been eliminated by the inner join operation are retained.

- **Full outer join** Rows from both the left and right tables (both tables listed in the join operation) that would have been eliminated by the inner join operation are retained.

The basic idea behind an outer join is as follows. Suppose Table A and Table B are joined by an ordinary (inner) join. Any row in either Table A or Table B that does not match a row in the other table (under the rules of the join condition) is left out of the result data set produced. By contrast, if Table A and Table B are joined by an outer join, any row in either Table A or Table B that does not contain a matching row in the other table is included in the result data set (exactly once) and columns in that row that would have contained matching values from the other table are empty. Thus, an outer join adds nonmatching rows to a result data set where an inner join would exclude them. A left outer join of Table A with Table B preserves nonmatching rows from Table A, a right outer join of Table A with Table B preserves nonmatching rows from Table B, and a full outer join preserves nonmatching rows from both Table A and Table B.

The syntax for the simplest form of a SELECT SQL statement using an inner join is

```
SELECT [Item ,...] FROM [TableReference_1] <<AS> CorrelationName>
<INNER> JOIN [TableReference_2] <<AS> CorrelationName> ON
[JoinCondition]
```

The syntax for the simplest form of a SELECT SQL statement using an outer join is

```
SELECT [Item ,...] FROM [TableReference_1] <<AS> CorrelationName>
[LEFT | RIGHT | FULL] OUTER JOIN [TableReference_2] <<AS>
CorrelationName> ON [JoinCondition]
```

where:

Item	Identifies one or more column names (specified alone or with an alias), literals, expressions, and/or scalar functions whose values are to be retrieved.
TableReference_1	Identifies the name of the first table that values are to be obtained from. This table is considered the Left table in an outer join.
TableReference_2	Identifies the name of the second table that values are to be obtained from. This table is considered the Right table in an outer join.
CorrelationName	Identifies a correlation (shorthand) name that is to be assigned to the table specified (that can be used within a search condition to refer to the table or view).
JoinCondition	Identifies the condition that is to be used to join the two tables specified.

For example, if the following SQL statement were executed

```
SELECT E.EMPNO, E.NAME, D.DEPTNAME FROM EMPLOYEE E RIGHT OUTER
JOIN DEPARTMENT D ON E.DEPTNO = D.DEPTNO
```

and if a table named EMPLOYEE looked like this

EMPLOYEE

EMPNO	NAME	DEPT	HIREDATE	SALARY	BONUS
000010	BOGART	D01	1980-11-01	52000.00	1800.00
000020	CAGNEY	D11	1980-12-01	38000.00	1200.00
000030	BACALL	D21	1981-01-15	48500.00	1450.00
000040	GRANT	D31	1981-02-01	36500.00	1000.00

and a table named DEPARTMENT looked like this

DEPARTMENT

DEPTNO	DEPTNAME
D01	PURCHASING
D21	ACCOUNTING

the result data set produced would look like this:

EMPNO	NAME	DEPTNAME
000010	BOGART	PURCHASING
000020	CAGNEY	
000030	BACALL	ACCOUNTING
000040	GRANT	

 NOTE DB2 Universal Database allows up to 15 tables to be joined within a single **SELECT** statement.

The WHERE Clause

The WHERE clause is used to tell the DB2 Database Manager how to search one or more tables for specific data. The WHERE clause is always followed by a search condition that contains one or more predicates that define how the DB2 Database Manager is to choose the information that will be contained in the result data set produced. DB2 Universal Database supports six types of WHERE clause predicates. They are

- Relational predicates (comparisons)
- BETWEEN
- LIKE
- IN
- EXISTS
- NULL

Each predicate specifies a test that, when applied to a row of data by the DB2 Database Manager, will evaluate to "TRUE," "FALSE," or "Unknown." If a predicate results in TRUE, it means that the operation is to be applied to that row; if the predicate results in FALSE, no operation is performed for that row. Predicates can be used to compare a column with a value, one column with another column from the same table, or a column in one table with a column from another table (just to name a few). A basic predicate compares two values; a quantified predicate compares a value with a collection of values. One or more predicates can be combined by using parentheses or boolean operators such as AND, OR, and NOT. The following is a list of comparison operators that can only be used with predicates:

- **ALL**   This is used in predicates that involve subqueries. In this case, a predicate is TRUE when the specified relationship is TRUE for all rows returned by a subquery. It is also TRUE if no rows are returned by a subquery.

- **SOME or ANY**   These are used in predicates that involve subqueries. The result of this predicate is TRUE when the specified relationship is TRUE for *at least one* row returned by a subquery.

- **EXCEPT**   This generates a result table consisting of all unique rows from the first SELECT statement that are not generated by the second SELECT statement.

- **INTERSECT**   This generates a result table consisting of unique rows that are common in the results of two SELECT statements.

All values specified in predicates must be of compatible data types.

Relational Predicates The relational predicates (otherwise known as comparison operators) are the operators that can be used to define a comparison relationship between two values. DB2 Universal Database recognizes the following comparison operators:

- < (less than)
- > (greater than)
- <= (less than or equal to)
- >= (greater than or equal to)
- = (equal to)
- <> (not equal to)
- NOT

Relational predicates are used to include or exclude rows from the final result data set produced. Therefore, they are typically used to specify a condition in which the value of a column is less than, greater than, equal to, or not equal to a specified literal value. For example, when executed, the SQL statement

```
SELECT LASTNAME FROM EMPLOYEES WHERE SALARY > 50000
```

would produce a result data set that contains the last name of all employees whose salary is greater than $50,000.

It is up to the application to ensure that the data type of the comparison column and the data type of the literal, or other value being checked, are compatible. If necessary, scalar functions can be embedded in the SELECT statement to achieve this result.

The BETWEEN Predicate The BETWEEN predicate is used to define a comparison relationship in which a value is checked to see whether it falls within a range of values. For example, when executed, the SQL statement

```
SELECT LASTNAME FROM EMPLOYEES WHERE EMPID BETWEEN 100 AND 120
```

would produce a result data set that contains the last name of all employees whose employee number is greater than or equal to 100 and less than or equal to 120.

If the NOT negation operator is applied to the BETWEEN predicate, a value is checked to see whether or not it falls outside a range of values. For example, when executed, the SQL statement

```
SELECT LASTNAME FROM EMPLOYEES WHERE EMPID NOT BETWEEN 100 AND 120
```

would produce a result data set that contains the last name of all employees whose employee number is less than 100 and greater than 120.

The LIKE Predicate   The LIKE predicate is used to define a comparison relationship in which a character value is checked to see whether or not it contains a prescribed pattern. The prescribed pattern is any arbitrary character string. Characters in the pattern string are interpreted as follows:

- The underscore character (_) is treated as a wildcard that stands for any single character.

- The percent character (%) is treated as a wildcard that stands for any sequence of characters.

- All other characters are treated as normal characters (they stand for themselves).

For example, when executed, the SQL statement

```
SELECT LASTNAME, FIRSTNAME FROM EMPLOYEES WHERE LASTNAME LIKE
"La%"
```

would produce a result data set that contains the last name and first name of all employees whose last name begins with the letters "La" (for example Larson, Layton, Lawson, and so on).

When using wildcard characters, care must be taken to ensure that they are placed in the appropriate location in the pattern string. Note that in the preceding example, only records for employees whose last name begins with the characters "La" would be returned. If the pattern specified had been "%La%", records for employees whose last name contains the characters "La" (anywhere in the name) would have been returned.

Likewise, you must also be careful about using uppercase and lowercase letters in pattern strings. If the data being examined is stored in a case-sensitive manner, the characters used in a pattern string must match the case used to store the data in the column being searched.

NOTE   Although the LIKE predicate can be an appealingly easy method to use to search for needed data, it should be used with caution; processing a LIKE predicate is one of the slowest type of operations that can be performed, and it can be extremely resource-intensive. For this reason, LIKE predicates should only be used when you cannot locate the data needed any other way.

The IN Predicate   The IN predicate is used to define a comparison relationship in which a value is checked to see whether or not it matches a value in a finite list of values. IN predicates come in two different formats: one simple and the other quite complex.

In its simplest form, the IN predicate can compare a value against a finite set of literal values. For example, when executed, the SQL statement

```
SELECT LASTNAME FROM CUSTOMERS WHERE STATE IN ("CA", "NY", "IL")
```

would produce a result data set that contains the last name of all customers that live in California, New York, and Illinois.

In its more complex form, the IN predicate can compare a value against a finite set of values that are generated by another query (otherwise known as a subquery). For example, when executed, the SQL statement

```
SELECT CUSTID FROM CUSTOMERS WHERE STATE IN (SELECT STATE FROM
REGIONS WHERE REGIONID = 1)
```

would produce a result data set containing the customer ID of all customers that lived in any state that was considered to be part of Region 1. In this example, the subquery `SELECT STATE FROM REGIONS WHERE REGIONID = 1` will produce a list of all states found in the territory that a company has identified as Region 1. Then the outer or main query will check each STATE value in the CUSTOMERS table to see if it exists in the set of values returned by the subquery.

The EXISTS Predicate   The EXISTS predicate is used to determine whether or not a particular row of data exists in a table. The EXISTS predicate is always followed by a subquery; therefore, it returns a "TRUE" or "FALSE" value indicating whether or not a particular row of data is found in the result data set generated by the subquery. For example, when executed, the SQL statement

```
SELECT COMPANYNAME FROM SUPPLIERS WHERE EXISTS (SELECT * FROM
ACTSPAYABLE WHERE AMTDUE > 10000 AND ACTSPAYABLE.CUSTID =
SUPPLIERS.CUSTID)
```

would produce a result data set that contains the company names of all suppliers that are owed $10,000 or more.

EXISTS predicates are often ANDed with other conditions to determine final row selection.

The NULL Predicate   The NULL predicate is used to determine whether or not a particular column in a row of data contains a value. For example, when executed, the SQL statement

```
SELECT EMPID FROM EMPLOYEES WHERE MIDDLEINITIAL IS NULL
```

would produce a result data set that contains the employee IDs of all employees whose record does not contain a value for the MIDDLEINITIAL column.

 NOTE NULL and zero (0) or blank (" ") are not the same. NULL is a special marker that is used to represent missing information. On the other hand, zero or blank (empty string) are actual values that can be placed in a column to indicate a specific value (or lack thereof). DB2 Universal Database enables the creator to decide whether or not each individual column in a table will support null values. Before writing SQL statements that check for null values, make sure that the column(s) specified are nullable.

The GROUP BY Clause

The GROUP BY clause is used to organize the rows of data in a result data set produced by the values contained in the column(s) specified. The GROUP BY clause is also used to specify what column to break on for control breaks when using aggregate functions such as SUM() and AVG(). For example, when executed, the SQL statement

```
SELECT DEPTNAME, SUM(SALESAMT) FROM DEPARTMENTS D, SALESHISTORY S
WHERE D.DEPTID = S.DEPTID GROUP BY DEPTNAME
```

would produce a result data set that contains one row for each department that has rows in the sales history table. Each row in the result data set produced would contain the department name and the total sales amount for that department.

A common mistake that is often made with this type of query is the addition of nonaggregate columns to the GROUP BY clause. Because grouping is performed by combining all of the nonaggregate columns together into a single concatenated key and breaking whenever that key value changes, extraneous columns can cause unexpected breaks.

The GROUP BY ROLLUP Clause   The GROUP BY ROLLUP clause is used to analyze a collection of data in a single dimension, but at more than one level of detail. For example, when executed, the SQL statement

```
SELECT STATE, AVG(INCOME) FROM CENSUS GROUP BY ROLLUP (STATE)
```

would produce a result data set that contains average income information for each state found in the CENSUS table, as well as the combined average income of all states listed.

In this example, only one expression (known as the grouping expression) is specified in the GROUP BY ROLLUP clause (the expression is STATE). However, one or more grouping expressions can be specified in a GROUP BY ROLLUP clause. When multiple grouping expressions are specified, the DB2 Database Manager groups the data by all grouping expressions used, then by all but the last grouping expression used, and so on. Then, it makes one final grouping that consists of the whole table. When specifying multiple grouping expressions, it is important to ensure that they are listed in the appropriate order. If one kind of group is logically contained inside another (for example, counties are inside a state), then that group should be listed after the group that it is contained in is listed, not before.

The GROUP BY CUBE Clause The GROUP BY CUBE clause is used to analyze a collection of data by organizing it into groups in more than one dimension. For example, when executed, the SQL statement

```
SELECT SEX, YEAR(HIREDATE), MAX(INCOME) FROM EMPLOYEES GROUP BY
CUBE (SEX, YEAR(HIREDATE))
```

would produce a result data set in which the data is grouped every way possible:

- By sex only
- By hire date only
- By sex and hire date
- As a single group that contains all sexes and hire dates

The term CUBE is intended to suggest that data is being analyzed in more than one dimension. In the previous example, data analysis was performed in two dimensions, which resulted in four types of groups. If the clause GROUP BY CUBE(ED_LEVEL, SEX, YEAR(HIREDATE)) had been used instead, data analysis would have been performed in three dimensions and the data would have been broken into eight types of groups. Thus, the number of types of groups produced by a CUBE operation can be determined by the formula 2^n where n is the number of expressions used in the GROUP BY CUBE clause.

The HAVING Clause

The HAVING clause is used to apply further selection criteria to columns that are referenced in a GROUP BY clause. The HAVING clause uses the same syntax as the WHERE clause except that it refers to grouped data rather than raw data. Like the WHERE clause, the HAVING clause is commonly used to tell the DB2 Database Manager how to search one or more tables for specific data. For example, when executed, the SQL statement

```
SELECT DeptName, SUM(SALESAMT) FROM DEPARTMENTS D, SALESHISTORY
S WHERE D.DEPTID = S.DEPTID GROUP BY DEPTNAME HAVING SUM(SALESAMT)
> 1000000
```

would produce a result data set that contains one row for every department that has rows in the sales history table whose total sales amount exceeds 1 million dollars.

The UNION Clause

The UNION clause is used to combine two separate and individual result data sets to produce one single result data set. In order for two result data sets to be combined with a UNION clause, they both must have the same number of columns and each of those columns must have the exact same data types assigned to them.

For example, suppose a company keeps employee information in a special table that is archived at the end of each year. Just before the table is archived, a new table is created and the records for all employees who are still employed by the company are copied to it. Throughout the year, as new employees are hired, they are added to the new table. To obtain a list of all employees who were employed by the company in 1996 and 1997, each archived table would have to be queried, and the results would have to be combined. You could perform such an operation by using the UNION clause in an SQL statement. For example, when executed, the SQL statement

```
SELECT LASTNAME, EMPID FROM EMPLOYEES96 UNION SELECT LASTNAME,
EMPID FROM EMPLOYEES97
```

would produce a result data set that contains the last name and the employee ID of all employees who worked for the company in 1996 and 1997.

By default, when two result data sets are combined, all duplicate rows are removed. However, if the keyword ALL follows the UNION clause (UNION ALL), all rows of data in both result data sets (including duplicates) will be copied to the combined result data set.

The ORDER BY Clause

The ORDER BY clause is used to sort and order the rows of data in a result data set by the values contained in the column(s) specified. Multiple columns can be used for ordering and each column used can be ordered in either ascending or descending order. If the keyword ASC follows the column name, ascending order is used. If the keyword DESC follows the column name, descending order is used. When more than one column is specified in the ORDER BY clause, the result data set is sorted by the first column specified (the primary sort), then the sorted data is sorted again by the next column specified, and so on. For example, when executed, the SQL statement

```
SELECT LASTNAME, FIRSTNAME, DEPTID FROM EMPLOYEES ORDER BY DEPTID
ASC, LASTNAME ASC
```

would produce a result data set that contains employee last names, first names, and department IDs, ordered by department ID and employee last name (the department IDs would be in ascending alphabetical order and the employee last names associated with a each department would be in ascending alphabetical order).

If a column in the result data set produced by a query is a summary column or a result column that cannot be specified by name, an integer value that corresponds to the column number can be used in place of a column name. When integer values are used, the first or leftmost column in the result data set produced is treated as column one, the next is column two, and so on. For example, the previous SQL statement could also have been coded as follows:

```
SELECT LASTNAME, FIRSTNAME, DEPTID FROM EMPLOYEES ORDER BY 3 ASC,
1 ASC
```

Although integer values are primarily used in the ORDER BY clause to specify columns that cannot be specified by name, they can be used in place of any column name.

A Word about Subqueries

As mentioned earlier, a subquery is a query within a query. Subqueries usually appear within the search condition of a WHERE or a HAVING clause. A subquery can also be used within a search condition for insert, update, and delete operations. A subquery may include search conditions of its own, and these search conditions may in turn include subqueries. When subqueries are processed, the DB2 Database Manager first performs the innermost query and then uses the results to execute the next outer query, and so on until all queries have been processed. A subquery can return either a single value or a set of values. If a set of values are to be returned, the keywords IN, ALL, ANY, SOME, EXIST, or NOT EXIST cannot be used. In special cases, the innermost query may execute once for each result row in the outer query. These types of queries are known as correlated subqueries. Correlated subqueries are used to search for one or more values that can be different for each row.

Retrieving Multiple Rows Using a Cursor

DB2 Universal Database, like most relational database management systems, uses a mechanism called a cursor to retrieve multiple rows of data from a database. A cursor is a pointer to a temporary result data set or table that holds all rows retrieved by a SELECT statement. The name cursor, as it applies to databases, probably originated from the blinking cursor found on early computer screens. Just as that cursor indicated the current position on the screen and identified where typed words would appear next, a database cursor indicates the current position in the result data set (the current row) and identifies which row of data will be returned to the application next.

The steps involved in using a cursor in an application program are as follows:

1. Specify (define) the cursor by executing the DECLARE CURSOR SQL statement that has the desired query specified.

2. Execute the query and generate the result data set by executing the OPEN SQL statement.

3. Retrieve the rows in the result data set, one at a time until an end of data condition occurs, by executing the FETCH SQL statement. Each time the FETCH statement is executed, the cursor is automatically moved to the next row in the result data set.

4. If appropriate, modify or delete the current row with either the UPDATE or the DELETE SQL statement (provided the cursor is an updatable cursor).

5. Terminate the cursor and delete the result data set produced, by executing the CLOSE SQL statement.

An application can use several cursors concurrently; however, each cursor requires its own set of DECLARE CURSOR, OPEN, FETCH, and CLOSE statements.

Adding Data—The INSERT Statement

When a base table is first created, it does not contain data. Data is added to a base table by executing the INSERT SQL statement. The INSERT statement is easier to use than the SELECT SQL statement because it does not have as many optional clauses and predicates. The basic syntax for the INSERT SQL statement is

```
INSERT INTO [TableName | ViewName] < ( [ColumnName] ,... ) >
[VALUES ( [Value] , . . . ) | SelectStatement]
```

where:

TableName	Identifies the name of the table that data is to be added to.
ViewName	Identifies the name of the updatable view that data is to be added to.
ColumnName	Identifies one or more column names that data values are to be stored in. Each name specified must be an unqualified name that identifies a column in the table or updatable view specified.

Value	Identifies one or more data values that are to be inserted into the column(s), table, or updatable view specified.
SelectStatement	Identifies a SELECT SQL statement that is to be used to generate data values by retrieving one or more rows of data from other database tables and/or views.

For example, when executed, the SQL statement

```
INSERT INTO EMPLOYEE (EMPNO) VALUES ('000500')
```

would add a row to the table named EMPLOYEE (the value for the EMPNO column in that row would be 000500 and the values for the remaining columns in that row would either be null or an appropriate default value).

If values are provided for all columns in the table (in the VALUES clause), column names do not have to be provided. If the list of column names is omitted, the list of data values provided must be in the same order as the columns in the table into which they are to be inserted, and the number of values provided must equal the number of columns in the table. However, if the number of values in the VALUES clause does not match the actual number of columns in the table or if values in the VALUES clause are to be placed in specific columns in the table, the names of those columns must be explicitly stated in the INSERT statement. In either case, each value provided must be compatible with the data type of the column that the value is to be stored in.

Depending upon how a table was defined, null or some predefined default value will be inserted into columns for which no corresponding value is provided. A value must always be provided for any table column that was defined with the NOT NULL constraint specified.

Literal values for columns can be hardcoded directly into an INSERT statement or a SELECT statement (subselect) can be specified in place of literal values in the VALUES clause. This format of the INSERT statement creates a type of "cut and paste" action where values are retrieved from one table or view and inserted into another.

Changing Data—The UPDATE Statement

Once data has been added to a table, it can be modified at any time by executing the UPDATE SQL statement. The UPDATE statement can be used to change the value of any number of columns of any number of rows of data. Like the INSERT SQL statement, the UPDATE statement is easier to use than the SELECT statement even though it optionally uses the WHERE clause and its predicates; the WHERE clause is used to locate a specific row or group of rows that are to be updated.

The basic syntax for the UPDATE SQL statement is

```
UPDATE [TableName | ViewName] <<AS> CorrelationName> SET
[[ColumnName] = [Value] | [SelectStatement]] <WHERE
[WhereCondition]>
```

or

```
UPDATE [TableName | ViewName] <<AS> CorrelationName> SET
( [ColumnName] , . . . ) = ( [Value] , . . . )
<WHERE [WhereCondition]>
```

where:

TableName	Identifies the name of the table that data is to be modified in.
ViewName	Identifies the name of the updatable view that data is to be modified in.
CorrelationName	Identifies a correlation (shorthand) name that is to be assigned to the table or updatable view specified (that can be used within a search condition to refer to the table or view).
ColumnName	Identifies one or more column names that data values are to be stored in. Each name specified must be an unqualified name that identifies a column in the table or updatable view specified.
Value	Identifies one or more data values that are to be inserted into the column(s), table, or updatable view specified.
SelectStatement	Identifies a SELECT SQL statement that is to be used to generate data values by retrieving one or more rows of data from other base tables and/or views.
WhereCondition	Identifies the search criteria that is to be used to determine which rows of data are to be modified. If the WHERE clause is omitted, the DB2 Database Manager will attempt to update every row in the table or updatable view specified.

For example, when executed, the SQL statement

```
UPDATE EMPLOYEE SET SALARY = SALARY * 1.20 WHERE JOB = 'ANALYST''
```

would increase the salary of every employee who has a job title of ANALYST by 20 percent.

In addition to changing the values of one or more columns in a table or updatable view, the UPDATE statement can be used to remove values from nullable columns, by changing the column value to NULL.

For example, when executed, the SQL statement

```
UPDATE EMPLOYEE SET BONUS = NULL WHERE JOB = 'ANALYST'
```

would remove the bonus values assigned to employees who have the job title ANALYST.

Deleting Data—The DELETE Statement

Occasionally, existing data may need to be removed from a database. One or more rows can be removed from a table by executing the DELETE SQL statement. Like the UPDATE statement, the DELETE statement optionally uses the WHERE clause and its predicates; the WHERE clause is used to locate a specific row or group of rows that are to be deleted.

The basic syntax for the DELETE SQL statement is

```
DELETE FROM [TableName | ViewName] <<AS> CorrelationName>
<WHERE [WhereCondition]>
```

where:

TableName	Identifies the name of the table that data is to be removed from.
ViewName	Identifies the name of the updatable view that data is to be removed from.
CorrelationName	Identifies a correlation (shorthand) name that is to be assigned to the table or updatable view specified (that can be used within a search condition to refer to the table or view).
WhereCondition	Identifies the search criteria that is to be used to determine which rows of data are to be removed. If the WHERE clause is omitted, the DB2 Database Manager will attempt to remove every row in the table or updatable view specified.

For example, when executed, the SQL statement

```
DELETE FROM EMPLOYEE WHERE JOB = 'ANALYST'
```

would remove every record for employees who have the job title ANALYST from the table named EMPLOYEE.

 NOTE Because omitting the WHERE clause in a DELETE SQL statement causes the delete operation to be applied to all rows in the table or view specified, it is important to always provide a WHERE clause with a DELETE statement unless you explicitly want to erase all data stored in a table.

It is important to recognize that the DELETE statement does not remove the values of specific columns. Instead, when a row is deleted, the values of all columns associated with a row are destroyed. Once a row of data has been deleted, it can only be restored if the database was backed up before the DELETE operation was performed.

Summary

The goal of this chapter was to introduce you to Structured Query Language (SQL) and to show you the syntax for the SQL statements that make up the Data Definition Language and the Data Manipulation Language statements.

SQL is a standardized language that is used to define database objects and to store, manipulate, and retrieve data in a relational database management system. The majority of SQL statements available can be divided into the following categories:

- **Embedded SQL Application Construct statements**   Used to facilitate embedded SQL application development

- **Data Control Language (DCL) statements**   Used to grant and revoke authorizations and privileges

- **Data Definition Language (DDL) statements**   Used to create, modify, and destroy database objects

- **Data Manipulation Language (DML) statements**   Used to retrieve and/or modify the data stored in a database

- **Database Connection and Transaction Control statements**   Used to establish and terminate database connections and transactions

When a database is first created, all system catalog tables that are needed by that database are created and space is allocated for the recovery log files used. At this point, the database cannot be used to store data because no data objects have been defined. This is where the DDL statements come in. The DDL statements are used to create, modify, and delete objects in the database that will be used to store user data and to improve data access performance. The following SQL statements make up the DDL:

- CREATE NODEGROUP
- CREATE BUFFERPOOL
- CREATE TABLESPACE
- CREATE TABLE

- CREATE VIEW

- CREATE INDEX

- CREATE SCHEMA

- CREATE ALIAS

- COMMENT ON

- ALTER NODEGROUP

- ALTER BUFFERPOOL

- ALTER TABLESPACE

- ALTER TABLE

- RENAME TABLE

- DROP

Since Version 5.0, DB2 Universal Database has allowed the DB2 Database Manager to operate in a parallel, multinode (workstation) environment. This means that instead of having to be physically stored in one single location, databases can be broken into several parts (known as database partitions) and each part can be stored in a different physical location. In a multinode environment, a single database partition usually exists on each physical node (workstation) used and the DB2 Database Manager uses the processors found at each node to manage that partition's portion of the database.

Database partitions are often referred to as nodes and one or more of the nodes (partitions) that make up a partitioned database can be stored in a subset known as a nodegroup. Each nodegroup that contains more than one database partition is known as a multipartition nodegroup and each database partition referenced in a multipartition nodegroup must belong to the same DB2 Database Manager instance.

By default, the following nodegroups are defined whenever a database is created:

- IBMCATGROUP (for the SYSCATSPACE table space)

- IBMDEFAULTGROUP (for the USERSPACE1 table space)

- IBMTEMPGROUP (for the TEMPSPACE1 table space)

Additional nodegroups can be created by executing the CREATE NODEGROUP SQL statement. One or more database partitions (nodes) can be added to or removed from an existing nodegroup by executing the ALTER NODEGROUP SQL statement.

A buffer pool is an area of main memory that has been allocated to the DB2 Database Manager for the purpose of caching table and index data pages as they are read from disk or modified. The purpose of buffer pools is to improve overall database performance by reducing disk I/O—data can be accessed much faster from memory than from disk. In fact, how buffer pools are created and used is the single most important area where database performance can be improved.

By default, DB2 Universal Database creates one buffer pool (named IBMDEFAULTBP) of an appropriate size for the platform used whenever a database is created. Additional buffer pools can be created by selecting the appropriate action from the Buffer Pools menu found in the Control Center or by executing the CREATE BUFFERPOOL SQL statement. The size of an existing buffer pool can be changed, an existing buffer pool's use of extended memory can be turned on or off, or an existing buffer pool can be added to a new nodegroup by executing the ALTER BUFFERPOOL SQL statement.

Table spaces are used to specify where data in a database is physically stored and to provide a layer of indirection between the database and the specific directories, devices, or files (known as containers) in which the actual data resides. Table spaces can improve database and application performance, provide a more flexible database configuration, and provide better data integrity.

A table space can be either a System Managed Space (SMS) or a Database Managed Space (DMS). For an SMS table space, each container used is a directory that resides within the file space of the operating system, and the operating system's file manager is responsible for controlling the storage space. For a DMS table space, each container used is either a fixed-size, pre-allocated file or a physical raw device such as a disk, and the DB2 Database Manager is responsible for controlling the storage space.

By default, DB2 Universal Database creates three table spaces (named SYSCAT-SPACE, USERSPACE1, and TEMPSPACE1) whenever a database is created. Additional table spaces can be created by selecting the appropriate action from the *Table Spaces* menu found in the Control Center or by executing the CREATE TABLESPACE SQL statement. New containers can be added to an existing DMS table space, an existing table space's properties can be changed, or a new SMS table space can be added to a database partition that currently does not have any containers defined for it by executing the ALTER TABLESPACE SQL statement.

A table is a logical structure that is used to present data as a collection of unordered rows with a fixed number of columns. Each column contains a set of values of the same data type—the definitions of the columns in a table make up the table structure and the rows contain the actual table data.

Tables can be created by selecting the appropriate action from the *Tables* menu found in the Control Center or by executing the CREATE TABLE SQL statement. Additional columns and constraints can be added to an existing table, the length of an existing varying-length character data type column can be increased, or existing constraints can be removed by executing the ALTER TABLE SQL statement.

Because tables are the basic data objects used to store information in a DB2 Universal Database database, the CREATE TABLE statement is the most fundamental DDL statement available. The basic job of the CREATE TABLE statement is to assign a name to the table that is to be created and to identify the names, data types, and attributes of one or more of the table's columns in what is known as a table definition. Along with column declarations, a table definition can also include other information such as the definition of primary keys, unique constraints, referential constraints, and check constraints. In addition to creating a table that matches a specific definition, the CREATE TABLE statement can also control where the resulting table is placed in physical storage.

One of the nice things about a relational database is that even when users are sharing data, they do not have to see that data in the same way. Some users can work directly with base tables, whereas other users can work with views. A view is essentially a named specification of a result table that is produced by a query whenever the view is referenced in a DML statement. For this reason, a view can be thought of as having columns and rows, just like a base table, and in most cases, data can be retrieved directly from a view just as it can be retrieved from a base table. However, whether or not a view can be used to add, update, or delete data depends on how it is defined. Views can be created by selecting the appropriate action from the *Views* menu found in the Control Center or by executing the CREATE VIEW SQL statement.

Based on their definition, some views are classified as read-only, whereas others are classified as insertable, updatable, or deletable. Read-only views can only be queried, but insertable, updatable, and deletable views can be both queried and used in insert, update, and delete operations. In general, a view is considered updatable if each row in the view can be uniquely mapped onto one row of a base table. (This makes it possible for the DB2 Database Manager to map insert, update, and delete operations that are performed on the view into matching operations that are performed on the underlying base table.) A view is considered insertable if every column of the view is updatable and if the SELECT statement of the view does not include a UNION ALL operation. Finally, a view is considered read-only if it is not deletable.

An inoperative view is one in which the view definition has been unintentionally dropped. When a view is made inoperative, all views that are dependent on the inoperative view are also made inoperative and packages that are dependent on the inoperative view are no longer valid. Until an inoperative view is explicitly recreated or dropped, all SQL statements that reference the inoperative view cannot be precompiled (with the exception of the CREATE ALIAS, CREATE VIEW, DROP VIEW, and COMMENT ON TABLE statements), and its qualified name cannot be used to name another view, table, or alias.

An index is an object that contains an ordered set of pointers that refer to a key in a base table. When indexes are used, the DB2 Database Manager can access data directly and more efficiently because the index provides a direct path to the data through pointers that have been ordered based on the values of the columns that the index(es) is associated with. If an index is created for an empty table, that index will not have any entries stored in it until the table is populated. However, if an index is created for a table that already contains data, index entries are made for the existing data as soon as the index is created. Indexes can be created by selecting the appropriate action from the *Indexes* menu found in the Control Center or by executing the CREATE INDEX SQL statement.

Any number of indexes can be created for a table, using various combinations of columns as keys. However, each index does not come without a cost. Part of this cost is paid in storage space requirements; each index replicates its key values and this replication requires additional storage space. The rest of this cost is paid in a slight reduction in performance for insert, update, and delete operations because each modification to a table results in a similar modification to all indexes that are defined on the table.

A schema is an identifier that helps provide a means of classifying or grouping objects that are stored in a database. A schema is also an object itself; therefore, an individual can own it and can control access to both the data and the objects that reside within it. Whenever a data object (for example, a table, view, or index) is created, it is always assigned, either implicitly or explicitly, to a schema.

Schemas are implicitly created whenever a data object is created and assigned a qualifier name that does not match any existing schema in the database. (If a schema is not included in the name provided when an object is created, the authorization ID of the user creating the object is used as the schema, by default.) Schemas can be explicitly created by selecting the appropriate action from the *Schemas* menu found in the Control Center or by executing the CREATE SCHEMA SQL statement.

An alias is simply an alternate name for a table, view, or nickname. Once created, aliases can be referenced in the same way any table, view, or nickname can be referenced. However, an alias cannot be used in every context that a table, view, or nickname can be used in. For example, an alias cannot be used in the check condition of a check constraint and it cannot reference a user-defined temporary table. Aliases can be created by selecting the appropriate action from the *Aliases* menu found in the Control Center or by executing the CREATE ALIAS SQL statement.

The system catalog tables that are created when a database is created are used to store descriptions of all objects that are defined for that particular database. However, the information stored in the system catalog tables only pertains to the definition of a specific object; it does not provide descriptive information about the object itself. To overcome this, many of the system catalog tables have a column named REMARKS in which a user can store a description or a comment (of up to 254 characters in length) about the object a record refers to. Descriptions/comments on various types of objects can be entered into the system catalog tables by executing the COMMENT ON SQL statement.

Just as it is important to be able to add objects to a database, it is also important to be able to remove objects that are no longer needed. Objects can be removed from a database by selecting the appropriate action from the object menus found in the Control Center or by executing the DROP SQL statement.

When designing and developing a relational database, it is common practice to give tables names that help identify the kind of data stored in them. However, because the number of characters that can be used to name a table is limited, and because we all think differently, sometimes a name that makes perfect sense to one person makes absolutely no sense to another. Likewise, sometimes a table that started out with one definition has been modified so many times that its original name no longer makes sense. If either of these are the case, an existing table can be given a new name (within a schema—a renamed table keeps its original schema name) by executing the RENAME TABLE SQL statement.

Eventually, almost every database application and/or database user needs to retrieve specific pieces of information (data) from the database they are interacting with. The operation that is used to retrieve data from a database is called a query (because it searches the database, usually to find the answer to some question). The answer returned by a query is expressed in two forms: either as a single row of data values or as a set of rows, otherwise known as a result data set (or result set).

In addition to being able to retrieve data from a database, applications and users often need to be able to add new information to, change information already stored in, or remove information from one or more base tables. A group of SQL statements known as Data Manipulation Language (DML) statements are used to accomplish these tasks.

The following SQL statements make up the DML:

- SELECT
- INSERT
- UPDATE
- DELETE

The SELECT SQL statement is the heart of all queries and it is used specifically for retrieving information. The power of the SELECT statement lies in its capability to be used to construct complex queries with an infinite number of variations (using a finite set of rules). The SELECT verb is recursive, meaning that the input of most DML statements can be the output of a successive number of nested SELECT statements (also known as subqueries).

Because the SELECT statement is the primary statement used to retrieve data, it can be the most complex and the most complicated DML statement used. Six different clauses can be used with a SELECT statement and each of these clauses has its own set of predicates. DB2 Universal Database recognizes the following SELECT statement clauses:

- **FROM**   The FROM clause is used, in conjunction with one or more references, to tell the DB2 Database Manager where to retrieve data from.

- **WHERE**   The WHERE clause is used to tell the DB2 Database Manager how to search one or more tables for specific data.

- **GROUP BY**   The GROUP BY clause is used to organize the rows of data in a result data set produced by the values contained in the column(s) specified. The GROUP BY clause is also used to specify what column to break on for control breaks when using aggregate functions such as SUM() and AVG().The GROUP BY ROLLUP clause is used to analyze a collection of data in a single dimension, but at more than one level of detail. The GROUP BY CUBE clause is used to analyze a collection of data by organizing it into groups in more than one dimension.

- **HAVING**   The HAVING clause is used to apply further selection criteria to columns that are referenced in a GROUP BY clause.

- **UNION**   The UNION clause is used to combine two separate and individual result data sets to produce one single result data set. In order for two result data sets to be combined with a UNION clause, they both must have the same number of columns and each of those columns must have the exact same data types assigned to them.

- **ORDER BY**   The ORDER BY clause is used to sort and order the rows of data in a result data set by the values contained in the column(s) specified. Multiple columns can be used for ordering and each column used can be ordered in either ascending or descending order. If the keyword ASC follows the column name, ascending order is used. If the keyword DESC follows the column name, descending order is used.

The WHERE clause is always followed by a search condition that contains one or more predicates that define how the DB2 Database Manager is to choose the information that will be contained in the result data set produced. DB2 Universal Database supports six types of WHERE clause predicates. They are

- **Relational predicates** Relational predicates are used to include or exclude rows from the final result data set produced. The following comparison operators are recognized: $<$ (less than), $>$ (greater than), $<=$ (less than or equal to), $>=$ (greater than or equal to), $=$ (equal to), $<>$ (not equal to), and NOT.

- **BETWEEN** The BETWEEN predicate is used to define a comparison relationship in which a value is checked to see whether it falls within a range of values.

- **LIKE** The LIKE predicate is used to define a comparison relationship in which a character value is checked to see whether or not it contains a prescribed pattern. The prescribed pattern is any arbitrary character string.

- **IN** The IN predicate is used to define a comparison relationship in which a value is checked to see whether or not it matches a value in a finite list of values.

- **EXISTS** The EXISTS predicate is used to determine whether or not a particular row of data exists in a table. The EXISTS predicate is always followed by a subquery; therefore, it returns a "TRUE" or "FALSE" value indicating whether or not a particular row of data is found in the result data set generated by the subquery.

- **NULL** The NULL predicate is used to determine whether or not a particular column in a row of data contains a value.

Each predicate specifies a test that, when applied to a row of data by the DB2 Database Manager, will evaluate to "TRUE," "FALSE," or "Unknown." If a predicate results in TRUE, it means that the operation is to be applied to that row; if the predicate results in FALSE, no operation is performed for that row. Predicates can be used to compare a column with a value, one column with another column from the same table, or a column in one table with a column from another table (just to name a few). A basic predicate compares two values; a quantified predicate compares a value with a collection of values. One or more predicates can be combined by using parentheses or boolean operators such as AND, OR, and NOT. The following is a list of comparison operators that can only be used with predicates:

- **ALL** This is used in predicates that involve subqueries. In this case, a predicate is TRUE when the specified relationship is TRUE for all rows returned by a subquery. It is also TRUE if no rows are returned by a subquery.

- **SOME or ANY** This is used in predicates that involve subqueries. The result of this predicate is TRUE when the specified relationship is TRUE for *at least one* row returned by a subquery.

PART II

- **EXCEPT** This generates a result table consisting of all unique rows from the first SELECT statement that are not generated by the second SELECT statement.

- **INTERSECT** This generates a result table consisting of unique rows that are common in the results of two SELECT statements.

All values specified in predicates must be of compatible data types.

When a base table is first created, it does not contain data. Data is added to a base table by executing the INSERT SQL statement. The INSERT statement is easier to use than the SELECT SQL statement because it does not have as many optional clauses and predicates.

Once data has been added to a table, it can be modified at any time by executing the UPDATE SQL statement. The UPDATE statement can be used to change the value of any number of columns of any number of rows of data. Like the INSERT SQL statement, the UPDATE statement is easier to use than the SELECT statement even though it optionally uses the WHERE clause and its predicates; the WHERE clause is used to locate a specific row or group of rows that are to be updated.

Occasionally, existing data may need to be removed from a database. One or more rows can be removed from a table by executing the DELETE SQL statement. Like the UPDATE statement, the DELETE statement optionally uses the WHERE clause and its predicates; the WHERE clause is used to locate a specific row or group of rows that are to be deleted.

Questions

1. Given the statement:

```
CREATE INDEX NAME_INDX ON TABLE1 (NAME)
```

In which of the following is the index data stored?
a. The catalog table space
b. The log file directory
c. The temporary table space
d. The user table space

2. The DMS table space TS1 has been created. Which of the following is NOT accurate?
a. Buffer pools can now be associated with this table space.
b. Containers may be added to TS1 using the ALTER statement.
c. Space for all containers used is not pre-allocated.
d. Tables may be split across this and other table spaces.

3. Given the following statements and operations:

```
CREATE TABLE T1 (C1 SMALLINT)
CREATE VIEW V1 AS SELECT * FROM T1
```

The following rows are inserted into T1: 2, 4, 6, and 8.

```
DROP TABLE T1
```

Which of the following will occur?

a. Both table T1 and view V1 will be destroyed.

b. Every row in Table T1 will be deleted, but table T1 will not be destroyed.

c. Table T1 will be destroyed; view V1 will still contain data and can still be accessed.

d. Table T1 will be destroyed; view V1 will be made inoperative.

4. Given the following table definitions:

```
DEPARTMENT:
DEPTNO          CHAR(3)
DEPTNAME        CHAR(30)
MGRNO           INTEGER
ADMRDEPT        CHAR(3)

EMPLOYEE:
EMPNO           INTEGER
FIRSTNAME       CHAR(30)
MIDINIT         CHAR
LASTNAME        CHAR(30)
WORKDEPT        CHAR(3)
```

Which of the following statements will list every employee's number and last name, along with the employee number and last name of his or her manager, including employees without a manager?

a. SELECT E.EMPNO, E.LASTNAME, M.EMPNO, M.LASTNAME FROM
    EMPLOYEE E LEFT INNER JOIN DEPARTMENT INNER JOIN
    EMPLOYEE M ON MGRNO=M.EMPNO ON E.WORKDEPT=DEPTNO

b. SELECT E.EMPNO, E.LASTNAME, M.EMPNO, M.LASTNAME FROM
    EMPLOYEE E LEFT OUTER JOIN DEPARTMENT INNER JOIN
    EMPLOYEE M ON MGRNO=M.EMPNO ON E.WORKDEPT=DEPTNO

c. SELECT E.EMPNO, E.LASTNAME, M.EMPNO, M.LASTNAME FROM
    EMPLOYEE E RIGHT OUTER JOIN DEPARTMENT INNER JOIN
    EMPLOYEE M ON MGRNO=M.EMPNO ON E.WORKDEPT=DEPTNO

    d. `SELECT E.EMPNO, E.LASTNAME, M.EMPNO, M.LASTNAME FROM`
       `EMPLOYEE E RIGHT INNER JOIN DEPARTMENT INNER JOIN`
       `EMPLOYEE M ON MGRNO=M.EMPNO ON E.WORKDEPT=DEPTNO`

5. Which of the following SQL statements updates the system catalog tables?

    a. `TERMINATE`

    b. `COMMENT ON`

    c. `DESCRIBE`

    d. `CONNECT`

6. Given the following statements and operations:

```
CREATE TABLE T1 (C1 CHAR(1))
```

The following rows are inserted into T1: 'a', 'b', 'c', 'd', 'e', and 'f'.

```
SET INTEGRITY FOR T1 OFF
ALTER TABLE T1 ADD CONSTRAINT CON1 CHECK (C1 = 'a')
SET INTEGRITY FOR T1 IMMEDIATE CHECKED FOR EXCEPTION IN T1
    USE T1EXP
```

Which of the following describes what happens to the rows with values of 'b', 'c', 'd', 'e', and 'f'?

    a. They are deleted from T1 only.

    b. They are deleted from T1 and written to the file db2diag.log.

    c. They are deleted from T1 and written to the file T1EXP.

    d. They are deleted from T1 and inserted into the table T1EXP.

    e. They are deleted from T1 and inserted into the table SYSCAT.CHECKS.

7. Given the statement:

```
CREATE VIEW V1 AS SELECT C1 FROM T1 WHERE C1 = 'c' WITH CHECK
OPTION
```

Which of the following SQL statements will insert data into the table T1?

    a. `INSERT INTO V1 VALUES ('ca')`

    b. `INSERT INTO V1 VALUES ('c')`

    c. `INSERT INTO V1 VALUES ('d')`

    d. `INSERT INTO V1 VALUES (c)`

8. Given the following table definition:

```
STAFF:
ID              INT
LASTNAME        CHAR(30)
```

Which of the following statements removes all rows from the STAFF table where a NULL value exists for LASTNAME?

a. `DELETE ALL FROM STAFF WHERE LASTNAME IS NULL`

b. `DELETE ALL FROM STAFF WHERE LASTNAME = NULL`

c. `DELETE FROM STAFF WHERE LASTNAME = 'NULL'`

d. `DELETE FROM STAFF WHERE LASTNAME IS NULL`

9. Given the following tables:

COUNTRY

ID	NAME	PERSON	CITIES
1	United States	2	20
2	Canada	2	10
3	Germany	1	0
4	France	7	5

STAFF

ID	NAME
1	Bogart
2	Bacall

If the following statement is executed

```
INSERT INTO STAFF SELECT PERSON, 'Greyson', FROM COUNTRY WHERE
PERSON > 2
```

how many rows will be inserted into the STAFF table?

a. 0

b. 1

c. 2

d. 3

e. 4

10. Which of the following commands can be used to update information stored in the system catalog tables so that the DB2 optimizer will choose the best access plan?

a. RUNSTATS

b. REORGCHK

    c. OPTIMIZE

    d. OPTPLANS

11. Given the following table:

EMPLOYEES

ID	NAME
1	Bogart, Humphrey
2	Bacall, Lauren

If the following query were issued

```
SELECT * FROM EMPLOYEES
```

the order of the rows returned would be based on which of the following?

    a. The primary key order

    b. The order that the rows were inserted into the table

    c. The order based on the index used the last time the REORG command was executed for the table

    d. No guaranteed order

12. If the following statement is executed

```
CREATE BUFFERPOOL MYPOOL SIZE 10
```

how much memory will be allocated for buffer pool MYPOOL?

    a. None; the statement will fail.

    b. 10 bytes

    c. 10,240 bytes

    d. 40,920 bytes

13. Given the following table definitions:

```
TABLE1:
ID          INT
NAME        CHAR(30)
PERSON      INT
CITIES      INT

TABLE2:
ID          INT
LASTNAME    CHAR(30)
```

Which of the following statements removes all rows from the TABLE1 table that have PERSONs in the TABLE2 table?

a. `DELETE FROM TABLE1 WHERE ID IN (SELECT ID FROM TABLE2)`

b. `DELETE FROM TABLE1 WHERE ID IN (SELECT PERSON FROM TABLE2)`

c. `DELETE FROM TABLE1 WHERE PERSON IN (SELECT ID FROM TABLE2)`

d. `DELETE FROM TABLE1 WHERE PERSON IN (SELECT PERSON FROM TABLE2)`

14. Given the following statements and operations:

```
CREATE TABLE T1 (C1 SMALLINT)
```

The following rows are inserted into T1: 10, 20, 30, 40, and 50.

```
ALTER TABLE T1 ADD CONSTRAINT CON1 CHECK (C1 < 50)
```

Which of the following describes what happens to the row with the value of 50?

a. Nothing; the ALTER statement will fail.

b. It is deleted from T1.

c. It is deleted from T1 and written to the file db2diag.log.

d. It is changed to 49.

15. Given the following table:

COUNTRY

ID	NAME	PERSON	CITIES
1	United States	1	10
2	Canada	2	20
3	Germany	2	10
4	France	1	0
5	Australia	7	5

Which of the following statements does NOT return a single row result data set?

a. `SELECT COUNT(*) FROM COUNTRY`

b. `SELECT PERSON FROM COUNTRY WHERE NAME LIKE '%a%'`

c. `SELECT NAME FROM COUNTRY WHERE CITIES < 10`

d. `SELECT ID, NAME FROM COUNTRY WHERE PERSON BETWEEN 5 AND 7`

16. Given the following table definitions:

```
TABLE1:
DEPTID          INTEGER
DEPTNAME        CHAR(30)
MGR             INTEGER
TABLE2:
ID              INTEGER
NAME            CHAR(30)
DEPT            INTEGER
COMM            DECIMAL(10,2)
```

Which of the following statements will display each department, alphabetically by name, and the name of the department manager?

   a. `SELECT A.DEPTNAME, B.NAME FROM TABLE1 A, TABLE2 B WHERE A.MGR=B.ID`

   b. `SELECT A.DEPTNAME, B.NAME FROM TABLE1 A, TABLE2 B WHERE A.MGR=A.ID GROUP BY A.DEPTNAME, B.NAME`

   c. `SELECT A.DEPTNAME, B.NAME FROM TABLE1 A, TABLE2 B WHERE A.MGR=B.ID GROUP BY A.DEPTNAME, B.NAME`

   d. `SELECT A.DEPTNAME, B.NAME FROM TABLE1 A, TABLE2 B WHERE B.MGR=A.ID`

17. Given the following statements and operations:

```
CREATE SCHEMA PAYROLL AUTHORIZATION ADMIN
CREATE TABLE EMPLOYEES (EMPID INT NOT NULL PRIMARY KEY,
                        SALARY DECIMAL(7,2))
```

Which of the following has the authority to add the column

```
BONUS       DECIMAL(7,2)
```

to the PAYROLL.EMPLOYEES table?

   a. Only the person who created the EMPLOYEES table

   b. Only the person who created the PAYROLL schema

   c. Only the person who created the EMPLOYEES table and the user ADMIN

   d. Only the person who created the PAYROLL schema and the user ADMIN

   e. Only the user ADMIN

18. Given the following tables:

EMPLOYEE

ID	NAME	DEPT
I	Bogart	I
2	Bacall	I
3	Monroe	2
4	Grant	I

DEPT

DEPTID	NAME
I	Planning
2	Support

If the following statements are executed

```
ALTER TABLE EMPLOYEE ADD FOREIGN KEY (DEPT) REFERENCES (DEPTID)
     ON DELETE CASCADE
DELETE FROM DEPT WHERE DEPTID = 2
```

how many rows will be deleted?

 a. 1
 b. 2
 c. 3
 d. 4

19. Which of the following statements eliminates all but one of each set of duplicate rows in the final result data set produced?

 a. `SELECT UNIQUE * FROM TABLE1`
 b. `SELECT DISTINCT * FROM TABLE1`
 c. `SELECT UNIQUE(*) FROM TABLE1`
 d. `SELECT DISTINCT(*) FROM TABLE1`

20. How many indexes will the following statement create?

```
CREATE TABLE MYTAB (COL1    INTEGER NOT NULL PRIMARY KEY,
                    COL2    CHAR(64),
                    COL3    CHAR(32),
                    COL4    INTEGER NOT NULL,
          CONSTRAINT C4 UNIQUE (COL4, COL1))
```

   a. 0

   b. 1

   c. 2

   d. 3

21. Given the following table definition:

```
STOCK:
TYPE       CHAR(1)
STATUS     CHAR(1)
QUANTITY   INTEGER
PRICE      DEC(7,2)
```

If items are indicated to be out of stock by setting STATUS to NULL and QUAN-TITY and PRICE to zero, which of the following statements updates the STOCK table to indicate that all items except those with TYPE of 'S' are temporarily out of stock?

   a. UPDATE STOCK SET STATUS='NULL', QUANTITY=0, PRICE=0
      WHERE TYPE <> 'S'

   b. UPDATE STOCK SET STATUS=NULL, SET QUANTITY=0,
      SET PRICE=0 WHERE TYPE <> 'S'

   c. UPDATE STOCK SET (STATUS, QUANTITY, PRICE) =
      ('NULL', 0, 0) WHERE TYPE <> 'S'

   d. UPDATE STOCK SET (STATUS, QUANTITY, PRICE) =
      (NULL, 0, 0) WHERE TYPE <> 'S'

22. Given the following statements:

```
CREATE TABLE TAB1 (ID INTEGER, CONSTRAINT CHKID CHECK (ID<100))
INSERT INTO TAB1 VALUES(100)
```

Which of the following will occur?

   a. The row is inserted with a NULL value.

   b. The row is inserted with a value of 100.

   c. The row insertion with a value of 100 is rejected.

   d. A trigger called CHKID is fired to validate the data.

23. Given the following tables:

NAMES

NAME	NUMBER
Wayne Gretzky	99
Jaromir Jagr	68
Bobby Orr	4
Bobby Hull	23
Brett Hull	16
Mario Lemieux	66
Steve Yzerman	19
Claude Lemieux	19
Mark Messier	11
Mats Sundin	13

POINTS

NAME	POINTS
Wayne Gretzky	244
Jaromir Jagr	168
Bobby Orr	129
Bobby Hull	93
Brett Hull	121
Mario Lemieux	189

PIM

NAME	PIM
Mats Sundin	14
Jaromir Jagr	18
Bobby Orr	12
Mark Messier	32
Brett Hull	66
Mario Lemieux	23
Joe Sakic	94

Which of the following statements will display player names, numbers, points, and PIM for all players who have an entry in all three tables?

a. SELECT NAMES.NAME, NAMES.NUMBER, POINTS.POINTS, PIM.PIM
   FROM NAMES INNER JOIN POINTS ON NAMES.NAME=POINTS.NAME
   INNER JOIN PIM ON PIM.NAME=NAMES.NAME

b. SELECT NAMES.NAME, NAMES.NUMBER, POINTS.POINTS, PIM.PIM
   FROM NAMES FULL OUTER JOIN POINTS ON
   NAMES.NAME=POINTS.NAME FULL OUTER JOIN PIM ON
   PIM.NAME=NAMES.NAME

c. SELECT NAMES.NAME, NAMES.NUMBER, POINTS.POINTS, PIM.PIM
   FROM NAMES LEFT OUTER JOIN POINTS ON
   NAMES.NAME=POINTS.NAME LEFT OUTER JOIN PIM ON
   PIM.NAME=NAMES.NAME

d. SELECT NAMES.NAME, NAMES.NUMBER, POINTS.POINTS, PIM.PIM
   FROM NAMES RIGHT OUTER JOIN POINTS ON
   NAMES.NAME=POINTS.NAME RIGHT OUTER JOIN PIM ON
   PIM.NAME=NAMES.NAME

24. Given the following statements:

```
CREATE TABLE TABLE1 (C1 SMALLINT)
CREATE TABLE TABLE2 (C1 INTEGER NOT NULL)
CREATE ALIAS T1 FOR TABLE1
CREATE VIEW V1 AS SELECT C1 FROM T1
CREATE ALIAS T1 FOR TABLE2
```

Which of the following is NOT correct?

a. View V1 will now reference table T2.

b. View V1 will now be inoperative.

c. Applications that reference alias T1 must be rebound.

d. A value must be provided for rows that are inserted into view V1.

25. Given the following table:

COUNTRY

ID	NAME	PERSON	CITIES
1	Canada	2	20
2	Cuba	2	10
3	Costa Rica	4	0
4	Columbia	7	5

Which of the following statements does NOT return the row for Canada?

a. SELECT NAME FROM COUNTRY WHERE CITIES > 10

b. SELECT NAME FROM COUNTRY WHERE NAME LIKE 'C%'

c. SELECT NAME FROM COUNTRY WHERE CITIES BETWEEN 10 AND 20

d. SELECT NAME FROM COUNTRY WHERE CITIES NOT BETWEEN 0
   AND 30

26. Given the following tables:

TABLE1

ID	NAME	DEPT
1	Bogart	1
2	Bacall	1
3	Monroe	2
4	Grant	1

TABLE2

ID	NAME	DEPT
1	Bogart	1
4	Grant	1
30	Robinson	2
40	Barrymore	1

Which of the following statements would return all values, including duplicates, shown in TABLE 1 and TABLE2?

a. SELECT ID, NAME, DEPT FROM TABLE1 UNION SELECT ID,
   NAME, DEPT FROM TABLE2

b. SELECT ID, NAME, DEPT FROM TABLE1 UNION ALL SELECT ID,
   NAME, DEPT FROM TABLE2

c. SELECT ID, NAME, DEPT FROM TABLE1 LEFT OUTER JOIN
   TABLE2 ON TABLE1.ID = TABLE2.ID

d. SELECT ID, NAME, DEPT FROM TABLE1 RIGHT OUTER JOIN
   TABLE2 ON TABLE1.ID = TABLE2.ID

Answers

1. **D.** Indexes are always created in user table spaces. This can be the default user space (USERSPACE1) or a user space that was created with the CREATE TABLESPACE statement.

2. **C.** Space must be allocated for containers that are part of a DMS table space. (Space does not have to be allocated for containers that are part of SMS table spaces.)

3. **D.** When a table that a view is dependant upon is dropped, that view becomes inoperative (and the table is destroyed).

4. **B.** Because we want to get employee records for employees that do not have a manager and because the EMPLOYEE table is listed before the OUTER JOIN clause, the LEFT OUTER JOIN is the correct join to use. (A RIGHT INNER JOIN or a LEFT INNER JOIN does not exist so statements A and D are invalid statements.)

5. **B.** The COMMENT ON SQL statement is used to store descriptions or comments about various types of objects in the system catalog tables.

6. **D.** When constraint checking is turned off and then back on with the SET INTEGRITY statement, all rows in the table specified that violate constraints that were added while constraint checking was turned off are deleted from the original table and inserted into the exception table specified.

7. **B.** By examining the SELECT statement used to create the view, you can tell that the data type for column C1 is CHAR(1). Because of this and the check constraint specified, the only valid value that can be inserted into V1 is the value 'c'.

8. **D.** The NULL predicate, which is used to determine whether or not a particular column in a row of data contains a value, must be coded like statement D.

9. **B.** Only one row, a row with the value 7, 'Greyson', will be added to the STAFF table; the value 7 comes from the only row in the COUNTRY table that matches the search criteria specified and the value 'Greyson' is hardcoded in the statement.

10. **A.** When the RUNSTATS command is executed, statistics about a table are updated and those statistics are used to find the best access plan for a query. The RUNSTATS command should be executed each time a new index is created.

11. **D.** Because the SQL statement used does not have an ORDER BY clause, no guarantee is made on what order the data will be returned in.

12. **D**. Because no page size was specified, the default page size 4,096 is used. Because 10 pages were specified, the total amount of memory used is $4,096 \times 10 = 40,920$ bytes.

13. **C**. Because we are looking for PERSONs in TABLE1 that have a matching ID in TABLE2, statement C is the only statement that is correct. (Statements B and D are incorrect because no PERSON column is in TABLE2; statement A is incorrect because it is looking for values that match the ID column in TABLE1, not the PER-SON column.)

14. **A**. A check constraint cannot be added to an existing table if any of its rows violate the check constraint. Because the row containing the value 50 violates the check constraint specified, the ALTER statement will fail and the table/data will be left as it was before the ALTER statement was executed.

15. **B**. With this statement, all rows that have the letter 'a' anywhere in the NAME value will be returned. In this case, every row would be returned so the result data set produced would contain five rows.

16. **C**. Statement C has the correct WHERE clause and GROUP BY clause. Statement A needs a GROUP BY clause and the WHERE clause is wrong in statements B and D.

17. **E**. Because the AUTHORIZATION option was specified with the CREATE SCHEMA statement, the user ADMIN is the only one who is allowed to modify objects in the PAYROLL schema.

18. **B**. Two rows will be deleted; one row will be deleted from the DEPT table and because that row has a dependant row in the EMPLOYEE table, the dependant row will also be deleted (because the referential constraint was defined as DELETE CASCADE.)

19. **B**. The word UNIQUE is used to assign the Unique constraint to a column and DISTINCT(*) would be treated as a function (that does not exist) so statement B is the correct statement.

20. **C**. Two indexes will be created; one index will be created for the COL1 column because it is the primary key, and one unique index will be created for the combined columns COL4 and COL1.

21. **D**. 'NULL' would be treated as a string, not as a null value so statements A and C would not set the STATUS to NULL and statement B is invalid because the SET keyword is only used once in the UPDATE statement. Therefore, statement D is the only UPDATE statement shown that will accomplish the desired task.

22. **C.** Because the value 100 violates the CHKID check constraint, the record is not inserted.

23. **A.** An INNER join will exclude records in both tables that do not have a matching column value. OUTER JOINS include missing rows from the first table (LEFT OUTER JOIN), the second table (RIGHT OUTER JOIN), or both tables (FULL OUTER JOIN).

24. **B.** When the target of an alias changes, views that reference that alias are not made inoperative.

25. **D.** When the NOT operator is placed before the BETWEEN predicate, values that are outside the range provided are returned.

26. **B.** By default, when two result data sets are combined with a UNION, all duplicate rows are removed unless the keyword ALL follows the UNION clause (for example, UNION ALL), in which case all rows of data in both result data sets (including duplicates) will be copied to the combined result data set.

Database Concurrency

In this chapter, you will learn

- What data consistency is
- What transactions are and how transactions are initiated and terminated
- How transactions are isolated from each other in a multi-user environment
- How DB2 Universal Database provides concurrency control through the use of locks
- What types of locks are available and how locks are acquired

The last objective of the DB2 Universal Database Family Fundamentals exam is to test your knowledge of the various mechanisms that are used by DB2 Universal Database to enable users and/or applications to interact concurrently with a database without sacrificing data consistency. This portion of the DB2 Universal Database Family Fundamentals exam is also designed to evaluate your ability to identify the factors that affect how these mechanisms are used.

This chapter is designed to introduce you to the concept of data consistency and to the various mechanisms that are used by DB2 Universal Database to maintain database consistency in both single- and multi-user environments.

TIP Eleven percent of the DB2 Universal Database Family Fundamentals exam is designed to test your knowledge of the mechanisms that affect database consistency and concurrency.

What Is Data Consistency?

The best way to define data consistency is by example. Suppose your company owns a chain of restaurants, and you have a database that is designed to keep track of supplies stored at each of those restaurants. To facilitate the purchasing process of supplies, your database contains an inventory table for each restaurant in the chain. Whenever supplies are received or used by a restaurant, the inventory table for that restaurant is updated. Now, suppose some bottles of ketchup are physically moved from one restaurant to another. The ketchup bottle count value stored in the donating restaurant's table needs to be lowered and the ketchup bottle count value stored in the receiving restaurant's table needs to be raised in order to accurately represent this inventory move. If a user lowers the ketchup bottle count in the donating restaurant's inventory table, but fails to raise the ketchup bottle count in the receiving restaurant's inventory table, the data will become inconsistent. Now, the total ketchup bottle inventory for the chain of restaurants is no longer accurate.

A database can become inconsistent if the database user forgets to make all the necessary changes (as in the previous example), if the system crashes when the user is in the middle of making changes, or if a database application, for some reason, stops prematurely. Inconsistency can also occur when several users are accessing the same database tables at the same time. For example, one user might read another user's changes before all tables have been properly updated and take some inappropriate action or make an incorrect change based on the premature data values read.

In order to properly maintain database consistency, solutions must be provided for the following questions:

- How can you maintain generic consistency of a database when you do not know what each individual database owner/user wants?

- How can you keep a single application from accidentally destroying database consistency?

- How can you ensure that multiple applications accessing the same data at the same time will not destroy database consistency?

- If the system fails while a database is in use, how can you restore it to a consistent state?

DB2 Universal Database addresses these questions with its transaction support, and its locking and logging mechanisms. From a certification viewpoint, understanding logging concepts is one of the objectives of the DB2 UDB V7.1 for the Windows, UNIX, and OS/2 Database Administration exam (Test 513). Therefore, logging mechanisms are covered in Chapter 13 and the remainder of this chapter will focus on transaction support and locking.

Transactions

Transactions are a relational database concept that has been around for quite some time. A *transaction*, or a unit of work, is a recoverable sequence of one or more SQL operations that are grouped together as a single unit, usually within an application process. The initiation and termination of a transaction define the points of database consistency; either the effects of all SQL operations performed within a transaction are applied to the database, or the effects of all SQL operations performed are completely "undone" and thrown away.

With embedded SQL applications and SQL scripts, transactions are automatically initiated when an SQL statement is executed immediately after a connection has been made to a database or when an SQL statement is executed immediately after an existing transaction has been terminated. With Open Database Connectivity (ODBC) and Call Level Interface (CLI) applications, transactions are started as soon as the application begins working with a data source or when an SQL statement is executed immediately after an existing transaction has been terminated. Regardless of how transactions are initiated, they must be explicitly terminated by the user or application that initiated them.

With embedded SQL applications and SQL scripts, transactions are terminated by executing either the COMMIT or the ROLLBACK SQL statement. The syntax for these two statements is

```
COMMIT <WORK>
ROLLBACK <WORK>
```

When the COMMIT statement is used to terminate a transaction, all changes made to the database since the transaction was initiated are made permanent. When the ROLLBACK statement is used to terminate a transaction, all changes made to the database since the transaction was initiated are backed out and the data is returned to the state it was in before the transaction began. In either case, the database is guaranteed to be in a consistent state at the completion of each transaction.

For example, if the following SQL statements were executed in the order shown:

```
CONNECT TO MY_DB
CREATE TABLE DEPT (DEPT_ID INTEGER NOT NULL,
                   DEPT_NAME VARCHAR(20))
INSERT INTO DEPT VALUES(100, 'PAYROLL')
```

```
INSERT INTO DEPT VALUES(200, 'ACCOUNTING')
COMMIT
INSERT INTO DEPT VALUES(300, 'SALES')
ROLLBACK
INSERT INTO DEPT VALUES(500, 'MARKETING')
COMMIT
```

the table that would be created and populated would look like this:

DEPT

DEPT_ID	DEPT_NAME
100	PAYROLL
200	ACCOUNTING
500	MARKETING

In this example, when the first COMMIT statement was executed, the creation of the table DEPT and the insertion of two records into the DEPT table were made permanent. When the ROLLBACK statement was executed, the third record inserted into the DEPT table was removed and the table was returned to the state it was in before the insert operation was performed. Finally, when the second COMMIT statement was executed, the change made to the DEPT table after the fourth record that was inserted was made permanent.

As you can see from this example, a commit or rollback operation only affects changes that were made within the transaction it ends. As long as data changes remain uncommitted, other users and applications are usually unable to see them (there are exceptions, which we will look at later), and they can be backed out with a rollback operation. However, once data changes are committed, they become accessible by other users and applications and can no longer be removed by a rollback operation. If a failure occurs before a transaction can be completed, the DB2 Database Manager will back out all uncommitted changes in order to restore the database consistency that it assumes existed when the transaction was initiated. Figure 7-1 shows the effects of a successful transaction; Figure 7-2 shows the effects of a transaction that fails.

It is important to note that although transactions provide generic database consistency by ensuring that data changes only become permanent after a transaction has been successfully committed, it is up to the user or application to ensure that the sequence of SQL operations within each transaction will always result in a consistent database. Going back to our restaurant example, this rule would be followed if the operation that lowers the ketchup bottle count value stored in the donating restaurant's table and the operation that raises the ketchup bottle count value stored in the receiving restaurant's

A Successful Transaction

START TRANSACTION   END TRANSACTION

SQL Operation
SQL Operation
SQL Operation
Commit

| Locks are acquired at the start of, and throughout the life of the transaction. | When the COMMIT statement is executed, all changes are made perrmanent. | Locks are released when the transaction is terminated (by the COMMIT statement). |

Time

Figure 7-1 Events that take place during the execution of a successful transaction

An Unsuccessful Transaction

START TRANSACTION

SQL Operation
SQL Operation
ERROR Condition
Rollback

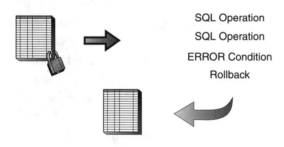

END TRANSACTION

| Locks are acquired at the start of, and throughout the life of the transaction. | When an error condition occurs, the DB2 Database Manager removes all changes made by the transaction. | Locks are released when the transaction is terminated (by the ROLLBACK statement). |

Time

Figure 7-2 Events that take place during the execution of an unsuccessful transaction

table are performed in the same transaction. This rule would be violated if the same operations were performed in two separate transactions.

Concurrency and Isolation Levels

So far, we have only looked at transactions from a single-user database point of view. With single-user databases, each transaction occurs serially and does not have to contend with interference from other transactions. However, with multi-user databases, transactions can occur simultaneously and each transaction has the potential to interfere with other transactions. Transactions that have the potential of interfering with one another are said to be *interleaved*, or *parallel*, transactions. Transactions that run isolated from each other are said to be *serializable*, which means that the results of running them simultaneously will be the same as the results of running them one right after another (serially). Ideally, all transactions should be serializable.

So why is it important that transactions be serializable? Consider the following: Suppose a salesman is entering orders on a database system at the same time an accountant is sending out bills. Now, suppose the salesman enters an order from Company X, but does not commit it (the salesman is still talking to the representative from Company X). While the salesman is on the phone, the accountant queries the database for a list of all outstanding orders, sees an order for Company X, and sends Company X a bill. Now, suppose the representative from Company X decides not to place the order at this time. The salesman rolls back the transaction because the representative changed his mind, and the order information is removed from the database. A week later, Company X receives a bill for parts they never ordered. If the salesman's transaction and the clerk's transaction had been isolated from each other (serialized), this problem would not have occurred. Either the salesman's transaction would have finished before the clerk's transaction started or the clerk's transaction would have finished before the salesman's transaction started; in either case, Company X would not have received a bill.

When transactions are not isolated from each other in multi-user environments, the following three types of events (or phenomena) can occur:

- **Dirty reads** This event occurs when a transaction reads data that has not yet been committed. For example, Transaction 1 changes a row of data and Transaction 2 reads the changed row before Transaction 1 commits the change. If Transaction 1 rolls back the change, Transaction 2 will have read data that is considered never to have existed.

- **Nonrepeatable reads** This event occurs when a transaction reads the same row of data twice, but gets different data values each time. For example, Transaction 1 reads a row of data and Transaction 2 changes or deletes that row and commits the change. When Transaction 1 attempts to reread the row, it will retrieve different data values (if the row was updated) or discover that the row no longer exists (if the row was deleted).

- **Phantoms**   This event occurs when a row of data matches a search criteria, but initially is not seen. For example, Transaction 1 reads a set of rows that satisfy some search criteria and Transaction 2 inserts a new row that matches Transaction 1's search criteria. If Transaction 1 re-executes the query that produced the original set of rows, a different set of rows will be retrieved.

Maintaining database consistency and data integrity while allowing more than one application to access the same data at the same time is known as *concurrency*. With DB2 Universal Database, concurrency is enforced through the use of *isolation levels*. An isolation level determines how data used in one transaction is locked or isolated from other transactions while it is being accessed. Table 7-1 shows the isolation levels that are available with DB2 Universal Database, along with the type of phenomena that can occur when each is used.

Repeatable Read

When used, the *Repeatable Read* isolation level locks all rows retrieved by a single transaction. By using the Repeatable Read isolation level, SELECT SQL statements issued multiple times within the same transaction will always yield the same result. A transaction using the Repeatable Read isolation level can retrieve and perform operations on the same set of rows as many times as needed until it is terminated. However, no other transactions can perform an insert, update, or delete operation that would affect the result table being accessed until the isolating transaction terminates. Transactions running

Table 7-1   Isolation Levels Used by DB2 Universal Database and the Phenomena That Can Occur When Each Is Used

Isolation Level	Dirty Reads	Nonrepeatable Reads	Phantoms
Repeatable Read	No	No	No
Read Stability	No	No	Yes
Cursor Stability	No	Yes	Yes
Uncommitted Read	Yes	Yes	Yes

under the Repeatable Read isolation level cannot see uncommitted changes made by other transactions. (The Repeatable Read isolation level does not let phantom rows be seen.)

Read Stability

Like the Repeatable Read isolation level, the *Read Stability* isolation level locks all rows retrieved by a single transaction. Unlike the Repeatable Read isolation level, the Read Stability isolation level does not completely isolate one transaction from the effects of other concurrent transactions. Thus, when the Read Stability isolation level is used and SELECT SQL statements are issued multiple times within the same transaction, they might not always yield the same result. (The Read Stability isolation level lets phantom rows be seen and nonrepeatable reads occur.)

Cursor Stability

When used, the *Cursor Stability* isolation level locks any row that is being accessed by a transaction, provided the cursor is positioned on that row. This lock remains in effect until either a new row is retrieved (fetched) or the transaction is terminated. If a transaction using the Cursor Stability isolation level has retrieved a row from a table, no other transactions can update or delete that row as long as the cursor is positioned on it. However, other transactions can perform insert, update, or delete operations on rows positioned on either side of the locked row, provided the locked row itself was not accessed via an index. Additionally, if a transaction using the Cursor Stability isolation level changes a row it retrieved, no other transactions can update or delete that row until the transaction that made the change is terminated. Therefore, when the Cursor Stability isolation level is used, the same SELECT SQL statement, issued twice within a single transaction, might not always yield the same results. Transactions running under the Cursor Stability isolation level cannot see uncommitted changes made by other transactions; both nonrepeatable reads and phantom reads are possible.

Uncommitted Read

When used, the *Uncommitted Read* isolation level enables a transaction to access uncommitted changes that have been made by other transactions. However, transactions running under the Uncommitted Read isolation level are not able to access tables, views, and indexes that are being created or dropped by other transactions until those transactions have been committed. A transaction using the Uncommitted Read isolation level does not lock other applications out of the row it is reading unless another transaction is attempting to drop or alter the table the row is in.

If a transaction running under the Uncommitted Read isolation level is using a read-only cursor, it will be able to access most uncommitted changes made by other transactions. (If a transaction running under the Uncommitted Read isolation level is accessing an updateable cursor, it will behave as if the Cursor Stability isolation level is being used.) All other changes made by other transactions can be read before they are committed or rolled back. With the Uncommitted Read isolation level, both nonrepeatable reads and phantom reads are possible.

Specifying the Isolation Level

Although isolation levels pertain to transactions, they are set at the application level. For embedded SQL applications, the isolation level is specified when the application is precompiled or when the application is bound to a database. In most cases, embedded SQL applications written in a supported, compilable language (such as C and C++) have their isolation level set through the ISOLATION option of PRECOMPILE PROGRAM or BIND commands. For CLI applications, the isolation level is determined by the attributes of the CLI statement handle being used. In either case, when no isolation level is specified, the Cursor Stability isolation level is used as the default.

Choosing the Proper Isolation Level

Choosing the proper isolation level to use is very important because the isolation level used influences not only concurrency, but also the overall performance of an application. Basically, when a more restrictive isolation level is used, less concurrency is available.

The best way to determine which isolation level to use is to decide which concurrency problems that can arise are unacceptable; then, select the isolation level that will prevent these problems from occurring. For example,

- Use the Uncommitted Read isolation level only if you are executing queries on read-only databases or if you are executing queries and do not care if those queries return uncommitted data values.

- Use the Cursor Stability isolation level when you want maximum concurrency without seeing uncommitted data values.

- Use the Read Stability isolation level when you want concurrency and you want qualified rows to remain stable for the duration of an individual transaction.

- Use the Repeatable Read isolation level if you are executing queries and changes to the result data sets produced are unacceptable.

Locking

Along with isolation levels, DB2 Universal Database provides concurrency control and prevents uncontrolled data access through the use of *locks*. A lock is a mechanism that associates a data resource with a single transaction, with the purpose of controlling how other transactions interact with that resource while it is associated with the transaction that acquired the lock. The transaction that the resource is associated with is said to hold, or own, the lock. The DB2 Database Manager imposes locks to prohibit owning transactions from accessing uncommitted data that is written by other transactions (unless the Uncommitted Read isolation level is used) or to prohibit the updating of rows by other transactions when the owning transaction is using the Repeatable Read isolation level. Once the owning transaction is terminated (either committed or rolled back), any changes made to the data resource are either made permanent or removed, and the data resource is unlocked so that it can be used by other transactions. Figure 7-3 illustrates the principles of data resource locking.

If one transaction attempts to access a data resource in a way that is incompatible with the lock being held by another transaction (we'll look at this subject later in the "Lock Compatibility" section), that transaction must wait until the owning transaction has ended. This is known as a *lock wait* and when a lock wait event occurs, the transaction attempting to access the data resource simply stops execution until the owning transaction has terminated and the incompatible lock is released.

Lock Attributes and Lock States

All locks have the following basic attributes:

- **Object** The *object* attribute identifies the data resource that is being locked. The DB2 Database Manager acquires locks on data resources, such as rows, tables, and indexes, whenever they are needed.

- **Size** The *size* attribute specifies the physical size of the portion of the data resource that is being locked. A lock does not always have to control an entire data resource. For example, rather than giving an application exclusive control over an entire table, the DB2 Database Manager can give an application exclusive control over a specific row in a table.

- **Duration** The *duration* attribute specifies the length of time a lock is held. A transaction's isolation level usually controls the duration of a lock.

- **Mode** The *mode* attribute specifies the type of access allowed for the lock owner as well as the type of access permitted for concurrent users of the locked data

PART II

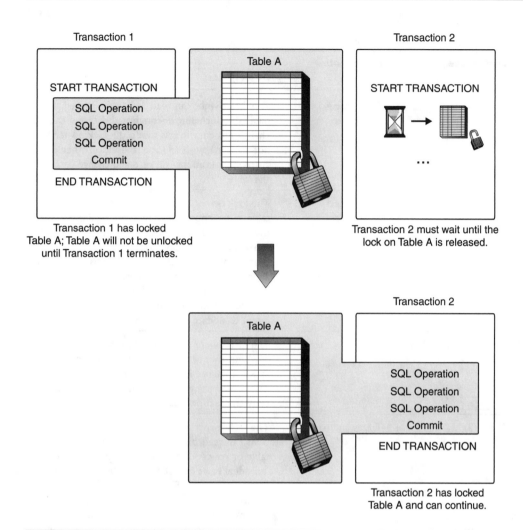

Figure 7-3 How DB2 Universal Database prevents uncontrolled concurrent access through the use of locks

resource. This attribute is commonly referred to as the *state* of the lock. Table 7-2 shows the various lock states available (and their effects) in order of increasing control over data resources.

Lock Compatibility

If the state of one lock placed on a data resource enables another lock to be placed on the same resource, the two locks (or states) are said to be *compatible*. Whenever one

Table 7-2 Lock States

Lock State (Mode)	Applicable Objects	Description
Intent None (IN)	Table spaces and tables	The lock owner can read data in the locked data table, including uncommitted data, but cannot change this data. In this mode, the lock owner does not acquire row-level locks; therefore, other concurrent applications can read and change data in the table.
Intent Share (IS)	Table spaces and tables	The lock owner can read data in the locked data table, but cannot change this data. Again, because the lock owner does not acquire row-level locks, other concurrent applications can both read and change data in the table. When a transaction owns an Intent Share lock on a table, it acquires a Share lock on each row it reads. This intent lock is acquired when a transaction does not convey the intent to update any rows in the table.
Next Key Share (NS)	Rows	The lock owner and all concurrent transactions can read, but cannot change data in the locked row. This lock is acquired in place of a Share lock on data that is read using the Read Stability or Cursor Stability transaction isolation level.
Share (S)	Tables and rows	The lock owner and any other concurrent transactions can read, but cannot change data in the locked table or row. As long as a table is not Share locked, individual rows in that table can be Share locked. If, however, a table is Share locked, the lock owner cannot acquire row Share locks in that table. If either a table or a row is Share locked, other concurrent transactions can read the data, but they cannot change it.
Intent Exclusive (IX)	Table spaces and tables	The lock owner and any other concurrent applications can read and change data in the locked data table. When the lock owner reads data from the data table, it acquires a Share lock on each row it reads, and it acquires an Update and an Exclusive lock on each row that it updates. Other concurrent applications can both read and update the locked data table. This intent lock is acquired when a transaction conveys the intent to update rows in the table. The SELECT FOR UPDATE, UPDATE WHERE, and INSERT SQL statements convey the intent to update.

Lock State (Mode)	Applicable Objects	Description
Share With Intent Exclusive (SIX)	Tables	The lock owner can both read and change data in the locked data table. The lock owner acquires Exclusive locks on the rows it updates, but does not acquire locks on rows that it reads; therefore, other concurrent applications can read, but cannot update the data in the locked table.
Update (U)	Tables and rows	The lock owner can update data in the locked data table and the lock owner automatically acquires Exclusive locks on the rows it updates. Other concurrent applications can read, but not update the data in the locked table.
Next Key Exclusive (NX)	Rows	The lock owner can read, but not change the locked row. Only individual rows can be locked in the Next Key Exclusive state. This lock is acquired on the next row in a table when a row is deleted from or inserted into the index for a table.
Next Key Weak Exclusive (NW)	Rows	The lock owner can read, but not change the locked row. Only individual rows can be locked in the Next Key Weak Exclusive state. This lock is acquired on the next row in a table when a row is inserted into the index of a noncatalog table.
Exclusive (X)	Tables and rows	The lock owner can both read and change data in the locked table. If a lock is set using the Exclusive state, only Uncommitted Read applications can access the locked table or row(s). Exclusive locks are acquired for data resources that are going to be manipulated with the INSERT, UPDATE, and/or DELETE SQL statements.
Weak Exclusive (WE)	Rows	The lock owner can read and change the locked row. Only individual rows can be locked in the Weak Exclusive state. This lock is acquired on a row when it is inserted into a noncatalog table.
Super Exclusive (Z)	Table spaces and tables	The lock owner can alter a table, drop a table, create an index, or drop an index. This lock is automatically acquired on a table, whenever an application attempts any one of these operations. No other concurrent applications can read or update the table until this lock is removed.

transaction holds a lock on a data resource and a second transaction requests a lock on the same resource, the first thing the DB2 Database Manager does is examine the two lock states to determine whether or not they are compatible. If the locks are compatible, the lock is granted to the second transaction (provided no other transaction is waiting for the data resource). If, however, the locks are incompatible, the second transaction must wait until the first transaction releases its lock (in fact, the second transaction must wait until *all* existing incompatible locks are released) before it can gain access to the resource and continue processing. Table 7-3 shows a lock compatibility matrix that identifies which locks are compatible and which are not.

Lock Conversion

When a transaction accesses a data resource that it already holds a lock on, and the mode of access needed requires a more restrictive lock than the one already held, the state of the lock is changed to the more restrictive state. The operation of changing the state of a lock already held to a more restrictive state is known as a *lock conversion*. Lock conversion occurs because a transaction can hold only one lock on a data resource at a time.

NOTE The DB2 Database Manager performs lock conversion operations whenever appropriate—no user intervention is necessary.

By examining the different lock states available (shown in Table 7-2), it quickly becomes apparent that there are distinct lock states that are only applicable for rows and distinct lock states that are only applicable for tables. In most cases, lock conversion is performed for locks that are acquired for rows, and the conversion process is usually straightforward. For example, if a Share (S) or an Update (U) lock is held and an Exclusive (X) lock is needed, the held lock will be converted to an Exclusive (X) lock. Intent Exclusive (IX) locks and Share (S) locks are special cases, however, because neither is considered to be more restrictive than the other. Therefore, if one of these locks is held and the other is requested, the held lock is converted to a Share With Intent Exclusive (SIX) lock. All other conversions result in the requested lock state becoming the new lock state of the lock being held, provided the requested lock state is more restrictive. (Lock conversion only occurs if a held lock can increase its restriction.) Once a lock has been converted, it stays at the highest level obtained until the transaction holding the lock is terminated.

Table 7-3   Lock Compatibility Matrix

Lock Requested by Second Transaction

Lock Type	Lock Held by First Transaction												
	None	IN	IS	NS	S	IX	SIX	U	NX	NW	X	WE	Z
None		YES	YES	YES	YES	YES	YES	YES	YES	YES	YES	YES	YES
IN	YES	YES	YES	YES	YES	YES	YES	YES	YES	YES	YES	YES	NO
IS	YES	YES	YES	YES	YES	YES	YES	YES	NO	NO	NO	NO	NO
NS	YES	YES	YES	YES	YES	YES	NO	YES	YES	YES	NO	NO	NO
S	YES	YES	YES	YES	YES	NO	NO	YES	NO	NO	NO	NO	NO
IX	YES	YES	YES	YES	NO	YES	NO	NO	NO	NO	NO	NO	NO
SIX	YES	YES	YES	NO	NO	NO	NO	NO	NO	NO	NO	NO	NO
U	YES	YES	YES	YES	YES	NO	NO	NO	NO	NO	NO	NO	NO
NX	YES	YES	NO	YES	NO	NO	NO	NO	NO	NO	NO	NO	NO
NW	YES	YES	NO	YES	NO	NO	NO	NO	NO	YES	NO	YES	NO
X	YES	YES	NO	NO	NO	NO	NO	NO	NO	NO	NO	NO	NO
WE	YES	YES	NO	NO	NO	NO	NO	NO	NO	YES	NO	NO	NO
Z	YES	NO	NO	NO	NO	NO	NO	NO	NO	NO	NO	NO	NO

YES   Locks are compatible; therefore, lock request is granted.
NO   Locks are not compatible; the requesting transaction must wait for the held lock to be released or for a timeout to occur.

Lock types:

IN	Intent None	U	Update
IS	Intent Share	NX	Next Key Exclusive
NS	Next Key Share	NW	Next Key Weak Exclusive
S	Share	X	Exclusive
IX	Intent Exclusive	WE	Weak Exclusive
SIX	Share With Intent Exclusive	Z	Super Exclusive

Although a transaction can hold only one lock on a data resource at a time, it can request a lock on the same data resource many times, indirectly, through a query. In addition, a transaction that is processing a query that is designed to update a row can inadvertently produce a *dual lock conversion*. For example, suppose a row was read via an index and as a result, the row was locked with a Share (S) lock. The table containing the row would have a covering intention lock—for this example, suppose that this is an Intent Share (IS) table-level lock. If the row is subsequently changed, the table-level lock will be converted to an Intent Exclusive (IX) lock, and the row-level lock will be converted to an Exclusive (X) lock.

 TIP The application of locks usually takes place implicitly during the execution of a query. Understanding the kinds of locks obtained for different queries and table and index combinations can assist you in designing and tuning your application.

Lock Escalation

All locks require space for storage and, because this space is not infinite, the DB2 Database Manager limits the amount of space that can be used for locks. Furthermore, the DB2 Database Manager limits the amount of space each transaction can use for its own locks. In order to prevent a specific database agent from exceeding these space limitations, a process known as *lock escalation* is performed whenever too many locks (of any type) have been acquired. Lock escalation is the conversion of several individual row-level locks on rows in a single table into one table-level lock on the table. Because lock escalation is handled internally, the only externally detectable result might be a reduction in concurrent access on one or more tables. Lock escalation rarely occurs in a properly configured database.

Here's how lock escalation works: When a transaction requests a lock and the lock storage space is full, one of the tables associated with the transaction is selected, a table-level lock is acquired, all row-level locks for that table are released to create space in the lock list data structure, and the table-level lock is added to the lock list. If this process does not free up enough space, another table is selected and the process is repeated until enough free space is available. At that point, the requested lock is acquired and the transaction resumes execution. However, if the necessary lock space is still unavailable after all locks associated with the transaction's tables have been escalated, the transaction is asked to either commit or roll back any changes that have been made since its initiation (that is, an SQL error code is generated) and the transaction is terminated.

An important point to remember is that lock escalation only occurs for the transaction that encounters a full lock storage buffer. This is because, in most cases, the lock storage space will be filled when that transaction reaches its own transaction lock limit. However, when a lock storage space buffer is exhausted, a transaction that is holding a relatively few number of locks might try to escalate, fail, and then be terminated. This means that transactions that hold many locks over a long period of time run the risk of causing other transactions to terminate prematurely. If lock escalation becomes objectionable, there are several ways to solve the problem:

- Increase the number of locks allowed by increasing the value of the *maxlocks* and/or the *locklist* parameter(s) in the database configuration file. This might be the best solution if the need to support concurrent access to one or more tables is very important. However, the overhead required to obtain record-level locks can cause a decrease in performance, which may cause more of a delay to other processes than is saved by providing concurrent access to a table.

- Locate and adjust any offending transaction (which may or may not be a transaction that terminates prematurely) and explicitly acquire table-level locks within it (by using the LOCK TABLE SQL statement).

- Change the degree of isolation being used. (Note that this may lead to decreased concurrency support.)

- Increase the frequency of commit operations. This tends to reduce the number of locks being held at a given point in time.

Deadlocks

Contention for locks by two or more transactions can result in a situation that is known as a *deadlock*. The best way to illustrate how a deadlock can occur is by example. Suppose Transaction 1 acquires an Exclusive (X) lock on Table A and Transaction 2 acquires an Exclusive (X) lock on Table B. Now, suppose Transaction 1 attempts to acquire an Exclusive (X) lock on Table B and Transaction 2 attempts to acquire an Exclusive (X) lock on Table A. Processing by both transactions is suspended until their second lock request is granted. However, because neither lock request can be granted until one of the transactions releases the lock it currently holds by performing a commit or rollback operation, and because neither transaction can perform a commit or rollback operation because they are both suspended (and waiting on locks), a deadlock situation occurs. Figure 7-4 illustrates this deadlock scenario.

A deadlock is more precisely referred to as a *deadlock cycle* because the transactions involved in a deadlock form a circle of wait states; each transaction in the circle is

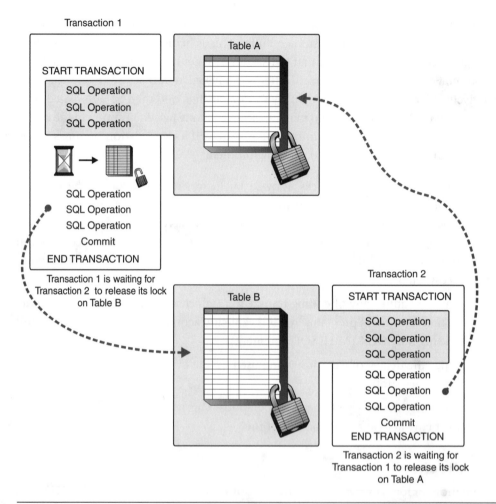

Transaction 1

START TRANSACTION

SQL Operation
SQL Operation
SQL Operation

Table A

SQL Operation
SQL Operation
SQL Operation
Commit

END TRANSACTION

Transaction 1 is waiting for
Transaction 2 to release its lock
on Table B

Table B

Transaction 2

START TRANSACTION

SQL Operation
SQL Operation
SQL Operation

SQL Operation
SQL Operation
SQL Operation
Commit
END TRANSACTION

Transaction 2 is waiting for
Transaction 1 to release its lock
on Table A

Figure 7-4   Example deadlock scenario

waiting for a lock held by one of the other transactions in the circle to be released. When a deadlock cycle occurs, all transactions involved will wait indefinitely for a lock to be released, unless some outside agent takes action to break the cycle. DB2 Universal Database's approach to combating deadlocks is an asynchronous system background process whose sole responsibility is to locate and resolve any deadlocks found in the locking subsystem. This background process, known as the *deadlock detector*, is started when a database becomes active. (A deadlock detector is associated with a specific database; therefore, a new one is launched as part of the database initialization process.) The deadlock detector stays "asleep" most of the time, but "wakes up" at preset intervals to determine whether or not deadlocks exist between transactions in the database. Normally, the deadlock detector wakes up, sees that there are no deadlocks in the locking subsystem, and goes back to sleep.

If the deadlock detector discovers a deadlock in the locking system, it selects one of the transactions in the deadlock cycle to roll back and terminate. The transaction that is rolled back and terminated receives an SQL error code, and all locks it had acquired are released. The remaining transaction(s) can now proceed because the deadlock cycle has been broken. It is possible, but very unlikely, that more than one deadlock cycle exists in a database's locking subsystem. If more than one deadlock cycle exists, the detector locates each remaining cycle and terminates one of the offending transactions in the same manner, until all deadlock cycles are broken.

Although most deadlock cycles involve two or more resources, a special type of deadlock, known as a *conversion deadlock*, can occur on a single database object. A conversion deadlock occurs when two or more transactions already hold compatible locks on an object, and then each transaction requests new, incompatible locks on that same object. A conversion deadlock usually occurs between two transactions that are searching for rows via an index scan. For example, suppose two different transactions acquire a Share (S) lock on a row when they read the row, and acquire an Exclusive (X) lock on a row when they update the row. If each transaction reads the same row, and then attempts to update that row, a conversion deadlock situation will occur.

Application designers should plan for different deadlock scenarios when designing high-concurrency applications that are to be run by multiple users. In situations where it is likely that the same set of rows may be read, and then updated by multiple copies of the same application program, the program should be designed to roll back and retry any transactions that might be terminated as a result of a deadlock cycle. A general rule of thumb is that the shorter the transaction, the less likely it is to get into a deadlock situation. Selecting the proper interval for the deadlock detector to wake up and look for deadlock cycles is also necessary to ensure good concurrent application performance. An interval that is too short will cause unnecessary overhead, and one that is too long will cause a deadlock cycle to delay a process for an unacceptable amount of time. Application designers must balance the possible delays in resolving deadlock cycles with the overhead of detecting them.

Lock Waits and Timeouts

Anytime a transaction holds a lock on a particular data resource (for example, a table or row), other transactions may be denied access to that resource until the owning transaction terminates and frees all the locks it has acquired. Without some sort of lock timeout detection mechanism in place, a transaction might wait indefinitely for a lock to be released in an abnormal situation. Such a situation might occur, for example, when a transaction is waiting for a lock that is held by another user's application to be released, and the other user has left his or her workstation without performing some interaction that would enable his or her application to commit the owning transaction. Obviously, these types of situations can cause poor application performance. To avoid stalling other applications in these types of situations, a lock timeout value can be specified in the database configuration file (the *locktimeout* configuration parameter). When used, this parameter value controls the amount of time that any transaction will wait to obtain a requested lock. If the requested lock is not acquired before the time interval specified in the *locktimeout* configuration parameter has elapsed, the waiting application receives an error and the transaction requesting the lock is rolled back. By specifying a lock timeout period, global deadlocks can be avoided, especially in distributed transaction applications.

How Locks Are Acquired

To maintain data integrity, the DB2 Database Manager acquires locks implicitly (and these locks remain under the DB2 Database Manager's control). These locks can be placed on a table space, an index, a table, a row (or multiple rows), or on both a table and a row (or multiple rows). Except for when the Uncommitted Read isolation level is used, it is never necessary for a transaction to explicitly request a lock. In fact, the only object that can be explicitly locked by a transaction is a table. Figure 7-5 illustrates the logic DB2 uses to determine the type of lock to acquire on a referenced data object.

Unless otherwise specified, the DB2 Database Manager always attempts to use row-level locks. However, the DB2 Database Manager can be forced to acquire table-level locks for a particular table by executing a special form of the ALTER TABLE SQL statement. The following shows the syntax for this form of the ALTER TABLE statement:

```
ALTER TABLE [TableName] LOCKSIZE [ROW | TABLE]
```

where:

TableName   Identifies the name of an existing table for which the level of locking that all transactions are to use when accessing it is to be specified.

For example, when executed, the SQL statement

```
ALTER TABLE EMPLOYEE LOCKSIZE TABLE
```

would force the DB2 Database Manager to acquire a table-level lock (provided no other transaction has an incompatible lock on this table) for any transaction that accesses the table named EMPLOYEE. On the other hand, if the SQL statement

```
ALTER TABLE EMPLOYEE LOCKSIZE ROW
```

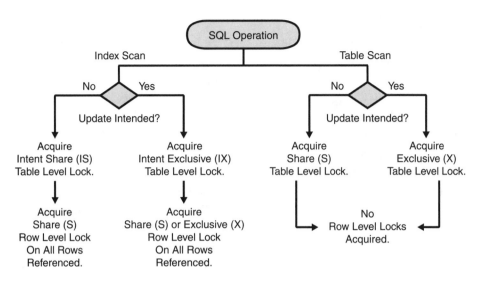

Figure 7-5 Logic used by the DB2 Database Manager to determine which type of lock(s) to acquire

were executed, the DB2 Database Manager would acquire row-level locks (the default behavior) for any transaction that accesses the table named EMPLOYEE.

The DB2 Database Manager can also be forced to acquire a table-level lock for a particular table by executing the LOCK TABLE SQL statement. The syntax for this statement is

```
LOCK TABLE [TableName] IN [SHARE | EXCLUSIVE] MODE
```

where:

TableName Identifies the name of an existing table that is to be locked.

For example, when executed, the SQL statement

```
LOCK TABLE EMPLOYEE IN SHARE MODE
```

would enable the current transaction to acquire a table-level lock on the EMPLOYEE table (provided no other transaction had a lock on this table), which would let other transactions read, but not change the data stored in it. On the other hand, if the SQL statement

```
LOCK TABLE EMPLOYEE IN EXCLUSIVE MODE
```

were executed, the table-level lock acquired would not let other transactions read or modify data stored in the EMPLOYEE table.

Concurrency and Granularity

It was mentioned earlier that anytime a transaction holds a lock on a particular data resource (for example, a table or row), other transactions might be denied access to that resource until the owning transaction is terminated. Therefore, to optimize for maximum concurrency, row-level locks are usually better than table-level locks because they limit access to a much smaller resource. However, because each lock acquired requires some amount of storage space and processing time (to manage), a table-level lock will require less overhead than several individual row-level locks.

As we have just seen, the granularity of locks (that is, whether row-level locks or table-level locks are used) can be controlled through the use of the ALTER TABLE and the LOCK TABLE SQL statements. Using the ALTER TABLE statement to control granularity is a global approach that will result in table-level locks being acquired by all transactions that access one particular table. On the other hand, using the LOCK TABLE statement to control granularity enables table-level locks to be acquired at a single-transaction level rather than at a global database level. In either case, only Share (S) and Exclusive (X) locks are acquired. As a result, overall performance is usually improved because transactions do not have to acquire and release several different row-level locks.

It may be preferable to acquire a permanent table-level lock using the ALTER TABLE statement rather than a single-transaction table-level lock using the LOCK TABLE statement in the following cases:

- The table to be accessed is read-only; therefore, only Share (S) locks will be needed. In this case, a table-level lock will improve overall performance, yet enable other transactions to obtain their own Share (S) locks on the table.

- The table will be accessed by a single transaction for maintenance purposes (in which case the transaction will need an Exclusive [X] lock for a limited period of time). Changing a table-level lock with the ALTER TABLE statement will provide such a transaction with an Exclusive (X) lock at the table level. Once the transaction has completed, the ALTER TABLE statement can be used again to return the table to row-level locking.

NOTE Use of the ALTER TABLE statement or the LOCK TABLE statement to control granularity does not prevent normal lock escalation from occurring.

Factors That Affect Locking

The state and granularity of locks that are acquired are determined by a combination of factors: the type of processing a transaction performs, how a transaction accesses data, and how the database is designed.

Transaction Processing

For the purpose of determining the lock attributes needed, all transactions typically fall under one of the following categories:

- **Read-Only** This refers to transactions that contain SELECT statements (which are intrinsically read-only), SELECT statements that have the FOR READ ONLY clause specified, or SQL statements that are ambiguous, but are presumed to be read-only because of the BLOCKING option specified as part of the precompile and/or bind process. Read-Only transactions only use Intent Share (IS) and/or Share (S) locks.

- **Intent To Change** This refers to transactions that contain SELECT statements that have the FOR UPDATE clause specified, or SQL statements that are ambiguous, but are presumed to be intended for change because of the way they are interpreted by the SQL precompiler. Intent To Change transactions use Share (S), Update (U), and Exclusive (X) locks for rows, and Update (U), Intent Exclusive (IX), and Exclusive (X) locks for tables.

- **Change** This refers to transactions that contain INSERT, UPDATE, and/or DELETE statements, but not UPDATE WHERE CURRENT OF or DELETE WHERE CURRENT OF statements. Change transactions only use Intent Exclusive (IX) and/or Exclusive (X) locks.

- **Cursor Controlled** This refers to transactions that contain UPDATE WHERE CURRENT OF and DELETE WHERE CURRENT OF statements. Cursor Controlled transactions only use Intent Exclusive (IX) and/or Exclusive (X) locks.

Keep in mind that transactions containing SQL statements that perform insert, update, or delete operations against one or more tables based on the result from a subquery perform two types of processing. Therefore, the locks needed for the tables returned in the subquery are determined by the rules for Read-Only transactions and the locks needed for the target table are determined by the rules for Change transactions.

Data Access Paths

When an SQL statement is precompiled, the DB2 Optimizer explores various ways to satisfy the statement's request and estimates the execution cost involved for each approach. Based on this evaluation, the DB2 Optimizer then selects what it believes to be the optimal access plan to use. An *access plan* specifies the operations required and the order those operations are to be performed in to resolve an SQL statement. When an application program is bound to a database (usually as part of the precompile process), a *package* is created. This package contains access plans for all of the static SQL statements contained in that application program. (Access plans for dynamic SQL statements are created at application run time.)

There are two ways to access data in a table: by directly reading the table (which is known as performing a *table* or *relation scan*) or by first accessing an index on that table (which is known as performing an *index scan*). A table scan occurs when the DB2 Database Manager must sequentially access every row in a table. An index scan occurs when the DB2 Database Manager accesses an index to do any or all of the following:

- Narrow down the set of qualifying rows (by scanning the rows in a certain range of the index) before accessing the base table. The index *scan range* (the start and stop points of the scan) is determined by the values in the query against which index columns are being compared.

- Order the output (for a SORT BY clause).

- Fully retrieve the requested data. If all of the requested data is in the index, the base table will not be accessed. This is known as an *index-only access*.

The access path chosen by the DB2 Optimizer, which is often determined by the database's design, can have a significant effect on the lock state used. For example, when an index scan is used to locate a specific row, the DB2 Database Manager will most likely acquire one or more Intent Share (IS) row-level locks. However, if a table scan is used, the entire table must be scanned in sequence to find the selected rows, and the DB2 Database Manager may acquire a single Share (S) table-level lock.

Keep in mind that simply creating indexes on every table does not guarantee that a less restrictive lock will always be acquired. Because the DB2 Optimizer decides whether or not indexes are used to process an SQL statement, even if you have indexes defined, the optimizer may choose to perform a table scan for any of the following reasons:

- No index is defined for the search criteria specified (in the WHERE clause). The index key must match the columns used in the WHERE clause in order for the optimizer to use the index to locate the desired row(s). If you choose to optimize for high concurrency, you should ensure that your table design includes a primary key for each table that will be updated. These primary keys should then be used whenever these tables are referenced by UPDATE SQL statements.

- Direct access may be faster than access via an index. The table must be large enough so that the DB2 Optimizer thinks it is worthwhile to take the extra step of going through the index, rather than just searching all the rows in the table. For example, the DB2 Optimizer would probably not use an index on a table that only had four rows of data in it.

- A large number of row-level locks would be acquired. If many rows in a table would be accessed by the transaction, the DB2 Optimizer would probably select a path that required a table-level lock.

Summary

The goal of this chapter was to introduce you to the concept of data consistency and to the various mechanisms that are used by DB2 Universal Database to maintain database consistency in both single- and multi-user environments.

A database can become inconsistent if a user forgets to make all the necessary changes, if the system crashes while a user is in the middle of making changes, or if a database application, for some reason, stops prematurely. Inconsistency can also occur when several users are accessing the same database tables at the same time. For example, one user might read another user's changes before all tables have been properly updated and take some inappropriate action or make an incorrect change based on the premature data values read.

In order to properly maintain database consistency, solutions must be provided for the following questions:

- How can you maintain generic consistency of a database when you do not know what each individual database owner/user wants?

- How can you keep a single application from accidentally destroying database consistency?

- How can you ensure that multiple applications accessing the same data at the same time will not destroy database consistency?

- If the system fails while a database is in use, how can you restore it to a consistent state?

DB2 Universal Database addresses these questions with its transaction support, and its locking and logging mechanisms.

A transaction (otherwise known as a unit of work) is a recoverable sequence of one or more SQL operations that are grouped together as a single unit, usually within an application process. The initiation and termination of a transaction define the points of database consistency; either the effects of all SQL operations performed within a transaction are applied to the database, or the effects of all SQL operations performed are completely undone and thrown away.

With embedded SQL applications and SQL scripts, transactions are automatically initiated when an SQL statement is executed immediately after a connection has been made to a database or when an SQL statement is executed immediately after an existing transaction has been terminated. With Open Database Connectivity (ODBC) and Call Level Interface (CLI) applications, transactions are started as soon as the application begins working with a data source or when an SQL statement is executed immediately after an existing transaction has been terminated. Regardless of how transactions are initiated, they must be explicitly terminated by the user or application that initiated them. With embedded SQL applications and SQL scripts, transactions are terminated by executing either the COMMIT or the ROLLBACK SQL statement.

When the COMMIT statement is used to terminate a transaction, all changes made to the database since the transaction was initiated are made permanent. When the ROLLBACK statement is used to terminate a transaction, all changes made to the database since the transaction was initiated are backed out and the data is returned to the state it was in before the transaction began. In either case, the database is guaranteed to be in a consistent state at the completion of each transaction.

With single-user databases, each transaction occurs serially and does not have to contend with interference from other transactions. With multi-user databases, however, transactions can occur simultaneously and each transaction has the potential to interfere with other transactions. Transactions that have the potential of interfering with one another are said to be interleaved or parallel transactions. Transactions that run isolated from each other are said to be serializable, which means that the results of running them simultaneously will be the same as the results of running them one right after another (serially). Ideally, all transactions should be serializable.

When transactions are not isolated from each other in multi-user environments, the following three types of events (or phenomena) can occur:

- Dirty reads
- Nonrepeatable reads
- Phantoms

Maintaining database consistency and data integrity while allowing more than one application to access the same data at the same time is known as concurrency. In DB2 Universal Database, concurrency is enforced through the use of isolation levels. An isolation level determines how data used in one transaction is locked or isolated from other transactions while it is being accessed. Four different isolation levels are available with DB2 Universal Database. They are

- **Repeatable Read**   All rows retrieved by a single transaction are locked; transactions are completely isolated and phantom rows are not seen.

- **Read Stability**   All rows retrieved by a single transaction are locked; transactions are not completely isolated and phantom rows can be seen and nonrepeatable reads can occur.

- **Cursor Stability**   Any row being accessed by a transaction is locked, provided the cursor is positioned on that row; transactions are not completely isolated. Although uncommitted changes cannot be seen, phantom rows can be seen and nonrepeatable reads can occur.

- **Uncommitted Read**   Transactions can access uncommitted changes made by other transactions; transactions are not isolated and nonrepeatable reads and phantom reads are possible.

Although isolation levels pertain to transactions, they are set at the application level. For embedded SQL applications, the isolation level is specified when the application is precompiled or when the application is bound to a database. For CLI applications, the isolation level is determined by the attributes of the CLI statement handle being used. In either case, when no isolation level is specified, the Cursor Stability isolation level is used as the default.

Along with isolation levels, DB2 Universal Database provides concurrency control and prevents uncontrolled data access through the use of locks. A lock is a mechanism that associates a data resource with a single transaction, with the purpose of controlling how other transactions interact with that resource while it is associated with the transaction that acquired the lock. The transaction that the resource is associated with is said to hold, or own, the lock. The DB2 Database Manager imposes locks to prohibit owning transactions from accessing uncommitted data that is written by other transactions (unless the Uncommitted Read isolation level is used) or to prohibit the updating of rows by other transactions when the owning transaction is using the Repeatable Read isolation level. Once the owning transaction is terminated (either committed or rolled back), any changes made to the data resource are either made permanent or removed, and the data resource is unlocked so that it can be used by other transactions. If one transaction attempts to access a data resource in a way that is incompatible with the lock being held by another transaction, that transaction must wait until the owning transaction has ended. This is known as a lock wait and when a lock wait event occurs, the transaction attempting to access the data resource simply stops execution until the owning transaction has terminated and the incompatible lock is released.

All locks have the following basic attributes:

- **Object**   Identifies the data resource that is being locked.
- **Size**   Specifies the physical size of the portion of the data resource that is being locked.
- **Duration**   Specifies the length of time a lock is held. A transaction's isolation level usually controls the duration of a lock.
- **Mode**   Specifies the type of access allowed for the lock owner as well as the type of access permitted for concurrent users of the locked data resource. This attribute is also known as the state of the lock.

Twelve different lock states are available. They are

- Intent None (IN)
- Intent Share (IS)
- Next Key Share (NS)
- Share (S)
- Intent Exclusive (IX)
- Share With Intent Exclusive (SIX)
- Update (U)
- Next Key Exclusive (NX)
- Next Key Weak Exclusive (NW)
- Exclusive (X)
- Weak Exclusive (WE)
- Super Exclusive (Z)

If the state of one lock placed on a data resource enables another lock to be placed on the same resource, the two locks (or states) are said to be compatible. Whenever one transaction holds a lock on a data resource and a second transaction requests a lock on the same resource, the first thing the DB2 Database Manager does is examine the two lock states to determine whether or not they are compatible. If the locks are compatible, the lock is granted to the second transaction (provided no other transaction is waiting for the data resource). If, however, the locks are incompatible, the second transaction must wait until the first transaction releases its lock (in fact, the second transaction must wait until *all* existing incompatible locks are released) before it can gain access to the resource and continue processing.

When a transaction accesses a data resource that it already holds a lock on, and the mode of access needed requires a more restrictive lock than the one already held, the state of the lock is changed to the more restrictive state. The operation of changing the state of a lock already held to a more restrictive state is known as a lock conversion. Lock conversion occurs because a transaction can hold only one lock on a data resource at a time.

All locks require space for storage and, because this space is not infinite, the DB2 Database Manager limits the amount of space that can be used for locks. Furthermore, the DB2 Database Manager limits the amount of space each transaction can use for its own locks. In order to prevent a specific database agent from exceeding these space limitations, a process known as lock escalation is performed whenever too many locks (of any type) have been acquired. Lock escalation is the conversion of several individual row-level locks on rows in a single table into one table-level lock. Because lock escalation is handled internally, the only externally detectable result might be a reduction in concurrent access on one or more tables. Lock escalation rarely occurs in a properly configured database.

Contention for locks by two or more transactions can result in a situation that is known as a deadlock. A deadlock is more precisely referred to as a deadlock cycle because the transactions involved in a deadlock form a circle of wait states; each transaction in the circle is waiting for a lock held by one of the other transactions in the circle to be released. When a deadlock cycle occurs, all transactions involved will wait indefinitely for a lock to be released, unless some outside agent takes action to break the cycle. DB2 Universal Database's approach to combating deadlocks is an asynchronous system background process whose sole responsibility is to locate and resolve any deadlocks found in the locking subsystem. This background process, known as the deadlock detector, is started when a database becomes active. The deadlock detector stays asleep most of the time but wakes up at preset intervals to determine whether or not deadlocks exist between transactions in the database. Normally, the deadlock detector wakes up, sees that there are no deadlocks in the locking subsystem, and goes back to sleep. If the deadlock detector discovers a deadlock in the locking subsystem, it selects one of the transactions in the deadlock cycle to roll back and terminate. The transaction that is rolled back and terminated receives an SQL error code, and all locks it had acquired are released. The remaining transaction(s) can now proceed because the deadlock cycle has been broken.

Anytime a transaction holds a lock on a particular data resource (for example, a table or row), other transactions may be denied access to that resource until the owning transaction terminates and frees all the locks it has acquired. Without some sort of lock timeout detection mechanism in place, a transaction might wait indefinitely for a lock to be released in an abnormal situation. To avoid stalling other applications in a multi-user environment, a lock timeout value can be specified in the database configuration file. When used, this value controls the amount of time that any transaction will wait to obtain a requested lock. If the requested lock is not acquired before the time interval specified has elapsed, the waiting application receives an error and the transaction requesting the lock is rolled back. By specifying a lock timeout period, global deadlocks can be avoided, especially in distributed transaction applications.

To maintain data integrity, the DB2 Database Manager acquires locks implicitly (and these locks remain under the DB2 Database Manager's control). These locks can be placed on a table space, an index, a table, a row (or multiple rows), or on both a table and a row (or multiple rows). Except for when the Uncommitted Read isolation level is used, it is never necessary for a transaction to explicitly request a lock. In fact, the only object that can be explicitly locked by a transaction is a table. Table locks can be explicitly acquired by executing a special form of the ALTER TABLE SQL statement or by executing the LOCK TABLE SQL statement.

To optimize for maximum concurrency, row-level locks are usually better than table-level locks because they limit access to a much smaller resource. However, because each lock acquired requires some amount of storage space and processing time (to manage), a table-level lock requires less overhead than several individual row-level locks. The state and size (row verses table) of locks that are acquired are determined by a combination of factors: the type of processing a transaction performs, how a transaction accesses data, and how the database is designed.

Questions

1. Given the following statements:

```
INSERT INTO STAFF VALUES (3, 'Cooper', 'Hollywood', 8)
ROLLBACK WORK
INSERT INTO STAFF VALUES (1, 'Monroe', 'Los Angeles', 1)
INSERT INTO STAFF VALUES (2, 'Grant', 'Pasadena', 21)
COMMIT
```

How many rows will be added to the STAFF table?

a. 0

b. 1

c. 2

d. 3

2. Which of the following database configuration parameters affects when lock escalation will occur?
   a. *numlocks*
   b. *maxlocks*
   c. *locktimeout*
   d. *lockthresh*

3. Which of the following objects can locks NOT be acquired for?
   a. An index key
   b. A table
   c. A row
   d. A column

4. Which of the following isolation levels may lock all of the rows that have been read in order to build a result data set?
   a. Repeatable Read
   b. Read Stability
   c. Cursor Stability
   d. Uncommitted Read

5. If an application acquires a Share (S) lock on a row in a table and then decides to delete that row, which of the following is most likely to happen, provided no other transactions are interacting with that table?
   a. An Update (U) lock will be acquired by lock escalation.
   b. An Exclusive (X) lock will be acquired by lock escalation.
   c. An Update (U) lock will be acquired by lock conversion.
   d. An Exclusive (X) lock will be acquired by lock conversion.

6. Which of the following isolation levels is most likely to acquire a table-level lock during an index scan?
   a. Repeatable Read
   b. Read Stability
   c. Cursor Stability
   d. Uncommitted Read

7. An Update (U) lock gets released by an application using the Repeatable Read isolation level during which of the following?
   a. If the cursor accessing the row is closed
   b. If the cursor accessing the row is moved to the next row

   c. If the transaction is committed

   d. If the transaction changes are made with an UPDATE statement rather than an UPDATE WHERE CURRENT OF statement

8. Which of the following processes can occur when a transaction using the Uncommitted Read isolation level scans through the same table multiple times?

   a. Uncommitted changes made by other processes can be accessed.

   b. Uncommitted changes made by other processes can be updated.

   c. Rows in a result data set can be updated; however, those updates can not be changed by other processes from one scan to the next.

   d. Rows in a result data set can be updated and those updates can be changed by other processes from one scan to the next.

9. Given the requirement of providing a read-only database, applications accessing the database should be run with which of the following isolation levels in order to provide the most read concurrency?

   a. Repeatable Read

   b. Read Stability

   c. Cursor Stability

   d. Uncommitted Read

10. Which of the following releases a lock that is held by an application using the Cursor Stability isolation level?

   a. If the cursor accessing the row is moved to the next row

   b. If the cursor accessing the row is used to update the row

   c. If the cursor's current row is deleted by the application

   d. If the cursor's current row needs to be updated by another application

Answers

1. **C.** The row with the values 3, 'Cooper', 'Hollywood', 8 would be removed when the first transaction was terminated with the ROLLBACK WORK statement. However, the remaining rows would be added when the second transaction was terminated with the COMMIT statement. Therefore, only two rows would be added.

2. **B.** By increasing the value of the *maxlocks* and/or the *locklist* parameter(s) in the database configuration file, the number of locks allowed will be increased; because lock escalation takes place when the lock storage buffer becomes full, increasing the value of these database configuration parameters should extend the size of the lock storage buffer and reduce lock escalation events.

3. **D.** Locks can only be acquired for table spaces, tables, rows, and indexes.

4. **B.** The key word here is *may*. The Repeatable Read isolation level will lock all rows read, whereas the Read Stability *may* lock all rows read.

5. **D.** Because an Exclusive (X) lock must be acquired before a row can be deleted and because the transaction already holds a Share (S) row-level lock, that lock will be converted to an Exclusive (X) lock.

6. **A.** Because the Repeatable Read isolation level is the most restrictive isolation level available, a transaction using this isolation level would most likely acquire a table-level lock to prevent data from changing (because changes to the table would be mirrored in the index) while performing an index scan.

7. **C.** All locks are released when the transaction holding them is terminated with either a commit or a rollback operation.

8. **A.** Uncommitted changes made by other processes can be seen by a transaction that is using the Uncommitted Read isolation level. However, the transaction cannot do anything with uncommitted data other than see it.

9. **D.** If a database is read-only, there is no need to use a restrictive isolation level because no transaction will be able to modify its data. Therefore, if the least restrictive isolation level (Uncommitted Read) is used, more applications can access the database at the same time (concurrently).

10. **A.** If a row-level lock is held by an application using the Cursor Stability isolation level, that lock remains in effect until either a new row is retrieved (fetched) or the transaction is terminated.

PART III

DB2 UDB Administration (Test 513)

Server Management

In this chapter, you will learn

- What an instance is and how instances are used
- The purpose of the DB2 Administration Server (DAS) instance
- How distributed connections enable clients to communicate with servers
- How to configure communications for a client and a server workstation
- What DB2 Discovery is and how it is used
- How (and where) users are authenticated
- How authorization levels and privileges determine what a user can and cannot do
- How authorization levels and privileges are given to (granted) and taken away from (revoked) an individual or a group of users

The first objective of the DB2 Universal Database—Database Administration for UNIX, Windows, and OS/2 exam is to evaluate your knowledge of server management—particularly your understanding of instances and your ability to configure communications—and to test your knowledge of the authorization levels and privileges used by DB2 Universal Database to protect data and database objects against unauthorized access and modification. Knowing how to establish communications between client and server workstations is only the beginning. You must also know how DB2 Discovery can be used to control what servers, instances, and databases can be seen by client workstations. In addition, knowing what authorization levels and privileges are available is just as important as knowing how to give a user the right combination of authorizations and privileges to control exactly what he or she can and cannot do while working with an instance or database. This chapter is designed to introduce you to the concept of instances, provide you with information about configuring communications for client and server workstations, and provide an in-depth look at the various authorization levels and privileges that are provided by DB2 Universal Database, Version 7.x.

 TIP Eighteen percent of the DB2 Universal Database—Database Administration for UNIX, Windows, and OS/2 exam is designed to test your knowledge of server management.

Instances

In Chapter 3, we saw that when any edition of DB2 Universal Database is installed on a workstation (system), program files for the DB2 Database Manager are physically copied to a specific location on that workstation, and one instance of the DB2 Database Manager is created and assigned to the system as part of the installation process. If needed, additional instances can be created once the DB2 Universal Database product is installed. Each time a new instance is created, it references the DB2 Database Manager program files that were copied to the workstation during the installation process; thus, each instance behaves like a separate installation of DB2 Universal Database, even though all instances within a particular system share the same binary code. Although all instances share the same physical code, they can be run concurrently, and each has its own environment (which can be modified by altering the contents of its configuration file).

Attaching to an Instance

The default instance for a particular system is defined by the *DB2INSTANCE* environment variable—that is the instance that is used for most operations. However, you can attach to any other instance available (including instances that exist on other systems) by selecting the *Attach* action from the *Instances* menu found in the Control Center and providing the appropriate user ID and password when the Attach dialog is displayed. Figure 8-1 shows the Control Center menu items that must be selected in order to activate the Attach dialog. Figure 8-2 shows how this dialog might look after its input fields have been populated.

An application or user can also attach to a specific instance by executing the ATTACH command, either from the Command Center or from the Command Line Processor. The syntax for this command is

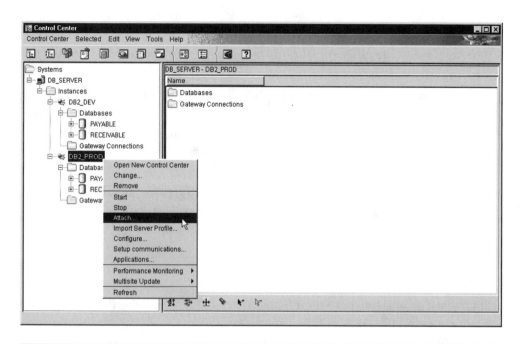

Figure 8-1   Invoking the Attach dialog from the Control Center

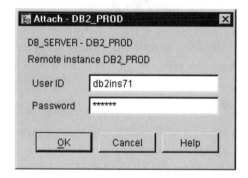

Figure 8-2   The Attach dialog

```
ATTACH <TO [InstanceName]> <USER [AuthorizationID] <USING
[Password] <NEW [NewPassword] CONFIRM [NewPassword]>>>
```

or

```
ATTACH <TO [InstanceName]> <USER [AuthorizationID] <CHANGE
PASSWORD>>
```

where:

InstanceName	Identifies the alias of the instance that the user/application will attach to.
AuthorizationID	Identifies the authorization ID of the user that the instance attachment will be made under.
Password	Identifies the password (that corresponds to the authorization ID specified) of the user that the instance attachment will be made under.
NewPassword	Identifies the new password that will replace the existing password that corresponds to the authorization ID specified for the user that the instance attachment will be made under.

For example, when executed, the command

```
ATTACH TO DB2_PROD USER DB2INS71 USING IBMDB2
```

will establish an attachment to the instance named DB2_PROD for the user who has the authentication ID "DB2INS71."

Once attached to an instance, maintenance and utility tasks that can only be done at the instance level (for example, create a new database, force applications off a database, monitor database activity, or change the contents of the DB2 Database Manager configuration file that is associated with that particular instance) can be performed.

Keep in mind that unless you have explicitly attached to a particular instance, all instance-level commands that are executed are done so against the current instance, which is identified by the *DB2INSTANCE* environment variable.

Detaching from an Instance

After an attachment to an instance has been made and all necessary maintenance and/or utility tasks have been performed, it is a good idea to terminate the attachment —by terminating the attachment, you eliminate the potential of accidentally performing new operations on the wrong instance. The easiest way to terminate an attachment to an instance is by attaching to another instance from the Control Center or by executing the DETACH command, either from the Command Center or from the Command Line Processor. The syntax for this command is

```
DETACH
```

As you can see, the DETACH command does not require any additional parameters. That's because you can only be attached to one instance at a time—when the DETACH command is executed, it terminates the current instance attachment.

The DB2 Administration Server (DAS) Instance

Most of the tools that are provided with DB2 Universal Database (such as the Control Center, the Client Configuration Assistant, the Script Center, and so on) require their own instance that operates concurrently with all other instances that have been defined for a system. To accommodate this need, a special instance, known as the DB2 Administration Server (DAS) instance, is automatically created as part of the DB2 Universal Database installation process. Once created, the DAS instance runs continuously as a background process whenever the system it was created on is online. (The DAS instance is started automatically each time the system is rebooted.)

The DAS instance is primarily responsible for

- Obtaining the configuration of the operating system being used by the workstation that DB2 Universal Database is installed on
- Obtaining user and group authentication information
- Starting and stopping instances (other than the DAS instance)
- Setting up communications for DB2 Universal Database servers
- Enabling remote administration of DB2 Universal Database servers
- Attaching to instances (other than the DAS instance)

The DAS instance is also responsible for assisting the Control Center and the Client Configuration Assistant when performing the following administration tasks:

- Enabling the administration of DB2 database servers from other client and/or server workstations.
- Providing the facility for job management, including the capability to schedule the execution of both DB2 and operating system user-defined command scripts. The Control Center is used to schedule jobs, view the results of completed jobs, and perform other administrative tasks against jobs that are executed either remotely or locally in conjunction with the DAS instance.
- Providing a means for discovering information about the configuration of DB2 instances, databases, and other DAS instances in conjunction with the DB2 Discovery utility (which we will look at shortly). The Client Configuration Assistant and the Control Center use this information to simplify and automate the configuration of client connections to DB2 database servers.

You must have a DAS instance running in order to use the Client Configuration Assistant or the Control Center and if you want to use the Control Center or the Client

Configuration Assistant in a client/server environment, each instance, including the DAS instance, must be configured to use one or more communications protocols.

Distributed Connections

In a client/server environment, DB2 Universal Database databases stored on servers are accessed by applications that reside on other workstations (remote clients) through what is known as a distributed connection. In addition to providing remote clients with access to a centralized database running on a server, distributed connections also enable Database Administrators to perform administrative tasks on a database server from any client workstation that has the DB2 Administration Client software installed. Figure 8-3 illustrates how distributed communications enable a remote client to interact with a DB2 server.

All remote clients use some type of communications product that provides support for one or more communications protocols to access a DB2 server. Likewise, DB2 servers

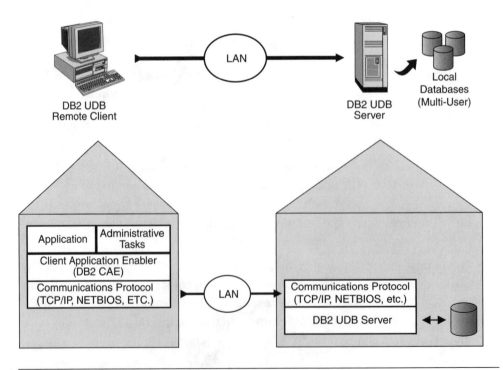

Figure 8-3   How a remote client communicates with a DB2 server

use some type of communications product to detect inbound requests from remote clients. Often, communications protocol support is provided as part of the operating system being used on both the client and server workstation; however, in some cases, it may be provided by a separate add-on product. In either case, both clients and servers must be configured to use a communications protocol that DB2 Universal Database supports. DB2 Universal Database supports the following communications protocols:

- Advanced Program-to-Program (APPC)
- Network Basic Input/Output System (NetBIOS)
- Transmission Control Protocol/Internet Protocol (TCP/IP)
- Internet Packet Exchange/Sequenced Packet Exchange (IPX/SPX)
- Named Pipe

Configuring Communications

When most editions of DB2 Universal Database are installed on a workstation, the communications protocols that are supported by that workstation are automatically detected and DB2 is configured to use those protocols—provided they are supported by DB2. At this time, information about each supported communications protocol found is collected and stored in the configuration file for the DAS instance and in the DB2 Database Manager configuration file for the initial instance that is created on the workstation. Unfortunately, this information is not automatically updated if you install a new communications protocol or if you reconfigure an existing communications protocol after DB2 Universal Database has been installed. In situations such as these, you must manually reconfigure communications for the DB2 Database Manager before the new protocol information can be used.

The easiest way to manually configure communications for one or more instances on a workstation is by selecting the *Setup Communications* action from the *Instances* menu found in the Control Center and then selecting the appropriate communications protocol Properties push button when the Setup Communications dialog is displayed. Figure 8-4 shows the Control Center menu items that must be selected in order to activate the Setup Communications dialog. Figure 8-5 shows how this dialog can be used to configure communications for the TCP/IP protocol.

On systems where the Control Center is not available, you can manually configure communications for an instance by updating the appropriate parameters of the DB2 Database Manager configuration file that is associated with that instance. Table 8-1 shows the modifiable DB2 Database Manager configuration parameters that affect communications.

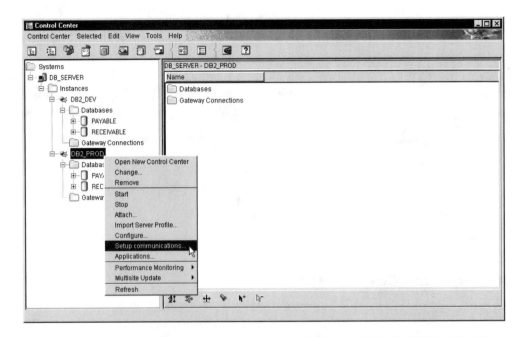

Figure 8-4 Invoking the Setup Communications dialog from the Control Center

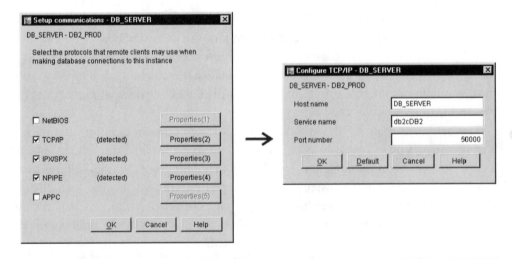

Figure 8-5 The Setup Communications and Configure TCP/IP dialogs

Table 8-1 DB2 Database Manager Configuration Parameters That Affect Communications

Parameter	Description	Range (Default)
Communication Protocols		
nname	Name assigned to the workstation (in a NetBIOS local area network [LAN] environment). If no value has been specified for this parameter, the server is not configured to use the NetBIOS communication protocol.	Any valid unique name (empty string)
svcename	Name of the TCP/IP port that the server will monitor for communications from remote client workstations. If no value has been specified for this parameter, the server is not configured to use the TCP/IP communication protocol.	Any valid port name/number (empty string)
tpname	Name of the remote transaction program client workstations must use when issuing allocate requests to the server (in an APPC environment). If no value has been specified for this parameter, the server is not configured to use the APPC protocol.	Any valid name (empty string)
fileserver	Name of the Novell NetWare file server where the internetwork address of the DB2 Database Manager is registered. If no value has been specified for this parameter, the server is not configured to use the IPX/SPX communication protocol.	Any valid name (empty string)
objectname	Name of the DB2 Database Manager instance in a Novell NetWare environment. If no value has been specified for this parameter, the server is not configured to use the IPX/SPX communication protocol.	Any valid unique name (empty string)
ipx_socket	Identifies the socket number that represents the connection end point in a DB2 server's Novell NetWare internetwork address. If no value has been specified for this parameter, the server is not configured to use the IPX/SPX communication protocol.	879E to 87A2 (879E)

(continued)

PART III

Table 8-1 DB2 Database Manager Configuration Parameters That Affect
Communications (*continued*)

Parameter	Description	Range (Default)
Distributed Services		
dir_type	Indicates whether or not Distributed Computing Environment (DCE) directory services are used.	None | DCE (None)
dir_path_name	Identifies the first part of the unique name of the DB2 Database Manager instance in the global namespace. (The complete name is made up of the combination of this value and the value of the *dir_obj_name* parameter.)	Any valid directory path (/.:/subsys/database/)
dir_obj_name	Identifies the second part of the unique name of the DB2 Database Manager instance in the global namespace. (The complete name is made up of the combination of this value and the value of the *dir_path_name* parameter—complete name must be less than 255 characters.)	Any valid unique name (empty string)
route_obj_name	Name of the default routing information object entry that will be used by all client applications attempting to access a Distributed Relational Database Architecture (DRDA) server.	Any valid unique name (null)
dft_client_comm	Identifies the communications protocols that client applications can use to issue remote requests to a DRDA server.	Null; IPXSPX; NETBIOS; TCPIP — separate with a comma if specifying more than one (Null)
dft_client_adpt	Default client adapter number for the NetBIOS protocol that has a server extracted from DCE directory services. (This parameter is only applicable to servers running on the OS/2 operating system.)	0 to 15 (0)

Setting the DB2COMM Registry Variable

If you configure communications for an instance by updating the appropriate parameters of its DB2 Database Manager configuration file, you must also update the value of the DB2COMM registry variable. The value stored in the DB2COMM registry variable determines which protocol's connection managers will be enabled when the DB2 Database Manager is started. (If this variable is not updated, one or more errors may be generated when the DB2 Database Manager attempts to start protocol support during instance initialization.)

The value of the DB2COMM registry variable can be set by issuing the following command, either from the Command Center or from the Command Line Processor:

```
db2set -i db2comm=[Protocol, ...]
```

where:

Protocol   Identifies one or more communications protocols that are to be started when the DB2 Database Manager is started. Any combination of the following values can be specified for this parameter: APPC, NETBIOS, TCPIP, or IPXSPX.

For example, when executed, the command

```
db2set -i db2comm=TCPIP, NETBIOS
```

will set the DB2COMM instance-level registry variable such that the DB2 Database Manager will start connection managers for TCP/IP and NetBIOS communication protocols each time the instance is started. Note that because the connection managers for the protocols specified are started when the instance is started, the DB2 Database Manager (instance) must be stopped and restarted before any changes made to the DB2COMM registry variable will take effect.

NOTE In order for a DB2 client to be able to communicate with a DB2 server, the DB2 server must be configured to accept inbound requests for the communications protocol the client plans to use. Therefore, in order for a communications protocol to be used between a client and a server, the DB2COMM registry variable at the server must include that protocol.

DB2 Discovery

As you can see, manually configuring communications can be an involved process, especially in complex network environments. Communications configuration is only the beginning. Before a client can send requests to a DB2 server for processing, both the server and the database stored on the server must be cataloged on the client workstation.

This is where DB2 Discovery comes in. With DB2 Discovery, you can easily catalog a remote server and a database without having to know any detailed communication-specific information. Here's how DB2 Discovery works. When invoked from the client workstation, DB2 Discovery broadcasts a discovery request over the network, and each DB2 server on the network that has been configured to support the discovery process responds by returning the following information:

- A list of instances found on the server that have discovery enabled, along with information about the communication protocol each instance supports
- A list of databases found within each instance that have discovery enabled

Both the Control Center and the Client Configuration Assistant can then use the information returned by DB2 Discovery to catalog any instance or database found by the discovery process.

DB2 Discovery can use one of two different methods to process a discovery request. These two methods are referred to as *search* and *known*. When the search discovery method is used, the entire network is searched for valid DB2 servers/databases and a list of the valid servers, instances, and databases found is returned to the client, along with the communications information needed to catalog each one. Because the communications protocol used by each server found may be different, specific communications information does not have to be provided for discovery requests that use the search discovery method. Figure 8-6 illustrates how the search DB2 Discovery method works.

In contrast, when the known discovery method is used, the network is searched only to locate a specific server that is using a specific communications protocol. (Because the client knows both the name of the server and the communications protocol it is using, the server is said to be "known" by the client.) Once the specified server is located, a list of the valid instances and databases found is returned to the client, along with the information needed to catalog each one. Figure 8-7 illustrates how the known DB2 Discovery works.

Configuration Parameters That Affect DB2 Discovery

Whether or not (and if so, how) a client can launch a DB2 Discovery request and whether or not (and if so, how) a particular DB2 server will respond to a discovery request is determined by the values of parameters found in the configuration file for the DAS instance, in the DB2 Database Manager configuration files for each instance (both on the client and on the server), and in the database configuration files for each database within an instance. Specifically, these parameters can control the following:

- Whether or not a client can launch a DB2 Discovery request

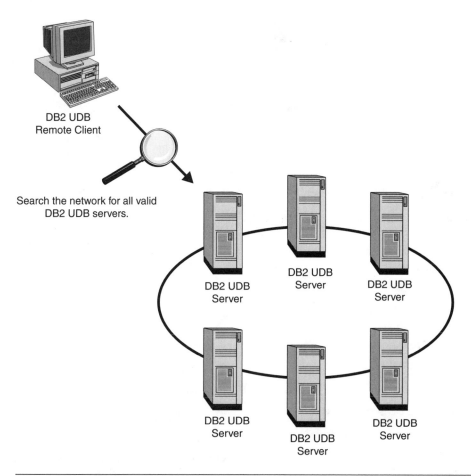

DB2 UDB
Remote Client

Search the network for all valid
DB2 UDB servers.

DB2 UDB
Server

DB2 UDB
Server

DB2 UDB
Server

DB2 UDB
Server

DB2 UDB
Server

DB2 UDB
Server

Figure 8-6   DB2 Discovery's search method

- The communications protocol(s) that a client will use when broadcasting search discovery requests

- Whether or not a server can be located by DB2 Discovery, and if so,

  - Whether the server can only be located when the search discovery method is used

  - Whether or not the server can only be located when the known discovery method is used

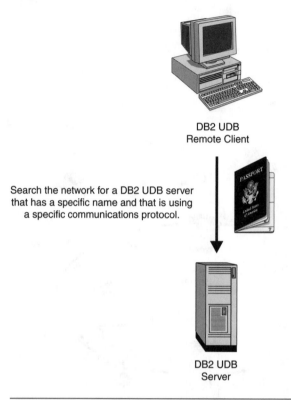

DB2 UDB
Remote Client

Search the network for a DB2 UDB server
that has a specific name and that is using
a specific communications protocol.

DB2 UDB
Server

Figure 8-7 DB2 Discovery's known method

- The communications protocol(s) that a server will use to listen for and respond to search discovery requests

- Whether or not an instance can be located with a discovery request

- Whether or not a database can be located with a discovery request

Table 8-2 shows the modifiable configuration parameters that affect DB2 Discovery.

Table 8-2   Configuration Parameters That Affect DB2 Discovery

Parameter	Description	Range (Default)
Client DB2 Instance **(DB2 Database Manager Configuration File)**		
discover	Identifies the default DB2 Discovery action that will be used by the client instance. If this parameter is set to SEARCH, the client instance can issue either search or known discovery requests. If this parameter is set to KNOWN, the client instance can only issue known discovery requests. If this parameter is set to DISABLE, the client instance cannot issue discovery requests.	DISABLE | KNOWN | SEARCH (SEARCH)
discover_comm	Identifies the communications protocols that the client instance will use to issue search discovery requests. (This parameter has no effect on known discovery requests.)	None; NETBIOS; TCPIP—separate with a comma if specifying more than one (None)
Server DAS Instance **(DAS Configuration File)**		
discover	Identifies the default DB2 Discovery action that will be used when the server is started. If this parameter is set to SEARCH, the server can respond to both search and known discovery requests. If this parameter is set to KNOWN, the server can only respond to known discovery requests. If this parameter is set to DISABLE, the server will ignore all discovery requests.	DISABLE | KNOWN | SEARCH (SEARCH)
discover_comm	Identifies the communications protocols that the DAS instance at the server will listen to for search discovery requests. (This parameter has no effect on known discovery requests.)	None; NETBIOS; TCPIP— separate with a comma if specifying more than one (None)

(continued)

PART III

Table 8-2 Configuration Parameters That Affect DB2 Discovery (*continued*)

Parameter	Description	Range (Default)
	Server DB2 Instance **(DB2 Database Manager Configuration File)**	
discover_inst	Identifies whether or not information about an instance (at the server) is included in the server's response to a discovery request. If this parameter is set to ENABLE, the server can include information about the instance in its response to both search and known discovery requests. If this parameter is set to DISABLE, the server cannot include information about the instance in its response discovery requests (or information about any database that is associated with the instance in its response to discovery requests). This parameter provides a way to hide an instance and all of its databases from DB2 Discovery.	ENABLE | DISABLE (ENABLE)
	Server Database **(Database Configuration File)**	
discover_db	Identifies whether or not information about a database (at the server) is included in the server's response to a discovery request. If this parameter is set to ENABLE, the server can include information about the database in its response to both search and known discovery requests. If this parameter is set to DISABLE, the server cannot include information about the database in its response to discovery requests. This parameter provides a way to hide an individual database from DB2 Discovery.	ENABLE | DISABLE (ENABLE)

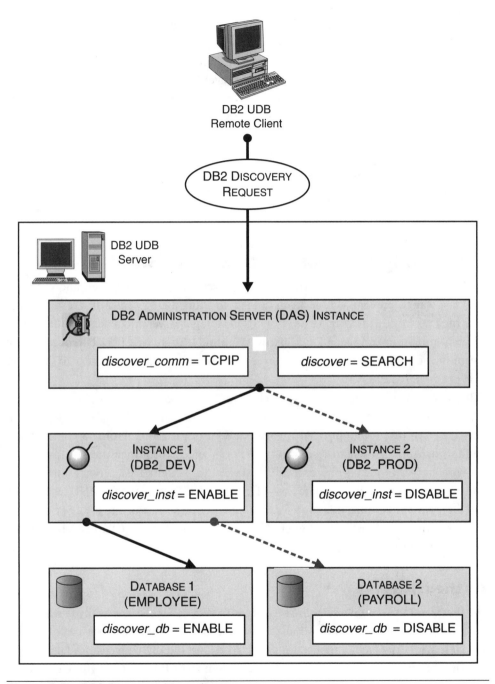

Figure 8-8   DB2 Discovery hierarchy

As you can see from Table 8-2, it is possible to configure a server in such a way that it will not be seen by DB2 Discovery when discovery requests are made. It is also possible to configure DB2 Discovery on a server in a hierarchical manner (that is, you can enable or disable DB2 Discovery at the server level, instance level, and database level). This enables you to allow DB2 Discovery to locate a particular server and at the same time prevent DB2 Discovery from seeing certain instances and/or databases at that server. Figure 8-8 illustrates how the configuration parameters that affect DB2 Discovery are used to create a selective DB2 Discovery environment. In this scenario, the server, Instance 1, and Database 1 can be located by discovery requests; Instance 2 and Database 2 cannot.

Controlling Database Access—Revisited

Enabling or disabling DB2 Discovery at the server level, instance level, and database level is a way to prevent a client from quickly locating a DB2 server or a remote database on a network. However, a savvy user can catalog a server and a database at a client workstation and avoid using DB2 Discovery entirely. Therefore, DB2 Discovery is not the only method used to keep unauthorized users from gaining access to sensitive servers and databases.

If you recall, in Chapter 3 we took a close look at the combination of external security services and internal access control measures DB2 Universal Database uses to protect data against unauthorized access and modification. From a certification standpoint, knowing what these security services and control measures are, as well as knowing how they are used, is crucial if you want to pass the DB2 Server Management portion of the DB2 Universal Database—Database Administration for UNIX, Windows, and OS/2 exam. Because this topic is such an important part of the DB2 Server Management objective, most of the material presented on security in Chapter 3 is repeated in this section for your convenience.

Authentication

The first step in managing database security is to verify that the user really is who he or she says he or she is. This step is called *authentication*. Authentication is performed by an external security facility that is not provided as part of DB2 Universal Database. This security facility may be part of the operating system (which is the case with UNIX, Windows NT, and many others), a separate product (such as DCE Security Services), or it may not exist at all (which, by default, is the case with Windows 95 and Windows 98). Most security facilities require two items in order to authenticate a user: a unique user

ID and a corresponding password. The user ID identifies the user to the security facility; the password, which is information that is only known by the user and the security facility, is used to verify the user during the authentication process.

How and where authentication takes place is determined by the authentication type being used by an instance. The authentication type is stored at the server (and sometimes at the client as well) in DB2 Database Manager configuration files that are associated with each instance. (The actual value is stored in the *authentication* parameter.) The following authentication types are available:

- **SERVER** Authentication occurs on the server using the security facility that is provided by the server's operating system. When a user ID and password are specified during an attempt to attach to an instance or connect to a database, they are checked at the server to determine whether or not the user is permitted to access the instance. By default, this is the authentication type used when an instance is first created.

- **SERVER_ENCRYPT** This is similar to SERVER in the sense that authentication occurs on the server using the security facility that is provided by the server's operating system. However, with this authentication type, all passwords are encrypted at the client before they are sent to the server.

- **CLIENT** Authentication typically occurs on the client workstation or database partition where a client application is invoked using the security facility that is provided by the client's operating system. When a user ID and password are specified during an attempt to attach to an instance or connect to a database, they are checked at the client/node to determine whether or not the user is permitted to access the instance. If the server indicates that CLIENT authentication will be used, two other parameters (which we will look at shortly) are used to determine the final authentication type.

- **DCS** Primarily used to catalog a database that is accessed using DB2 Connect, this authentication type is similar to SERVER in the sense that authentication occurs on the server using the security facility that is provided by the server's operating system—unless the server is being accessed via DRDA Application Server (AS) architecture using the APPC protocol. In this case, the DCS authentication type indicates that authentication will occur at the server, but only in the APPC layer.

- **DCS_ENCRYPT** This is similar to DCS; however, with this authentication type, all passwords are encrypted at the client level before they are sent to the server.

- **DCE** Authentication occurs on the server using the security facility that is provided by the DCE Security Services.

PART III

- **DCE_SERVER_ENCRYPT**   This is similar to DCE; however, with this authentication type, all passwords are encrypted at the client before they are sent to the server.

- **KERBEROS**   This can be used when both the client and the server are using the Windows 2000 operating system, which supports the Kerberos security protocol. The Kerberos security protocol performs authentication as a third-party authentication service by using conventional cryptography to create a shared secret key. This key becomes a user's credential and is used to verify the identity of users during all occasions when local or network services are requested; the key eliminates the need to pass the user ID and password across the network as text.

- **KRB_SERVER_ENCRYPT**   The server recognizes and accepts either the KERBEROS or the SERVER_ENCRYPT authentication scheme. If the client's authentication type is KERBEROS, authentication is performed using the Kerberos security system. If the client's authentication type is not KERBEROS, the server acts as if the SERVER_ENCRYPT authentication type was specified.

NOTE   The authentication type used by the default instance for a particular system (which is defined by the **DB2INSTANCE** environment variable) determines how access to the database server and to all databases under its control will be authenticated.

Trusted Versus Untrusted Clients

We saw earlier that if a client uses the CLIENT authentication type, authentication occurs on the client workstation or database partition where a client application is invoked by using the security facility that is provided by the client's operating system. However, if a server uses the CLIENT authentication type, additional information must be provided so the DB2 Database Manager will know which clients are responsible for validating users and which clients depend on the server for user authentication. To help make this determination, clients are placed into one of two groups:

- **Trusted clients**   Clients that use an operating system that provides an integrated security facility (for example, Windows NT, Windows 2000, OS/2, all supported versions of UNIX, MVS, OS/390, VM, VSE, and AS/400)

- **Untrusted clients**   Clients that use an operating system that does not provide an integrated security facility (for example, Windows 95 and Windows 98)

How and where authentication for both trusted clients and untrusted clients takes place is also specified in the DB2 Database Manager configuration files that are associated with each instance. (The actual values are stored in the *trust_allclnts* and *trust_clntauth* parameters.) If the *trust_allclnts* configuration parameter is set to YES (which is the default), the DB2 Database Manager for that instance assumes that all clients that will access the server are trusted clients. This implies that all clients can validate the user on behalf of the server. However, if this configuration parameter is set to NO, the DB2 Database Manager assumes that one or more untrusted clients will access the server; therefore, all users must be authenticated at the server. (If this configuration parameter is set to DRDAONLY, only MVS, OS/390, VM, VSE, and OS/400 clients will be treated as trusted clients.)

In some cases, it may be desirable to perform authentication at the server, even for trusted clients. For this reason, the *trust_clntauth* configuration parameter is used to indicate where trusted clients will be validated. By accepting the default value for this parameter (which is CLIENT), all users of trusted clients are validated at the client workstation. By setting this configuration parameter to SERVER, all users of trusted clients will be authenticated at the server.

A Word about Users and Groups

As you begin to look at the different authorities and privileges that are available with DB2 Universal Database, you will see several references to users and groups. A *user* is any individual who can be authenticated, either by the server or by the client workstation. A *group* is a collection of two or more users. If a user belongs to a group and the group is given specific authorities and privileges, the user will receive those same authorities and privileges.

At first glance, it appears that users and groups are synonymous. However, there is one distinct difference between the two: In some cases, if a user has acquired the authority or privileges needed to grant specific privileges to other users through group membership, he or she is not allowed to grant those privileges.

Authorities

Once a user has been authenticated, the DB2 Database Manager must determine whether or not the user has the authority needed to perform the task requested. This determination is made by evaluating the set of authorities and privileges that have either been assigned to an individual or that have been assigned to a group that an individual is a member of. Authorities convey rights that are required in order to perform certain kinds of administrative and maintenance operations. Privileges convey rights that are required in order to perform certain actions on a specific database or database object.

With DB2 Universal Database, five authorization levels are used to control which administrative and maintenance operations a user can perform. Three of these authorization levels apply to the DB2 Database Manager instance (and all databases that are managed by that instance), whereas the remaining two only apply to a specific database. The following are five levels of authority that are recognized by DB2 Universal Database:

- System Administrator (SYSADM) authority
- System Control (SYSCTRL) authority
- System Maintenance (SYSMAINT) authority
- Database Administrator (DBADM) authority
- Load (LOAD) authority

Figure 8-9 shows the relationship among these five authorities, as well as their span of control (that is, instance versus database).

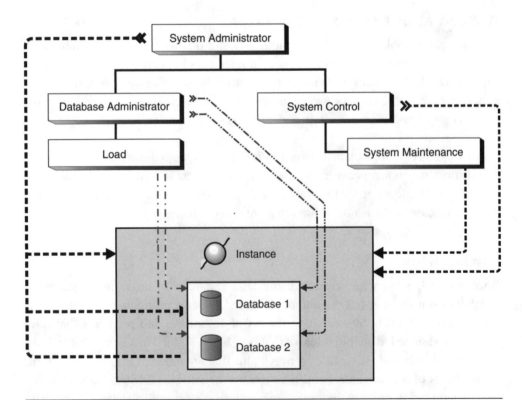

Figure 8-9 The hierarchy and relationship of DB2 Universal Database authorities

Each of the instance-level authorities can only be given to a group of users (rather than to one or more individuals), and the names of the groups that have been given these authorities are recorded in the DB2 Database Manager configuration files that are associated with each instance. On the other hand, the two database-level authorities can be held by a group of users and/or by one or more individuals. Groups and individuals that have been given these authorities are recorded in the system catalog table SYSCAT.DBAUTH, which is part of the database that the authority applies to.

TIP   Names of the groups that have been given instance-level authorities can be seen by executing the **GET DATABASE MANAGER CONFIGURATION** command and examining the values shown for the *sysadm_group*, *sysctrl_group*, and *sysmaint_group* parameters. The names of the users and groups that have been given database-level authorities can be seen by running a query against the appropriate SYSCAT.DBAUTH system catalog table.

System Administrator (SYSADM) Authority

System Administrator (SYSADM) authority is the highest level of administrative authority recognized by DB2 Universal Database. Users who belong to the group that has this authority have the ability to run any DB2 Universal Database utility, execute any DB2 command, SQL statement, or application programming interface (API) function call, and may access any database or database object that is being managed by a specific DB2 Database Manager instance. Additionally, users with SYSADM authority may perform the following tasks:

- Migrate a database.
- Modify the values stored in the DB2 Database Manager configuration file that is associated with the instance. (This includes specifying the groups that have System Control and/or System Maintenance authority.)
- Give (grant) an individual or a group of users DBADM authority.

Users with SYSADM authority may also perform the same functions that users with System Control authority, System Maintenance authority, and DBADM authority may perform.

NOTE   When a user with SYSADM authority creates a database, he or she is automatically given Database Manager authority on that database. If the user is removed from the SYSADM group, he or she can still access any database he or she created, as a Database Administrator, unless that authority is explicitly removed (revoked).

System Control (SYSCTRL) Authority

System Control (SYSCTRL) authority is the highest level of instance control authority recognized by DB2 Universal Database. Users who belong to the group that has this authority have the ability to perform maintenance and utility operations against a specific DB2 Database Manager instance and against any databases that fall under that instance's control. However, users with SYSCTRL authority are not automatically given the right to access or modify data stored in any database that is controlled by the instance. SYSCTRL authority is designed to enable special users to administer an instance that contains sensitive data that they most likely do not have access to.

Users with SYSCTRL authority or higher may perform the following tasks:

- Update a database, node, or distributed connection services (DCS) directory.
- Force users off the system.
- Create or destroy (drop) a database.
- Create, alter, or drop a table space.
- Create a new database from an existing database backup image.

Users with SYSCTRL authority may perform the same functions that users with System Maintenance authority may perform. In addition, users with SYSCTRL authority are automatically given the CONNECT privilege for every database that is being managed by the instance.

NOTE When a user with SYSCTRL authority creates a database, he or she is automatically given Database Manager authority on that database. If the user is removed from the SYSCTRL group, he or she can still access any database he or she created, as a Database Administrator, unless that authority is explicitly revoked.

System Maintenance (SYSMAINT) Authority

System Maintenance (SYSMAINT) authority is the second highest level of instance control authority recognized by DB2 Universal Database. Users who belong to the group that has this authority have the ability to perform maintenance and utility operations against a specific DB2 Database Manager instance and against any databases that fall under that instance's control. However, users with SYSMAINT authority are not allowed to create new databases and/or drop existing databases, and are not automatically given the right to access or modify data stored in any of the databases that already exist. Like SYSCTRL authority, SYSMAINT authority is designed to enable special users to administer an instance that contains sensitive data that they most likely do not have access to.

Users with SYSMAINT authority or higher may perform the following tasks:

- Modify the values stored in database configuration files.

- Make a backup image of a database or a table space.

- Restore a database using a backup image (the database must already exist).

- Restore a table space using a backup image.

- Perform a roll-forward recovery operation.

- Start or stop a DB2 Database Manager instance.

- Run a trace.

- Take database system monitor snapshots of a DB2 Database Manager instance or its databases.

- Query the state of a table space.

- Update log history files.

- Quiesce (restrict access to) a table space.

- Reorganize a table.

- Collect catalog statistics using the Run Statistics (RUNSTATS) utility.

In addition, users with SYSMAINT authority are automatically given the CONNECT privilege for every database that is being managed by a particular instance.

Database Administrator (DBADM) Authority

Database Administrator (DBADM) authority is the second highest level of administrative authority recognized by DB2 Universal Database. Users who have this authority have the ability to run most DB2 Universal Database utilities, issue database-specific DB2 commands, and access data and/or database objects that are stored in a specific database. However, they can only perform these functions on the database for which DBADM authority is held.

Users with DBADM authority or higher may perform the following tasks:

- Query the state of a table space.

- Update log history files.

- Quiesce (restrict access to) a table space.
- Reorganize a table.
- Collect catalog statistics using the RUNSTATS utility.

Users with DBADM or SYSADM authority may also

- Read database log files.
- Create, activate, and drop event monitors.

In addition, users with DBADM authority may perform the same functions that users who hold all of the database privileges available may perform. (In fact, when a user is given DBADM authority, he or she receives all but one of the database privileges available as well.)

 NOTE When a user creates a new database, he or she is automatically given DBADM authority (along with the appropriate privileges) on that database.

Load (LOAD) Authority

Load (LOAD) authority is a special level of database authority that is used to determine whether a user holds the right to bulk load data into an existing table, using either the AutoLoader utility or the LOAD command/API. In previous releases, the LOAD authority was only available with DB2 Universal Database for OS/390; now it is available for the entire DB2 Universal Database family. LOAD authority is designed to enable users to perform bulk load operations without having to have SYSADM or DBADM authority. This enables users to perform more DB2 functions, while giving Database Administrators more granular control over the administration of their database.

In addition to being able to bulk load data, users with LOAD authority or higher may

- Query the state of a table space.
- Quiesce (restrict access to) a table space.
- Collect catalog statistics using the RUNSTATS utility.

In addition to holding LOAD authority, users wanting to perform bulk load operations must also hold the following:

- The INSERT privilege on the table data will be loaded when the load utility is invoked in INSERT mode, TERMINATE mode (to terminate a previous load insert operation), or RESTART mode (to restart a previous load insert operation).

- The INSERT and DELETE privilege on the table data will be loaded when the load utility is invoked in REPLACE mode, TERMINATE mode (to terminate a previous load replace operation), or RESTART mode (to restart a previous load replace operation).

- The INSERT privilege on the exception table will be used, if such a table is used as part of the load operation.

Privileges

As mentioned earlier, privileges are used to convey the right to perform certain actions on a specific object (for example, a table, a view, an index, and so on) within a database to an individual or a group of users. With DB2 Universal Database, two types of privileges exist: database and object privileges.

Database Privileges

Database privileges apply to a database as a whole, rather than to a specific object within a database. Figure 8-10 shows the different types of database privileges available.

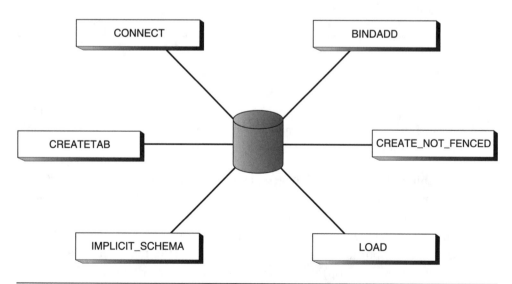

Figure 8-10   Database privileges

As you can see in Figure 8-10, six different database privileges exist:

- **CONNECT**   Conveys the right to establish a connection to (and access) a database.

- **CREATETAB**   Conveys the right to create new tables in a database.

- **BINDADD**   Conveys the right to create packages in a database when precompiling and/or binding application program files to that database.

- **CREATE_NOT_FENCED**   Conveys the right to create user-defined functions (UDFs) that are considered safe enough to run in the DB2 Database Manager operating environment's process or address space. If a function is registered as FENCED, the DB2 Database Manager insulates its internal resources (for example, data buffers and control blocks) such that they cannot be accessed by that function. Most functions will have the option of running as FENCED or NOT FENCED.

- **IMPLICIT_SCHEMA**   Conveys the right to implicitly create a new schema by creating an object with a schema name that is different from the schema names that already exist in a database.

- **LOAD**   Conveys the right to load data into existing tables.

 NOTE   When a user is given DBADM authority, he or she automatically receives the **CONNECT, CREATETAB, BINDADD, CREATE_NOT_FENCED,** and **IMPLICIT_SCHEMA** privileges.

Object Privileges

Unlike database privileges, which apply to a database as a whole, object privileges apply only to a specific object within a database. The object privileges that are available with DB2 Universal Database are categorized as follows:

- **Ownership or CONTROL privileges**   Usually, when an individual creates a database object, he or she receives full control of that object. Control of an object is given to a user through a special ownership privilege, known as the CONTROL privilege. The CONTROL privilege is like a master privilege that includes all privileges that are applicable to a given object. The CONTROL privilege also conveys the right to remove (drop) the object from the database and the right to grant or revoke any applicable privilege for that particular object (other than the CON-

TROL privilege) to/from other users and groups. In most cases, the creator of a database object automatically receives the CONTROL privilege for that object. This rule has one exception: The creator of a view will only receive the CONTROL privilege for that view if he or she also has the CONTROL privilege for each base table that is referenced by the view.

- **Individual privileges**   Individual privileges convey the right to perform a specific operation on a specific object.

- **Implicit privileges**   Implicit privileges are privileges that are automatically given to a user when a higher-level privilege is explicitly given to a user (refer to the section on the Database Administrator privilege for an example). It is important to remember that implicit privileges are not automatically revoked when the higher-level privilege that caused them to be granted is revoked.

- **Indirect privileges**   Indirect privileges are typically associated with packages. When a user executes a package that requires additional privileges (for example, a package that deletes a row of data from a table requires the DELETE privilege on that table), the user is indirectly given those privileges while he or she is executing the package. Indirect privileges are temporary and do not exist outside the scope in which they are granted.

Figure 8-11 shows the ownership and individual object privileges that are available.

As you can see in Figure 8-11, individual privileges vary among database objects. The following sections describe the individual privileges that are available for a particular object.

Schema Privileges   Schema privileges are designed to control what users can (and cannot) do with a particular schema. The following schema privileges are available:

- **CREATEIN**   Conveys the right to create objects within a schema

- **ALTERIN**   Conveys the right to change the comment associated with any database object in a schema or alter any table within a schema

- **DROPIN**   Conveys the right to remove (drop) any database object stored in a schema

The owner of a schema (typically the creator) is implicitly given these privileges along with the ability to grant any combination of these privileges to other users and groups. The database objects that are manipulated within a schema include tables, views, indexes, packages, user-defined data types, UDFs, triggers, stored procedures, and aliases.

PART III

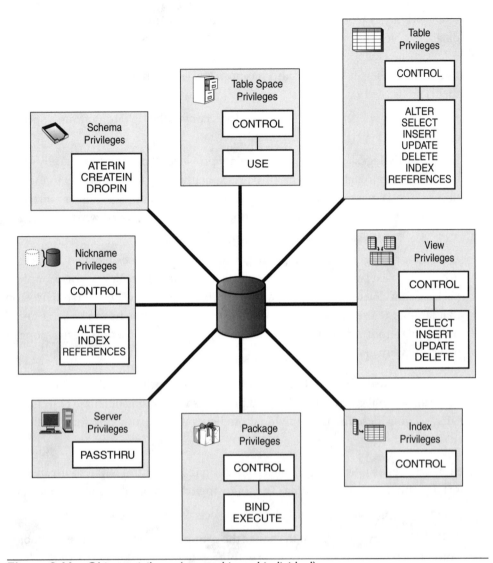

Figure 8-11   Object privileges (ownership and individual)

Table Space Privileges   Table space privileges are designed to control what users can (and cannot) do with a particular table space. In addition to the CONTROL privilege, the following table space privilege is available:

- **USE**   Conveys the right to create tables within a table space

In previous releases, the USE table space privilege was only available with DB2 Universal Database for OS/390; now it is available for the entire DB2 Universal Database family. The USE privilege prevents users from creating tables in table spaces that they have not been given access to. It also provides administrators with more control over a database. The owner of a table space (typically the creator who must have SYSADM or SYSCTRL authority) is implicitly given both the CONTROL privilege and the USE privilege along with the ability to grant the USE privilege to other users and groups.

> **NOTE** The USE privilege cannot be used to convey the right to create tables within the SYSCATSPACE table space or within any system temporary table space. By default, when a database is created, the USE privilege for table space USERSPACE1 is given to the group PUBLIC; however, this privilege can be revoked.

Table Privileges Table privileges are designed to control what users can (and cannot) do with a particular database table. In addition to the CONTROL privilege, the following table privileges are available:

- **ALTER** Conveys the right to add columns to a table, add or change comments associated with a table and/or any of its columns, create a primary key for a table, create a unique constraint for a table, and create or drop a check constraint for a table. Users who have been given this privilege also have the right to create triggers for the table (however, additional object privileges may be required).

- **SELECT** Conveys the right to retrieve data from a table, create a view that references the table, and run the EXPORT utility.

- **INSERT** Conveys the right to add data to a table and to run the IMPORT utility.

- **UPDATE** Conveys the right to modify data in a table. This privilege can be granted for the entire table, or it can be restricted to one or more specific columns within the table.

- **DELETE** Conveys the right to remove rows of data from a table.

- **INDEX** Conveys the right to create an index for a table.

- **REFERENCES** Conveys the right to create and drop foreign key constraints that reference a table in a parent relationship. This privilege can be granted for the entire table, or it can be restricted to one or more specific columns within the table.

The owner of a table (typically the creator) is implicitly given these privileges, along with the CONTROL privilege, and the ability to grant any combination of these privileges (excluding the CONTROL privilege) to other users and groups.

> **NOTE** A user must have the **CONNECT** privilege on the database before he or she can use any of the table privileges available.

View Privileges   View privileges are designed to control what users can (and cannot) do with a particular view. In addition to the CONTROL privilege, the following view privileges are available:

- **SELECT**   Conveys the right to retrieve data from a view, create a view that references the view, and run the EXPORT utility.

- **INSERT**   Conveys the right to add data to an updateable table and run the IMPORT utility.

- **UPDATE**   Conveys the right to modify data in an updateable view. This privilege can be granted for the entire view, or it can be restricted to one or more specific columns within the view.

- **DELETE**   Conveys the right to remove rows of data from an updateable view.

The owner of a view (typically the creator) is implicitly given these privileges, the CONTROL privilege for the view if he or she holds the CONTROL privilege on every table that the view references, and the ability to grant any combination of these privileges (excluding the CONTROL privilege) to other users and groups.

> **NOTE** A user must have the **CONNECT** privilege on the database before he or she can use any of the view privileges available.

Index Privileges   Only one index privilege is available. That privilege is the CONTROL privilege, which in this case conveys the right to remove (drop) an index from the database. The owner of an index (typically the creator) is implicitly given the CONTROL privilege. However, the owner is not given the ability to grant that privilege to other users and groups unless they hold SYSADM or DBADM authority.

Package Privileges   A package is a database object that contains the information needed by the DB2 Database Manager to access data in the most efficient way possible for a particular application program. Package privileges are designed to control what users can (and cannot) do with a particular package. In addition to the CONTROL privilege (which in this case provides the user with the ability to rebind, drop, or execute a package as well as the ability to grant those privileges to others), the following package privileges are available:

- **BIND** Conveys the right to rebind a package that has already been bound to a database. However, in order to rebind a package, a user must have, in addition to the BIND privilege for that package, the privileges that are needed to execute each SQL statement stored in the package.

- **EXECUTE** Conveys the right to execute a package. A user who has the EXECUTE privilege for a particular package can execute that package, even if he or she does not have the privileges that are needed to execute the SQL statements stored in the package. That's because any privileges needed to execute the SQL statements are implicitly granted to the package user. It is important to note that in order for privileges to be implicitly granted, the creator of the package must hold privileges as an individual user or as a member of the group PUBLIC—not as a member of a named group.

The owner of a package (typically the creator) is implicitly given these privileges, along with the CONTROL privilege, and the ability to grant any combination of these privileges (excluding the CONTROL privilege) to other users and groups.

NOTE A user must have the **CONNECT** privilege on the database before he or she can use any of the package privileges available.

Users who have the authority to execute a package containing nicknames don't need additional authorities or privileges for the nicknames within the package; however, they must be able to pass any authentication checks performed at the data source(s) in which the objects that are referenced by the nicknames are stored. Additionally, users must hold the appropriate authorizations and privileges for all referenced objects at the data source itself.

Server Privileges A DB2 federated system is a distributed computing system that consists of a DB2 server, known as a *federated server* (in a DB2 installation, any number of DB2 instances can be configured to function as federated servers), and one or more data sources to which the federated server sends queries. Each data source consists of an instance of a relational database management system (RDBMS) plus the database or databases that the instance supports. The data sources in a DB2 federated system can include Oracle instances as well as instances of any member of the DB2 family.

Server privileges are designed to control what users can (and cannot) do with a particular federated server. Only one server privilege is available—the PASSTHRU privilege, which conveys the right to issue Data Definition Language (DDL) and Data Manipulation Language (DML) SQL statements directly to a data source (as pass-through operations).

Nickname Privileges   When a client application submits a distributed request to a federated database server, the server sends the request to the appropriate data source for processing. Such a request does not identify the data source itself; instead, it references tables and views within the data source by using nicknames that map to specific table and view names at the data source. Nicknames are not alternate names for tables and views in the same way that aliases are; instead, they are pointers by which a federated server references these objects.

Nickname privileges are designed to control what users can (and cannot) do with a particular nickname. Nickname privileges do not affect any privileges that might exist for the data source objects that are referenced by a nickname. In addition to the CONTROL privilege, the following nickname privileges are available:

- **ALTER**   Conveys the right to change column names in a nickname, add or change the DB2 data type that a nickname column's data type maps to, and specify column options for a particular nickname column.

- **INDEX**   Conveys the right to create an index specification on a nickname.

- **REFERENCES**   Conveys the right to create and drop a foreign key that specifies a nickname as the parent in a relationship. This privilege can be granted for the entire nickname, or it can be restricted to one or more specific columns within the nickname.

The owner of a nickname (typically the creator) is implicitly given these privileges, along with the CONTROL privilege, and the ability to grant any combination of these privileges (excluding the CONTROL privilege) to other users and groups.

NOTE   A user must have the CONNECT privilege on the database before he or she can use any of the nickname privileges available.

Granting and Revoking Authorities and Privileges

During the DB2 Universal Database installation process, SYSADM authority is granted to the following users, by default (according to the operating system being used):

- **Windows 95/98**   Any Windows 95 or Windows 98 user
- **Windows NT/2000**   A valid DB2 username that belongs to the Administrators group
- **OS/2**   A valid DB2 user ID that belongs to the User Profile Management (UPM) Administrator or Local Administrator group
- **UNIX**   A valid DB2 username that belongs to the primary group of the instance owner's user ID

Once DB2 Universal Database is successfully installed, the individual who will act as the system administrator should create new usernames, group names, and passwords before creating the instances where the databases will reside. This action serves two purposes:

1. As mentioned earlier, the instance-level authorities (SYSADM, SYSCTRL, and SYS-MAINT authority) can only be given to a group of users. By creating new groups and storing the names of those groups in the DB2 Database Manager configuration file, the system administrator can control who gets instance-level authority.

2. By creating new usernames, group names, and passwords, the risk of a user other than the system administrator learning of the defaults and using them in an improper fashion is minimized.

Database-level authorities, database privileges, and object privileges can be given to (or taken from) an individual user or a group of users by any user who has the authority to do so. Database-level authorities, database privileges, and object privileges can be given to (granted) and taken away from (revoked) a user or a group of users by selecting Authorities or Privileges from the database and object menus found in the Control Center. Figure 8-12 shows how the Table Privileges dialog, which is used to grant and revoke table privileges, might look after it is activated by the Control Center.

Authorities and privileges can also be given to a user or a group of users by executing the appropriate form of the GRANT SQL statement. Authorities and privileges can be taken away from a user or group of users by executing the appropriate form of the REVOKE SQL statement. The syntax for these two statements are

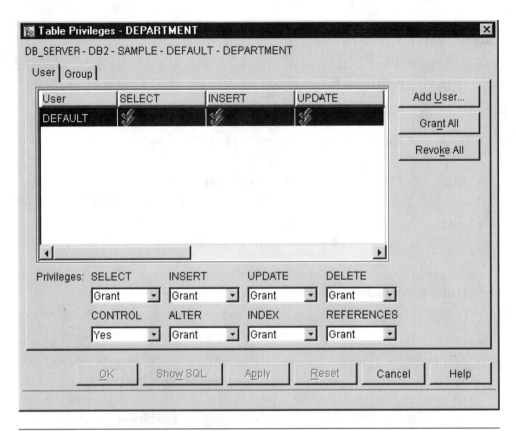

Figure 8-12   The Control Center tool for granting and revoking table privileges

```
GRANT [Authority | Privilege,...] ON [DATABASE | Object
[ObjectName] ] TO [Recipient,...] <WITH GRANT OPTION>

REVOKE [Authority | Privilege, ...] ON [DATABASE | Object
[ObjectName] ] FROM [Forfeiter, . . . ]
```

where:

Authority	Identifies the authority(ies) to be given to or taken from a specific user, a specific group of users, or all users.
Privilege	Identifies the privilege(s) to be given to or taken from a specific user, a specific group of users, or all users.
Object	Identifies the type of object that the specified privilege(s) is associated with.

ObjectName	Identifies the specific object (by name) that the specified privilege(s) is associated with.
Recipient - Forfeiter	Identifies the user(s) and/or group(s) that is to receive/lose the privileges specified. This can be any of the following values:

- USER [*UserName*]
  Identifies a specific user that the specified authority(ies) and/or privilege(s) are to be given to.

- GROUP [*GroupName*]
  Identifies a specific group of users that the specified authority(ies) and/or privilege(s) are to be given to.

- PUBLIC
  Indicates that the specified authority(ies) and/or privilege(s) are to be given to the group PUBLIC (all users).

(If the WITH GRANT OPTION option is specified, the *Recipient* will be able to grant the schema, table, view, or nickname privilege(s) received to other users or group of users.)

For example, the following GRANT statement would give USER_1 the ability to retrieve rows of data from a table named EMPLOYEE, along with the ability to give this privilege to other users:

```
GRANT SELECT ON TABLE EMPLOYEE TO USER_1 WITH GRANT OPTION
```

On the other hand, the following REVOKE statement would take this ability away:

```
REVOKE SELECT ON TABLE EMPLOYEE FROM USER_1
```

Not only do authorization levels and privileges control what a user can and cannot do, but they also control what authorities and privileges a user can and cannot grant and revoke to/from other users and groups. Table 8-3 shows the authorization requirements for granting and revoking database-level authorities, database privileges, and object privileges.

Taking Control of a Server to Perform Maintenance Operations

Because there is no limit to the number of users and groups that can be granted access to a database, it can be difficult, if not impossible, to coordinate the work efforts of

Table 8-3 Authorization Requirements for Granting and Revoking Authorities and
Privileges

If a User Holds . . .	He or She Can Grant . . .	He or She Can Revoke . . .
System Administrator (SYSADM) authority	Database Administrator (DBADM) authority Load (LOAD) authority Any database privilege Any CONTROL privilege Any object privilege	Database Administrator (DBADM) authority Load (LOAD) authority Any database privilege Any CONTROL privilege Any object privilege
System Control (SYSCTRL) authority	Table space privileges	Table space privileges
System Maintenance (SYSMAINT) authority		
Database Administrator (DBADM) authority	Any database privilege Any CONTROL privilege Any object privilege	Any database privilege Any CONTROL privilege Any object privilege
CONTROL privilege on an object	Any object privilege associated with the object the user holds CONTROL privilege for	Any table, view, nickname, or package privilege associated with the table, view, nickname, or package the user holds CONTROL privilege for
An object privilege that was assigned with WITH GRANT OPTION specified	The object privilege that was assigned with WITH GRANT OPTION specified	

everyone who is using a particular database at any given point in time. Most of the time, such coordination is not necessary. However, in order to bring a server or an instance down to make changes to it or perform routine maintenance, it often becomes necessary to get everyone to stop using one or more databases for a short period of time. (In fact, if you attempt to stop the DB2 Database Manager for an instance while one or more applications/users are attached to that instance or connected to a database within that instance, you will receive an error message.)

If your organization is small, it may be relatively easy to contact every user and ask them to disconnect so you can perform any tasks that are necessary. But what if your organization is large? Or what if an employee went home and inadvertently left an instance attachment or a database connection open? Wouldn't it be nice if you had a way to find out who is using an instance or a database on a server and terminate attachments to that instance and/or connections to databases in that instance?

If you have SYSADM or SYSCTRL authority for a server, you can find out what applications are attached to an instance (or connected to a database within that instance) on the server by selecting the *Applications* action from the *Instances* menu found in the Control Center. Figure 8-13 shows the Control Center menu items that must be selected in order to activate the Applications dialog. Figure 8-14 shows how this dialog might look if an application is connected to a database within the instance specified.

You can terminate attachments to instances and/or connections to databases in an instance by highlighting one or more entries in the list shown on the Applications dialog and selecting the Force push button (or you can terminate all attachments by selecting the Force All push button) shown on the dialog.

NOTE When an application's connection to a database is terminated because the application was forced off the server, all uncommitted SQL operations that had been performed by the application are rolled back.

You can also find out what applications are attached to an instance or connected to a database within that instance by executing the LIST APPLICATIONS command, either

Figure 8-13 Invoking the Applications dialog from the Control Center

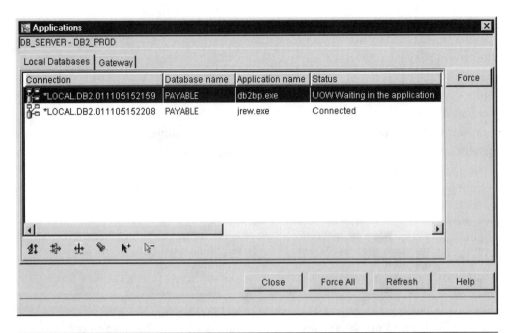

Figure 8-14   The Applications dialog

from the Command Center or from the Command Line Processor. The syntax for this command is

```
LIST APPLICATIONS <FOR [DATABASE | DB] [DatabaseName]>
<GLOBAL | AT NODE [NodeNumber]> <SHOW DETAIL>
```

where:

>   *DatabaseName*   Identifies a specific database that application information will be obtained for.

>   *NodeNumber*   Identifies a specific node number that application information will be obtained and displayed for.

For example, when executed, the command

```
LIST APPLICATIONS
```

will produce output that looks something like this:

```
Auth Id   Application   Appl.    Application Id              DB      #of
          Name          Handle                              Name    Agents
----------------------------------------------------------------------------
smith     db2bp_32      12       *LOCAL.smith.970220191502   TEST    1
smith     db2bp_32      11       *LOCAL.smith.970220191453   SAMPLE  1
```

Once you know what applications are attached to an instance or connected to a database within that instance, you can terminate their attachments/connections by executing the FORCE APPLICATIONS command, either from the Command Center or from the Command Line Processor. The syntax for this command is

```
FORCE APPLICATION ( [ApplicationHandle] ,... ) <MODE ASYNC>
```

or

```
FORCE APPLICATION ALL <MODE ASYNC>
```

where:

ApplicationHandle   Identifies one or more applications (by application ID number) that will be forced off the system.

Using the output shown in the previous LIST APPLICATIONS example, if the command

```
FORCE APPLICATION (12)
```

was executed, the first instance attachment/database connection being held by the first application in the list (which has an application ID of 12) would be terminated, and the application would be forced off the system.

NOTE   In order to preserve database integrity, only applications/users that are idle or that are performing interruptible database operations can be terminated when the **FORCE APPLICATIONS** command is processed. (For example, applications or users in the process of creating or backing up a database would not be terminated.) In addition, the DB2 Database Manager for the instance cannot be stopped (by the db2stop command) during a force; the DB2 Database Manager must remain active so that subsequent DB2 Database Manager operations can be handled without the need for a restart. Finally, because the **FORCE APPLICATION** command is run asynchronously, other applications/users can attach to the instance or connect to a database within the instance after this command has been executed. Additional **FORCE APPLICATION** commands may be required to completely force all users/applications off an instance.

Scheduling Maintenance with the Journal

An alternative to forcing users and applications off an instance in order to perform routine maintenance is to schedule maintenance jobs to run at a time when there is little or no database activity. Such scheduled jobs can be created automatically by some of the tools launched from the Control Center (for example, the Backup Database Wizard will create a scheduled database backup job), or they can be created from the Script Center and scheduled with the Journal. In addition to performing its own set of tasks, a scheduled job can launch a command script to do additional work upon its completion (or failure).

If you recall, in Chapter 2 we saw that the Script Center is a tool that enables users to create scripts consisting of DB2 commands, system commands, and SQL statements. With the Script Center, users can also

- View information about all command scripts that are known to the system.
- Run a saved command script immediately.
- Schedule a script to run unattended at a later date or at a regular interval.
- Import a script that was created outside the Script Center or that was saved in the Command Center.
- Edit a saved command script. (When a saved script is modified, all jobs dependent on the saved script inherit the new modified behavior.)
- Copy a command script.
- Remove a saved command script.
- Access the Journal to see the results that were logged when a particular script was run and to see the status of all scheduled jobs.

The Journal, on the other hand, is a notebook that provides a way for users to monitor jobs and review information that has been generated, either by jobs that have completed execution or by other administrative tools. The Journal notebook consists of the following pages:

- The Jobs page
- The Recovery page
- The Alerts page
- The Messages page

The *Jobs* page is used to monitor pending jobs, running jobs, and job histories. This page is also used to perform actions on a pending job (for example, to reschedule it), show the scripts associated with a job, or run a pending job immediately. The *Recovery* page is used to display the details from backup, restore, and load operations (such as the contents of the recovery history file) and to restore a database's recovery log file. The *Alerts* page shows any alert messages that have been generated by the Performance Monitor, and the *Messages* page shows a running history of messages that have been generated by the other DB2 administration tools. (A success or failure message can also be sent to the Messages page of the Journal by a scheduled job that has completed exe-

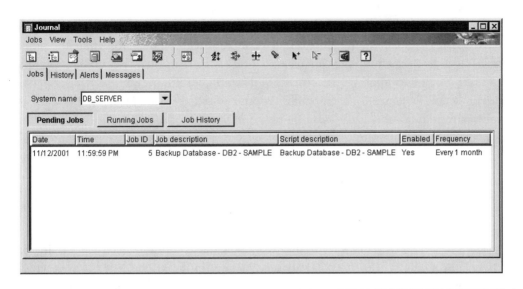

Figure 8-15 A scheduled backup database job that will be executed by the Journal

cution.) Figure 8-15 shows how the Pending Jobs page of the Journal might look on a Windows NT server after a scheduled database backup job has been created by the Backup Database Wizard.

By scheduling jobs to run during periods of low activity, the impact on users can be greatly reduced, and the need to force users off a server may be eliminated.

Summary

The goal of this chapter was to introduce you to concepts of DB2 Universal Database server management and review the authorization levels and privileges that are used by DB2 Universal Database to protect data and database objects against unauthorized access and modification.

When any edition of DB2 Universal Database is installed on a workstation (system), program files for the DB2 Database Manager are physically copied to a specific location on that workstation and one instance of the DB2 Database Manager is created and assigned to the system as part of the installation process. If needed, additional instances can be created once the DB2 Universal Database product is installed. Each time a new instance is created, it references the DB2 Database Manager program files that were copied to the workstation during the installation process; thus, each instance behaves like a separate installation of DB2 Universal Database, even though all instances within a particular system share the same binary code. Although all instances share the same physical code, they can be run concurrently, and each has its own environment (which can be modified by altering the contents of its configuration file).

The default instance for a particular system is defined by the *DB2INSTANCE* environment variable—this is the instance that is used for most operations. However, you can attach to any other instance available (including instances that exist on other systems) by selecting the *Attach* action from the *Instances* menu found in the Control Center and providing the appropriate user ID and password when the Attach dialog is displayed or by executing the ATTACH command, either from the Command Center or from the Command Line Processor. Once attached to an instance, you can perform maintenance and utility tasks that can only be done at the instance level (for example, create a new database, force applications off a database, monitor database activity, or change the contents of the DB2 Database Manager configuration file that is associated with that particular instance). Unless you have explicitly attached to a particular instance, all instance-level commands that are executed are done so against the current instance, which is identified by the *DB2INSTANCE* environment variable.

Most of the tools that are provided with DB2 Universal Database (such as the Control Center, the Client Configuration Assistant, the Script Center, and so on) require their own instance that operates concurrently with all other instances that have been defined for a system. To accommodate this need, a special instance, known as the DB2 Administration Server (DAS) instance, is automatically created as part of the DB2 Universal Database installation process. Once created, the DAS instance runs continuously as a background process whenever the system it was created on is online. (The DAS instance is started automatically each time the system is rebooted.)

The DAS instance is primarily responsible for

- Obtaining the configuration of the operating system being used by the workstation that DB2 Universal Database is installed on
- Obtaining user and group authentication information
- Starting and stopping instances (other than the DAS instance)
- Setting up communications for DB2 Universal Database servers
- Enabling remote administration of DB2 Universal Database servers
- Attaching to instances (other than the DAS instance)

The DAS instance is also responsible for assisting the Control Center and the Client Configuration Assistant when performing the following administration tasks:

- Enabling the administration of DB2 database servers from other client and/or server workstations.

- Providing the facility for job management, including the ability to schedule the execution of both DB2 and operating system user-defined command scripts. The Control Center is used to schedule jobs, view the results of completed jobs, and perform other administrative tasks against jobs that are executed either remotely or locally in conjunction with the DAS instance.

- Providing a means for discovering information about the configuration of DB2 instances, databases, and other DAS instances in conjunction with the DB2 Discovery utility. The Client Configuration Assistant and the Control Center use this information to simplify and automate the configuration of client connections to DB2 database servers.

You must have a DAS instance running in order to use the Client Configuration Assistant or the Control Center.

In a client/server environment, DB2 Universal Database databases stored on servers are accessed by applications that reside on other workstations (remote clients) through what is known as a distributed connection. In addition to providing remote clients access to a centralized database running on a server, distributed connections also enable Database Administrators to perform administrative tasks on a database server from any client workstation that has the DB2 Administration Client software installed.

All remote clients use some type of communications product that provides support for one or more communications protocols to access a DB2 server. Likewise, DB2 servers use some type of communications product to detect inbound requests from remote clients. Often, communications protocol support is provided as part of the operating system being used on both the client and the server workstation; however, in some cases, it may be provided by a separate add-on product. In either case, both clients and servers must be configured to use a communications protocol that DB2 Universal Database supports. The following communications protocols are supported by DB2 Universal Database are supported by:

- Advanced Program-to-Program Communications (APPC)
- Network Basic Input/Output System (NetBIOS)
- Transmission Control Protocol/Internet Protocol (TCP/IP)
- Internet Packet Exchange/Sequenced Packet Exchange (IPX/SPX)
- Named Pipe

When most editions of DB2 Universal Database are installed on a workstation, the communications protocols that are supported by that workstation are automatically detected and DB2 is configured to use those protocols—provided they are supported by DB2. At this time, information about each supported communications protocol found is collected and stored in the configuration file for the DAS instance and in the DB2 Database Manager configuration file for the initial instance that is created on the workstation. Unfortunately, this information is not automatically updated if you install a new communications protocol or if you reconfigure an existing communications protocol after DB2 Universal Database has been installed. In situations such as these, you must manually reconfigure communications for DB2 before the new protocol information can be used. You can manually configure communications for one or more instances on a workstation by selecting the *Setup Communications* action from the *Instances* menu found in the Control Center and then selecting the appropriate communications protocol Properties push button from the Setup Communications dialog that is displayed, or by updating the appropriate parameters of the DB2 Database Manager configuration file that is associated with that instance. The following are the DB2 Database Manager configuration parameters that affect communications:

- *nname*
- *svcename*
- *tpname*
- *fileserver*
- *objectname*
- *ipx_socket*
- *dir_type*
- *dir_path_name*
- *dir_obj_name*
- *route_obj_name*
- *dft_client_comm*
- *dft_client_adpt*

If you configure communications for an instance by updating the appropriate parameters of its DB2 Database Manager configuration file, you must also update the value of the DB2COMM registry variable. The value of the DB2COMM registry variable can be set by issuing the command db2set -i db2comm=[*Protocol*] from either the Command Center or the Command Line Processor.

Before a client can send requests to a DB2 server for processing, both the server and the database stored on the server must be cataloged on the client workstation. With DB2 Discovery, you can easily catalog a remote server and a database without having to know any detailed communication-specific information. The way DB2 Discovery works is simple. When invoked from the client workstation, DB2 Discovery broadcasts a discovery request over the network, and each DB2 server on the network that has been configured to support the discovery process responds by returning the following information:

- A list of instances found on the server that have discovery enabled, along with information about the communication protocol each instance supports

- A list of databases found within each instance that have discovery enabled

Both the Control Center and the Client Configuration Assistant can then use the information returned by DB2 Discovery to catalog any instance or database found by the discovery process.

DB2 Discovery can use one of two different methods to process a discovery request. These two methods are referred to as search and known. When the search discovery method is used, the entire network is searched for valid DB2 servers/databases and a list of the valid servers, instances, and databases found is returned to the client, along with the communications information needed to catalog each one. When the known discovery method is used, the network is searched only to locate a specific server that is using a specific communications protocol. Once the specified server is located, a list of the valid instances and databases found is returned to the client, along with the information needed to catalog each one.

Whether or not (and if so, how) a client can launch a DB2 Discovery request and whether or not (and if so, how) a particular DB2 server will respond to a discovery request is determined by the values of parameters found in the configuration file for the DAS instance, in the DB2 Database Manager configuration files for each instance (both on the client and on the server), and in the database configuration files for each database within an instance. Specifically, these parameters can control the following:

- Whether or not a client can launch a DB2 Discovery request

- The communications protocol(s) that a client will use when broadcasting search discovery requests

- Whether or not a server can be located by DB2 Discovery, and if so,

    - Whether or not the server can only be located when the search discovery method is used

- Whether or not the server can only be located when the known discovery method is used

- The communications protocol(s) that a server will use to listen for and respond to search discovery requests

- Whether or not an instance can be located with a discovery request

- Whether or not a database can be located with a discovery request

DB2 Universal Database uses a combination of external security services and internal access control measures to protect data against unauthorized access and modification. The first step in managing database security is to verify that the user really is who he or she says he or she is. This step is called authentication. Authentication is performed by an external security facility that is not provided as part of DB2 Universal Database. This security facility may be part of the operating system (which is the case with UNIX, Windows NT, and many others), a separate product (such as Distributed Computing Environment [DCE] Security Services), or it may not exist at all (which, by default, is the case with Windows 95 and Windows 98). Most security facilities require two items in order to authenticate a user: a unique user ID and a corresponding password. The user ID identifies the user to the security facility; the password, which is information that is only known by both the user and the security facility, is used to verify the user during the authentication process. How and where authentication takes place is determined by the authentication type being used by an instance.

Once a user has been authenticated, the DB2 Database Manager must determine whether or not the user has the authority needed to perform the task requested. This determination is made by evaluating the set of authorities and privileges that have either been assigned to an individual or that have been assigned to a group that an individual is a member of. Authorities convey rights that are required in order to perform certain kinds of administrative and maintenance operations. Privileges convey rights that are required in order to perform certain actions on a specific database or database object.

The following are five levels of authority that are recognized by DB2 Universal Database:

- System Administrator (SYSADM) authority

- System Control (SYSCTRL) authority

- System Maintenance (SYSMAINT) authority

- Database Administrator (DBADM) authority

- Load (LOAD) authority

Six different database privileges exist:

- CONNECT
- CREATETAB
- BINDADD
- CREATE_NOT_FENCED
- IMPLICIT_SCHEMA
- LOAD

Fifteen different object privileges exist:

- ALTER (Table and Nickname)
- ALTERIN (Schema)
- BIND (Package)
- CONTROL (Table Space, Table, View, Index, Package, and Nickname)
- CREATEIN (Schema)
- DELETE (Table and View)
- DROPIN (Schema)
- EXECUTE (Package)
- INDEX (Table and Nickname)
- INSERT (Table and View)
- PASSTHRU (Server)
- REFERENCES (Table and Nickname)
- SELECT (Table and View)
- UPDATE (Table and View)
- USE (Table Space)

Database-level authorities, database privileges, and object privileges can be given to (or taken from) an individual user or a group of users by any user who has the authority to do so. These authorities and privileges are given (granted) to a user or a group of users by executing the appropriate form of the GRANT SQL statement. These authorities and privileges are taken away (revoked) from a user or group of users by executing the appropriate form of the REVOKE SQL statement.

Because there is no limit to the number of users and groups that can be granted access to a database, it can be difficult, if not impossible, to coordinate the work efforts of everyone who is using a particular database at any given point in time. This can present a problem if it becomes necessary to bring a server or an instance down to make changes to it or to perform routine maintenance. If you have SYSADM or SYSCTRL authority for a server, you can find out what applications are attached to an instance (or connected to a database within that instance) on the server by selecting the *Applications* action from the *Instances* menu found in the Control Center or by executing the LIST APPLICATIONS command, either from the Command Center or from the Command Line Processor. You can terminate attachments to instances and/or connections to databases within an instance by highlighting one or more entries in the list shown on the Applications dialog and selecting the Force push button (or you can terminate all attachments by selecting the Force All push button) shown on the dialog. You can also terminate attachments to instances and/or connections to databases within an instance by executing the FORCE APPLICATIONS command, either from the Command Center or from the Command Line Processor.

In order to preserve database integrity, only applications/users that are idle or that are performing interruptible database operations can be terminated when the FORCE APPLICATIONS command is processed. (For example, applications or users in the process of creating or backing up a database would not be terminated.) In addition, the DB2 Database Manager for the instance cannot be stopped (by the **db2stop** command) during a force; the DB2 Database Manager must remain active so that subsequent DB2 Database Manager operations can be handled without the need for a restart. Finally, because the FORCE APPLICATION command is run asynchronously, other applications/users can attach to the instance or connect to a database within the instance after this command has been executed. Additional FORCE APPLICATION commands may be required to completely force all users/applications off an instance.

An alternative to forcing users and applications off an instance in order to perform routine maintenance is to schedule maintenance jobs to run at a time when there is little or no database activity. Such scheduled jobs can be created automatically by some of the tools launched from the Control Center (for example, the Backup Database Wizard will create a scheduled database backup job), or they can be created from the Script Center and scheduled with the Journal.

Questions

1. Two databases, MYDB1 and MYDB2, will reside in different instances on the same DB2 Universal Database server. Which of the following actions provides a

user with SYSADM authority on MYDB1, but no authority on MYDB2?

a. Grant SYSADM authority to the user on MYDB1.

b. Revoke SYSADM authority from the user on MYDB2.

c. Specify different SYSADM groups for the instances.

d. Specify different SYSADM groups for the databases.

2. Given the statements:

```
GRANT SELECT ON Table1 TO User1
GRANT UPDATE ON Table1 TO User1 WITH GRANT OPTION
```

Which of the following privileges can User1 grant to User2?

a. DBADM on DATABASE to User2

b. CONTROL on TABLE Table1 to User2

c. SELECT on TABLE Table1 to User2

d. UPDATE on TABLE Table1 to User2

3. Which two of the following are required in order to set up a DB2 UDB server that allows remote client access using APPC and TCP/IP?

a. Update the DB2 Database Manager configuration.

b. Catalog the client workstation.

c. Set the DB2COMM registry variable.

d. Create a DB2 instance for each protocol.

e. Update the database configuration for each database.

4. Which of the following actions is required in order to force a user off a remote database?

a. Catalog the remote database.

b. Quiesce the remote database.

c. Connect to the remote database.

d. Attach to the remote DB2 instance.

e. Update the *DB2INSTANCE* environment variable.

5. Given the following statements:

```
CONNECT TO SAMPLE
GRANT SELECT ON TABLE T1 TO PUBLIC
```

Who can create a view based on the table T1?

a. No one

b. Anyone who can connect to SAMPLE

c. Only the creator of table of T1

d. Anyone with DBADM authority

6. Which two of the following must be done to enable DB2 UDB databases on servers to be automatically detected by DB2 clients?
   a. Run the Client Configuration Assistant at the database server.
   b. Set AUTHENTICATION=CLIENT in the DB2 Database Manager configuration on the server.
   c. Set DISCOVER_DB=ENABLE in the database configuration.
   d. Set DISCOVER=ENABLE in the DB2 Database Manager configuration on the server.
   e. Set DISCOVER_INST=ENABLE in the DB2 Database Manager configuration on the server.

7. Given an application with the following embedded static SQL statement:

   ```
   INSERT INTO HR.PAYROLL(EMPID, SALARY) VALUES ("John Doe", 30000.00)
   ```

   Which of the following must have the INSERT privilege on the table HR.PAYROLL in order for the application to bind successfully?
   a. Each person who binds the application
   b. Each person who executes the application
   c. Each person who executes this section of the package
   d. Each person who is a member of the same non-PUBLIC group as the person binding the package

8. Suppose the following statement:

   ```
   CREATE TABLE HR.PAYROLL
   ```

   returns the following message when executed:

   ```
   SQL0551N "USER1" does not have the privilege to perform
   operation "CREATE" on object "HR.PAYROLL"
   ```

   Which of the following statements will correct the situation assuming USER1 does not have the IMPLICIT_SCHEMA database privilege?
   a. GRANT CREATETAB ON DATABASE MYDB1 TO USER1
   b. GRANT CREATEIN ON SCHEMA USER1 TO USER1
   c. GRANT CREATEIN ON SCHEMA HR TO USER1
   d. GRANT CREATEIN ON SCHEMA PAYROLL TO USER1

9. Which two of the following is true if the command FORCE APPLICATIONS ALL is executed?
   a. No new database connections are allowed.
   b. Uncommitted transactions are rolled back.
   c. Uncommitted transactions are committed.
   d. The DB2 Database Manager cannot be stopped.
   e. Users attempting to create a database are stopped.

10. A DB2 server needs to have user IDs and passwords validated at the server. In addition, the passwords and all data should be encrypted. Which of the following authentication levels provides these requirements?
   a. SERVER
   b. SERVER_ENCRYPT
   c. DCS_ENCRYPT
   d. DCE_SERVER_ENCRYPT
   e. None

11. Assuming support for the NetBIOS protocol exists on both workstations, which two of the following are required before a server can receive NetBIOS requests from a client?
   a. A named pipe must be established between the client and the server.
   b. Both the client and the server must be running on the same operating system.
   c. The registry variable DB2COMM at the server must contain the value NET-BIOS.
   d. The registry variable DB2COMM at the client must contain the value NET-BIOS.
   e. The *nname* parameter of the server DB2 Database Manager configuration must contain a unique name.

12. Which of the following can be used to schedule jobs built by the Script Center?
   a. The Command Center
   b. The Control Center
   c. The Journal
   d. The Command Line Processor

13. Given the following:

```
NNAME       =
SVCENAME    =
TPNAME      =
FILESERVER  = dbserve
OBJECTNAME  = OBJ1
IPX_SOCKET  = 879E
```

Which of the following DB2COMM registry variable values enables the configured protocol(s)?

a. DB2COMM=IPXSPX

b. DB2COMM=TCPIP, IPXSPX

c. DB2COMM=NETBIOS, IPXSPX

d. DB2COMM=TCPIP, NETBIOS

14. There are two instances on a server that DB2 Discovery must be able to locate. However, there is a need to restrict one client from locating the instances with the search discovery method—all other clients will use the search discovery method. Which of the following should be performed?

a. Set each of the server's *discover_inst* instance parameters to SEARCH and set the client's DAS instance *discover* parameter to DISABLE.

b. Set each of the server's *discover_inst* instance parameters to ENABLE and set the client's DAS instance *discover* parameter to KNOWN.

c. Set the server's DAS instance *discover* parameter to KNOWN and set the client's DAS instance *discover* parameter to DISABLE.

d. Set the server's DAS instance *discover* parameter to KNOWN, set the client's DAS instance *discover* parameter to KNOWN, and set all remaining client's DAS instance *discover* parameter to SEARCH.

Answers

1. **C.** Because the group that holds SYSADM authority for an instance is stored in the DB2 Database Manager configuration file for the instance, and because MYDB1 and MYDB2 reside in two different instances, if a user is only added to the SYSADM group for the instance MYDB1 is stored in, he or she will have no authority on MYDB2.

2. **D.** Because User1 was given UPDATE authority and the WITH GRANT OPTION, this is the only privilege he or she is allowed to give to User2.

3. **A and C.** In order for a server to accept client requests using both APPC and TCP/IP protocols, the appropriate DB2 Database Manager configuration parameters must contain values needed for the protocols selected and the DB2COMM registry variable must be set to reflect the protocols the server is configured for.

4. **D.** In order to force a user off a remote database, you must first attach to the remote instance that the database is stored in. Remember that unless you have explicitly attached to a particular instance, all instance-level commands that are executed (FORCE APPLICATIONS is an instance-level command) are done so against the current instance, which is identified by the *DB2INSTANCE* environment variable.

5. **B.** Because the SELECT privilege for table T1 has been granted to the group PUBLIC, anyone who can connect to the SAMPLE database is allowed to create a view that is based on table T1.

6. **C and E.** In order for a DB2 database to be detected by DB2 Discovery, the *discover_inst* configuration parameter for the instance the database is stored in (on the server) needs to be set to ENABLE and the *discover_db* configuration parameter for the database itself also needs to be set to ENABLE.

7. **B.** Because the SQL statement is static, the privileges of the person who executes the statement are checked at run time. Therefore, each person who executes the application must have INSERT privileges on the table HR.PAYROLL.

8. **C.** The error message indicates that the person does not have the privilege needed to create a table in the schema named HR. Because the user does not have the IMPLICIT_SCHEMA privilege, he/she must be granted the CREATEIN schema privilege before the table can be created.

9. **B and D.** When an application's connection to a database is terminated because the application was forced off the server, all uncommitted SQL operations that had been performed by the application are rolled back. In addition, in order to preserve database integrity, only applications/users that are idle or that are performing interruptible database operations can be terminated when the FORCE APPLICATIONS command is processed. (For example, applications or users in the process of creating or backing up a database would not be terminated.) In addition, the DB2 Database Manager for the instance cannot be stopped (by the **db2stop** command) during a force; the DB2 Database Manager must remain active so that subsequent DB2 Database Manager operations can be handled without the need for a restart. However, because the FORCE APPLICATION

command is run asynchronously, other applications/users can attach to the instance or connect to a database within the instance after this command has been executed.

10. E. This question is a little tricky. Because only passwords are encrypted when any of the _ENCRYPT authentication types are specified, none of the authentication types shown will meet the requirements of having both passwords and data encrypted. (The SERVER_ENCRYPT method would encrypt the passwords, but the data would be unencrypted.)

11. C and E. In order for a server to accept requests using the NetBIOS communications protocol information, the value NETBIOS must be stored in the DB2COMM registry variable, and the unique name of the server must be stored in the *nname* DB2 Database Manager configuration parameter.

12. C. Scheduled jobs can be created automatically by some of the tools launched from the Control Center, or they can be created from the Script Center—in either case they are scheduled with the Journal.

13. A. Because the NNAME (NetBIOS), SVCENAME (TCP/IP), and TPNAME (APPC) parameter values are empty, only IPX/SPX is a recognized communications protocol. Therefore, the DB2COMM registry variable should be set to IPXSPX.

14. B. By setting each of the server's *discover_inst* instance parameters to ENABLE and leaving the server's DAS instance *discover* parameter set to SEARCH (the default), both instances can be located by both search and known discovery methods. However, by setting the client's DAS instance *discover* parameter to KNOWN, the client can only use the known discovery method to look for the server. All other clients can use the search discovery method because, by default, their DAS instance *discover* parameter is set to SEARCH.

Data Placement

In this chapter, you will learn

- What buffer pools are, how buffer pools are created, and how they are used
- What table spaces are, how table spaces are created, and how they are used
- The differences between system managed space (SMS) and database managed space (DMS) table spaces
- How a table space's page size, extent size, and prefetch size affect a database's performance
- How to obtain information about existing table spaces without querying the system catalog tables

The second objective of the DB2 Universal Database—Database Administration for UNIX, Windows, and OS/2 exam is to evaluate your knowledge of how data in a database is physically stored and to test your understanding of the basic objects that are available with DB2 Universal Database. Understanding how data is physically stored is only the beginning. It is also important to know how the components that make up DB2 Universal Database's storage model are created and modified, as well as how some of their characteristics influence database performance.

Because the basic objects that are available with DB2 Universal Database were covered in Chapter 4 and the SQL statements used to create them were covered in Chapter 6, they will not be addressed again in this chapter. Instead, this chapter will focus on providing you with everything you need to know about how data in a database is stored and accessed.

TIP Fifteen percent of the DB2 Universal Database—Database Administration for UNIX, Windows, and OS/2 exam is designed to test your knowledge of how data in a database is physically stored.

Creating a DB2 Universal Database Database—A Review

In Chapter 4, we saw that when you create a DB2 Universal Database database, you are establishing an administrative relational database entity that provides an underlying structure for an eventual collection of database objects (such as tables, views, indexes, and so on). This underlying structure consists of a set of system catalog tables (along with a set of corresponding views), a set of table spaces in which both the system catalog tables and the eventual collection of database objects will reside, and a set of files that will be used to handle database recovery and other bookkeeping details.

Databases can be created by selecting the appropriate action from the Database menu found in the Control Center (refer to Chapter 4 for more information) or by executing the CREATE DATABASE SQL statement, either from the Command Center, the Command Line Processor, or an application program. The syntax for this command is also shown in Chapter 4.

NOTE Only users with System Administrator (SYSADM) authority or System Control (SYSCTRL) authority are allowed to create a new database.

Regardless of how the process is initiated, whenever a new database is created, the DB2 Database Manager performs the following set of tasks in the order shown:

1. It creates the physical directories needed in the appropriate location.

2. It creates files that are needed for database recovery and other bookkeeping tasks.

3. It creates three table spaces and assigns them the names SYSCATSPACE, USERSPACE1, and TEMPSPACE1.

4. It creates all the system catalog tables and views in the catalog table space and populates the tables as appropriate. Initially, this set of tables and views will occupy about 3.5 megabytes of disk space.

5. It initializes the database configuration file for the new database. Some of the parameters in this file will be set using values that were specified as input for the Create Database Wizard or CREATE DATABASE command; others will be assigned system default values.

6. It binds a set of utility programs to the new database so that the packages that are required before those programs can be executed will be created.

7. It grants Database Administrator (DBADM) authority to the user who created the database.

8. It grants CONNECT, CREATETAB, and BINDADD privileges to the group PUBLIC. This step enables all users to connect to the new database, create tables in the new database, and bind application programs to the new database. Once the database has been created, these privileges can be explicitly revoked.

The DB2 Universal Database Storage Model

All DB2 Universal Database databases use a storage model that consists of three distinct components:

- Buffer pools

- Table spaces

- Containers

Figure 9-1 illustrates the relationship between each of these components.

In order to control how data is stored and accessed, it is important to understand what each of these components are and how they are used.

Buffer Pools

In Chapter 4, we saw that a buffer pool is an area of main memory that has been allocated to the DB2 Database Manager for the purpose of caching table and index data pages as they are read from disk and/or modified. Using a set of heuristic algorithms, the DB2 Database Manager prefetches pages of data that it thinks a user is about to need into one or more buffer pools and it moves pages of data that it thinks are no longer needed back to disk. This approach improves overall system performance because data can be accessed much faster from memory than from disk. (The fewer times the DB2 Database Manager needs to perform disk input/output [I/O], the better the performance.)

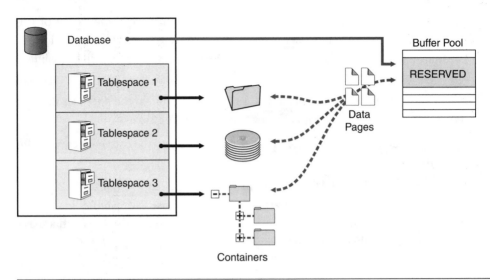

Figure 9-1 Relationship between buffer pools, table spaces, and containers

Each time a new database is created, one buffer pool, named IBMDEFAULTBP, is also created as part of the database initialization process. On UNIX platforms, this buffer pool consists of 1,000 4K (kilobyte) pages of memory; on all other platforms, this buffer pool consists of 250 4K pages of memory. The actual memory used by this buffer pool (and by any other buffer pools that may exist) is allocated when the first connection to the database is established and it is freed when all connections to the database have been terminated.

Additional buffer pools can be created, dropped, and modified by selecting the appropriate action from the Buffer Pools menu found in the Control Center (refer to Chapter 4 for more information) or by executing the CREATE BUFFERPOOL, DROP BUFFERPOOL, and ALTER BUFFERPOOL SQL statements, either from the Command Center, the Command Line Processor, or an application program. The syntax for these SQL statements is shown in Chapter 6.

A Word about Page Cleaning

Over time, as pages accumulate in the buffer pool, the buffer pool becomes full. If the buffer pool is full of unmodified pages, this situation does not pose a problem because one of those pages can be overwritten the next time a new page is read. However, if the buffer pool is full of modified pages, one of these pages must be written out to the disk before a new page can be read in. Such a situation can cause a noticeable decrease in performance.

To prevent a buffer pool from becoming full, page cleaner agents are used to write modified pages to disk at a predetermined interval (by default, when the buffer pool is 60 percent full) to guarantee the availability of buffer pool pages for future read operations. The interval at which modified pages are removed from a buffer pool is determined by the value of the *num_iocleaners* database configuration parameter.

Table Spaces

When setting up a new database, one of the first tasks that must be performed is to map the logical database design to physical storage on a system. This is where table spaces come into play. Table spaces are used to control where data in a database is physically stored on a system and to provide a layer of indirection between the database and the container objects in which the actual data resides. Because every table in a database must reside in a table space, table spaces enable you to create a physical database design that fits your particular environment. For example, frequently accessed data can be stored on newer, faster devices, whereas legacy data can reside on older, slower devices.

When a database is created, the following three table spaces are also created and associated with the buffer pool IBMDEFAULTBP as part of the database initialization process:

- A *catalog* table space named SYSCATSPACE, which is used to store the system catalog tables and views associated with the database

- A *user* table space named USERSPACE1, which is used to store all user-defined objects (such as tables, indexes, and so on) along with user data

- A *temporary* table space named TEMPSPACE1, which is used to store temporary tables that might be created in order to resolve a query

Additional user and temporary table spaces can be created, dropped, and modified by selecting the appropriate action from the Table Spaces menu found in the Control Center (refer to Chapter 4 for more information) or by executing the CREATE TABLESPACE, DROP TABLESPACE, and ALTER TABLESPACE SQL statements, either from the Command Center, the Command Line Processor, or an application program. The syntax for these SQL statements is shown in Chapter 6.

Regardless of how they are created, all table spaces are classified according to how their storage space is managed: A table space can be either a system managed space (SMS) or a database managed space (DMS).

System Managed Space (SMS) Table Spaces

With system managed space (SMS) table spaces, the operating system's file manager is responsible for allocating and managing the storage space used by the table space. SMS table spaces typically consist of several individual files (representing data objects such as tables and indexes) that are stored in the file system. The table space creator designates the locations of these files, the DB2 Database Manager controls when they are created, and the operating system's file manager manages how they are stored on disk. Unless otherwise specified as input for the Create Table Space Wizard/dialog or the CREATE TABLESPACE command, all table spaces are created as SMS table spaces by default.

Database Managed Space (DMS) Table Spaces

With database managed space (DMS) table spaces, the table space creator (and in some cases, the DB2 Database Manager) is responsible for allocating the storage space used and the DB2 Database Manager is responsible for managing it. Essentially, a DMS table space is an implementation of a special-purpose file system that has been designed specifically to meet the needs of the DB2 Database Manager. The table space creator designates one or more locations that are to contain this special file system, along with the amount of memory that has been (or that is to be) allocated for each and the DB2 Database Manager allocates the amount of space specified (if appropriate) and manages its use. In most situations, DMS table spaces are more efficient than SMS table spaces.

Additional differences between SMS table spaces and DMS table spaces are shown in Table 9-1.

Containers

Every table space is made up of at least one container, which is essentially an allocation of physical storage that the DB2 Database Manager is given unique access to. Containers can be identified by a directory name, a filename, or by the name of a particular device (such as a hard disk). A single table space can span many containers, but each container can only belong to one table space.

Directory Containers

Directory containers are references to specific directories that may or may not already exist in a file system. When defining directory containers, absolute or relative directory names can be provided—when a relative directory name is provided, the directory is expected to be relative to the directory that the database itself resides in. If any compo-

Table 9-1   Characteristics of SMS and DMS Table Spaces

Characteristics	SMS Table Spaces	DMS Table Spaces
The number of storage locations (containers) used can be increased after the table space has been created.	No	Yes
Each storage location (container) used must be the same size.	Yes	No
Storage location (container) size can be changed after the table space has been created.	No	Yes
Index data for a table can be stored in a separate table space.	No	Yes
Long data for a table can be stored in a separate table space.	No	Yes
One table can span multiple table spaces.	No	Yes
Storage space is allocated only when it is needed.	Yes	No
Table space can span multiple disks.	Yes	Yes
Extent size can be changed after table space is created.	No	No
Prefetch size can be changed after table space is created.	Yes	Yes

nent of the directory name specified does not exist, the DB2 Database Manager will automatically create that component. If every component does exist, however, the directory name specified must not refer to a directory that already contains files or subdirectories.

Directory containers can only be used by SMS table spaces. Likewise, SMS table spaces are only allowed to use directory containers. However, an SMS table space can be defined such that it uses multiple directory containers (in which case, each directory container used could be mapped to a directory that resides on a different physical disk drive to balance the table space's I/O workload.)

File Containers

File containers are fixed-size, pre-allocated files that may or may not already exist in a file system. Like directory containers, absolute or relative directory names can be used to identify the location of the file to be used—if a relative directory name is provided, the file is expected to be relative to the directory that the database itself resides in. Again, if any component of the directory name specified does not exist, the DB2 Database Manager will automatically create that component. Similarly, if no file that has the filename specified can be found, a file with that name will be created and initialized to the size specified when the table space is created, provided the appropriate amount of disk space is available. (The amount of space that is to be allocated for a file container can be specified in pages, kilobytes, megabytes, or gigabytes.)

File containers can only be used by DMS table spaces. DMS table spaces, on the other hand, can use both file and device containers.

Device Containers

Device containers are physical (raw) devices that are recognized by the operating system being used. On AIX and Solaris operating systems, a physical device can be any logical volume that uses a *character special interface*. On Windows NT and Windows 2000 operating systems, a physical device is any unformatted partition or any physical disk. When device containers are used, the amount of storage space available on the device must be provided as part of the container reference. (The amount of space a device container consumes can be specified in pages, kilobytes, megabytes, or gigabytes.) Because a device that is used as a table space container cannot be used by anything else, it is important to make sure that *all* available space on that device is specified when it is assigned to a table space; all unused space remaining will be wasted.

Device containers can only be used by DMS table spaces. DMS table spaces, on the other hand, can use both device and file containers.

Basic Buffer Pool and Table Space Requirements

At a minimum, every DB2 Universal Database database must contain the following:

- One or more buffer pools.

- One catalog table space, which is used to store the system catalog tables and views associated with the database. This table space must be named SYSCATSPACE; however, it can be an SMS or a DMS table space.

  By default, an SMS catalog table space (named SYSCATSPACE) is automatically created whenever a new database is created.

- One or more user table spaces, which are used to store all user-defined objects (such as tables, indexes, and so on) along with user data. User table spaces can be assigned any name that meets DB2 Universal Database's object naming requirements (provided the name has not already been assigned to another table space in the database) and any combination of SMS and DMS table spaces can be used.

If DMS user table spaces are used, two types can exist: regular and long. Tables that contain user data reside in one or more regular table spaces. Indexes are stored in regular table spaces as well and they can reside in the same table space as the data they are associated with or they can reside in separate regular table spaces. Long field data or large object (LOB) data stored in a table may reside in long table spaces to improve performance. The use of long table spaces is optional because long data can also reside in regular table spaces.

The maximum size of a regular table space is dependent upon the table space page size used: 64G (gigabytes) if 4K pages are used, 128G if 8K pages are used, 256G if 16K pages are used, and 512G if 32K pages are used. The maximum size of a long table space is 2T (terabytes).

By default, one SMS user table space (named USERSPACE1) is automatically created whenever a new database is created.

- One or more temporary table spaces, which are used to store temporary tables. Like user table spaces, temporary table spaces can be assigned any name that meets DB2 Universal Database's object naming requirements (provided the name has not already been assigned to another table space in the database) and any combination of SMS and DMS table spaces can be used.

Two types of temporary table spaces can exist: system and user. The DB2 Database Manager uses system temporary table spaces during SQL operations to store transient data such as intermediate tables that might be created during sorting, table reorganization, index creation, and table joins. User temporary table spaces are used to store declared global temporary tables that in turn are used to store application-specific temporary data.

The maximum size of a temporary table space is 2T.

By default, one SMS system temporary table space (named TEMPSPACE1) is automatically created whenever a new database is created.

NOTE Because a hierarchic relationship exists between buffer pools, table spaces, and the objects that reside in table spaces, each must be created in a specific order—buffer pools must be created before table spaces that reference them are created and table spaces must be created before objects that reside in them are created.

Characteristics That Affect Table Space Performance

We have already seen that the management style chosen for a particular table space can have an impact on how efficiently (or how inefficiently) I/O operations are performed. In addition to how a table space is managed, three other table space characteristics must be taken into consideration in order to design a database for optimum performance. These characteristics are

- Page size
- Extent size
- Prefetch size

Page Size

With DB2 Universal Database, rows of data in a table are organized into blocks called *pages*. The size of the page determines the size of a single row—the length of a single row of data cannot exceed the size of a single page. The actual page size used by a particular table is determined by the page size of the table space the table is assigned to. Four different page sizes are available: 4K, 8K, 16K, and 32K. By default, all table spaces that are created by the database creation process are assigned a 4K page size.

 NOTE In order to create a table space that uses a page size larger than 4K, you must first create a buffer pool that uses the desired page size. The table space must then be associated with this buffer pool during the table space creation process.

Regardless of the page size used, the first 76 bytes of a page are reserved for the DB2 Database Manager's use and the remaining bytes are available for user data. (Keep in mind that because LOB data is not stored directly in a row, LOB columns only take up 24 bytes of a page—the amount of space required to store a reference to the LOB data value's location.)

Extent Size

An *extent* is a unit of space within a container that makes up a table space. When a table space spans multiple containers, data associated with that table space is stored on all of its respective containers in a round-robin fashion; the extent size of a table space represents the number of pages of table data that are to be written to one container before

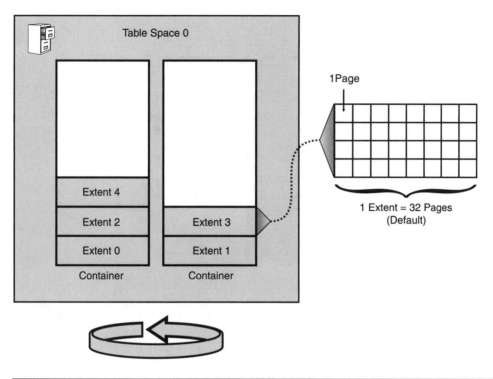

Figure 9-2 Containers and extents

moving to the next container in the list. This helps balance data across all containers that belong to a given table space (assuming all extent sizes specified are equal). Figure 9-2 illustrates how extents are used to balance data across containers; Figure 9-3 illustrates how data from two tables named EMPLOYEE and DEPARTMENT might be stored in table space HR (which uses three containers and has an extent size of two 4K pages) if both tables have five pages of data.

If you look closely at how table data is stored in a database, you will find that it is stored as three separate objects: as a data object, which is where regular column data (user data) is stored; as an index object, which is where indexes defined on the table are stored; and as a long field object, which is where long field data is stored if the table contains one or more long data columns. Each of these three objects is stored separately and each can be stored in its own table space provided DMS table spaces are used. Figure 9-4 illustrates how user data, index data, and long data can be physically stored in three separate DMS table spaces.

Each object is also paired with a metadata object known as an *extent map*, which is used to keep track of all extents in the table space that belong to the object. Space for

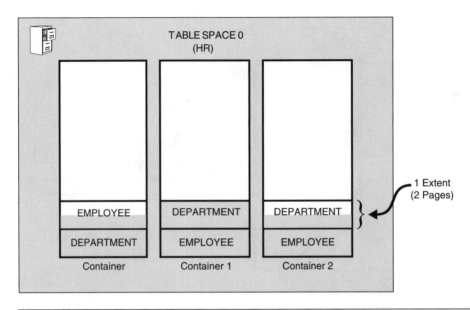

Figure 9-3   How containers and extents control where table data is physically stored

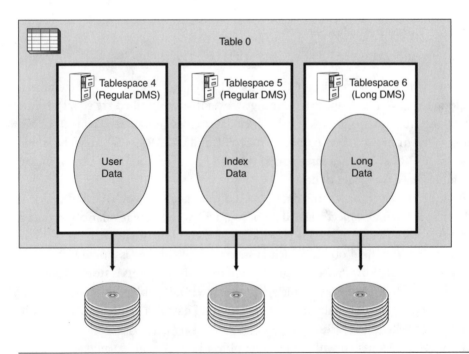

Figure 9-4   How user data, index data, and long data can be stored in different DMS table spaces

these objects and space for their extent maps are acquired (one extent at a time) as they are needed. Thus, each time a new table is added to a table space, at least two extents are acquired: one for the table's data object and one for the data object's extent map. (When a DMS table space is created, three extents that the DB2 Database Manager uses for storing overhead and control information are also acquired.)

Choosing the Proper Extent Size

As you might imagine, the efficiency of read and write operations is affected by the way extents are stored on disk. Therefore, it is imperative that the proper extent size is specified during the table space creation process, especially since a table space's extent size cannot be modified once the table space has been created. Generally, if many small tables are to be stored in a table space, that table space should use a relatively small extent size (or be an SMS table space, which allocates needed space one page at a time). On the other hand, if only a few very large tables are to be stored in a table space, that table space should use a relatively large extent size to reduce the amount of overhead needed to allocate new extents.

In addition, how the tables stored in the table space are to be accessed should also be taken into consideration. Sequential table scans (which is how data is typically accessed in a data warehousing environment) typically access a large percentage of rows in a table. Therefore, in this type of environment, a larger extent size may help reduce the number of I/O operations the DB2 Database Manager has to perform. In contrast, an environment in which tables are accessed in a random manner using key values (for example, an online transaction processing environment) might benefit from a smaller extent size; a large extent would cause a large amount of data pages that are not needed by the application to be copied to the buffer pool.

Prefetch Size

We saw earlier that the DB2 Database Manager uses a set of heuristic algorithms to fetch pages of data that it thinks a user is about to need into one or more buffer pools before requests for the data are actually made. The prefetch size of a table space identifies the number of pages of table data that are to be read in advance of the pages currently being referenced by a query, in anticipation that they will be needed to resolve the query. The overall objective of sequential prefetching is to reduce query response time. This can be achieved if page prefetching can occur asynchronously to query execution.

 NOTE   In order for prefetching to be efficient, a sufficient number of clean buffer pool pages must exist.

Choosing the Proper Prefetch Size

For optimum performance, the prefetch size specified for a particular table space should be a multiple of the extent size specified. Usually, the number of containers used by the table space determines the value of this multiple. For example, suppose you have a table space that uses three devices. If you specify a prefetch size that is three times the extent size used, the DB2 Database Manager can retrieve several pages in a single request (in parallel), thereby significantly increasing I/O throughput. (This assumes that each device is a separate physical device, and that the controller has sufficient bandwidth to handle the data stream returned from each device.)

A Word about Data Fragmentation

When DMS table spaces use device containers, the data stored in those table spaces tends to be contiguous on disk, and can be read in a minimum amount of time. However, when DMS table spaces use file containers, the data stored in those table spaces may have been broken up by the file system and stored in more than one location on disk. (Data in a large file that has been pre-allocated for use by a DMS table space tends to be contiguous on disk, especially if the file was allocated in a clean file space.) Data fragmentation occurs most often when SMS table spaces are used, where files are extended one page at a time.

Obtaining Information about Existing Table Spaces

Like all data objects, when a table space is created, information about that table space is recorded in the database's system catalog tables. Thus, you can view specific information about every table space in a database by querying the appropriate system catalog tables or system catalog views. You can also view specific information about table spaces by issuing the following command from either the Command Center or the Command Line Processor:

```
LIST TABLESPACES <SHOW DETAIL>
```

When executed, this command obtains and displays the following information about every table space that has been defined for a particular database:

- The internal ID that the DB2 Database Manager assigned the table space when it was created

- The name that was assigned to the table space when it was created

- The method used to manage the table space's storage space (SMS or DMS)

- The type of data the table space was designed to hold (regular data, long data, or temporary data)

- The current state of the table space (refer to the "Table Space States" section in this chapter for more information)

If the SHOW DETAIL option is specified when the LIST TABLESPACES command is executed, the following additional information will be displayed:

- The total number of pages the table space is designed to hold. For DMS table spaces, this is the sum of all pages of all container spaces specified. For SMS table spaces, this is the total amount of file space currently being used.

- The number of pages in the table space that user data can be stored in. For DMS table spaces, this value is determined by subtracting the number of pages needed for overhead from the total number of pages available. For SMS table spaces, this value is equal to the total number of pages the table space is designed to hold.

- The number of pages in the table space that already contain data. (For SMS table spaces, this value is equal to the total number of pages the table space is designed to hold.)

- The number of pages in the table space that are currently empty. (This information is only applicable to DMS table spaces.)

- The number of pages that mark the current "high water mark" or end of the table space's address space (that is, the page number of the first free page following the last allocated extent of the table space). (This information is only applicable to DMS table spaces.)

- The size, in bytes, that one page of data in the table space will occupy.

- The number of pages that are contained in one extent of the table space.

- The number of pages of data that will be read from the table space in advance of those pages currently being referenced by a query, in anticipation that they will be needed to resolve the query.

- The number of containers used by the table space.

- The earliest point in time that may be specified if a point-in-time roll-forward recovery operation is to be performed on the table space. (This information is only displayed if the value is not zero.)

- The ID of the table space that caused the table space being queried to be placed in the "Load Pending" or "Delete Pending" state. (This information is only displayed if the table space being queried has been placed in the "Load Pending" or "Delete Pending" state.)

- The ID of the object that caused the table space being queried to be placed in the "Load Pending" or "Delete Pending" state. (This information is only displayed if the table space being queried has been placed in the "Load Pending" or "Delete Pending" state.)

- The number of users and/or applications that have placed the table space in a "Quiesced" (restricted access) state. (This information is only displayed if the table space being queried has been placed in the "Quiesced:SHARE", "Quiesced: UPDATE", or "Quiesced:EXCLUSIVE" state.)

- The ID of the table space(s) and object(s) that caused the table space being queried to be placed in a "Quiesced" state. (This information is only displayed if the table space being queried has been placed in the "Quiesced:SHARE", "Quiesced: UPDATE", or "Quiesced:EXCLUSIVE" state.)

For example, if the command

```
LIST TABLESPACES SHOW DETAIL
```

is executed after a connection to the SAMPLE database that is provided with DB2 Universal Database has been established, the following information might be returned:

```
           Tablespaces for Current Database

Tablespace ID                          = 0
Name                                   = SYSCATSPACE
Type                                   = System managed space
Contents                               = Any data
State                                  = 0x0000
   Detailed explanation:
      Normal
Total pages                            = 1757
Useable pages                          = 1757
Used pages                             = 1757
Free pages                             = Not applicable
High water mark (pages)                = Not applicable
Page size (bytes)                      = 4096
Extent size (pages)                    = 32
Prefetch size (pages)                  = 16
Number of containers                   = 1

Tablespace ID                          = 1
Name                                   = TEMPSPACE1
Type                                   = System managed space
```

```
Contents                      = System Temporary data
State                         = 0x0000
   Detailed explanation:
      Normal
Total pages                   = 1
Useable pages                 = 1
Used pages                    = 1
Free pages                    = Not applicable
High water mark (pages)       = Not applicable
Page size (bytes)             = 4096
Extent size (pages)           = 32
Prefetch size (pages)         = 16
Number of containers          = 1

Tablespace ID                 = 2
Name                          = USERSPACE1
Type                          = System managed space
Contents                      = Any data
State                         = 0x0000
   Detailed explanation:
      Normal
Total pages                   = 336
Useable pages                 = 336
Used pages                    = 336
Free pages                    = Not applicable
High water mark (pages)       = Not applicable
Page size (bytes)             = 4096
Extent size (pages)           = 32
Prefetch size (pages)         = 16
Number of containers          = 1
```

Table Space States

Because a table space plays such an important role in the storage of data, the DB2 Database Manager keeps track of the current condition of a table space in order to prevent SQL operations from accessing and manipulating data while a table space is in anything other than a "Normal" state. A table space can be in several states, and it can be in more than one state at a given point in time. Because of this, table space states are stored as hexadecimal numbers that can be ANDed together to keep track of multiple states. Table 9-2 shows the various states that a table space can be in, along with the hexadecimal bit definitions that are used to identify each state.

Both the hexadecimal value and the corresponding description of a table space's state are included in the output generated by the LIST TABLESPACES command. Generally, a table space remains in the "Normal" state unless it is affected by a load, backup, or recovery operation or unless it is placed in a "Quiesced" state (in preparation for a load operation).

Table 9-2   Table Space States and Their Hexadecimal Values

Table Space State	Hexadecimal Value
Normal	0x0000 0000
Quiesced:SHARE	0x0000 0001
Quiesced:UPDATE	0x0000 0002
Quiesced:EXCLUSIVE	0x0000 0004
Load Pending	0x0000 0008
Delete Pending	0x0000 0010
Backup Pending	0x0000 0020
Roll-Forward In Progress	0x0000 0040
Roll-Forward Pending	0x0000 0080
Restore/Recovery Pending	0x0000 0100
Disable Pending	0x0000 0200
Reorg In Progress	0x0000 0400
Backup In Progress	0x0000 0800
Storage Must Be Defined	0x0000 1000
Restore In Progress	0x0000 2000
Offline And Not Accessible	0x0000 4000
Drop Pending	0x0000 8000
Storage May Be Defined	0x2000 0000
StoreDef In "Final" State	0x4000 0000
StoreDef Was Changed Prior To Roll-Forward	0x8000 0000
DMS Rebalancer Is Active	0x1000 0000 0
Table Space Deletion In Progress	0x2000 0000 0
Table Space Creation In Progress	0x4000 0000 0

Obtaining Information about Table Space Containers

Information about containers that have been assigned to a specific table space can be obtained by issuing the following command from either the Command Center or the Command Line Processor:

```
LIST TABLESPACE CONTAINERS FOR [TableSpaceID] <SHOW DETAIL>
```

where:

TableSpaceID   Identifies the table space (by the ID that was assigned to it by the DB2 Database Manager when the table space was created) that container information is to be obtained for.

When executed, this command obtains and displays the following information about every container that is associated with the table space specified:

- The internal ID that the DB2 Database Manager assigned the container when the table space it is associated with was created

- The name that was used to reference the container when it was assigned to the table space

- The container type (directory/path, file, or device)

If the SHOW DETAIL option is specified when the LIST TABLESPACE CONTAINERS command is executed, the following additional information will be displayed:

- The total number of pages the table space container is designed to hold. For SMS table spaces, this is the total amount of file space currently being used by the container.

- The number of pages in the table space container that user data can be stored in. For DMS table spaces, this value is determined by subtracting the number of pages needed for overhead from the total number of pages available. For SMS table spaces, this value is equal to the total number of pages the table space container is designed to hold.

- An indication of whether or not the container is accessible.

For example, if the command

```
LIST TABLESPACE CONTAINERS FOR 0 SHOW DETAIL
```

is executed after a connection to the SAMPLE database that is provided with DB2 Universal Database has been established, the following information might be returned:

```
          Tablespace Containers for Tablespace 0

Container ID           = 0
Name                   = C:\DB2\NODE0000\SQL00001\SQLT0000.0
Type                   = Path
Total pages            = 1757
Useable pages          = 1757
Accessible             = Yes
```

NOTE   If a particular container is not accessible, the DB2 Database Manager will place the table space that is associated with that container in the "Offline" state. Once the problem that made the container inaccessible has been resolved, the ALTER TABLESPACE SQL statement can be extended with the SWITCH ONLINE option specified to return the affected table space to the "Normal" state. (Refer to Chapter 6 for more information about the ALTER TABLESPACE SQL statement.)

Altering an Existing Table Space

Because SMS table spaces rely on the operating system to manage their physical storage requirements, very few changes can be made to them after they have been created. Specifically, only the buffer pool a table space is associated with and the number of pages that are prefetched when prefetching is performed can be changed for an existing SMS table space. On the other hand, because DMS table spaces use either a fixed-size, pre-allocated file, or a physical raw device such as a disk for storage, they have to be monitored closely (and possibly be modified) to ensure that they are always large enough to meet the database's storage requirements—the size of a DMS table space can be increased either by increasing the size of one or more of its containers or by adding one or more new containers to it.

New containers can be added to an existing DMS table space and some of the characteristics of existing DMS or SMS table spaces can be changed by executing the ALTER TABLESPACE SQL statement. The syntax for this SQL statement is shown in Chapter 6.

Summary

The primary goal of this chapter was to provide you with an understanding of how a DB2 Universal Database database is created and to introduce you to the components that make up DB2 Universal Database's storage model.

In its simplest form, a DB2 Universal Database database is a set of related database objects. In fact, when you create a DB2 Universal Database database, you are establishing an administrative relational database entity that provides an underlying structure for an eventual collection of database objects (such as tables, views, indexes, and so on). This underlying structure consists of a set of system catalog tables (along with a set of corresponding views), a set of table spaces in which both the system catalog tables and the eventual collection of database objects will reside, and a set of files that will be used to handle database recovery and other bookkeeping details.

The easiest way to create a DB2 Universal Database database is by using the Create Database Wizard, which is invoked from the Control Center. A database can also be created by executing the CREATE DATABASE command, either from the Command Center or from the Command Line Processor. Regardless of how the process is initiated, whenever a new database is created, the DB2 Database Manager performs the following set of tasks in the order shown:

1. It creates the physical directories needed in the appropriate location.

2. It creates files that are needed for database recovery and other bookkeeping tasks.

3. It creates three table spaces and assigns them the names SYSCATSPACE, USERSPACE1, and TEMPSPACE1.

4. It creates all the system catalog tables and views in the catalog table space and populates the tables as appropriate. Initially, this set of tables and views will occupy about 3.5 megabytes of disk space.

5. It initializes the database configuration file for the new database. Some of the parameters in this file will be set using values that were specified as input for the Create Database Wizard or CREATE DATABASE command; others will be assigned system default values.

6. It binds a set of utility programs to the new database so that the packages that are required before those programs can be executed will be created.

7. It grants Database Administrator (DBADM) authority to the user who created the database.

8. It grants CONNECT, CREATETAB, and BINDADD privileges to the group PUBLIC. This step enables all users to connect to the new database, create tables in the new database, and bind application programs to the new database. Once the database has been created, these privileges can be explicitly revoked.

All DB2 Universal Database databases use a storage model that consists of three distinct components:

- Buffer pools
- Table spaces
- Containers

A buffer pool is an area of main memory that has been allocated to the DB2 Database Manager for the purpose of caching table and index data pages as they are read from disk and/or modified. Using a set of heuristic algorithms, the DB2 Database Manager prefetches pages of data that it thinks a user is about to need into one or more buffer pools and it moves pages of data that it thinks are no longer needed back to disk. This approach improves overall system performance because data can be accessed much faster from memory than from disk.

Each time a new database is created, one buffer pool, named IBMDEFAULTBP, is also created as part of the database initialization process. Additional buffer pools can be created, dropped, and modified by selecting the appropriate action from the Buffer Pools menu found in the Control Center or by executing the CREATE BUFFERPOOL, DROP BUFFERPOOL, and ALTER BUFFERPOOL SQL statements, either from the Command Center, the Command Line Processor, or an application program.

Table spaces are used to control where data in a database is physically stored on a system and to provide a layer of indirection between the database and the container objects in which the actual data resides. Because every table in a database must reside in a table space, table spaces enable you to create a physical database design that fits your particular environment.

When a database is created, the following three table spaces are also created and associated with the buffer pool IBMDEFAULTBP as part of the database initialization process:

- A catalog table space named SYSCATSPACE, which is used to store the system catalog tables and views associated with the database
- A user table space named USERSPACE1, which is used to store all user-defined objects (such as tables, indexes, and so on) along with user data
- A temporary table space named TEMPSPACE1, which is used to store temporary tables that might be created in order to resolve a query

Additional user and temporary table spaces can be created, dropped, and modified by selecting the appropriate action from the Table Spaces menu found in the Control

Center or by executing the CREATE TABLESPACE, DROP TABLESPACE, and ALTER TABLESPACE SQL statements, either from the Command Center, the Command Line Processor, or an application program.

All table spaces are classified according to how their storage space is managed; a table space can be either a system managed space (SMS) or a database managed space (DMS).

With SMS table spaces, the operating system's file manager is responsible for allocating and managing the storage space used by the table space. SMS table spaces typically consist of several individual files (representing data objects such as tables and indexes) that are stored in the file system. The table space creator designates the locations of these files, the DB2 Database Manager controls when they are created, and the operating system's file manager manages how they are stored on disk.

With DMS table spaces, the table space creator (and in some cases, the DB2 Database Manager) is responsible for allocating the storage space used and the DB2 Database Manager is responsible for managing it. Essentially, a DMS table space is an implementation of a special-purpose file system that has been designed specifically to meet the needs of the DB2 Database Manager. The table space creator designates one or more locations that are to contain this special file system, along with the amount of memory that has been (or that is to be) allocated for each and the DB2 Database Manager allocates the amount of space specified (if appropriate) and manages its use. In most situations, DMS table spaces are more efficient than SMS table spaces.

Every table space is made up of at least one container, which is essentially an allocation of physical storage that the DB2 Database Manager is given unique access to. Containers can be identified by a directory name, by a filename, or by the name of a particular device (such as a hard disk). A single table space can span many containers, but each container can only belong to one table space.

Three types of containers exist:

- Directory containers
- File containers
- Device containers

Directory containers are references to specific directories that may or may not already exist in a file system. File containers are fixed-size, pre-allocated files that may or may not already exist in a file system. Device containers are physical (raw) devices that are recognized by the operating system being used. On AIX and Solaris operating systems, a physical device can be any logical volume that uses a character special interface. On Windows NT and Windows 2000 operating systems, a physical device is any unformatted partition or any physical disk.

At a minimum, every DB2 Universal Database database must contain the following:

- One or more buffer pools.

- One catalog table space, which is used to store the system catalog tables and views associated with the database. This table space must be named SYSCATSPACE, however, it can be an SMS or a DMS table space.

- One or more user table spaces, which are used to store all user-defined objects (such as tables, indexes, and so on) along with user data. User table spaces can be assigned any name that meets DB2 Universal Database's object naming requirements (provided the name has not already been assigned to another table space in the database) and any combination of SMS and DMS table spaces can be used.

- One or more temporary table spaces, which are used to store temporary tables. Like user table spaces, temporary table spaces can be assigned any name that meets DB2 Universal Database's object naming requirements (provided the name has not already been assigned to another table space in the database) and any combination of SMS and DMS table spaces can be used.

Because a hierarchic relationship exists between buffer pools, table spaces, and the objects that reside in table spaces, each must be created in a specific order—buffer pools must be created before table spaces that reference them are created and table spaces must be created before objects that reside in them are created.

In addition to how a table space is managed, three other table space characteristics must be taken into consideration in order to design a database for optimum performance. These characteristics are

- Page size
- Extent size
- Prefetch size

With DB2 Universal Database, rows of data in a table are organized into blocks, called pages. The size of the page determines the size of a single row—the length of a single row of data cannot exceed the size of a single page. The actual page size used by a particular table is determined by the page size of the table space the table is assigned to. Four different page sizes are available: 4K, 8K, 16K, and 32K.

An extent is a unit of space within a container that makes up a table space. When a table space spans multiple containers, data associated with that table space is stored on all of its respective containers in a round-robin fashion; the extent size of a table space represents the number of pages of table data that are to be written to one container before moving to the next container in the list. This helps balance data across all containers that belong to a given table space (assuming all extent sizes specified are equal).

The prefetch size of a table space identifies the number of pages of table data that are to be read in advance of the pages currently being referenced by a query, in anticipation that they will be needed to resolve the query. The overall objective of sequential prefetching is to reduce query response time. This can be achieved if page prefetching can occur asynchronously to query execution.

Like all data objects, when a table space is created, information about that table space is recorded in the database's system catalog tables. Therefore, you can view specific information about every table space in a database by querying the appropriate system catalog tables or system catalog views. You can also view specific information about table spaces by issuing the LIST TABLESPACES command from either the Command Center or the Command Line Processor. You can view information about containers that have been assigned to a specific table space by issuing the LIST TABLESPACE CONTAINERS command from either the Command Center or the Command Line Processor.

The DB2 Database Manager keeps track of the current condition of a table space in order to prevent SQL operations from accessing and manipulating data while a table space is in anything other than a "Normal" state. Because of this, a table space can be in any of the following states at any given point in time:

- Normal
- Quiesced:SHARE
- Quiesced:UPDATE
- Quiesced:EXCLUSIVE
- Load Pending
- Delete Pending
- Backup Pending
- Roll-Forward In Progress
- Roll-Forward Pending
- Restore/Recovery Pending
- Disable Pending
- Reorg In Progress
- Backup In Progress
- Storage Must Be Defined
- Restore In Progress

- Offline And Not Accessible
- Drop Pending
- Storage May Be Defined
- StoreDef In 'Final' State
- StoreDef Was Changed Prior To Roll-Forward
- DMS Rebalancer Is Active
- Table Space Deletion In Progress
- Table Space Creation In Progress

Because SMS table spaces rely on the operating system to manage their physical storage requirements, very few changes can be made to them after they have been created. Specifically, only the buffer pool a table space is associated with and the number of pages that are prefetched when prefetching is performed can be changed for an existing SMS table space. On the other hand, because DMS table spaces use either a fixed-size, pre-allocated file, or a physical raw device such as a disk for storage, they have to be monitored closely (and possibly be modified) to ensure that they are always large enough to meet the database's storage requirements. The size of a DMS table space can be increased either by increasing the size of one or more of its containers or by adding one or more new containers to it. New containers can be added to an existing DMS table space and some of the characteristics of existing DMS or SMS table spaces can be changed by executing the ALTER TABLESPACE SQL statement.

Questions

1. Which of the following can be optionally specified when a new database is created?
   a. The location of log files
   b. The location of user tables
   c. The location of table spaces
   d. The location of stored procedures

2. If the following command is executed:

```
CREATE DATABASE TEST_DB
    CATALOG TABLESPACE MANAGED BY SYSTEM USING (FILE 'Temp' 1024)
    EXTENTSIZE 16 PREFETCHSIZE 32
    USER TABLESPACE MANAGED BY SYSTEM USING ('C:\UserData')
    TEMPORARY TABLESPACE MANAGED BY DATABASE USING
    ('C:\SysCat1', 'C:\SysCat2')
    EXTENTSIZE 10
```

What will the extent size of the system catalog space be?

a. 1,024 16K pages

b. 16 4K pages

c. 16 32K pages

d. 10 4K pages

3. If a CREATE TABLESPACE statement is executed and the size of its container(s) was not specified, which of the following types of table spaces will be created?

a. SMS

b. DMS

c. SYSTEM TEMPORARY

d. USER TEMPORARY

4. In order to store regular table data in one table space and corresponding index data in another table space, which of the following must be used?

a. Two SMS table spaces that use directory containers

b. Two SMS table spaces that use file containers

c. Two DMS table spaces that use directory containers

d. Two DMS table spaces that use file containers

5. Which of the following CREATE TABLESPACE statements will create a table space that allocates space as required?

a. CREATE TABLESPACE TS1 MANAGED BY SYSTEM USING ('D:\Container1', 'E:\Container2')

b. CREATE INCREMENTAL TABLESPACE TS1 MANAGED BY SYSTEM USING ('D:\Container1', 'E:\Container2') EXTENTSIZE 1

c. CREATE TABLESPACE TS1 MANAGED BY DATABASE USING (DEVICE '/dev/rdev11' 150000) EXTENTSIZE 1

d. CREATE INCREMENTAL TABLESPACE TS1 MANAGED BY DATABASE USING (DEVICE '/dev/rdev11' 150000)

6. If the following statement is executed:

```
CREATE DATABASE DB1 DFT_EXTENT_SZ 2 NUMSEGS 4
```

How many DMS table spaces will be created?

a. 0

b. 1

c. 2

d. 3

e. 4

7. Given the following table space information:

```
Tablespace ID = 0
Name = USERSPACE1
Type = System managed space
Contents = Any data
State = 0x0010
Total pages = 0
Useable pages = 0
Page size (bytes) = 4096
Extent size (pages) = 32
Prefetch size (pages) = 16
Number of containers = 1
```

Which of the following describes the current state of the USERSPACE1 table space?

a. Accessible

b. Backup Pending

c. Restore Pending

d. Delete Pending

e. Offline

8. Given the following scenario:

A system has twelve 9G disks that can be used by a database.

The database will need to have a table named MYTAB.

The data portion of the MYTAB table will require 20G of storage.

The index portion of the MYTAB table will require 12G of storage.

Two table spaces (MYDATA_TS and MYINDEX_TS) have been defined.

If the table MYTAB is created by executing the following statement:

```
CREATE TABLE MYTAB (...) IN MYDATA_TS
```

How many containers must be created (for all table spaces) in order to hold the amount of data expected?

a. 2

b. 3

c. 4

d. 5

e. 6

9. Which table space characteristic may be altered for both system managed space (SMS) and database managed space (DMS) table spaces?

a. Extent size

b. Prefetch size

c. Location of an existing container

d. Size of an existing container

10. Which of the following can be used as a container in an SMS table space?

a. Directory

b. File

c. Logical volume

d. Raw device

11. Which command will show you how many free pages are left in a DMS table space?

a. SHOW TABLESPACES WITH DETAIL

b. LIST TABLESPACES

c. LIST TABLESPACES SHOW DETAIL

d. LIST TABLESPACE CONTAINERS

12. How many buffer pools can be assigned to an individual table space?

a. 1

b. 2

c. 4

d. 8

13. When is memory allocated for a buffer pool?

a. When the instance for the database is started

b. Each time an SQL statement is executed against the database

c. Each time a transaction is terminated by a commit operation

d. When the first connection to the database is made

Answers

1. C. By default, when a DB2 Universal Database database is created, three SMS table spaces are also created and stored in subdirectories of the directory the database is created in. However, the location of these table spaces, along with their storage management type, can be provided as input for the Create Database Wizard or CREATE DATABASE command.

2. B. The default page size for the three table spaces that are created when a new database is created is 4K. Because an extent size of 16 was specified for the system catalog table space, the extent size is 16 4K pages.

3. **A.** If no container size is specified for a container, the container is treated as a directory container. Because directory containers can only be used with SMS table spaces, an SMS table space will be created.

4. **D.** Index data can only be stored in a separate table space if DMS regular table spaces are used. Because directory containers can only be used with SMS table spaces, the correct answer is D.

5. **A.** Statements B and D are invalid—INCREMENTAL is not part of the syntax for the CREATE TABLESPACE statement. Therefore, because SMS table spaces acquire space as needed whereas space must be pre-allocated for DMS table spaces, the correct answer is A.

6. **A.** Unless otherwise specified, three SMS table spaces are created when a new database is created. No DMS table spaces are created.

7. **D.** The table space state value 0x0010 indicates the "Delete Pending" state. (Refer to Table 9-2 for details.)

8. **C.** This question is a little tricky. The key is that, although two table spaces exist, only one will be used to store both table and index data. Therefore, one table space that can hold 32G (20G + 12G) of data is needed. Because the disks available can hold 9G each, four disks (containers) are needed (4 × 9 = 36G). If the data portion of MYTAB were to be stored in the MYDATA_TS table space and if the index portion of MYTAB were to be stored in the MYINDEX_TS table space, five containers would be needed—three for the MYDATA_TS table space and two for the MYINDEX_TS table space.

9. **B.** With SMS table spaces, only the prefetch size and the buffer pool associated with the table space can be changed (with the ALTER TABLESPACE statement).

10. **A.** Only directory containers can be used with SMS table spaces.

11. **C.** In order to obtain detailed information about a table space, the LIST TABLESPACES command must be executed with the SHOW DETAIL option specified.

12. **A.** Only one buffer pool can be assigned to a particular table space. However, several table spaces can use the same buffer pool.

13. **D.** Buffer pools are allocated when the first connection to a database is established; buffer pools are freed when all connections to the database have been terminated.

Data Access

In this chapter, you will learn

- How to use views to control what data a user can and cannot access
- What types of indexes are available and how to choose the right type for a given situation
- What referential integrity constraints are and how they can be used to maintain data consistency between two tables
- The purpose of the system catalog tables and views
- The purpose of the Script Center
- How to examine the contents of tables and views without using queries
- The purpose of the DB2LOOK tool
- The purpose of a federated system

The third objective of the DB2 Universal Database—Database Administration for UNIX, Windows, and OS/2 exam is to evaluate your understanding of the objects that can be used to control data access and the constraints that can be used to ensure that data integrity is maintained as data is manipulated. This portion of the Database Administration for UNIX, Windows, and OS/2 exam is also designed to evaluate your knowledge about some of the tools that are provided by DB2 Universal Database for accessing data and duplicating data objects, and is meant to test your ability to interpret the information stored in the system catalog tables and views.

Knowing what objects and constraints are available is just as important as knowing how to incorporate the right combination of objects and constraints to ensure that users only have access to data they need, that data integrity is always maintained, and that optimum performance is achieved whenever possible. This chapter is designed to enforce and enhance your knowledge of views, indexes, and constraints and provide in-depth coverage of the tools that are available for viewing the contents of tables and views, performing repetitive operations against database objects, and reverse-engineering a database to produce Data Definition Language (DDL) script files.

TIP   Twenty-three percent of the DB2 Universal Database—Database Administration for UNIX, Windows, and OS/2 exam is designed to test your knowledge of the tools you can use to control data access.

Tables—A Review

The heart of all data storage and access in a DB2 Universal Database database is the table data object. If you recall, in Chapter 4 we saw that tables are logical structures that are used to present data as a collection of unordered rows with a fixed number of columns. Each column contains a set of values of the same data type or one of its sub-types—the definition of the columns in a table make up the *table structure*, and the rows contain the actual *table data*. The storage representation of a row is called a *record*, and the storage representation of a column is called a *field*. At each intersection of a row and column in a database table, there is a specific data item called a *value*. Figure 10-1 shows the structure of a simple database table.

Typically, data in a table is logically related and, as we will soon see, additional relationships can be defined between tables.

Views

One of the nice things about a relational database is that even when users are sharing the same data, each user can see the data in a different way. Some users can work directly with the base tables that make up a database, whereas other users may only be allowed to work with views, which act as virtual tables that have been derived in some way from one or more base tables. For example, suppose a company has a database that contains a table that is populated with information about each employee of the company. One user might use a view that only enables him or her to see information about the employees he or she manages; another user might use a view that enables him or her to see everything about an employee except salary information; and a third user

Table A

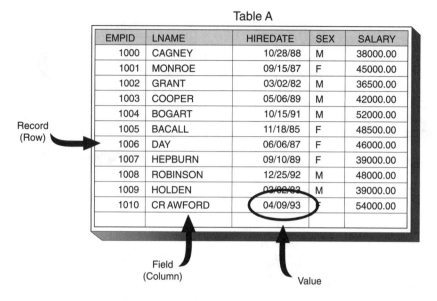

EMPID	LNAME	HIREDATE	SEX	SALARY
1000	CAGNEY	10/28/88	M	38000.00
1001	MONROE	09/15/87	F	45000.00
1002	GRANT	03/02/82	M	36500.00
1003	COOPER	05/06/89	M	42000.00
1004	BOGART	10/15/91	M	52000.00
1005	BACALL	11/18/85	F	48500.00
1006	DAY	06/06/87	F	46000.00
1007	HEPBURN	09/10/89	F	39000.00
1008	ROBINSON	12/25/92	M	48000.00
1009	HOLDEN	02/02/83	M	39000.00
1010	CRAWFORD	04/09/93	F	54000.00

Record
(Row)

Field
(Column)

Value

Figure 10-1   A simple database table

might use a view that only enables him or her to see the average salary for a particular department. Views such as these aid application development and provide a valuable degree of control over who is given access to data.

In Chapter 4, we saw that a view is essentially a named specification of a result table that is produced whenever the view is referenced in a Structured Query Language (SQL) statement. For this reason, a view can be thought of as having columns and rows, just like a base table, and in most cases, data can be retrieved from a view just as it can be retrieved from a base table. However, whether or not a view can be used to add, update, or delete data depends on how it was defined. Although a view looks like a base table, it does not exist as a table in physical storage; therefore, it does not contain data. Instead, a view refers to data stored in other base tables (a view may refer to another view, but ultimately the reference will be resolved to data stored in one or more base tables). A view can include any or all of the columns or rows contained in the table(s) on which it is based, any number of columns from other views, or a combination of columns from both tables and other views. When a view is referenced in an SQL statement, the definition of that view is merged into the SQL statement to form a new statement that is sent to a database for processing. Figure 10-2 illustrates the basic relationship between base tables and views.

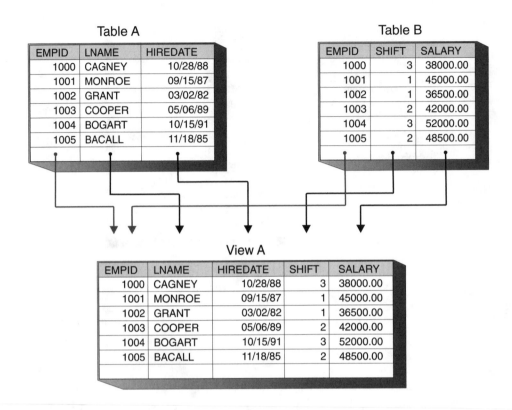

Table A

EMPID	LNAME	HIREDATE
1000	CAGNEY	10/28/88
1001	MONROE	09/15/87
1002	GRANT	03/02/82
1003	COOPER	05/06/89
1004	BOGART	10/15/91
1005	BACALL	11/18/85

Table B

EMPID	SHIFT	SALARY
1000	3	38000.00
1001	1	45000.00
1002	1	36500.00
1003	2	42000.00
1004	3	52000.00
1005	2	48500.00

View A

EMPID	LNAME	HIREDATE	SHIFT	SALARY
1000	CAGNEY	10/28/88	3	38000.00
1001	MONROE	09/15/87	1	45000.00
1002	GRANT	03/02/82	1	36500.00
1003	COOPER	05/06/89	2	42000.00
1004	BOGART	10/15/91	3	52000.00
1005	BACALL	11/18/85	2	48500.00

Figure 10-2   A simple view

In Figure 10-2, a view is created from two separate base tables. Because the EMPID column is common in both tables, that column is used to join the tables to create a single view that contains all columns.

When a column of a view is derived from a column of a base table, that column inherits all of its characteristics (such as the data type and whether or not the column is nullable) from the column of the underlying base table. Like base tables, the rows of virtual base tables that are defined by views have no intrinsic ordering sequence. However, a SELECT statement that is used to retrieve rows from a view can contain an ORDER BY clause that specifies a desired order.

Types of Views

Based on their definition, some views are classified as read-only, whereas other views are classified as insertable, updatable, or deletable. Read-only views can only be queried, but insertable, updatable, and deletable views can be both queried and used in insert, update, and delete operations. In general, a view is updatable if each row in the view can be uniquely mapped to a single row of data in one base table. (This makes it possible for the DB2 Database Manager to map insert, update, and delete operations that are performed on the view into matching operations that are performed on the underlying base table.) On the other hand, if any of the following is included in the outermost query that makes up the view definition, the view is read-only:

- A VALUES, DISTINCT, GROUP BY, or HAVING clause.
- Any column function.
- Any type of join.
- A reference to another read-only view.
- A call to a table function.
- A UNION, INTERSECT, or EXCEPT clause. (Views defined using UNION ALL can be used in update and delete operations provided their corresponding columns have the exact same data types—including lengths and default values.)

Even when a view is updatable, some of its columns may not be updatable because they do not map directly to columns of the underlying table. For example, the following statement will create an updatable view named ALLPARTS in which the PARTNO and DESCRIPTION columns are updatable, but the QUANTITY column is not:

```
CREATE VIEW ALLPARTS (PARTNO, DESCRIPTION, QUANTITY) AS SELECT
PARTNO, DESCRIPTION, QUANT_ON_HAND + QUANT_ON_ORDER FROM PARTS
```

You should keep in mind that when insert, update, or delete operations are performed against a view, those operations are really performed on rows stored in underlying base tables. For example, when you delete a row from a view, all information in the underlying table's row is deleted—including information in columns that are not visible in the view. Similarly, when you insert a row into a view, all columns in the underlying table that are not included in the view receive default values (if any of these columns were not defined with the WITH DEFAULT attribute, you would not be able to insert a row into the view).

Imposing Restrictions on Views with the WITH CHECK OPTION clause

Suppose a view was created using the following CREATE VIEW statement:

```
CREATE VIEW FAST_ORDERS AS SELECT PARTNO, UNIT_PRICE, QUANTITY,
TURNAROUND_TIME FROM ORDERS WHERE TURNAROUND_TIME < 4
```

Now suppose the following INSERT statement was used to add data to this updatable view:

```
INSERT INTO FAST_ORDERS VALUES ('P2251', 12.97, 2, 6)
```

This creates an interesting situation because the INSERT statement will attempt to insert a row with a turnaround time of six hours into a view with a definition that only includes rows with a turnaround time of less than four hours. So what will happen when this statement is executed? Well, because the FAST_ORDERS view definition does not include query features that make it a read-only view, the DB2 Database Manager is able to insert the row into the underlying ORDERS table (provided default values exist for columns that are not included in the view). However, if the INSERT statement was followed immediately by a query against the FAST_ORDERS view, the new row would not be seen. This raises a question on policy: Should an updatable view support insert and update operations whose results that will not be visible to the view?

Rather than dictate policy in such situations, DB2 Universal Database enables the creator of each view to answer this question by specifying (or ignoring) the WITH CHECK OPTION clause. If a view is created with the WITH CHECK OPTION clause specified, each row that is inserted or updated using the view must conform to the view's definition. For example, if the FAST_ORDERS view was created using the following CREATE VIEW statement:

```
CREATE VIEW FAST_ORDERS AS SELECT PARTNO, UNIT_PRICE, QUANTITY,
TURNAROUND_TIME FROM ORDERS WHERE TURNAROUND_TIME < 4 WITH CHECK
OPTION
```

the INSERT statement used earlier would no longer be valid. (Because the INSERT statement fails to satisfy the new definition of the FAST_ORDERS view, its effects are rolled back and the statement has no effect on the underlying table.)

NOTE A view that is defined with the **WITH CHECK OPTION** clause specified is called a symmetric view because everything that can be inserted into it can also be retrieved from it.

If you look at the syntax for the CREATE VIEW statement (which is shown in Chapter 6), you will notice that the WITH CHECK OPTION clause has two forms: cascaded and local. The difference between these two forms is only meaningful when one view is created on top of another one. In this case, if the topmost view is created with the local form of the WITH CHECK OPTION clause specified, insert and update operations performed on the topmost view must satisfy the definitions of the topmost view and all of the underlying views that also have check options specified (however, they do not have to satisfy the definitions of underlying views that do not have a check option). On the other hand, if the topmost view is created with the cascaded form of the WITH CHECK OPTION clause specified, insert and update operations performed on the topmost view must satisfy the definitions of the topmost view and all of the underlying views, regardless of whether or not the underlying views have a check option.

Indexes and Constraints

Because we have seen how views can be used to control what data a user can or cannot access and how views that are created with the WITH CHECK OPTION clause can impose restrictions on insert, update, and delete operations performed against those views, an obvious question at this point might be, How can a database administrator impose similar control over users who work directly with base tables as opposed to views? In many cases, restrictions on insert, update, and delete operations performed against base tables (and views derived from base tables) are imposed through one or more constraints. Most constraints are defined as part of the table creation process (constraints were covered in great detail in Chapter 5); however, the constraints that relate specifically to data access are tied closer to indexes than to the tables the indexes are based on. We need to take a closer look at these constraints in order to understand how restrictions can be imposed on insert, update, and delete operations that are performed against a base table. But before we look at these constraints, let's review what an index is.

Indexes—A Review

In Chapter 4, we saw that an index is an object that contains an ordered set of pointers that refer to a key (one or more columns) in a base table. When indexes are used, the DB2 Database Manager can access data directly and more efficiently because the index provides a direct path to the data through pointers that have been ordered based on the values of the columns that the index(es) is associated with. Figure 10-3 illustrates the basic relationship between an index and a base table.

If an index is created for frequently used columns in a table, performance can often be greatly improved on data access and update operations. In addition, indexes provide greater concurrency when more than one transaction is accessing the same table— because row retrieval is faster, locks do not have to be held as long.

Table A

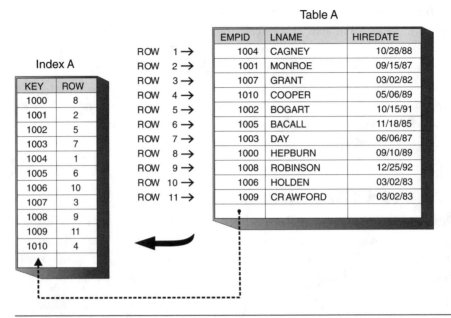

Index A

KEY	ROW
1000	8
1001	2
1002	5
1003	7
1004	1
1005	6
1006	10
1007	3
1008	9
1009	11
1010	4

	EMPID	LNAME	HIREDATE
ROW 1 →	1004	CAGNEY	10/28/88
ROW 2 →	1001	MONROE	09/15/87
ROW 3 →	1007	GRANT	03/02/82
ROW 4 →	1010	COOPER	05/06/89
ROW 5 →	1002	BOGART	10/15/91
ROW 6 →	1005	BACALL	11/18/85
ROW 7 →	1003	DAY	06/06/87
ROW 8 →	1000	HEPBURN	09/10/89
ROW 9 →	1008	ROBINSON	12/25/92
ROW 10 →	1006	HOLDEN	03/02/83
ROW 11 →	1009	CRAWFORD	03/02/83

Figure 10-3 A simple index

In DB2 Universal Database, indexes are implemented using balanced binary trees (B-tree), which are hierarchical data structures in which each element may have at most one predecessor, but may have many successors. These B-trees are optimized using an efficient and high-concurrency index management method that uses write-ahead logging. Every optimized index has bidirectional pointers on each leaf page (an index page that refers to an actual page of data) that enable the index to support scans in either a forward or reverse direction—but not both directions at the same time.

NOTE To allow an index to directly obtain rows in sequence in both forward and reverse directions, the **ALLOW REVERSE SCANS** option of the **CREATE INDEX** statement must be specified when the index is created. (The **DISALLOW REVERSE SCANS** option is used by default, and values in an index can only be obtained by searching in the forward direction.)

Keys

As mentioned earlier, a key is a single column or a set of columns in a table or index that can be used to identify and/or access a specific row of data. Any column can be part of a key and the same column can be part of more than one key. A key that consists of a single column is called an *atomic key*; a key that is composed of more than one column is called a *composite key*. In addition to having atomic or composite attributes, keys are classified according to how they are used to implement constraints:

- A *unique* key is used to implement unique constraints.

- A *primary* key is used to implement entity integrity constraints. (A primary key is a special type of unique key that does not support null values.)

- A *foreign* key is used to implement referential integrity constraints. (Foreign keys must reference primary keys or unique keys; foreign keys do not have corresponding indexes.)

Keys are normally specified during the declaration of a table, an index, or a referential constraint definition.

Understanding Constraints

Within most businesses, data often must adhere to certain restrictions or rules. Such restrictions may apply to single pieces of information such as which format and sequence to use for purchase order numbers, or they may apply to several pieces of information such as which employees are members of which departments and which employees manage those departments. Constraints are DB2 Universal Database's way of enforcing such rules within the confines of the database system. Essentially, constraints are rules that govern or influence the way in which data values can be added and/or modified.

Constraints are associated with base tables and are either defined as part of the table creation process or are added to a table's definition after the table has been created. However, once a constraint has been created, there is no special way to change its definition to reflect any changes in business rules. Instead, the existing constraint must be deleted and a new constraint that reflects the new business rules must be created. Although constraints are only associated with base table objects, they are often enforced through the use of one or more unique or primary key indexes.

Unique (and Nonunique) Indexes

So just what are unique indexes? Unique indexes are indexes that help maintain data integrity by ensuring that no two rows of data in a base table have identical key values. (When attempting to create a unique index for a table that already contains data, values in the column(s) that comprise the index are checked for uniqueness—if the table contains rows with duplicate key values, the index creation process fails.) Once a unique index has been defined for a table, uniqueness is enforced during insert and update operations. In addition to enforcing the uniqueness of data values, a unique index can also be used to improve data retrieval performance during query processing.

Nonunique indexes, on the other hand, are not used to enforce constraints on the base tables they are associated with. Instead, nonunique indexes are used solely to improve query performance by maintaining a sorted order of data values that are used frequently.

Differences Between Primary Key/Unique Key Constraints and Unique Indexes

It is important to understand that there is a significant difference between a primary/ unique key constraint and a unique index. DB2 Universal Database uses a combination of a unique index and the NOT NULL constraint to implement the relational database concept of primary and unique key constraints. Therefore, unique indexes do not enforce primary key constraints by themselves because they allow null values. (Although null values represent unknown values, when it comes to indexing, a null value is treated as being equal to other null values.) Therefore, if a unique index consists of a single column, only one null value is allowed—more than one null value would violate the unique constraint. Likewise, if a unique index consists of multiple columns, a specific combination of values and nulls can be used only once.

A Word about Indexes and Optimization

When creating an index, it is important to keep in mind that indexes are never used directly by an application or a user. Instead, the decision of whether or not to use an index, and which index to use, is made by the DB2 Optimizer when Data Manipulation Language (DML) SQL statements are processed. The DB2 Optimizer bases its decision on statistical information such as the number of rows in a table, the indexes that exist for a table, and the overall size of a table. However, you can help control how well (or how poorly) the DB2 Optimizer works in two ways. The first is to make sure that the statistical information used by the DB2 is kept up-to-date. This is accomplished by running the Run Statistics (RUNSTATS) utility on a regular basis. (The RUNSTATS utility is covered in great detail in Chapter 12.)

The second way to control how the DB2 Optimizer works is by controlling the optimization level that is used when optimization is performed. The optimization level used is specified by executing the SET CURRENT QUERY OPTIMIZATION SQL statement, either from the Command Center or from the Command Line Processor. The syntax for this statement is

```
SET CURRENT QUERY OPTIMIZATION <=> [0 | 1 | 2 | 3 | 5 | 7 | 9]
```

where:

0   Indicates that a minimal amount of optimization techniques will be used when the optimizer generates an access plan.

1   Indicates that the amount of optimization techniques that will be used when the optimizer generates an access plan should be roughly equal to that provided by DB2 Version 1.

2   Indicates that the amount of optimization techniques that will be used when the optimizer generates an access plan should be higher than that provided by DB2 Version 1, but significantly lower than level 3 and above.

3   Indicates that a moderate amount of optimization techniques will be used when the optimizer generates an access plan.

5   Indicates that a significant amount of optimization techniques will be used when the optimizer generates an access plan. This is the default optimization class used by the DB2 Optimizer.

9   Indicates that the maximum amount of optimization techniques will be used when the optimizer generates an access plan. This optimization class can greatly expand the number of possible access paths that are evaluated before an access plan is created.

Generally, higher optimization class levels require more memory and time when optimization is performed, potentially resulting in better overall performance when the optimized statement is executed. When dynamic SQL is used [in both embedded SQL and Call Level Interface/Open Database Connectivity (CLI/ODBC) applications], class 3 and above is typically used. Class 0 is most suitable for very simple SQL statements that access small, well-indexed tables in environments in which it is desirable to keep optimization costs to a minimum. Class 9 is typically reserved for specific problem queries or very complex and long-running queries that access very large tables.

Referential Constraints Revisited

In Chapter 5, we saw that a referential constraint (also known as a foreign key constraint) is used to define a required relationship between and within base tables. For example, a referential constraint could be used to ensure that every record stored in the EMPLOYEE table of a company's database reflects that the employee is a member of a department that exists in the DEPARTMENT table of that database. The relationship between these two tables is based on matching values between the set of columns that make up the primary key in the DEPARTMENT table and the set of columns in the

PART III

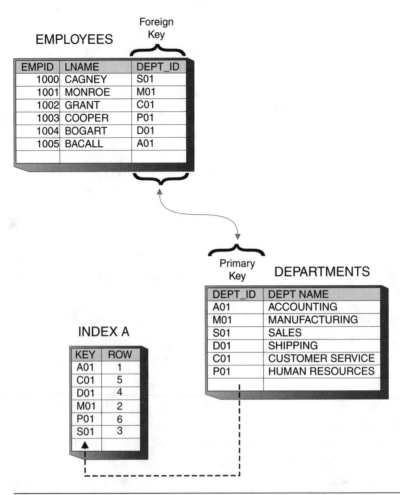

Figure 10-4   Example referential constraint and corresponding primary key index

EMPLOYEE table that make up the foreign key. Figure 10-4 illustrates how such a referential constraint might look. Keep in mind that although a unique index exists for the
primary key in the parent table, no corresponding index exists for the foreign key in the
child table.

 NOTE   Only users with System Administrator (SYSADM) authority, Database
Administrator (DBADMN) authority, the **CONTROL** privilege on the parent table,
or the **REFERENCES** privilege on either the parent table or on each column of
the specified parent key are allowed to define a referential constraint.

As long as a referential constraint is in effect, the DB2 Database Manager guarantees that for each row in a child table that has a non-null value in its foreign key columns, there is a row in a corresponding parent table that has a matching value in its parent key. So what happens when an SQL operation attempts to change data in such a way that referential integrity will be compromised? In order to answer this question, it helps to understand the ways a referential constraint could be violated:

- An insert operation could attempt to add a row of data to a child table that has a value in its foreign key columns that does not match a value in the corresponding parent table's parent key.

- An update operation could attempt to change the value in a child table's foreign key columns to a value that has no matching value in the corresponding parent table's parent key.

- An update operation could attempt to change the value in a parent table's parent key to a value that does not have a matching value in a child table's foreign key columns.

- A delete operation could attempt to remove a record from a parent table that has a matching value in a child table's foreign key columns.

The DB2 Database Manager handles these types of situations by enforcing a set of rules that are associated with each referential constraint. This set of rules consists of the following:

- An insert rule
- An update rule
- A delete rule

The Insert Rule

The insert rule of a referential constraint ensures that non-null values are only inserted into the columns that make up a foreign key in a child table if a parent key containing the same values exists in the parent table. If a null value is inserted into any of the columns that make up a foreign key in a child table, the value of the foreign key for that record is null. Any attempt to insert values into a child table that violate the insert rule will result in an error. On the other hand, non-null values can be inserted into the columns that make up the parent key of a parent table at any time; no checking will be performed on the child table.

PART III

The insert rule is implicitly created when a referential constraint is created and the DB2 Database Manager enforces it whenever an insert operation is performed on the child table of the constraint.

The Update Rule

The update rule of a referential constraint controls how referential integrity checks will be performed when the values of the columns that make up a foreign key in a child table or the values of the columns that make up a parent key in a parent table are changed. How the update rule of a referential constraint was specified when the constraint was defined determines how referential integrity violation checking is conducted when an update operation is performed on either table. The update rule for a referential constraint can be specified in one of two ways:

- **ON UPDATE NO ACTION**   This specification ensures that when an update operation is performed, every row in the child table that contains non-null values in the columns that make up its foreign key will have *some* matching value in the parent key of the associated parent table, but not necessarily the same matching value that it had before the update operation occurred. If this condition is not met, the update operation will fail and all changes made will be rolled back.

- **ON UPDATE RESTRICT**   This specification ensures that when an update operation is performed, every row in the child table that contains non-null values in the columns that make up its foreign key will have the same matching value in the parent key of the associated parent table that it had before the update operation occurred. If this condition is not met, the update operation will fail and all changes made will be rolled back.

By default, the ON UPDATE NO ACTION specification is enforced when a value in a column of a foreign key or a parent key is updated. If the ON UPDATE RESTRICT specification is used, it is only enforced when a value in a column of a parent key is updated. When a value in a column of a foreign key is updated, the ON UPDATE NO ACTION specification is enforced. As you can see, the ON UPDATE RESTRICT specification is more restrictive than the ON UPDATE NO ACTION specification. For example, an update operation that is designed to exchange the parent key values of two rows in a parent table could violate an ON UPDATE RESTRICT specification, but not an ON UPDATE NO ACTION specification.

The update rule is implicitly created with the ON UPDATE NO ACTION specification when a referential constraint is created. Like the insert rule, this rule is enforced by the DB2 Database Manager.

The Delete Rule

The delete rule of a referential constraint controls how referential integrity checks will be performed and, in some cases, how integrity violations will be resolved when a row is deleted from a parent table. More precisely, the delete rule controls what happens when a row of the parent table is the object of a delete or propagated delete operation (defined in the following sections) and when the row has dependents in the dependent table of the referential constraint. Again, how the delete rule of a referential constraint was specified when the constraint was defined determines how referential integrity violation checking/resolution is conducted when a delete operation is performed on a parent table. The delete rule for a referential constraint can be specified in one of four ways:

- **ON DELETE CASCADE** This specification ensures that when a parent row is deleted from a parent table, every row in the child table that contains matching values in the columns that make up its foreign key will also be deleted. (If the deletion of a parent row causes the deletion of a dependent row, the delete operation on the parent table is *propagated* to the child table. If the child table is also a parent table, the delete operation may also be propagated to another child table. Therefore, any table that may be involved in a delete operation on a parent table is *delete-connected* to that parent table. Thus, a table is delete-connected to a parent table if it is a dependent of that parent table or if it is a dependent of a table to which delete operations from the parent table cascade.)

- **ON DELETE SET NULL** This specification ensures that when a parent row is deleted from a parent table, every nullable column in every row in the child table that contains matching values in the columns that make up its foreign key will be set to null. (Of course, in order for this specification to work, at least one of the columns in the foreign key must be nullable.)

- **ON DELETE NO ACTION** This specification ensures that when a delete operation is performed, every row in the child table that contains non-null values in the columns that make up its foreign key will have *some* matching value in the parent key of the associated parent table, but not necessarily the same matching value that it had before the delete operation occurred. If this condition is not met, the delete operation will fail and all changes made will be rolled back.

- **ON DELETE RESTRICT** This specification ensures that when a delete operation is performed, every row in the child table that contains non-null values in the columns that make up its foreign key will have the same matching value in the parent key of the associated parent table that it had before the delete operation occurred. If this condition is not met, the delete operation will fail and all changes made will be rolled back.

By default, the ON DELETE NO ACTION specification is enforced when a row in a parent table is deleted. When a delete operation is performed on a parent table, the DB2 Database Manager looks for rows in the corresponding child table that has values in the columns that make up its foreign key that are the same as the values in the parent key of the row that is about to be deleted.

Each referential constraint in which a table is a parent has its own delete rule, and all applicable delete rules are used to determine the end result of a delete operation. Thus, a row cannot be deleted if it has dependents in a referential constraint with a delete rule specification of ON DELETE RESTRICT or ON DELETE NO ACTION or if the deletion cascades to any of its descendents that are dependents in a referential constraint with the delete rule specification of ON DELETE RESTRICT or ON DELETE NO ACTION.

Examples of Referential Constraints

Now that we've seen how the insert, update, and delete rules that are associated with referential constraints are used to prevent constraint violations, let's take a look at two examples of how these rules are implemented. In addition to examining the syntax used to implement these rules, we will also examine the tables involved in a referential constraint before and after a DML statement is executed to see what effects the insert, update, and delete rules had on the tables.

Example 1

If the following CREATE TABLE SQL statements were executed

```
CREATE TABLE DEPARTMENT
(DEPT_NO     CHAR(3) PRIMARY KEY NOT NULL,
 DEPT_NAME   VARCHAR(40) NOT NULL,
 MGR_ID      SMALLINT)

CREATE TABLE EMPLOYEE
(EMP_ID      SMALLINT PRIMARY KEY NOT NULL,
 NAME        VARCHAR(40),
 DEPT_ID     CHAR(3),
 HIREDATE    DATE WITH DEFAULT,
 CONSTRAINT FK_DEPT FOREIGN KEY (DEPT_ID)
     REFERENCES DEPARTMENT (DEPT_NO) ON DELETE SET NULL)
```

the following tables would be created:

DEPARTMENT

DEPT_NO	DEPT_NAME	MGR_ID

EMPLOYEE

EMP_ID	NAME	DEPT_ID	HIREDATE

Now, suppose these tables were populated as follows:

DEPARTMENT

DEPT_NO	DEPT_NAME	MGR_ID
A00	PLANNING	100
B00	DEVELOPMENT	—
C00	OPERATIONS	—

EMPLOYEE

EMP_ID	NAME	DEPT_ID	HIREDATE
100	CAGNEY	A00	10/28/88
120	MONROE	A00	09/15/87
130	GRANT	B00	03/02/82
140	COOPER	C00	05/06/89

If the following DELETE SQL statement is executed

```
DELETE FROM DEPARTMENT WHERE DEPT_ID = 'A00'
```

the row in the DEPARTMENT table that has the value A00 assigned to its DEPT_ID column will be deleted and all rows in the EMPLOYEE table that have the value A00 assigned to their DEPT_ID column will be modified such that the value A00 will be replaced with the null value. As a result, the tables will look like this:

DEPARTMENT

DEPT_NO	DEPT_NAME	MGR_ID
B00	DEVELOPMENT	—
C00	OPERATIONS	—

EMPLOYEE

EMP_ID	NAME	DEPT_ID	HIREDATE
100	CAGNEY	-	10/28/88
120	MONROE	-	09/15/87
130	GRANT	B00	03/02/82
140	COOPER	C00	05/06/89

Example 2

If the following CREATE TABLE SQL statements were executed

```
CREATE TABLE PARTS
(PART_NO           CHAR(10) PRIMARY KEY NOT NULL,
 DESCRIPTION       VARCHAR(30),
 PRICE             DECIMAL(10,2))

CREATE TABLE ORDERS
(ORDER_NO          SMALLINT PRIMARY KEY NOT NULL,
 PO_NUM            CHAR(12) NOT NULL,
 PART_NO           CHAR(10),
 ORDER_DATE        DATE WITH DEFAULT,
 CONSTRAINT FK_PART FOREIGN KEY (PART_NO)
      REFERENCES PARTS (PART_NO) ON UPDATE CASCADE)
```

the following tables would be created:

PARTS

PART_NO	DESCRIPTION	PRICE

ORDERS

ORDER_NO	PO_NUM	PART_NO	ORDER_DATE

Now, suppose these tables were populated as follows:

PARTS

PART_NO	DESCRIPTION	PRICE
JE204	STARTER	87.93
PR928	BRAKE PADS	39.20
CW463	FAN BELT	14.59

ORDERS

ORDER_NO	PO_NUM	PART_NO	ORDER_DATE
100	ZY-00345	JE204	10/28/01
100	AN-0087	CW463	10/28/01
110	TR-0104	JE204	03/02/01
120	KT-2076	PR928	05/06/01

If the following UPDATE SQL statement is executed

```
UPDATE PARTS SET PART_NO = 'JF207' WHERE PART_NO = 'JE204'
```

the row in the PARTS table that has the value JE204 assigned to its PART_NO column will be modified (the value JE204 will be changed to JF207), and all rows in the ORDERS table that have the value JE204 assigned to their PART_NO column will be modified such that the value JE204 will be replaced with the value JF207. As a result, the tables will look like this:

PARTS

PART_NO	DESCRIPTION	PRICE
JF207	STARTER	87.93
PR928	BRAKE PADS	39.20
CW463	FAN BELT	14.59

ORDERS

ORDER_NO	PO_NUM	PART_NO	ORDER_DATE
100	ZY-00345	JF207	10/28/01
100	AN-0087	CW463	10/28/01
110	TR-0104	JF207	03/02/01
120	KT-2076	PR928	05/06/01

Improving Performance with a Clustering Index

Whenever data is added to a base table (by an insert operation), a special insert search algorithm is used to find an appropriate physical location to store the data. This algorithm begins by examining the Free Space Control Records (FSCRs) for the table, which are managed by the DB2 Database Manager, in an attempt to locate a page with enough free space available. (This may not always return a valid page because sometimes, even when the FSCR says a page has enough free space, that space may not be usable because it has been reserved by an uncommitted delete operation that has been performed by another transaction. For this reason, you should ensure that all transactions are committed frequently so that any space that has been freed will be usable immediately.)

By default, only the first five FSCRs in a table are searched (the *DB2MAXF-SCRSEARCH* registry variable controls the number of FSCRs that are searched) the first time an insert operation is performed against a table. If no space is found within the first five FSCRs, the record being inserted is appended to the end of the table. To optimize the performance of multiple insert operations, subsequent records are also appended to the end of the table until two extents are filled. Once two extents have been filled, the next insert operation will resume searching FSCRs where the last FSCR search ended. Once all FSCRs for a table have been searched, all remaining records to be inserted are appended to the end of the table and no additional searching using FSCRs is done again until space is created somewhere in the table (for example, by a delete operation).

This behavior is altered somewhat if a special type of index known as a *clustering index* is defined for the base table. When an insert operation is performed against a table and a clustering index exists for that table, the DB2 Database Manager attempts to store records on the same page that other records with similar index key values are already stored on. If no space is available on that page, the DB2 Database Manager makes an attempt to put the record into one of the surrounding pages. If no space is available on either of those pages, the FSCR search algorithm is used—with one small difference: A worst-fit approach is used rather than a first-fit approach when looking for a storage location. The worst-fit approach is taken so pages with more free space available will be chosen; the unused space will become a new clustering area for rows with similar index key values.

As you might imagine, clustering indexes can also improve the performance of most query operations because they provide a more linear access path to data (which has been stored in pages). In addition, because rows with similar index key values are stored together, prefetching is usually more efficient when clustering indexes are used.

Unfortunately, clustering indexes cannot be specified as part of the table definition used with the CREATE TABLE statement. Instead, clustering indexes are only created by executing the CREATE INDEX statement with the CLUSTER option specified. Therefore, if you want the primary key index for a table to be a clustering index, you should not include a primary key specification as part of the table definition used with a CREATE TABLE statement—once a primary key is created, its associated index cannot be modified. Instead, the table should be created without a primary key, the CREATE INDEX . . . CLUSTER statement should be used to create a clustering index, and finally, the ALTER TABLE statement should be used to add a primary key that corresponds to the clustering index created to the table. This clustering index will then be used as the table's primary key index. Generally, clustering is more effectively maintained if the clustering index is unique.

System Catalog Tables and Views

In Chapter 5, we saw that when a database is created, a special set of tables known as the *system catalog tables* is constructed and initialized as part of the database creation process. These tables contain information about the definitions of all database objects (for example, tables, views, indexes, and packages), as well as information about the type of security access that users have to the database objects available. The system catalog tables are automatically updated during normal operation in response to SQL DDL statements, environment routines, and certain utilities. You cannot explicitly create, drop, or modify the information stored in these tables; however, you can query and view their content.

In addition to the system catalog tables, the following database objects are also defined and stored in the system catalog as part of the database creation process:

- A set of user-defined functions (UDFs), which are created in the SYSFUN schema.
- A set of read-only views for the system catalog tables, which are created in the SYSCAT schema. Table 10-1 lists the read-only system catalog views that are available with DB2 Universal Database, Version 7.1.

Table 10-1 Read-Only System Catalog Views

System Catalog View Name	Contents
SYSCAT.ATTRIBUTES	Attributes of structured data types
SYSCAT.BUFFERPOOLS	Buffer pool configuration for a nodegroup
SYSCAT.BUFFERPOOLNODES	Buffer pool size information for a node
SYSCAT.CHECKS	Check constraints
SYSCAT.COLAUTH	Column privileges
SYSCAT.COLUMNS	Columns
SYSCAT.COLCHECKS	Columns referenced by check constraints
SYSCAT.COLOPTIONS	Detailed column options
SYSCAT.COLDIST	Detailed column statistics
SYSCAT.CONSTDEP	Constraint dependencies
SYSCAT.DATATYPES	Data types
SYSCAT.DBAUTH	Authorities on a database
SYSCAT.EVENTMONITORS	Event monitor definitions
SYSCAT.EVENTS	Events currently being monitored
SYSCAT.FULLHIERARCHIES	Type, table, and view hierarchies
SYSCAT.FUNCDEP	Function dependencies
SYSCAT.FUNCMAPPINGS	Function mapping
SYSCAT.FUNCMAPOPTIONS	Function mapping options
SYSCAT.FUNCMAPPARMOPTIONS	Function mapping parameter options
SYSCAT.FUNCPARMS	Function parameters
SYSCAT.FUNCTIONS	User-defined functions (UDFs)
SYSCAT.HIERARCHIES	Type, table, and view hierarchies
SYSCAT.INDEXAUTH	Index privileges
SYSCAT.INDEXCOLUSE	Index columns
SYSCAT.INDEXDEP	Index dependencies
SYSCAT.INDEXES	Indexes
SYSCAT.INDEXOPTIONS	Index options

System Catalog View Name	Contents
SYSCAT.KEYCOLUSE	Columns used in keys
SYSCAT.NODEGROUPS	Nodegroup definitions
SYSCAT.NODEGROUPDEF	Nodegroup partitions
SYSCAT.NAMEMAPPINGS	Object mapping
SYSCAT.PACKAGEDEP	Package dependencies
SYSCAT.PACKAGEAUTH	Package privileges
SYSCAT.PACKAGES	Packages
SYSCAT.PARTITIONMAPS	Partitioning maps
SYSCAT.PASSTHRUAUTH	Pass-through privileges
SYSCAT.PROCEDURES	Stored procedures
SYSCAT.PROCOPTIONS	Procedure options
SYSCAT.PROCPARMOPTIONS	Procedure parameter options
SYSCAT.PROCPARMS	Procedure parameters
SYSCAT.REFERENCES	Referential constraints
SYSCAT.REVTYPEMAPPINGS	Reverse data type mapping
SYSCAT.SCHEMAAUTH	Schema privileges
SYSCAT.SCHEMATA	Schemas
SYSCAT.SERVEROPTIONS	Server options
SYSCAT.SERVERS	System servers
SYSCAT.STATEMENTS	Statements in packages
SYSCAT.SYSCASTFUNCTIONS	Cast functions
SYSCAT.TABAUTH	Table privileges
SYSCAT.TABCONST	Table constraints
SYSCAT.TABLES	Tables
SYSCAT.TABLESPACES	Table spaces
SYSCAT.TABOPTIONS	Remote table options
SYSCAT.TBSPACEAUTH	Table space use privileges
SYSCAT.TRIGDEP	Trigger dependencies

continued

PART III

Table 10-1   Read-Only System Catalog Views *(continued)*

System Catalog View Name	Contents
SYSCAT.TRIGGERS	Triggers
SYSCAT.TYPEMAPPINGS	Type mapping information
SYSCAT.USEROPTIONS	Server options values
SYSCAT.VIEWDEP	View dependencies
SYSCAT.VIEWS	Views
SYSCAT.WRAPOPTIONS	Wrapper options
SYSCAT.WRAPPERS	Wrappers

- A set of updatable views for the system catalog tables, which are created in the SYS-STAT schema. These updatable views enable you to update statistical information about a table without using the RUNSTATS utility. Table 10-2 lists the updatable system catalog views that are available with DB2 Universal Database, Version 7.1.

Application programs should be written to work with these views as opposed to working directly with base system catalog tables. This is because the system catalog views are designed to use more consistent conventions than the underlying system catalog base tables.

NOTE   The order of columns in the system catalog tables and views may change from release to release. To prevent such changes from affecting programming logic, always explicitly specify column names in a SELECT statement rather than letting them default by using SELECT *.

Table 10-2   Updatable System Catalog Views

System Catalog View Name	Contents
SYSSTAT.COLDIST	Detailed column statistics
SYSSTAT.COLUMNS	Columns
SYSSTAT.FUNCTIONS	User-defined functions (UDFs)
SYSSTAT.INDEXES	Indexes
SYSSTAT.TABLES	Tables

A description of each system catalog view available, including column names and data types, can be found in Appendix A. From a certification viewpoint, knowing what system catalog views are available is not as important as knowing what system catalog view (and in some cases, what column within a system catalog view) will be modified by a particular operation.

> **TIP** It is strongly recommended that you become familiar with the information presented in Appendix A—particularly for the more common views (such as SYSCAT.TABLES, SYSCAT.VIEWS, and so on)—before you attempt to take the DB2 Universal Database—Database Administration for UNIX, Windows, and OS/2 exam. It has been my experience that several questions on this exam and on other certification exams are designed to test your ability to evaluate and interpret information stored in the system catalog views.

Using the Script Center

One of the tools provided with DB2 Universal Database that can be used to examine the contents of a system catalog table or view (or for that matter, any table or view) is the Script Center. The Script Center enables you to write scripts that consist of one or more DB2 commands, system commands, and/or SQL statements, which can then be executed immediately or scheduled to run unattended at a later date or at a regular interval. With the Script Center, you can also do the following:

- Import a script that was created outside the Script Center or that was saved in the Command Center.

- Edit a saved command script. (When a saved script is modified, all jobs dependent on the saved script inherit the new modified behavior.)

- View information about all command scripts that are known to the system.

- Copy or edit existing scripts to create new scripts.

- Remove saved scripts that are no longer needed.

Figure 10-5 shows how the Script Center looks on a Windows NT server; Figure 10-6 shows how stored scripts can be executed immediately from the Script Center; and Figure 10-7 shows how stored scripts can be scheduled from the Script Center. Figure 10-8 shows how a script that is used to update statistics for all tables in the SAMPLE database would be scheduled to run at 1:00 A.M. each weekday using the Script Center.

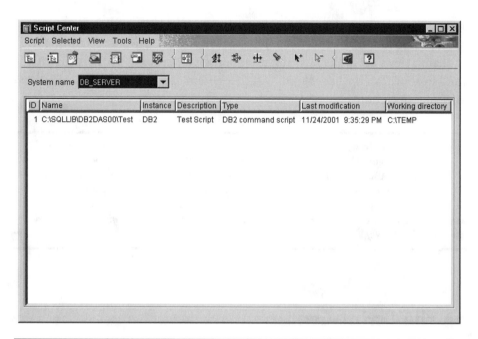

Figure 10-5 The Script Center

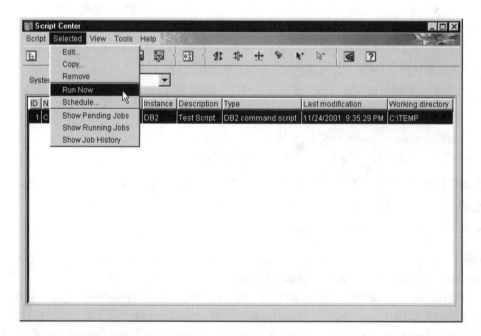

Figure 10-6 Executing a script immediately

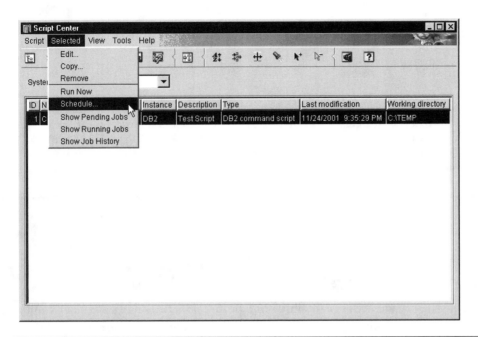

Figure 10-7   Scheduling a script for later execution

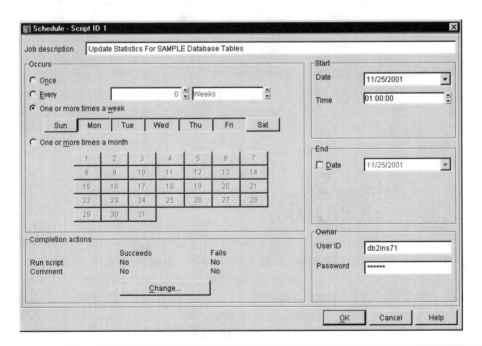

Figure 10-8   Scheduling a script to run each weekday at 1:00 A.M.

Scripts can be composed and edited inside the Script Center, or they can be created using an editor of your choice and imported into the Script Center for scheduling or immediate execution.

> **NOTE** Although many script files can be executed directly from the Command Center or the Command Line Processor, if they are run from within the Script Center, you get the added advantage of having the results logged in the Journal. This is because a job is automatically created whenever you schedule or run a script from the Script Center; this is not the case when scripts are executed outside of the Script Center.

An Alternative Method for Viewing Information Stored in Tables and Views

Although queries and scripts containing one or more SELECT SQL statements can be used to retrieve the contents of any table that a user has SELECT privileges on, an alternate way to view the contents of a table or view quickly is by highlighting the table or view shown in the Control Center and selecting the *Sample Contents* action from either the *Tables* menu or the *Views* menu when that menu is made available. Figure 10-9 shows the Control Center menu items that must be selected in order to view the information stored in a table quickly (in this case, the system catalog table SYSIBM.SYSTA-BLES). Figure 10-10 shows how the Sample Contents dialog (which is activated by the Control Center) might look after it has been populated with data that has been retrieved from the table specified (again, in this example, the system catalog table SYSIBM.SYSTABLES).

Reverse-Engineering a Database with DB2LOOK

DB2 Universal Database provides a special tool named DB2LOOK that can be used to generate the DDL SQL statements needed to re-create existing objects in a given database. In addition to generating DDL statements, DB2LOOK can also collect statistical information that has been generated for objects in a database from the system catalog tables and save it (in readable format) in an external file. In fact, by using DB2LOOK, it is possible to create a clone of an existing database that contains both its data objects and current statistical information about each of those objects.

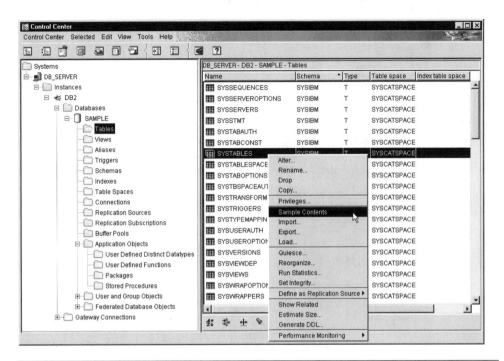

Figure 10-9   Viewing the contents of a table from the Control Center

Figure 10-10   Sample Contents dialog

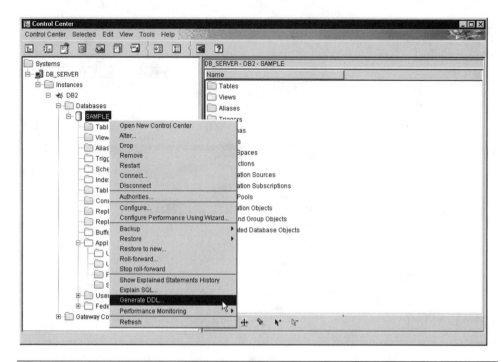

Figure 10-11 Invoking the Generate DDL dialog from the Control Center

The easiest way to use DB2LOOK is by selecting the *Generate DDL* action from the *Database* menu found in the Control Center. Figure 10-11 shows the Control Center menu items that must be selected in order to display the Generate DDL dialog (which in turn invokes the DB2LOOK tool). Figure 10-12 shows how the Generate DDL dialog (which is activated by the Control Center) might look after its input fields have been populated.

DB2LOOK can also be invoked by executing the DB2LOOK system command from the system command prompt. The syntax for this command is the following:

```
DB2LOOK -d [DatabaseAlias] <-u [Creator]> <-s> <-g> <-a> <-h> <-r>
<-c> <-p> <-o [OutputFileName]> <-e <-t [TableName]>> <-m <-t
[TableName]>> <-l> <-x> <-i [AuthorizationID]> <-w [Password]> <-f>
```

where:

DatabaseAlias   Identifies the alias name that has been assigned to the database whose system catalog tables will be queried.

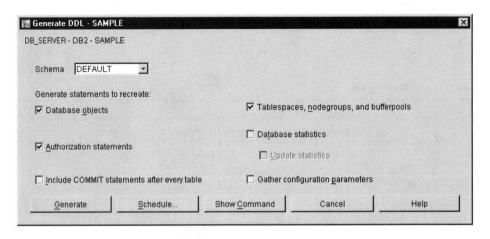

Figure 10-12   Generate DDL dialog

Creator	Identifies the creator ID that will be used as criteria when obtaining information from the system catalog tables; if used, only information about objects that were created by the creator ID specified will be obtained.
OutputFileName	Identifies the location and name of the external file that all information collected will be written to.
TableName	Identifies a specific table that information will be obtained for.
AuthorizationID	Identifies the authorization ID of the user that a database connection will be established for (if the alias for a remote database is specified in the *DatabaseAlias* parameter).
Password	Identifies the password (that corresponds to the authorization ID specified) of the user that a database connection will be established for (if the alias for a remote database is specified in the *DatabaseAlias* parameter).

The options shown with this command are described in Table 10-3.

For example, when executed, the system command

```
DB2LOOK -d SAMPLE -a -e -m -o SAMPLE.DDL
```

will create a file named SAMPLE.DDL that contains the DDL statements needed to re-create all tables and indexes found in the SAMPLE database, along with the UPDATE SQL statements needed to update the system catalog tables with information that is

Table 10-3   Options Recognized by the DB2LOOK System Command

DB2LOOK System Command Option	Description
-d	Indicates that the alias name that has been assigned to the database whose system catalog tables will be queried is specified in the *DatabaseAlias* parameter.
-u	Indicates that the creator ID that will be used as criteria when obtaining information from the system catalog tables is specified in the *Creator* parameter.
-s	Indicates that the output file produced will be in PostScript format.
-g	Indicates that a graph will be used to show fetch page pairs for indices.
-a	Indicates that information about all objects (regardless of who they were created by) will be collected.
-h	Indicates that help information for the DB2LOOK system command will be displayed.
-r	Indicates that the RUNSTATS utility will NOT be invoked when the -m option is specified. By default, the RUNSTATS utility is always invoked when the -m option is specified.
-c	Indicates that CONNECT, COMMIT, and CONNECT RESET statements will not be generated when the -m option is specified. By default, these statements are included in the output file produced when the -m option is specified.
-p	Indicates that the output file produced will be in plain text format.
-o	Indicates that the location and name of the external file that all information collected will be written to is specified in the *OutputFileName* parameter.
-e	Indicates that DDL statements will be extracted for the appropriate objects and written to the output file produced.
-t	Indicates that the DDL statements and/or statistics information to be collected will be limited to the table specified in the *TableName* parameter.
-m	Indicates that the UPDATE statements needed to replicate the statistics on tables, columns, and indexes will be generated and included in the output file produced. When the -m option is specified, the -p, -g, and -s options are ignored.
-l	Indicates that DDL statements will be generated for user-defined table spaces, nodegroups, and buffer pools and written to the output file produced.
-x	Indicates that authorization statements (such as GRANT and REVOKE) will be generated and written to the output file produced.

DB2LOOK System Command Option	Description
-i	Indicates that the authorization ID of the user that a database connection will be established for is specified in the *AuthorizationID* parameter.
-w	Indicates that the password that corresponds to the authorization ID specified in the *AuthorizationID* parameter is specified in the *Password* parameter.
-f	Indicates that database configuration parameter values and registry variable values will be collected and written to the output file produced.

needed in order to duplicate the statistical information that was collected from the SAMPLE database.

Expanding a Database's Boundaries with Federated Systems

When DB2 Universal Database, Version 7.1 was released, a new concept known as *federated systems*, along with a set of SQL statements designed to support this new concept, was introduced. A federated system provides a way for the DB2 Database Manager to interact with data stored in tables that are managed by other relational database management systems (RDBMSs). For example, using a federated system, you could perform a join operation between a DB2 Universal Database base table and an Oracle view.

So just what is a federated system? A federated system is a computing system that consists of the following:

- A DB2 Universal Database server (otherwise referred to as a federated server).

- One or more semiautonomous data sources that the federated server can forward SQL operations to. Each data source consists of an instance of an RDBMS, along with the database or databases that the instance supports. Supported RDBMSs include DB2 Universal Database, members of the DB2 Family (such as DB2 for OS/390 and DB2 for AS/400), and Oracle.

To end users and client applications, data sources in a federated system appear as a single collective database. In reality, users and applications actually interact with a database called a *federated database*, which contains catalog entries that identify data sources and their characteristics. Specifically, federated database catalog entries contain information such as what a data source object is called, what information it contains, and information about the conditions under which the data source can be used. The actual RDBMSs being referenced, modules used to communicate with the data source, and DBMS data objects (such as tables) that will be accessed reside outside of the federated database system.

Federated systems consist of three distinct objects, which can be created by accessing the appropriate menu item from the Control Center or by executing the appropriate DDL SQL statements from the Command Center, the Command Line Processor, or an application program. These objects are as follows:

- **Wrappers**   Identify the modules (.DLL, library, and so on) that will be used to access particular data sources.

- **Servers**   Identify the server that the data source is managed by. Server data includes a wrapper name, a server name, the server type, the server version, authorization information, and any server options desired.

- **Nicknames**   Identify specific data source objects such as tables, aliases, views, and so on. Users and applications reference nicknames in SQL statements just as they reference base tables and views.

In addition to these required objects, the following additional objects may or may not need to be created, depending upon your specific needs:

- **User mappings**   Identify how DB2 Universal Database authentication information will be customized for a specific data source.

- **Data type mappings**   Identify how data source-specific data types will be mapped to DB2 Universal Database data types.

- **Function mappings**   Identify how data source-specific functions will be mapped to DB2 Universal Database's built-in functions.

- **Index specifications**   Identify how a data source-specific index looks so the DB2 Optimizer can take advantage of it to improve performance.

Once objects for a federated system have been created, the data stored in the data sources the federated system objects reference can be accessed as though it were stored in one large DB2 Universal Database database. To retrieve data from a federated data source, users/applications connect to the federated database just as they would connect to any other database and submit queries that have been written using DB2 Universal Database SQL (that reference tables and views in the data source by the nicknames that they were assigned). The DB2 Database Manager then optimizes and distributes the queries to the appropriate data sources for processing, collects the data requested as it is returned from the data source, and returns it to the requestor. During this process, DB2 does not monopolize or restrict access to the data source itself, other than to enforce locking and integrity constraints. In other words, DB2 queries that contain references to Oracle objects, for example, can be submitted while Oracle applications are accessing the same objects. Applications can use DB2 SQL to retrieve values from any data source column that has a DB2-supported data type with one exception—binary large object (BLOB), character large object (CLOB), and double-byte character large object (DBCLOB) data types are not supported.

To send data values to a federated data source (that is to perform insert, update, and/or delete operations on a data source table), users/applications connect to the federated database just as they would connect to any other database and submit queries that have been written using the data source's SQL dialect—not DB2 Universal Database's SQL dialect—in a special mode called *pass-through* mode. In a pass-through mode session, an SQL statement is sent to the data source for processing if it is dynamically prepared and executed during the session through the execution of either (1) an EXECUTE IMMEDIATE statement or (2) a PREPARE statement followed by an EXECUTE statement. (Pass-through mode can also be used to submit queries to a data source in that data source's SQL dialect.)

Summary

The goal of this chapter was to introduce you to the objects that can be used to control data access and provide you with an in-depth understanding of the constraints that can be used to ensure that data integrity is maintained as data is manipulated. This chapter was also designed to provide you with information about the system catalog and introduce you to some of the tools that are provided by DB2 Universal Database for accessing data and duplicating data objects.

The heart of all data storage and access in a DB2 Universal Database database is the table data object. Tables are logical structures that are used to present data as a collection of unordered rows with a fixed number of columns. Each column contains a set of values of the same data type or one of its subtypes—the definition of the columns in a table make up the table structure, and the rows contain the actual table data. The storage representation of a row is called a record, and the storage representation of a column is called a field. At each intersection of a row and column in a database table, there is a specific data item called a value.

One of the nice things about a relational database is that even when users are sharing the same data, each user can see the data in a different way. Some users can work directly with the base tables that make up a database, whereas other users may only be allowed to work with views, which act as virtual tables that have been derived in some way from one or more base tables. Views often aid application development because they can be used to provide a valuable degree of control over who is given access to data.

A view is essentially a named specification of a result table that is produced whenever the view is referenced in an SQL statement. For this reason, a view can be thought of as having columns and rows, just like a base table, and in most cases, data can be retrieved from a view just as it can be retrieved from a base table. However, whether or not a view can be used to add, update, or delete data depends on how it was defined. Although a view looks like a base table, it does not exist as a table in physical storage; therefore, it does not contain data. Instead, a view refers to data stored in other base tables (a view may refer to another view, but ultimately the reference will be resolved to data stored in one or more base tables).

Based on their definition, some views are classified as read-only, whereas others views are classified as insertable, updatable, or deletable. Read-only views can only be queried, but insertable, updatable, and deletable views can be both queried and used in insert, update, and delete operations. In general, a view is updatable if each row in the view can be uniquely mapped to a single row of data in one base table.

Views that are created with the WITH CHECK OPTION clause specified can impose restrictions on insert, update, and delete operations that are performed against them. Such views are called symmetric views because everything that can be inserted into them can also be retrieved from them. The WITH CHECK OPTION clause has two forms: cascaded and local. The difference between these two forms is only meaningful when one view is created on top of another one. In this case, if the topmost view is created with the local form of the WITH CHECK OPTION clause specified, insert and update operations performed on the topmost view must satisfy the definitions of the topmost view and all of the underlying views that also have check options specified (however, they do not have to satisfy the definitions of underlying views that do not have a check option). On the other hand, if the topmost view is created with the cascaded form of the WITH CHECK OPTION clause specified, insert and update operations performed on the topmost view must satisfy the definitions of the topmost view and all of the underlying views, regardless of whether or not the underlying views have a check option.

An index is an object that contains an ordered set of pointers that refer to a key (one or more columns) in a base table. When indexes are used, the DB2 Database Manager can access data directly and more efficiently because the index provides a direct path to the data through pointers that have been ordered based on the values of the columns that the index(es) is associated with. In many cases, restrictions on insert, update, and delete operations performed against base tables (and views derived from base tables) are imposed through one or more constraints. Most constraints are defined as part of the table creation process; however, the constraints that relate specifically to data access are tied closer to indexes than to the tables the indexes are based on.

By default, indexes are only scanned in the forward direction. To allow an index to directly obtain rows in sequence in both forward and reverse directions, the ALLOW REVERSE SCANS option of the CREATE INDEX statement must be specified when the index is created.

A key is a single column or a set of columns in a table or index that can be used to identify and/or access a specific row of data. Any column can be part of a key and the same column can be part of more than one key. A key that consists of a single column is called an atomic key; a key that is composed of more than one column is called a composite key. In addition to having atomic or composite attributes, keys are classified according to how they are used to implement constraints:

- A unique key is used to implement unique constraints.

- A primary key is used to implement entity integrity constraints. (A primary key is a special type of unique key that does not support null values.)

- A foreign key is used to implement referential integrity constraints. (Foreign keys must reference primary keys or unique keys; foreign keys do not have corresponding indexes.)

Keys are normally specified during the declaration of a table, an index, or a referential constraint definition.

Within most businesses, data often must adhere to certain restrictions or rules. Such restrictions may apply to single pieces of information such as which format and sequence to use for purchase order numbers, or they may apply to several pieces of information such as which employees are members of which departments and which employees manage those departments. Constraints are DB2 Universal Database's way of enforcing such rules within the confines of the database system. Essentially, constraints are rules that govern or influence the way in which data values can be added and/or modified. Although constraints are only associated with base table objects, they are often enforced through the use of one or more unique or primary key indexes.

Unique indexes are indexes that help maintain data integrity by ensuring that no two rows of data in a base table have identical key values. (When attempting to create a unique index for a table that already contains data, values in the column(s) that comprise the index are checked for uniqueness—if the table contains rows with duplicate key values, the index creation process fails.) Once a unique index has been defined for a table, uniqueness is enforced during insert and update operations. In addition to enforcing the uniqueness of data values, a unique index can also be used to improve data retrieval performance during query processing.

Nonunique indexes, on the other hand, are not used to enforce constraints on the base tables they are associated with. Instead, nonunique indexes are used solely to improve query performance by maintaining a sorted order of data values that are used frequently.

It is important to understand that there is a significant difference between a primary/unique key constraint and a unique index. DB2 Universal Database uses a combination of a unique index and the NOT NULL constraint to implement the relational database concept of primary and unique key constraints. Therefore, unique indexes do not enforce primary key constraints by themselves because they allow null values.

When creating an index, it is important to keep in mind that indexes are never used directly by an application or a user. Instead, the decision of whether or not to use an index, and which index to use, is made by the DB2 Optimizer when Data Manipulation Language (DML) SQL statements are processed. The DB2 Optimizer bases its decision on statistical information such as the number of rows in a table, the indexes that exist for a table, and the overall size of a table. However, you can help control how well (or how poorly) the DB2 Optimizer works in two ways. The first is to make sure that the statistical information used by the DB2 is kept up-to-date. This is accomplished by running the RUNSTATS utility on a regular basis. The second way to control how the DB2 Optimizer works is by controlling the optimization level that is used when optimization is performed. The optimization level to be used is specified by executing the SET CURRENT QUERY OPTIMIZATION SQL statement, either from the Command Center or from the Command Line Processor. Generally, higher optimization class levels require more memory and time when optimization is performed, potentially resulting in better overall performance when the optimized statement is executed.

A referential constraint (also known as a foreign key constraint) is used to define a required relationship between and within base tables—a referential constraint guarantees that table relationships are maintained and that data entry rules are always followed. As long as a referential constraint is in effect, the DB2 Database Manager guarantees that for each row in a child table that has a non-null value in its foreign key columns, there is a row in a corresponding parent table that has a matching value in its parent key.

A set of rules that are used to maintain referential integrity is associated with every referential constraint defined. This set of rules consists of the following:

- An insert rule

- An update rule

- A delete rule

The insert rule of a referential constraint ensures that non-null values are only inserted into the columns that make up a foreign key in a child table if a parent key containing the same values exists in the parent table. The update rule of a referential constraint controls how referential integrity checks will be performed when the values of the columns that make up a foreign key in a child table or the values of the columns that make up a parent key in a parent table are changed. The delete rule of a referential constraint controls how referential integrity checks will be performed and, in some cases, how integrity violations will be resolved when a row is deleted from a parent table. More precisely, the delete rule controls what happens when a row of the parent table is the object of a delete or propagated delete operation and when the row has dependents in the dependent table of the referential constraint.

Whenever data is added to a base table (by an insert operation), a special insert search algorithm is used to find an appropriate physical location to store the data. The behavior of the search algorithm is altered somewhat if a special type of index known as a clustering index is defined for the base table. When an insert operation is performed against a table and a clustering index exists for that table, the DB2 Database Manager attempts to store records on the same page that other records with similar index key values are stored on. If no space is available on that page, the DB2 Database Manager tries to put the record into one of the surrounding pages. If it is still not successful, it stores the record on a new page and preallocates enough space on that page to hold additional clustered records. Clustering indexes can improve the performance of most query operations because they provide a more linear access path to data (which has been stored in pages). In addition, because rows with similar index key values are stored together, prefetching is usually more efficient when clustering indexes are used.

When a database is created, a special set of tables known as the system catalog tables is constructed and initialized as part of the database creation process. These tables contain information about the definitions of all database objects (for example, tables, views, indexes, and packages), as well as information about the type of security access that users have to the database objects available. The system catalog tables are automatically updated during normal operation in response to SQL Data Definition Language (DDL) statements, environment routines, and certain utilities. You cannot explicitly create, drop, or modify the information stored in these tables; however, you can query and view their content.

In addition to the system catalog tables, the following database objects are also defined and stored in the system catalog as part of the database creation process:

- A set of user-defined functions (UDFs), which are created in the SYSFUN schema.

- A set of read-only views for the system catalog tables, which are created in the SYSCAT schema.

- A set of updatable views for the system catalog tables, which are created in the SYS-STAT schema. These updatable views enable you to update statistical information about a table without using the RUNSTATS utility.

A description of each system catalog view available, including column names and data types, can be found in Appendix A.

One of the tools provided with DB2 Universal Database that can be used to examine the contents of a system catalog table or view (or for that matter, any table or view) is the Script Center. The Script Center enables you to write scripts that consist of one or more DB2 commands, system commands, and/or SQL statements, which can then be executed immediately or scheduled to run unattended at a later date or at a regular interval. With the Script Center, you can also do the following:

- Import a script that was created outside the Script Center or that was saved in the Command Center.

- Edit a saved command script. (When a saved script is modified, all jobs dependent on the saved script inherit the new modified behavior.)

- View information about all command scripts that are known to the system.

- Copy or edit existing scripts to create new scripts.

- Remove saved scripts that are no longer needed.

Scripts can be composed and edited inside the Script Center, or they can be created using an editor of your choice and imported into the Script Center for scheduling or immediate execution.

DB2 Universal Database provides a special tool named DB2LOOK that can be used to generate the DDL SQL statements needed to re-create existing objects in a given database. In addition to generating DDL statements, DB2LOOK can also collect statistical information that has been generated for objects in a database from the system catalog tables and save it (in readable format) in an external file. In fact, by using DB2LOOK, it is possible to create a clone of an existing database that contains both its data objects and current statistical information about each of those objects. DB2LOOK can be invoked by selecting the *Generate DDL* action from the *Database* menu found in the

Control Center or by executing the DB2LOOK system command from the system command prompt.

When DB2 Universal Database, Version 7.1 was released, a new concept known as federated systems, along with a set of SQL statements designed to support this new concept, was introduced. A federated system provides a way for the DB2 Database Manager to interact with data stored in tables that are managed by other relational database management systems (RDBMSs). For example, using a federated system, you could perform a join operation between a DB2 Universal Database base table and an Oracle view.

Specifically, a federated system is a computing system that consists of the following:

- A DB2 Universal Database server (otherwise referred to as a federated server).

- One or more semiautonomous data sources that the federated server can forward SQL operations to. Each data source consists of an instance of an RDBMS, along with the database or databases that the instance supports. Supported RDBMSs include DB2 Universal Database, members of the DB2 Family (such as DB2 for OS/390 and DB2 for AS/400), and Oracle.

To end users and client applications, data sources in a federated system appear as a single collective database. In reality, users and applications actually interface with a database called a federated database, which contains catalog entries that identify data sources and their characteristics.

Federated systems consist of three distinct objects, which can be created by accessing the appropriate menu item from the Control Center or by executing the appropriate DDL SQL statements from the Command Center, the Command Line Processor, or an application program. These objects include the following:

- Wrappers
- Servers
- Nicknames

In addition to these required objects, the following additional objects may or may not need to be created, depending upon your specific needs:

- User mappings
- Data type mappings
- Function mappings
- Index specifications

PART III

Once objects for a federated system have been created, the data stored in the data sources the federated system objects reference can be accessed as though it were stored in one large DB2 Universal Database database. To retrieve data from a federated data source, users/applications connect to the federated database just as they would connect to any other database and submit queries that have been written using DB2 Universal Database SQL (that reference tables and views in the data source by the nicknames that they were assigned). To send data values to a federated data source (that is, to perform insert, update, and/or delete operations on a data source table), users/applications connect to the federated database just as they would connect to any other database and submit queries that have been written using the data source's SQL dialect—not DB2 Universal Database's SQL dialect—in a special mode called pass-through mode.

Questions

1. Which of the following will occur when a view is created on a table?
    a. Memory usage is reduced.
    b. Data access time is increased.
    c. Data access control is increased.
    d. Query compilation time is reduced.

2. In which of the following are definitions of tables stored in a DB2 Universal Database database?
    a. The system catalogs
    b. The DB2DIAG.LOG file
    c. The recovery history file
    d. The database configuration file

3. Given the following:

```
CREATE TABLE TAB1 (COL1  INT  CONSTRAINT NOT NUL CHECK(COL1 IS NOT NULL),
                   COL2  CHAR(10))
```

Which of the following will enforce uniqueness of COL1, which currently does not contain duplicate values?
    a. Create a primary key on COL1.
    b. Create a unique index on COL1.
    c. Create a cluster index on COL1.
    d. Create a unique constraint on COL1.

4. Which of the following enables tables in heterogeneous databases to be joined?

   a. The join columns in the two tables must have the exact same data type.

   b. The user or database administrator may have to override some mappings of data types from one database before the join can be successful.

   c. The DB2 Database Manager will automatically map all data types in each database to the same data type.

   d. The join operation must be an inner join or a full outer join.

5. Given the following statements:

```
CREATE TABLE ID.PC (SERIAL_NUM   INT  NOT NULL PRIMARY KEY,
                    MODEL_NUM    INT  NOT NULL,
                    OWNER_ID     INT,
                    FOREIGN KEY (OWNER_ID) REFERENCES ID.EMPLOYEES
                        ON DELETE CASCADE)

CREATE TABLE ID.EMPLOYEES (EMPLOYEE_NUM   INT  NOT NULL PRIMARY KEY,
                           EMPLOYEE_NAME  CHAR(20))

DELETE FROM ID.EMPLOYEES WHERE EMPLOYEE_NUM = 12345
```

   Which of the following occurs to data stored in the table ID.PC?

   a. OWNER_ID is not null for all rows where OWNER_ID was 12345.

   b. OWNER_ID is null for all rows where OWNER_ID was 12345.

   c. All rows where OWNER_ID was 12345 are deleted.

   d. All rows where OWNER_ID was 12345 are copied to an exception table.

6. Which of the following occurs when a view is created on a base table?

   a. View columns may inherit any NOT NULL WITH DEFAULT attributes from the base table.

   b. Memory usage is reduced and access time is increased.

   c. Query compilation time is reduced when applications use the view instead of the table.

   d. The creator of the view always receives the CONTROL privilege on the view.

7. Which of the following tools does not allow users to schedule batch table update operations?

   a. Command Center

   b. Script Center

   c. Journal

   d. Control Center

8. Given the following DDL statements:

```
CREATE TABLE ID.PC (SERIAL_NUM   INT  NOT NULL PRIMARY KEY,
                    MODEL_NUM    INT  NOT NULL,
                    OWNER_ID     INT)

CREATE TABLE ID.EMPLOYEES (EMPLOYEE_NUM   INT  NOT NULL PRIMARY KEY,
                           EMPLOYEE_NAME  CHAR(20))
```

and the query:

```
SELECT EMPLOYEE_NAME, SERIAL_NUM
FROM ID.EMPLOYEES, ID.PC
WHERE OWNER_ID = EMPLOYEE_NUM
```

Creating an index on which of the following will cause the query to run faster (assuming the query is executed after the ID.PC and ID.EMPLOYEES tables have been populated)?

a. EMPLOYEE_NUM

b. EMPLOYEE_NAME

c. OWNER_ID

d. SERIAL_NUM

9. Which of the following tools allows you to view the contents of a table?

a. Control Center

b. Script Center

c. Visual Explain

d. Journal

10. Given the following table definitions:

```
Table: TEST_TAKEN
TEST_NAME     CHAR(50)  NOT NULL
TEST_NUMBER   INT       NOT NULL
TEST_SCORE    INT       NOT NULL
CANDIDATE_ID  INT       NOT NULL

Table: CANDIDATE
CANDIDATE_ID       INT        NOT NULL
CANDIDATE_NAME     CHAR(50)   NOT NULL
ADDRESS            CHAR(100)  NOT NULL
PHONE              CHAR(14)
```

and the following requirements:

- Candidate IDs can only be assigned once.

- A query that returns all names and addresses of individuals who have taken a test is needed.

Which of the following indexes should be created so that the optimizer will perform an index scan, reading a minimum number of physical pages, when executing the query shown?

  a. A unique clustered index on CANDIDATE_NAME (TEST_TAKEN)

  b. A unique clustered index on CANDIDATE_ID, CANDIDATE_NAME (CANDIDATE)

  c. A primary key on CANDIDATE_ID (CANDIDATE)

  d. A unique index on CANDIDATE_ID, CANDIDATE_NAME (CANDIDATE)

  e. A unique index on CANDIDATE_ID, TEST_NUMBER (TEST_TAKEN)

11. Which of the following can NOT be performed by the Script Center?

  a. Create a script.

  b. Delete a script.

  c. Explain a script.

  d. Schedule a script.

  e. Execute a script.

12. How can you tell if a check constraint was validated after a load operation was performed against a table?

  a. Locate the record for the table in the SYSCAT.TABLES system catalog view and look for the value N in the STATUS column.

  b. Locate the record for the table in the SYSCAT.TABLES system catalog view and look for the value C in the STATUS column.

  c. Locate the record for the table in the SYSCAT.TABCONST system catalog view and look for the value N in the STATUS column.

  d. Locate the record for the table in the SYSCAT.TABCONST system catalog view and look for the value C in the STATUS column.

13. Which of the following cannot be obtained by DB2LOOK?

  a. DDL statements

  b. Statistical information

  c. Database Manager configuration parameter values

  d. Database configuration parameter values

  e. Registry value

14. Which of the following can be used to control optimization for DB2 CLI applications?
    a. An environment variable
    b. The SET CURRENT QUERY OPTIMIZATION statement
    c. The system catalog
    d. A database configuration parameter

15. Which of the following delete rules will allow a row to be deleted from the parent table if a row with a corresponding key value still exists in the child table?
    a. DELETE
    b. RESTRICT
    c. CASCADE
    d. SET NULL

16. Which of the following when used in a view definition does not cause the view to be read-only?
    a. A column function
    b. A DISTINCT clause
    c. A join
    d. An INTERSECT clause
    e. A UNION ALL clause

Answers

1. **C.** Because each view has its own set of privileges, data access control is increased when a view is created; views provide a valuable degree of control over who is given access to data and who is not.

2. **A.** Definitions of all objects in a database are stored in the system catalog tables.

3. **B.** Unique indexes help maintain data integrity by ensuring that no two rows of data in a base table have identical key values. Remember that DB2 Universal Database uses a combination of a unique index and the NOT NULL constraint to implement the relational database concept of primary keys.

4. **B.** In a federated system (which allows tables in heterogeneous databases to be joined), data type mappings are used to identify how data source-specific data types will be mapped to DB2 Universal Database data types. When performing a join operation in a federated system, one or more data type mappings may be required.

5. **C.** Because the referential constraint between the ID.PC table and the ID.EMPLOYEES table was defined with the ON DELETE CASCADE rule specified, when rows with EMPLOYEE_NUM = 12345 are deleted from the ID.EMPLOYEE table, the delete operation is duplicated in the ID.PC table.

6. **A.** When a column of a view is derived from a column of a base table, that column inherits all characteristics (such as the data type and whether or not the column is nullable) from the column of the underlying base table.

7. **D.** A script that performs batch table update operations can be (1) generated and scheduled from the Command Center, (2) generated and scheduled from the Script Center, (3) generated from the Command Center and scheduled from the Journal, (4) generated from the Script Center and scheduled from the Journal, or (5) generated from any editor and scheduled from the Journal.

8. **C.** Because SERIAL_NUM and EMPLOYEE_NUM are primary keys for the ID.PC and ID.EMPLOYEES tables, respectively, unique indexes have already been created for these two columns. In addition, because OWNER_ID is used to join the two tables and no index currently exists for this column, creating a nonunique index for OWNER_ID will cause the query to run faster.

9. **A.** Although queries containing one or more SELECT SQL statements can be used to retrieve the contents of any table that a user has SELECT privileges on, an alternate way to quickly view the contents of a table or view is by highlighting that table or a view in the Control Center and selecting the *Sample Contents* action from either the *Tables* menu or the *Views* menu when that menu is made available.

10. **B.** When a clustering index exists for a table, the DB2 Database Manager attempts to store records on the same page that other records with similar index key values are stored on, which often reduces the number of physical pages that need to be read in order to satisfy a query. In this example, because CANDIDATE_ID is used to join the two tables and because CANDIDATE_NAME is part of the information needed to satisfy the query, a clustering index on these two columns will cause the DB2 Optimizer to perform an index scan—and fewer physical pages will need to be read.

11. **C.** The Script Center cannot be used to generate Explain information for a script. (The Visual Explain tool, which is activated from the Command Center, can generate Explain information for individual SQL statements that might be included in a script.)

PART III

12. **A.** Appendix A would have helped you here. A table can be left in "Check Pending" state following a load operation (which is covered in more detail in Chapter 12) if one or more check constraints or referential integrity constraints defined for it could not be validated. If the STATUS column of the entry for the loaded table in the SYSCAT.TABLES system catalog table contains the value N (indicating the table is in a "Normal" state), all constraints on the table were validated. If the STATUS column contains the value C, the opposite is true.

13. **C.** Because DB2LOOK obtains information about a specific database and not about the instance that a database exists under, it does not obtain information about the DB2 Database Manager configuration. All of the other information shown can be obtained by executing the DB2LOOK system command with the -e, -m, and -f options specified.

14. **B.** If a clustering index is not used, the optimization level used to generate access plans for applications is specified by executing the SET CURRENT QUERY OPTIMIZATION SQL statement, either from the Command Center or from the Command Line Processor.

15. **D.** If the ON DELETE SET NULL rule is used with a referential constraint, rows can be deleted from the parent table if a row with a corresponding key value still exists in the child table. The corresponding key values in the child table will be replaced with nulls.

16. **E.** Views defined using the UNION ALL clause can be used in update and delete operations provided their corresponding columns have the exact same data types —including lengths and default values.

Monitoring Database Activity

In this chapter, you will learn

- How to use the snapshot monitor
- How to create and control one or more event monitors
- How to analyze event monitor output
- How to use the Performance Monitor
- How to collect, view, and analyze Explain information
- How to obtain and modify DB2 Database Manager configuration information
- How to obtain and modify configuration information for a specific database

The fourth objective of the DB2 Universal Database—Database Administration for UNIX, Windows, and OS/2 exam is to evaluate your understanding of database monitoring and test your knowledge of the various monitoring tools that are provided with DB2 Universal Database. From a certification viewpoint, knowing what monitoring tools are available is just as important as knowing how to use the information provided by those tools to determine how well (or how poorly) a DB2 Database Manager instance and/or one or more of the databases under its control are performing.

This chapter is designed to introduce you to the tools that come with DB2 Universal Database that are used to monitor the events that take place in a database system. This chapter is also designed to introduce you to the tool that can be used to analyze Structured Query Language (SQL) operations to locate weaknesses in an application or database design that results in poor performance.

TIP Sixteen percent of the DB2 Universal Database—Database Administration for UNIX, Windows, and OS/2 exam is designed to test your knowledge of database and performance monitoring.

The Database System Monitor

Along with tools like the Control Center and the Command Line Processor, DB2 Universal Database provides a powerful tool known as the Database System Monitor that can acquire information about the current state of a database system or about the state of a database system over a specified period of time. Once collected, this information can be used to do the following:

- Monitor database activity.
- Assist in problem determination.
- Analyze database system performance.
- Aid in configuring/tuning the database system.

Although the Database System Monitor is often referred to as a single monitor, in reality it consists of several individual monitors that have distinct, but related purposes. One of these individual monitors is known as the *snapshot monitor;* the rest are known as *event monitors.* Both types of monitors can be controlled using commands, administrative application programming interface (API) functions, and/or interfaces that are available with the Control Center.

The Snapshot Monitor

The snapshot monitor is designed to provide information about the state of a DB2 Universal Database instance and the data it controls, and call attention to situations that appear to be peculiar, irregular, abnormal, or difficult to classify. This information is provided in the form of a series of snapshots, each of which represents what the system looks like at a specific point in time. Table 11-1 shows the various types of information that can be obtained by the snapshot monitor.

Table 11-1   Information Obtained by the Snapshot Monitor

Item	Information Type
State	
The current status of the database	Value
The current number of connections to a database	Value
Information about the current or most recent transaction [unit of work (UOW)]	Timestamp
Run-time values for configurable system parameters	Value
The current status of an application	Value
A list of locks being held by an application	Value
Information about the most recent SQL statement executed by an application	Timestamp
Anomalous Situations	
The number of deadlocks that have occurred from the time monitoring started until the time the snapshot is taken	Count
The number of transactions processed by a database from the time monitoring started until the time the snapshot is taken	Count
The total amount of time an application has waited on locks (from the time monitoring started until the time the snapshot is taken)	Count

> **NOTE**   Only users with System Administrator (SYSADM) authority, System Control (SYSCTRL) authority, or System Maintenance (SYSMAINT) authority are allowed to use the snapshot monitor.

Snapshot Monitor Switches

Obtaining some of the data collected by the snapshot monitor requires additional processing overhead. For example, in order to calculate the execution time of an SQL statement, the DB2 Database Manager must make a call to the operating system to obtain timestamps before and after the statement is executed. Such system calls are generally expensive. Fortunately, the snapshot monitor provides system administrators with a great deal of flexibility in choosing what information is collected when a snapshot is

Table 11-2 Snapshot Monitor Switches

Monitor Group	Monitor Switch Name (DB2 Database Manager Configuration Parameter)	Information Provided
Buffer pools	BUFFERPOOL (*dft_mon_bufferpool*)	Amount of buffer pool activity (that is, number of read and write operations performed and the amount of time taken for each read/write operation)
Locks	LOCK (*dft_mon_lock*)	Number of locks held and number of deadlock cycles encountered
Sorts	SORT (*dft_mon_sort*)	Number of heaps used, overflows encountered, and sort operations performed
SQL statements	STATEMENT (*dft_mon_stmt*)	Statement processing start time, statement processing end time, and statement ID
Tables	TABLE (*dft_mon_table*)	Amount of table activity performed (that is, number of rows read and number of rows written)
Transactions (UOWs)	UOW (*dft_mon_uow*)	Transaction start times, transaction completion times, and transaction completion status

taken—the type and amount of information returned (and the amount of overhead required) when a snapshot is taken is determined by the way one or more snapshot monitor switches have been set. Table 11-2 shows the snapshot monitor switches available, along with a description of the information collected when each one is turned on.

As you can see from the information shown in Table 11-2, each snapshot monitor switch available has a corresponding parameter value in the DB2 Database Manager configuration file. In a few moments, we will look at the difference between setting a snapshot monitor switch and setting that monitor switch's corresponding DB2 Database Manager configuration parameter.

Examining the Current State of the Snapshot Monitor Switches Before a snapshot is taken, one or more snapshot monitor switches must be turned on (if all snapshot monitor switches available are turned off, only very basic snapshot monitor information will be collected). But before a particular snapshot monitor switch is turned on, it's a good idea to examine the current state of snapshot monitor switches available.

The easiest way to examine the current state of the snapshot monitor switches available is by executing the GET MONITOR SWITCHES command, either from the Command Center or from the Command Line Processor. The syntax for this command is

```
GET MONITOR SWITCHES <AT NODE [NodeNumber] | GLOBAL>
```

where:

> *NodeNumber* Identifies a specific node in a partitioned database system that the status of snapshot monitor switches will be obtained and displayed for.

For example, when executed, the following GET MONITOR SWITCHES command

```
GET MONITOR SWITCHES
```

will produce the following output (for a single-partition database) if no snapshot monitor switches have been turned on:

```
                Monitor Recording Switches

Switch list for node 0
Buffer Pool Activity Information   (BUFFERPOOL) = OFF
Lock Information                         (LOCK) = OFF
Sorting Information                      (SORT) = OFF
SQL Statement Information           (STATEMENT) = OFF
Table Activity Information              (TABLE) = OFF
Unit of Work Information                  (UOW) = OFF
```

On the other hand, the same GET MONITOR SWITCHES statement will produce output similar to the following output if one of the snapshot monitor switches available (in this case, the TABLE snapshot monitor switch) has been turned on:

```
                Monitor Recording Switches

Switch list for node 0
Buffer Pool Activity Information   (BUFFERPOOL) = OFF
Lock Information                         (LOCK) = OFF
Sorting Information                      (SORT) = OFF
SQL Statement Information           (STATEMENT) = OFF
Table Activity Information              (TABLE) = ON  12-01-2001
                                                      10:00:20.097996
Unit of Work Information                  (UOW) = OFF
```

From this output, you can see that the TABLE snapshot monitor switch has been turned on (and that it was turned on December 1, 2001, at 10:00 A.M.).

PART III

Changing the State of a Snapshot Monitor Switch   Once the current state of all snapshot monitor switches is known, you can tell the snapshot monitor to start (or stop) collecting specific snapshot monitor information by changing the state of one or more of the snapshot monitor switches available. The easiest way to change the state of a particular snapshot monitor switch is by executing the UPDATE MONITOR SWITCHES command, either from the Command Center or from the Command Line Processor. The syntax for this command is

```
UPDATE MONITOR SWITCHES USING [[SwitchName] ON | OFF ,...] <AT
NODE [NodeNumber] | GLOBAL>
```

where:

> *SwitchName*   Identifies one or more snapshot monitor switches whose current states are to be changed. This parameter can contain any or all of the following values: BUFFERPOOL, LOCK, SORT, STATEMENT, TABLE, and UOW.

> *NodeNumber*   Identifies a specific node in a partitioned database system where the state of the snapshot monitor switch(es) specified will be changed.

For example, when executed, the following UPDATE MONITOR SWITCHES command

```
UPDATE MONITOR SWITCHES USING TABLE ON
```

will tell the snapshot monitor to begin collecting snapshot information about table activity (for example, the number of rows read, the number of rows written, and so on).

The Difference Between Updating Snapshot Monitor Switches and Updating the DB2 Database Manager Configuration   When the UPDATE MONITOR SWITCHES command is used to turn a snapshot monitor switch on, the snapshot monitor information that is collected is only applicable for the application that activated the switch (for example, the Command Center or the Command Line Processor session in which the UPDATE MONITOR SWITCHES statement is executed). To tell the snapshot monitor to collect information for all applications that access any database within an instance, the parameter value in the DB2 Database Manager configuration file that corresponds to the snapshot monitor switch specified must be updated instead. It's important to note that when the value of one of these configuration parameters is changed, the DB2 Database Manager must be stopped and restarted before the change takes effect. (This is true for most DB2 Database Manager configuration parameters.) On the other hand, when the state of a snapshot monitor switch is changed by executing the UPDATE MONITOR SWITCHES command, the change takes effect immediately.

Capturing Snapshot Information

Once a snapshot monitor switch has been turned on, the snapshot monitor begins collecting appropriate monitor data. To capture and view this data at a specific point in time, a snapshot must be taken. Snapshots can be taken by embedding the appropriate API in an application program or by executing the GET SNAPSHOT command, either from the Command Center or from the Command Line Processor. The syntax for this command is

```
GET SNAPSHOT FOR [DATABASE MANAGER | DB MANAGER | DBM ] <AT NODE
[NodeNumber] | GLOBAL>
```

or

```
GET SNAPSHOT FOR [<ALL DCS> DATABASES | <ALL DCS> APPLICATIONS |
ALL BUFFERPOOLS | ALL REMOTE_DATABASES | ALL REMOTE_APPLICATIONS |
FCM FOR ALL NODES] <AT NODE [NodeNumber] | GLOBAL>
```

or

```
GET SNAPSHOT FOR [<DCS> APPLICATION | LOCKS FOR APPLICATION]
[APPLID [ApplicationID] | AGENTID [ApplicationHandle]] <AT NODE
[NodeNumber] | GLOBAL>
```

or

```
GET SNAPSHOT FOR [ALL | <DCS> [DATABASE | DB] <DCS> APPLICATIONS |
TABLES | TABLESPACES | LOCKS | BUFFERPOOLS | REMOTE_DATABASES |
REMOTE_APPLICATIONS | DYNAMIC SQL <WRITE TO FILE>] ON [Data-
baseAlias] <AT NODE [NodeNumber] | GLOBAL>
```

where:

NodeNumber	Identifies a specific node in a partitioned database system where snapshot information will be collected from.
ApplicationID	Identifies a specific application by ID that snapshot information will be collected for.
ApplicationHandle	Identifies a specific application by handle that snapshot information will be collected for.
DatabaseAlias	Identifies a database, by alias, that snapshot information will be collected for.

For example, when executed, the following GET SNAPSHOT command

```
GET SNAPSHOT FOR BUFFERPOOLS ON SAMPLE
```

will produce output information (for a single-partition database) similar to the following—provided the BUFFERPOOL snapshot monitor switch was turned on before the snapshot was taken:

```
Bufferpool Snapshot

Bufferpool name                                = IBMDEFAULTBP
Database name                                  = SAMPLE
Database path                                  = C:\DB2\NODE0000\
                                                 SQL00001\
Input database alias                           = SAMPLE
Buffer pool data logical reads                 = 63
Buffer pool data physical reads                = 27
Buffer pool data writes                        = 0
Buffer pool index logical reads                = 84
Buffer pool index physical reads               = 44
Total buffer pool read time (ms)               = 36
Total buffer pool write time (ms)              = 0
Asynchronous pool data page reads              = 0
Asynchronous pool data page writes             = 0
Buffer pool index writes                       = 0
Asynchronous pool index page reads             = 0
Asynchronous pool index page writes            = 0
Total elapsed asynchronous read time           = 0
Total elapsed asynchronous write time          = 0
Asynchronous read requests                     = 0
Direct reads                                   = 54
Direct writes                                  = 0
Direct read requests                           = 8
Direct write requests                          = 0
Direct reads elapsed time (ms)                 = 20
Direct write elapsed time (ms)                 = 0
Database files closed                          = 0
Data pages copied to extended storage          = 0
Index pages copied to extended storage         = 0
Data pages copied from extended storage        = 0
Index pages copied from extended storage       = 0
```

Resetting the Snapshot Monitor Counters

As you can see from the example just provided, the output produced by a snapshot contains, among other things, cumulative information about how often a particular activity was performed within some time frame window. This cumulative information is collected and stored in a wide variety of activity counters whose contents are retrieved at the time a snapshot is taken. So when does the counting start exactly? Counting begins

- When a snapshot monitor switch is turned on (or when the DB2 Database Manager is restarted after one or more of its configuration parameters that correspond to a snapshot monitor switch have been turned on)
- Each time the counters are manually reset

To use the snapshot monitor effectively, it is usually desirable to obtain snapshot information after a specific period of time has elapsed. To control the window of time that is monitored, reset the counters to zero when monitoring is to begin and then take a snapshot once the desired period of time has expired.

Although snapshot monitor counters can be set to zero by turning all appropriate snapshot monitor switches off and back on, the easiest way to reset all snapshot monitor counters to zero is by executing the RESET MONITOR command, either from the Command Center or from the Command Line Processor. The syntax for this command is

```
RESET MONITOR ALL <DCS> <AT NODE [NodeNumber] | GLOBAL>
```

or

```
RESET MONITOR FOR <DCS> [DATABASE | DB] [DatabaseAlias] <AT NODE
[NodeNumber] | GLOBAL>
```

where:

NodeNumber Identifies a specific node in a partitioned database system where snapshot monitor counters will be reset to zero.

DatabaseAlias Identifies a database, by alias, that snapshot monitor counters will be zeroed for.

For example, when executed, the following RESET MONITOR command

```
RESET MONITOR FOR DATABASE SAMPLE
```

will reset the counters for all active snapshot monitor switches to zero.

It is important to note that you cannot selectively reset counters for a particular group (controlled by a snapshot monitor switch) by executing the RESET MONITOR command. Instead, if you only want to reset the counters associated with a specific snapshot monitor switch, you must turn that snapshot monitor switch off and back on.

Event Monitors

Unfortunately, some database activities cannot be monitored easily with the snapshot monitor. Take, for example, when a deadlock cycle occurs. In Chapter 7, we saw that if the deadlock detector "awakes" and discovers that a deadlock exists in the locking system, it randomly selects, rolls back, and terminates one of the transactions involved in the deadlock cycle. (The transaction that is rolled back and terminated receives an SQL error code, all locks it had acquired are released, and the remaining transaction(s) are then allowed to proceed.) Information about this series of events cannot be easily captured by the snapshot monitor because in all likelihood, the deadlock cycle will have been broken long before a snapshot can be taken. An event monitor, on the other hand, could be used to capture such information. This is because unlike the snapshot monitor, which is used to record the state of database activity at a specific point in time, an event monitor is used to record database activity as soon as a specific event or transition occurs.

Although event monitors return information that is very similar to the information returned by the snapshot monitor, the event controls when the snapshot is taken. Specifically, event monitors can capture and write system monitor data to a file or a named pipe whenever any of the following events occur:

- A transaction is terminated.
- An SQL statement is executed.
- A deadlock cycle is detected.
- A connection to a database is established.
- A connection to a database is terminated.
- A database is activated.
- A database is deactivated.
- An SQL statement's subsection completes processing (when a database is partitioned).
- The FLUSH EVENT MONITOR SQL statement is executed.

Unlike the snapshot monitor, which resides in the background and is controlled by the settings of the snapshot monitor switches (or corresponding DB2 Database Manager configuration parameter values), event monitors are created using Data Definition Language (DDL) statements. Because of this, event monitors only gather information for the database in which they have been defined; event monitors cannot be used to collect information at the DB2 Database Manager instance level.

When an event monitor is created, the event types that will be monitored must be included as part of the event monitor's definition; a single event monitor can be defined for more than one event type. Table 11-3 shows the event types available, along with a description of what (and when) information is collected for each type.

PART III

Table 11-3 Event Monitor Types

Event Type	When Data Is Collected	Information Provided
Database	When the database is deactivated or when the last application connected to the database disconnects	The values of all database-level counters.
Buffer pools	When the database is deactivated or when the last application connected to the database disconnects	The values of all buffer pool ounters, prefetchers, page cleaners, and direct input/output (I/O) for each buffer pool used.
Tables	When the database is deactivated or when the last application connected to the database disconnects	Number of rows read and number of rows written for each table.
Table spaces	When the database is deactivated or when the last application connected to the database disconnects	The values of all buffer pool counters, prefetchers, page cleaners, and direct I/O for each table space used.
Deadlocks	When a deadlock cycle is detected	The applications involved and the types of locks that are in contention.
Connections	When an application that is connected to the database disconnects	The values of all application-level counters.

(continued)

Table 11-3 Event Monitor Types *(continued)*

Event Type	When Data Is Collected	Information Provided
SQL statements	When an SQL statement (static or dynamic) is processed or when an SQL statement's subsection completes processing (in a partitioned database environment)	Statement start/stop time, amount of CPU consumed, text of dynamic SQL statements, SQL Communications Area (SQLCA) (return code of the SQL statement), and other metrics such as fetch count.
		For partitioned databases, the amount of CPU consumed, execution time, table and table queue information.
Transactions (UOW)	When a transaction is terminated (by a COMMIT or a ROLLBACK statement)	Transaction start/stop time, previous transaction time, amount of CPU consumed, and locking and logging metrics. (Transaction records are not generated if database is using two-phase commit processing and an X/Open XA Interface.)

NOTE   Only users with SYSADM authority, SYSCTRL authority, SYSMAINT authority, or Database Administrator (DBADM) authority are allowed to create and use an event monitor.

Creating an Event Monitor

Now that you know the basic differences between the snapshot monitor and an event monitor and what types of events can be monitored, let's look at how an event monitor is created. The easiest way to create an event monitor is by using the Create Event Monitor dialog, which is invoked by selecting the *Create* action from the *Event monitor* menu found in the Event Monitors GUI tool. [The Event Monitors GUI tool is activated by entering the command db2emcrt at the system command prompt or by selecting the Event Monitors entry from the DB2 folder (non-UNIX platforms only).] Figure 11-1 shows the menu items that must be selected in order to activate the Create Event Monitor dialog. Figure 11-2 shows how the Create Event Monitor dialog might look after its input fields have been populated.

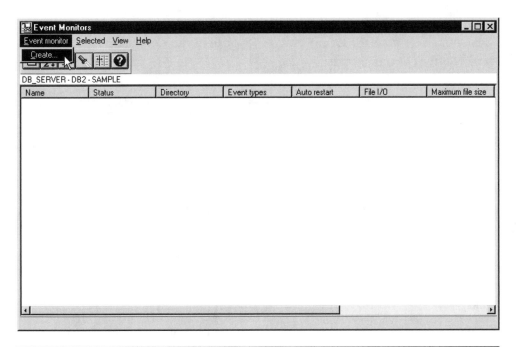

Figure 11-1   Creating an Event Monitor from the Event Monitors GUI tool

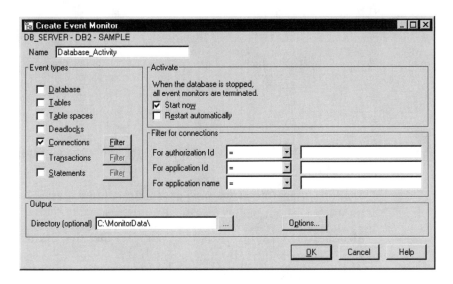

Figure 11-2   Sample Create Event Monitor dialog

Event monitors can also be created by executing the CREATE EVENT MONITOR SQL statement, either from the Command Center or from the Command Line Processor. The syntax for this statement is

```
CREATE EVENT MONITOR [EventMonitorName] FOR [DATABASE |
BUFFERPOOLS | TABLES | TABLESPACES | DEADLOCKS] WRITE TO PIPE
[PipeName] <MANUALSTART | AUTOSTART> <ON NODE [NodeNumber] <LOCAL
| GLOBAL>>
```

or

```
CREATE EVENT MONITOR [EventMonitorName] FOR [DATABASE | BUFFER-
POOLS | TABLES | TABLESPACES | DEADLOCKS] WRITE TO FILE
[DirectoryName] <MAXFILES [NONE | [NumberOfFiles]]> <MAXFILESIZE
[NONE | [MaxFileSize]]> <BUFFERSIZE [NumBufferPages]> <BLOCKED |
NONBLOCKED> <APPEND | REPLACE> <MANUALSTART | AUTOSTART> <ON NODE
[NodeNumber] <LOCAL | GLOBAL>>
```

or

```
CREATE EVENT MONITOR [EventMonitorName] FOR [CONNECTIONS |
STATEMENTS | TRANSACTIONS] <WHERE [<NOT> [APPL_ID | AUTH_ID |
APPL_NAME] [ComparisonOperator] [ComparisonString] <AND | OR> ,
. . . ]> WRITE TO PIPE [PipeName] <MANUALSTART | AUTOSTART> <ON
NODE [NodeNumber] <LOCAL | GLOBAL>>
```

or

```
CREATE EVENT MONITOR [EventMonitorName] FOR [CONNECTIONS |
STATEMENTS | TRANSACTIONS] <WHERE [<NOT> [APPL_ID | AUTH_ID |
APPL_NAME] [ComparisonOperator] [ComparisonString] <AND | OR> ,
. . . ]> WRITE TO FILE [DirectoryName] <MAXFILES [NONE |
[NumberOfFiles]]> <MAXFILESIZE [NONE | [MaxFileSize]]> <BUFFERSIZE
[NumBufferPages]> <BLOCKED | NONBLOCKED> <APPEND | REPLACE>
<MANUALSTART | AUTOSTART> <ON NODE [NodeNumber] <LOCAL | GLOBAL>>
```

where:

EventMonitorName	Identifies the name that will be assigned to the event monitor that will be created.
PipeName	Identifies the name of the pipe that information collected by the event monitor being created will be written to.
DirectoryName	Identifies the location where the event data files that created and populated with information collected by the event monitor being created will be stored.
NumberOfFiles	Identifies the maximum number of event data files the event monitor will create.

MaxFileSize	Identifies the maximum size (in 4K pages) that a single event data file can be.
NumBufferPages	Identifies the maximum size (in 4K pages) that the I/O buffer the event monitor being created will be. (All event monitor file I/O is buffered to improve performance.)
ComparisonOperator	Specifies how the application ID (APPL_ID), authorization ID (AUTH_ID), or application name (APPL_NAME) will be compared with the value specified in the *ComparisonString* parameter. Valid values for this parameter are =, <>, >, >=, <, <=, LIKE, or NOT LIKE.
ComparisonString	The value that will be compared with the application ID (APPL_ID), authorization ID (AUTH_ID), or application name (APPL_NAME) to determine whether or not a particular connection, statement, or transaction event will be recorded.
NodeNumber	Identifies a specific node in a partitioned database system where the event monitor being created will run and record event data.

For example, when executed, the following CREATE EVENT MONITOR statement

```
CREATE EVENT MONITOR Deadlock_Events FOR DEADLOCKS WRITE TO FILE
C:\MonitorData MAXFILES 4 MAXFILESIZE 1000
```

will create an event monitor that

- Has been assigned the name Deadlock_Events.

- Is activated whenever a deadlock cycle is detected in the database's locking system.

- Will allocate four files for output, each of which is 4M in size (for a total storage area of 16M).

- Will store information on drive C: in a directory named MonitorData. The files themselves will be named 00000000.evt, 00000001.evt, and so on.

 NOTE Although any number of event monitors can be created for a database, no more than 32 event monitors per instance can be active at any one time.

Starting and Stopping Event Monitors

Just as one or more snapshot monitor switches must be turned on before a snapshot is taken, one or more event monitors must be turned on before event monitor data will be collected. (An event monitor will be turned on, or made active, automatically each time the database is started if the AUTOSTART option was specified when the event monitor was created.) As soon as an event monitor is created with the Create Event Monitor dialog, it is made active by default. However, if you choose to override this default behavior, you can activate the event monitor at any time (once it has been created) by highlighting the event monitor in the list of available event monitors shown in the Event Monitors GUI tool and selecting the *Start Event Monitoring* action from the *Event monitor* menu. Figure 11-3 shows the menu items that must be selected in order to activate an event monitor from the Event Monitors GUI tool.

Event monitors can also be activated by executing the SET EVENT MONITOR STATE SQL statement, either from the Command Center or from the Command Line Processor. The syntax for this statement is

```
SET EVENT MONITOR [EventMonitorName] STATE < = > [MonitorState]
```

where:

EventMonitorName   Identifies the name of the event monitor that will be activated or deactivated.

MonitorState   Identifies the state the event monitor will be placed in. Valid values for this parameter are 0 (the event monitor will be placed in the inactive state) and 1 (the event monitor will be placed in the active state).

For example, when executed, the following SET EVENT MONITOR STATE statement

```
SET EVENT MONITOR Deadlock_Events STATE = 1
```

will activate an event monitor named Deadlock_Events, whereas the statement

```
SET EVENT MONITOR Deadlock_Events STATE = 0
```

will deactivate the event monitor named Deadlock_Events.

Once an event monitor is activated, it sits quietly in the background and waits for one of the events it is associated with to occur. When such an event takes place, the event monitor collects information that is appropriate for the event that fired it and writes that information to the event monitor's target location. If the target location is a named pipe, a stream of data will be written directly to the named pipe. If the target location is

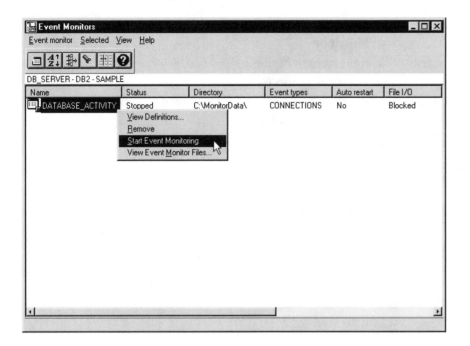

Figure 11-3   Activating an event monitor from the Event Monitors GUI tool

a directory, the stream of data will be written directly to one or more files. (As mentioned earlier, these files are sequentially numbered and have the extension .evt.)

NOTE   The output directory specified as the target location for an event monitor must exist and the DB2 Database Manager instance owner must have read and write permission for this directory. Otherwise, the event monitor will fail when it attempts to store the data collected in a file.

The application at the receiving end of the named pipe an event monitor is writing to is responsible for promptly reading the information written. Otherwise, the event monitor will turn off if the pipe becomes full. Likewise, an event monitor will turn off if the file space that was allocated for its output when the event monitor was created is consumed.

Determining the Current State of an Event Monitor

The current state of an event monitor can be determined by viewing the value stored in the Status column of the Event Monitors GUI tool for the event monitor in question or by using the SQL function EVENT_MON_STATE( ) in a query. The syntax for this function is

```
EVENT_MON_STATE ( [EventMonitorName] )
```

where:

> *EventMonitorName*   Identifies the name of the event monitor whose state will be determined.

This function returns the value 0 if the event monitor specified is not active and the value 1 if the event monitor specified is active. For example, when executed, the following query will determine the current state of all event monitors that have been defined for a particular database:

```
SELECT EVMONNAME,
    CASE
    WHEN EVENT_MON_STATE (EVMONNAME)=0 THEN 'Inactive'
    WHEN EVENT_MON_STATE (EVMONNAME)=1 THEN 'Active'
    END
FROM SYSCAT.EVENTMONITORS
```

Forcing an Event Monitor to Generate Output before It Is Triggered

Because some events, such as database events, do not activate event monitors as frequently as others, it can often be desirable to have an event monitor to write its current monitor values to its target location before the monitor triggering event occurs. In such situations, a system administrator can force an event monitor to write all information collected so far to the appropriate output location by executing the FLUSH EVENT MONITOR SQL statement, either from the Command Center or from the Command Line Processor. The syntax for this statement is

```
FLUSH EVENT MONITOR [EventMonitorName] < BUFFER >
```

where:

> *EventMonitorName*   Identifies the name of the event monitor whose information will be written to its target location prematurely.

For example, when executed, the following FLUSH EVENT MONITOR statement

```
FLUSH EVENT MONITOR Deadlock_Events
```

will cause the event monitor named Deadlock_Events to write its current values to its I/O target.

Records that are written to an event monitor's target location are logged prematurely in the event monitor log and assigned the identifier *partial record* unless the BUFFER option is specified when the FLUSH EVENT MONITOR statement is executed. In this case, only data that is already present in the event monitor buffers is written out; partial records are not generated.

NOTE   When an event monitor is flushed, the event monitor values are not reset. This means that the event monitor record that would have been generated if the **FLUSH EVENT MONITOR** statement had not been executed will still be generated when the event monitor is triggered normally.

Viewing Event Monitor Data

Because data files that are produced by an event monitor are written in binary format, their contents cannot be viewed directly with a text editor. Instead, one of two special utilities that are provided with DB2 Universal Database must be used:

- **Event Analyzer**   A GUI tool that will read the information stored in an event monitor data file and produce a listing

- **db2evmon**   A text-based tool that will read the information stored in an event monitor data file and generate a report

The Event Analyzer is activated by entering the command db2eva at the system command prompt or by highlighting the event monitor in the list of available event monitors shown in the Event Monitors GUI tool and selecting the *View Event Monitor Files* action from the *Event monitor* menu. Figure 11-4 shows the menu items that must be selected in order to activate the Event Analyzer from the Event Monitors GUI tool. Figure 11-5 shows how the initial input screen of the Event Analyzer might look after it has been populated (this screen is not shown if the Event Analyzer is invoked from the Event Monitors GUI tool). Figure 11-6 shows how the Event Analyzer might look after it has examined the contents of one or more data files that have been produced by an event monitor (in this example, an event monitor that monitored connection events was used).

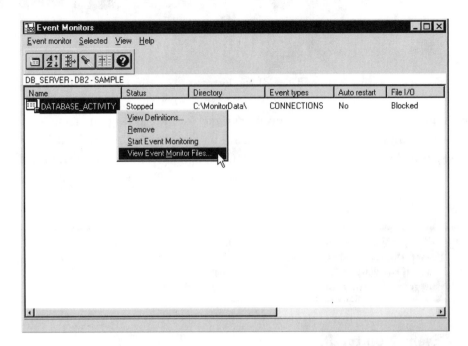

Figure 11-4 Activating the Event Analyzer from the Event Monitors GUI tool

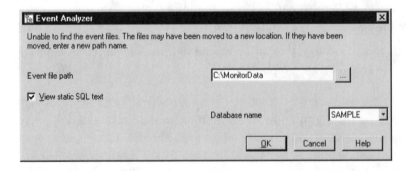

Figure 11-5 The initial screen of the Event Analyzer (only shown when the Event Analyzer is activated from the system command prompt)

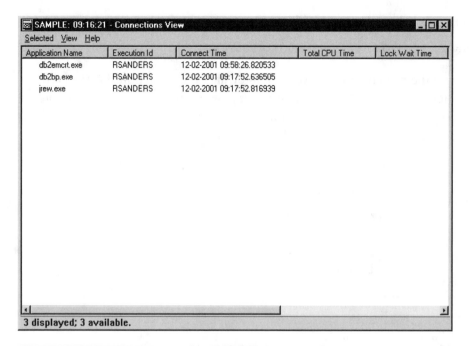

Figure 11-6   Sample Event Analyzer screen

The db2evmon tool is activated by entering the command db2evmon at the system command prompt. The syntax for this command is

```
db2evmon MONITOR -db [DatabaseAlias] -ev [EventMonitorName]
```

or

```
db2evmon MONITOR -path [MonitorFilesLocation]
```

where:

DatabaseAlias	Identifies the database by alias where the event monitor that generated the data files whose contents will be displayed is defined.
EventMonitorName	Identifies the name of the event monitor that generated the data files whose contents will be displayed.
MonitorFilesLocation	Identifies the location where the event monitor data files whose contents will be displayed are stored.

For example, when executed, the following db2evmon command

```
db2evmon MONITOR -path C:\MonitorData
```

will retrieve the contents of the event monitor data files stored in the MonitorData directory located on disk drive C: and produce a report. In this particular example, an event monitor that monitored connection events was used to produce the event monitor data files and the report generated looked like this:

```
------------------------------------------------------------------
                          EVENT LOG HEADER
    Event Monitor name: DATABASE_ACTIVITY
    Server Product ID: SQL07010
    Version of event monitor data: 6
    Byte order: LITTLE ENDIAN
    Number of nodes in db2 instance: 1
    Codepage of database: 1252
    Country code of database: 1
    Server instance name: DB2
------------------------------------------------------------------


------------------------------------------------------------------
    Database Name: SAMPLE
    Database Path: C:\DB2\NODE0000\SQL00001\
    First connection timestamp: 12-02-2001 09:14:16.062830
    Event Monitor Start time:   12-02-2001 09:16:21.432604
------------------------------------------------------------------

3) Connection Header Event ...
    Appl Handle: 2
    Appl Id: *LOCAL.DB2.011202141416
    Appl Seq number: 0001
    DRDA AS Correlation Token: *LOCAL.DB2.011202141416
    Program Name    : db2emcrt.exe
    Authorization Id: RSANDERS
    Execution Id    : RSANDERS
    Codepage Id: 1252
    Country code: 1
    Client Process Id: 286
    Client Database Alias: SAMPLE
    Client Product Id: SQL07010
    Client Platform: Unknown
    Client Communication Protocol: Local
    Client Network Name:
    Connect timestamp: 12-02-2001 09:14:16.062830


------------------------------------------------------------------
    Database Name: SAMPLE
    Database Path: C:\DB2\NODE0000\SQL00001\
    First connection timestamp: 12-02-2001 09:14:16.062830
    Event Monitor Start time:   12-02-2001 09:16:40.602970
------------------------------------------------------------------
```

```
6) Connection Header Event ...
   Appl Handle: 2
   Appl Id: *LOCAL.DB2.011202141416
   Appl Seq number: 0001
   DRDA AS Correlation Token: *LOCAL.DB2.011202141416
   Program Name    : db2emcrt.exe
   Authorization Id: RSANDERS
   Execution Id     : RSANDERS
   Codepage Id: 1252
   Country code: 1
   Client Process Id: 286
   Client Database Alias: SAMPLE
   Client Product Id: SQL07010
   Client Platform: Unknown
   Client Communication Protocol: Local
   Client Network Name:
   Connect timestamp: 12-02-2001 09:14:16.062830
```

NOTE By default, the report produced by the db2evmon utility is always displayed on the screen. However, if the report is quite long, you may find it to your advantage to redirect the output to a file, which can then be opened with a scrollable text editor or printed.

Deleting an Event Monitor

When an event monitor is no longer needed, it can be removed (dropped) from the database just like any other object. The easiest way to delete an existing event monitor is by selecting the *Remove* action from the *Event monitor* menu found in the Event Monitors GUI tool. Figure 11-7 shows the Event Monitors menu items that must be selected in order to drop an existing event monitor.

An event monitor can also be destroyed by executing the DROP EVENT MONITOR SQL statement, either from the Command Center or from the Command Line Processor. The syntax for this statement is

```
DROP EVENT MONITOR [EventMonitorName]
```

where:

EventMonitorName   Identifies the name that has been assigned to the event monitor that will be destroyed.

For example, when executed, the following DROP EVENT MONITOR statement would destroy an event monitor named Deadlock_Events:

```
DROP EVENT MONITOR Deadlock_Events
```

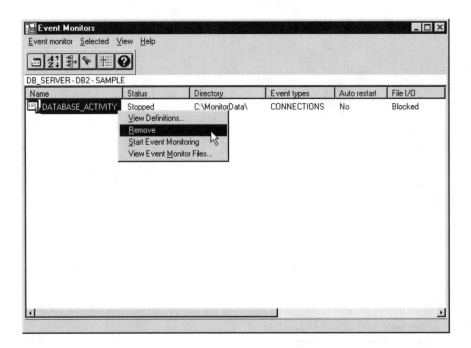

Figure 11-7 Dropping an event monitor from the Event Monitors GUI tool

The Performance Monitor

In addition to the snapshot monitor and the event monitors that comprise the Database System Monitor, DB2 Universal Database provides a special monitor known as the Performance Monitor that can be used to take snapshots of one or more performance monitor variables at predefined intervals. The Performance Monitor runs using a predefined configuration that is composed of up to 212 different performance monitor variables, which are grouped by level (Instance, Database, Table, Table Space, and Connection) and category (Agents, Connections, Sorts, Buffer Pool and I/O, Lock and Deadlocks, Table, and SQL Statement Activity) according to the type of information they provide. (For example, the Table level and Table category performance monitor variables include "Rows written per second," "Rows read per second," and "Accesses to overflowed records.")

Eighteen predefined Performance Monitor configurations are provided when DB2 Universal Database is installed. You can use any of these configurations as they are, you can copy and modify them to meet your specific needs, or you can create new configurations from scratch, using the Performance Monitor GUI tools that can be invoked from the Control Center menus. (However, it is recommended that you stick with using one of the predefined monitor configurations until you are comfortable with how the Performance Monitor is used.)

One nice feature the Performance Monitor tool provides is the capability to take a series of snapshots of the variables being monitored over a period of time and graph the information obtained from each snapshot so that significant changes can be seen quickly. A second feature is its capability to assign threshold values to each performance monitor variable being monitored. Once one or more threshold values have been assigned to a performance monitor variable, the display colors of that particular item will change from green to yellow (lower threshold values) or red (higher threshold values) when those threshold values are exceeded and, if desired, a message can be generated or a command script can be executed.

Starting, Stopping, and Viewing the Performance Monitor

The Performance Monitor can be started, stopped, or graphically viewed by selecting the appropriate action from the *Performance Monitoring* menu found in the Control Center. Figure 11-8 shows the Control Center menu items that must be selected in order to display the Performance Monitor. Figure 11-9 shows how the Performance Monitor can be used to set threshold values for a particular performance monitor variable.

Sending Messages to the Journal

If you recall, in Chapter 2 we learned that the Journal is a notebook that provides a way for users to monitor jobs and review various information that has been generated by completed jobs or other administrative tools and that the Journal notebook consists of four pages: the Jobs page, the Recovery page, the Alerts page, and the Messages page.

When the Performance Monitor is running and one or more threshold values have been assigned to a performance monitor variable, a message can be sent to the Alerts page of the Journal (and to the Alert Center) when one or more threshold values are exceeded. Figure 11-9 shows how to tell the Performance Monitor to send a message to the Alert Center and to the Alerts page of the Journal; Figure 11-10 shows how the Alerts page of the Journal might look on a Windows NT server after the threshold value for the number of local database connections allowed has been exceeded.

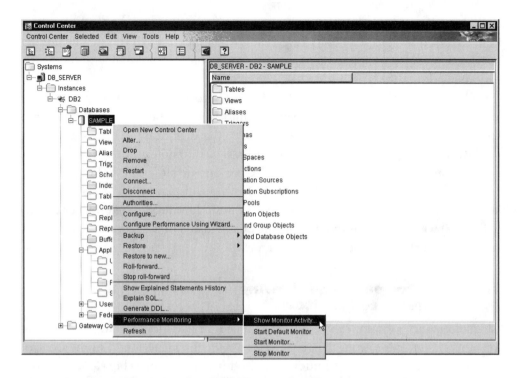

Figure 11-8 Invoking the Performance Monitor from the Control Center

A Word about the Query Patroller Tracker

In Chapter 2, we saw that the DB2 Query Patroller provides a way for database administrators to govern the execution of queries and manage the resources required by those queries so that hundreds of users can safely submit queries on multiterabyte class systems and receive results within an acceptable time frame. DB2 Query Patroller also enables administrators to set individual user and group priorities, as well as user query cost threshold limits. This enables a data warehouse to deliver query results to its most important users first. It also has the capability to limit usage of system resources by stopping runaway queries before they start. In addition, DB2 Query Patroller captures information such as the requesting user's ID, I/O cost, result data set/table size, and elapsed query run time each time a query is processed. This information makes it easy to charge end-user departments for their use of the data warehouse.

The DB2 Query Patroller Tracker is a tool that provides two key features that enable a system administrator to manage databases in a data warehouse. First, it gives the system administrator the ability to monitor the database load and activity over a specified

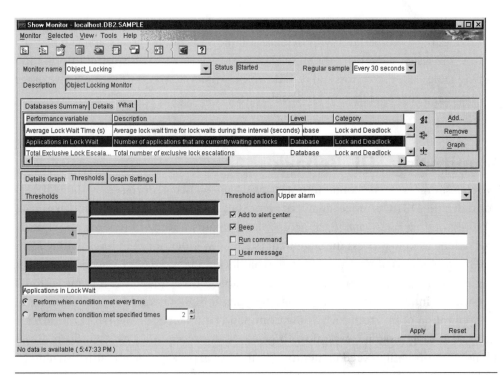

Figure 11-9   Setting threshold values for a performance monitor variable

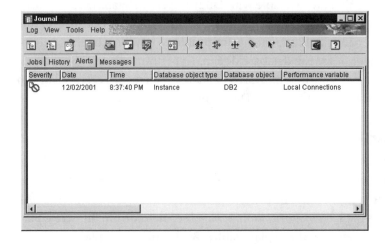

Figure 11-10   The Alerts page of the Journal

period of time by displaying usage history in a graphical, user-friendly format. Second, it provides the administrator with details on table and column access that can be used to tune the system. Because the Query Patroller server stores the historical information in DB2 tables, administrators can drill down on whatever aspects of the database usage they desire, using the query tool of their choice.

Monitoring SQL Behavior

When a source code file containing static SQL statements is processed by the SQL Pre-compiler, the DB2 Optimizer analyzes every SQL statement encountered and generates a corresponding *access plan*. Each access plan contains information about the strategy that will be used to process the statement (such as whether or not indexes will be used, what sort methods, if any, are required, what locking semantics are needed, and what join methods, if any, will be used). The executable form of these access plans is stored as packages in the system catalog tables. If dynamic SQL statements are used, either in an application or by a tool such as the Command Line Processor, the DB2 Optimizer is invoked during program execution to generate the access plan needed. Such access plans are temporarily stored in memory (in the global package cache) rather than in the system catalog. (If an SQL statement is executed and its access plan already exists in the global package cache, the existing access plan is reused and the DB2 Optimizer is not called again.)

Although the monitors that are available with DB2 Universal Database can be used to obtain information about how SQL operations perform, they do not provide the information needed to analyze SQL statements for problems that may be the result of a poorly written statement or a weak database design. To perform this type of analysis, you must be able to view the information stored in an SQL statement's access plan—to view a statement's access plan, you must use DB2 Universal Database's Explain Facility.

The Explain Facility

DB2 Universal Database provides one of the most comprehensive Explain Facilities in the industry. With the Explain Facility, detailed optimizer information on the access plan chosen for an SQL statement can be collected and viewed. When such information is collected for an access plan, that information is stored separately from the access plan in a special set of tables known as the Explain tables. By default, the Explain tables are not created as part of the database creation process. Instead, they must be manually created in the database that the Explain Facility will be used with before any component of the Explain Facility is invoked. [A DB2 Command Line Processor script (named

EXPLAIN.DDL) that creates the Explain tables can be found in the *misc* subdirectory of the *sqllib* directory where the DB2 Universal Database product was installed.]

Collecting Explain Data

In addition to the Explain tables just described, DB2 Universal Database's Explain Facility consists of several different interface tools, which have their own data requirements. Because of this, two basic types of data can be collected from an SQL statement's access plan:

- **Explain data** Contains detailed information about an SQL statement's access plan and stores this information in the appropriate Explain tables.

- **Explain snapshot data** Contains information about the current internal representation of an SQL statement and any related information. (This information is stored in the SNAPSHOT column of the EXPLAIN_SNAPSHOT table.)

As with the Database System Monitor, both types of Explain Facility data can be collected in a variety of ways. Some ways to collect Explain Facility data include

- The EXPLAIN SQL statement

- The CURRENT EXPLAIN MODE and CURRENT EXPLAIN SNAPSHOT special registers

- The EXPLAIN and EXPLSNAP bind options

The EXPLAIN SQL Statement The easiest way to collect explain and/or explain snapshot information for a single dynamic SQL statement is by executing the EXPLAIN SQL statement from an application directly, from the Command Center, or from the Command Line Processor. The syntax for this command is the following:

```
EXPLAIN [ALL | PLAN SELECTION | PLAN] <FOR SNAPSHOT | WITH
SNAPSHOT> <SET QUERYNO = [QueryNumber]> <SET QUERYTAG =
[QueryTag]> FOR [SQLStatement]
```

where:

QueryNumber	Identifies an integer value that will be placed in the QUERYNO column of the EXPLAIN_STATEMENT table when Explain information for the SQL statement specified is collected.
QueryTag	Identifies a character value that will be placed in the QUERYTAG column of the EXPLAIN_STATEMENT table when Explain information for the SQL statement specified is collected.

SQLStatement   The INSERT, UPDATE, DELETE, SELECT, SELECT INTO, VALUES, or VALUES INTO SQL statement that Explain information will be collected for.

For example, when executed, the following EXPLAIN statement

```
EXPLAIN ALL WITH SNAPSHOT FOR "SELECT * FROM EMPLOYEE"
```

will collect information about the access plan generated for the SELECT statement specified, and it will populate the Explain tables with the explain data and explain snapshot data collected. (However, it will not execute the SELECT statement or display the Explain information collected—another tool of the Explain Facility will have to be used to view this information.)

The CURRENT EXPLAIN MODE and CURRENT EXPLAIN SNAPSHOT Special Registers   Another way to collect explain and/or explain snapshot information for dynamic SQL statements is by using two special registers, the CURRENT EXPLAIN SNAPSHOT special register and the CURRENT EXPLAIN MODE special register, which exist specifically to provide support for the Explain Facility. (DB2 Universal Database uses 14 special registers to keep track of specific pieces of information that are used to describe or control the environment in which SQL statements are executed.)

The CURRENT EXPLAIN SNAPSHOT special register controls the behavior of the Explain Facility with respect to the collection of explain snapshot data. If the value of this special register is NO, the Explain Facility is disabled and no explain snapshot data is captured. On the other hand, if the value of this special register is EXPLAIN, the Explain Facility is turned on and explain snapshot data is collected for each dynamic INSERT, UPDATE, DELETE, SELECT, SELECT INTO, VALUES, or VALUES INTO SQL statement used when it is prepared for execution. The statements themselves, however, are not executed. If the value of the CURRENT EXPLAIN SNAPSHOT special register is YES, the Explain Facility behaves the same as it would if the value was EXPLAIN with one exception—all statements that explain snapshot data is collected for are executed as if the Explain Facility was not being used.

The CURRENT EXPLAIN MODE special register controls the behavior of the Explain Facility with respect to the collection of explain data. It can function exactly as the CURRENT EXPLAIN SNAPSHOT special register (except that explain data rather than explain snapshot data is collected); therefore, it can contain the value NO, YES, or EXPLAIN. However, one of the advantages the Explain Facility can provide when the CURRENT EXPLAIN MODE special register is used is the capability to recommend when and where one or more indexes might improve query performance. If the value of this special register is RECOMMEND INDEXES, explain data is collected as if the value was EXPLAIN and additional data is collected that can be used to reveal how additional indexes could be used to improve query performance. If the value of the CURRENT EXPLAIN MODE special register is EVALUATE INDEXES, not only will additional information that can be used to recommend indexes be collected, but that information will also be used to create virtual indexes and the virtual indexes themselves will be incorporated into a reevaluation to determine whether or not they do indeed improve performance as expected.

The values of the CURRENT EXPLAIN SNAPSHOT and CURRENT EXPLAIN MODE special registers can be set or modified by executing the SET CURRENT EXPLAIN SNAPSHOT or SET CURRENT EXPLAIN MODE SQL statements, respectively.

Table 11-4 shows how the various values of the CURRENT EXPLAIN MODE and CURRENT EXPLAIN SNAPSHOT special registers control the Explain Facility.

Table II-4 The Effects the CURRENT EXPLAIN MODE and CURRENT EXPLAIN SNAPSHOT Special Registers Have on the Explain Facility

Special Register Value	Static SQL Statements	Dynamic SQL Statements
CURRENT EXPLAIN MODE		
NO	No explain data collected	No explain data collected
YES	No explain data collected	Explain data collected; SQL statement executed
EXPLAIN	No explain data collected	Explain data collected; SQL statement not executed
RECOMMEND INDEXES	No explain data collected	Explain data collected; additional index data collected; SQL statement not executed
EVALUATE INDEXES	No explain data collected	Explain data collected; additional index data collected; virtual indexes created and evaluated; SQL statement not executed
CURRENT EXPLAIN SNAPSHOT		
NO	No explain snapshot data collected	No explain snapshot data collected
YES	No explain snapshot data collected	Explain snapshot data collected; SQL statement executed
EXPLAIN	No explain snapshot data collected	Explain snapshot data collected; SQL statement not executed

The EXPLAIN and EXPLSNAP Bind Options   To collect explain and/or explain snapshot information for static and/or dynamic SQL statements embedded in applications, two special bind options, the EXPLAIN option and the EXPLSNAP option, can be specified when the application that contains the SQL statements is bound to a specific database. As you might imagine, the EXPLAIN bind option controls the behavior of the Explain Facility with respect to the collection of explain data, and the EXPLSNAP bind option controls the behavior of the Explain Facility with respect to the collection of explain snapshot data. Aside from that, there is no other difference between the two.

If either option is specified along with the keyword NO (EXPLAIN NO), the Explain Facility is disabled and no explain/explain snapshot data is captured when the application is bound to the database. On the other hand, if either option is specified along with the keyword YES (EXPLSNAP YES), the Explain Facility is turned on and explain/explain snapshot data is collected for each static INSERT, UPDATE, DELETE, SELECT, SELECT INTO, VALUES, or VALUES INTO SQL statement used in the application being bound. If either option is specified along with the keyword ALL (EXPLAIN ALL), the Explain Facility is turned on and explain/explain snapshot data is collected for every INSERT, UPDATE, DELETE, SELECT, SELECT INTO, VALUES, or VALUES INTO SQL statement used in the application being bound, regardless of whether it is static or dynamic.

Table 11-5 shows how the various forms of the EXPLAIN and EXPLSNAP bind options available control what type of explain/explain snapshot data is collected at application bind time.

Table 11-5   The Effects the EXPLAIN and EXPLSNAP Bind Options Have on the Explain Facility

Bind Option	Static SQL Statements	Dynamic SQL Statements
EXPLAIN		
EXPLAIN NO	No explain data collected	No explain data collected
EXPLAIN YES	Explain data collected	No explain data collected
EXPLAIN ALL	Explain data collected	Explain data collected
EXPLSNAP		
EXPLSNAP NO	No explain snapshot data collected	No explain snapshot data collected
EXPLSNAP YES	Explain snapshot data collected	No explain snapshot data collected
EXPLSNAP ALL	Explain snapshot data collected	Explain snapshot data collected

Examining Explain Data

Once explain and/or explain snapshot data has been collected and stored in the Explain tables by the Explain Facility, the data collected can be retrieved and presented for evaluation in several ways:

- By using customized queries that poll the one or more of the Explain tables
- By using the db2expln tool
- By using the dynexpln tool
- By using the db2exfmt tool
- By using Visual Explain

Because the Explain tables have the same characteristics as other base tables in the database, it is relatively easy to construct custom queries, either from the Command Center or from the Script Center, that retrieve specific information from those tables and return it to the display. (By creating the queries in the Command Center or the Script Center, they can be saved and reexecuted as necessary.) However, if you want the information stored in the Explain tables to be presented in a predefined format, you must use one of the Explain display tools available.

Table 11-6 shows the various Explain Facility tools that can be used to examine explain and explain snapshot data, and indicates what each tool can and cannot do.

Table 11-6   The Explain Facility Data Examination Tools

Desired Characteristics	Visual Explain	db2expln	dynexpln	db2exfmt
Graphical user interface (GUI)	Yes	No	No	No
Text output	No	Yes	Yes	Yes
Static SQL supported	Yes	Yes	No	Yes
Dynamic SQL supported	Yes	No	Yes	Yes
"Quick-and-dirty" static SQL analysis	No	Yes	No	No
Call Level Interface (CLI) applications supported	Yes	No	No	Yes
Detailed optimizer information	Yes	No	No	Yes
Suited for analysis of multiple statements	No	Yes	Yes	Yes

The db2expln Tool   It was mentioned earlier that when a source code file containing SQL statements is bound to a database, the DB2 Optimizer analyzes every static SQL statement encountered and generates a corresponding access plan, which is then stored in the database in the form of a package. The db2expln tool is an Explain Facility tool that generates Explain information for and describes the access plan selected for each static SQL statement referenced by a package that has been stored in the system catalog tables. (It is typically used to obtain a quick explanation of the access plans chosen by packages for which explain data was not captured at bind time.)

When executed from the system command prompt, db2expln shows the actual implementation of the access plan chosen for a particular SQL statement stored in a package. However, it does not show information about how that SQL statement was optimized.

The dynexpln Tool   The dynexpln tool is similar to the db2expln tool except for the following:

- It does not show the actual implementation of the access plan chosen for a particular SQL statement stored in a package.
- It is used to obtain a quick explanation of the access plan selected for dynamic SQL statements that do not contain parameter markers.

When executed from the system command prompt, dynexpln creates a static package for the statements specified (either at the command prompt or from a text file) and then uses the db2expln tool to describe them.

The db2exfmt Tool   The db2exfmt tool is used to format and display the data stored in the Explain tables. When executed from the system command prompt, this tool can generate a graph that shows the total cost of an operation, the I/O cost associated with processing an SQL statement, and the expected output cardinality.

Visual Explain   Visual Explain is a GUI-based tool that enables database administrators and application developers to view a graphical representation of the access plan that has been selected for a particular SQL statement by the DB2 Optimizer. Compared to the other tools available, Visual Explain can be used to study queries in more detail, especially those queries that contain complex sequences of operations. Visual Explain can also be used to do the following:

- View the statistics that were used at the time of optimization. You can then compare these statistics to the current catalog statistics to help you determine whether rebinding the package might improve performance.

- Determine whether or not an index was used to access a table. If an index was not used, Visual Explain can help you determine which columns might benefit from being indexed.

- View the effects of performing various tuning techniques by comparing the before and after versions of the access plan graph for a query.

- Obtain information about each operation in the access plan, including the total estimated cost and number of rows retrieved (cardinality).

Both static and dynamic SQL statements can be analyzed with Visual Explain; however, the output from Visual Explain cannot be easily manipulated for further analysis and the information provided is not accessible to other applications. Unfortunately, Visual Explain is also not available on all platforms that are supported by DB2 Universal Database.

Visual Explain can be activated by entering an SQL statement that will be explained in the Explain SQL Statement dialog, which can be invoked by selecting the *Explain SQL* action from the *Database* menu found in the Control Center. Figure 11-11 shows the

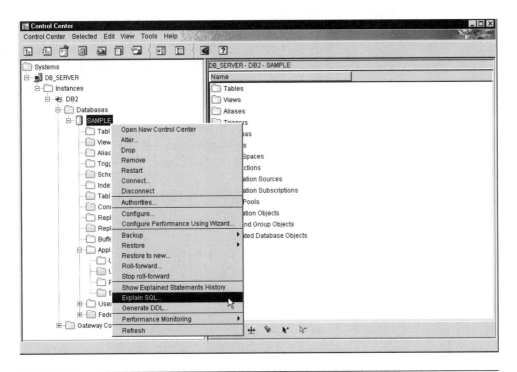

Figure 11-11   Invoking the Explain SQL Statement dialog from the Control Center

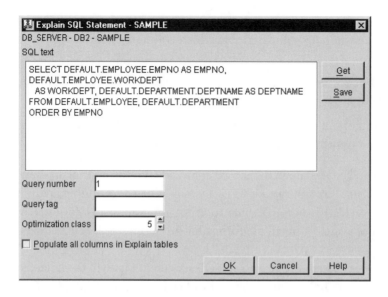

Figure 11-12   Sample Explain SQL Statement dialog

Control Center menu items that must be selected in order to display the Explain SQL Statement dialog. Figure 11-12 shows how the Explain SQL Statement dialog (which is activated by the Control Center) might look after its input fields have been populated. Figure 11-13 shows how a graphical view of the access plan selected for the SQL statement provided might be presented by Visual Explain.

The output produced by Visual Explain consists of a hierarchical graph that represents the various components needed to process the SQL statement specified. Each component is represented by a graphical object and each object is known as a node. Basically, there are two types of nodes: operator nodes, which indicate that an action is performed on a group of data, and operand nodes, which identify the object the operator is acting upon. Operand nodes are typically tables and indexes, which are represented in the graph by rectangles and diamonds, respectively. Operator nodes, on the other hand, can be anything from an SQL statement or clause to an index or table scan. Operator nodes, which are represented in the graph by ovals, indicate how data is accessed (IXSCAN, TBSCAN, RIDSCN, and IXAND), how tables are joined (MSJOIN and NLJOIN), and other factors such as whether or not a sort operation will be performed. (Specific information about the operators available can be found in the Visual Explain Online Help.) All nodes shown in the Visual Explain output are connected by arrows that show the flow of data from one node to the next. The end of an access plan is always the RETURN operator.

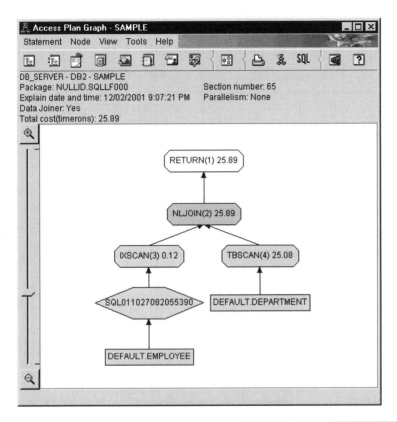

Figure 11-13   Visual Explain's graphical access plan for an SQL statement

Using this information, you can see that the access plan shown in Figure 11-13 is fairly simple. In this example, there are four operators and three operands. The operands are the tables DEFAULT.EMPLOYEE and DEFAULT.DEPARTMENT and the index SQL011027082055390, which is an index for the DEFAULT.EMPLOYEE table. The operators include a table scan (TBSCAN), an index scan (IXSCAN), a nested-loop join (NLJOIN), and of course, the RETURN operator.

Each node shown in an access plan graph has detailed information that can be accessed by double-clicking the left mouse button while the mouse pointer is on the node or by selecting the *Show details* action from the *Node* menu. Figure 11-14 shows how the Operator Details dialog looks for the IXSCAN operator shown in Figure 11-13.

Although Visual Explain can be used to dynamically generate graphical access plans for SQL statements that have been entered on the Explain SQL Statements dialog, it can also be used to view explain snapshot data that was captured using any of the methods

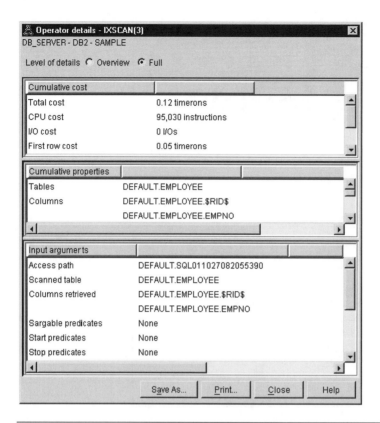

Figure 11-14 Sample Operator Details dialog

discussed earlier. The easiest way to use Visual Explain for this purpose is by invoking the Explained Statement History dialog first, which can be done by selecting the *Show Explained Statements History* action from the *Database* menu found in the Control Center. Figure 11-15 shows the Control Center menu items that must be selected in order to display the Explained Statements History dialog, and Figure 11-16 shows how the Explained Statements History dialog might look once it is displayed.

Once the Explained Statements History dialog is displayed, the graphical access plan for a particular SQL statement (for which explain snapshot data was collected earlier) can be displayed by highlighting the package that was created for the statement and selecting the *Show Access Plan* action from the *Statement* menu found in the Explained Statements History dialog.

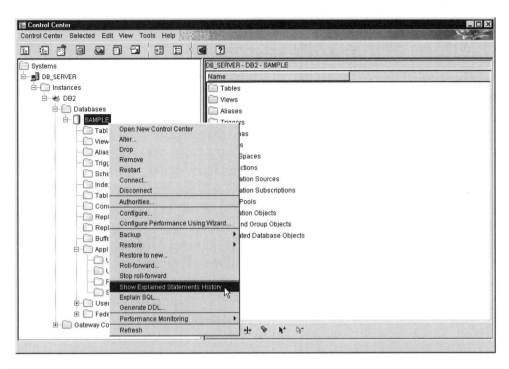

Figure 11-15 Invoking the Explained Statements History dialog from the Control Center

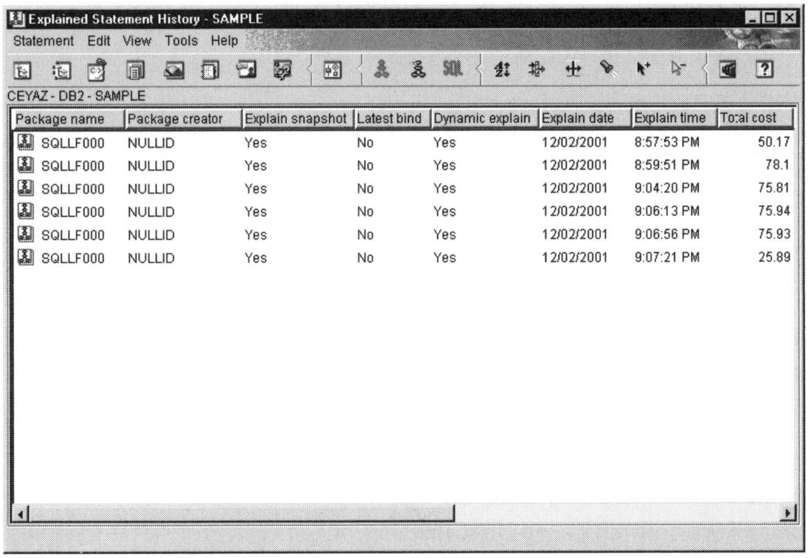

Figure 11-16 Sample Explained Statements History dialog

Configuring Database and Database Manager Resources

Because monitoring adds additional processing overhead, the amount of time spent monitoring a system should be limited, and monitoring should always be performed with some purpose in mind. Often the purpose for monitoring is to provide greater concurrency and eliminate potential bottlenecks that can slow down database response time. However, monitoring can also be used to provide input into how a DB2 Database Manager instance or a database under an instance should be configured so that resource utilization is optimized.

DB2 Universal Database uses an extensive array of configuration parameters to control how a DB2 Database Manager instance or a specific database allocates system resources (such as disk space and memory). In many cases, the default values provided for these configuration parameters are sufficient to meet an application's needs. However, because the default values provided are oriented toward database systems that have relatively small amounts of memory and that are dedicated database servers, overall system and application performance can often be greatly improved by changing one or more configuration parameter values.

In fact, DB2 Database Manager and/or DB2 database configuration parameter values should always be modified if your database environment contains one or more of the following elements:

- Large databases
- Databases that normally service large numbers of concurrent connections
- One or more special applications that have high performance requirements
- A special hardware configuration
- Unique query and/or transaction loads
- Unique query and/or transaction types

Viewing the DB2 Database Manager's Configuration

Configuration parameter values for the DB2 Database Manager instance are stored in a file named *db2systm* that is located in the *sqllib* directory where the DB2 Universal Database product was installed. (This file is created along with the DB2 Database Manager during the DB2 Universal Database product installation process.) Most values (parameters) in this file control the amount of system resources that will be allocated to a single instance of the DB2 Database Manager. Other values contain information about the DB2 Database Manager instance itself and cannot be changed.

The easiest way to examine the current values of the parameters of the DB2 Database Manager configuration file is by executing the GET DATABASE MANAGER CONFIGURATION command, either from the Command Center or from the Command Line Processor. The syntax for this command is

```
GET [DATABASE MANAGER | DB MANAGER | DBM] [CONFIGURATION |
CONFIG | CFG]
```

For example, when executed, the following GET DATABASE MANAGER CONFIGURATION command

```
GET DBM CFG
```

will produce output information similar to the following:

```
        Database Manager Configuration

    Node type = Database Server with local and remote clients

Database manager configuration release level       = 0x0900
Maximum total of files open          (MAXTOTFILOP) = 16000
CPU speed (millisec/instruction)        (CPUSPEED) = 1.267457e-006
Max number of concurrently active databases  (NUMDB) = 8
Data Links support                    (DATALINKS) = NO
Federated Database System Support     (FEDERATED) = YES
Transaction processor monitor name   (TP_MON_NAME) =
Default charge-back account        (DFT_ACCOUNT_STR) =
Java Development Kit 1.1 installation path (JDK11_PATH) =
Diagnostic error capture level        (DIAGLEVEL) = 3
Notify Level                         (NOTIFYLEVEL) = 2
Diagnostic data directory path         (DIAGPATH) =
Default database monitor switches
   Buffer pool                    (DFT_MON_BUFPOOL) = OFF
   Lock                              (DFT_MON_LOCK) = OFF
   Sort                              (DFT_MON_SORT) = OFF
   Statement                         (DFT_MON_STMT) = OFF
   Table                            (DFT_MON_TABLE) = OFF
   Unit of work                      (DFT_MON_UOW) = OFF
SYSADM group name                    (SYSADM_GROUP) =
SYSCTRL group name                   (SYSCTRL_GROUP) =
SYSMAINT group name                  (SYSMAINT_GROUP) =
Database manager authentication     (AUTHENTICATION) = SERVER
Cataloging allowed without authority (CATALOG_NOAUTH) = YES
Trust all clients                   (TRUST_ALLCLNTS) = YES
Trusted client authentication       (TRUST_CLNTAUTH) = CLIENT
Default database path                  (DFTDBPATH) = C:
Database monitor heap size (4KB)       (MON_HEAP_SZ) = 32
UDF shared memory set size (4KB)       (UDF_MEM_SZ) = 256
Java Virtual Machine heap size (4KB)  (JAVA_HEAP_SZ) = 512
Audit buffer size (4KB)               (AUDIT_BUF_SZ) = 0
Backup buffer default size (4KB)         (BACKBUFSZ) = 1024
```

```
Restore buffer default size (4KB)            (RESTBUFSZ) = 1024
Agent stack size                         (AGENT_STACK_SZ) = 16
Minimum committed private memory (4KB)    (MIN_PRIV_MEM) = 32
Private memory threshold (4KB)         (PRIV_MEM_THRESH) = 1296
Sort heap threshold (4KB)                   (SHEAPTHRES) = 10000
Directory cache support                      (DIR_CACHE) = YES
Application support layer heap size (4KB)    (ASLHEAPSZ) = 15
Max requester I/O block size (bytes)          (RQRIOBLK) = 32767
DOS requester I/O block size (bytes)      (DOS_RQRIOBLK) = 4096
Query heap size (4KB)                     (QUERY_HEAP_SZ) = 1000
DRDA services heap size (4KB)              (DRDA_HEAP_SZ) = 128
Priority of agents                            (AGENTPRI) = SYSTEM
Max number of existing agents                (MAXAGENTS) = 200
Agent pool size  (calculated)            (NUM_POOLAGENTS) = 4
Initial number of agents in pool         (NUM_INITAGENTS) = 0
Max number of coordinating agents        (MAX_COORDAGENTS) = MAXAGENTS
Max no. of concurrent coordinating agents  (MAXCAGENTS) = MAX_COORDAGENTS
Max number of logical agents             (MAX_LOGICAGENTS) = MAX_COORDAGENTS
Keep DARI process                            (KEEPDARI) = YES
Max number of DARI processes                  (MAXDARI) = MAX_COORDAGENTS
Initialize DARI process with JVM          (INITDARI_JVM) = NO
Initial number of fenced DARI process    (NUM_INITDARIS) = 0
Index re-creation time                       (INDEXREC) = ACCESS
Transaction manager database name         (TM_DATABASE) = 1ST_CONN
Transaction resync interval (sec)      (RESYNC_INTERVAL) = 180
SPM name                                     (SPM_NAME) = ESPATOLA
SPM log size                             (SPM_LOG_FILE_SZ) = 256
SPM resync agent limit                   (SPM_MAX_RESYNC) = 20
SPM log path                              (SPM_LOG_PATH) =
NetBIOS Workstation name                        (NNAME) =
TCP/IP Service name                           (SVCENAME) = db2cDB2
APPC Transaction program name                  (TPNAME) =
IPX/SPX File server name                    (FILESERVER) =
IPX/SPX DB2 server object name              (OBJECTNAME) =
IPX/SPX Socket number                       (IPX_SOCKET) = 879E
Discovery mode                               (DISCOVER) = SEARCH
Discovery communication protocols       (DISCOVER_COMM) = TCPIP
Discover server instance                (DISCOVER_INST) = ENABLE
Directory services type                      (DIR_TYPE) = NONE
Directory path name                     (DIR_PATH_NAME) = /.:/subsys/
                                                          database/

Directory object name                      (DIR_OBJ_NAME) =
Routing information object name          (ROUTE_OBJ_NAME) =
Default client comm. protocols          (DFT_CLIENT_COMM) =
Default client adapter number           (DFT_CLIENT_ADPT) = 0
Maximum query degree of parallelism      (MAX_QUERYDEGREE) = ANY
Enable intra-partition parallelism       (INTRA_PARALLEL) = NO
No. of int. communication buffers(4KB) (FCM_NUM_BUFFERS) = 1024
Number of FCM request blocks                 (FCM_NUM_RQB) = 512
Number of FCM connection entries         (FCM_NUM_CONNECT) = (FCM_NUM_RQB * 0.75)
Number of FCM message anchors            (FCM_NUM_ANCHORS) = (FCM_NUM_RQB * 0.75)
```

Viewing a Database's Configuration

Configuration parameter values for an individual database are stored in a file named *SQLDBCON* that is located in the *SQLxxxxx* directory that was created when the database was created (*xxxxx* represents the number assigned by the DB2 Database Manager during the database creation process). Many of the values (parameters) in this file control the amount of system resources that will be allocated to the associated database during normal operation. Other values contain information about the database itself (such as the current state of the database) and cannot be changed.

The easiest way to examine the current values of the parameters of a particular database's configuration file is by executing the GET DATABASE CONFIGURATION command, either from the Command Center or from the Command Line Processor. The syntax for this command is the following:

```
GET [DATABASE | DB] [CONFIGURATION | CONFIG | CFG] FOR
[DatabaseAlias]
```

where:

DatabaseAlias   Identifies a database by alias that configuration parameter values will be retrieved for

For example, when executed, the following GET DATABASE CONFIGURATION command

```
GET DB CFG FOR SAMPLE
```

will produce output information (for a single-partition database) similar to the following:

```
        Database Configuration for Database SAMPLE

Database configuration release level                    = 0x0900
Database release level                                  = 0x0900
Database territory                                      = US
Database code page                                      = 1252
Database code set                                       = IBM-1252
Database country code                                   = 1
Dynamic SQL Query management         (DYN_QUERY_MGMT)   = DISABLE
Directory object name                 (DIR_OBJ_NAME)   =
Discovery support for this database     (DISCOVER_DB)   = ENABLE
Default query optimization class       (DFT_QUERYOPT)   = 5
Degree of parallelism                     (DFT_DEGREE)   = 1
Continue upon arithmetic exceptions  (DFT_SQLMATHWARN)   = NO
```

```
Default refresh age                        (DFT_REFRESH_AGE) = 0
Number of frequent values retained         (NUM_FREQVALUES) = 10
Number of quantiles retained               (NUM_QUANTILES) = 20
Backup pending                                             = NO
Database is consistent                                     = YES
Rollforward pending                                        = NO
Restore pending                                            = NO
Multi-page file allocation enabled                         = NO
Log retain for recovery status                             = NO
User exit for logging status                               = NO
Data Links Token Expiry Interval (sec)     (DL_EXPINT) = 60
Data Links Number of Copies                (DL_NUM_COPIES) = 1
Data Links Time after Drop (days)          (DL_TIME_DROP) = 1
Data Links Token in Uppercase              (DL_UPPER) = NO
Data Links Token Algorithm                 (DL_TOKEN) = MAC0
Database heap (4KB)                        (DBHEAP) = 600
Catalog cache size (4KB)                   (CATALOGCACHE_SZ) = 32
Log buffer size (4KB)                      (LOGBUFSZ) = 8
Utilities heap size (4KB)                  (UTIL_HEAP_SZ) = 5000
Buffer pool size (pages)                   (BUFFPAGE) = 250
Extended storage segments size (4KB)       (ESTORE_SEG_SZ) = 16000
Number of extended storage segments        (NUM_ESTORE_SEGS) = 0
Max storage for lock list (4KB)            (LOCKLIST) = 50
Max appl. control heap size (4KB)          (APP_CTL_HEAP_SZ) = 128
Sort list heap (4KB)                       (SORTHEAP) = 256
SQL statement heap (4KB)                   (STMTHEAP) = 2048
Default application heap (4KB)             (APPLHEAPSZ) = 128
Package cache size (4KB)                   (PCKCACHESZ) = (MAXAP-
                                                              PLS*8)
Statistics heap size (4KB)                 (STAT_HEAP_SZ) = 4384
Interval for checking deadlock (ms)        (DLCHKTIME) = 10000
Percent. of lock lists per application     (MAXLOCKS) = 22
Lock timeout (sec)                         (LOCKTIMEOUT) = -1
Changed pages threshold                    (CHNGPGS_THRESH) = 60
Number of asynchronous page cleaners       (NUM_IOCLEANERS) = 1
Number of I/O servers                      (NUM_IOSERVERS) = 3
Index sort flag                            (INDEXSORT) = YES
Sequential detect flag                     (SEQDETECT) = YES
Default prefetch size (pages)              (DFT_PREFETCH_SZ) = 16
Default number of containers                               = 1
Default tablespace extentsize (pages)      (DFT_EXTENT_SZ) = 32
Max number of active applications          (MAXAPPLS) = 40
Average number of active applications      (AVG_APPLS) = 1
Max DB files open per application          (MAXFILOP) = 64
Log file size (4KB)                        (LOGFILSIZ) = 250
Number of primary log files                (LOGPRIMARY) = 3
Number of secondary log files              (LOGSECOND) = 2
Changed path to log files                  (NEWLOGPATH) =
Path to log files                                          =
                   C:\DB2\NODE0000\SQL00001\SQLOGDIR\
First active log file                                      =
Group commit count                         (MINCOMMIT) = 1
```

```
Percent log file reclaimed before soft chckpt (SOFTMAX) = 100
Log retain for recovery enabled              (LOGRETAIN) = OFF
User exit for logging enabled                 (USEREXIT) = OFF
Auto restart enabled                       (AUTORESTART) = ON
Index re-creation time                        (INDEXREC) = SYSTEM
(ACCESS)
Default number of loadrec sessions      (DFT_LOADREC_SES) = 1
Number of database backups to retain    (NUM_DB_BACKUPS) = 12
Recovery history retention (days)       (REC_HIS_RETENTN) = 366
TSM management class                      (TSM_MGMTCLASS) =
TSM node name                              (TSM_NODENAME) =
TSM owner                                     (TSM_OWNER) =
TSM password                               (TSM_PASSWORD) =
```

Changing the Value of a DB2 Database Manager Configuration Parameter

The value of one or more DB2 Database Manager configuration parameters can be changed by using the Configure Instance dialog, which is invoked by selecting the *Configure* action from the *Instances* menu found in the Control Center. Figure 11-17 shows the menu items that must be selected in order to activate the Configure Instance dialog. Figure 11-18 shows how the Configure Instance dialog typically looks after it has been activated.

The value of one or more DB2 Database Manager configuration parameters can also be changed by executing the UPDATE DATABASE MANAGER CONFIGURATION command, either from the Command Center or from the Command Line Processor. The syntax for this command is the following:

```
UPDATE [DATABASE MANAGER | DB MANAGER | DBM] [CONFIGURATION |
CONFIG | CFG] USING [[Keyword] [Value], . . . ]
```

where:

Keyword   Identifies one or more DB2 Database Manager configuration parameters (by a special keyword) whose values will be updated. Table 11-7 shows the list of possible keywords.

Value   Identifies the new value that will be assigned to the configuration parameter specified.

For example, when executed, the following UPDATE DATABASE MANAGER CONFIGURATION command will change the value of the *numdb* DB2 Database Manager configuration parameter to 12:

```
UPDATE DBM CFG USING NUMDB 4
```

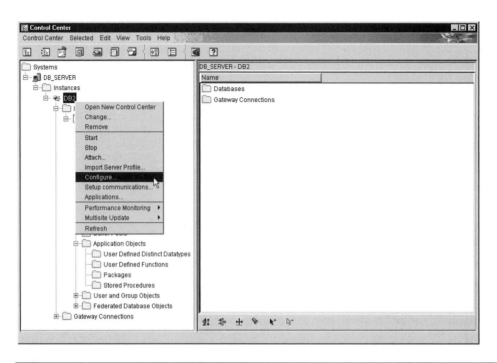

Figure 11-17 Invoking the Configure Instance dialog from the Control Center

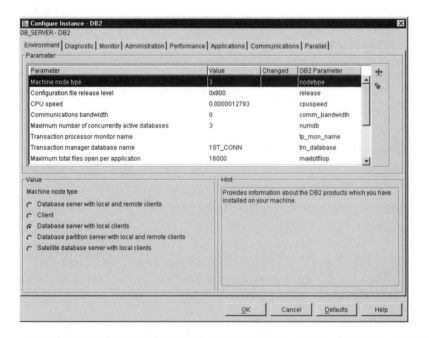

Figure 11-18 The Configure Instance dialog

Table 11-7 Keywords Recognized by the UPDATE DATABASE MANAGER CONFIGURATION SQL Statement

Keyword	Parameter Name	Description
AGENT_STACK_SZ	agent_stack_sz	Specifies the amount of memory that is allocated and committed by the operating system for each agent. This parameter specifies the number of pages for each agent stack on an OS/2 server.
AGENTPRI	agentpri	Specifies the execution priority that will be assigned to DB2 Database Manager processes and threads on a particular workstation.
ASLHEAPSZ	aslheapsz	Specifies the size (in pages) of the memory shared between a local client application and a DB2 Database Manager agent.
AUTHENTICATION	authentication	Specifies how and where authentication of a user takes place. If this parameter is set to CLIENT, then all authentication takes place at the client workstation. If this parameter is set to SERVER, the user ID and password are sent from the client workstation to the server workstation so that authentication can take place at the server.
BACKBUFSZ	backbufsz	Specifies the size (in 4K pages) of the buffer that is used for backing up a database (if the buffer size is not specified when the backup utility is invoked).
CATALOG_NOAUTH	catalog_noauth	Specifies whether or not users without SYSADM authority are able to catalog and uncatalog nodes, databases, or distributed connection services (DCS) and Open Database Connectivity (ODBC) directories.
COMM_BANDWIDTH	comm._bandwidth	Specifies the calculated value for the communications bandwidth (in megabytes per second) that will be used by the SQL optimizer to estimate the cost of performing certain operations between the database partition servers of a partitioned database system.

(continued)

PART III

Table 11-7 Keywords Recognized by the UPDATE DATABASE MANAGER CONFIGURATION SQL Statement *(continued)*

Keyword	Parameter Name	Description
CONN_ELAPSE	*conn_elapse*	Specifies the number of seconds that a Transmission Control Protocol/Internet Protocol (TCP/IP) connection between two nodes will be established in. If a connection is established within the time specified by this parameter, communications are established. If not, another attempt is made to establish communications. If attempts exceed the time specified by the *max_connretries* parameter, an error is returned.
CPUSPEED	*cpuspeed*	Specifies the CPU speed (in milliseconds per instruction) that will be used by the SQL optimizer to estimate the cost of performing certain operations.
DATALINKS	*datalinks*	Specifies whether or not DataLinks support is enabled.
DFT_ACCOUNT_STR	*dft_account_str*	Specifies the default accounting string to be used when connecting to Distributed Relational Database Architecture (DRDA) servers.
DFT_CLIENT_COMM	*dft_client_comm*	Specifies the communication protocols that all client applications attached to a specific DB2 Database Manager instance can use for establishing remote connections.
MON_BUFPOOL	*dft_mon_bufpool*	Specifies the default value of the snapshot monitor's buffer pool switch.
DFT_MON_LOCK	*dft_mon_lock*	Specifies the default value of the snapshot monitor's lock switch.
DFT_MON_SORT	*dft_mon_sort*	Specifies the default value of the snapshot monitor's sort switch.
DFT_MON_STMT	*dft_mon_stmt*	Specifies the default value of the snapshot monitor's statement switch.
DFT_MON_TABLE	*dft_mon_table*	Specifies the default value of the snapshot monitor's table switch.
DFT_MON_UOW	*dft_mon_uow*	Specifies the default value of the snapshot monitor's UOW.

Keyword	Parameter Name	Description
DFTDBPATH	*dftdbpath*	Specifies the default drive (OS/2 or Windows) or directory path (UNIX) used to store new databases. If no path is specified when a database is created, the database is created in the location specified by this parameter.
DIAGLEVEL	*diaglevel*	Specifies the diagnostic error capture level that is used to determine the severity of diagnostic errors that get recorded in the error log file (db2diag.log).
DIAGPATH	*diagpath*	Specifies the fully qualified path where DB2 diagnostic information is stored.
DIR_CACHE	*dir_cache*	Specifies whether or not directory cache support is enabled. If this parameter is set to YES, node, database, and DCS directory files are cached in memory. This reduces connect overhead by eliminating directory file I/O and minimizing the directory searches required to retrieve directory information.
DIR_OBJ_NAME	*dir_obj_name*	Specifies the object name that represents a DB2 Database Manager instance (or a database) in the DCE directory name space. The concatenation of this value and the *dir_path_name* value yields a global name that uniquely identifies the DB2 Database Manager instance or database in the name space governed by the directory services specified in the *dir_type* parameter.
DIR_PATH_NAME	*dir_path_name*	Specifies the directory path name in the Distributed Computing Environment (DCE) name space. The unique name of the DB2 Database Manager instance in the global name space is made up of this value and the value in the *dir_obj_name* parameter.
DIR_TYPE	*dir_type*	Specifies the type of directory services used (indicates whether or not the DB2 Database Manager instance uses the DCE global directory services).

(continued)

PART III

Table 11-7   Keywords Recognized by the UPDATE DATABASE MANAGER CONFIGURATION SQL Statement *(continued)*

Keyword	Parameter Name	Description
DISCOVER	*discover*	Specifies the type of DB2 Discovery requests supported on a client or server. If this parameter is set to SEARCH, search discovery, in which the DB2 client searches the network for DB2 databases, is supported. If this parameter is set to KNOWN, known discovery, in which the discovery request is issued against the administration server specified by the user, is supported. If this parameter is set to DISABLE, the client or server will not respond to any type of discovery request.
DISCOVER_COMM	*discover_comm*	Specifies the communications protocols that clients use to issue search discovery requests and that servers use to listen for search discovery requests.
DISCOVER_INST	*discover_inst*	Specifies whether or not client discovery of an instance is enabled.
DOS_RQRIOBLK	*dos_rqrioblk*	Specifies the DOS requester I/O block size (which controls the size of the I/O blocks that are allocated on both the client and the server workstations). This parameter is only applicable on DOS clients, including DOS clients running under OS/2.
DRDA_HEAP_SZ	*drda_heap_sz*	Specifies the size (in pages) of the DRDA heap. This heap is used by the DRDA AS clause and by DB2 Connect.
FCM_NUM_ANCHORS	*fcm_num_anchors*	Specifies the number of Fast Communications Manager (FCM) message anchors used. Agents use the message anchors to send messages among themselves.
FCM_NUM_BUFFERS	*fcm_num_anchors*	Specifies the number of 4K buffers that are used for internal communications (messages) among the nodes in an instance.
FCM_NUM_CONNECT	*fcm_num_connect*	Specifies the number of FCM connection entries available. Agents use connection entries to pass data among themselves.

Keyword	Parameter Name	Description
FCM_NUM_RQB	*fcm_num_rqb*	Specifies the number of FCM request blocks used. Request blocks are the media through which information is passed between the FCM daemon and an agent.
FEDERATED	*federated*	Specifies whether or not federated database object support is enabled. If this parameter is set to YES, the DB2 Database Manager instance can use nicknames to access data managed by the DB2 family and by other database management systems (DBMSs).
FILESERVER	*fileserver*	Specifies the Internet Packet Exchange/Sequenced Packet Exchange (IPX/SPX) file server name used. This is the name of the Novell NetWare file server where the internetwork address of the DB2 Database Manager instance is registered.
INDEXREC	*indexrec*	Specifies when invalid database indexes should be re-created. This parameter is used if the database configuration parameter *indexrec* is set to SYSTEM. Possible values for this parameter are ACCESS and RESTART.
INITDARI_JVM	*initdari_jvm*	Specifies whether or not whether each fenced Database Application Remote Interface (DARI) process will load the Java Virtual Machine (JVM) when starting (which will reduce the initial startup time for fenced Java stored procedures, especially when used in conjunction with the *num_initdaris* parameter).
INTRA_PARALLEL	*intra_parallel*	Specifies whether or not the DB2 Database Manager instance can use intrapartition parallelism.
IPX_SQCKET	*ipx_socket*	Specifies a well-known IPX/SPX socket number and represents the connection end point in a DB2 server's NetWare internetwork address.
JAVA_HEAP_SZ	*java_heap_sz*	Specifies the maximum size of the heap used by the Java interpreter. For nonpartitioned database systems, one heap is allocated for the instance; for partitioned database systems, one heap is allocated for each database partition server.

(continued)

Table 11-7 Keywords Recognized by the UPDATE DATABASE MANAGER CONFIGURATION SQL Statement *(continued)*

Keyword	Parameter Name	Description
JDK11_PATH	*jdk11_path*	Specifies the directory where the Java Development Kit 1.1 has been installed. CLASSPATH and other environment variables used by the Java interpreter are computed using the value of this parameter.
KEEPDARI	*keepdari*	Specifies whether or not a DARI processes will be kept after each DARI call. If this parameter is set to NO, a new DARI process is created and terminated for each DARI invocation. If this parameter is set to YES, a DARI process is reused for subsequent DARI calls and is terminated only when the associated user application exits.
MAX_CONNRETRIES	*max_connretries*	Specifies the number of connection retries that can be made to a node—if an attempt to establish communication between two nodes fails because the value specified by the *conn_elapse* parameter has been reached.
MAX_COORDAGENTS	*max_coordagents*	Specifies the maximum number of coordinating agents that can exist at one time on a node.
MAX_LOGICAGENTS	*max_logicagents*	Specifies the maximum number of applications that can be connected to the instance.
MAX_QUERYDEGREE	*max_querydegree*	Specifies the maximum degree of parallelism used for any SQL statement executing on this instance of the DB2 Database Manager. For a multinode system, this parameter applies to the degree of parallelism used within a single node.
MAX_TIME_DIFF	*max_timediff*	Specifies the maximum time difference (in minutes) that is permitted among the system clocks of the nodes listed in the file db2nodes.cfg.
MAXAGENTS	*maxagents*	Specifies the maximum number of DB2 Database Manager agents that can exist simultaneously, regardless of which database is being used.
MAXCAGENTS	*maxcagents*	Specifies the maximum number of DB2 Database Manager agents that can be concurrently executing a DB2 Database Manager transaction. This parameter can be set to the same value as the *maxagents* parameter.

Keyword	Parameter Name	Description
MAXDARI	*maxdari*	Specifies the maximum number of DARI processes that can reside at the database server. The value of this parameter cannot exceed the value of the *maxagents* parameter.
MAXTOTFILOP	*maxtotfilop*	Specifies the maximum number of files that can be open per OS/2 application. The value specified in this parameter defines the total database and application file handles that can be used by a specific process connected to a database (OS/2 only).
MIN_PRIV_MEM	*min_pri_mem*	Specifies the number of pages that the database server process will reserve as private virtual memory when a DB2 Database Manager instance is started (OS/2 only).
MON_HEAP_SZ	*mon_heap_sz*	Specifies the amount of memory (in 4K pages) to allocate for Database System Monitor data (Database System Monitor heap size).
NNAME	*nname*	Specifies the name of the node or workstation. Database clients use this value to access database server workstations using NetBIOS. If the database server workstation changes the name specified in *nname*, all clients that access the database server workstation must catalog it again and specify the new name.
N/A	*nodetype*	Specifies whether the node is configured as a server with local and remote clients, a client, or a server with local clients. This parameter is not updateable.
NOTIFYLEVEL	*notifylevel*	Specifies the severity level used to determine which messages that are written to the notification files (on a Windows system).
NUM_INITAGENTS	*num_initagents*	Specifies the initial number of agents that are created in the agent pool when the DB2 Database Manager is started.
NUM_INITDARIS	*num_initdaris*	Specifies the initial number of idle fenced DARI processes that are created in the DARI pool when the DB2 Database Manager is started. This parameter is ignored if a value is not specified for the *keepdari* parameter.

(continued)

PART III

Table 11-7 Keywords Recognized by the UPDATE DATABASE MANAGER CONFIGURATION SQL Statement *(continued)*

Keyword	Parameter Name	Description
NUM_POOLAGENTS	*num_poolagents*	Specifies the size to which the agent pool is allowed to grow.
NUMDB	*numdb*	Specifies the maximum number of local databases that can be active (that is, that can have applications connected to them) at the same time.
OBJECTNAME	*objectname*	Specifies the IPX/SPX object name of the DB2 Database Manager instance in a Novell NetWare network.
PRIV_MEM_THRESH	*priv_mem_thresh*	Specifies a threshold below which a server will not release the memory associated with a client when that client's connection is terminated.
QUERY_HEAP_SZ	*query_heap_sz*	Specifies the maximum amount of memory (in pages) that can be allocated for the query heap. The query heap is used to store each query in the agent's private memory.
N/A	*release*	Specifies the release level of the DB2 Database Manager configuration file. This parameter is not updateable.
RESTBUFSZ	*restbufsz*	Specifies the size (in 4K pages) of the buffer that is used for restoring a database (if the buffer size is not specified when the restore utility is invoked).
RESYNC_INTERVAL	resync_interval	Specifies the time interval (in seconds) after which a transaction manager (TM) or a resource manager (RM) retries to recover any outstanding in-doubt transactions found in the TM or the RM. This parameter value is only used when transactions are running in a distributed unit of work (DUOW) environment.
ROUTE_OBJ_NAME	*route_obj_name*	Specifies the name of the default routing information object entry that will be used by all client applications attempting to access a DRDA server.
RQRIOBLK	*rqrioblk*	Specifies the size (in bytes) of the communication buffer used between remote applications and their database agents on the database server.

Keyword	Parameter Name	Description
SHEAPTHRES	*sheapthres*	Specifies the limit on the total amount of memory (in pages) available for sorting across the entire DB2 Database Manager instance.
SPM_LOG_FILE_SZ	*spm_log_file_sz*	Specifies the size (in 4K pages) of the Sync Point Manager (SPM) log file.
SPM_LOG_PATH	*spm_log_path*	Specifies the directory where SPM log files are written.
SPM_MAX_RESYNC	*spm_max_resync*	Specifies the number of simultaneous agents that can perform resynchronization operations.
SPM_NAME	*spm_name*	Specifies the name of the SPM instance that will be used by the DB2 Database Manager.
SS_LOGON	*ss_logon*	Specifies whether or not a user ID and password are required in order to start and stop the DB2 Database Manager instance.
START_STOP_TIME	*start_stop_time*	Specifies the time (in minutes) within which all nodes of a partitioned database must respond to START DATABASE MANAGER, STOP DATABASE MANAGER, and ADD NODE commands.
SVCENAME	*svcename*	Specifies a service name that represents the DB2 Database Manager instance in a TCP/IP network. This value must be the same as the Connection Service name specified in the services file.
SYSADM_GROUP	*sysadm_group*	Specifies the group name that has SYSADM authority for the DB2 Database Manager instance.
SYSCTRL_GROUP	*sysctrl_group*	Specifies the group name that has SYSCTRL authority for the DB2 Database Manager instance.
SYSMAINT_GROUP	*sysmaint_group*	Specifies the group name that has SYSMAINT authority for the DB2 Database Manager instance.
TM_DATABASE	*tm_database*	Specifies the name of the TM database for each DB2 Database Manager instance.
TP_MON_NAME	*tp_mon_name*	Specifies the name of the transaction processing (TP) monitor product being used.

(continued)

Table 11-7 Keywords Recognized by the UPDATE DATABASE MANAGER CONFIGURATION SQL Statement *(continued)*

Keyword	Parameter Name	Description
TPNAME	*tpname*	Specifies the name of the remote transaction program that the database client must use when it issues an allocate request to the DB2 Database Manager instance using the Advanced Program-to-Program (APPC) communication protocol.
TRUST_ALLCLNTS	*trust_allclnts*	Specifies whether or not all clients are treated as trusted clients (that is, whether or not a level of security is available at the client that is used to validate users at the client).
TRUST_CLNTAUTH	*trust_clntauth*	Specifies whether or not all users of trusted clients are validated at the client.
UDF_MEM_SZ	*udf_mem_sz*	For a fenced user-defined function (UDF), this parameter specifies the default allocation for memory to be shared between the database process and the UDF. For an unfenced process, this parameter specifies the size of the private memory set. In both cases, this memory is used to pass data to a UDF and back to a database.

Changing the Value of a Database's Configuration Parameter

The value of one or more database configuration parameters can be changed by using the Configure Database dialog, which is invoked by selecting the *Configure* action from the *Databases* menu found in the Control Center. Figure 11-19 shows the menu items that must be selected in order to activate the Configure Database dialog. Figure 11-20 shows how the Configure Database dialog typically looks after it has been activated.

The value of one or more database configuration parameters can also be changed by executing the UPDATE DATABASE CONFIGURATION command, either from the Command Center or from the Command Line Processor. The syntax for this command is the following:

```
UPDATE [DATABASE | DB] [CONFIGURATION | CONFIG | CFG] FOR
[DatabaseAlias] USING [[Keyword] [Value], . . . ]
```

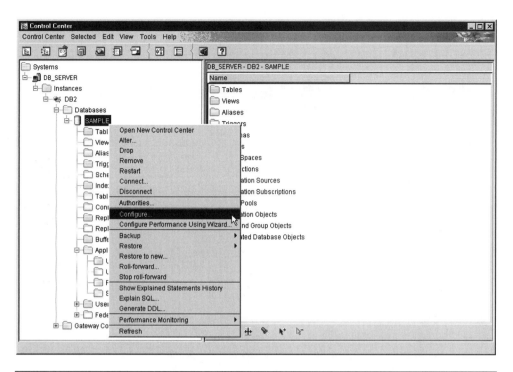

Figure 11-19   Invoking the Configure Database dialog from the Control Center

where:

DatabaseAlias   Identifies a database by alias that configuration information will be updated for.

Keyword   Identifies one or more database configuration parameters (by a special keyword) whose values will be updated. Table 11-8 shows the list of possible keywords.

Value   Identifies the new value that will be assigned to the configuration parameter specified.

For example, when executed, the following UPDATE DATABASE CONFIGURATION command will change the value of the *autorestart* database configuration parameter for the SAMPLE database to OFF:

```
UPDATE DB CFG USING AUTORESTART OFF
```

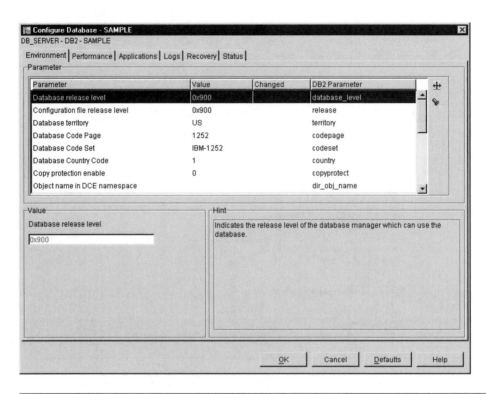

Figure 11-20   The Configure Database dialog

Table 11-8   Keywords Recognized by the UPDATE DATABASE CONFIGURATION SQL Statement

Keyword	Parameter Name	Description
APP_CTL_HEAP_SZ	app_ctl_heap_sz	Specifies the maximum size (in 4K pages) of memory that will be allocated for the application control heap. The application control heap is used to share information among agents working on behalf of the same application at a node in a Massively Parallel Processor (MPP) or a Symmetrical Multiprocessor (SMP) system.
APPLHEAPSZ	applheapsz	Specifies the size (in pages) of the application heap that is available for each individual agent. Memory that will be used for caching packages (specified by the pckcachesz parameter) is allocated from the application heap.

Keyword	Parameter Name	Description
AUDIT_BUF_SZ	*audit_buf_sz*	Specifies the size (in pages) of the application heap that is available for each individual agent.
AUTO_RESTART	*autorestart*	Specifies whether or not the DB2 Database Manager can automatically issue a RESTART DATABASE command when a connection is attempted when the database in an inconsistent state (which is the case if the last database connection was disrupted or if the database was not terminated normally during the previous session). If this parameter is set to ON, a database is restarted automatically, if necessary. If this parameter is set to OFF, a database must be restarted manually.
AVG_APPLS	*avg_appls*	Specifies the average number of active applications that normally access the database. This parameter is used by the SQL optimizer to help estimate how much buffer pool memory will be available for the chosen access plan at application run time.
N/A	*backup_pending*	Specifies whether or not a database needs to be backed up. If this parameter is set to NO, the database is in a usable state. If this parameter is set to YES, an OFFLINE backup must be performed before the database can be used. This parameter is not updateable.
BUFF_PAGE	*buff_page*	Specifies the size (in pages) of the buffer pool that is used to store and manipulate data read from the database.
CATALOGCACHE_SZ	*catalogcache_sz*	Specifies the size (in pages) of the internal catalog cache (allocated from the *dbheap*) that is used by the SQL Precompiler to hold the packed descriptors for commonly referenced objects such as tables and constraints.
CHNGPGS_THRESH	*chngpgs_thresh*	Specifies the level (percentage) of pages that must be changed before the asynchronous page cleaners used by DB2 will be started, if they are not already active.
N/A	*codepage*	Specifies the code page used by the database. This parameter is not updateable.
N/A	*codeset*	Specifies the code set used by the database. This parameter is not updateable.

(continued)

Table 11-8 Keywords Recognized by the UPDATE DATABASE CONFIGURATION SQL Statement *(continued)*

Keyword	Parameter Name	Description
COPY_PROTECT	*copyprotect*	Specifies whether or not the database copy-protection attribute for the database is enabled (OS/2 only).
N/A	*country*	Specifies the country code used by the database. This parameter is not updateable.
N/A	*database_consistent*	Specifies whether or not the database is in a consistent state. If this parameter is set to YES, all transactions have been committed or rolled back and the data in the database is consistent. If this parameter is set to NO, a transaction or some other task is pending on the database and the data in the database is not consistent at this time. This parameter is not updateable.
database_level		Specifies the release level of the DB2 Database Manager that can access the database. This parameter is not updateable.
DBHEAP	*dbheap*	Specifies the size (in pages) of the database heap that is used to hold control information on all open cursors accessing the database. Both log buffers and catalog cache buffers are allocated from the database heap.
DFT_DEGREE	*dft_degree*	Specifies the default value for the CURRENT DEGREE special register and the DEGREE bind option.
DFT_EXTENT_SZ	*dft_extent_sz*	Specifies the default extent size (in pages) that will be used when new table spaces are created if no extent size is specified.
DFT_LOADREC_SES	*dft_loadrec_ses*	Specifies the default number of load recovery sessions that will be used during the recovery of a table load operation. This parameter is only applicable if roll-forward recovery is enabled.
DFT_PREFETCH_SZ	*dft_prefetch_sz*	Specifies the default prefetch size (in pages) that will be used when new table spaces are created if no prefetch size is specified.
DFT_QUERYOPT	*dft_queryopt*	Specifies the default query optimization class the DB2 Optimizer will use when compiling SQL

queries.

Keyword	Parameter Name	Description
DFT_REFRESH_AGE	dft_refresh_age	Specifies the default value that will be used for the refresh age of summary tables if the CURRENT REFRESH AGE special register has not been set. This parameter is used to determine whether summary tables will be considered when optimizing the processing of dynamic SQL queries.
DFT_SQLMATHWARN	dft_sqlmathwarn	Specifies whether or not arithmetic errors and retrieval conversion errors are handled as errors or as warnings during SQL statement compilation.
DIR_OBJ_NAME	dir_obj_name	Specifies the object name in the DCE name space that represents a DB2 Database Manager instance (or database) in the directory.
DISCOVER_DB	discover_db	Specifies whether or not information about a database from is returned to a client when a discovery request is issued by the client against the server.
DL_EXPINT	dl_expint	Specifies the interval of time (in seconds) for which the DB2 DataLinks Manager file access token generated is valid.
DL_NUM_COPIES	dl_num_copies	Specifies the number of additional copies of a file to be made in the archive server [such as a Tivoli Storage Manager (TSM) server] when a file is linked to the database (DB2 DataLinks Manager only).
DL_TIME_DROP	dl_time_drop	Specifies the interval of time (in days) files will be retained on an archive server (such as a TSM server) after a DROP TABLE, DROP DATABASE, or DROP TABLESPACE statement is issued (DB2 DataLinks Manager only).
DL_TOKEN	dl_token	Specifies the algorithm used in the generation of DATALINK file access control tokens (DB2 DataLinks Manager only).
DL_UPPER	dl_upper	Specifies whether file access control tokens use uppercase letters only or can contain both uppercase and lowercase letters (DB2 DataLinks Manager only).

(continued)

Table 11-8 Keywords Recognized by the UPDATE DATABASE CONFIGURATION SQL Statement *(continued)*

Keyword	Parameter Name	Description
DLCHKTIME	*dlchktime*	Specifies the time interval frequency (in milliseconds) at which the DB2 Database Manager is to check for deadlocks among all the applications connected to a database.
DYN_QUERY_MGMT	*dyn_query_mgmt*	Specifies whether or not queries that exceed thresholds are trapped by DB2 Query Patroller. If this parameter is set to ENABLE and the cost of the dynamic query exceeds the trap threshold for the user or group (as specified in the Query Patroller user profile table), the query will be trapped by DB2 Query Patroller. If this parameter is set to DISABLE, no queries are trapped.
ESTORE_SEG_SZ	*estore_seg_sz*	Specifies the number of pages to be stored in the extended memory segments available to the database.
INDEXREC	*indexrec*	Specifies when invalid indexes will be re-created. This parameter can be set to any of the following values: SYSTEM, SYSTEM, ACCESS, or RESTART. The default setting is SYSTEM, which specifies that the value of the DB2 Database Manager configuration parameter *indexrec* will be used.
INDEXSQRT	*indexsort*	Specifies whether or not sorting of index keys is to occur during index creation.
LOCKLIST	*locklist*	Specifies the maximum amount of storage (in pages) that will be allocated for the lock list.
LOCKTIMEOUT	*locktimeout*	Specifies the number of seconds that an application will wait to obtain a lock before timing out.
LOGBUFSZ	*logbufsz*	Specifies the number of pages that are used to buffer log records before they are written to disk. This buffer is allocated from the database heap.
LOGFILSIZ	*logfilsiz*	Specifies the amount of disk storage space (in pages) that will be allocated to log files that are used for data recovery. This parameter defines the size of each primary and secondary log file.
N/A	*loghead*	Specifies the name of the log file that contains the head of the active log. The next log record written will start at head of the active log file. This parameter is not updateable.

Keyword	Parameter Name	Description
LOGFILSIZ	*logpath*	Specifies the current path being used to access log files. This parameter is not updateable.
LOGPRIMARY	*logprimary*	Specifies the number of primary log files that will be used for database recovery.
LOG_RETAIN	*logretain*	Specifies whether or not active log files will be retained as archived log files for use in roll-forward recovery (also known as archival logging).
N/A	*log_retain_status*	Specifies whether or not log files are being retained for use in roll-forward recovery. This parameter is not updateable.
LOGSECOND	*logsecond*	Specifies the number of secondary log files that can be used for database recovery.
MAXAPPLS	*maxappls*	Specifies the maximum number of application programs (both local and remote) that can connect to the database at one time.
MAXFILOP	*maxfilop*	Specifies the maximum number of database files that an application program can have open at one time.
MAXLOCKS	*maxlocks*	Specifies the maximum percentage of the lock list that any application program can use.
MINCOMMIT	*mincommit*	Specifies the number of SQL commits that can be grouped for the database. Better control of I/O and log activity can be achieved by grouping SQL commits.
N/A	*multipage_alloc*	Specifies whether or not multipage file allocation is used to when additional space is needed for system managed space (SMS) table spaces.
NEWLOGPATH	*newlogpath*	Specifies an alternate path to use for storing recovery log files.
NUM_DB_BACKUPS	*num_db_backups*	Specifies the number of database backups to retain for a database. After the specified number of backups is reached, old backups are marked as expired in the recovery history file.
NUM_ESTORE_SEGS	*num_estore_segs*	Specifies the number of extended storage memory segments available to the database.

PART III

(continued)

Table 11-8 Keywords Recognized by the UPDATE DATABASE CONFIGURATION SQL Statement *(continued)*

Keyword	Parameter Name	Description
NUM_FREQVALUES	*num_freqvalues*	Specifies the number of most frequent values that will be collected when the WITH DISTRIBUTION option is specified with the RUN STATISTICS command (or function).
NUM_IOCLEANERS	*num_iocleaners*	Specifies the number of asynchronous page cleaners that are used by a database.
NUM_IOSERVERS	*num_ioservers*	Specifies the number of I/O servers for a database. I/O servers are used on behalf of database agents to perform prefetch I/O and asynchronous I/O needed by utilities such as backup and restore.
NUM_QUANTILES	*num_quantiles*	Specifies the number of quantiles (values in a column that satisfy a RANGE predicate) that will be collected when the WITH DISTRIBUTION option is specified with the RUN STATISTICS command (or function).
N/A	*numsegs*	Specifies the number of containers that will be created within the default SMS table spaces of the database. This parameter is not updateable.
PCKCACHESZ	*pckcachesz*	Specifies the amount of application heap memory that will be used for caching packages.
REC_HIS_RETENTN	*rec_his_retentn*	Specifies the number of days that historical information on backups will be retained.
N/A	*release*	Specifies the release level of the database configuration file. This parameter is not updateable.
N/A	*restore_pending*	Specifies whether or not the database is in "Restore Pending" state. This parameter is not updateable.
N/A	*rollfwd_pending*	Specifies whether or not a roll-forward recovery procedure needs to be performed before the database can be used. If this parameter is set to NO, neither the database nor any of its table space is in "Roll-forward Pending" state. If this parameter is set to DATABASE, the database needs to be rolled forward before it can be used. If this parameter is set to TABLESPACES, one or more table spaces in the database need to be rolled forward. This parameter is not updateable.

Keyword	Parameter Name	Description
SEQDETECT	seqdetect	Specifies whether or not sequential detection for the database is enabled.
SOFTMAX	softmax	Specifies the maximum percentage of log file space to be consumed before a soft checkpoint is taken.
SORT_HEAP	sortheap	Specifies the number of private memory pages that are available for each sort operation in an application program.
STAT_HEAP_SZ	stat_heap_sz	Specifies the maximum size of the heap space (in pages) that will be used in creating and collecting all table statistics when distribution statistics are gathered.
STMTHEAP	stmtheap	Specifies the heap size (in pages) that will be used for compiling SQL statements.
N/A	territory	Specifies the territory of the database. This parameter is not updateable.
TSM_MGMTCLASS	tsm_mgmtclass	Specifies how the server should manage backup versions or archive copies of the objects being backed up. The TSM management class is assigned from the TSM administrator.
TSM_NODENAME	tsm_nodename	Specifies the node name associated with the TSM product (used to override the default setting).
TSM_OWNER	tsm_owner	Specifies the owner associated with the TSM product (used to override the default setting).
TSM_PASSWORD	tsm_password	Specifies the password associated with the TSM product (used to override the default setting).
USER_EXIT	userexit	Specifies whether or not a user exit function for archiving or retrieving log files can be called the next time the database is opened. If this parameter is set to OFF, a user exit function cannot be called. If this parameter is set to ON, a user exit function can be called.
N/A	user_exit_status	Specifies whether or not a user exit function can be called to store archive log files. If this parameter is set to OFF, a user exit function cannot be called to store archive log files. If this parameter is set to ON, a user exit function can be called to store archive log files. This parameter is not updateable.

(continued)

Table 11-8   Keywords Recognized by the UPDATE DATABASE CONFIGURATION SQL
Statement *(continued)*

Keyword	Parameter Name	Description
UTIL_HEAP_SZ	*util_heap_sz*	Specifies the maximum amount of shared memory that can be used simultaneously by the backup, restore, and load utilities.

Changing the Value of a DB2 Registry or Environment Variable

In addition to DB2 Database Manager and database configuration parameters, DB2 Universal Database utilizes several registry and environment variables that can be used to configure the system where DB2 Universal Database has been installed. Because changes made to registry and environment variables impact the entire system, changes should be carefully considered before they are made.

From a certification standpoint, knowing what registry and environment variables are available is not as important as knowing how the value of a registry or an environment variable can be changed. The system command DB2SET is used to display, set, or remove DB2 registry profile variables. The syntax for this command is

```
DB2SET <[Variable] = [Value]> <-g> <-i [Instance] <NodeNumber>>
<-all> <-null> <-r [Instance] <NodeNumber>> <-n [DASNode]
<-u [UserID] <-p [Password]>>> <-l | -lr> <-v> <-ul | -ur>
<-h | -?>
```

where:

Variable   Identifies the registry or environment variable whose value will be displayed, set, or removed.

Value   Identifies the value that will be assigned to the registry or environment variable specified. If no value is specified, but a registry or environment variable is specified, the registry or environment specified is deleted.

Instance   Identifies the instance profile that the registry or environment variable specified is associated with.

NodeNumber   Identifies a specific node that is listed in the file db2nodes.cfg.

DASNode   Identifies the name of the node where the remote DB2 Administration Server instance resides.

PART III

UserID   Identifies the authentication ID that will be used to attach to the DB2 Administration Server instance.

Password   Identifies the password (for the authentication ID) that will be used to attach to the DB2 Administration Server instance.

Table 11-9 describes the options shown with this command.

For example, when executed, the system command

```
DB2SET -all DB2COMM
```

will display all values that have been defined for the DB2COMM variable of the current instance.

After changing the value of a registry variable, the DB2 Database Manager must be stopped and then restarted before the changes take effect. After changing the value of any environment variable, the system must be rebooted before the changes take effect.

Table 11-9   Options Recognized by the DB2SET System Command

DB2SET System Command Option	Description
-g	Indicates that a global profile variable will be displayed, set, or removed.
-i	Indicates that an instance profile variable will be displayed, set, or removed.
-all	Indicates that all occurrences of the local environment variables as defined in the following are displayed: • The environment, denoted by [-e] • The node-level registry, denoted by [-n] • The instance-level registry, denoted by [-i] • The global-level registry, denoted by [-g]
-null	Indicates that the value of the variable at the specified registry level will be set to NULL. (This avoids having to look up the value in the next registry level, as defined by the search order.)
-r	Indicates that the profile registry for the given instance is reset.
-n	Indicates that a remote DB2 Administration Server instance node name is specified.
-u	Indicates that an authentication ID that will be used to attach to the DB2 Administration Server instance is specified.

(continued)

Table 11-9 Options Recognized by the DB2SET System Command

DB2SET System Command Option	Description
-p	Indicates that a password for the authentication ID specified is provided.
-l	Indicates that all instance profiles will be listed.
-lr	Indicates that all registry variables supported will be listed.
-v	Indicates that verbose mode will be used.
-ul	Indicates that user profile variables will be accessed. (This parameter is only valid on Windows operating systems.)
-ur	Indicates that user profile variables will be refreshed. (This parameter is only valid on Windows operating systems.)
-h or -?	Indicates that help information for the DB2SET command will be displayed. If this option is specified, all other options are ignored and help information is displayed.

Summary

The goal of this chapter was to introduce you to the set of tools that come with DB2 Universal Database that are used to monitor the events that take place in a database system and introduce you to the tool that can be used to analyze SQL operations.

Along with tools like the Control Center and the Command Line Processor, DB2 Universal Database provides a powerful tool known as the Database System Monitor that can acquire information about the current state of a database system or about the state of a database system over a specified period of time. Once collected, this information can be used to do the following:

- Monitor database activity.
- Assist in problem determination.
- Analyze database system performance.
- Aid in configuring/tuning the database system.

Although the Database System Monitor is often referred to as a single monitor, in reality it consists of several individual monitors that have distinct, but related purposes. One of these individual monitors is known as the snapshot monitor; the rest are known as event monitors. Both types of monitors can be controlled using commands, administrative application programming interface (API) functions, and/or interfaces that are available with the Control Center.

The snapshot monitor is designed to provide information about the state of a DB2 Universal Database instance and the data it controls, and call attention to situations that appear to be peculiar, irregular, abnormal, or difficult to classify. This information is provided in the form of a series of snapshots, each of which represents what the system looks like at a specific point in time.

Obtaining some of the data collected by the snapshot monitor requires additional processing overhead. For example, in order to calculate the execution time of an SQL statement, the DB2 Database Manager must make a call to the operating system to obtain timestamps before and after the statement is executed. Such system calls are generally expensive. Fortunately, the snapshot monitor provides system administrators with a great deal of flexibility in choosing what information is collected when a snapshot is taken—the type and amount of information returned (and the amount of overhead required) when a snapshot is taken is determined by the way one or more snapshot monitor switches have been set. The following snapshot monitor switches are available:

- BUFFERPOOL
- LOCK
- SORT
- STATEMENT
- TABLE
- UOW (transaction)

Before a snapshot is taken, one or more snapshot monitor switches must be turned on (if all snapshot monitor switches available are turned off, only very basic snapshot monitor information will be collected). But before a particular snapshot monitor switch is turned on, it's a good idea to examine the current state of snapshot monitor switches available. The easiest way to examine the current state of the snapshot monitor switches available is by executing the GET MONITOR SWITCHES command, either from the Command Center or from the Command Line Processor. Once the current state of all snapshot monitor switches is known, you can tell the snapshot monitor to start (or stop) collecting specific snapshot monitor information by changing the state of one or more of the snapshot monitor switches available. The easiest way to change the state of a particular snapshot monitor switch is by executing the UPDATE MONITOR SWITCHES command, either from the Command Center or from the Command Line Processor.

When the UPDATE MONITOR SWITCHES command is used to turn a snapshot monitor switch on, the snapshot monitor information that is collected is only applicable for the application that activated the switch (for example, the Command Center or the Command Line Processor session in which the UPDATE MONITOR SWITCHES statement is executed). To tell the snapshot monitor to collect information for all applications that access any database within an instance, a DB2 Database Manager configuration file parameter must be used instead (there is a DB2 Database Manager configuration file parameter that corresponds to each snapshot monitor switch available).

Once a snapshot monitor switch has been turned on, the snapshot monitor begins collecting appropriate monitor data. To capture and view this data at a specific point in time, a snapshot must be taken. Snapshots can be taken by embedding the appropriate API in an application program or by executing the GET SNAPSHOT command, either from the Command Center or from the Command Line Processor.

The output produced by a snapshot contains, among other things, cumulative information about how often a particular activity was performed within some time frame window. This cumulative information is collected and stored in a wide variety of activity counters whose contents are retrieved at the time a snapshot is taken. So when does the counting start exactly? Counting begins

- When a snapshot monitor switch is turned on (or when the DB2 Database Manager is restarted after one or more of its configuration parameters that correspond to a snapshot monitor switch have been turned on)
- Each time the counters are manually reset

To use the snapshot monitor effectively, it is usually desirable to obtain snapshot information after a specific period of time has elapsed. To control the window of time that is monitored, reset the counters to zero when monitoring is to begin and then take a snapshot once the desired period of time has expired. Although snapshot monitor counters can be set to zero by turning all appropriate snapshot monitor switches off and back on, the easiest way to reset all snapshot monitor counters to zero is by executing the RESET MONITOR command, either from the Command Center or from the Command Line Processor.

It is important to note that you cannot selectively reset counters for a particular group (controlled by a snapshot monitor switch) by executing the RESET MONITOR command. Instead, if you only want to reset the counters associated with a specific snapshot monitor switch, you must turn that snapshot monitor switch off and back on.

Unfortunately, some database activities cannot be monitored easily with the snapshot monitor. Take, for example, when a deadlock cycle occurs. In Chapter 7, we saw that if the deadlock detector "awakes" and discovers that a deadlock exists in the locking system, it randomly selects, rolls back, and terminates one of the transactions involved in the deadlock cycle. (The transaction that is rolled back and terminated receives an SQL error code, all locks it had acquired are released, and the remaining transaction(s) are then allowed to proceed.) Information about this series of events cannot be easily captured by the snapshot monitor because in all likelihood, the deadlock cycle will have been broken long before a snapshot can be taken. An event monitor, on the other hand, could be used to capture such information. This is because unlike the snapshot monitor, which is used to record the state of database activity at a specific point in time, an event monitor is used to record database activity as soon as a specific event or transition occurs.

Although event monitors return information that is very similar to the information returned by the snapshot monitor, the event controls when the snapshot is taken. Specifically, event monitors can capture and write system monitor data to a file or a named pipe whenever any of the following events occur:

- A transaction is terminated.

- An SQL statement is executed.

- A deadlock cycle is detected.

- A connection to a database is established.

- A connection to a database is terminated.

- A database is activated.

- A database is deactivated.

- An SQL statement's subsection completes processing (when a database is partitioned).

- The FLUSH EVENT MONITOR SQL statement is executed.

Unlike the snapshot monitor, which resides in the background and is controlled by the settings of the snapshot monitor switches (or corresponding DB2 Database Manager configuration parameter values), event monitors are created using Data Definition Language (DDL) statements. Because of this, event monitors only gather information for the database in which they have been defined; event monitors cannot be used to collect information at the DB2 Database Manager instance level.

The easiest way to create an event monitor is by using the Create Event Monitor dialog, which is invoked by selecting the *Create* action from the *Event monitor* menu found in the Event Monitors GUI tool. [The Event Monitors GUI tool is activated by entering the command db2emcrt at the system command prompt or by selecting the Event Monitors entry from the DB2 folder (non-UNIX platforms only).] Event monitors can also be created by executing the CREATE EVENT MONITOR SQL statement, either from the Command Center or from the Command Line Processor.

Just as one or more snapshot monitor switches must be turned on before a snapshot is taken, one or more event monitors must be turned on before event monitor data will be collected. (An event monitor will be turned on, or made active, automatically each time the database is started if the AUTOSTART option was specified when the event monitor was created.) As soon as an event monitor is created with the Create Event Monitor dialog, it is made active by default. However, if you choose to override this default behavior, you can activate the event monitor at any time (once it has been created) by highlighting the event monitor in the list of available event monitors shown in the Event Monitors GUI tool and selecting the *Start Event Monitoring* action from the *Event monitor* menu. Event monitors can also be activated by executing the SET EVENT MONITOR STATE SQL statement, either from the Command Center or from the Command Line Processor.

Once an event monitor is activated, it sits quietly in the background and waits for one of the events it is associated with to occur. When such an event takes place, the event monitor collects information that is appropriate for the event that fired it and writes that information to the event monitor's target location. If the target location is a named pipe, a stream of data will be written directly to the named pipe. If the target location is a directory, the stream of data will be written directly to one or more files.

Because some events, such as database events, do not activate event monitors as frequently as others, it can often be desirable to have an event monitor to write its current monitor values to its target location before the monitor triggering event occurs. In such situations, a system administrator can force an event monitor to write all information collected so far to the appropriate output location by executing the FLUSH EVENT MONITOR SQL statement, either from the Command Center or from the Command Line Processor.

Records that are written to an event monitor's target location prematurely are logged in the event monitor log and assigned the identifier "partial record" unless the BUFFER option is specified when the FLUSH EVENT MONITOR statement is executed. In this case, only data that is already present in the event monitor buffers is written out; a partial record is not generated.

Because data files that are produced by an event monitor are written in binary format, their contents cannot be viewed directly with a text editor. Instead, one of two special utilities that are provided with DB2 Universal Database must be used:

- **Event Analyzer** A GUI tool that will read the information stored in an event monitor data file and produce a listing

- **db2evmon** A text-based tool that will read the information stored in an event monitor data file and generate a report

When an event monitor is no longer needed, it can be removed (dropped) from the database just like any other object. The easiest way to delete an existing event monitor is by selecting the *Remove* action from the *Event monitor* menu found in the Event Monitors GUI tool. An event monitor can also be destroyed by executing the DROP EVENT MONITOR SQL statement, either from the Command Center or from the Command Line Processor.

In addition to the snapshot monitor and the event monitors that comprise the Database System Monitor, DB2 Universal Database provides a special monitor known as the Performance Monitor that can be used to take snapshots of one or more performance monitor variables at predefined intervals. The Performance Monitor runs using a predefined configuration that is composed of up to 212 different performance monitor variables, which are grouped by level (Instance, Database, Table, Table Space, Connection) and category (Agents, Connections, Sorts, Buffer Pool and I/O, Lock and Deadlocks, Table, SQL Statement Activity) according to the type of information they provide. Eighteen predefined Performance Monitor configurations are provided when DB2 Universal Database is installed. You can use any of these configurations as they are, you can copy and modify them to meet your specific needs, or you can create new configurations from scratch, using the Performance Monitor GUI tools that can be invoked from the Control Center menus.

One nice feature the Performance Monitor tool provides is the capability to take a series of snapshots of the variables being monitored over a period of time and graph the information obtained from each snapshot so that significant changes can be seen quickly. A second feature is its capability to assign threshold values to each performance monitor variable being monitored. Once one or more threshold values have been assigned to a performance monitor variable, the display colors of that particular item will change from green to yellow (lower threshold values) or red (higher threshold values) when those threshold values are exceeded and, if desired, a message can be generated or a command script can be executed.

The DB2 Query Patroller provides a way for database administrators to govern the execution of queries and manage the resources required by those queries so that hundreds of users can safely submit queries on multiterabyte class systems and receive results within an acceptable time frame. DB2 Query Patroller also enables administrators to set individual user and group priorities, as well as user query cost threshold limits. This enables a data warehouse to deliver query results to its most important users first. It also has the capability to limit usage of system resources by stopping runaway queries before they start. In addition, DB2 Query Patroller captures information such as the requesting user's ID, I/O cost, result data set/table size, and elapsed query run time each time a query is processed.

The DB2 Query Patroller Tracker is a tool that provides two key features that enable a system administrator to manage databases in a data warehouse. First, it gives the system administrator the ability to monitor the database load and activity over a specified period of time by displaying usage history in a graphical, user-friendly format. Second, it provides the administrator with details on table and column access that can be used to tune the system. Because the Query Patroller server stores the historical information in DB2 tables, administrators can drill down on whatever aspects of the database usage they desire, using the query tool of their choice.

When a source code file containing static SQL statements is processed by the SQL Precompiler, the DB2 Optimizer analyzes every SQL statement encountered and generates a corresponding access plan. Each access plan contains information about the strategy that will be used to process the statement (such as whether or not indexes will be used, what sort methods, if any, are required, what locking semantics are needed, and what join methods, if any, will be used.) The executable form of these access plans is stored as packages in the system catalog tables. If dynamic SQL statements are used, either in an application or by a tool such as the Command Line Processor, the DB2 Optimizer is invoked during program execution to generate the access plan needed. Such access plans are temporarily stored in memory (in the global package cache) rather than in the system catalog. (If an SQL statement is executed and its access plan already exists in the global package cache, the existing access plan is reused and the DB2 Optimizer is not called again.)

Although the monitors that are available with DB2 Universal Database can be used to obtain information about how SQL operations perform, they do not provide the information needed to analyze SQL statements for problems that may be the result of a poorly written statement or a weak database design. To perform this type of analysis, you must be able to view the information stored in an SQL statement's access plan—to view a statement's access plan, you must use DB2 Universal Database's Explain Facility.

With the Explain Facility, detailed optimizer information on the access plan chosen for an SQL statement can be both collected and viewed. When such information is collected for an access plan, that information is stored separately from the access plan in a special set of tables known as the Explain tables. By default, the Explain tables are not created as part of the database creation process. They must be manually created in the database that the Explain Facility will be used with before any component of the Explain Facility is invoked.

DB2 Universal Database's Explain Facility consists of several different interface tools, which have their own data requirements. Because of this, two basic types of data can be collected from an SQL statement's access plan:

- **Explain data** Contains detailed information about an SQL statement's access plan and stores this information in the appropriate Explain tables.

- **Explain snapshot data** Contains information about the current internal representation of an SQL statement and any related information. (This information is stored in the SNAPSHOT column of the EXPLAIN_SNAPSHOT table.)

As with the Database System Monitor, both types of Explain Facility data can be collected through a variety of ways. Some ways to collect Explain Facility data include

- The EXPLAIN SQL statement
- The CURRENT EXPLAIN MODE and CURRENT EXPLAIN SNAPSHOT special registers
- The EXPLAIN and EXPLSNAP bind options

The easiest way to collect explain and/or explain snapshot information for a single dynamic SQL statement is by executing the EXPLAIN SQL statement from an application directly, from the Command Center, or from the Command Line Processor.

Another way to collect explain and/or explain snapshot information for dynamic SQL statements is by using two special registers, the CURRENT EXPLAIN SNAPSHOT special register and the CURRENT EXPLAIN MODE special register, which exist specifically to provide support for the Explain Facility. (DB2 Universal Database uses 14 special registers to keep track of specific pieces of information that are used to describe or control the environment in which SQL statements are executed.) The CURRENT EXPLAIN SNAPSHOT special register controls the behavior of the Explain Facility with respect to the collection of explain snapshot data; the CURRENT EXPLAIN MODE special register controls the behavior of the Explain Facility with respect to the collection of explain data.

To collect explain and/or explain snapshot information for static and/or dynamic SQL statements embedded in applications, two special bind options, the EXPLAIN option and the EXPLSNAP option, can be specified when the application that contains the SQL statements is bound to a specific database. As you might imagine, the EXPLAIN bind option controls the behavior of the Explain Facility with respect to the collection of explain data, and the EXPLSNAP bind option controls the behavior of the Explain

Facility with respect to the collection of explain snapshot data. Aside from that, there is no other difference between the two.

Once explain and/or explain snapshot data has been collected and stored in the Explain tables by the Explain Facility, the data collected can be retrieved and presented for evaluation in several ways:

- By using customized queries that poll the one or more of the Explain tables
- By using the `db2expln` tool
- By using the `dynexpln` tool
- By using the `db2exfmt` tool
- By using Visual Explain

Because monitoring adds additional processing overhead, the amount of time spent monitoring a system should be limited, and monitoring should always be performed with some purpose in mind. Often the purpose for monitoring is to provide greater concurrency and eliminate potential bottlenecks that can slow down database response time. However, monitoring can also be used to provide input into how a DB2 Database Manager instance or a database under an instance should be configured so that resource utilization is optimized.

DB2 Universal Database uses an extensive array of configuration parameters to control how a DB2 Database Manager instance or a specific database allocates system resources (such as disk space and memory). In many cases, the default values provided for these configuration parameters are sufficient to meet an application's needs. However, because the default values provided are oriented toward database systems that have relatively small amounts of memory and that are dedicated database servers, overall system and application performance can often be greatly improved by changing one or more configuration parameter values.

Configuration parameter values for the DB2 Database Manager instance are stored in a file named *db2systm* that is located in the *sqllib* directory where the DB2 Universal Database product was installed. (This file is created along with the DB2 Database Manager during the DB2 Universal Database product installation process.) Most values (parameters) in this file control the amount of system resources that will be allocated to a single instance of the DB2 Database Manager. Other values contain information about the DB2 Database Manager instance itself and cannot be changed.

The easiest way to examine the current values of the parameters of the DB2 Database Manager configuration file is by executing the GET DATABASE MANAGER CONFIGU-RATION command, either from the Command Center or from the Command Line

Processor. The easiest way to change the value of one or more DB2 Database Manager configuration parameters is by using the Configure Instance dialog, which is invoked by selecting the *Configure* action from the *Instances* menu found in the Control Center. The value of one or more DB2 Database Manager configuration parameters can also be changed by executing the UPDATE DATABASE MANAGER CONFIGURATION command, either from the Command Center or from the Command Line Processor.

Configuration parameter values for an individual database are stored in a file named *SQLDBCON* that is located in the *SQLxxxxx* directory that was created when the database was created (*xxxxx* represents the number assigned by the DB2 Database Manager during the database creation process). Many of the values (parameters) in this file control the amount of system resources that will be allocated to the associated database during normal operation. Other values contain information about the database itself (such as the current state of the database) and cannot be changed.

The easiest way to examine the current values of the parameters of a particular database's configuration file is by executing the GET DATABASE CONFIGURATION command, either from the Command Center or from the Command Line Processor. The easiest way to change the value of one or more database configuration parameters is by using the Configure Database dialog, which is invoked by selecting the *Configure* action from the *Databases* menu found in the Control Center. The value of one or more database configuration parameters can also be changed by executing the UPDATE DATABASE CONFIGURATION command, either from the Command Center or from the Command Line Processor.

In addition to DB2 Database Manager and database configuration parameters, DB2 Universal Database utilizes several registry and environment variables that can be used to configure the system where DB2 Universal Database has been installed. The system command DB2SET is used to display, set, or remove DB2 registry profile variables. After changing the value of a registry variable, the DB2 Database Manager must be stopped and then restarted before the changes take effect. After changing the value of any environment variable, the system must be rebooted before the changes take effect.

Questions

1. Which of the following will capture dynamic SQL explain snapshots for an application?
   a. The SET CURRENT EXPLAIN SNAPSHOT YES statement
   b. The SET CURRENT EXPLAIN SNAPSHOT NO statement
   c. The EXPLSNAP YES bind option
   d. The EXPLAIN YES bind option

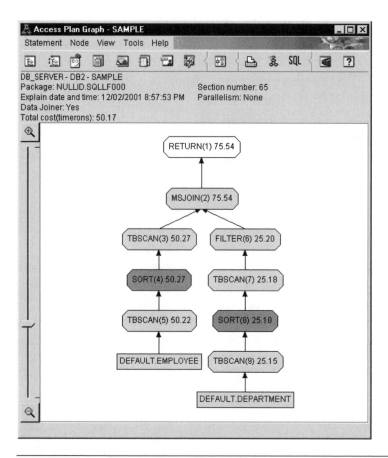

Figure 11-21   Visual Explain output

2. According to the Visual Explain output shown in Figure 11-21, how many index scans were performed?
   a. Zero
   b. One
   c. Two
   d. Three

3. What must be done prior to capturing an explain snapshot?
   a. Update the Explain directory.
   b. Create the Explain database.
   c. Rebind the Explain tool.
   d. Create the Explain tables.

4. Which SQL statement can be analyzed using the Explain Facility?

    a. COMMIT

    b. DESCRIBE

    c. ROLLBACK

    d. UPDATE

    e. GRANT

5. What is the minimum authority required to obtain a DB2 monitor snapshot?

    a. SYSADM

    b. DBCTRL

    c. DBADM

    d. PUBLIC

6. Given the following snapshot monitor output:

```
Total sort time (ms)                        = 153
Total buffer pool read time (ms)            = 3015
Total elapsed asynchronous read time (ms)   = 1960
Direct reads elapsed time (ms)              = 81
```

    How much time was spent prefetching data?

    a. 153 ms

    b. 3,015 ms

    c. 1,960 ms

    d. 81 ms

7. If a query is to provide a sorted result, how might DB2 perform the sorting operation?

    a. DB2 will not sort the result.

    b. DB2 will sort the data within the buffer pool.

    c. DB2 will always sort the data on disk.

    d. DB2 will attempt to perform the sort in memory.

8. If a DB2 event monitor has been defined for a database and it is active, where would its output be found?

    a. In the TEMPSPACE1 table space

    b. In a user-defined database table

    c. In the Explain tables

    d. In a user-defined directory location

9. If you wanted to record details of each occurrence of a deadlock within a database, what should be performed?

   a. Obtain a periodic database monitor snapshot.

   b. Use the Explain Facility.

   c. Examine the db2diag.log for each occurrence.

   d. Create an event monitor and examine its output.

10. Which of the following would be used to set the DB2_STRIPPED_CONTAINERS registry value to indicate that RAID devices will be used for table space containers?

    a. `UPDATE DBM CFG USING DB2_STRIPPED_CONTAINERS ON`

    b. `UPDATE DB CFG FOR ALL USING DB2_STRIPPED_CONTAINERS ON`

    c. `DB2SET DB2_STRIPPED_CONTAINERS=ON`

    d. `DB2 SET DB2_STRIPPED_CONTAINERS ON`

11. When will a specific performance monitor variable enter one of the red zones in the performance monitor graph?

    a. When a variable exceeds a threshold defined by the DB2 server

    b. When too many variables have been defined

    c. When too many users have connected to the database

    d. When a variable exceeds a threshold defined by the user

    e. When too much swapping occurs

Answers

1. **A.** The SET CURRENT EXPLAIN SNAPSHOT YES statement enables the explain snapshot facility and creates a snapshot of the internal representation for each eligible dynamic SQL statement. (This information is inserted in the SNAPSHOT column of the EXPLAIN_STATEMENT table.)

2. **A.** Apparently no indexes exist for the two tables that were used in this join operation—only table scans were performed. (The performance of this query could most likely be improved by creating indexes for both tables.)

3. **D.** Before any of the Explain tools can be used, the Explain tables must be created for the database that SQL statements will be explained for.

4. **D.** The Explain utility is designed to analyze SELECT, SELECT INTO, UPDATE, INSERT, VALUES, VALUES INTO, and DELETE SQL statements (the primary use is to observe the access paths for the SELECT parts of these statements).

5. **A.** Only users with System Administrator (SYSADM) authority, System Control (SYSCTRL) authority, or System Maintenance (SYSMAINT) authority are allowed to use the snapshot monitor.

6. **C.** Prefetching is viewed as asynchronous read operations by the snapshot monitor and the monitor output shown indicates that 1,960 milliseconds were spent performing asynchronous read operations.

7. **D.** The DB2 Database Manager always attempts to perform sorting operations in memory. If not enough memory is available, the sort will take place on disk (in the container(s) that makes up the system temporary table space used by the sort operation).

8. **D.** The location that output from a DB2 event monitor will be written to is specified with the WRITE TO clause of the CREATE EVENT MONITOR SQL statement.

9. **D.** The only way to record details of deadlocks as they occur is by creating an event monitor that monitors deadlock events.

10. **C.** The DB2SET command is used to set or change the values of registry and environment variables.

11. **D.** Users are responsible for setting threshold values for items that are monitored by the performance monitor. When the value for a variable exceeds the threshold value set, the monitor will chart the variable in the red zone.

PART III

CHAPTER 12

DB2 Universal Database's Data Movement and Data Management Utilities

In this chapter, you will learn

- What file formats are recognized by DB2 Universal Database's data movement utilities

- How to use the Export utility to extract specific portions of data from a database and externalize it to a file

- How to use the Import utility to make data stored in external files available to a database

- How to use the Load utility to bulk load a table using data stored in external files

- How to use the DB2MOVE utility to copy a database from one platform to another

- How to optimize the physical distribution of all data stored in a table

- How to update the information stored in the system catalog tables so that the DB2 Optimizer can choose the best data access path available when resolving a query

The fifth objective of the DB2 Universal Database—Database Administration for UNIX, Windows, and OS/2 exam is to test your knowledge about the data movement and data management utilities that are available with DB2 Universal Database. Knowing what tools are available is just as important as knowing which tool to use to perform a specific task. This chapter is designed to introduce you to the data movement and data management utilities that are provided by DB2 Universal Database, Version 7.x.

 TIP Eighteen percent of the DB2 Universal Database—Database Administration for UNIX, Windows, and OS/2 exam is designed to test your knowledge of DB2 Universal Database's data movement and data management utilities.

DB2 Universal Database's Data Movement Utilities

Although a database is normally thought of as a single self-contained entity, there are times when it becomes necessary for a database to exchange data with the outside world. For this reason, DB2 Universal Database provides four different utilities that are used to move data between databases and external files. Specifically, these utilities are the

- Export utility
- Import utility
- Load utility
- DB2MOVE utility

In a few moments, we will take a closer look at each of these utilities. However, before we do, it is important to become familiar with the different file formats that each utility supports because the file format plays a large part in how these utilities process data.

Supported File Formats

Whenever data is moved between databases and external files, care must be taken to ensure that data that resides in an external file that is accessed by one of DB2 Universal Database's data movement utilities has been stored in a format that can be easily processed. Otherwise, more time may be spent correcting data after it has been moved than was required to actually move the data! To assist in this regard, DB2 Universal Database recognizes and supports the following data file formats (a file's format determines how data is physically stored in the file):

- **Delimited ASCII (DEL)**   This format consists of data values (variable in length) that are separated by a delimiting (field separator) character. Because commas (,) are typically used as the field separator character, this format is sometimes referred to as Comma-Separated Variable (CSV) format.

- **Nondelimited ASCII (ASC)**   This format consists of fixed-length data values that are column aligned.

- **Worksheet Format (WSF)**   This format defines the layout of data that has been stored in a file format that is compatible with IBM's Lotus 1-2-3 and Lotus Symphony products.

- **PC Integrated Exchange Format (IXF)**   This format consists of data values that are stored in a format that is compatible with all DB2 Universal Database products.

Delimited ASCII (DEL) Format

The delimited ASCII (DEL) format is used extensively in relational database management systems (RDBMSs) and many software applications for exchanging data with a wide variety of application products (especially with other database products). With this format, a delimiter (which is a unique character that is not found in the data values themselves) is used to identify the beginning or end of each data element in a file. Some of the more common delimiters that are used in DEL files include

- **Column delimiters**   Column delimiters are used to mark the end of a data value that is associated with a particular column (based on its position in the file). In most cases, the comma (,) character is used as the column delimiter for a file.

- **Row delimiters**   Row delimiters are used to mark the end of a record or row. On UNIX systems, the newline character (0x0A) is often used as the row delimiter for a file. On Windows and OS/2 systems, the carriage return/linefeed characters (0x0D to 0x0A) are often used as the row delimiter for a file.

- **Character delimiters**   Character delimiters are used to mark the beginning and end of character data values. In most cases, the double quote character (") is used as the character delimiter for a file.

Typically, when data is written to a DEL file, rows are streamed into the file (one after another)—the specified column delimiter separates each column's data value and the specified row delimiter separates each row. If a column's data value is a character value, it is preceded and followed by the specified character delimiter. Numeric values are represented by their ASCII equivalent—the period character (.) is used to denote the

PART III

decimal point, if appropriate; real values are represented with scientific notation (E); negative values are preceded by the minus character (−); and positive values may be preceded by the plus character (+).

For example, if the contents of the ORG table of the SAMPLE database (which is shipped with the DB2 Universal Database Product) were stored in a DEL format file and if the comma character was used as the column delimiter, the carriage return/line-feed character was used as the row delimiter, and the double quote character was used as the character delimiter, the contents of the file would look something like this:

```
10,"Head Office",160,"Corporate","New York"
15,"New England",50,"Eastern","Boston"
20,"Mid Atlantic",10,"Eastern","Washington"
38,"South Atlantic",30,"Eastern","Atlanta"
42,"Great Lakes",100,"Midwest","Chicago"
51,"Plains",140,"Midwest","Dallas"
66,"Pacific",270,"Western","San Francisco"
84,"Mountain",290,"Western","Denver"
```

Nondelimited ASCII (ASC) Format

The nondelimited ASCII (ASC) format, sometimes referred to as the fixed-length ASCII format, is also used to exchange data with a wide variety of application products. With this format, the position of each data element in a file determines which column and row it belongs to. When data is written to an ASC file, rows are streamed into the file (one after another)—all column values are written using a fixed length and either the newline characters (UNIX systems) or the carriage return/linefeed characters (Windows and OS/2 systems) separate each row. If a column's data value is a character value, it is padded with blanks, if appropriate, to meet the fixed length for the column—character delimiters are not used. As with DEL files, numeric values are represented by their ASCII equivalent—the period character (.) is used to denote the decimal point, if appropriate; real values are represented with scientific notation (E); negative values are preceded by the minus character (−); and positive values may be preceded by the plus character (+).

Using the example from earlier, if the contents of the ORG table of the SAMPLE database were stored in a ASC format, the contents of the file would look something like this:

```
10Head Office    160CorporateNew York
15New England    50 Eastern   Boston
20Mid Atlantic   10 Eastern   Washington
38South Atlantic30 Eastern    Atlanta
42Great Lakes    100Midwest    Chicago
51Plains         140Midwest    Dallas
66Pacific        270Western    San Francisco
84Mountain       290Western    Denver
```

NOTE Although the Load utility and the Import utility support this format, the Export utility does not.

Worksheet Format (WSF)

The worksheet format (WSF) is a special file format that is used exclusively by the Lotus 1-2-3 and Lotus Symphony spreadsheet products. Although different releases of these products have incorporated different features in the file formats they use for data storage, a subset of features still resides within each, and it is this subset that is recognized and used by DB2 Universal Database's data movement utilities. Worksheet files cannot be edited with a normal text editor.

NOTE Although the Export utility and the Import utility support this format, the Load utility does not.

PC Integrated Exchange Format (PC/IXF)

PC Integrated Exchange Format (PC/IXF or IXF) is a special file format that is used almost exclusively by DB2 Universal Database to move data between different DB2 Universal Database databases. In general, data is written to a IXF file as an unbroken sequence of variable-length records. Character data values are stored in their ASCII representation without additional padding; numeric values are stored as packed decimal or binary values, depending upon their original data type. Table definitions (including associated index definitions) are also stored in IXF files; thus, tables and associated indexes can be created and populated, if necessary, when this format is used.

NOTE If a table contains packed character data, the data will have to be unpacked before it can be written to a IXF file. The simplest way to unpack packed character data is to create a view on the table that contains the packed data. Because such a view will automatically form character data from packed character data, the view itself can then be used to write the data to a IXF file.

Like worksheet files, IXF files cannot be edited with a normal text editor.

Obtaining Columnar Data from External Files

As you can see, the file format determines how data is physically stored in an external file. Likewise, the file format determines the method that must be used with the DB2 data movement in order to correctly identify how data values in a file are mapped to the columns of a table. Three methods are available for mapping data values to columns:

- The location method (coded as METHOD L)
- The name method (coded as METHOD N)
- The position method (coded as METHOD P)

The Location Method

With the location method, columnar data values are identified by a series of beginning and ending byte position values that when used together identify the location of a column value within a single row. Each byte position value is treated as an offset from the beginning of the row (which is byte position 1). Figure 12-1 illustrates how the location method is used to identify how specific data values in a file are mapped to columns in a table. The location method can only be used with files that are stored in ASC format.

The Name Method

With the name method, columnar data values are identified by the name of the column they are associated with in the file. That's because when this method is used, the DB2 data management utilities expect column names and information about which column each data value is associated with to be stored in the file along with the data values themselves. Figure 12-2 illustrates how the name method is used to identify how specific data values in a file are mapped to columns in a table. The name method can only be used with files that are stored in IXF format.

The Position Method

With the position method, columnar data values are identified by their indexed position within a single row—the first data value found in a row has the index position 1, the second value found has the index position 2, and so on. Figure 12-3 illustrates how the position method is used to identify how specific data values in a file are mapped to columns in a table.

The position method can be used with files that are stored in DEL or IXF format. The position method must be used if files are stored in DEL format.

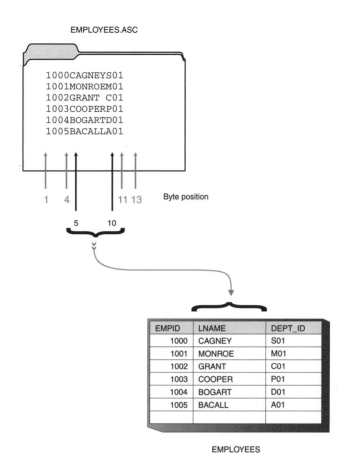

Figure 12-1   Obtaining columnar data with the location method

The Export Utility

DB2 Universal Database's Export utility is used to extract specific portions of data from a database and externalize it to DEL, WSF, or IXF formatted files. Such files can then be used to populate tables in a variety of databases (including the database the data was extracted from) or provide input to software applications such as spreadsheets and word processors.

At a minimum, the following information must be provided when the Export utility is invoked:

- A valid SQL SELECT statement that will retrieve the specific data that will be exported

- The location and name of the file that all data retrieved by the SELECT statement specified will be written to

- The format that data is written to the file in

- The location and name of the file that messages generated by the Export utility will be written to

Figure 12-4 illustrates how these elements are used to perform a simple export operation.

When the data that is exported contains large object (LOB) values, by default, only the first 32KB of each LOB value are actually written to the file that contains the exported data. This is not a problem if every LOB data value being exported is less than 32KB in size. However, if the default behavior is used and LOB data that is greater than

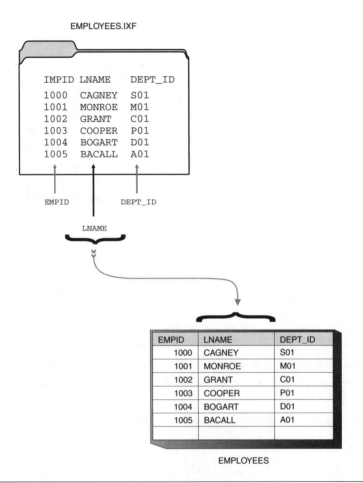

Figure 12-2 Obtaining columnar data with the name method

EMPLOYEES.IXF

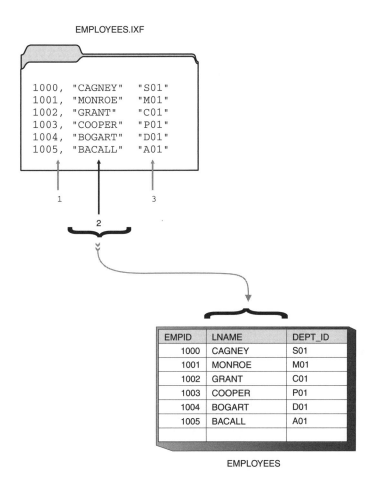

Figure 12-3   Obtaining columnar data with the position method

---

32KB in size is exported, the data will be truncated. Usually, this is undesirable behavior. By overriding this default behavior and by providing the Export utility with one or more locations that LOB data is written to, each LOB data value encountered will be stored in its entirety in its own individual file (that is assigned a name that either the user or the Export utility provides) instead. Figure 12-5 illustrates a simple export operation in which LOB data is processed in this manner.

Default behavior can also be overridden when exporting data stored in Typed tables. However, from a certification viewpoint, knowing how to export Typed tables as well as knowing the EXPORT command options available for exporting Typed tables is not important. Therefore, these topics will not be addressed.

EMPLOYEES

EMPID	LNAME	DEPT_ID
1000	CAGNEY	S01
1001	MONROE	M01
1002	GRANT	C01
1003	COOPER	P01
1004	BOGART	D01
1005	BACALL	A01

EMPLOYEES.IXF

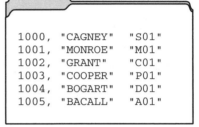

```
1000,  "CAGNEY"   "S01"
1001,  "MONROE"   "M01"
1002,  "GRANT"    "C01"
1003,  "COOPER"   "P01"
1004,  "BOGART"   "D01"
1005,  "BACALL"   "A01"
```

EXPORT TO EMPLOYEES.DEL OF DEL
SELECT * FROM EMPLOYEES

EMPLOYEES.DEL

Figure 12-4   A simple export operation

Performing an Export Operation

The easiest way to perform an export operation is by selecting the *Export* action from the *Table* menu found in the Control Center and providing the appropriate information when the Export Table dialog is displayed. Figure 12-6 shows the Control Center menu items that must be selected in order to activate the Export Table dialog. Figure 12-7 shows how the first page of this dialog might look after its input fields have been populated.

The Export utility can also be invoked by executing the EXPORT command, either from the Command Center or from the Command Line Processor. The syntax for this command is

```
EXPORT TO [FileName] OF [DEL | WSF | IXF] <LOBS TO [LOBPath ,...]>
<LOBFILE [LOBFileName ,...]> <MODIFIED BY [Modifier ,...]> <METHOD
N ( [ColumnName ,...] )> <MESSAGES [MessageFileName]>
[SelectStatement]
```

where:

FileName   Identifies the name and location of the file that exported data will be written to.

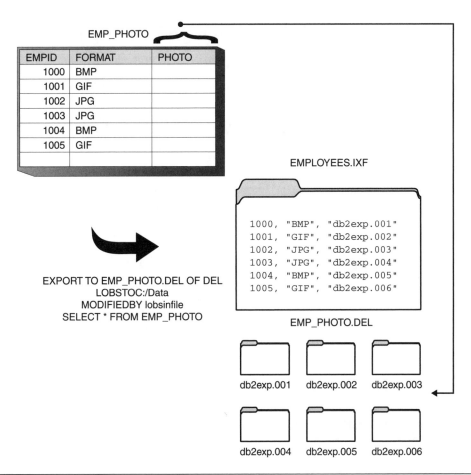

EMP_PHOTO

EMPID	FORMAT	PHOTO
1000	BMP	
1001	GIF	
1002	JPG	
1003	JPG	
1004	BMP	
1005	GIF	

EMPLOYEES.IXF

```
1000,  "BMP",  "db2exp.001"
1001,  "GIF",  "db2exp.002"
1002,  "JPG",  "db2exp.003"
1003,  "JPG",  "db2exp.004"
1004,  "BMP",  "db2exp.005"
1005,  "GIF",  "db2exp.006"
```

EXPORT TO EMP_PHOTO.DEL OF DEL
LOBSTOC:/Data
MODIFIEDBY lobsinfile
SELECT * FROM EMP_PHOTO

EMP_PHOTO.DEL

db2exp.001   db2exp.002   db2exp.003

db2exp.004   db2exp.005   db2exp.006

Figure 12-5   A simple export operation in which LOB data is stored in individual files

LOBPath   Identifies one or more locations where files containing LOB data will
                 be stored.

LOBFileName Identifies one or more base filenames that are used to name the files
                 that LOB data values will be written to. During an export operation,
                 filenames are constructed by appending a period (.) and a three-digit
                 sequence number to the current base filename in this list, and then
                 appending the generated filename to the LOB data path specified (in
                 LOBPath). For example, if the current LOB path is the directory
                 C:\Data Files and the current LOB filename is Value, the LOB files
                 created will be C:\Data Files\Value.001, C:\Data Files\Value.002, and
                 so on.

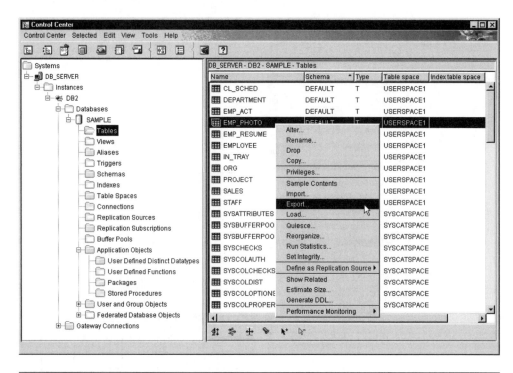

Figure 12-6 Invoking the Export Table dialog from the Control Center

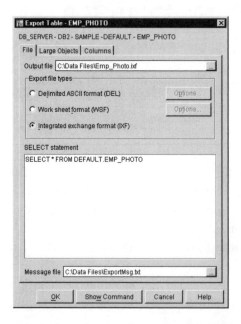

Figure 12-7 The first page of the Export Table dialog

Modifier	Identifies one or more options that are used to override one or more default behaviors of the Export utility. Table 12-1 shows the list of possible modifiers.
ColumnName	Identifies one or more column names that will be written to the file that exported data is written to. If this option is not used, the column names in the table are written to the file.
MessageFileName	Identifies the name and location of the file that messages generated by the Export utility will be written to during the export operation.
SelectStatement	Identifies a valid dynamic SELECT statement that when executed, will retrieve the data from the database that will be written to an external file.

PART III

Table 12-1   File Type Modifiers Recognized by the Export Utility

Modifier	Description
All File Formats	
lobsinfile	Indicates that LOB data values will be written to individual files.
Delimited ASCII (DEL) Format	
chardel*x* (where *x* is any valid delimiter character)	Identifies a specific character that will be used as a character delimiter. The default character delimiter is a double quotation mark (") character. The character specified is used in place of double quotation marks to enclose a character string.
coldel*x* (where *x* is any valid delimiter character)	Identifies a specific character that will be used as a column delimiter. The default column delimiter is a comma (,) character. The character specified is used in place of a comma to signal the end of a column.
datesiso	Indicates that all DATE data values will be exported in International Standards Organization (ISO) format (YYYY-MM-DD). By default, the Export utility normally writes the following: • DATE data in YYYYMMDD format • CHAR(date) data in YYYY-MM-DD format • TIME data in HH.MM.SS format • TIMESTAMP data in YYYY-MM-DD-HH.MM.SS.uuuuuu format
decplusblank	Indicates that positive decimal values are will be prefixed with a blank space instead of a plus sign (+). The default action prefixes positive decimal values with a plus sign.
decpt*x* (where *x* is any valid delimiter character)	Identifies a specific character that will be used as a decimal point character. The default decimal point character is a period (.) character. The character specified is used in place of a period as a decimal point character.

(continued)

Table 12-1 File Type Modifiers Recognized by the Export Utility (*continued*)

Modifier	Description
dldel*x* (where *x* is any valid delimiter character)	Identifies a specific character that is will be used as a DATALINK delimiter. The default DATALINK delimiter is a semicolon (;) character. The character specified is used in place of a semicolon as the interfield separator for a DATALINK value. It is needed because a DATALINK value may have more than one subvalue. It is important to note that the character specified must not be the same as the row, column, or character delimiter used.
nodoubledel	Indicates that double character delimiters should not be recognized.
Worksheet Format (WSF)	
1	Indicates that a WSF file that is compatible with Lotus 1-2-3 Release 1 or Lotus 1-2-3 Release 1a will be created. By default, WSF files that are compatible with Lotus 1-2-3 Release 1 or Lotus 1-2-3 Release 1a are generated unless otherwise specified.
2	Indicates that a WSF file that is compatible with Lotus Symphony Release 1.0 will be created.
3	Indicates that a WSF file that is compatible with Lotus 1-2-3 Version 2 or Lotus Symphony Release 1.1 will be created.
4	Indicates that a WSF file that contains double-byte character system (DBCS) characters will be created.

For example, when executed, the commands

```
CONNECT TO SAMPLE
EXPORT TO C:\Data Files\Emp_Photo.ixf OF IXF LOBS TO C:\Data
Files\ MODIFIED BY lobsinfile MESSAGES C:\Data Files\ExportMsg.txt
SELECT * FROM EMP_PHOTO
```

will

- Establish a connection to the SAMPLE database (which is shipped with the DB2 Universal Database Product). A connection to a database must exist before data can be exported.

- Retrieve all data values found in the EMP_PHOTO table of the SAMPLE database.

- Write any value that is *not* an LOB data value to an external file, using the IXF format. This file will be assigned the name Emp_Photo.ixf, and it will reside in a directory named Data Files that is located on drive C:.

- Write all LOB data values found to their own individual file; each file created will reside in a directory named Data Files that is located on drive C:.

- Write any messages produced by the Export utility to a file named ExportMsg.txt that will reside in a directory named Data Files that is located on drive C:.

NOTE Only users with System Administrator (SYSADM) authority or Database Administrator (DBADMN) authority are allowed to invoke the Export utility.

The Import Utility

Just as there may be times when data in a database needs to be copied to external files, there may times when it is necessary to make data stored in external files available to a database. This is where DB2 Universal Database's Import utility comes in. The Import utility provides a way to read data directly from DEL, ASC, WSF, or IXF formatted files and store it in a specific database table.

At a minimum, the following information must be provided when the Import utility is invoked:

- The location and name of the file that data will be copied from

- The format that data in the file is stored in

- The name of the table that data stored in the file will be copied to

- An indication of how data will be copied to the table specified

- The location and name of the file that messages generated by the Import utility will be written to

Figure 12-8 illustrates how these elements are used to perform a simple import operation.

Ways to Import Data

When the Export utility is used to externalize data in a table to a IXF formatted file, the table structure and definitions of all of the table's associated indexes are written to the file along with the data. Because of this, the Import utility can create/re-create a table and its indexes as well as populate the table if data is being imported from a IXF formatted file. When any other file format is used, if the table or updateable view receiving the data already contains data values, the data being imported can either replace or

EMPLOYEES

EMPID	LNAME	DEPT_ID
1000	CAGNEY	S01
1001	MONROE	M01
1002	GRANT	C01
1003	COOPER	P01
1004	BOGART	D01
1005	BACALL	A01

EMPLOYEES.IXF

```
1000,  "CAGNEY"   "S01"
1001,  "MONROE"   "M01"
1002,  "GRANT"    "C01"
1003,  "COOPER"   "P01"
1004,  "BOGART"   "D01"
1005,  "BACALL"   "A01"
```

EMPLOYEES.DEL

EXPORT TO EMPLOYEES.DEL OF DEL
INSERT INTO EMPLOYEES

Figure 12-8   A simple import operation

be appended to the existing data, provided the base table receiving the data does not contain a primary key that is referenced by a foreign key of another table. (If the base table contains a primary key that is referenced by a foreign key, imported data can only be appended to the existing table.) In some situations, data being imported can also be used to update existing rows in a base table.

NOTE   Data can also be imported directly into a hierarchical structure that exists due to the relationship between two or more Typed tables. However, from a certification viewpoint, knowing how to import data into a Typed table hierarchy as well as knowing the IMPORT command options available for importing data into a Typed table hierarchy is not important. Therefore, these topics will not be addressed.

Importing LOB Data

Earlier we saw that when data that will be exported contains LOB values, by default, only the first 32KB bytes of each LOB value are actually written to the file that contains the exported data, and that by overriding this default behavior and providing the Export utility with one or more locations that LOB data will be written to, each LOB data value encountered will be stored in its entirety in its own individual file (that is assigned a name that either the user or the Export utility provides).

Thus, LOB data can reside in a source data file, or it can reside in one or more separate external files that a source data file references. If the latter is the case, they do not have to be provided as input to the Import utility because the names of the files that contain LOB data are stored in the source data file.

Figure 12-9 illustrates a simple import operation in which LOB data resides in individual files.

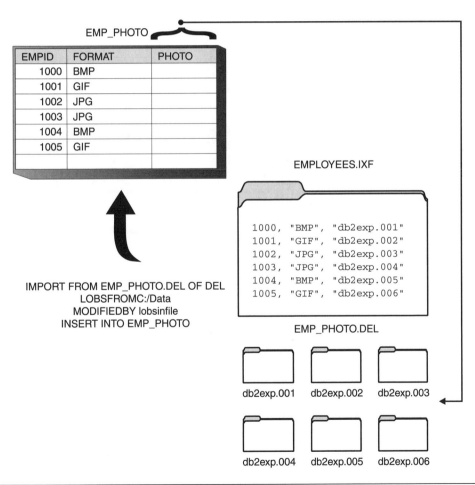

Figure 12-9   A simple import operation in which LOB data is stored in individual files

Performing an Import Operation

The easiest way to perform an import operation is by selecting the *Import* action from the *Table* menu found in the Control Center and providing the appropriate information when the Import Table dialog is displayed. Figure 12-10 shows the Control Center menu items that must be selected in order to activate the Import Table dialog. Figure 12-11 shows how the first page of this dialog might look after its input fields have been populated.

The Import utility can also be invoked by executing the IMPORT command, either from the Command Center or from the Command Line Processor. The syntax for this command is

```
IMPORT FROM [FileName] OF [DEL | WSF | IXF] <LOBS FROM [LOBPath
,...]> <MODIFIED BY [Modifier ,...]> <METHOD L ( [ColumnStart]
[ColumnEnd] ,... )> <NULL INDICATORS ( [NullIndColNumber ,...] )>
<COMMITCOUNT [CommitValue]> <RESTARTCOUNT [RestartValue]>
<MESSAGES [MessageFileName]> [CREATE INTO [TableName]
< ( [TableColName ,...] )> <IN [TableSpaceName] <INDEX IN
[IndexTSName]> <LONG IN [LongTSName]>> | [INSERT | INSERT_UPDATE |
REPLACE | REPLACE_CREATE] INTO [TableName]
< ( [TableColName ,...] )>]
```

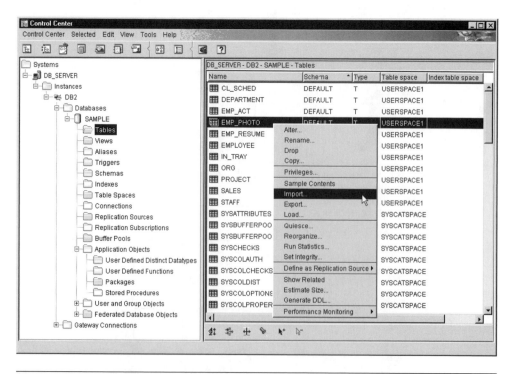

Figure 12-10   Invoking the Import Table dialog from the Control Center

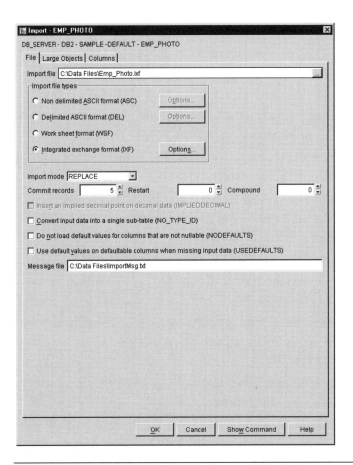

Figure 12-11 The first page of the Import Table dialog

or

```
IMPORT FROM [FileName] OF [DEL | WSF | IXF] <LOBS FROM [LOBPath ,...]>
<MODIFIED BY [Modifier ,...]> <METHOD N ( [ColumnName ,...] )>
<COMMITCOUNT [CommitValue]> <RESTARTCOUNT [RestartValue]>
<MESSAGES [MessageFileName]> [CREATE INTO [TableName]
< ( [TableColName ,...] )> <IN [TableSpaceName] <INDEX IN
[IndexTSName]> <LONG IN [LongTSName]>> | [INSERT | INSERT_UPDATE |
REPLACE | REPLACE_CREATE] INTO [TableName] < ( [TableColName ,...] )>]
```

or

```
IMPORT FROM [FileName] OF [DEL | WSF | IXF] <LOBS FROM [LOBPath ,...]>
<MODIFIED BY [Modifier ,...]> <METHOD P ( [ColumnPosition ,...] )>
<COMMITCOUNT [CommitValue]> <RESTARTCOUNT [RestartValue]>
<MESSAGES [MessageFileName]> [CREATE INTO [TableName]
```

```
< ( [TableColName ,...] )> <IN [TableSpaceName] <INDEX IN
[IndexTSName]> <LONG IN [LongTSName]>> | [INSERT | INSERT_UPDATE |
REPLACE | REPLACE_CREATE] INTO [TableName] < ( [TableColName ,...] )>]
```

where:

FileName	Identifies the name and location of the file that contains data that will be imported.
LOBPath	Identifies one or more locations where files containing LOB data that will be imported are stored.
Modifier	Identifies one or more options that are used to override one or more default behaviors of the Import utility. Table 12-2 shows the list of possible modifiers.
ColumnStart	Identifies the starting position of one or more data values (which marks the beginning of a column) that will be imported from a ASC format file.
ColumnEnd	Identifies the ending position of one or more data values (which marks the end of a column) that will be imported from a ASC format file.
ColumnName	Identifies the name of one or more columns that will be imported from a IXF formatted file.
ColumnPosition	Identifies the index position (starting at 1) of one or more columns that will be imported from a IXF or a DEL formatted file.
NullIndColNumber	Identifies the position of one or more data values that will be treated as null indicator variables for column data that is imported from a ASC format file.
CommitValue	Identifies the number of rows of data that will be read from the input data file specified and copied to the receiving table specified before a commit operation is performed.
RestartValue	Identifies the number of rows of data found in the input data file specified that will be skipped. This parameter is typically used when an earlier import operation fails midway through processing—by skipping rows that have already been successfully imported, a restarted import operation can essentially continue where it left off.

MessageFileName	Identifies the name and location of the file that messages generated by the Import utility will be written to during the import operation.
TableName	Identifies the name of the table (or updatable view) that imported data will be written to.
TableColName	Identifies one or more specific columns in the table or updatable view that imported data will be written to.
TableSpaceName	Identifies the table space that the table that will be created from the information stored in the IXF formatted file specified will be stored in.
IndexTSName	Identifies the database managed space (DMS) table space that all indexes for the table that will be created will be stored in.
LongTSName	Identifies the DMS table space that all long data for the table that will be created will be stored in.

Table 12-2 File Type Modifiers Recognized by the Import Utility

Modifier	Description
All File Formats	
compound=*x* where *x* is any number between 1 and 100	Indicates that nonatomic compound SQL should be used to insert the data read from a file into a table or updateable view and that a specific number of statements (between 1 and 100) will be included in the compound SQL block. This modifier is incompatible with INSERT_UPDATE mode, hierarchical tables, and the following modifiers: usedefaults, identitymissing, identityignore, generatedmissing, and generatedignore.
generatedignore	Indicates that data for all generated columns is present in the file being imported; however, that data should be ignored—instead, the Import utility should generate an appropriate value or set of values for each row.
generatedmissing	Indicates that data for all generated columns is missing from the file being imported—instead, the Import utility should generate an appropriate value or set of values for each row.
identityignore	Indicates that data for all identity columns is present in the file being imported; however, that data should be ignored—instead, the Import utility should generate an appropriate value or set of values for each row.
identitymissing	Indicates that data for all identity columns is missing from the file being imported—instead, the Import utility should generate an appropriate value or set of values for each row.

(continued)

Table 12-2   File Type Modifiers Recognized by the Import Utility (*continued*)

Modifier	Description
lobsinfile	Indicates that LOB data values will be read from individual files.
no_type_id	Indicates that data for Typed tables should be converted to a single nontyped subtable. This modifier is only valid when importing data into a single subtable.
nodefaults	Indicates that if the source column data for a target table column is not explicitly specified and the table column is not nullable, default values should not be loaded. If this modifier is not used and a source column data value for one of the target table columns is not explicitly specified, one of the following occurs: • If a default value can be specified for a column, the default value is loaded. • If the column is nullable and a default value cannot be specified for that column, a NULL is loaded. • If the column is not nullable and a default value cannot be specified, an error is returned and the Import utility stops processing.
usedefaults	Indicates that if a source column for a target table column has been specified, but the data file does not contain data for that column for one or more row, default values will be loaded. Examples of missing data include the following: • **For DEL format files** "„" is specified for the column. • **For ASC format files** The NULL indicator is set to yes for the column. • **For DEL/ASC/WSF format files** A row that does not have enough columns or is not long enough for the original specification. If this modifier is not used and a source column does not contain a data value for a row, one of the following occurs: • If the column is nullable, a NULL is loaded. • If the column is not nullable, the row is rejected.
Delimited/Nondelimited ASCII (DEL/ASC) Format	
dateformat="*x*" (where *x* is any valid combination of date format elements)	Identifies how date values in the source file are formatted. The following date elements can be used to create the format string provided with this modifier: • **YYYY** Year (four digits ranging from 0000 to 9999) • **M** Month (one or two digits ranging from 1 to 12) • **MM** Month (two digits ranging from 1 to 12; mutually exclusive with M) • **D** Day (one or two digits ranging from 1 to 31) • **DD** Day (two digits ranging from 1 to 31; mutually exclusive with D) • **DDD** Day of the year (three digits ranging from 001 to 366; mutually exclusive with other day or month elements) Some examples of date format strings are • D-M-YYYY • MM.DD.YYYY • YYYYDDD

Modifier	Description
implieddecimal	Indicates that the location of an implied decimal point is determined by the column definition—the Import utility should not assume that the decimal point is at the end of the value (default behavior). For example, if this modifier is specified, the value 12345 would be loaded into a DECIMAL(8,2) column as 123.45, *not* as 12345.00.
noeofchar	Indicates that the optional end-of-file character 0x1A is not to be treated as an end-of-file character. Instead, this character should be treated as a normal character if it is encountered.
timeformat="*x*" (where *x* is any valid combination of time format elements)	Identifies how time values in the source file are formatted. The following time elements can be used to create the format string provided with this modifier: • **H** Hour (one or two digits ranging from 0 to 12 for a 12-hour system and 0 to 24 for a 24-hour system) • **HH** Hour (two digits ranging from 0 to 12 for a 12-hour system and 0 to 24 for a 24-hour system; mutually exclusive with H) • **M** Minute (one or two digits ranging from 0 to 59) • **MM** Minute (two digits ranging from 0 to 59; mutually exclusive with M) • **S** Second (one or two digits ranging from 0 to 59) • **SS** Second (two digits ranging from 0 to 59; mutually exclusive with S) • **SSSSS** Second of the day after midnight (five digits ranging from 00000 to 86399; mutually exclusive with other time elements) • **TT** Meridian indicator (A.M. or P.M.) Some examples of time format strings are • HH:MM:SS • HH.MM TT • SSSSS
timestampformat="*x*" (where *x* is any valid combination of date and time format elements)	Identifies how timestamp values in the source file are formatted. The following date and time elements can be used to create the format string provided with this modifier: • **YYYY** Year (four digits ranging from 0000 to 9999) • **M** Month (one or two digits ranging from 1 to 12) • **MM** Month (two digits ranging from 1 to 12; mutually exclusive with M) • **D** Day (one or two digits ranging from 1 to 31) • **DD** Day (two digits ranging from 1 to 31; mutually exclusive with D) • **DDD** Day of the year (three digits ranging from 001 to 366; mutually exclusive with other day or month elements) • **H** Hour (one or two digits ranging from 0 to 12 for a 12-hour system and 0 to 24 for a 24-hour system) • **HH** Hour (two digits ranging from 0 to 12 for a 12-hour system and 0 to 24 for a 24-hour system; mutually exclusive with H) • **M** Minute (one or two digits ranging from 0 to 59) • **MM** Minute (two digits ranging from 0 to 59; mutually exclusive with M) • **S** Second (one or two digits ranging from 0 to 59)

(continued)

PART III

Table 12-2   File Type Modifiers Recognized by the Import Utility (*continued*)

Modifier	Description
timestampformat="x" (where x is any valid combination of date and time format elements)	• **SS** Second (two digits ranging from 0 to 59; mutually exclusive with S) • **SSSSS** Second of the day after midnight (five digits ranging from 00000 to 86399; mutually exclusive with other time elements) • **UUUUUU** Microsecond (six digits ranging from 000000 to 999999) • **TT** Meridian indicator (A.M. or P.M.) An example of a timestamp format string is • YYYY/MM/DD HH:MM:SS.UUUUUU
Nondelimited ASCII (ASC) Format	
nochecklengths	Indicates that the Import utility should attempt to import every row in the source file, even if the source data has a column definition that exceeds the size of the target column in the table. Such rows can be successfully imported if code page conversion causes the source data to shrink in size; for example, 4-byte EUC data in a source file could shrink to 2-byte DBCS data in the target table and require half the space. This option is particularly useful if it is known that the source data will fit in all cases despite mismatched column definitions.
nullindchar=x (where x is any valid character)	Identifies a specific character that will be used as a null indicator value. The default null indicator is the letter Y. The character specified is used in place of double quotation marks to enclose a character string. This modifier is case sensitive for Extended Binary Coded Decimal Interchange Code (EBCDIC) data files, except when the character is an English letter. For example, if the null indicator character is specified to be the letter N, then the letter n is also recognized as a null indicator.
reclen=x (where x is any number between 1 and 32767)	Indicates that a specific number of characters will be read from the source file for each row—newline characters should not be used to indicate the end of a row.
striptblanks	Indicates that trailing blank spaces will be truncated from values that are loaded into variable-length character fields. This modifier cannot be specified together with the striptnulls modifier; these are mutually exclusive options.
striptnulls	Indicates that trailing nulls (0x00 characters) will be truncated from values that are loaded into variable-length character fields. This modifier cannot be specified together with the striptblanks modifier; these are mutually exclusive options.
Delimited ASCII (DEL) Format	
chardelx (where x is any valid delimiter character)	Identifies a specific character that will be used as a character delimiter. The default character delimiter is a double quotation mark (") character. The character specified is used in place of double quotation marks to enclose a character string.

Modifier	Description
coldelx (where x is any valid delimiter character)	Identifies a specific character that will be used as a column delimiter. The default column delimiter is a comma (,) character. The character specified is used in place of a comma to signal the end of a column.
datesiso	Indicates that all DATE data values will be exported in ISO format (YYYY-MM-DD). By default, the Export utility normally writes • DATE data in YYYYMMDD format • CHAR(date) data in YYYY-MM-DD format • TIME data in HH.MM.SS format • TIMESTAMP data in YYYY-MM-DD-HH.MM.SS.uuuuuu format
decplusblank	Indicates that positive decimal values will be prefixed with a blank space instead of a plus sign (+). The default action prefixes positive decimal values with a plus sign.
decptx (where x is any valid delimiter character)	Identifies a specific character that will be used as a decimal point character. The default decimal point character is a period (.) character. The character specified is used in place of a period as a decimal point character.
delprioritychar	Indicates that the priority for evaluating delimiters is character delimiter, record delimiter, or column delimiter, rather than record delimiter, character delimiter, or column delimiter (which is the default). This modifier is typically used with older applications that depend on the older priority.
dldelx (where x is any valid delimiter character)	Identifies a specific character that will be used as a DATALINK delimiter. The default DATALINK delimiter is a semicolon (;) character. The character specified is used in place of a semicolon as the interfield separator for a DATALINK value. It is needed because a DATALINK value may have more than one subvalue. It is important to note that the character specified must not be the same as the row, column, or character delimiter used.
keepblanks	Indicates that all the leading and trailing blanks found for each column of type CHAR, VARCHAR, LONG VARCHAR, or CLOB must be retained. If this modifier is not specified, all leading and trailing blanks that are not inside character delimiters are removed, and a NULL is inserted into the table for all blank source columns found.
nodoubledel	Indicates that double character delimiters should not be recognized.
PC Integrated Exchange Format (IXF)	
forcein	Indicates that the Import utility should accept data despite code page mismatches (in other words, to suppress translation between code pages).
indexixf	Indicates that the Import utility will drop all indexes currently defined on the existing table and create new indexes using the index definitions stored in the IXF formatted source file. This modifier can only be used when the contents of a table are being replaced, and it cannot be used with a view.

(continued)

PART III

Table 12-2   File Type Modifiers Recognized by the Import Utility (*continued*)

Modifier	Description
indexschema or indexschema="*x*" (where *x* is a valid schema name)	Indicates that the Import utility will assign all indexes created to the schema specified. If this modifier is used and no schema name is specified, all indexes created will be assigned to the default schema for the user ID that is associated with the current database connection. If this modifier is not used, all indexes created will be assigned to the schema identified in the IXF formatted source file.
nochecklengths	Indicates that the Import utility will attempt to import every row in the source file, even if the source data has a column definition that exceeds the size of the target column in the table. Such rows can be successfully imported if code page conversion causes the source data to shrink in size; for example, 4-byte Extended UNIX Code (EUC) data in a source file could shrink to 2-byte DBCS data in the target table and require half the space. This option is particularly useful if it is known that the source data will fit in all cases despite mismatched column definitions.

For example, when executed, the commands

```
CONNECT TO SAMPLE
IMPORT FROM C:\Data Files\Emp_Photo.ixf OF IXF LOBS FROM C:\Data
Files\ MODIFIED BY lobsinfile indexschema=PERSONNEL COMMITCOUNT 5
MESSAGES C:\Data Files\ImportMsg.txt REPLACE INTO
DEFAULT.EMP_PHOTO
```

will

- Establish a connection to the SAMPLE database (which is shipped with the DB2 Universal Database Product). A connection to a database must exist before data can be imported.

- Retrieve all data values found in the file Emp_Photo.ixf that resides in a directory named Data Files that is located on drive C:. (This file was written using the IXF format.)

- Retrieve all LOB data values referenced in the file Emp_Photo.ixf from their own individual files; each LOB data file resides in a directory named Data Files that is located on drive C:.

- Replace the data found in the table EMP_PHOTO table of the SAMPLE database (which is stored in the schema DEFAULT) with the data retrieved from the file Emp_Photo.ixf and from LOB data files referenced by the file Emp_Photo.ixf.

- Assign any indexes created for the table EMP_PHOTO to the schema PERSONNEL.

- Perform a commit operation each time five rows of data have been added to the EMP_PHOTO table.

- Write any messages produced by the Import utility to a file named ImportMsg.txt that resides in a directory named Data Files that is located on drive C:.

 NOTE   Only users with SYSADM authority, DBADMN authority, the **CONTROL** privilege on all referenced tables and views, or the **INSERT** and **SELECT** privilege on all referenced tables and views are allowed to use the Import utility to perform **INSERT** operations.

Only users with SYSADM authority, DBADMN authority, or the **CONTROL** privilege on all referenced tables and views are allowed to use the Import utility to perform **INSERT_UPDATE**, **REPLACE**, or **REPLACE_CREATE** operations on existing tables.

Only users with SYSADM authority, DBADMN authority, the **CREATETAB** privilege and **IMPLICIT_SCHEMA** on the database if the schema of the table does not exist, or the **CREATEIN** privilege on the schema if the schema of the table does exist are allowed to use the Import utility to perform **CREATE** or **REPLACE_CREATE** operations on new tables.

The Load Utility

Like the Import utility, the Load utility is designed to read data directly from DEL, ASC, or IXF formatted files and store it in a specific database table. However, unlike when the Import utility is used, the table that the data is stored in must already exist in the database before the load operation is initiated—the Load utility ignores the table structure and index definition information stored in IXF formatted files. Likewise, the Load utility does not create new indexes for a table—it only rebuilds indexes that have already been defined for the table being loaded. Other functional differences between the Import utility and the Load utility can be seen in Table 12-3.

The most important difference between the Import utility and the Load utility relates to performance. Because the Import utility inserts data into a table one row at a time, each row inserted must be checked for constraint compliance (such as foreign key constraints and table check constraints) and all activity performed must be recorded in the database's transaction log files.

Table 12-3 Differences Between the Import Utility and the Load Utility

Import Utility	Load Utility
Significantly slower than the Load utility when processing large amounts of data.	Significantly faster than the Import utility when processing large amounts of data.
Tables and indexes can be created from IXF format files.	Tables and indexes must exist before data can be loaded into them.
WSF formatted files are supported.	WSF formatted files are not supported.
Data can be imported into tables, views, or aliases that refer to tables or views.	Data can only be loaded into tables—data cannot be loaded into views or aliases.
Table spaces that the table and its indexes reside in remain online during an import operation.	Table spaces that the table and its indexes reside in are taken offline during a load operation.
All row transactions are written to the active log file(s).	Minimal logging is performed—row transactions are not written to the active log file(s).
Triggers can be fired during an import operation.	Triggers are not fired during a load operation.
If an import operation is interrupted and a commit frequency value was specified, the table will remain usable and it will contain all rows that were inserted up to the moment the last commit operation was performed. The user has the option to restart the import operation or leave the table as it is.	If a load operation was interrupted and a consistency point (commit frequency) value was specified, the table remains in the "Load Pending" state and cannot be used until the load process is restarted to continue the load operation or the table space that the table resides in is restored from a backup image that was created before the load operation was initiated.
The amount of free disk space needed to import data is approximately the size of the largest index being imported plus about 10 percent. This space is allocated from the system temporary table space(s) that has been defined for the database.	The amount of free disk space needed to load data is approximately the size of the sum of all indexes for the table being loaded. This space is temporarily allocated outside the database environment.
All constraint checking is performed during an import operation.	Only uniqueness checking is performed during a load operation. All other constraint checking must be performed after the load operation has completed (by calling the SET INTEGRITY SQL statement).
Full referential integrity/constraint checking is performed on user-supplied data.	The amount of referential integrity/constraint checking performed on user-supplied data can be controlled.

continued

Import Utility	Load Utility
The keys of each row are inserted into the appropriate index during an import operation.	All keys are sorted during a load operation and the indexes are rebuilt when the load phase of the load operation has completed.
Statistics for the affected table must be manually collected (by issuing the RUNSTATS command) after an import operation is performed.	Statistics for the affected table can be collected and updated during a load operation.
Data can be imported into a host database through DB2 Connect.	Data cannot be loaded into a host database.
Data files to be imported must reside on the same workstation that the import facility is invoked from.	Data files and named pipes that will provide the data to be loaded must reside on the same workstation that the database receiving the data resides on.
A backup image is not created during an import operation.	A backup image (copy) can be created during a load operation.
The Import utility makes limited use of intrapartition parallelism.	The Load utility takes full advantage of intrapartition parallelism on symmetric multi-processor (SMP) workstations.
Data conversion between code pages is not performed by the Import utility.	Character data (and numeric data expressed as characters) can be converted from one code page to another during a load operation.
Hierarchical data can be imported.	Hierarchical data cannot be loaded.
Numeric data must be stored as character representations.	Numeric data (other than DECIMAL data) can be stored and loaded in either binary form or as character representations. DECIMAL data can be stored and loaded in packed decimal or zoned decimal form or as character representations.

The Load utility inserts data into a table much faster than the Import utility because instead of inserting data into a table one row of data at a time, it builds data pages using several individual rows of data and then writes those pages directly to the table space container that the table's structure and any preexisting data have been stored in. Existing primary/unique indexes are then rebuilt once all data pages constructed have been written to the container and duplicate rows that violate primary or unique key constraints are deleted (and copied to an exception table, if appropriate). In addition, because pages of data are written instead of individual rows, changes made to a table by

PART III

a load operation are not recorded in the database's transaction log files. Unfortunately, because changes made to a table by the Load utility are not logged, changes cannot be reapplied by performing a roll-forward recovery operation if a database failure occurs. To get around this problem, the Load utility can automatically make a backup copy of all data loaded so it can be reloaded quickly if necessary.

The Three Phases of a Load Operation

Unlike the import process, the load process consists of three separate phases that make up a single operation:

- The load phase
- The build phase
- The delete phase

The Load Phase   Two things happen during the load phase: Data is read from the source file specified and loaded into the appropriate database table, and index key values are collected and sorted.

When a load operation is initiated, the interval that the Load utility is to generate a point of consistency is specified, and each time the appropriate number of rows are processed (within the load phase), the point of consistency information is updated. The point of consistency information serves as a checkpoint for the Load utility—in the event a load operation is interrupted during its execution of the load phase and restarted, the operation will continue from the last consistency point established. As part of updating the point of consistency information, the Load utility writes a message to the appropriate message file identifying the current number of records that have been successfully loaded. This information can be used by the individual who started the load operation to monitor the operation's progress. (Specifically, the LOAD QUERY command is used to monitor the progress of a load operation.)

The Build Phase   As soon as the load phase of a load operation is complete, the build phase is started. During the build phase, indexes that are associated with primary and/or unique keys that have been defined for the table that was loaded are updated with the index key values that were collected and sorted during the load phase. This is also where statistical information about the table and its indexes is updated, if appropriate.

Because the beginning of the build phase serves as a consistency point, if a load operation is interrupted during its execution of the build phase and restarted, the operation will continue from the beginning of the build phase—the load phase does not have to be repeated.

The Delete Phase   When the build phase of a load operation is complete, the delete phase is started. During the delete phase, all rows that violated a primary and/or unique key constraint are removed from the table and copied to an exception table (provided one was specified), and a message about each offending row is written to a message file so it can be corrected and manually moved to the table at some future point in time. These are the only types of constraints that are checked. In order to check loaded data for additional constraint violations, constraint checking should be turned off (with the SET INTEGRITY SQL statement) before the load operation is started and then turned back on and performed immediately (again, with the SET INTEGRITY SQL statement) after the load operation has completed.

Like the beginning of the build phase, the beginning of the delete phase serves as another consistency point. Therefore, if a load operation is interrupted during its execution of the delete phase and restarted, the operation will continue from the beginning of the delete phase—the load phase and the build phase do not have to be repeated.

A Word about Loading LOB Data

Earlier we saw that LOB data can reside in a source data file, or it can reside in one or more separate external files that a source data file references. If the latter is the case, they do not have to be provided as input to the Load utility because the names of the files that contain LOB data are stored in the source data file. Keep in mind that this only holds true if data is loaded from a file. If data is loaded from a named pipe, the LOB data itself must be sent across the pipe—not the name of the file that contains the LOB data.

Performing a Load Operation

The easiest way to perform a load operation is by selecting the *Load* action from the *Table* menu found in the Control Center and providing the appropriate information when the Load dialog is displayed. Figure 12-12 shows the Control Center menu items that must be selected in order to activate the Load dialog. Figure 12-13 shows how the first page of this dialog might look after its input fields have been populated.

The Load utility can also be invoked by executing the LOAD command, either from the Command Center or from the Command Line Processor. The syntax for this command is

```
LOAD <CLIENT> FROM [FileName | PipeName | Device ,...] <LOBS FROM
[LOBPath ,...]> <MODIFIED BY [Modifier ,...]> <METHOD L
( [ColumnStart] [ColumnEnd] ,... )> <NULL INDICATORS
( [NullIndColNumber ,...] )> <SAVECOUNT [SaveCount]>
```

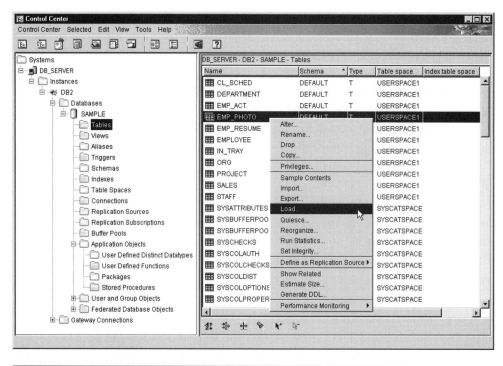

Figure 12-12   Invoking the Load dialog from the Control Center

```
<ROWCOUNT [RowCount]> <WARNINGCOUNT [WarningCount]> <MESSAGES
[MessageFileName]> <TEMPFILES PATH [TempFilesPath]> [INSERT |
REPLACE | RESTART | TERMINATE] INTO [TableName] <( [TableColName
,...] )> <FOR EXCEPTION [ExceptionTableName]> <STATISTICS NO |
STATISTICS YES | STATISTICS YES WITH DISTRIBUTION <AND <DETAILED>
INDEXES ALL> | STATISTICS YES [AND | FOR] <DETAILED> INDEXES ALL>
<NONRECOVERABLE | COPY NO | COPY YES USE TSM OPEN [NumTSMSessions]
SESSIONS | COPY YES TO [CopyDevice | CopyDirectory ,...] | COPY
YES LOAD [LibraryName] <OPEN [NumLibSessions] SESSIONS>> <HOLD
QUIESCE> <WITHOUT PROMPTING> <DATA BUFFER [BufferSize]>
<CPU_PARALLELISM [NumCPUProcesses]> <DISK_PARALLELISM
[NumDiskProcesses]> <INDEXING MODE [AUTOSELECT | REBUILD |
INCREMENTAL | DEFERRED]>
```

or

```
LOAD <CLIENT> FROM [FileName | PipeName | Device ,...] <LOBS FROM
[LOBPath ,...]> <MODIFIED BY [Modifier ,...]> <METHOD N
( [ColumnName ,...] )> <SAVECOUNT [SaveCount]> <ROWCOUNT
[RowCount]> <WARNINGCOUNT [WarningCount]> <MESSAGES
[MessageFileName]> <TEMPFILES PATH [TempFilesPath]> [INSERT |
REPLACE | RESTART | TERMINATE] INTO [TableName] <( [TableColName
```

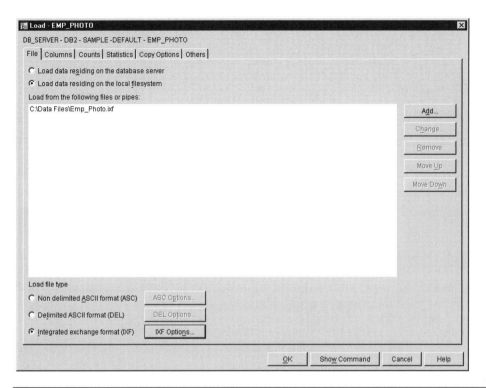

Figure 12-13 The first page of the Load dialog

```
,...] )> <FOR EXCEPTION [ExceptionTableName]> <STATISTICS NO |
STATISTICS YES | STATISTICS YES WITH DISTRIBUTION <AND <DETAILED>
INDEXES ALL> | STATISTICS YES [AND | FOR] <DETAILED> INDEXES ALL>
<NONRECOVERABLE | COPY NO | COPY YES USE TSM OPEN [NumTSMSessions]
SESSIONS | COPY YES TO [CopyDevice | CopyDirectory ,...] | COPY
YES LOAD [LibraryName] <OPEN [NumLibSessions] SESSIONS>> <HOLD
QUIESCE> <WITHOUT PROMPTING> <DATA BUFFER [BufferSize]>
<CPU_PARALLELISM [NumCPUProcesses]> <DISK_PARALLELISM
[NumDiskProcesses]> <INDEXING MODE [AUTOSELECT | REBUILD |
INCREMENTAL | DEFERRED]>
```

or

```
LOAD <CLIENT> FROM [FileName | PipeName | Device ,...] <LOBS FROM
[LOBPath ,...]> <MODIFIED BY [Modifier ,...]> <METHOD P
( [ColumnPosition ,...] )> <SAVECOUNT [SaveCount]> <ROWCOUNT
[RowCount]> <WARNINGCOUNT [WarningCount]> <MESSAGES
[MessageFileName]> <TEMPFILES PATH [TempFilesPath]> [INSERT |
REPLACE | RESTART | TERMINATE] INTO [TableName] <( [TableColName
,...] )> <FOR EXCEPTION [ExceptionTableName]> <STATISTICS NO |
STATISTICS YES | STATISTICS YES WITH DISTRIBUTION <AND <DETAILED>
```

```
INDEXES ALL> | STATISTICS YES [AND | FOR] <DETAILED> INDEXES ALL>
<NONRECOVERABLE | COPY NO | COPY YES USE TSM OPEN [NumTSMSessions]
SESSIONS | COPY YES TO [CopyDevice | CopyDirectory ,...] | COPY
YES LOAD [LibraryName] <OPEN [NumLibSessions] SESSIONS>> <HOLD
QUIESCE> <WITHOUT PROMPTING> <DATA BUFFER [BufferSize]>
<CPU_PARALLELISM [NumCPUProcesses]> <DISK_PARALLELISM
[NumDiskProcesses]> <INDEXING MODE [AUTOSELECT | REBUILD |
INCREMENTAL | DEFERRED]>
```

where:

FileName	Identifies the name and location of a file that data will be loaded from.
PipeName	Identifies the name of a named pipe that data will be loaded from.
Device	Identifies the name of a device that data will be loaded from.
LOBPath	Identifies one or more locations where files containing LOB data that will be loaded are stored.
Modifier	Identifies one or more options that are used to override one or more default behaviors of the Load utility. Table 12-4 shows the list of possible modifiers.
ColumnStart	Identifies the starting position of one or more data values (which marks the beginning of a column) that will be loaded from a ASC format file.
ColumnEnd	Identifies the ending position of one or more data values (which marks the end of a column) that will be loaded from a ASC format file.
ColumnName	Identifies the name of one or more columns that will be loaded from a IXF formatted file.
ColumnPosition	Identifies the index position (starting at 1) of one or more columns that will be loaded from a IXF or a DEL formatted file.
NullIndColNumber	Identifies the position of one or more data values that will be treated as null indicator variables for column data that will be loaded from a ASC format file.
SaveCount	Identifies the number of rows of data that will be processed before the Load utility establishes a new consistency point. The value specified for this parameter is converted to a page count

and rounded up to intervals of the extent size of the table space the table being loaded is stored in.

RowCount	Identifies the number of physical records in the file that will be loaded.
WarningCount	Identifies the number of warnings that are allowed to occur before the Load utility will abort the load operation.
MessageFileName	Identifies the name and location of the file that messages generated by the Load utility will be written to during the load operation.
TempFilesPath	Identifies the location where temporary files that might be needed by the Load utility during the load operation will be placed.
TableName	Identifies the name of the table (or updatable view) that loaded data will be written to.
TableColName	Identifies one or more specific columns in the table or updatable view that loaded data will be written to.
ExecptionTableName	Identifies the exception table that all rows that violate unique index or primary key index constraints will be copied to.
NumTSMSessions	Identifies the number of I/O sessions that will be used with Tivoli Storage Manager.
CopyDevice	Identifies the device that a backup copy of all data loaded will be written to.
CopyDirectory	Identifies the directory location that a backup copy of all data loaded will be written to.
LibraryName	Identifies the name and location of the shared library (dynamic link library on OS/2 and Windows) that contains vendor-specific backup and restore I/O functions that will be used to create a backup copy of all data loaded.
NumLibSessions	Identifies the number of I/O sessions that will be used by the shared library (dynamic link library on OS/2 and Windows) that contains vendor-specific backup and restore I/O functions that are used to create a backup copy of all data loaded.
BufferSize	Identifies the number of 4K pages (regardless of the degree of parallelism used) that is used as buffered space for transferring data within the Load utility.

Table 12-4   File Type Modifiers Recognized by the Load Utility

Modifier	Description
All File Formats	
anyorder	Indicates that the preservation of source data order is not required. (This will yield significant performance increases on SMP systems.) If the value specified for the *NumCPUProcesses* parameter is 1, this modifier will be ignored. This modifier is not supported if SAVECOUNT > 0, because data must be loaded in sequence in order for crash recovery (after a consistency point has been taken) to work properly.
fastparse	Indicates that reduced syntax checking will be performed on user-supplied column values. (This can yield significant performance increases.) When this modifier is used, tables are guaranteed to be architecturally correct, and the Load utility only performs sufficient data checking to prevent a segmentation violation or trap from occurring. Data that is in the correct format will be loaded correctly.
generatedignore	Indicates that data for all generated columns is present in the file being loaded; however, that data should be ignored—instead, the Load utility should generate an appropriate value or set of values for each row. This modifier cannot be used with either the generatedmissing or the generatedoverride modifier.
generatedmissing	Indicates that data for all generated columns is missing from the file being loaded—instead, the Load utility should generate an appropriate value or set of values for each row. This modifier cannot be used with either the generatedignore or the generatedoverride modifier.
generatedoverride	Indicates that the Load utility is to accept explicit, non-NULL data values for all generated columns in the table (contrary to the normal rules for these types of columns). This modifier is useful when migrating data from another database system or when loading a table from data that was recovered using the DROPPED TABLE RECOVERY option of the ROLLFORWARD DATABASE command. This modifier cannot be used with either the generatedmissing or the generatedignore modifier.
identityignore	Indicates that data for all identity columns is present in the file being loaded; however, that data should be ignored—instead, the Load utility should generate an appropriate value or set of values for each row. This modifier cannot be used with either the identitymissing or the identityoverride modifier.

Modifier	Description
identitymissing	Indicates that data for all identity columns is missing from the file being loaded—instead, the Load utility should generate an appropriate value or set of values for each row. This modifier cannot be used with either the identityignore or the identityoverride modifier.
identityoverride	Indicates that the Load utility will accept explicit, non-NULL data values for all identity columns in the table (contrary to the normal rules for these types of columns). This modifier is useful when migrating data from another database system or when loading a table from data that was recovered using the DROPPED TABLE RECOVERY option of the ROLLFORWARD DATABASE command. This modifier should be used only when an identity column that was defined as GENERATED ALWAYS is present in the table that will be loaded. This modifier cannot be used with either the identitymissing or the identityignore modifier.
indexfreespace=x (where x is a number between 0 and 99 [percent])	Indicates that a percentage of each index page will be left as free space when loading any index that is associated with the table being loaded.
lobsinfile	Indicates that LOB data values will be written to individual files.
noheader	Indicates that the Load utility will skip the header verification code (applicable only to load operations into tables that reside in a single-node nodegroup) when processing the source data file.
norowwarnings	Indicates that warning messages about rejected rows should be suppressed.
pagefreespace=x (where x is a number between 0 and 100 [percent])	Indicates that a percentage of each data page associated with the table being loaded will be left as free space.
totalfreespace=x (where x is a number between 0 and 100 [percent])	Indicates that a percentage of the total number of data pages used by the table being loaded will be appended to the end of the table and treated as free space.

(continued)

PART III

Table 12-4   File Type Modifiers Recognized by the Load Utility (*continued*)

Modifier	Description
usedefaults	Indicates that if a source column for a target table column has been speci- fied, but the data file does not contain data for that column for one or more row, default values should be loaded. Examples of missing data include

	• **For DEL format files**	",," is specified for the column.
	• **For ASC format files**	The NULL indicator is set to yes for the column.
	• **For DEL/ASC/WSF format files**	A row that does not have enough columns or is not long enough for the original specification.

If this modifier is not used and a source column does not contain a data value for a row, one of the following occurs:
- If the column is nullable, a NULL is loaded.
- If the column is not nullable, the row is rejected.

Delimited/Nondelimited ASCII (DEL/ASC) Format

Modifier	Description
codepage=*x* (where *x* is any valid code page value)	Identifies the code page of the data in the source data file. This modifier informs the Load utility that character data (and numeric data specified in characters) should be converted from the code page specified to the database code page during the load operation. When this modifier is used, the following rules apply: • For pure DBCS (graphic), mixed DBCS, and EUC, delimiters are restricted to the range of x00 to x3F, inclusive. • For DEL data specified in an EBCDIC code page, the delimiters may not coincide with the shift-in and shift-out DBCS characters. • nullindchar must specify symbols included in the standard ASCII set between code points x20 and x7F, inclusive. This refers to ASCII symbols and code points. EBCDIC data can use the corresponding symbols, even though the code points will be different.
dateformat="*x*" (where *x* is any valid combination of date format elements)	Identifies how date values in the source file are formatted. The following date elements can be used to create the format string provided with this modifier: • **YYYY** Year (four digits ranging from 0000 to 9999) • **M** Month (one or two digits ranging from 1 to 12) • **MM** Month (two digits ranging from 1 to 12; mutually exclusive with M) • **D** Day (one or two digits ranging from 1 to 31) • **DD** Day (two digits ranging from 1 to 31; mutually exclusive with D) • **DDD** Day of the year (three digits ranging from 001 to 366; mutually exclusive with other day or month elements) Some examples of date format strings are • D-M-YYYY • MM.DD.YYYY • YYYYDDD

Modifier	Description
dumpfile=x (where x is a fully qualified name of a file)	Identifies the name and location of an exception file to which rejected rows will be written. The contents of a dump file are written to disk in an asynchronous buffered mode. In the event a load operation fails or is interrupted, the number of records committed to disk cannot be known with certainty, and consistency cannot be guaranteed after a LOAD RESTART. A dump file can only be assumed to be complete for load operations that start and complete in a single pass. This modifier does not support filenames with multiple file extensions. For example, dumpfile=/export/home/DUMP.FILE is acceptable; dumpfile=/export/home/DUMP.LOAD.FILE is not.
implieddecimal	Indicates that the location of an implied decimal point is determined by the column definition—the Load utility should not assume that the decimal point is at the end of the value (default behavior). For example, if this modifier is specified, the value 12345 would be loaded into a DECIMAL(8,2) column as 123.45, not as 12345.00.
noeofchar	Indicates that the optional end-of-file character 0x1A should not be treated as an end-of-file character. Instead, this character should be treated as a normal character if it is encountered.
timeformat="x" (where x is any valid combination of time format elements)	Identifies how time values in the source file are formatted. The following time elements can be used to create the format string provided with this modifier: • **H** Hour (one or two digits ranging from 0 to 12 for a 12-hour system and 0 to 24 for a 24-hour system) • **HH** Hour (two digits ranging from 0 to 12 for a 12-hour system and 0 to 24 for a 24-hour system; mutually exclusive with H) • **M** Minute (one or two digits ranging from 0 to 59) • **MM** Minute (two digits ranging from 0 to 59; mutually exclusive with M) • **S** Second (one or two digits ranging from 0 to 59) • **SS** Second (two digits ranging from 0 to 59; mutually exclusive with S) • **SSSSS** Second of the day after midnight (five digits ranging from 00000 to 86399; mutually exclusive with other time elements) • **TT** Meridian indicator (A.M. or P.M.) Some examples of time format strings are • HH:MM:SS • HH.MM TT • SSSSS

PART III

continued

Table 12-4 File Type Modifiers Recognized by the Load Utility (*continued*)

Modifier	Description
timestampformat="x" (where *x* is any valid combination of date and time format elements)	Identifies how timestamp values in the source file are formatted. The following date and time elements can be used to create the format string provided with this modifier: • **YYYY** Year (four digits ranging from 0000 to 9999) • **M** Month (one or two digits ranging from 1 to 12) • **MM** Month (two digits ranging from 1 to 12; mutually exclusive with M) • **D** Day (one or two digits ranging from 1 to 31) • **DD** Day (two digits ranging from 1 to 31; mutually exclusive with D) • **DDD** Day of the year (three digits ranging from 001 to 366; mutually exclusive with other day or month elements) • **H** Hour (one or two digits ranging from 0 to 12 for a 12-hour system and 0 to 24 for a 24-hour system) • **HH** Hour (two digits ranging from 0 to 12 for a 12-hour system and 0 to 24 for a 24-hour system; mutually exclusive with H) • **M** Minute (one or two digits ranging from 0 to 59) • **MM** Minute (two digits ranging from 0 to 59; mutually exclusive with M) • **S** Second (one or two digits ranging from 0 to 59) • **SS** Second (two digits ranging from 0 to 59; mutually exclusive with S) • **SSSSS** Second of the day after midnight (five digits ranging from 00000 to 86399; mutually exclusive with other time elements) • **UUUUUU** Microsecond (six digits ranging from 000000 to 999999) • **TT** Meridian indicator (A.M. or P.M.) An example of a timestamp format string is • YYYY/MM/DD HH:MM:SS.UUUUUU
Nondelimited ASCII (ASC) Format	
binarynumerics	Indicates that numeric (but not DECIMAL) data is stored in binary format rather than as character representations. When this modifier is used, • No conversion between data types is performed, with the exception of BIGINT, INTEGER, and SMALLINT. • Data lengths must match their target column definitions. • FLOAT values must be in IEEE Floating Point format. • The byte order of the binary data stored in the source file is assumed to be big endian, regardless of the server platform used. (Little-endian computers [such as Intel-based PCs, VAX workstations, and so on] store the least significant byte [LSB] of a multibyte word at the lowest address in a word and the most significant byte [MSB] at the highest address. Big-endian computers [such as machines based on the Motorola 68000a series of central processing units [CPUs]—Sun, Macintosh, and so on] do the opposite—the MSB is stored at the lowest address and the LSB is stored at the highest address.)

Modifier	Description
	• NULLs cannot be present in the data for columns that are affected by this modifier. Blanks (normally interpreted as NULL) are interpreted as a binary value when this modifier is used. • The noeofchar modifier must also be used.
nochecklengths	Indicates that the Load utility should attempt to load every row in the source file, even if the source data has a column definition that exceeds the size of the target column in the table. Such rows can be successfully loaded if code page conversion causes the source data to shrink in size; for example, 4-byte EUC data in a source file could shrink to 2-byte DBCS data in the target table and require half the space. This option is particularly useful if it is known that the source data will fit in all cases despite mismatched column definitions.
packeddecimal	Indicates that numeric DECIMAL data is stored in packed decimal format rather than as character representations. When this modifier is used, • The byte order of the binary data stored in the source file is assumed to be big endian, regardless of the server platform used. • NULLs cannot be present in the data for columns that are affected by this modifier. Blanks (normally interpreted as NULL) are interpreted as a binary value when this modifier is used. • The noeofchar modifier must also be used.
nullindchar=x (where x is any valid character)	Identifies a specific character that will be used as a null indicator value. The default null indicator is the letter Y. The character specified is used in place of double quotation marks to enclose a character string. This modifier is case sensitive for EBCDIC data files, except when the character is an English letter. For example, if the null indicator character is specified to be the letter N, then the letter n is also recognized as a null indicator.
reclen=x (where x is any number between 1 and 32767)	Indicates that a specific number of characters will be read from the source file for each row—newline characters should not be used to indicate the end of a row.
striptblanks	Indicates that trailing blank spaces will be truncated from values that are loaded into variable-length character fields. This modifier cannot be specified together with the striptnulls modifier; these are mutually exclusive options.
striptnulls	Indicates that trailing nulls (0x00 characters) will be truncated from values that are loaded into variable-length character fields. This modifier cannot be specified together with the striptblanks modifier; these are mutually exclusive options.

(continued)

PART III

Table 12-4   File Type Modifiers Recognized by the Load Utility (*continued*)

Modifier	Description
zoneddecimal	Indicates that numeric DECIMAL data is stored in zoned decimal format rather than as character representations. When this modifier is used, • Half-byte sign values can be one of the following: "+" = 0xC 0xA 0xE 0xF "−" = 0xD 0xB • Supported values for digits are 0x0 to 0x9. • Supported values for zones are 0x3 and 0xF. • The noeofchar modifier must also be used.
Delimited ASCII (DEL) Format	
chardel*x* (where *x* is any valid delimiter character)	Identifies a specific character that will be used as a character delimiter. The default character delimiter is a double quotation mark (") character. The character specified is used in place of double quotation marks to enclose a character string.
coldel*x* (where *x* is any valid delimiter character)	Identifies a specific character that will be used as a column delimiter. The default column delimiter is a comma (,) character. The character specified is used in place of a comma to signal the end of a column.
datesiso	Indicates that all DATE data values will be exported in ISO format (YYYY-MM-DD). By default, the Export utility normally writes • DATE data in YYYYMMDD format • CHAR(date) data in YYYY-MM-DD format • TIME data in HH.MM.SS format • TIMESTAMP data in YYYY-MM-DD-HH.MM.SS.uuuuuu format
decplusblank	Indicates that positive decimal values will be prefixed with a blank space instead of a plus sign (+). The default action prefixes positive decimal values with a plus sign.
decpt*x* (where *x* is any valid delimiter character)	Identifies a specific character that will be used as a decimal point character. The default decimal point character is a period (.) character. The character specified is used in place of a period as a decimal point character.
delprioritychar	Indicates that the priority for evaluating delimiters is character delimiter, record delimiter, or column delimiter, rather than record delimiter, character delimiter, or column delimiter (which is the default). This modifier is typically used with older applications that depend on the older priority.

Modifier	Description
dldel*x* (where *x* is any valid delimiter character)	Identifies a specific character that will be used as a DATALINK delimiter. The default DATALINK delimiter is a semicolon (;) character. The character specified is used in place of a semicolon as the interfield separator for a DATALINK value. It is needed because a DATALINK value may have more than one subvalue. It is important to note that the character specified must not be the same as the row, column, or character delimiter used.
keepblanks	Indicates that all the leading and trailing blanks found for each column of type CHAR, VARCHAR, LONG VARCHAR, or CLOB will be retained. If this modifier is not specified, all leading and trailing blanks that are not inside character delimiters are removed, and a NULL is inserted into the table for all blank source columns found.
nodoubledel	Indicates that double character delimiters should not be recognized.
PC Integrated Exchange Format (IXF)	
forcein	Indicates that the Load utility is to accept data despite code page mismatches (in other words, to suppress translation between code pages).
nochecklengths	Indicates that the Load utility will attempt to load every row in the source file, even if the source data has a column definition that exceeds the size of the target column in the table. Such rows can be successfully loaded if code page conversion causes the source data to shrink in size; for example, 4-byte EUC data in a source file could shrink to 2-byte DBCS data in the target table and require half the space. This option is particularly useful if it is known that the source data will fit in all cases despite mismatched column definitions.
NumCPUProcesses	Identifies the number of processes or threads that the Load utility spawns for parsing, converting, and formatting records when building table objects. This parameter is designed to exploit intrapartition parallelism.
NumDiskProcesses	Identifies the number of processes or threads that the Load utility spawns for writing data to the table space containers that the target table is stored in.

NOTE It is always a good idea to restrict access to all table spaces associated with the table that receives data during a load operation. Table space access can be restricted by executing the QUIESCE TABLESPACES FOR TABLE command before the load operation is started. Restrictions placed on table space access can be removed by executing the QUIESCE TABLESPACES FOR TABLE command again immediately after the load operation has completed.

For example, when executed, the commands

```
CONNECT TO SAMPLE
LOAD FROM C:\Data Files\Emp_Photo.ixf OF IXF LOBS FROM C:\Data
Files\ MODIFIED BY lobsinfile pagefreespace=0 totalfreespace=0
MESSAGES C:\Data Files\LoadMsg.txt REPLACE INTO DEFAULT.EMP_PHOTO
STATISTICS YES COPY NO INDEXING MODE REBUILD
```

will

- Establish a connection to the SAMPLE database (which is shipped with the DB2 Universal Database Product). A connection to a database must exist before data can be loaded.

- Retrieve all data values found in the file Emp_Photo.ixf that resides in a directory named Data Files that is located on drive C:. (This file was written using the IXF format.)

- Retrieve all LOB data values referenced in the file Emp_Photo.ixf from their own individual files; each LOB data file resides in a directory named Data Files that is located on drive C:.

- Replace the data found in the table EMP_PHOTO table of the SAMPLE database (which is stored in the schema DEFAULT) with the data retrieved from the file Emp_Photo.ixf and from LOB data files referenced by the file Emp_Photo.ixf.

- Update the statistics for the table EMP_PHOTO and its indexes.

- Rebuild all indexes associated with the EMP_PHOTO table.

- Write any messages produced by the Load utility to a file named LoadMsg.txt that resides in a directory named Data Files that is located on drive C:.

NOTE   Only users with SYSADM authority, DBADMN authority, or Load (LOAD) authority, and the INSERT privilege on all referenced tables are allowed to use the Load utility to perform INSERT load operations (or to restart/terminate INSERT load operations).
Only users with SYSADM authority, DBADMN authority, or LOAD authority, and the INSERT privilege and DELETE privilege on all referenced tables are allowed to use the Load utility to perform REPLACE load operations (or to restart/terminate REPLACE load operations).
Only users with SYSADM authority, DBADMN authority, or the INSERT privilege on the exception table used are allowed to have invalid rows written to an exception table by the Load utility.

The DB2MOVE Utility

It's easy to see how the Export utility, when used together with the Import utility or the Load utility, provides a way to copy a table from one database to another. But what if you want to copy several tables or an entire database? To perform this kind of operation, you could run a set of export and import operations for every table that needs to be copied or you could let the DB2MOVE utility do most of the work for you. The DB2MOVE utility facilitates the movement of a large number of tables between DB2 databases. This utility queries the system catalog tables for a particular database and compiles a list of all user tables found. It then exports the contents and table structure of each table found to a IXF formatted file. The set of files produced can then be imported or loaded to another DB2 database on the same system, or they can be transferred to another workstation platform and imported or loaded to a DB2 database that resides on that platform. (This is the best method to use when copying or moving an existing database from one platform to another.)

The DB2MOVE utility can be run in one of three modes: EXPORT, IMPORT, or LOAD. When run in EXPORT mode, the DB2MOVE utility invokes the Export utility to extract data from one or more tables and externalize it to IXF formatted files. It also creates a file named *db2move.lst* that contains the names of all tables processed, along with the names of the files that the table's data was written to. In addition, the DB2MOVE utility may produce one or more message files that contain warning or error messages that were generated as a result of an export operation.

When run in IMPORT mode, the DB2MOVE utility invokes the Import utility to re-create a table and its indexes from data stored in IXF formatted files. In this mode, the file *db2move.lst* is used to establish a link between the IXF formatted files needed and the tables into which data will be imported.

When run in LOAD mode, the DB2MOVE utility invokes the Load utility to populate tables that have already been created with data stored in IXF formatted files. Again, the file *db2move.lst* is used to establish a link between the IXF formatted files needed and the tables into which data will be imported.

Invoking the DB2MOVE Utility

The DB2MOVE utility is invoked by executing the DB2MOVE command, from the system command prompt. The syntax for this command is

```
DB2MOVE [DatabaseName] [EXPORT | IMPORT | LOAD] <Option, ...>
```

where:

DatabaseName	Identifies the name of the database that data will be retrieved from or copied to.
Option	Identifies one or more options that are used to control behavior of the Export, Import, or Load utility (when called by the DB2MOVE utility). Table 12-5 shows the list of possible options.

Table 12-5 Options Recognized by the DB2MOVE Utility

Option	Description
EXPORT, IMPORT, and LOAD Options	
-l *x* (where *x* is a list of valid pathnames)	Specifies the absolute pathnames where LOB files are created (as part of EXPORT) or retrieved from (as part of IMPORT or LOAD). When specifying multiple LOB paths, each must be separated by commas; no blanks are allowed between LOB paths. If the first path runs out of space (during EXPORT) or the files are not found in the path (during IMPORT or LOAD), the second path will be used and so on. If the action is EXPORT and LOB paths are specified, all files in the LOB path directories are deleted, the directories are removed, and new directories are created. If no LOB path is specified, the current directory is used for the LOB path.
-u *x* (where *x* is a valid user ID)	Specifies the user ID that will be used for authentication. If the DB2MOVE utility is run on a client workstation that communicates with a remote server, a user ID and password should be specified. If no user ID is specified, the current logged-on user ID is used as the default. Both user ID and password are optional. However, if one is specified, the other must be specified.
-p *x* (where *x* is a valid password)	Specifies the password that will be used for authentication. If the DB2MOVE utility is run on a client workstation that communicates with a remote server, a user ID and password should be specified. If no password is specified, the current logged-on user password is used as the default. Both user ID and password are optional. However, if one is specified, the other must be specified.
EXPORT Options	
-tc *x* (where *x* is a list of table creator user IDs)	Indicates that only the tables that were created by the creators listed with this option should be exported. When specifying multiple table creators, a comma must separate each; no blanks are allowed between creator IDs. An asterisk (*) can be used as a wildcard character that can be placed anywhere in the creator name list. The maximum number of creators that can be specified is ten.

Option	Description
EXPORT Options	
-tn *x* where *x* is a list of table names	Indicates that only the table names that match exactly with those listed with this option will be exported. When specifying multiple table names, a comma must separate each; no blanks are allowed between table names. An asterisk (*) can be used as a wildcard character that can be placed anywhere in the table name list.
	The maximum number of table names that can be specified is ten.
-io *x* (where *x* is a valid Import utility action)	Specifies the Import utility action to take. Valid actions are INSERT, INSERT_UPDATE, REPLACE, CREATE, and REPLACE_CREATE. If no Import utility action is specified, the REPLACE_CREATE action is used by default.
LOAD Options	
-lo *x* (where *x* is a valid Load utility action)	Specifies the Load utility action to take. Valid actions are INSERT and REPLACE. If no Load utility action is specified, the INSERT action is used by default.

For example, when executed, the command

```
DB2MOVE SAMPLE EXPORT
```

will query the system catalog tables for the SAMPLE database, compile a list of all user tables found, and produce the following set of files:

- **EXPORT.out**   Contains the summarized result of the EXPORT action.

- **db2move.lst**   Contains a list of original table names, along with their corresponding IXF format filenames (tab*nnn*.ixf) and message filenames (tab*nnn*.msg). This list, the exported IXF files, and the LOB files (tab*nnnc.yyy*) are used as input to a subsequent DB2MOVE . . . IMPORT or DB2MOVE . . . LOAD command.

- **tab*nnn*.ixf**   The exported IXF file of a specific table. (*nnn* is the table number.)

- **tab*nnn*.msg**   The export message file of the corresponding table. (*nnn* is the table number.)

- **tab*nnnc.yyy***   The exported LOB files of a specific table. (*nnn* is the table number, *c* is a letter of the alphabet, and *yyy* is a number ranging from 001 to 999.) These files are only created if one or more tables being exported contain LOB data. If created, these LOB files are placed in the LOB paths (directories) specified. There are a total of 26,000 possible names for the LOB files.

- **system.msg** A message file containing system messages for creating or deleting file or directory commands. This is only used if an LOB path is specified.

DB2 Universal Database's Data Maintenance Utilities

The way data stored in tables is physically distributed across table space containers can have a significant impact on the performance of applications that access the data. How data is stored in a table is affected by insert, update, and delete operations that are performed on the table. For example, a delete operation may leave empty pages that for some reason never get reused. Or update operations performed on variable-length columns may result in larger column values that cause an entire row to be moved to a different page because they no longer fit on the original page. In both scenarios, internal gaps are created in the underlying table space containers. As a consequence, the DB2 Database Manager may have to read more physical pages into memory in order to retrieve the data needed to satisfy a query.

Because situations such as these are almost unavoidable, DB2 Universal Database provides three different data maintenance utilities that can be used to optimize the physical distribution of all data stored in a table:

- The Reorganize Check utility
- The Reorganize Table utility
- The Run Statistics utility

The Reorganize Check Utility

Now that you know it is almost impossible to work with a database without creating gaps in one or more of its table space containers, you are probably wondering how you can determine what the physical organization of your tables and/or indexes looks like. More importantly, you may wonder how much storage space is currently being utilized and how much is free because of internal gaps in one or more table space containers.

Questions like these can be answered by running the Reorganize Check utility. When executed, this utility optionally generates statistics and analyzes all statistics available to determine whether or not one or more tables need to be reorganized—which is an action that will cause existing internal gaps to be removed.

The Reorganize Check utility is invoked by executing the REORGCHK command, either from the Command Center or from the Command Line Processor. The syntax for this command is

```
REORGCHK <UPDATE STATISTICS | CURRENT STATISTICS> <ON TABLE [USER
| SYSTEM | ALL | [TableName]]>
```

where:

TableName Identifies the name of a specific table that will be analyzed to determine whether or not it needs to be reorganized.

For example, when executed, the command

```
REORGCHK UPDATE STATISTICS ON TABLE DEFAULT.EMPLOYEE
```

might produce the following output:

```
Doing RUNSTATS ....

Table statistics:

F1: 100 * OVERFLOW / CARD < 5
F2: 100 * TSIZE / ((FPAGES-1) * (TABLEPAGESIZE-76)) > 70
F3: 100 * NPAGES / FPAGES > 80

CREATOR    NAME       CARD   OV   NP   FP    TSIZE   F1  F2 F3  REORG
--------------------------------------------------------------------
DEFAULT    EMPLOYEE     32    0    2    2     2784    0  69 100  -*-
--------------------------------------------------------------------


Index statistics:

F4: CLUSTERRATIO or normalized CLUSTERFACTOR > 80
F5: 100 * (KEYS * (ISIZE+8)+(CARD-KEYS) * 4)/(NLEAF * INDEXPAGESIZE)
    > 50
F6: (100-PCTFREE) * (INDEXPAGESIZE-96) / (ISIZE+12) ** (NLEVELS-2) *
    (INDEXPAGESIZE-96) / (KEYS * (ISIZE+8) + (CARD-KEYS) * 4) < 100

CREATOR   NAME    CARD LEAF  LVLS  ISIZE   KEYS  F4   F5   F6   REORG
--------------------------------------------------------------------
Table: DEFAULT.EMPLOYEE

SYSIBM    EMPNO_KEY  32    1    1      6     32  100   -    -    ---


--------------------------------------------------------------------

CLUSTERRATIO or normalized CLUSTERFACTOR (F4) will indicate REORG is
necessary for indexes that are not in the same sequence as the base
table. When multiple indexes are defined on a table, one or more
indexes may be flagged as needing REORG.  Specify the most important
index for REORG sequencing.
```

NOTE Only users with SYSADM authority, DBADMN authority, or the CONTROL privilege on the table being evaluated are allowed to invoke the Reorganize Check utility.

Interpreting the Output Generated by the Reorganize Check Utility

As you can see, the output generated by the Reorganize Check utility is divided into two sections. The first section shows the table statistics and formulas used to determine if a table reorganization is necessary; the second section shows information about the table's indexes and the formulas used to determine if an index reorganization is necessary.

Table Statistics If you examine the preceding sample output from the Reorganize Check utility, the first thing you will see after the heading Table Statistics are the formulas F1, F2, and F3. These formulas are used to provide guidelines for determining whether or not table reorganization is necessary:

- *Formula F1 works with the number of overflow rows encountered.* It recommends reorganizing a table if 5 percent or more of the total number of rows in the table are overflow rows. (Overflow rows are rows that have been moved to new pages because an update operation made them too large to be stored in the page they were written to originally or because new columns were added to an existing table.)

- *Formula F2 works with free/unused space.* It recommends reorganizing a table if the table size (TSIZE) is less than or equal to 70 percent of the size of the total storage space allocated for that table—in other words, if more than 30 percent of the total storage space allocated for the table is unused.

- *Formula F3 works with free pages.* It recommends reorganizing a table if 20 percent or more of the pages for that table are free. (A page is considered free when it does not contain any rows.)

Immediately following these three formulas is a table that contains information about the values used in the formulas for each table processed, along with the results. This table contains the following columns:

- **CREATOR** The name of the schema that the table belongs to.

- **NAME** The name of the table that was evaluated to determine whether or not reorganization is necessary.

- **CARD**   The number of rows found in the table.

- **OV (OVERHEAD)**   The number of overflow rows found in the table.

- **NP (NPAGES)**   The number of pages (allocated for the table) that contain data.

- **FP (FPAGES)**   The total number of pages that have been allocated for the table.

- **TSIZE**   The size of the table in bytes. This value is calculated by multiplying the number of rows found in the table (CARD) by the average row length. The average row length is computed as the sum of the average column lengths (the AVG-COLLEN column in the system catalog table SYSCAT.SYSCOLUMNS) of all columns defined for the table plus 10 bytes for row overhead. For long data and LOB data columns, only the approximate length of the descriptor is used—the actual size of long data and LOB data columns is not included in TSIZE.

- **F1**   The results of formula F1.

- **F2**   The results of formula F2.

- **F3**   The results of formula F3.

- **REORG**   Each hyphen (-) displayed in this column indicates that the calculated results were within the set bounds of the corresponding formula, and each asterisk (*) indicates that the calculated results exceeded the set bounds of its corresponding formula. The first - or * corresponds to formula F1, the second - or * corresponds to formula F2, and the third - or * corresponds to formula F3. Table reorganization is recommended when the results of the calculations exceed the bounds set for the formula. For example, the value --- indicates that because the results of F1, F2, and F3 are within the set bounds of each formula, no table reorganization is necessary. The notation -*- indicates that the results of F2 recommend reorganizing the table, even though the results of F2 and F3 are within their set bounds.

You may have noticed that most of these columns correspond to elements in the first three formulas shown. In fact, the one element in the formulas that is not represented in the table is the TABLEPAGESIZE element, which reflects the page size of the table space that the table data resides in.

NOTE   Because the **CARD, OVERFLOW, NPAGES,** and **FPAGES** information is stored in the system catalog table **SYSCAT.TABLES** after table statistics have been generated, a determination of whether or not a table needs to be reorganized can often be made by examining the values stored in these columns for a particular table.

Index Statistics   Immediately following the table statistics results table, you will see the heading Index Statistics, followed by the formulas F4, F5, and F6. These formulas are used to provide guidelines for determining whether or not table reorganization is necessary by examining the table's indexes:

- *Formula F4 works with the cluster ratio or normalized cluster factor of an index.* This ratio identifies the percentage of table data rows that are stored in the same physical sequence as the indexed data for the table. It recommends reorganizing a table if the cluster ratio for the index is less than 80 percent. (Often, the cluster ratio is not optimal for indexes that contain several duplicate keys and a large number of entries.)

- *Formula F5 works with storage space that has been reserved for index entries.* It recommends reorganizing a table if 50 percent or more of the storage space allocated for an index is empty.

- *Formula F6 measures the usage of the index's pages.* It recommends reorganizing a table if the actual number of entries found in the index is less than 90 percent of the number of entries (NLEVELS) the index tree can handle.

Immediately following these three formulas is a table that contains information about the values used in the formulas for each index processed, along with the results. This table contains the following columns:

- **CREATOR**   The name of the schema that the index belongs to.
- **NAME**   The name of the index that was evaluated to determine whether or not table reorganization is necessary.
- **CARD**   The number of rows found in the base table the index is associated with.
- **LEAF**   The total number of index leafs (pages) that have been allocated for the index.
- **LVLS (LEVELS)**   The total number of levels the index has.
- **ISIZE**   The size of the index in bytes. This value is calculated by multiplying the number of rows found in the index (CARD) by the average row length. The average row length is computed as the sum of the average column lengths (the AVG-COLLEN column in the system catalog table SYSCAT.SYSCOLUMNS) of all columns participating in the index.
- **KEYS (FULLKEYCARD)**   The number of unique entries found in the index.
- **F4**   The results of formula F4.

- **F5** The results of formula F5. (The notation $+++$ indicates that the result exceeds 999, and is invalid, in which case the Reorganize Check utility should be run again with the UPDATE STATISTICS option specified.)

- **F6** The results of formula F6. (The notation $+++$ indicates that the result exceeds 999, and is invalid, in which case the Reorganize Check utility should be run again with the UPDATE STATISTICS option specified.)

- **REORG** Each hyphen (-) displayed in this column indicates that the calculated results were within the set bounds of the corresponding formula, and each asterisk (*) indicates that the calculated results exceeded the set bounds of its corresponding formula. The first - or * corresponds to formula F4, the second - or * corresponds to formula F5, and the third - or * corresponds to formula F6. Table reorganization is recommended when the results of the calculations exceed the bounds set for the formula. For example, the value —- indicates that because the results of F4, F5, and F6 are within the set bounds of each formula, no table reorganization is necessary. The notation -*- indicates that the results of F5 recommend reorganizing the table, even though the results of F4 and F6 are within their set bounds.

Again, most of these columns correspond to elements in the second set of formulas shown. The two elements in the formulas that are not represented in the table are the INDEXPAGESIZE element, which reflects the page size of the table space that the index data resides in, and the PCTFREE element, which reflects the percentage of each index page that will be left free. Values for the PCTFREE element can range from 0 to 99; the default value is 10.

The Reorganize Table Utility

After evaluating the output of the Reorganize Check utility, you may find it necessary to reorganize the physical layout of one or more tables. This is where the Reorganize Table utility comes in. When executed, the Reorganize Table utility eliminates gaps in table space containers by rewriting the data associated with a table to contiguous pages in storage (similar to the way a disk defragmenter works). With the help of an index, the Reorganize Table utility can also place the data rows of a table in the same physical sequence as the index specified, thereby increasing the cluster ratio of the selected index. This approach also has an attractive side effect—if the DB2 Database Manager finds the data needed to satisfy a query stored in contiguous space and in the desired sort order, the overall performance of the query will be improved because the seek time needed to read the data will be shorter and a sort operation may no longer be necessary.

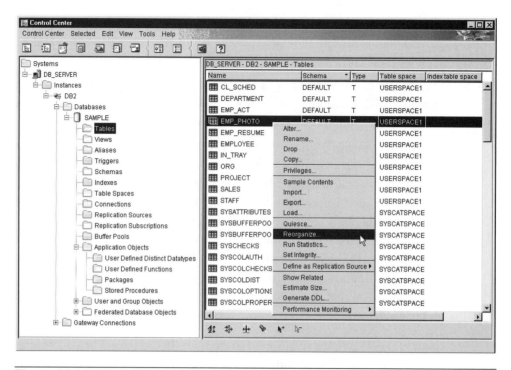

Figure 12-14   Invoking the Reorganize Table dialog from the Control Center

Figure 12-15   The Reorganize Table dialog

The easiest way to invoke the Reorganize Table utility is by using the Reorganize Table dialog. Figure 12-14 shows the Control Center menu items that must be selected in order to activate the Reorganize Table dialog. Figure 12-15 shows how this dialog might look after its input fields have been populated.

The Reorganize Table utility can also be invoked by executing the REORG command, either from the Command Center or from the Command Line Processor. The syntax for this command is

```
REORG TABLE [TableName] <INDEX [IndexName]> <USE TABLESPACE
[SysTempTSName]>
```

where:

TableName	Identifies the name of the table whose physical layout will be reorganized.
IndexName	Identifies the associated index that will be used to order the data stored in the table that will be reorganized. If an index name is not provided, the data stored in the table is reorganized without regard to order.
SysTempTSName	Identifies a temporary table space where the DB2 Database Manager can temporarily store a copy of the table that will be reorganized. If a table space name is not provided, the DB2 Database Manager will store a working copy of the table that will be reorganized in the same table space(s) that the table currently resides in.

For example, when executed, the command

```
REORG TABLE DEFAULT.EMPLOYEE INDEX EMPNO_KEY USE TEMPSPACE1
```

will

1. Copy the table DEFAULT.EMPLOYEE to the temporary table space named TEMP-SPACE1.

2. Reorganize the data in the table DEFAULT.EMPLOYEE so that it is stored in contiguous pages and ordered to match the records in the EMPNO_KEY index.

3. Delete the copy of the table DEFAULT.EMPLOYEE that was copied to the temporary table space named TEMPSPACE1.

NOTE Only users with SYSADM authority, System Control (SYSCTRL) authority, System Maintenance (SYSMAINT) authority, DBADMN authority, or the CONTROL privilege on the table being reorganized are allowed to invoke the Reorganize Table utility.

Index Reorganization

Now that you have seen how a table can be reorganized, you are probably wondering if it is necessary to reorganize indexes as well. After all, information about indexes shows up in the output provided by Reorganize Check utility, right? Indexes can be reorganized as well as tables; however, there is no utility for performing such an operation. Instead, the DB2 Database Manager is responsible for automatically reorganizing indexes—provided the index was created in such a way that automatic reorganization is possible.

Whether or not an index will automatically be reorganized and when reorganization will occur is determined by the MINPCTUSED option that is part of the CREATE INDEX SQL statement. If the MINPCTUSED option is not specified, the index being created will not be automatically reorganized when the DB2 Database Manager has deemed it appropriate to do so. On the other hand, if the MINPCTUSED option is used, the threshold for the minimum percentage of space used on an index leaf page is specified as part of the MINPCTUSED option (for example, MINPCTUSED 80) and if the percentage of space used on the page is at or below the percentage specified after a key is deleted from an index leaf page, an attempt is made to merge the remaining keys on the page with those of a neighboring page. If sufficient space is available on either of these pages, the merge is performed and one of the pages is deleted. The value specified for the minimum percentage of space used can be from 0 to 99. However, for performance reasons, a value of 50 or below is recommended.

The Run Statistics Utility

Although the system catalog tables contain information such as the number of rows in a table, the way storage space is utilized by tables and indexes, and the number of different values found in a column, this information is not automatically kept up-to-date. Instead, it has to be generated periodically by running the Run Statistics utility.

The information that is collected by the Run Statistics utility is used in two ways: to provide information about the physical organization of the data in a table and provide information that the DB2 Optimizer can use when selecting the best path to use to access data that will satisfy the requirements of a query. Earlier we saw how information about the physical organization of the data in a table can be used to determine whether or not fragmentation has occurred. Now let's look at how the information that is collected by the Run Statistics utility is used by the DB2 Optimizer.

Whenever an SQL statement is sent to the DB2 Database Manager for processing, the DB2 Optimizer reads the system catalog tables to determine the size of each table referenced by the statement, the characteristics of the columns that are referenced by the statement, and whether or not indexes have been defined for the table(s) that are referenced by the statement, and to obtain other similar information. Using this information, the DB2 Optimizer then determines the best access path to take to satisfy the needs of the SQL statement. Therefore, if the information needed by the DB2 Optimizer is missing or out-of-date, it may choose an access plan that will cause the SQL statement to take longer to execute than is necessary. Having valid information available becomes more crucial as the complexity of the SQL statement increases; when only one table (that has no indexes defined for it) is referenced, there are only a limited number of choices available to the DB2 Optimizer. However, when several tables (each of which has one or more indexes defined) are referenced, the number of choices available to the DB2 Optimizer increases dramatically.

The easiest way to invoke the Run Statistics utility is by using the Run Statistics dialog. Figure 12-16 shows the Control Center menu items that must be selected in order to activate the Run Statistics dialog. Figure 12-17 shows how this dialog might look after its input fields have been populated.

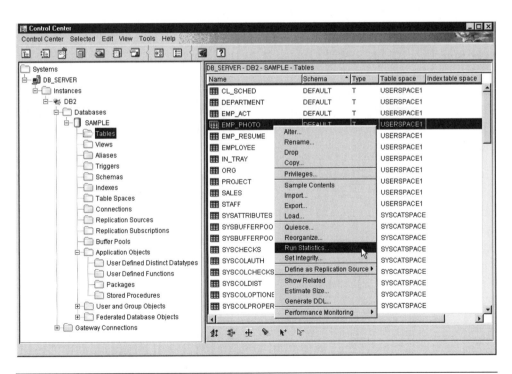

Figure 12-16   Invoking the Run Statistics dialog from the Control Center

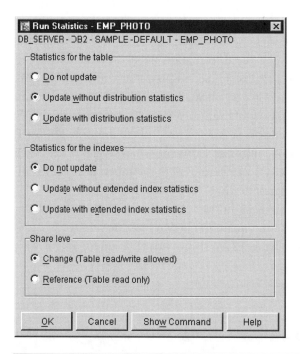

Figure 12-17 The Run Statistics dialog

The Run Statistics utility can also be invoked by executing the RUNSTATS command, either from the Command Center or from the Command Line Processor. The syntax for this command is

```
RUNSTATS ON TABLE [TableName] <WITH DISTRIBUTION | WITH
DISTRIBUTION AND <DETAILED> INDEXES ALL | WITH DISTRIBUTION AND
<DETAILED> INDEX [IndexName]> <SHRLEVEL [CHANGE | REFERENCE]>
```

or

```
RUNSTATS ON TABLE [TableName] <[AND | FOR] <DETAILED> INDEXES ALL
| [AND | FOR] <DETAILED> INDEX [IndexName]> <SHRLEVEL [CHANGE |
REFERENCE]>
```

where:

TableName   Identifies the name of the table that statistical information will be collected and updated for.

IndexName   Identifies the name of the index that statistical information will be collected and updated for.

For example, when executed, the command

```
RUNSTATS ON TABLE DEFAULT.EMPLOYEE WITH DISTRIBUTION AND INDEXES
ALL SHRLEVEL CHANGE
```

will update the statistical information stored in the system catalog tables for the table named DEFAULT.EMPLOYEE. It is important to note that the Run Statistics utility does not produce output information. However, its results can be seen by querying the CARD, OVERFLOW, NPAGES, and FPAGES columns of the system catalog table SYSCAT.TABLES. (If the values of these columns are set to -1, statistical information has not been produced for the object identified by that particular row.)

 NOTE Only users with SYSADM authority, SYSCTRL authority, SYSMAINT authority, DBADMN authority, or the CONTROL privilege on the table that statistics are to be collected for are allowed to invoke the Run Statistics utility.

Recommendations on When to Use the Run Statistics Utility

So just how often should the statistics for a table be collected? Ideally, the Run Statistics utility should be used to update the statistics for a table as soon as possible after the following events occur:

- A large number of insert, update, or delete operations have been performed against a table.
- An import operation is performed against a table.
- A load operation is performed against a table.
- One or more columns are added to an existing table.
- A new index is created for a table.
- A table has been reorganized.

It is important to note that whenever statistics for a table are collected/updated, all packages that reference the table should be rebound so that the DB2 Optimizer can evaluate the new information and formulate new access plans that may improve application performance.

Summary

The goal of this chapter was to introduce you to the data movement and data management utilities that are available with DB2 Universal Database and to show you the different file formats that are recognized by the data movement utilities.

Whenever data is moved between databases and external files, care must be taken to ensure that data that resides in an external file that will be accessed by one of DB2 Universal Database's data movement utilities has been stored in a format that can be easily processed. Otherwise, more time may have to be spent correcting data after it has been moved than was required to actually move the data! To assist in this regard, DB2 Universal Database recognizes and supports the following data file formats (a file's format determines how data is physically stored in the file):

- **Delimited ASCII (DEL)**   This format consists of data values (variable in length) that are separated by a delimiting (field separator) character. Because commas (,) are typically used as the field separator character, this format is sometimes referred to as Comma-Separated Variable (CSV) format.

- **Nondelimited ASCII (ASC)**   This format consists of fixed-length data values that are column aligned.

- **Worksheet Format (WSF)**   This format defines the layout of data that has been stored in a file format that is compatible with IBM's Lotus 1-2-3 and Lotus Symphony products.

- **PC Integrated Exchange Format (PC/IXF or IXF)**   This format consists of data values that are stored in a format that is compatible with all DB2 Universal Database products.

The file format determines how data is physically stored in an external file. It also determines the method that must be used with the DB2 data movement in order to correctly identify how data values in a file are mapped to the columns of a table. Three methods are available for mapping data values to columns:

- The location method (coded as METHOD L)
- The name method (coded as METHOD N)
- The position method (coded as METHOD P)

With the location method, columnar data values are identified by a series of beginning and ending byte position values that when used together identify the location of a column value within a single row. With the name method, columnar data values are identified by the name of the column they are associated with in the file. That's because when this method is used, the DB2 data management utilities expect column names and information about which column each data value is associated with to be stored in the file along with the data values themselves. With the position method, columnar data values are identified by their indexed position within a single row—the first data value found in a row has the index position 1, the second value found has the index position 2, and so on.

Although a database is normally thought of as a single self-contained entity, there are times when it becomes necessary for a database to exchange data with the outside world. For this reason, DB2 Universal Database provides four different utilities that are used to move data between databases and external files. Specifically, these utilities are the following:

- The Export utility
- The Import utility
- The Load utility
- The DB2MOVE utility

DB2 Universal Database's Export utility is used to extract specific portions of data from a database and externalize it to DEL, WSF, or IXF formatted files. Such files can then be used to populate tables in a variety of databases (including the database the data was extracted from) or provide input to software applications such as spreadsheets and word processors.

At a minimum, the following information must be provided when the Export utility is invoked:

- A valid SQL SELECT statement that will retrieve the specific data that will be exported
- The location and name of the file that all data retrieved by the SELECT statement specified will be written to
- The format that data will be written to the file in
- The location and name of the file that messages generated by the Export utility will be written to

When the data that will be exported contains large object (LOB) values, by default, only the first 32KB of each LOB value are actually written to the file that contains the exported data. This is not a problem if every LOB data value being exported is less than 32KB in size. However, if the default behavior is used and LOB data that is greater than

32KB in size is exported, the data will be truncated. Usually, this is undesirable behavior. By overriding this default behavior and by providing the Export utility with one or more locations that LOB data will be written to, each LOB data value encountered will be stored in its entirety in its own individual file (that is, assigned a name that either the user or the Export utility provides) instead.

An export operation can be performed by selecting the *Export* action from the *Table* menu found in the Control Center or by executing the EXPORT command, either from the Command Center or from the Command Line Processor.

Just as there may be times when data in a database needs to be copied to external files, there may times when it is necessary to make data stored in external files available to a database. This is where DB2 Universal Database's Import utility comes in. The Import utility provides a way to read data directly from DEL, ASC, WSF, or IXF formatted files and store it in a specific database table.

At a minimum, the following information must be provided when the Import utility is invoked:

- The location and name of the file that data will be copied from
- The format that data in the file is stored in
- The name of the table that data stored in the file will be copied to
- An indication of how data will be copied to the table specified
- The location and name of the file that messages generated by the Import utility will be written to

When the Export utility is used to externalize data in a table to a IXF formatted file, the table structure and definitions of all of the table's associated indexes are written to the file along with the data. Because of this, the Import utility can create/re-create a table and its indexes as well as populate the table if data is being imported from a IXF formatted file. When any other file format is used, if the table or updateable view receiving the data already contains data values, the data being imported can either replace or be appended to the existing data provided the base table receiving the data does not contain a primary key that is referenced by a foreign key of another table. (If the base table contains a primary key that is referenced by a foreign key, imported data can only be appended to the existing table.) In some situations, data being imported can also be used to update existing rows in a base table.

An import operation can be performed by selecting the *Import* action from the *Table* menu found in the Control Center or by executing the IMPORT command, either from the Command Center or from the Command Line Processor.

Like the Import utility, the Load utility is designed to read data directly from DEL, ASC, or IXF formatted files and store it in a specific database table. However, unlike when the Import utility is used, the table that the data will be stored in must already exist in the database before the load operation is initiated—the Load utility ignores the table structure and index definition information stored in IXF formatted files. Likewise, the Load utility does not create new indexes for a table—it only rebuilds indexes that have already been defined for the table being loaded.

The most important difference between the Import utility and the Load utility relates to performance. Because the Import utility inserts data into a table one row at a time, each row inserted must be checked for constraint compliance (such as foreign key constraints and table check constraints) and all activity performed must be recorded in the database's transaction log files.

The Load utility inserts data into a table much faster than the Import utility because instead of inserting data into a table one row of data at a time, it builds data pages using several individual rows of data and then writes those pages directly to the table space container that the table's structure and any preexisting data have been stored in. Existing primary/unique indexes are then rebuilt once all data pages constructed have been written to the container and duplicate rows that violate primary or unique key constraints are deleted (and copied to an exception table, if appropriate). In addition, because pages of data are written instead of individual rows, changes made to a table by a load operation are not recorded in the database's transaction log files.

Unlike the import process, the load process consists of three separate phases that make up a single operation:

- The load phase
- The build phase
- The delete phase

Two things happen during the load phase: Data is read from the source file specified and loaded into the appropriate database table, and index key values are collected and sorted. As soon as the load phase of a load operation is complete, the build phase is started. During the build phase, indexes that are associated with primary and/or unique keys that have been defined for the table that was loaded are updated with the index key values that were collected and sorted during the load phase. This is also where statistical information about the table and its indexes is updated, if appropriate.

When the build phase of a load operation is complete, the delete phase is started. During the delete phase, all rows that violated a primary and/or unique key constraint are removed from the table and copied to an exception table (provided one was specified), and a message about each offending row is written to a message file so it can be corrected and manually moved to the table at some future point in time. These are the only types of constraints that are checked. In order to check loaded data for additional constraint violations, constraint checking should be turned off (with the SET INTEGRITY SQL statement) before the load operation is started, and then turned back on and performed immediately (again, with the SET INTEGRITY SQL statement) after the load operation has completed.

A load operation can be performed by selecting the *Load* action from the *Table* menu found in the Control Center or by executing the LOAD command, either from the Command Center or from the Command Line Processor.

The DB2MOVE utility facilitates the movement of a large number of tables between DB2 databases. This utility queries the system catalog tables for a particular database and compiles a list of all user tables found. It then exports the contents and table structure of each table found to a IXF formatted file. The set of files produced can then be imported or loaded to another DB2 database on the same system, or they can be transferred to another workstation platform and imported or loaded to a DB2 database that resides on that platform. (This is the best method to use when copying or moving an existing database from one platform to another.)

The DB2MOVE utility can be run in one of three modes: EXPORT, IMPORT, or LOAD. When run in EXPORT mode, the DB2MOVE utility invokes the Export utility to extract data from one or more tables and externalize it to IXF formatted files. It also creates a file named *db2move.lst* that contains the names of all tables processed, along with the names of the files that the table's data was written to. In addition, the DB2MOVE utility may produce one or more message files that contain warning or error messages that were generated as a result of an export operation.

When run in IMPORT mode, the DB2MOVE utility invokes the Import utility to re-create a table and its indexes from data stored in IXF formatted files. In this mode, the file *db2move.lst* is used to establish a link between the IXF formatted files needed and the tables into which data will be imported.

When run in LOAD mode, the DB2MOVE utility invokes the Load utility to populate tables that have already been created with data stored in IXF formatted files. Again, the file *db2move.lst* is used to establish a link between the IXF formatted files needed and the tables into which data will be imported.

The DB2MOVE utility is invoked by executing the DB2MOVE command, either from the Command Center or from the Command Line Processor.

The way data stored in tables is physically distributed across table space containers can have a significant impact on the performance of applications that access the data. How data is stored in a table is affected by insert, update, and delete operations that are performed on the table. For example, a delete operation may leave empty pages that for some reason never get reused. Or update operations performed on variable-length columns may result in larger column values that cause an entire row to be moved to a different page because they no longer fit on the original page. In both scenarios, internal gaps are created in the underlying table space containers. As a consequence, the DB2 Database Manager may have to read more physical pages into memory in order to retrieve the data needed to satisfy a query.

Because situations such as these are almost unavoidable, DB2 Universal Database provides three different data maintenance utilities that are used to optimize the physical distribution of all data stored in a table:

- The Reorganize Check utility

- The Reorganize Table utility

- The Run Statistics utility

You can determine what the physical organization of tables and indexes look like, as well as how much storage space is utilized and how much is by running the Reorganize Check utility. When executed, this utility optionally generates statistics and analyzes all statistics available to determine whether or not one or more tables need to be reorganized—which is an action that will cause existing internal gaps to be removed. The Reorganize Check utility is invoked by executing the REORGCHK command, either from the Command Center or from the Command Line Processor.

After evaluating the output of the Reorganize Check utility, you may find it necessary to reorganize the physical layout of one or more tables. This is where the Reorganize Table utility comes in. When executed, the Reorganize Table utility eliminates gaps in table space containers by rewriting the data associated with a table to contiguous pages in storage (similar to the way a disk defragmenter works). With the help of an index, the Reorganize Table utility can also place the data rows of a table in the same physical sequence as the index specified, thereby increasing the cluster ratio of the selected index. This approach also has an attractive side effect—if the DB2 Database Manager finds the data needed to satisfy a query stored in contiguous space and in the desired sort order, the overall performance of the query will be improved because the seek time needed to read the data will be shorter and a sort operation may no longer be necessary.

The Reorganize Table utility can be invoked by selecting the Reorganize action from the Table menu found in the Control Center or by executing the REORG command, either from the Command Center or from the Command Line Processor.

Although the system catalog tables contain information such as the number of rows in a table, the way storage space is utilized by tables and indexes, and the number of different values found in a column, this information is not automatically kept up-to-date. Instead, it has to be generated periodically by running the Run Statistics utility.

The information that is collected by the Run Statistics utility is used in two ways: to provide information about the physical organization of the data in a table and provide information that the DB2 Optimizer can use when selecting the best path to use to access data that will satisfy the requirements of a query.

The Run Statistics utility can be invoked by selecting the *Run Statistics* action from the *Table* menu found in the Control Center or by executing the RUNSTATS command, either from the Command Center or from the Command Line Processor.

Questions

1. Which of the following file formats contains the information needed to create a table during an import operation?
   a. Delimited ASCII (ASC)
   b. Nondelimited ASCII (ASC)
   c. PC Integrated Exchange Format (IXF)
   d. Text (TXT)
   e. Worksheet Format (WSF)

2. To export a table from one database that will be imported into another database where the table already exists, which of the following file formats cannot be used?
   a. ASC
   b. DEL
   c. IXF
   d. WSF

3. Which of the following utilities can insert data into a DB2 for OS/390 database?
   a. LOAD
   b. EXPORT
   c. IMPORT
   d. UPLOAD
   e. DB2MOVE

4. Which of the following tasks is performed by the Load utility?
   a. Reorganizing data
   b. Creating the table
   c. Altering table structure
   d. Collecting table statistics

5. Which of the following utilities can add data to a table with a primary key defined and have all rows that violate the primary key constraint stored in an exception table?

   a. LOAD
   b. FORCE
   c. EXPORT
   d. IMPORT
   e. UPLOAD

6. Given the following catalog view:

SYSCAT.TABLES

TABSCHEMA	TABNAME	CARD	OVERFLOW	NPAGES	FPAGES
ADMIN	PAYROLL1	-1	-1	-1 -1	
ADMIN	PAYROLL2	-1	-1	-1 -1	

Which of the following is the first step towards improving query response time?
   a. Drop existing indexes on PAYROLL1.
   b. Drop existing indexes on PAYROLL2.
   c. Reorganize the table based on an index for PAYROLL1.
   d. Reorganize the table based on an index for PAYROLL2.
   e. Run statistics on the base tables PAYROLL1 and PAYROLL2.

7. Which of the following must be used to move a DB2 database from Windows NT to Linux?
   a. Back up the database on Windows NT and restore it on Linux.
   b. Use Relational Connect to move the data using INSERT statements that contain subselects.
   c. Use DB2MOVE to automate exporting the tables on Windows NT and loading them on Linux.
   d. Use DB2LOOK with the -e option specified to capture the DDL and data for each table in a format that can be imported to DB2 on Linux.

8. Having just completed a reorganization of a DB2 table, which of the following steps may improve query performance?
   a. Run statistics on the table.
   b. Reorganize each remaining index on the table.
   c. Drop and re-create each index on the table.
   d. Update the database configuration.

9. Which two of the following does REORGCHK provide?
   a. Date of last table reorg
   b. Index size
   c. Number of rows in the table
   d. Support of nicknames
   e. Table page size

10. Online index reorganization provides the capability to reclaim index free space after the deletion of an index key. Which of the following options gives an index this capability?
    a. `CREATE INDEX . . . . ONLINE`
    b. `CREATE INDEX . . . . RECLAIM`
    c. `CREATE INDEX . . . . MINPCTUSED`
    d. `CREATE INDEX . . . . REORGSPACE`

11. What action may be specified from the LOAD command?
    a. REORG of the table.
    b. Roll-forward of the database.
    c. COPY the loaded data (BACKUP).
    d. Create the table if it does not exist.

12. Why might data exist in an exception table following a LOAD operation?
    a. Primary key constraint violations may have occurred.
    b. Triggers may have been fired and populated the exception table.
    c. Referential integrity constraint violations may have occurred.
    d. The data types in the LOAD file do not match the table definition.

13. Which database objects can be reorganized using the REORG command?
    a. Table spaces
    b. Containers
    c. Tables
    d. Indexes

14. Following a successful RUNSTATS execution, what should be performed?
    a. RESTORE a previous database backup image.
    b. REORG for all database objects.
    c. REBIND applications.
    d. RESTART the database.

15. What dictates where errors encountered during an EXPORT are reported?
  a. The DB2MESSAGES environment variable.
  b. The MESSAGES parameter specified during EXPORT.
  c. The database configuration file.
  d. The errors are placed in the specified exception file.

Answers

1. C. Because table definitions (including associated index definitions) are stored in PC Integrated Exchange Format (IXF) files along with data, tables and associated indexes can be created and populated, if necessary, when this format is used.

2. A. The Export utility does not support nondelimited ASCII (ASC) format files.

3. C. The Import utility is the only utility that can insert data into a host database through DB2 Connect. (Refer to Table 12-3.)

4. D. If specified, the Load utility can invoke the Run Statistics utility as part of its build phase.

5. A. During the delete phase of a load operation, all rows that violated a primary and/or unique key constraint are removed from the table and copied to an exception table (provided one was specified), and a message about each offending row is written to a message file so it can be corrected and manually moved to the table at some future point in time.

6. E. If the values of the CARD, OVERFLOW, NPAGES, and FPAGES columns of the system catalog table SYSCAT.TABLES are set to -1, statistical information has not been produced for the object identified by that particular row. The first step towards improving query response time is to update the statistics for these tables.

7. C. The DB2MOVE utility queries the system catalog tables for a particular database and compiles a list of all user tables found. It then exports the contents and table structure of each table found to a IXF formatted file. The set of files produced can then be imported or loaded to another DB2 database on the same system, or they can be transferred to another workstation platform and imported or loaded to a DB2 database that resides on that platform. This is the best method to use when copying or moving an existing database from one platform to another.

8. **A.** Ideally, the Run Statistics utility should be used to update the statistics for a table after the table has been reorganized.

9. **B** and **C.** Among other things, the Reorganize Check utility provides the size of each index that has been defined for a table (ISIZE) and the number of rows in the table (CARD).

10. **C.** Whether or not an index will automatically be reorganized and when reorganization will occur is determined by the MINPCTUSED option that is part of the CREATE INDEX SQL statement. If the MINPCTUSED option is used, the threshold for the minimum percentage of space used on an index leaf page is specified as part of the MINPCTUSED option (for example, MINPCTUSED 80) and if the percentage of space used on the page is at or below the percentage specified after a key is deleted from an index leaf page, an attempt is made to merge the remaining keys on the page with those of a neighboring page.

11. **C.** Because changes made to a table by the Load utility are not logged, they cannot be reapplied by performing a roll-forward recovery operation if a database failure occurs. To get around this problem, the Load utility can automatically make a backup copy of all data loaded so it can be reloaded quickly if necessary.

12. **A.** During a load operation, all rows that violate a primary and/or unique key constraint are removed from the table and copied to an exception table (provided one is specified). These are the only types of constraints that are checked by the Load utility.

13. **C.** Only tables can be reorganized by the Reorganize Table utility—which is invoked by the REORG command.

14. **C.** Whenever statistics for a table are collected/updated, all packages that reference the table should be rebound so that the DB2 Optimizer can evaluate the new information and formulate new access plans that may improve application performance.

15. **B.** The MESSAGES [*MessageFileName*] option of the EXPORT command is used to identify the name and location of the file that messages generated by the Export utility will be written to during the export operation.

CHAPTER 13

Database Recovery and Maintenance

In this chapter, you will learn

- What transaction logging is and how it is performed
- How to return a database that has been placed in an inconsistent state to a consistent state
- How to create a backup image of a database
- How to return a database to the state it was in when a backup image was made (by restoring it from a backup image)
- How to reapply (or roll-forward) some or all changes made to a database since the last backup image was made once the database has been returned to the state it was in when the backup image was made
- Which database configuration parameters affect logging and data recovery

The sixth objective of the DB2 Universal Database—Database Administration for UNIX, Windows, and OS/2 exam is to evaluate your understanding of transaction logging, particularly the types of logging available, and to test your knowledge about the database recovery mechanisms that are available. This chapter is designed to introduce you to the concept of transaction logging and to provide an in-depth look at the various tools that are used to return an inconsistent database to a consistent state and a corrupted database to the state it was in at a specific point in time.

TIP Seven percent of the DB2 Universal Database—Database Administration for UNIX, Windows, and OS/2 exam is designed to test your knowledge of logging concepts and database recovery.

Transaction Logging

In Chapter 7, we saw how transactions and locks are used to maintain database consistency when two or more users and/or applications access a database concurrently. These two mechanisms resolve most concurrency issues, provided applications and hardware perform as expected. But what happens if a power interruption occurs or an application abends while a database is in use? DB2 Universal Database uses a mechanism known as *transaction logging* to restore data consistency when these types of situations occur.

Transaction logging is simply a process that is used to keep track of changes that are made to a database, as they are made. Each time a change is made to a row in a table (by an insert, update, or delete operation), records that reflect that change are written to a log buffer, which is simply a designated area in memory. If an insert operation is performed, a record containing the new row is written to the log buffer; if an update operation is performed, a record containing the row's original values is written to the log buffer, along with a record containing the row's new values (two separate records are written); and if a delete operation is performed, a record containing the row's original values is written to the log buffer. These types of records, along with records that indicate whether a transaction was committed or rolled back, make up the majority of the records stored in the log buffer.

When a transaction terminates by executing a COMMIT or a ROLLBACK SQL statement, all log records associated with that transaction are immediately written from the log buffer to one or more log files stored on disk. Only after all log records associated with the transaction have been externalized to one or more log files does the transaction receive confirmation that the commit or rollback operation has been successfully completed. This ensures that all log records of a completed transaction will not be lost due to a system failure. The transaction logging process is illustrated in Figure 13-1.

Log records may be written to disk before a commit or a rollback operation is performed: for example, if the log buffer becomes full. However, such "early-writes" do not affect data consistency because the execution of the COMMIT or ROLLBACK statement itself is logged eventually. (A transaction that has started and that has been externalized

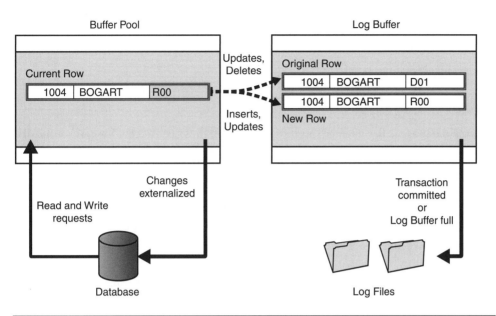

Buffer Pool

Log Buffer

Figure 13-1   Transaction logging

to a log file is not considered complete until the commit or rollback operation that terminates that transaction is also externalized to the log file.)

NOTE   Pages of data in a buffer pool that have been changed by a transaction that has been committed do not have to be externalized to disk when that transaction performs a commit operation. Instead, such pages may remain in memory if the data they contain is accessed frequently.

Because more than one transaction may be using a database at a given time, a log file may contain log records for multiple transactions. Therefore, to keep everything straight, each log record is assigned a special ID that identifies the transaction that created it. In addition, all log records for a single transaction are chained together whenever possible. If a transaction was committed, all log records associated with that transaction are eventually written to the database, at which time they are no longer needed. However, if a transaction was rolled back, the DB2 Database Manager processes each log record associated with that transaction in reverse order and backs out all changes made. That is why "before" and "after" records are written for all update operations.

DB2 Universal Database uses two types of logging strategies. They are

- Circular logging
- Archival logging

Circular Logging

When a database is first created, a set of *primary* log files are allocated as part of the creation process. When circular logging is used, records stored in the log buffer are written to these primary log files, in a circular sequence. Once all records stored in a primary log file are applied to the corresponding database (after the transaction they are associated with has been committed or rolled back), that log file is marked as *reusable* because its records are no longer needed. When this log file becomes the next log file in the sequence, its contents are overwritten with new log records and the process repeats itself. (Overwritten log records are not recoverable.)

If the DB2 Database Manager attempts to acquire the next primary log file in the sequence and it is not yet available for reuse, a *secondary* log file will be allocated automatically and new log records are written to this secondary log file. When this secondary log file becomes full, the DB2 Database Manager will poll the primary log file again and if it is still not available, another secondary log file will be allocated and filled. This process will continue until the desired primary log file becomes reusable or until the number of secondary log files created exceeds the number of secondary log files permitted; if the latter occurs, all database activity will halt until the desired primary log file becomes reusable. When all log records stored in a secondary log file are applied to the corresponding database, that log file is deallocated and its contents are destroyed. Circular logging is illustrated in Figure 13-2.

Archival Logging

Like circular logging, when archival logging (also known as log retention logging) is used, records stored in the log buffer are written to one or more primary log files. However, when archival logging is used, primary log files are not reused; instead, when a primary log file becomes full, it is archived and a new primary log file is allocated. This process continues as long as log files are needed or until primary log files consume all the disk space available.

With archival logging, secondary log files are not used. Instead, three types of primary log files are used:

- **Active** Active log files contain records that are associated with transactions that have not yet been committed or rolled back. Active log files also contain records

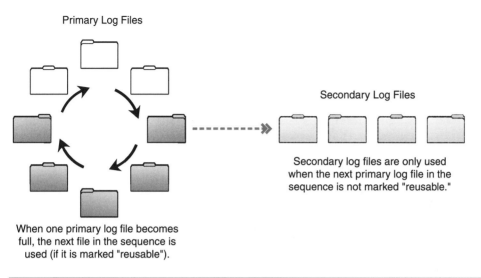

Figure 13-2 Circular logging

for transactions that have been committed, but whose changes have not yet been written to the corresponding database's files.

- **Online archive**   Online archive log files contain records that are associated with completed transactions that have been written to the corresponding database's files. These log files are termed "online" because they reside in the same subdirectory as the active log files and "archive" because they are no longer needed for normal processing.

- **Offline archive**   Like online archive log files, offline archive log files contain records that are associated with completed transactions that have been written to the corresponding database's files. However, rather than residing in the same subdirectory as active log files, these log files have been moved to another storage location, either manually or by a user-exit routine.

Figure 13-3 illustrates archival logging, along with the three types of log files used.

Returning a Database to a Consistent State

Whenever one or more transactions are unexpectedly interrupted (either by a power interruption or an application failure), all databases being accessed at the time

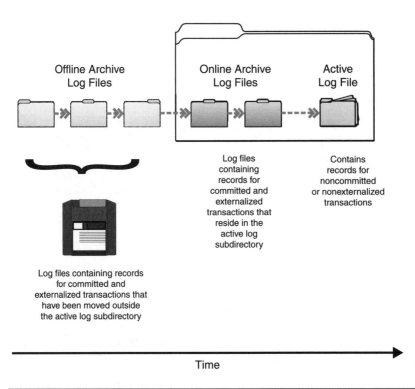

Offline Archive
Log Files

Online Archive
Log Files

Active
Log File

Log files
containing
records for
committed and
externalized
transactions that
reside in the
active log
subdirectory

Contains
records for
noncommitted
or nonexternalized
transactions

Log files containing records
for committed and
externalized transactions that
have been moved outside
the active log subdirectory

Time

Figure 13-3 Archival logging

the interruption occurred are placed in an *inconsistent* or unstable state. Such databases remain in an inconsistent state until some action is taken to return them to a consistent state. (A database that is in an inconsistent state notifies users and applications that it is unusable via a specific return code that is generated when either a user or an application attempts to establish a connection to it.) A database that has been placed in an inconsistent state can be returned to a consistent state by selecting the *Restart Database* action from the Control Center menu. Figure 13-4 shows the Control Center menu item that must be selected in order to restart an inconsistent database.

A database can also be returned to a consistent state by executing the RESTART DATABASE command, either from the Command Center or from the Command Line Processor. The syntax for this command is

```
RESTART [DATABASE | DB] [DatabaseName] <USER [AuthorizationID]
<USING [Password]>> <DROP PENDING TABLESPACES
( [TableSpaceName] , . . . )>
```

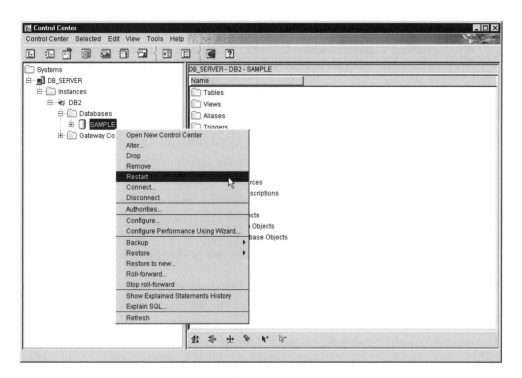

Figure 13-4   Restarting a database from the Control Center

where:

DatabaseName	Identifies the database that is to be returned to a consistent state.
AuthorizationID	Identifies the authorization ID of the user that the database is to be restarted under.
Password	Identifies the password (that corresponds to the authorization ID specified) of the user that the database is to be restarted under.
TableSpaceName	Identifies one or more table spaces that are to be disabled and placed in "Drop Pending" state if an error is encountered with them when the database is restarted.

For example, when executed, the command

```
RESTART DATABASE SAMPLEDB USER DB2INS71 USING IBMDB2
```

would return the database SAMPLEDB to a consistent state.

NOTE The DB2 Database Manager checks the state of a database when it first attempts to establish a connection to that database. If the autorestart parameter of a database's configuration file is set to **ON**, the **RESTART DATABASE** command is automatically executed if the DB2 Database Manager determines that the database is in an inconsistent state.

When the RESTART DATABASE command is executed, the DB2 Database Manager determines whether or not database recovery is needed by examining the active recovery log file(s) that isassociated with the database specified. If the log shows that the database was shut down abnormally, the database could be in an inconsistent state because changes made by completed transactions that were still in the buffer pool may have been lost. If the DB2 Database Manager determines that a database restart is necessary, it attempts to return the database to a consistent state by doing the following:

1. Removing any changes made by transactions that were in-flight (that is, that have not been committed or rolled back) from the database. Because the DB2 Database Manager follows the rule that changes are only consistent when they have been explicitly committed, all work done by in-flight transactions is considered inconsistent and must be backed out of the database to preserve database consistency.

2. Writing changes made by committed transactions found in the log file(s) that have not been written to the database to the database.

3. Rolling back any transactions that were in the process of being rolled back so that all changes made to the database by that transaction are removed.

Figure 13-5 illustrates how a database remains in a consistent state during normal operation; Figure 13-6 illustrates how a database is returned to a consistent state by the RESTART DATABASE command.

As you can see, during the recovery process, the DB2 Database Manager must scan all the log files available, along with the database itself, in order to return an inconsistent database to a consistent state. As you might imagine, if the log file(s) for a database is large, it could take quite a while to scan the whole log and read associated rows from the database. Fortunately, it's usually not necessary to scan the entire log because the chance is great that records recorded at the beginning of the log file are associated with transactions that have been completed and that have already been written to the database. Thus, if there were some way to skip these log records during the recovery process, the length of time needed to recover the entire database could be shortened.

That's where the *soft checkpoint* comes in. The soft checkpoint establishes a pointer in the database log at which database recovery is to begin—all records recorded before the

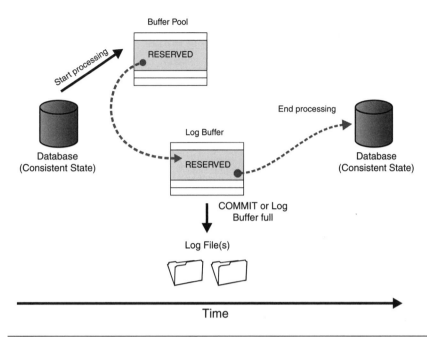

Figure 13-5   How a database remains in a consistent state during normal processing

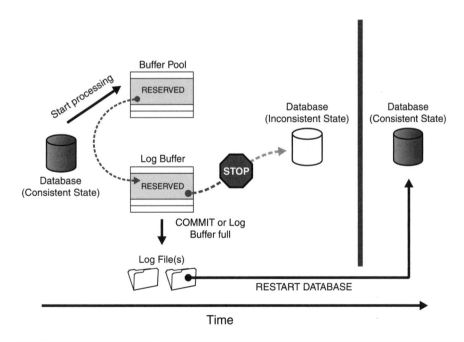

Figure 13-6   How a database is returned to a consistent state by the RESTART DATABASE command

soft checkpoint are assumed to be associated with completed transactions that have already been written to the database. A soft checkpoint is most useful when log files are large, because it can reduce the number of log records that are examined during database recovery. Obviously, the more often the soft checkpoint is updated, the faster a database recovery operation can be performed.

Managing Database Recovery

Although the RESTART DATABASE command in conjunction with transaction log files can be used to resolve database problems that are caused by power interruptions and/or application failures, these two items cannot be used to handle problems that can arise when the storage media being used to hold a database's files becomes corrupted or fails. To address these types of problems, some kind of backup (and recovery) program must be established. To help establish such a program, DB2 Universal Database provides a set of utilities that can be used to

- Create a backup image of a database.
- Return a database to the state it was in when a backup image was made (by restoring it from a backup image).
- Reapply (or roll-forward) some or all changes made to a database since the last backup image was made once the database has been returned to the state it was in when the backup image was made.

Creating a Backup Image of a Database

One of the basic tools used to prevent catastrophic data losses when media failures occur is a database backup image. A database backup image is essentially a copy of an entire database or of one or more table spaces that make up a database. Once created, a backup image can be used at any time to return a database to the state it was in at the time the image was made. A good backup/recovery program should ensure that backup images are created regularly, and that multiple backup copies of critical data are retained in a secure location. (Ideally, a database backup image should reside on one or more physical devices that do not contain the database itself or on removable media such as tape or diskettes.) Depending upon the type of logging used, database backup images can be made when a database is offline or while other users and applications are connected to it (online). (However, in order to create a backup image while a database is online, archival logging must be used.)

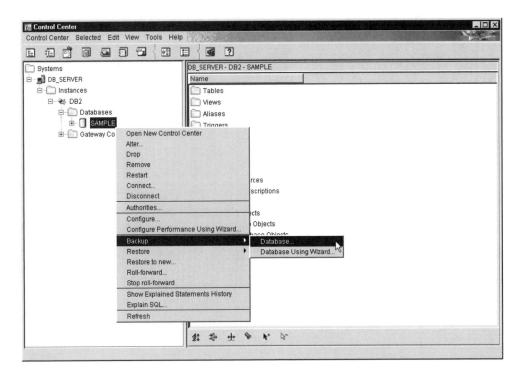

Figure 13-7   Invoking the Backup Database dialog from the Control Center

The easiest way to create a backup image of a DB2 Universal Database database (or of a specific table space within a database) is by using the Backup Database dialog. Figure 13-7 shows the Control Center menu items that must be selected in order to activate the Backup Database dialog. Figure 13-8 shows how the first page of the Backup Database dialog might look after its input fields have been populated.

A database or one of its table spaces can also be backed up by executing the BACKUP command, either from the Command Center or from the Command Line Processor. The syntax for this command is

```
BACKUP [DATABASE | DB] [DatabaseName] <USER [AuthorizationID]
<USING [Password]>> <TABLESPACE ( [TableSpaceName] , . . . )>
<ONLINE> <USE TSM <OPEN [NumSessions] SESSIONS> | TO [Directory] |
TO [Device] | LOAD [Library] <OPEN [NumSessions] SESSIONS>> <WITH
[NumBuffers] BUFFERS> <BUFFER [BufferSize]> <PARALLELISM
[ParallelNum]> <WITHOUT PROMPTING>
```

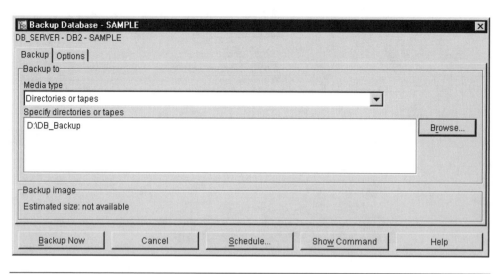

Figure 13-8   The first page of the Backup Database dialog

where:

DatabaseName	Identifies the database that is to be backed up.
AuthorizationID	Identifies the authorization ID of the user that the database is to be backed up under.
Password	Identifies the password (that corresponds to the authorization ID specified) of the user that the database is to be backed up under.
TableSpaceName	Identifies one or more table spaces that are to be backed up.
NumSessions	Identifies the number of I/O sessions that are to be created between DB2 Universal Database and Tivoli Storage Manager (formerly ASDM) or some other vendor backup product.
Directory	Identifies one or more directories that are to be used to store the backup image created.
Device	Identifies one or more raw devices that are to be used to store the backup image created.
Library	Identifies the name of the shared library (.DLL file on OS/2 or Windows) that contains vendor-specific backup and restore I/O functions that are to be used.

NumBuffers Identifies the number of buffers that are to be used to perform the backup operation. By default, two buffers are used if this option is not specified.

BufferSize Identifies the size in pages that each buffer used to perform the backup operation should be. By default, buffers that are 1,024 pages in size are used if this option is not specified.

ParallelNum Identifies the number of table spaces that can be read in parallel by the backup utility.

For example, when executed, the following BACKUP command would create a backup image of a database named SAMPLEDB (offline) and store it in a directory named BACKUPS on logical disk drive D:

```
BACKUP DATABASE SAMPLEDB USER DB2INS71 USING IBMDB2 TO D:\BACKUPS
```

NOTE Only users with System Administrator (SYSADM) authority, System Control (SYSCTRL) authority, or System Maintenance (SYSMAINT) authority are allowed to create a database backup image.

The Recovery History File

Along with the database configuration file, another important file that is produced during the database creation process is a file that is known as the recovery history file. The recovery history file is used to log historical information about certain actions that are performed against a database. Specifically, a record is automatically written to the recovery history file when any of the following activities are performed:

- A backup image of the database or one of its table spaces is created.

- A recovery (restore) operation is performed using a backup image of the database or one of its table spaces.

- A table is loaded using the load facility.

- A roll-forward recovery operation is performed on either the database or one of its table spaces.

- A table space is altered.

- A table space is quiesced.

- The data in a table is reorganized.

- The statistics for a table are updated.

- A table is deleted (dropped).

In addition to providing information about which type of activity was performed, each entry in the recovery history file contains the date and time the activity was performed, how a particular activity was performed, the specific table spaces and tables of the database that were affected by the activity, and the location of each backup image created, along with information on how to access the image (if the activity was a backup operation). In a moment, we'll see how this information is used when an attempt is made to restore a corrupted database.

The contents of a database's recovery history file can be seen by executing the LIST HISTORY command, either from the Command Center or from the Command Line Processor. The syntax for this command is

```
LIST HISTORY <BACKUP | ROLLFORWARD | ALTER TABLESPACE | DROPPED
TABLE | LOAD | RENAME TABLESPACE> <ALL | SINCE [DateTime] |
CONTAINING [<SchemaName.>ObjectName]> FOR <DATABASE | DB>
[DatabaseName]
```

where:

DateTime	Identifies a timestamp that is to be used as search criteria when listing entries in the recovery history file; only entries with timestamps that are less than or equal to the timestamp provided are listed.
SchemaName	Identifies the name of a schema that is to be used as search criteria when listing entries in the recovery history file; only entries that indicate that the object specified in the *ObjectName* parameter that resides in the schema specified are listed.
ObjectName	Identifies the name of an object that is to be used as search criteria when listing entries in the recovery history file; only entries that indicate that the object specified are listed.
DatabaseName	Identifies the name of the database whose recovery history file is to be queried.

For example, when executed, the following LIST HISTORY command would list the entire contents of the recovery history file that is associated with a database named SAMPLEDB:

```
LIST HISTORY ALL FOR SAMPLEDB
```

Entries in a database's recovery history file can be altered by executing the UPDATE HISTORY FILE command and entries can be removed by executing the PRUNE HISTORY command. From a certification viewpoint, knowing how to use these commands is not important. Instead, emphasis is placed on knowing how the recovery history file is used to facilitate the database recovery process.

Restoring a Database (or a Table Space) from a Backup Image

When a database or one of its table spaces becomes damaged or corrupt, it can be returned to a usable state provided one or more backup images exist. The backup image used may contain the contents of an entire database, or it may contain the contents of one or more of the database's table spaces. Restoring the contents of an entire database must be done while the database is offline; restoring the contents of one or more table spaces can be done while other users and applications are interacting with other table spaces in the database (that is, while the database is online).

Because the recovery history file contains summary and image location information for each backup image available, it is used as a tracking mechanism during restore operations. Each backup image file contains special information in its header that is checked against the records in the recovery history file to verify that the backup image being used corresponds to the database being restored. Each full database backup image also contains a copy of the database's recovery history file. However, when an existing database is restored from a full database backup image, that database's recovery history file is not overwritten. (A special form of the RESTORE DATABASE command can be used to restore *just* the recovery history file from a database backup image.) On the other hand, if a backup image is used to create a new database (a backup image can be used to create a new database that is an exact duplicate of the database that the backup image was created from), the recovery history file stored in the backup image becomes the recovery history file for the new database.

The easiest way to restore a DB2 Universal Database database (or a specific table space within a database) from a backup image is by using the Restore Database dialog. Figure 13-9 shows the Control Center menu items that must be selected in order to activate the Restore Database dialog. Figure 13-10 shows how the first page of the Restore Database dialog might look after its input fields have been populated.

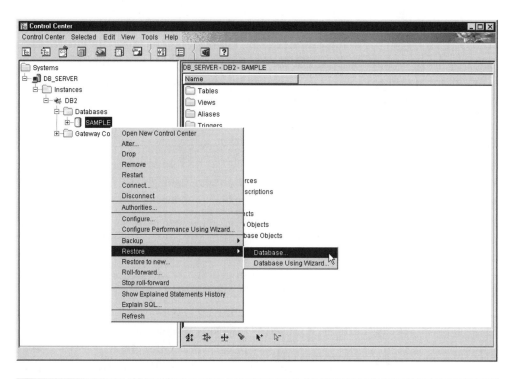

Figure 13-9   Invoking the Restore Database dialog from the Control Center

A database or one of its table spaces can also be restored from a backup image by executing the RESTORE command, either from the Command Center or from the Command Line Processor. The syntax for this command is

```
RESTORE [DATABASE | DB] [DatabaseName] <USER [AuthorizationID]
<USING [Password]>> <TABLESPACE ONLINE | TABLESPACE
( [TableSpaceName] , . . . ) <ONLINE> | HISTORY FILE <ONLINE>>
<USE TSM <OPEN [NumSessions] SESSIONS> | FROM [Directory] | FROM
[Device] | LOAD [Library] <OPEN [NumSessions] SESSIONS>> <TAKEN AT
[BackupDate]> <TO [TargetLocation]> <INTO [TargetAlias]>
<NEWLOGPATH [LogsLocation]> <WITH [NumBuffers] BUFFERS> <BUFFER
[BufferSize]> <DLREPORT [DLFileName]> <REPLACE EXISTING>
<REDIRECT> <PARALLELISM [ParallelNum]> <WITHOUT ROLLING FORWARD>
WITHOUT DATALINK> <WITHOUT PROMPTING>
```

or

```
RESTORE [DATABASE | DB] [DatabaseName] CONTINUE
```

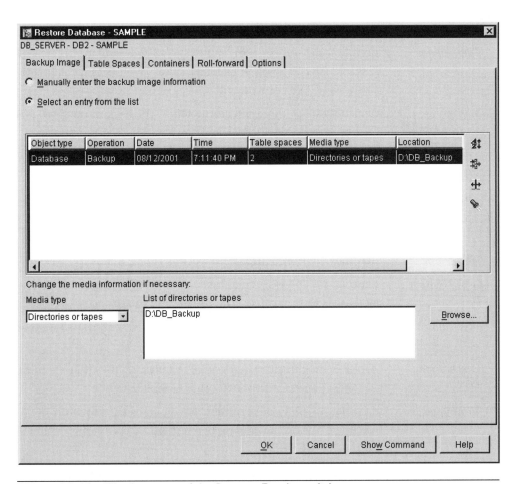

Figure 13-10   The first page of the Restore Database dialog

or

```
RESTORE [DATABASE | DB] [DatabaseName] ABORT
```

where:

DatabaseName	Identifies the database that is to be restored.
AuthorizationID	Identifies the authorization ID of the user that the database is to be restored under.
Password	Identifies the password (that corresponds to the authorization ID specified) of the user that the database is to be restored under.

TableSpaceName	Identifies one or more table spaces that are to be restored.
NumSessions	Identifies the number of I/O sessions that are to be created between DB2 Universal Database and Tivoli Storage Manager (formerly ASDM) or some other vendor backup product.
Directory	Identifies one or more directories where the backup image that is to be used is stored.
Device	Identifies one or more raw devices where the backup image to be used is stored.
Library	Identifies the name of the shared library (.DLL file on OS/2 or Windows) that contains vendor-specific backup and restore I/O functions that are to be used.
BackupDate	Identifies the timestamp of the backup image that is to be used.
TargetLocation	Identifies the directory that the database is to be stored in if a new database is to be created from the backup image specified.
TargetAlias	Identifies the alias name that is to be assigned to the database that is being restored.
LogsLocation	Identifies the directory that contains active log files that are to be used after the restore operation has completed.
NumBuffers	Identifies the number of buffers that are to be used to perform the backup operation. By default, two buffers are used if this option is not specified.
BufferSize	Identifies the size in pages that each buffer used to perform the backup operation should be. By default, buffers that are 1,024 pages in size are used if this option is not specified.
DLFileName	Identifies a file that will contain a list of all DataLink files that become unlinked as a result of the restore operation after the restore operation is completed.
ParallelNum	Identifies the number of table spaces that can be read in parallel by the backup utility.

For example, when executed, the following RESTORE command would restore a database named SAMPLEDB (offline) using a backup image stored in a directory named BACKUPS on logical disk drive D:

```
RESTORE DATABASE SAMPLEDB FROM C:\BACKUPS
```

> **NOTE**   Only users with System Administrator (SYSADM) authority, System Control (SYSCTRL) authority, or System Maintenance (SYSMAINT) authority are allowed to restore an existing database from a backup image; only users with SYSADM or SYSCTRL are allowed to create a new database from a backup image.

Redirected Restore Operations

A full backup image of a database contains, among other things, a list of all table space containers that were in use by the database at the time the backup image was made. During a restore operation, a check is performed to ensure that all table space containers listed in the backup image still exist and are accessible. If this check determines that one or more of the table space containers in the list is no longer available or is no longer accessible, the restore operation will fail. When such a condition exists, all invalid table space containers found can be redefined during the restore process by performing a special restore operation that is known as a *redirected restore*.

The easiest way to perform a redirected restore operation is by using the Containers page of the Restore Database dialog. Figure 13-11 shows how this page can be used to specify new table space containers for a redirected restore operation.

A redirected restore can also be performed by executing the RESTORE command with the REDIRECT option specified. When the RESTORE command is executed with this option specified, each invalid table space container found is flagged when table space containers are checked, and all table spaces that reference invalid table space containers are placed in the "Restore Pending" state. A list of all table spaces affected can be produced by executing the LIST TABLESPACES command (refer to Chapter 9 for more information). Once all affected table spaces have been identified, new table space containers can be defined by executing the SET TABLESPACE CONTAINERS command (again, refer to Chapter 9 for more information). After new table space containers have been created for every table space that was placed in the "Restore Pending" state, the redirected restore operation can be completed by executing the RESTORE command again; this time with the CONTINUE option specified.

> **NOTE**   When new table space containers are defined during a redirected restore operation, all previous table space containers defined for the specified table space become invalid. Unfortunately, DB2 does not automatically release the media storage used by invalid table space containers; the database administrator must perform this task after the redirected restore operation has completed.

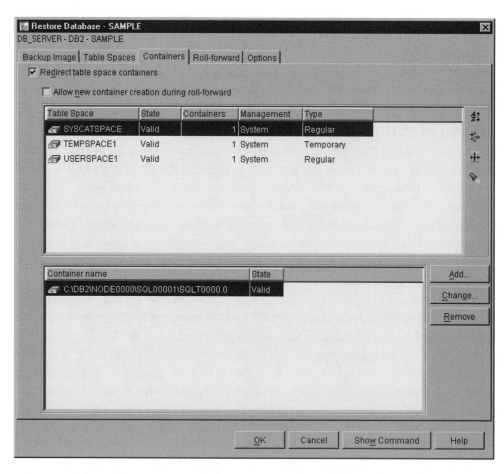

Figure 13-11   The Containers Page of the Restore Database Wizard

Roll-Forward Recovery

When a database is restored from a backup image, it is returned to the state it was in when the backup image used was created. This means that, unless special steps are taken, all changes made to a database after the backup image used was created will be lost after a restore operation is performed. To return a database to the state it was in at any given point in time (including the point in time just before the database files became corrupted), the database must be configured to support roll-forward recovery; roll-forward recovery uses archival logging in conjunction with a database's log files to reapply any or all changes made to a database since the last backup image was generated after a restore operation has been performed. Figure 13-12 illustrates how roll-

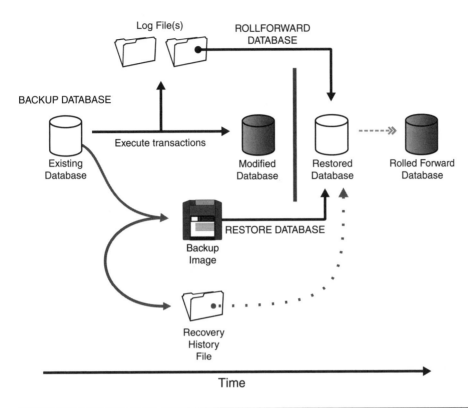

Figure 13-12 Roll-forward recovery

forward recovery is used in conjunction with the backup and restore utilities to return a database to the state it was in at a specific point in time.

As transactions are applied to the database, they are also written to one or more log files. When the database is restored from a backup image, all changes made to the database since the backup image was created are lost. When roll-forward recovery is applied (using log files), the database is returned to the state it was in before the restore operation began.

Roll-forward recovery is enabled by setting the *logretain* and/or the *userexit* parameter in the database configuration file to YES. If either of these configuration parameters is set, the database's transaction log files are configured in such a way that all entries that are needed to perform a roll-forward recovery operation are retained and archived for later use. (When both of these configuration parameters are set to NO, which is the default, circular logging is used and roll-forward recovery is not supported.) If the *logretain* parameter is set to YES, a new log file will be opened as soon as the current active log file becomes full and the database administrator must manually move older log files to an archive; otherwise, the server may eventually run out of storage space. If the *userexit* parameter is set to YES, a new log file will still be opened as soon as the current active log file becomes full, but a user-supplied program that examines the log file directory's contents and moves older log files to an archive will automatically be invoked (and the risk of running out of storage space on the server is eliminated). When either parameter is changed from NO to YES, the database is placed in the "Backup Pending" state and can no longer be used until a full backup image is created. (This backup image serves as the starting point for any future roll-forward recovery operations.)

Table 13-1 highlights some of the differences between a database that has roll-forward recovery enabled and a database that does not.

The easiest way to initiate a roll-forward recovery operation is by using the Roll-Forward Database dialog. Figure 13-13 shows the Control Center menu items that must be selected in order to activate the Roll-Forward Database dialog. Figure 13-14 shows how the first page of the Roll-Forward Database dialog might look after its input fields have been populated.

Table 13-1   Differences in Functionality When Roll-Forward Recovery Is Enabled

If Roll-Forward Recovery Is NOT Enabled	If Roll-Forward Recovery Is Enabled
The database can only be backed up when no applications are connected to it (that is, only offline backups are supported).	The database can be backed up at any time— when no applications are connected to it or while applications are connected to it and transactions are in progress (that is, offline and online backups are supported).
Each backup image created must contain the state of the entire database; table space backups are not supported.	A backup image may contain the current state of the database or the current state of one or more table spaces; table spaces within a database can be backed up and restored independently. This provides the ability to back up more active table spaces at a greater frequency than less active table spaces.
The database can be restored to the state it was in at the time any available backup images were taken. However, transactions that have occurred since the backup image was taken cannot be reapplied.	The database can be restored to the state it was in at the time any available backup images were taken. In addition, any or all subsequent transactions that have occurred since the last backup image was taken can be reapplied.

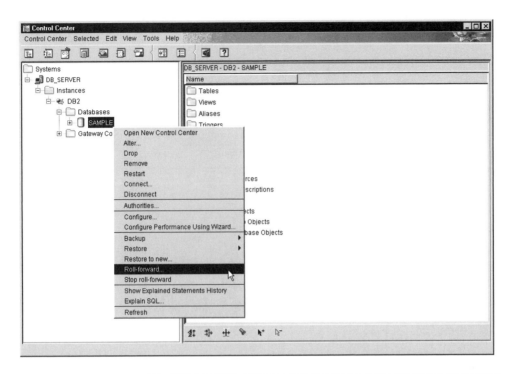

Figure 13-13   Invoking the Roll-Forward Database dialog from the Control Center

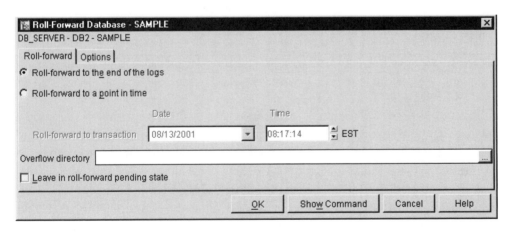

Figure 13-14   The first page of the Roll-Forward Database dialog

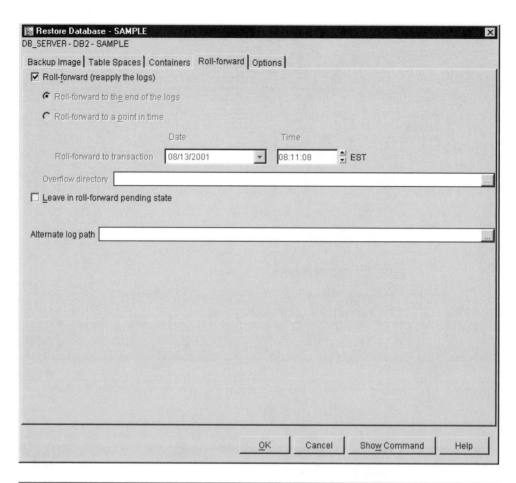

Figure 13-15 The Roll-Forward page of the Restore Database Dialog

Because a roll-forward recovery operation is typically performed immediately after a database has been restored from a backup image, a roll-forward recovery operation can also be initiated by providing the appropriate information on the Roll-Forward page of the Restore Database dialog. Figure 13-15 shows how the Roll-Forward page of the Restore Database dialog looks before its input fields have been populated.

A roll-forward recovery operation can also be initiated by executing the ROLLFOR-WARD command, either from the Command Center or from the Command Line Processor. The syntax for this command is

```
ROLLFORWARD [DATABASE | DB] [DatabaseName] <USER [AuthorizationID]
<USING [Password]>> <TO [PointInTime] <ON ALL NODES> <AND COMPLETE
| AND STOP>> <TABLESPACE ONLINE | TABLESPACE ( [TableSpaceName] ,
```

```
. . . ) <ONLINE>> <OVERFLOW LOG PATH ( [LogDirectory] <ON NODE
[NodeNumber]> , . . . )> <RECOVER DROPPED TABLE [DroppedTableID]
TO [ExportDirectory]>
```

or

```
ROLLFORWARD [DATABASE | DB] [DatabaseName] <USER [AuthorizationID]
<USING [Password]>> <TO END OF LOGS <ON ALL NODES | ON ALL NODES
EXCEPT ( [StartingNodeNumber] TO [EndingNodeNumber] ) | ON [NODE |
NODES] ( [StartingNodeNumber] TO [EndingNodeNumber] )> <AND
COMPLETE | AND STOP>> <TABLESPACE ONLINE | TABLESPACE (
[TableSpaceName] , . . . ) <ONLINE>> <OVERFLOW LOG PATH (
[LogDirectory] <ON NODE [NodeNumber]> , . . . )> <RECOVER DROPPED
TABLE [DroppedTableID] TO [ExportDirectory]>
```

or

```
ROLLFORWARD [DATABASE | DB] [DatabaseName] <USER [AuthorizationID]
<USING [Password]>> <<COMPLETE | STOP | CANCEL | QUERY STATUS> <ON
ALL NODES | ON ALL NODES EXCEPT ( [StartingNodeNumber] TO
[EndingNodeNumber] ) | ON [NODE | NODES] ( [StartingNodeNumber] TO
[EndingNodeNumber] )>> <TABLESPACE ONLINE | TABLESPACE (
[TableSpaceName] , . . . ) <ONLINE>> <OVERFLOW LOG PATH (
[LogDirectory] <ON NODE [NodeNumber]> , . . . )> <RECOVER DROPPED
TABLE [DroppedTableID] TO [ExportDirectory]>
```

where:

DatabaseName	Identifies the database that is to be rolled forward.
AuthorizationID	Identifies the authorization ID of the user that the database is to be rolled forward under.
Password	Identifies the password (that corresponds to the authorization ID specified) of the user that the database is to be rolled forward.
PointInTime	Identifies a specific point in time that all committed transactions (including any transactions committed precisely at that time) are to be rolled forward.
TableSpaceName	Identifies one or more table spaces that are to be rolled forward.
LogDirectory	Identifies a specific location that contains archived log files that are to be used to perform the roll-forward operation.
NodeNumber	Identifies one or more specific partition (node) numbers that the roll-forward recovery operation is to be performed on.

DroppedTableID	Identifies a specific table (by ID number) that has been dropped that is to be restored as part of the roll-forward recovery process.
ExportDirectory	Identifies a specific location that data that was stored in one or more tables that have been dropped since the backup image being used was made is to be written to. (This data will be written to one or more individual files in this location.)
StartingNodeNumber	A partition number that identifies the beginning of a range of partitions (nodes) that the roll-forward recovery operation is/is not to be performed on.
EndingNodeNumber	A partition number that identifies the end of a range of partitions (nodes) that the roll-forward recovery operation is/is not to be performed on.

For example, when executed, the following ROLLFORWARD command would reapply all transactions that were committed at or before 2001-07-04-14.21.56.245378 to a database named SAMPLEDB:

```
ROLLFORWARD DATABASE SAMPLEDB TO 2001-07-04-14.21.56.245378
AND STOP
```

A roll-forward recovery operation usually follows the completion of a full database or table space restore operation that has left the database or a table space in the "Roll-Forward Pending" state. When this is the case, all log files that will be used for roll-forward recovery must be copied to a separate directory *before* the restore operation is performed (otherwise, they will be replaced with the log files that are stored in the backup image). These log files must then be copied to the appropriate log directory (as specified in the database configuration file) after the restore operation is complete and before roll-forward recovery is initiated. (Alternately, the directory that they are stored in can be specified in the Overflow Directory entry field of the Roll-Forward Database/Restore Database dialog or the *LogDirectory* parameter of the ROLLFORWARD command.) If these log files cannot be accessed by the roll-forward recovery utility, the roll-forward recovery operation will fail!

NOTE Only users with System Administrator (SYSADM) authority, System Control (SYSCTRL) authority, or System Maintenance (SYSMAINT) authority are allowed to perform a roll-forward recovery operation.

Rebuilding Invalid Indexes

When the storage media being used to hold a database's files becomes corrupted or fails, indexes can become invalid, along with the data. However, if the data is unaffected and only the index is damaged (which would be the case if data and indexes were stored on two different devices and the device containing the indexes failed), the index can be recovered simply by recreating it. When the DB2 Database Manager detects that an index is no longer valid, it automatically attempts to rebuild it. When the DB2 Database Manager attempts to rebuild an invalid index, it is controlled by the *indexrec* parameter of the database (or the DB2 Database Manager) configuration file. There are three possible settings for this parameter:

- **SYSTEM** Invalid indexes are to be rebuilt at the time specified in the *indexrec* parameter of the DB2 Database Manager configuration file. (This setting is only valid for database configuration files.)

- **RESTART** Invalid indexes are to be rebuilt when the database is restarted (either explicitly or implicitly).

- **ACCESS** Invalid indexes are to be rebuilt the first time they are accessed after they have been marked invalid.

If database restart time is not a concern, it is better for invalid indexes to be rebuilt as part of the process of returning a database to a consistent state. When this approach is used, the time needed to restart a database will be longer due to the index recreation process; however, normal processing will not be impacted once the database has been returned to a consistent state. On the other hand, when indexes are rebuilt as they are accessed, the time taken to restart a database is faster, but an unexpected degradation in response time may occur as a result of an index being recreated—users accessing a table that uses an invalid index would have to wait for the index to be rebuilt. In addition, unexpected locks may be acquired and held long after an invalid index has been recreated, especially if the transaction that caused the index recreation to occur never terminates (that is, commits or rolls back changes made).

Configuration Parameters That Affect Logging and Data Recovery

It was mentioned earlier that each database has its own configuration file, and that many of the parameters in this file are used to specify the amount of resources that are to be allocated to that database. In addition, a number of the parameters in a database configuration file enable you to manage your environment to ensure that you can perform adequate recovery of your data or transactions in the event a power interruption or a media failure occurs. The modifiable database configuration parameters that affect logging and data recovery are shown in Table 13-2. The modifiable DB2 Database Manager configuration parameters that affect logging and data recovery are shown in Table 13-3.

Table 13-2 Database Configuration Parameters That Affect Logging and Data Recovery

Database Log Files		
Parameter	**Description**	**Range (Default)**
logprimary	Number of primary log files to preallocate	2–128 (3)
logsecond	Number of secondary log files to allocate and use when a primary log file is not available	0–126 (2)
logfilsiz	Size (in 4K pages) that all primary and secondary log files should be	4–65,535 (1,000)
newlogpath	Location where log files are stored or are to be stored	Any valid path (NULL)
Database Log Activity		
Parameter	**Description**	**Range (Default)**
logbufsz	Amount of memory (in 4K pages) that is to be used as a buffer for log records before they are written to disk	4–4,096 (8)
mincommit	Number of commit operations that are to be performed before log records are written to a log file	1–25 (1)
softmax	Number of log records to write to a log file before setting a soft checkpoint	1–100 * *logprimary* value (100)
logretain	Indicates whether or not log retention logging (archival logging) is to be used	No | Capture | Recovery (No)
userexit	Indicates whether or not log retention logging (archival logging) is to be used and if so, whether or not a user exit routine should be called when processing log file archive or retrieval requests	Yes | No (No)

PART III

Recovery

Parameter	Description	Range (Default)
autorestart	Indicates whether or not the RESTART DATABASE command is to be executed automatically whenever the DB2 Database Manager determines that the database is in an inconsistent state	Yes | No (Yes)
indexrec	Identifies when the DB2 Database Manager is to attempt to rebuild invalid indexes	SYSTEM | ACCESS | RESTART (SYSTEM)
dft_loadrec_ses	Identifies the number of sessions that are to be used to recover a table load operation	1–30,000 (1)
rec_his_retentn	Number of days that historical information on backup operations should be retained in the recovery history file	-1; 1–30,000 (365)
num_db_backups	Number of the most recent database backup images to retain	1–32,767 (12)

Table 13-3   DB2 Database Manager Configuration Parameters That Affect Logging and Data Recovery

Recovery

Parameter	Description	Range (Default)
backbufsz	Size (in 4K pages) of the buffer used to perform backup operations if the buffer size is not specified when the backup utility is invoked	16–524,288 (1,024)
restbufsz	Size (in 4K pages) of the buffer used to perform restore operations if the buffer size is not specified when the restore utility is invoked	16–524,288 (1,024)
indexrec	Identifies when the DB2 Database Manager is to attempt to rebuild invalid indexes	ACCESS | RESTART (ACCESS)

Summary

The goal of this chapter was to introduce you to the tools that DB2 Universal Database provides that enable you to return a database to a usable state, with minimal or no loss of data, in the event an unexpected loss of power or storage media occurs.

Although transactions and locks resolve most concurrency issues, provided applications and hardware perform as expected, they cannot resolve problems when a power interruption occurs or an application abends while a database is in use. To restore data consistency when these types of situations occur, DB2 Universal Database uses a mechanism known as transaction logging. Transaction logging is simply a process that is used to keep track of changes that are made to a database, as they are made. Each time a change is made to a row in a table (by an insert, update, or delete operation), records that reflect that change are written to a log buffer, which is nothing more than a designated area in memory.

When a transaction terminates by executing a COMMIT or a ROLLBACK SQL statement, all log records associated with that transaction are immediately written from the log buffer to one or more log files stored on disk. Only after all log records associated with the transaction have been externalized to one or more log files does the transaction receive confirmation that the commit or rollback operation has been successfully completed. This ensures that all log records of a completed transaction will not be lost due to a system failure.

Because more than one transaction may be using a database at a given time, a log file may contain log records for multiple transactions. Therefore, to keep everything straight, each log record is assigned a special ID that identifies the transaction that created it. In addition, all log records for a single transaction are chained together whenever possible. If a transaction was committed, all log records associated with that transaction are eventually written to the database, at which time they are no longer needed. However, if a transaction was rolled back, the DB2 Database Manager processes each log record associated with that transaction in reverse order and backs out all changes made.

DB2 Universal Database uses two types of logging strategies. They are

- Circular logging
- Archival logging

When circular logging is used, records stored in the log buffer are written to a set of preallocated primary log files, in a circular sequence. Once all records stored in a primary log file are applied to the corresponding database (after the transaction they are associated with has been committed or rolled back), that log file is marked as "reusable" because its records are no longer needed. When this log file becomes the next log file in the sequence, its contents are overwritten with new log records and the process repeats itself. (Overwritten log records are not recoverable.)

If the DB2 Database Manager attempts to acquire the next primary log file in the sequence and it is not yet available for reuse, a secondary log file will be allocated automatically and new log records are written to this secondary log file. When this secondary log file becomes full, the DB2 Database Manager will poll the primary log file again and if it is still not available, another secondary log file will be allocated and filled. This process will continue until the desired primary log file becomes reusable or until the number of secondary log files created exceeds the number of secondary log files permitted; if the latter occurs, all database activity will halt until the desired primary log file becomes reusable. When all log records stored in a secondary log file are applied to the corresponding database, that log file is deallocated and its contents are destroyed.

Like circular logging, when archival logging (also known as log retention logging) is used, records stored in the log buffer are written to one or more primary log files. However, when archival logging is used, primary log files are not reused; instead, when a primary log file becomes full, it is archived and a new primary log file is allocated. This process continues as long as log files are needed or until primary log files consume all disk space available.

With archival logging, secondary log files are not used. Instead, three types of primary log files are used:

- Active
- Online archive
- Offline archive

Whenever one or more transactions are unexpectedly interrupted, (either by a power interruption or an application failure) all databases being accessed at the time the interruption occurred are placed in an inconsistent or unstable state. Such databases remain in an inconsistent state until some action is taken to return them to a consistent state. (A database that is in an inconsistent state notifies users and applications that it is unusable via a specific return code that is generated when either a user or an application attempts to establish a connection to it.) A database that has been placed in an inconsistent state can be returned to a consistent state by selecting the Restart Database action from the Control Center menu or by executing the RESTART DATABASE command, either from the Command Center or from the Command Line Processor. (The DB2 Database Manager checks the state of a database when it first attempts to establish a connection to that database. If the *autorestart* parameter of a database's configuration file is set to ON, the RESTART DATABASE command is automatically executed if the DB2 Database Manager determines that the database is in an inconsistent state.)

When the RESTART DATABASE command is executed, the DB2 Database Manager determines whether or not database recovery is needed by examining the active recovery log file(s) that is associated with the database specified. If the log shows that the database was shut down abnormally, the database could be in an inconsistent state because changes made by completed transactions that were still in the buffer pool may have been lost. If the DB2 Database Manager determines that a database restart is necessary, it attempts to return the database to a consistent state by doing the following:

1. Removing any changes made by transactions that were in-flight (that is, that have not been committed or rolled back) from the database. Because the DB2 Database Manager follows the rule that changes are only consistent when they have been explicitly committed, all work done by in-flight transactions is considered inconsistent and must be backed out of the database to preserve database consistency.

2. Writing changes made by committed transactions found in the log file(s) that have not been written to the database to the database.

3. Rolling back any transactions that were in the process of being rolled back so that all changes made to the database by that transaction are removed.

Although the RESTART DATABASE command in conjunction with transaction log files can be used to resolve database problems that are caused by power interruptions and/or application failures, these two items cannot be used to handle problems that can arise when the storage media being used to hold a database's files becomes corrupted or fails. To address these types of problems, some kind of backup (and recovery) program must be established. To help establish such a program, DB2 Universal Database provides a set of utilities that can be used to

• Create a backup image of a database.

• Return a database to the state it was in when a backup image was made (by restoring it from a backup image).

• Reapply (or roll-forward) some or all changes made to a database since the last backup image was made once the database has been returned to the state it was in when the backup image was made.

One of the basic tools used to prevent catastrophic data losses when media failures occur is a database backup image. A database backup image is essentially a copy of an entire database or of one or more table spaces that make up a database. Once created, a backup image can be used at any time to return a database to the state it was in at the time the image was made. A good backup/recovery program should ensure that backup images are created regularly, and that multiple backup copies of critical data are retained in a secure location. A backup image of a DB2 Universal Database database (or of a specific table space within a database) can be made by invoking the Backup Database dialog from the Control Center or by executing the BACKUP command, either from the Command Center or from the Command Line Processor.

Along with the database configuration file, another important file that is produced during the database creation process is a file that is known as the recovery history file. The recovery history file is used to log historical information about certain actions that are performed against a database. Specifically, a record is automatically written to the recovery history file when any of the following activities are performed:

- A backup image of the database or one of its table spaces is created.
- A recovery (restore) operation is performed using a backup image of the database or one of its table spaces.
- A table is loaded using the load facility.
- A roll-forward recovery operation is performed on either the database or one of its table spaces.
- A table space is altered.
- A table space is quiesced.
- The data in a table is reorganized.
- The statistics for a table are updated.
- A table is deleted (dropped).

In addition to providing information about which type of activity was performed, each entry in the recovery history file contains the date and time the activity was performed, how a particular activity was performed, the specific table spaces and tables of the database that were affected by the activity, and the location of each backup image created, along with information on how to access the image (if the activity was a backup operation).

When a database or one of its table spaces becomes damaged or corrupt, it can be returned to a usable state provided one or more backup images exist. The backup image used may contain the contents of an entire database, or it may contain the contents of one or more of the database's table spaces. Because the recovery history file contains summary and image location information for each backup image available, it is used as a tracking mechanism during restore operations. Each backup image file contains special information in its header that is checked against the records in the recovery history file to verify that the backup image being used corresponds to the database being restored.

A DB2 Universal Database database (or a specific table space within a database) can be restored from a backup image by invoking the Restore Database dialog from the Control Center or by executing the RESTORE command, either from the Command Center or from the Command Line Processor.

A full backup image of a database contains, among other things, a list of all table space containers that were in use by the database at the time the backup image was made. During a restore operation, a check is performed to ensure that all table space containers listed in the backup image still exist and are accessible. If this check determines that one or more of the table space containers in the list is no longer available or is no longer accessible, the restore operation will fail. When such a condition exists, all invalid table space containers found can be redefined during the restore process by performing a special restore operation that is known as a redirected restore.

When a database is restored from a backup image, it is returned to the state it was in when the backup image used was created. This means that unless special steps are taken, all changes made to a database after the backup image used was created will be lost after a restore operation is performed. To return a database to the state it was in at any given point in time (including the point in time just before the database files became corrupted), the database must be configured to support roll-forward recovery; roll-forward recovery uses archival logging in conjunction with a database's log files to reapply any or all changes made to a database since the last backup image was generated after a restore operation has been performed. Roll-forward recovery is enabled by setting the *logretain* and/or the *userexit* parameter in the database configuration file to YES. If either of these configuration parameters is set, the database's transaction log files are configured in such a way that all entries needed to perform a roll-forward recovery operation are retained and archived for later use.

A roll-forward recovery operation can be initiated by invoking the Roll-Forward Database dialog from the Control Center, by providing the appropriate information on the Roll-Forward page of the Restore Database dialog, or by executing the ROLLFORWARD command, either from the Command Center or from the Command Line Processor.

When the storage media being used to hold a database's files becomes corrupted or fails, indexes can become invalid, along with the data. However, if the data is unaffected and only the index is damaged (which would be the case if data and indexes were stored on two different devices and the device containing the indexes failed), the index can be recovered simply by recreating it. When the DB2 Database Manager detects that an index is no longer valid, it automatically attempts to rebuild it. When the DB2 Database Manager attempts to rebuild an invalid index, it is controlled by the *indexrec* parameter of the database (or the DB2 Database Manager) configuration file. There are three possible settings for this parameter:

- SYSTEM

- RESTART

- ACCESS

If database restart time is not a concern, it is better for invalid indexes to be rebuilt as part of the process of returning a database to a consistent state.

A number of parameters in a database configuration file enable you to manage your environment to ensure that you can perform adequate recovery of your data or transactions in the event a power interruption or a media failure occurs. The modifiable database configuration parameters that affect logging and data recovery are

- *logprimary*

- *logsecond*

- *logfilsiz*

- *newlogpath*

- *logbufsz*

- *mincommit*

- *softmax*

- *logretain*

- *userexit*

- *autorestart*

- *indexrec*

- *dft_loadrec_ses*

- *rec_his_retentn*

- *num_db_backups*

The modifiable DB2 Database Manager configuration parameters that affect logging and data recovery are

- *backbufsz*

- *restbufsz*

- *indexrec*

Questions

1. When trying to back up the database named SAMPLE with the BACKUP command, the following message is generated:

```
SQL1035N The database is currently in use. SQLSTATE=57019
```

   Which of the following must be done in order to get the backup operation to run successfully?
   a. Issue DB2STOP.
   b. Issue CONNECT RESET.
   c. Issue QUIESCE SAMPLE.
   d. Reissue BACKUP command with the ONLINE option specified.
   e. Reissue BACKUP command with the OFFLINE option specified.

2. Which of the following commands, when executed, will update the recovery history file?
   a. EXPORT
   b. IMPORT
   c. BACKUP
   d. RUNSTATS
   e. REORG

3. Which of the following must be done before a redirected restore is performed for a database?
   a. All containers in the redirected restore must be untagged.
   b. An attachment must be made to an instance that is not the same as the instance that contains the original database.
   c. Container names provided in the redirected restore must not match the original container names being replaced.
   d. The output from a LIST TABLESPACE command that shows which table space containers are invalid must be obtained.

4. Which action establishes a point of consistency for database recovery?
   a. Performing a table space level RESTORE only
   b. Performing a database level RESTORE
   c. Performing a QUIESCE TABLESPACE command
   d. Performing a FORCE APPLICATIONS command

5. A database named SAMPLE exists in the instance PROD1 on workstation WORK2. Workstation WORK1 has cataloged the remote node N2 for WORK2 and

the database SAMPLE at that node. Which of the following commands will back up the database SAMPLE from workstation WORK2?

a. `ATTACH TO N2; BACKUP DATABASE SAMPLE`

b. `ATTACH TO PROD1; BACKUP DATABASE SAMPLE`

c. `BACKUP DATABASE SAMPLE REMOTE PROD1`

d. `CONNECT TO SAMPLE; BACKUP DATABASE SAMPLE`

6. Which of the following is the minimum authority needed to restore an existing database from a backup image?

a. SYSIBM

b. SYSCTRL

c. SYSMAINT

d. DBADMN

7. Which of the following configuration parameters is set to support online database backups?

a. backup_pending

b. userexit

c. logbufsz

d. backbufsz

8. Which of the following configuration parameters can be used to minimize the amount of time it takes to restart an inconsistent database?

a. indexrec

b. autorestart

c. softmax

d. minrestarttm

Answers

1. **D.** In order to create a backup image of a database while one or more users are connected to it, the backup operation must be performed online.

2. **C.** The recovery history file is updated whenever any of the following activities are performed: a backup image of the database or one of its table spaces is created; a recovery (restore) operation is performed using a backup image of the database or one of its table spaces; a table is loaded using the load facility; a roll-forward recovery operation is performed on either the database or one of its table spaces; a table space is altered; a table space is quiesced; the data in a table is reorganized; the statistics for a table are updated; and a table is deleted (dropped).

3. **D.** When the RESTORE command is executed with the REDIRECT option specified, each invalid table space container found is flagged when table space containers are checked, and all table spaces that reference invalid table space containers are placed in the "Restore Pending" state. A list of all table spaces affected can be produced by executing the LIST TABLESPACES command; once all affected table spaces have been identified, new table space containers can be defined by executing the SET TABLESPACE CONTAINERS command. After new table space containers have been created for every table space that was placed in the "Restore Pending" state, the redirected restore operation can be completed by executing the RESTORE command again; this time with the CONTINUE option specified.

4. **B.** By restoring a database from a full database backup image, a point of consistency is established for any roll-forward recovery operations that follow.

5. **D.** To back up a database stored on a server workstation from an administrative client workstation, you must first establish a connection to that database.

6. **C.** Only users with System Administrator (SYSADM) authority, System Control (SYSCTRL) authority, or System Maintenance (SYSMAINT) authority are allowed to restore an existing database from a backup image. Out of these three, SYSADM is the lowest level authority.

7. **B.** When the *userexit* configuration parameter is turned on, roll-forward recovery is enabled for a database; an online backup operation can only be performed if roll-forward recovery has been enabled.

8. **A.** If the *indexrec* configuration parameter is set to ACCESS, a database will be restarted faster because invalid indexes will be rebuilt when a user or application attempts to use them, rather than as part of the database restart process.

Problem Determination

In this chapter, you will learn

- The common types of problems and errors that can be encountered when using DB2 Universal Database
- What error codes are, how they are categorized, and how they are interpreted
- How First Failure Data Capture (FFDC) information is collected and where that information is stored
- How entries in the db2diag.log file are interpreted
- The purpose of the SQL Communications Area (SQLCA) structure, how its contents are interpreted, and how its contents are dumped to the db2diag.log file

The last objective of the DB2 Universal Database—Database Administration for UNIX, Windows, and OS/2 exam is to evaluate your understanding of how information about a particular problem can be obtained and to test your ability to locate and interpret First Failure Data Capture (FFDC) information captured by DB2 Universal Database when an error occurs. This chapter is designed to introduce you to the common types of errors that can be encountered when using DB2 Universal Database, and introduce you to some of the tools that are available to help identify the source of and provide resolutions for problems when they occur.

TIP Three percent of the DB2 Universal Database—Database Administration for UNIX, Windows, and OS/2 exam is designed to test your ability to determine the cause of a problem.

Common Types of Errors

Regardless of whether a simple or a complex database environment is used, the possibility that problems will be encountered can never be eliminated. Most problems or errors that occur fall under one of the following categories:

- Operating system-specific
- Hardware- or I/O-specific
- Application-specific
- Communications-specific

Because errors can never be completely eliminated, DB2 Universal Database provides a set of tools that can help pinpoint the cause when an error situation occurs. In many cases, these tools can also provide recommendations that, when followed, may resolve the situation that caused an error to be generated.

Error Codes

When an error occurs within a database system, the DB2 Database Manager notifies the user by generating a specific error code, which is then presented in a variety of ways. For example, if any of the administration tools that come with DB2 Universal Database are being used when an error occurs, the error code generated, and in many cases a corresponding error message, will be displayed in a pop-up dialog. The error code and message will then be recorded in the Journal, along with the date and time that the error occurred. Figure 14-1 shows an example of how errors are logged by the Journal.

As you might imagine, because the DB2 Universal Database environment can be quite complex, a large number of error codes (and corresponding error messages) are available. Each error code consists of a three-character (or in some cases, a four-character) prefix, followed by a four- or five-digit message number, followed by a single character (in most cases). The three-character (and in some cases, the four-character) prefix of each error code identifies what category that particular error code falls under:

- 'ASN0' DB2 Data Replication Capture errors
- 'ASN1' DB2 Data Replication Apply errors
- 'AUD' DB2 Audit Facility errors
- 'CCA' Client Configuration Assistant errors
- 'CLI' ODBC/Call Level Interface function errors

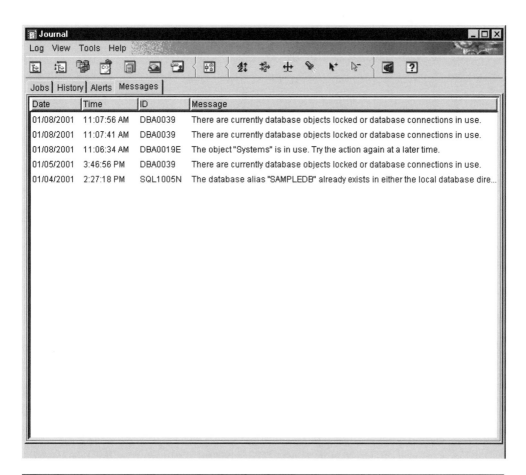

Figure 14-1   How error codes and messages are logged in the Journal

- **'DB2'**   Command Center/Command Line Processor errors
- **'DBA'**   Control Center/DBA Utility errors\
- **'DBI'**   DB2 Installation/Configuration errors
- **'DES'**   Text Extender errors
- **'DIA'**   Diagnostic errors
- **'DMB'**   Image, Audio, and Video Extender errors
- **'DWC'**   Data Warehouse Center errors
- **'FLG'**   Information Catalog Manager errors
- **'GOV'**   DB2 Governor Utility errors

- 'GSE'   Spatial Extender errors
- 'SAT'   DB2 Satellite Edition errors
- 'SPM'   Sync point manager errors
- 'SQJ'   Embedded SQL in Java (SQLJ) errors
- 'SQL'   Structured Query Language (SQL) errors

The one-character suffix, when supplied, helps identify the severity of the situation that caused the error code to be generated. This suffix can be any of the following:

- 'I'   Informational
- 'W'   Warning
- 'N'   Notification
- 'C' or 'E'   Critical error

Viewing Error Messages

If you receive a specific error code and you are not using one of the administration tools provided with DB2 Universal Database, there are several ways to view the error message that is associated with the error code received:

- By looking up the code in the *IBM DB2 Universal Database Message Reference Volume 1* or the *IBM DB2 Universal Database Message Reference Volume 2* documentation

- By executing the GET ERROR MESSAGE [sqlaintp()] API from an application program

- By asking the DB2 Database Manager to provide the message that is associated with the error code

You can ask the DB2 Database Manager to provide the error message for a specific error code by executing the following command, either from the Command Center or from the Command Line Processor:

```
<DB2> ? [ErrorCode]
```

where:

ErrorCode   Identifies the specific error code that error message information is to be obtained for.

For example, if the following command were executed,

```
DB2 ? CCA3002N
```

the following message would be displayed:

```
An I/O error occurred. Explanation: An error was encountered
attempting to open, read, change the file position or close a
file. User Response: If a file name was specified, verify that the
file name is valid and that the user has permission to access the
file. Also check for any disk and operating system errors.
```

Reason Codes

Sometimes an error message contains a reference to a reason code. For example, the message for error code SQL0866N might be "Connection redirection failed. Reason code: "01" ". Reason codes usually provide more detailed information to supplement the error message text. In most cases, this additional information can be obtained by looking up both the error code (first) and the reason code (second) in the *IBM DB2 Universal Database Message Reference Volume 1* or the *IBM DB2 Universal Database Message Reference Volume 2* documentation. However, in some cases, it may be necessary to consult other system documentation. Using the previous example, if you look up the error code SQL0866N in the *IBM DB2 Universal Database Message Reference Volume 2* documentation, you would see the message "A database connection involved more than one redirection from a server to another server; only one connection redirection is supported." for reason code 01.

First Failure Data Capture (FFDC) Information

First Failure Data Capture (FFDC) information is diagnostic information that is automatically captured by DB2 Universal Database whenever an error occurs. This information contains crucial details that may help in the diagnosis and resolution of problems. Because this information is gathered at the time an error occurs, the need to reproduce errors in order to get diagnostic information is reduced or eliminated.

The information captured by FFDC includes

- **db2diag.log entries**   db2diag.log is the primary diagnostic log file used by DB2 Universal Database. Whenever an error occurs, an entry containing diagnostic information about the particular error is automatically made in this file (as the error is occurring).

- **db2alert.log entries**   db2alert.log is the primary alert log file used by DB2 Universal Database. If the DB2 Database Manager determines that an error is an alert, an entry is made in this file and copied to the operating system or native logging facility. (An alert is an error notification that occurs when a severe error occurs.)

- **Dump files**   In some cases, when a DB2 Universal Database process or thread fails, extra information is logged in external binary dump files that are named after the failing process ID. These files are more-or-less unreadable and are designed to be forwarded to DB2 Customer Support for interpretation.

- **Trap files**   If the DB2 Database Manager cannot continue processing because of a trap, segmentation violation, or exception, it generates a trap file that contains the sequence of function calls made for the last steps executed before a problem occurred.

 NOTE   Alerts written to the db2alert.log file are not the same as alerts that are logged in the Alert Center or Journal. Those alerts are warnings that are generated by the DB2 Universal Database Snapshot Monitor, whereas alerts written to the db2alert.log file are notifications of severe system errors.

FFDC information is written to the directory specified in the *diagpath* parameter of the DB2 Database Manager configuration file. This parameter contains a null string when an instance is first created and, until the null string is changed, all FFDC information collected is placed in the following locations:

- For Windows and OS/2, if the location of the instance directory is not stored in the *DB2INSTPROF* environment variable, *DB2Path\DB2Instance*, where *DB2Path* is the path stored in the DB2PATH environment variable and *DB2Instance* is the value stored in the DB2INSTDEF environment variable (which is DB2 by default) or if the location of the instance directory is stored in the *DB2INSTPROF* environment variable, *Drive:\DB2InstProfile\DB2Instance*, where *Drive* is the drive referenced in the *DB2PATH* environment variable, *DB2InstProfile* is the name of the instance profile directory, and *DB2Instance* is the value stored in the *DB2INSTDEF* environment variable (which is DB2 by default)

- For UNIX, in *$HOME/sqllib/db2dump*, where *$HOME* is the home directory of the instance owner

Figure 14-2 illustrates how FFDC information might be stored in a Windows or OS/2 environment; Figure 14-3 illustrates how FFDC information might be stored in a UNIX environment.

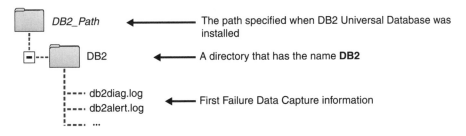

Figure 14-2   How FFDC information might be stored in a Windows or OS/2 environment

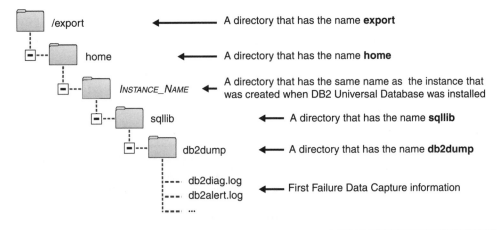

Figure 14-3   How FFDC information might be stored in a UNIX environment

NOTE   A db2diag.log file also exists for the Database Administration Server (DAS) instance. This file is located in a subdirectory named *db2das00* that can be found in the directory named *sqllib* that is located where the DB2 Universal Database product was installed. At this time, the location of this file cannot be changed.

Regardless of where FFDC information is stored, it is up to the system administrator to make sure the directory used is cleaned periodically; DB2 Universal Database does not contain a mechanism that automatically removes dump files and trap files that have been generated by the FFDC tool.

The level of diagnostic information obtained by FFDC is also controlled by a parameter in the DB2 Database Manager configuration file. This parameter, *diaglevel*, can be set to any of the following values:

- **0**   Do not collect diagnostic data (not recommended).
- **1**   Collect diagnostic data for severe errors only.
- **2**   Collect diagnostic data for all errors (both severe and not severe) but not for warnings.
- **3**   Collect diagnostic data for all errors and warnings.
- **4**   Collect diagnostic data for all errors and warnings; include informational messages and other internal diagnostic information.

When an instance is first created, the *diaglevel* parameter is set to 3 by default and diagnostic information for errors and warnings is collected whenever such events occur. Whenever possible, the *diaglevel* parameter should be set to 4 (except in a parallel environment where this setting will usually produce too much data), particularly when DB2 Universal Database is initially set up, when configuration parameters are changed, or when a large number of errors seem to be occurring.

NOTE   If the diaglevel configuration parameter is set to 4, DB2 Universal Database will run slower when the DB2 Database Manager is started, when an initial connection to a database is established, and when an error condition occurs.

The db2diag.log File

The db2diag.log file is an ASCII file that consists of diagnostic records that have been generated by the FFDC tool. Each record or *entry* in this file contains either information about a particular administrative event that has occurred or specific error information. Administrative event entries are valuable, because they indicate whether events such as backup and restore operations were started and if so, whether or not they finished successfully. Error information entries, on the other hand, are only useful when trying to diagnose an external symptom, or if the source of a particular error has been isolated and you are looking for more information. For example, if an application receives an unexpected SQL code or if a database crashes, error information such as pointers to dump files may exist as part of an error information entry. (If a database is behaving normally, error information entries are not important and can usually be ignored.)

NOTE Once created, the db2diag.log file grows continuously. As a result, the most recent entries are always found near the end of the file. If storage space for this file becomes an issue, a backup copy should be made (if it needs to be kept) and the file should be deleted. A new db2diag.log file will be created automatically the next time one is needed.

Interpreting db2diag.log Entry Headers

Every entry in the db2diag.log file begins with a specific set of values that are intended to help identify the particular event an entry corresponds to. Because this block of information is recorded for all entries and because it is always recorded in a specific order, it is referred to as the *entry header*. Figure 14-4 illustrates how a db2diag.log entry header looks; Figure 14-5 shows the same entry header with lettered bullets beside each value provided. The remainder of this section will focus on identifying each component found in a db2diag-log file entry header.

```
2001-05-16-10.58.58.046000    Instance:DB2    Node:000
PID:190(db2syscs.exe)    TID:346    Appid:*LOCAL.DB2.010807154913
data_protection  sqlpgint    Probe:40    Database:SAMPLE
DIA1568C Backup pending for database.
ZRC=FFFF85A1
```

Figure 14-4 Sample db2diag.log entry header

Ⓐ 2001-05-16-10.58.58.046000   **Ⓑ** Instance:DB2   **Ⓒ** Node:000

Ⓓ PID:190(db2syscs.exe)   **Ⓔ** TID:346   **Ⓕ** Appid:*LOCAL.DB2.010807154913

Ⓖ data_protection   **Ⓗ** sqlpgint   **Ⓘ** Probe:40   **Ⓙ** Database:SAMPLE

Ⓚ DIA1568C   **Ⓛ** Backup pending for database.

Ⓜ ZRC=FFFF85A1

Figure 14-5 Individual components of a db2diag.log entry header

Each entry header contains the following components (refer to Figure 14-5):

A.   A timestamp that identifies when the entry was made.

B.   The name of the instance that generated the entry.

C.   The number that corresponds to the node that generated the entry. If DB2 Universal Database Enterprise—Extended Edition is not being used or if a nonpartitioned environment is being used, the node number is always 000.

D.   The Process ID of the process that generated the entry. This value is more applicable in a UNIX environment where DB2 operates with multiple processes. In a Windows or OS/2 environment, DB2 operates with multiple threads rather than multiple processes; therefore, the Process ID is usually that of the main executable. In this example, the entry came from the process identified as 190. The name of this process is db2syscs.exe and it is connected to the database named SAMPLE.

NOTE   If the application is operating in a Distributed Unit Of Work (DUOW) environment, the Process ID shown is the DUOW correlation token.

E.   The unique transaction identifier of the transaction that generated the entry. In this example, the entry came from the transaction identified as 346.

F.   The application ID of the application for which the process is working. In this example, the process generating the entry is working on behalf of an application with the ID *LOCAL.DB2.010807154913. To find out more about a particular application ID, do the following:

- Execute the LIST APPLICATIONS command on a DB2 UDB server or execute the LIST DCS APPLICATIONS command on a DB2 UDB Connect gateway to obtain a list of all available application IDs. Then, using this list, you can determine information about the client experiencing the error, such as its node name and its TCP/IP address.

- Execute the GET SNAPSHOT FOR APPLICATION command to view information about a specific application.

G.   The DB2 component that produced the entry. If the entry was generated by a user application that executed the db2AdminMsgWrite() API, this component of the entry header will read "User Application."

H.   The name of the function that produced the entry. (This function operates within the DB2 Universal Database subcomponent that produced the entry.) If the entry was generated by a user application that executed the db2AdminMsgWrite() API, this component of the entry header will read "User Function."

To find out more about the type of activity performed by a function, look at the fourth letter of its name. The following list shows some of the letters used in the fourth position of the function name and the type of activity they identify:

- **b** Buffer pools
- **c** Communication between clients and servers
- **d** Data management
- **e** Engine processes
- **o** Operating system calls (such as opening and closing files)
- **p** Data protection (such as locking and logging)
- **r** Relational database services
- **s** Sorting
- **x** Indexing

In this example, the fourth letter of the function sqlpgint (*p*) indicates a data protection problem has occurred. (For example, the database is in "backup pending" mode.)

I.   The ID of the internal error that was reported.

J.   The database on which the error occurred.

K.   A diagnostic error code (beginning with the letters *DIA*) that attempts to explain the reason for the entry.

L.   A diagnostic error message that attempts to explain the reason for the entry.

M.   The hexadecimal representation of an internal return code.

Interpreting SQLCA Data Structure Value Entries

The SQL Communications Area (SQLCA) structure is a collection of variables that are updated each time an SQL statement or an administrative API function is executed. The individual variables (or fields) that make up this structure are shown in Table 14-1.

Table 14-1   Fields That Make Up the SQLCA Data Structure

Field Name	Data Type	Description
sqlcaid	CHAR(8)	An "eye catcher" for storage dumps that contain SQLCA information. This field contains the value "SQLCA" (or the value "SQLCAL" if line number information is returned from parsing an SQL procedure body).
sqlcabc	INTEGER	The size, in bytes, of the SQLCA data structure variable (which at this time is 136 bytes).
sqlcode	INTEGER	The SQL return code value. A value of 0 means "Successful Execution," a positive value means "Successful execution with warnings," and a negative value means "Error." Refer to the *IBM DB2 Universal Database Message Reference Volume 1* or the *IBM DB2 Universal Database Message Reference Volume 2* documentation for specific meanings of SQL return code values.
sqlerrml	SMALLINT	The size, in bytes, of the data stored in the sqlerrmc field of this structure. This value can be any number between 0 and 70. A value of 0 indicates that no data is stored in the sqlerrmc field.
sqlerrmc	CHAR(70)	One or more error message tokens, separated by the value 0xFF, that are substituted for variables in the descriptions of error conditions. This field is also used when a successful connection is established. (When a NOT ATOMIC compound SQL statement is issued, this field may contain information about up to seven errors.)
sqlerrp	CHAR(8)	A diagnostic value that begins with a three-letter code that identifies the product being used, followed by five digits that identify the version, release, and modification level of the product being used. For example, "SQL07010" means DB2 Universal Database, version 7, release 1, and modification level 0. If the sqlcode field contains a negative value, this field identifies the module that returned an error. This field is also used when a successful connection is completed.
sqlerrd	ARRAY of INTEGERs	An array of six integer values that provide additional diagnostic information. Table 14-2 identifies the types of diagnostic information that can be provided. (With the exception of sqlerrd(6), these values are usually empty if there are no errors.)

Field Name	Data Type	Description
sqlwarn	ARRAY of CHAR(1)s	An array of warning indicators, each of which contains either a blank or the letter 'W'. Table 14-3 identifies the types of warning information that can be provided. (When a compound SQL statement is issued, this field will contain an accumulation of any warning indicators set by all substatements.)
sqlstate	CHAR(5)	The SQLSTATE (the X/Open CLI and ISO/IEC 92 standardized diagnostic message code) that indicates the outcome of the most recently executed SQL statement.

Table 14-2   Elements of the sqlerrd Array

Array Element	Diagnostic Information Provided
sqlerrd(1)	If the SQLCA data reflects a successful connection, this element will contain the maximum expected difference in length of mixed character data when character data is converted from the application's code page to the database's code page. If there is no expected difference, this element will contain either 0 or 1; if an increase in length is anticipated, this element will contain a positive number (the anticipated increase in length of mixed character data when it is converted); if a decrease in length is anticipated, this element will contain a negative number (the anticipated decrease in length of mixed character data when it is converted). On successful return from an SQL procedure, this element contains the return status value from the SQL procedure.
sqlerrd(2)	If the SQLCA data reflects a successful connection, this element will contain the maximum expected difference in length of mixed character data when character data is converted from the application's code page to the database's code page. If there is no expected difference, this element will contain either 0 or 1; if an expansion is anticipated, this element will contain a positive number (the anticipated expansion length); if a contraction is anticipated, this element will contain a negative number (the anticipated contraction length). If the SQLCA data reflects a NOT ATOMIC compound SQL statement that encountered one or more errors, this element will contain a number that corresponds to the number of SQL substatements that failed.
sqlerrd(3)	If the SQLCA data reflects an SQL statement preparation operation that was successful, this element contains an estimate of the number of rows that will be returned when the SQL statement that was prepared is executed. If the SQLCA data reflects an insert, update, or delete operation, this element contains the actual number of rows affected.

(continued)

Table 14-2   Elements of the sqlerrd Array *(continued)*

Array Element	Diagnostic Information Provided
sqlerrd(3)	If the SQLCA data reflects a compound SQL statement that was executed successfully, this element contains an accumulation of all substatement rows. If the SQLCA data reflects a successful connection, this element contains 1 if the database is updateable and 2 if the database is read only.
	If CREATE PROCEDURE for an SQL procedure is invoked and an error is encountered parsing the SQL procedure body, this element contains the line number where the error was encountered. (The sqlcaid field of the SQLCA data must be set to SQLCAL for this to be a valid line number.)
sqlerrd(4)	If the SQLCA data reflects a PREPARE operation, this element contains a relative cost estimate of the resources that are required to process the statement.
	If the SQLCA data reflects a compound SQL statement that was executed successfully, this element contains a count of the number of substatements that were successfully executed.
	If the SQLCA data reflects a successful connection, this element contains 0 if a one-phase commit from a down-level client was executed; 1 if a one-phase commit was executed; 2 if a one-phase, read-only commit was executed; or 3 if a two-phase commit was executed.
sqlerrd(5)	This element contains the total number of rows deleted, inserted, or updated as a result of the enforcement of constraints after a successful delete operation and/or the processing of triggered SQL statements from activated triggers.
	If the SQLCA data reflects a compound SQL statement that was executed successfully, this element contains an accumulation of the number of such rows for all substatements.
	If the SQLCA data reflects a successful connection, this element contains 0 if authentication is to take place at the server; 1 if authentication is to take place at the client; 2 if authentication is to be performed by DB2 Connect; 3 if authentication is to be performed by DCE Security Services Authentication; or 255 if where authentication is to take place is unspecified.
sqlerrd(6)	For partitioned databases, this element contains the partition number of the partition that encountered an error or warning. If no errors or warnings were encountered, this element contains the partition number of the coordinator node.
	The number in this element is the same as that specified for the partition in the db2nodes.cfg file.

Table 14-3 Elements of the sqlwarn Array

Array Element	Warning Information
sqlwarn(1)	This element is blank if all other elements are blank; it contains a 'W' if at least one other element is not blank.
sqlwarn(2)	This element contains a 'W' if the value of a string column was truncated when assigned to a host variable; it contains an 'N' if the null terminator was truncated. This element contains an 'A' if a CONNECT or ATTACH operation is successful and the authentication ID specified for the connection was longer than 8 bytes.
sqlwarn(3)	This element contains a 'W' if NULL values were eliminated from the argument of a function.
sqlwarn(4)	This element contains a 'W' if the number of columns is not equal to the number of host variables provided.
sqlwarn(5)	This element contains a 'W' if a prepared UPDATE or DELETE statement does not include a WHERE clause.
sqlwarn(6)	Reserved for future use.
sqlwarn(7)	This element contains a 'W' if the result of a date calculation was adjusted to avoid an invalid date.
sqlwarn(8)	If a CONNECT operation was invoked and successful, this element contains an 'E' if the *dyn_query_mgmt* database configuration parameter is enabled.
sqlwarn(9)	This element contains a 'W' if a character that could not be converted was replaced with a substitution character.
sqlwarn(10)	This element contains a 'W' if arithmetic expressions containing errors were ignored during column function processing.
sqlwarn(11)	This element contains a 'W' if there was a conversion error while converting a character data value in one of the fields in the SQLCA data structure.

Application programs that contain embedded SQL statements (other than DECLARE, INCLUDE, and WHENEVER statements) or API function calls that are precompiled with the LANGLEVEL SAA1 option (the default) or the LANGLEVEL MIA option specified must define at least one SQLCA data structure variable that can be accessed by the DB2 Database Manager. (An SQLCA data structure variable can also be defined in each thread of a multithreaded application.)

An SQLCA data structure variable is also associated with the Command Line Processor. The values stored in this SQLCA data structure (which are updated each time a command is executed) can be seen by executing the following command at the beginning of a Command Line Processor session:

```
<DB2> -a.
```

Once this command is submitted, the contents of the SQLCA data structure used will be provided as part of the output returned each time subsequent commands are executed.

When severe errors occur, the contents of an SQL Communications Area (SQLCA) data structure are also written to the db2diag.log file. Figure 14-6 illustrates how a SQLCA structure "dump" to the db2diag.log looks; Figure 14-7 shows the same SQLCA structure dump with lettered bullets beside each value provided. The remainder of this section will focus on identifying each component found in an SQLCA structure dump entry.

Each SQLCA structure entry contains the following components (refer to Figure 14-7):

A. A title that marks the beginning of the SQLCA structure dump.

B. The eye catcher that identifies the beginning of the SQLCA data.

C. The SQL return code value. A value of 0 means "Successful execution," a positive value means "Successful execution with warnings," and a negative value means "Error."

```
2001-05-16-10.58.58.046000    Instance:DB2    Node:000
PID:1157(db2agent (instance))   Appid:none
relation_data_serv  sqlrerlg    Probe:17    Database:SAMPLE
DIA9999E An internal error occurred. Report the following error code:
"FFFF813C".

Data Title:SQLCA pid(14358)
Sqlcaid :SQLCA    sqlcabc:136    sqlcode:-=980    sqlerrml:0
sqlerrmc:
Sqlerrp :sqlrita
sqlerrd : (1)0xFFFFE101    (2)0x00000000    (3)0x00000000
          (4)0x00000000    (5)0x00000000    (6)0x00000000
sqlwarn : (1)      (2)      (3)      (4)      (5)      (6)
          (7)      (8)      (9)      (10)     (11)
sqlstate:
```

Figure 14-6 Sample SQLCA structure dump

```
Ⓐ Data Title:SQLCA pid(14358)
Ⓑ sqlcaid :SQLCA    sqlcabc:136  Ⓒ sqlcode:-980    sqlerrml:0
Ⓓ sqlerrmc:

   sqlerrp :sqlrita
Ⓔ sqlerrd : (1)0xFFFFE101   (2)0x00000000   (3)0x00000000
           (4)0x00000000   (5)0x00000000   (6)0x00000000
   sqlwarn : (1)      (2)      (3)      (4)      (5)      (6)
            (7)      (8)      (9)      (10)     (11)
   sqlstate:
```

Figure 14-7   Individual components of an SQLCA structure dump

D.   One or more reason codes, separated by the value 0xFF, that are associated with the SQL return code.

E.   A hexadecimal representation of up to six minor errors, which occurred in the sequence shown, that caused the final SQL error to be generated. (The next section describes how to interpret these values.)

Interpreting Hexadecimal Codes

For the most part, the information found in the db2diag.log file is easy to read. However, certain pieces of data such as hexadecimal dumps and internal DB2 codes can be difficult to interpret. Whenever hexadecimal values are found, they can be interpreted by performing the following steps:

1. If the hexadecimal value is in the form 0xFFFF*nnnn* (which will be the case on UNIX systems), proceed to step 3.

2. If the hexadecimal value is in the form 0x*nnnn*FFFF (which may be the case on Windows and OS/2 systems), it must be byte-reversed before it can be interpreted. To do this, switch the first four characters with the last four characters; then switch the fifth and sixth characters with the seventh and eighth characters. For example, the error code 0x0AE6FFFF would be changed to 0xFFFF0AE6, which would then be changed to 0xFFFFE60A.

3. When you have the error code in a meaningful form, convert it to decimal format using a hexadecimal calculator or some other conversion tool. For example, the error code 0xFFFFE60A would convert to -6646 decimal.

4. Try to locate the code in Appendix A (DB2 Internal Return Codes) of the *IBM DB2 Universal Database Troubleshooting Guide* documentation. If you can locate the code there, the error code is an internal return code. If you can't find the code there, it is an SQL return code—try to locate the error code in the *IBM DB2 Universal Database Message Reference Volume 2* documentation. (You may need to remove the sign, prefix the number with the characters *SQL*, and add the suffix *N* in order to locate the corresponding SQL code: for example, -6646 would become SQL6646N.)

Figure 14-8 illustrates the logic that is used to interpret hexadecimal codes found in the db2diag.log file.

Locating Failed Objects

Sometimes the information provided in the db2diag.log file identifies a specific object that failed. When that is the case, locating the object may give you additional insight as to why the error occurred. So how do you find the object?

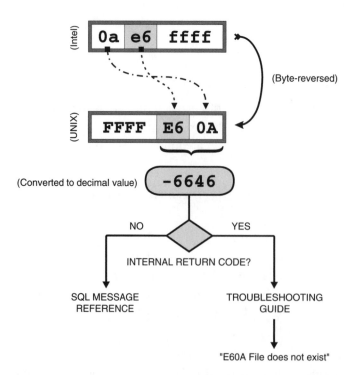

Figure 14-8 Logic used to interpret hexadecimal codes found in the db2diag.log file

```
2001-05-16-10.58.58.046000     Instance:DB2   Node:000
PID:906(db2syscs.exe)     TID:919    Appid:*LOCAL.DB2.010809155717
buffer_pool_services   sqlbcres    Probe:907    Database:TEST_DB
DIA3726C An invalidpage checksum was found for page "".

Obj={pool:2;obj:10;type:0}State=x274
Data Title :SQLB_OBJECT_DESC pid(104)tid(109)
0200 0a00 0200 0a00 0000 0000 0000 0000 ...............
0000 002e e00c 0000 0000 0000 0000 0000 ...............
0000 0000 0100 0000 2700 0000 0000 0000 ...............
0000 0000 0000 0000 ........
Dump File :C:\SQLLIB \DB2 \104109.dmp Data :SQLB_PAGE
```

Figure 14-9 Entry in the db2diag.log file that identifies an object that generated an error

You begin by locating a line of text in the db2diag.log file that begins with the letters "Obj=". Figure 14-9 shows a db2diag.log file entry that contains such a line.

The object that produced the db2diag.log file entry shown in Figure 14-9 can be located by performing the following steps:

1. Determine which table space owns the object. The text "pool:n" identifies the table space (by ID number) that the object is stored in. To find out the name of this table space, connect to the appropriate database and issue the following command from the Command Center or the Command Line Processor:

```
<DB2> LIST TABLESPACES
```

(For this example, assume that the table space in the database named SAMPLE whose table space ID is 2 is the table space named USERSPACE1.)

2. Determine which table in the table space owns the object. The text "obj:n" identifies the table (by ID number) that the object is stored in. To find out the name of this table, connect to the appropriate database and issue the following command from the Command Center or the Command Line Processor:

```
<DB2> "SELECT TABNAME, TABLEID, TBSPACEID FROM SYSCAT.TABLES WHERE
TABLEID = [TableID] and TBSPACEID = [TableSpaceID]">
```

where:

TableID　　　　Identifies the table ID number found in the db2diag.log file

TableSpaceID　Identifies the table ID number found in the db2diag.log file

(For this example, assume that the table in the database named SAMPLE whose table ID is 4 that is stored in the table space whose ID is 2 is the table named ARTISTS.)

3. Determine what type of data is stored in the object. The text "`type:n`" identifies the type of data stored in the object. The most common types are

- 1 User data
- 2 Index data
- 3 Long data

An Example Scenario

Now that we've seen how to interpret db2diag.log file entries, let's take a look at an example of how the db2diag.log file can be used to diagnose problems.

Problem

While attempting to connect to a database, we receive the following error:

```
SQL1004C There is not enough storage on the file system to process
the command.
```

How do we determine which file system is involved?

Approach

1. Look up the message code in the *IBM DB2 Universal Database Message Reference Volume 2* documentation. The documentation provides a detailed explanation for error code SQL1004C and recommends that we "`Choose a different file system or erase some non-database files from the specified file system to make space for the database manager functions.`"

2. Examine the db2diag.log on the server to find out exactly which file system is full and to see if additional information is available. For this example, assume the db2diag.log file contains the entries shown in Figure 14-10.

From these entries, we learn that

1. The function sqlpgifl encountered the error code 0xFFFFD60C (remember to byte-reverse error codes that are in the form 0x*nnnn*FFFF). Converting this code to decimal does not yield a valid SQL return code; therefore, the code is an internal return code. When we look up the return code in Appendix A of the *IBM DB2 Uni-*

```
2001-05-16-10.58.58.046000    Instance:DB2    Node:000
PID:226(db2syscs.exe)    TID:222    Appid:*LOCAL.DB2.010807154913
data_protection  sqlpgifl   Probe:146   Database:SAMPLE
DiagData
```
0cd6 ffff ◀❶

```
2001-05-16-10.58.58.046000    Instance:DB2    Node:000
PID:226(db2syscs.exe)    TID:222    Appid:*LOCAL.DB2.010807154913
data_protection  sqlpgifl ◀❷     Probe:36   Database:SAMPLE
DiagData
0cd6 ffff
```

```
2001-05-16-10.58.58.046000    Instance:DB2    Node:000
PID:226(db2syscs.exe)    TID:222    Appid:*LOCAL.DB2.010807154913
data_protection  sqlpgifl   Probe:145   Database:SAMPLE
DiagData
0cd6 ffff
```

Figure 14-10   Entries in the example's db2diag.log file

versal Database Troubleshooting Guide documentation, we see that the return code means "Disk full."

2. The sqlpgif1 function, which is a logging function (because the fourth character in its name is *p*), repeatedly encounters this error. The repeated failure of this function indicates that we should examine the log path to check available space.

Solution

1. Determine how much space is in the log path (by executing the command DIR on Windows or OS/2 systems; DF on UNIX-based systems).

2. Determine how much space may be required for logging. The amount of space (in bytes) required for log files can range from (*logprimary* $\times$ (*logfilsiz* $\times$ 4,096)) + 8,192 to ((*logprimary* + *logsecond*) $\times$ (*logfilsiz* + 2) $\times$ 4,096) + 8,192. This calculation shows the range of space that may be required by logs, assuming archival logging is not being used. If archival logging is being used, the number of log files created will grow continuously. (When archival logging is used, ensure that the log path specified has as much space available as possible.)

3. If you determine that the file system is full, do one of the following:

   a. Extend the size of the file system containing the logs (UNIX-based systems only).

b. Move the logs to another location that has enough available storage space.

c. Examine your logging configuration parameters to see if their values can be reduced.

Summary

The goal of this chapter was to discuss some of the common types of errors that can be encountered when using DB2 Universal Database, and introduce you to some of the tools that are available to help identify the source of and provide resolutions for problems when they occur.

Regardless of whether a simple or a complex database environment is used, the possibility that problems will be encountered can never be eliminated. Most problems or errors that occur fall under one of the following categories:

- Operating system-specific

- Hardware- or I/O-specific

- Application-specific

- Communications-specific

Whenever an error occurs within a database system, the DB2 Database Manager notifies the user by generating a specific error code, which is then presented to the user in a variety of ways. For example, if any of the administration tools that come with DB2 Universal Database are being used when an error occurs, the error code generated, and in many cases a corresponding error message, will be displayed in a pop-up dialog. The error code and message will then be recorded in the Journal, along with the date and time that the error occurred.

Because the DB2 Universal Database environment can be quite complex, a large number of error codes (and corresponding error messages) are available. Each error code consists of a three-character (or in some cases, a four-character) prefix, followed by a four- or five-digit message number, followed by a single character (in most cases). The three-character (and in some cases, four-character) prefix of each error code identifies what category that particular error code falls under. The one-character suffix, when supplied, helps identify the severity of the situation that caused the error code to be generated.

If you receive a specific error code and you are not using one of the administration tools that come with DB2 Universal Database, there are several ways to view the error message that is associated with that error code:

- By looking up the code in the *IBM DB2 Universal Database Message Reference Volume 1* or the *IBM DB2 Universal Database Message Reference Volume 2* documentation

- By executing the GET ERROR MESSAGE [sqlaintp()] API from an application program

- By asking the DB2 Database Manager to provide the message that is associated with the error code

Sometimes an error message contains a reference to a reason code. Reason codes usually provide more detailed information to supplement the error message text. In most cases, this additional information can be obtained by looking up both the error code (first) and the reason code (second) in the *IBM DB2 Universal Database Message Reference Volume 1* or the *IBM DB2 Universal Database Message Reference Volume 2* documentation. However, in some cases, it may be necessary to consult other system documentation.

First Failure Data Capture (FFDC) information is diagnostic information that is automatically captured by DB2 Universal Database whenever an error occurs. This information contains crucial information that may help in the diagnosis and resolution of problems. Because this information is gathered at the time an error occurs, the need to reproduce errors in order to get diagnostic information is reduced or eliminated.

The information captured by FFDC includes

- db2diag.log entries
- db2alert.log entries
- Dump files
- Trap files

FFDC information is written to the directory specified in the *diagpath* parameter of the DB2 Database Manager configuration file. Because DB2 Universal Database does not contain a mechanism that automatically removes dump files and trap files that have been generated by the FFDC tool, the system administrator must make sure this directory is cleaned periodically.

The level of diagnostic information obtained by FFDC is also controlled by a parameter in the DB2 Database Manager configuration file. This parameter, *diaglevel*, can be set to any of the following values:

- **0**   Do not collect diagnostic data (not recommended).
- **1**   Collect diagnostic data for severe errors only.

- **2** Collect diagnostic data for all errors (both severe and not severe) but not for warnings.

- **3** Collect diagnostic data for all errors and warnings.

- **4** Collect diagnostic data for all errors and warnings; include informational messages and other internal diagnostic information.

When an instance is first created, the *diaglevel* parameter is set to 3 by default and diagnostic information for errors and warnings is collected whenever such events occur. Whenever possible, the *diaglevel* parameter should be set to 4 (except in a parallel environment where this setting will usually produce too much data), particularly when DB2 Universal Database is initially set up, when configuration parameters are changed, or when a large number of errors seem to be occurring.

The db2diag.log file is an ASCII file that consists of diagnostic records that have been generated by the FFDC tool. Each record or entry in this file contains either information about a particular administrative event that has occurred or specific error information. Administrative event entries are valuable, because they indicate whether events such as backup and restore operations were started and if so, whether or not they finished successfully. Error information entries, on the other hand, are only useful when trying to diagnose an external symptom, or if the source of a particular error has been isolated and you are looking for more information.

Once created, the db2diag.log file grows continuously. As a result, the most recent entries are always found near the end of the file. If storage space for this file becomes an issue, a backup copy should be made (if it needs to be kept) and the file should be deleted. A new db2diag.log file will be created automatically the next time one is needed.

Every entry in the db2diag.log file begins with a specific set of values that are intended to help identify the particular event an entry corresponds to. Because this block of information is recorded for all entries and because it is always recorded in a specific order, it is referred to as the entry header. All entry headers contain, among other things, a timestamp that identifies when an error occurred, an application identifier that enables you to match up entries with specific applications, the name of the DB2 UDB subcomponent that produced the entry, and a diagnostic error message that attempts to explain the reason for the entry.

The SQL Communications Area (SQLCA) structure is a collection of variables that are updated each time an SQL statement or an administrative API function is executed. Application programs that contain embedded SQL statements (other than DECLARE, INCLUDE, and WHENEVER statements) or API function calls that are precompiled with the LANGLEVEL SAA1 option (the default) or the LANGLEVEL MIA option specified must define at least one SQLCA data structure variable that can be accessed by the

DB2 Database Manager. An SQLCA data structure variable is also associated with the Command Line Processor. When severe errors occur, the contents of an SQLCA data structure are also written to the db2diag.log file.

For the most part, the information found in the db2diag.log file is easy to read. However, certain pieces of data such as hexadecimal dumps and internal DB2 codes can be difficult to interpret. Whenever hexadecimal values are found, they can be interpreted by performing the following steps:

1. If the hexadecimal value is in the form 0xFFFF*nnnn* (which will be the case on UNIX systems), proceed to step 3.

2. If the hexadecimal value is in the form 0x*nnnn*FFFF (which may be the case on Windows and OS/2 systems), it must be byte-reversed before it can be interpreted. To do this, switch the first four characters with the last four characters; then switch the fifth and sixth characters with the seventh and eighth characters. For example, the error code 0x0AE6FFFF would be changed to 0xFFFF0AE6, which would then be changed to 0xFFFFE60A.

3. When you have the error code in a meaningful form, convert it to decimal format using a hexadecimal calculator or some other conversion tool. For example, the error code 0xFFFFE60A would convert to -6646 decimal.

4. Try to locate the code in Appendix A (DB2 Internal Return Codes) of the *IBM DB2 Universal Database Troubleshooting Guide* documentation. If you can locate the code there, the error code is an internal return code. If you can't find the code there, it is an SQL return code—try to locate the error code in the *IBM DB2 Universal Database Message Reference Volume 2* documentation.

Questions

1. The location of the db2diag.log file is specified in which of the following?
   a. db2.ini
   b. DB2 registry
   c. Database directory
   d. Database configuration
   e. Database Manager configuration

2. Given the following db2diag.log file entry header:

```
2001-07-16-20.52.42.001160 Instance:db2ins71 Node:000
PID:44829(db2sysc (SAMPLE))Appid:*LOCAL.db2ins71.970317140834
relation_data_serv sqlrerlg Probe:17 Database:SAMPLE
DIA9999E An internal return code occurred.Report the following
:"0xFFFFE101".
```

Which of the following type of activity was being performed by the function that produced this entry?

a. Buffer pool

b. Data management

c. Relational database services

d. Indexing

3. If the sqlcode element of the SQLCA data structure contains a positive value after an SQL statement is executed, which of the following statements is correct?

a. The statement executed successfully.

b. The statement executed, but one or more warnings occurred.

c. The statement executed, but one or more errors occurred.

d. The statement could not be executed.

Answers

1. **E.** First Failure Data Capture (FFDC) information is written to the directory specified in the *diagpath* parameter of the DB2 Database Manager. (The db2diag.log file is part of this information.)

2. **C.** To find out more about the type of activity performed by a function that produced an entry in the db2diag.log file, look at the fourth letter of its name. Because the fourth character in this function's name (sqlrerlg) is *r*, it performs relational database services activity.

3. **B.** An SQL return code value of 0 means "Successful execution," a positive value means "Successful execution with warnings," and a negative value means "Error."

System Catalog Views

When a database is created, a special set of tables known as the *system catalog tables* are constructed and initialized as part of the database creation process. These tables contain information about the definitions of all database objects (for example, tables, views, indexes, and packages), as well as information about the type of security access that users have to the database objects available. The system catalog tables are automatically updated during normal operation in response to SQL Data Definition Language (DDL) statements, environment routines, and certain utilities. You cannot explicitly create, drop, or modify the information stored in these tables; however, you can query and view the content of the tables.

In addition to the system catalog tables, the following database objects are also defined and stored in the system catalog as part of the database creation process:

- A set of user-defined functions (UDFs), which are created in the SYSFUN schema.

- A set of read-only views for the system catalog tables, which are created in the SYSCAT schema.

- A set of updatable views for the system catalog tables, which are created in the SYSSTAT schema. These updatable views enable you to update statistical information about a table without using the Run Statistics (RUNSTATS) utility.

This appendix contains a description of each read-only and updatable system catalog view available.

SYSIBM.SYSDUMMY1

This view is used by applications that must be compatible with DB2 Universal Database for OS/390.

Table A-1   SYSIBM.SYSDUMMY1 System Catalog View

Column Name	Data Type	Description
IBMREQD	CHAR(1)	The letter Y

SYSCAT.ATTRIBUTES

This view contains one row for each attribute (including inherited attributes, where applicable) that has been defined for a user-defined structured data type.

Table A-2   SYSCAT.ATTRIBUTES System Catalog View

Column Name	Data Type	Description
TYPESCHEMA	VARCHAR(128)	The qualified name of the structured data type that contains the attribute.
TYPENAME	VARCHAR(18)	
ATTR_NAME	VARCHAR(18)	The name of the attribute.
ATTR_TYPESCHEMA	VARCHAR(128)	The qualified name of the data type of the attribute.
ATTR_TYPENAME	VARCHAR(18)	
TARGET_TYPESCHEMA	VARCHAR(128)	The qualified name of the target data type, if the data type of the attribute is REFERENCE. (This contains a null value if the data type of the attribute is not REFERENCE.)
TARGET_TYPENAME	VARCHAR(18)	
SOURCE_TYPESCHEMA	VARCHAR(128)	The qualified name of the data type in the data type hierarchy where the attribute was was introduced. For noninherited attributes, these columns have the same values as TYPESCHEMA and TYPENAME.
SOURCE_TYPENAME	VARCHAR(18)	
ORDINAL	SMALLINT	The numeric position (starting at 0) of the attribute in the definition of the structured data type.
LENGTH	INTEGER	The maximum length allowed for data values (always 0 for distinct data types). The LENGTH column indicates precision for DECIMAL fields.
SCALE	SMALLINT	The number of digits allowed to the right of the decimal point if the data type of the attribute is DECIMAL. (This contains the value 0 if the data type of the attribute is not DECIMAL.)

(continued)

Table A-2   SYSCAT.ATTRIBUTES System Catalog View (continued)

Column Name	Data Type	Description
CODEPAGE	SMALLINT	The code page of the attribute. For character-string attributes not defined with the FOR BIT DATA attribute, the value is the database code page. For graphic-string attributes, the value is the double Byte character system (DBCS) code page implied by the (composite) database code page. (Otherwise, the value is 0.)
LOGGED	CHAR(I)	Indicates whether or not the attribute is logged: Y = Attribute is logged. N = Attribute is not logged. Applies only if the data type of the attribute is large object (LOB) or distinct based on LOB. (Otherwise, this is blank.)
COMPACT	CHAR(I)	Indicates whether or not the attribute is compacted in storage: Y = Attribute is compacted. N = Attribute is not compacted. Applies only if the data type of the attribute is LOB or distinct based on LOB. (Otherwise, this is blank.)
DL_FEATURES	CHAR(10)	Encoded DATALINK features such as link type, control mode, recovery, and unlink properties. Applies only if the data type of the attribute is DATALINK. (Otherwise, this is blank if the data type of the attribute is REFERENCE and null if the data type of the attribute is anything else.)

SYSCAT.BUFFERPOOLNODES

This view contains one row for each node in a buffer pool that has a node-specific buffer pool with a size that is different from the default size specified (for the buffer pool) in the NPAGES column of the SYSCAT.BUFFERPOOLS system catalog view.

Table A-3   SYSCAT.BUFFERPOOLNODES System Catalog View

Column Name	Data Type	Description
BUFFERPOOLID	INTEGER	A system-generated internal buffer pool identifier
NODENUM	SMALLINT	The number used to identify the node
NPAGES	INTEGER	The number of pages in the buffer pool found on this node

SYSCAT.BUFFERPOOLS

This view contains one row for each buffer pool (in every nodegroup) that has been defined.

Table A-4   SYSCAT.BUFFERPOOLS System Catalog View

Column Name	Data Type	Description
BPNAME	VARCHAR(18)	The name of the buffer pool.
BUFFERPOOLID	INTEGER	A system-generated internal buffer pool identifier.
NGNAME	VARCHAR(18)	The name of the nodegroup the buffer pool exists on. (The value is null if the buffer pool exists on all nodes in the database.)
NPAGES	INTEGER	The number of pages in the buffer pool.
PAGESIZE	INTEGER	The size of the pages used by the buffer pool.
ESTORE	CHAR(1)	Indicates whether or not the buffer pool uses extended storage: N = The buffer pool does not use extended storage. Y = The buffer pool uses extended storage.

SYSCAT.CASTFUNCTIONS

This view contains one row for each user-defined data type cast function that has been created. (Built-in data type cast functions are not included.)

Table A-5   SYSCAT.CASTFUNCTIONS System Catalog View

Column Name	Data Type	Description
FROM_TYPESCHEMA	VARCHAR(128)	The qualified name of the data type of the input parameter (before casting).
FROM_TYPENAME	VARCHAR(18)	
TO_TYPESCHEMA	VARCHAR(128)	The qualified name of the data type of the result (after casting).
TO_TYPENAME	VARCHAR(18)	
FUNCSCHEMA	VARCHAR(128)	The qualified name of the data type cast function.
FUNCNAME	VARCHAR(18)	
SPECIFICNAME	VARCHAR(18)	The specific name of the cast function instance.
ASSIGN_FUNCTION	CHAR(1)	Indicates whether or not the cast function is an implicit assignment function: Y = Function is an assignment function. N = Function is not an assignment function.

SYSCAT.CHECKS

This view contains one row for each check constraint that has been defined.

Table A-6 SYSCAT.CHECKS System Catalog View

Column Name	Data Type	Description
CONSTNAME	VARCHAR(18)	The name of the check constraint.
DEFINER	VARCHAR(128)	The authorization ID under which the check constraint was defined.
TABSCHEMA	VARCHAR(128)	The qualified name of the table to which the constraint applies.
TABNAME	VARCHAR(128)	
CREATE_TIME	TIMESTAMP	The date and time at which the constraint was defined. (This is used in resolving functions that are used in the constraint, if any. No functions will be chosen that were created after the constraint was defined.)
QUALIFIER	VARCHAR(128)	The value of the CURRENT SCHEMA special register variable at the time the constraint was defined. (This is used to resolve any unqualified references.)
TYPE	CHAR(1)	Indicates what type of check constraint the check constraint is: A = System-generated check constraint for a GENERATED ALWAYS column. C = User-defined check constraint.
FUNC_PATH	VARCHAR(254)	The value of the CURRENT PATH special register variable at the time the constraint was defined.
TEXT	CLOB(64K)	The text of the check constraint.

SYSCAT.COLAUTH

This view contains one row for each user or group that has been granted a column-level privilege.

Table A-7   SYSCAT.COLAUTH System Catalog View

Column Name	Data Type	Description
GRANTOR	VARCHAR(128)	The authorization ID of the user who granted the privilege. (Otherwise, the value is SYSIBM.)
GRANTEE	VARCHAR(128)	The authorization ID of the user or group that holds the privilege.
GRANTEETYPE	CHAR(1)	Indicates whether the grantee is a user or a group: U = The grantee is an individual user. G = The grantee is a group.
TABSCHEMA	VARCHAR(128)	The qualified name of the table or view the column resides in.
TABNAME	VARCHAR(128)	
COLNAME	VARCHAR(128)	The name of the column to which the privilege applies.
COLNO	SMALLINT	The ordinal position (starting at 0) of the column in the table or view.
PRIVTYPE	CHAR(1)	Indicates the type of privilege the grantee holds on the table or view: U = The grantee holds an UPDATE privilege. R = The grantee holds a REFERENCES privilege.
GRANTABLE	CHAR(1)	Indicates whether or not the privilege is grantable: G = The privilege is grantable. N = The privilege is not grantable.

SYSCAT.COLCHECKS

This view contains one row for each column that is referenced by a check constraint.

Table A-8   SYSCAT.COLCHECKS System Catalog View

Column Name	Data Type	Description
CONSTNAME	VARCHAR(18)	The name of the check constraint.
TABSCHEMA	VARCHAR(128)	The qualified name of the table that contains the referenced column.
TABNAME	VARCHAR(128)	
COLNAME	VARCHAR(128)	The name of the referenced column.
USAGE	CHAR(1)	Indicates how the column is used in the check constraint: R = The column is referenced in a check constraint. S = The column is a source column in a system-generated check constraint that supports a generated column. T = The column is a target column in a system-generated check constraint that supports a generated column.

SYSCAT.COLDIST

This view contains detailed column statistics that are used by the DB2 Optimizer. Each row describes the nth most frequent or the nth quantile value found for a column.

Table A-9   SYSCAT.COLDIST System Catalog View

Column Name	Data Type	Description
TABSCHEMA	VARCHAR(128)	The qualified name of the table that the entry applies to.
TABNAME	VARCHAR(128)	
COLNAME	VARCHAR(128)	The name of the column that the entry applies to.
TYPE	CHAR(1)	Indicates whether the record is for a frequency value or a quantile value: F = Frequency value. Q = Quantile value.
SEQNO	SMALLINT	The value for n is as follows: If TYPE = F, it identifies the n in the nth most frequent value. If TYPE = Q, it identifies the n in the nth quantile value.
COLVALUE	VARCHAR(254)	The data value, converted to either a character literal value or null.
VALCOUNT	BIGINT	The number of occurrences or rows found: If TYPE = F, it is the number of occurrences of COLVALUE in the column. If TYPE = Q, it is the number of rows with values less than or equal to COLVALUE.
DISTCOUNT	BIGINT	The number of distinct quantile values found: If TYPE = F, it is a null value. If TYPE = Q, it is the number of distinct values that are less than or equal to COLVALUE.

SYSCAT.COLOPTIONS

This view contains one row for each column-specific option defined.

Table A-10   SYSCAT.COLOPTIONS System Catalog View

Column Name	Data Type	Description
TABSCHEMA	VARCHAR(128)	The schema name of a table or nickname.
TABNAME	VARCHAR(128)	The unqualified name of a table or nickname.
COLNAME	VARCHAR(128)	The local column name.
OPTION	VARCHAR(128)	The name of the column option.
SETTING	VARCHAR(255)	The column option value.

SYSCAT.COLUMNS

This view contains one row for each column (including inherited columns, where applicable) that has been defined for a table or view.

Table A-11   SYSCAT.COLUMNS System Catalog View

Column Name	Data Type	Description
TABSCHEMA	VARCHAR(128)	The qualified name of the table or view that contains the column.
TABNAME	VARCHAR(128)	
COLNAME	VARCHAR(128)	The name of the column.
COLNO	SMALLINT	The ordinal position (starting at 0) of the column in the table or view.
TYPESCHEMA	VARCHAR(128)	The qualified name of the data type of the column, if the data type of the column is a distinct data type. (Otherwise, TYPESCHEMA contains the value SYSIBM and TYPENAME contains the data type of the column in long form—for example, CHARACTER.) Note: If FLOAT or FLOAT(n) with n greater than 24 was specified, TYPENAME would contain the value DOUBLE. If FLOAT(n) with n less than 25 was specified, TYPENAME would contain the value REAL. If NUMERIC was specified, TYPENAME would contain the value DECIMAL.
TYPENAME	VARCHAR(18)	
LENGTH	INTEGER	The maximum length allowed for data values (always 0 for distinct data types). The LENGTH column indicates precision for DECIMAL fields.
SCALE	SMALLINT	The number of digits allowed to the right of the decimal point if the data type of the column is DECIMAL. (This contains the value 0 if the data type of the column is not DECIMAL.)

(continued)

Table A-11 SYSCAT.COLUMNS System Catalog View *(continued)*

Column Name	Data Type	Description
DEFAULT	VARCHAR(254)	The default value for the column (expressed as a constant, special register, or a cast function that is appropriate for the data type of the column.) This may also be the keyword NULL. This is a null value if a DEFAULT clause is not specified or if the column is a column in a view. Values may be converted from what was specified as a default value. For example, date and time constants are presented in International Standards Organization (ISO) format; cast function names are qualified with schema name, and the identifiers are delimited.
NULLS	CHAR(1)	Indicates whether or not the column accepts null values (is nullable): Y = Column is nullable. N = Column is not nullable. Note: Although the value N may be displayed for a column in a view that is derived from an expression or function, such a column will accept nulls when the statement using the view is processed with warnings for arithmetic errors.
CODEPAGE	SMALLINT	The code page of the column. For character-string columns not defined with the FOR BIT DATA attribute, the value is the database code page. For graphic-string columns, the value is the DBCS code page implied by the (composite) database code page. (Otherwise, the value is 0.)
LOGGED	CHAR(1)	Indicates whether or not the column is logged: Y = Column is logged. N = Column is not logged. Applies only if the data type of the column is LOB or distinct based on LOB. (Otherwise, this is blank.)
COMPACT	CHAR(1)	Indicates whether or not the column is compacted in storage: Y = Column is compacted in storage. N = Column is not compacted. Applies only if the data type of the column is LOB or distinct based on LOB. (Otherwise, this is blank.)

Column Name	Data Type	Description
COLCARD	BIGINT	Identifies the number of distinct values found in the column. (Otherwise, the value is -1 if statistics have not been collected or -2 if the column is an inherited column or a column of a hierarchy table.)
HIGH2KEY	VARCHAR(254)	Identifies the second highest value found in the column. (Otherwise, this is empty if statistics have not been collected or if the column is an inherited column or a column of a hierarchy table.)
LOW2KEY	VARCHAR(254)	Identifies the second lowest value found in the column. (Otherwise, this is empty if statistics have not been collected or if the column is an inherited column or a column of a hierarchy table.)
AVGCOLLEN	INTEGER	The average length of data values in the column. (Otherwise, the value is -1 if the data type of the column is a long or LOB data type or if statistics have not been collected; the value is -2 if the column is an inherited column or a column of a hierarchy table.)
KEYSEQ	SMALLINT	The column's numerical position within the table's primary key. (Otherwise, the value is null if the table is a subtable or a hierarchical table.)
PARTKEYSEQ	SMALLINT	The column's numerical position within the table's partitioning key. (Otherwise, the value is null or 0 if the column is not part of a partitioning key or if the table is a subtable or a hierarchical table.)
NQUANTILES	SMALLINT	The number of quantile values recorded in SYSCAT.COLDIST for the column. (Otherwise, the value is -1 if statistics have not been collected or -2 if the column is an inherited column or a column of a hierarchy table.)
NMOSTFREQ	SMALLINT	The number of most frequent values recorded in SYSCAT.COLDIST for the column. (Otherwise, the value is -1 if statistics have not been collected or -2 if the column is an inherited column or a column of a hierarchy table.)

(continued)

Table A-11   SYSCAT.COLUMNS System Catalog View *(continued)*

Column Name	Data Type	Description
NUMNULLS	BIGINT	The number of null values found in the column. (Otherwise, the value is -1 if statistics have not been collected.)
TARGET_TYPESCHEMA	VARCHAR(128)	The qualified name of the target data type if the data type of the column is REFERENCE. (This contains a null value if the data type of the attribute is not REFERENCE.)
TARGET_TYPENAME	VARCHAR(18)	
SCOPE_TABSCHEMA	VARCHAR(128)	The qualified name of the scope (target table) if the data type of the column is REFERENCE. (This contains a null value if the data type of the attribute is not REFERENCE.)
SCOPE_TABNAME	VARCHAR(128)	
SOURCE_TABSCHEMA	VARCHAR(128)	The qualified name of the table or view in the respective hierarchy where the column was first introduced. For noninherited columns, these columns have the same values as TBCREATOR and TBNAME. (This contains a null value if the column does not belong to a Typed table or view.)
SOURCE_TABNAME	VARCHAR(128)	
DL_FEATURES	CHAR(10)	Encoded DATALINK features such as link type, control mode, recovery, and unlink properties. Each character position is defined as follows (numbers represent each position): 1. Link type (U for URL). 2. Link control (F for file and N for no). 3. Integrity (A for all and N for none). 4. Read permission (F for file system and D for database). 5. Write permission (F for file system and B for blocked). 6. Recovery (Y for yes and N for no). 7. On unlink (R for restore, D for delete, and N for not applicable). 8. Characters 8 through 10 are reserved for future use. Applies only if the data type of the column is DATALINK. (Otherwise, this is blank if the data type of the column is REFERENCE and null if the data type of the column is anything else.)

Column Name	Data Type	Description

SPECIAL_PROPS	CHAR(8)	Identifies special properties for columns if the data type of the column is REFERENCE. (Otherwise, the value is null.)
		Each character position is defined as follows (numbers represent each position):
		1. Object identifier (OID) column flag:
		  Y = Yes
		  N = No
		2. User-generated or system-generated flag:
		  U = User
		  S = System

HIDDEN	CHAR(1)	Indicates whether or not the column is a hidden column: S = Column is a system-managed hidden column. Blank = Column is not hidden.
INLINE_LENGTH	INTEGER	Length of structured data type column that can be kept with base table row. (This contains the value 0 if no value was explicitly set by ALTER/CREATE TABLE statement.)
IDENTITY	CHAR(1)	Indicates whether or not the column is an identity column: Y = The column is an identity column. N = The column is not an identity column.
GENERATED	CHAR(1)	Indicates whether or not the column's value is generated: A = Column value is always generated. D = Column value is generated by default. Blank = Column value is not generated.
TEXT	CLOB(64K)	The test used to create the column (if the column is generated), starting with the keyword AS.
REMARKS	VARCHAR(254)	A user-supplied comment.

SYSCAT.CONSTDEP

This view contains one row for each dependency a constraint has on some other object.

Table A-12   SYSCAT.CONSTDEP System Catalog View

Column Name	Data Type	Description
CONSTNAME	VARCHAR(18)	The name of the constraint.
TABSCHEMA	VARCHAR(128)	The qualified name of the table the constraint applies to.
TABNAME	VARCHAR(128)	
BTYPE	CHAR(1)	The type of object the constraint depends on includes the following: F = Function instance. I = Index instance. R = Structured data type.
BSCHEMA	VARCHAR(128)	The qualified name of the object the constraint depends on.
BNAME	VARCHAR(18)	

SYSCAT.DATATYPES

This view contains one row for each data type available (including built-in and user-defined data types).

Table A-13   SYSCAT.DATATYPES System Catalog View

Column Name	Data Type	Description
TYPESCHEMA	VARCHAR(128)	The qualified name of the data type. (The value is SYSIBM for built-in data types.)
TYPENAME	VARCHAR(18)	
DEFINER	VARCHAR(128)	The authorization ID under which the data type was created.
SOURCESCHEMA	VARCHAR(128)	The qualified name of the source data type used for distinct types.
SOURCENAME	VARCHAR(18)	The qualified name of the built-in data type used as the reference type that is used as the representation for references to structured data types. The value is null for all other data types.
METATYPE	CHAR(1)	Identifies what kind of data type the data type is: S = System predefined type. T = Distinct type. R = Structured type.
TYPEID	SMALLINT	A system-generated internal data type identifier.
SOURCETYPEID	SMALLINT	Internal data type ID of the source data type used for distinct data types. (Otherwise, the value is null.) For user-defined structured data types, this is the internal data type ID of the reference representation data type.
LENGTH	INTEGER	Maximum data length allowed by the data type (always 0 for system predefined parameterized types such as DECIMAL and VARCHAR). For user-defined structured data types, this indicates the length of the reference representation data type.

(continued)

Table A-13   SYSCAT.DATATYPES System Catalog View *(continued)*

Column Name	Data Type	Description
SCALE	SMALLINT	The number of digits allowed to the right of the decimal point for distinct data types or reference representation data types based on the system predefined DECIMAL type (always 0 for all other data types, including DECIMAL itself). For user-defined structured data types, this indicates the length of the reference representation data type.
CODEPAGE	SMALLINT	The code page used for character and graphic distinct data types or reference representation data types. (Otherwise, the value is 0.)
CREATE_TIME	TIMESTAMP	The date and time at which the data type was created.
ATTRCOUNT	SMALLINT	The number of attributes used in the data type if it is a structured data type. (Otherwise, the value is 0.)
INSTANTIABLE	CHAR(1)	Indicates whether or not the data type can be instantiated: Y = The data type can be instantiated. N = The data type cannot be instantiated.
WITH_FUNC_ACCESS	CHAR(1)	Indicates whether or not all methods for the data type can be invoked using function notation: Y = Methods for this data type can be invoked using function notation. N = Methods for this data type cannot be invoked using function notation.
FINAL	CHAR(1)	Indicates whether or not the data type can have subtypes: Y = The data type cannot have subtypes. N = The data type can have subtypes.
INLINE_LENGTH	INTEGER	The length of a structured data type that can be kept with a base table row. (It contains 0 if no value was explicitly set by the CREATE TYPE statement.)
REMARKS	VARCHAR(254)	A user-supplied comment.

SYSCAT.DBAUTH

This view contains one row for each user or group that has been granted a database-level privilege.

Table A-14   SYSCAT.DBAUTH System Catalog View

Column Name	Data Type	Description
GRANTOR	VARCHAR(128)	The authorization ID of the user who granted the privilege. (Otherwise, the value is SYSIBM.)
GRANTEE	VARCHAR(128)	The authorization ID of the user or group that holds the privilege.
GRANTEETYPE	CHAR(1)	Indicates whether the grantee is a user or a group: U = The grantee is an individual user. G = The grantee is a group.
DBADMAUTH	CHAR(1)	Indicates whether or not the grantee holds Database Administrator (DBADM) authority over the database: Y = The grantee holds DBADM authority. N = The grantee does not hold DBADM authority.
CREATETABAUTH	CHAR(1)	Indicates whether or not the grantee can create tables in the database (has the CREATETAB privilege): Y = The grantee holds the CREATETAB privilege. N = The grantee does not hold the CREATETAB privilege.
BINDADDAUTH	CHAR(1)	Indicates whether or not the grantee can create new packages in the database (has the BINDADD privilege): Y = The grantee holds the BINDADD privilege. N = The grantee does not hold the BINDADD privilege.
CONNECTAUTH	CHAR(1)	Indicates whether or not the grantee can connect to the database (has the CONNECT privilege): Y = The grantee holds the CONNECT privilege. N = The grantee does not hold the CONNECT privilege.

(continued)

Table A-14   SYSCAT.DBAUTH System Catalog View *(continued)*

Column Name	Data Type	Description
NOFENCEAUTH	CHAR(1)	Indicates whether or not the grantee can create nonfenced functions (has the CREATE_NOT_FENCED privilege): Y = The grantee holds the CREATE_NOT_FENCED privilege. N = The grantee does not hold the CREATE_NOT_FENCED privilege.
IMPLSCHEMAAUTH	CHAR(1)	Indicates whether or not the grantee can implicitly create schemas in the database (has the IMPLICIT_SCHEMA privilege): Y = The grantee holds the IMPLICIT_SCHEMA privilege. N = The grantee does not hold the IMPLICIT_SCHEMA privilege.
LOADAUTH	CHAR(1)	Indicates whether or not the grantee holds LOAD authority over the database: Y = The grantee holds LOAD authority. N = The grantee does not hold LOAD authority.

SYSCAT.EVENTMONITORS

This view contains one row for each event monitor that has been defined.

Table A-15   SYSCAT.EVENTMONITORS System Catalog View

Column Name	Data Type	Description
EVMONNAME	VARCHAR(18)	The name of the event monitor.
DEFINER	VARCHAR(128)	The authorization ID under which the event monitor was created.
TARGET_TYPE	CHAR(1)	Identifies the type of target all event monitor data collected will be written to: F = File. P = Pipe (named).
TARGET	VARCHAR(246)	The name of the target that all event monitor data collected will be written to (absolute pathname of file or absolute name of pipe).
MAXFILES	INTEGER	The maximum number of event files allowed in the TARGET path specified. (The value is null if there is no maximum or if TARGET_TYPE = N.)
MAXFILESIZE	INTEGER	The maximum size (in 4K pages) that each event file can grow to before the event monitor will create a new file. (The value is null if there is no maximum or if TARGET_TYPE = N.)
BUFFERSIZE	INTEGER	The size (in 4K pages) of the buffers used by the event monitor to write to a file. (The value is null if TARGET_TYPE = N.)
IO_MODE	CHAR(1)	Indicates the type of file I/O used by the event monitor to write to a file: B = Blocked. N = Not blocked. (The value is null if TARGET_TYPE = N.)
WRITE_MODE	CHAR(1)	Indicates how the monitor should handle existing event data when the monitor is activated: A = Append new data to existing data. R = Replace existing data. (The value is null if TARGET_TYPE = N.)

(continued)

Table A-15   SYSCAT.EVENTMONITORS System Catalog View *(continued)*

Column Name	Data Type	Description
AUTOSTART	CHAR(1)	Indicates whether or not the event monitor will be activated automatically when the database starts: Y = Yes. N = No.
NODENUM	SMALLINT	Identifies the number of the partition (or node) on which the event monitor runs and logs events.
MONSCOPE	CHAR(1)	Identifies the scope the event monitor should use: L = Local. G = Global.
REMARKS	VARCHAR(254)	Reserved for future use.

SYSCAT.EVENTS

This view contains one row for each event that is being monitored. (One event monitor can monitor multiple events.)

Table A-16   SYSCAT.EVENTS System Catalog View

Column Name	Data Type	Description
EVMONNAME	VARCHAR(18)	The name of the event monitor that is monitoring the event.
TYPE	VARCHAR(18)	Identifies the type of event being monitored: DATABASE CONNECTIONS TABLES STATEMENTS TRANSACTIONS DEADLOCKS TABLESPACES
FILTER	CLOB(32K)	The full text of the WHERE clause that applies to the event being monitored.

SYSCAT.FULLHIERARCHIES

This view contains one row for each relationship that exists between a subtype and a supertype; a subtable and a supertable; and a subview and a superview. (All hierarchical relationships, including immediate ones, are included in this view.)

Table A-17   SYSCAT.FULLHIERARCHIES System Catalog View

Column Name	Data Type	Description
METATYPE	CHAR(1)	Identifies the type of hierarchical relationship that exists: R = A relationship exists between structured data types. U = A relationship exists between Typed tables. W = A relationship exists between Typed views.
SUB_SCHEMA	VARCHAR(128)	The qualified name of the subtype, subtable, or subview in the relationship.
SUB_NAME	VARCHAR(128)	
SUPER_SCHEMA	VARCHAR(128)	The qualified name of the supertype, supertable, or superview in the relationship.
SUPER_NAME	VARCHAR(128)	
ROOT_SCHEMA	VARCHAR(128)	The qualified name of the structured data type, Typed table, or Typed view that is at the root of the hierarchy.
ROOT_NAME	VARCHAR(128)	

SYSCAT.FUNCDEP

This view contains one row for each dependency that exists between a function/method and any other object.

Table A-18 SYSCAT.FUNCDEP System Catalog View

Column Name	Data Type	Description
FUNCSCHEMA	VARCHAR(128)	The qualified name of the function or method that has dependencies on another object.
FUNCNAME	VARCHAR(18)	
BTYPE	CHAR(1)	Identifies the type of object the function or method is dependent upon: A = Alias F = Function or method instance O = Privilege dependency on all subtables or subviews in a table or view hierarchy R = Structured data type S = Summary table T = Table U = Typed table V = View W = Typed view X = Index extension
BSCHEMA	VARCHAR(128)	The qualified name of the object the function or method is dependent upon. (If BTYPE = F, this is the specific name of a function.)
BNAME	VARCHAR(128)	
TABAUTH	SMALLINT	If BTYPE = O, S, T, U, V, or W, the privileges (encoded) on the table or view that are required by the dependent function or the method. (Otherwise, the value is null.)

SYSCAT.FUNCMAPOPTIONS

This view contains one row for each function mapping option that has been defined.

Table A-19   SYSCAT.FUNCMAPOPTIONS System Catalog View

Column Name	Data Type	Description
FUNCTION_MAPPING	VARCHAR(18)	The name of the function mapping.
OPTION	VARCHAR(128)	The name of the function mapping option.
SETTING	VARCHAR(255)	The function mapping option value.

SYSCAT.FUNCMAPPARMOPTIONS

This view contains one row for each function mapping parameter option defined.

Table A-20   SYSCAT.FUNCMAPPARMOPTIONS System Catalog View

Column Name	Data Type	Description
FUNCTION_MAPPING	VARCHAR(18)	The name of the function mapping.
ORDINAL	SMALLINT	The numeric position (starting at 0) of the parameter in the definition of the function.
LOCATION	CHAR(1)	Indicates whether the mapping is local or remote: L = Local R = Remote
OPTION	VARCHAR(128)	The name of the function mapping parameter option.
SETTING	VARCHAR(255)	The function mapping parameter option value.

SYSCAT.FUNCMAPPINGS

This view contains one row for each function mapping that has been defined.

Table A-21 SYSCAT.FUNCMAPPINGS System Catalog View

Column Name	Data Type	Description
FUNCTION_MAPPING	VARCHAR(18)	The unqualified name of the function mapping (which may have been system generated).
FUNCSCHEMA	VARCHAR(128)	The schema that the function mapping was defined under. (This contains null if the mapping was system generated for a built-in function.)
FUNCNAME	VARCHAR(1024)	The name of the local built-in or UDF the mapping refers to.
FUNCID	INTEGER	A system-generated internal function identifier.
SPECIFICNAME	VARCHAR(18)	The name of the local function instance.
DEFINER	VARCHAR(128)	The authorization ID under which the function mapping was created.
WRAPNAME	VARCHAR(128)	The name of the wrapper that the function mapping has been applied to.
SERVERNAME	VARCHAR(128)	The name of the data source that the function mapping has been applied to.
SERVERTYPE	VARCHAR(30)	The type of data source that the function mapping has been applied to.
SERVERVERSION	VARCHAR(18)	The version of the data source server that the function mapping has been applied to.
CREATE_TIME	TIMESTAMP	The date and time at which the function mapping was defined.
REMARKS	VARCHAR(254)	A user-supplied comment.

SYSCAT.FUNCPARMS

This view contains one row for each parameter or result of a function or method that has been defined in the database.

Table A-22   SYSCAT.FUNCPARMS System Catalog View

Column Name	Data Type	Description
FUNCSCHEMA	VARCHAR(128)	The qualified name of the function or method.
FUNCNAME	VARCHAR(18)	
SPECIFICNAME	VARCHAR(18)	The specific name of the function instance.
ROWTYPE	CHAR(1)	Indicates whether the record is for a parameter or a result: P = The record is for a parameter. R = The record is for a result before casting. C = The record is for a result after casting.
ORDINAL	SMALLINT	If ROWTYPE = P, the numeric position (starting at 0) of the parameter in the function's parameter signature. If ROWTYPE = R and the function returns a table, the result column's numeric position (starting at 0) in the result table. (Otherwise, the value is 0.)
PARMNAME	VARCHAR(128)	The name of the parameter or result column. (The value is null if no name exists.)
TYPESCHEMA	VARCHAR(128)	The qualified name of the data type of the parameter or result.
TYPENAME	VARCHAR(18)	
LENGTH	INTEGER	The maximum length allowed for parameter or result data values (always 0 if the parameter or result is a distinct data type).
SCALE	SMALLINT	The number of digits allowed to the right of the decimal point of the parameter or result if the data type of the parameter or result is DECIMAL (always 0 if the parameter or result is a distinct data type).

(continued)

Table A-22 SYSCAT.FUNCPARMS System Catalog View *(continued)*

Column Name	Data Type	Description
CODEPAGE	SMALLINT	The code page of the parameter or result. For character-string data types not defined with the FOR BIT DATA attribute, the value is the database code page. (Otherwise, the value is 0.)
CAST_FUNCID	INTEGER	The system-generated internal identifier of the casting function used, if any.
AS_LOCATOR	CHAR(I)	Indicates whether the parameter or result is passed as a locator: Y = The parameter or result is passed in the form of a locator. N = The parameter or result is not passed in the form of a locator.
TARGET_TYPESCHEMA	VARCHAR(128)	The qualified name of the target data type, if the data type of the parameter or result is REFERENCE. (This contains a null value if the data type of the parameter or result is not REFERENCE.)
TARGET_TYPENAME	VARCHAR(18)	
SCOPE_TABSCHEMA	VARCHAR(128)	The qualified name of the scope (target table), if the data type of the parameter or result is REFERENCE. (This contains a null value if the data type of the parameter or result is not REFERENCE or if the scope is not defined.)
SCOPE_TABNAME	VARCHAR(128)	
TRANSFORM_GRPNAME	VARCHAR(18)	The name of the transform group used if the parameter is a structured data type.

SYSCAT.FUNCTIONS

This view contains one row for each UDF (scalar, table, or source), system-generated method, or user-defined method that has been created.

Table A-23   SYSCAT.FUNCTIONS System Catalog View

Column Name	Data Type	Description
FUNCSCHEMA	VARCHAR(128)	The qualified name of the function.
FUNCNAME	VARCHAR(18)	
SPECIFICNAME	VARCHAR(18)	The specific name of the function instance.
DEFINER	VARCHAR(128)	The authorization ID under which the function was created.
FUNCID	INTEGER	A system-generated internal function identifier.
RETURN_TYPE	SMALLINT	Internal type code of the function's return value data type.
ORIGIN	CHAR(1)	Identifies the source of the function: B = A built-in function E = A user-defined external function Q = A user-defined SQL function U = A UDF that is based on a source function S = A system-generated function
TYPE	CHAR(1)	Identifies the type of function the information is for: C = Column function R = Row function S = Scalar function T = Table function
METHOD	CHAR(1)	Indicates whether or not the information is for a system-generated method: Y = The function is for a method. N = The function is not for a method.
EFFECT	CHAR(2)	Identifies the type of method the method information is for: MU = Mutator method OB = Observer method CN = Constructor method
PARM_COUNT	SMALLINT	The number of parameters used by the function.

(continued)

Table A-23 SYSCAT.FUNCTIONS System Catalog View *(continued)*

Column Name	Data Type	Description
PARM_SIGNATURE	VARCHAR(180) FOR BIT DATA	A concatenation of up to 90 parameter data types, in internal format. (This has zero length if function takes no parameters.)
CREATE_TIME	TIMESTAMP	The date and time at which the function was created. (The value is 0 for Version 1 functions.)
QUALIFIER	VARCHAR(128)	The value of the CURRENT SCHEMA special register variable at the time the constraint was defined. (This is used to resolve any unqualified references.)
WITH_FUNC_ACCESS	CHAR(1)	Indicates whether or not the method can be invoked using functional notation: Y = The method can be invoked by using functional notation. N = The method cannot be invoked by using functional notation.
TYPE_PRESERVING	CHAR(1)	Indicates whether or not the method return value data type is governed by a type-preserving parameter: Y = Return value data type is governed by a type-preserving parameter. (All system-generated mutator methods are type preserving.) N = Return value data type is the declared return type of the method.
VARIANT	CHAR(1)	Indicates whether or not the function is a variant function: Y = The function is variant (results may differ). N = The function is invariant (results are consistent). (This is blank if ORIGIN is not E.)
SIDE_EFFECTS	CHAR(1)	Indicates whether or not the function has external side effects: E = The function has external side effects (number of invocations is important). N = The function has no side effects. (This is blank if ORIGIN is not E.)
FENCED	CHAR(1)	Indicates whether or not the function is fenced: Y = The function is fenced. N = The function is not fenced. (This is blank if ORIGIN is not E.)

Column Name	Data Type	Description
NULLCALL	CHAR(1)	Indicates how the function responds if called with a null parameter value: Y = The function will be called if a null parameter value is specified. N = The function will not be called if a null parameter value is specified (function result is implicitly null if operand(s) are null). (This is blank if ORIGIN is not E.)
CAST_FUNCTION	CHAR(1)	Indicates whether or not the function is a cast function: Y = The function is a cast function. N = The function is not a cast function.
ASSIGN_FUNCTION	CHAR(1)	Indicates whether or not the function is an implicit assignment function: Y = The function is an implicit assignment function. N = The function is not an implicit assignment function.
SCRATCHPAD	CHAR(1)	Indicates whether or not the function has a scratch pad: Y = The function has a scratch pad. N = The function does not have a scratch pad. (This is blank if ORIGIN is not E.)
FINAL_CALL	CHAR(1)	Indicates whether or not a final call is made to the function (at run-time end-of-statement): Y = A final call is made to the function. N = No final call is made to the function. (This is blank if ORIGIN is not E.)
PARALLELIZABLE	CHAR(1)	Indicates whether or not the function can be executed in parallel: Y = The function can be executed in parallel. N = The function cannot be executed in parallel. (This is blank if ORIGIN is not E.)
CONTAINS_SQL	CHAR(1)	Indicates whether or not the function or method contains SQL statements: C = The function contains SQL; only SQL that does not read or modify SQL data is allowed. N = The function does not contain SQL; SQL is not allowed. R = The function contains SQL; only SQL that reads SQL data is allowed.

(continued)

Table A-23 SYSCAT.FUNCTIONS System Catalog View (continued)

Column Name	Data Type	Description
DBINFO	CHAR(1)	Indicates whether or not a DBINFO parameter is passed to an external function: Y = DBINFO is passed. N = DBINFO is not passed. (This is blank if ORIGIN is not E.)
RESULT_COLS	SMALLINT	The number of columns in the result table produced by the function if the function is a table function (TYPE = T). (Otherwise, the value is 1.)
LANGUAGE	CHAR(8)	Implementation language (C, JAVA, OLE, or OLEDB) used to produce the body of the function. (This is blank if ORIGIN is not E or Q.)
IMPLEMENTATION	VARCHAR(254)	If ORIGIN = E, this identifies the path/module/function that is used to implement the function. If ORIGIN = U and the source function is a built-in function, this identifies the source function that implements the function by name and signature. (Otherwise, the value is null.)
CLASS	VARCHAR(128)	If LANGUAGE = JAVA, this identifies the class that implements the function. (Otherwise, the value is null.)
JAR_ID	VARCHAR(128)	If LANGUAGE = JAVA, this identifies the jar file that implements the function. (Otherwise, the value is null.)
PARM_STYLE	CHAR(8)	Identifies the parameter style declared for the function when it was created: DB2SQL DB2GENRL JAVA (This is blank if ORIGIN is not E.)

Column Name	Data Type	Description
SOURCE_SCHEMA	VARCHAR(128)	The qualified name of the source function used if ORIGIN = U and the source function is a UDF. If ORIGIN = U and the source function is a built-in function, SOURCE_SCHEMA is SYSIBM and SOURCE_SPECIFIC is N/A for built-in. (The value is null if ORIGIN is not U.)
SOURCE_SPECIFIC	VARCHAR(18)	
IOS_PER_INVOC	DOUBLE	Estimated number of I/Os required per invocation. (The value is -1 if not known.)
INSTS_PER_INVOC	DOUBLE	Estimated number of instructions performed per invocation. (The value is -1 if not known.)
IOS_PER_ARGBYTE	DOUBLE	Estimated number of I/Os required per input argument byte. (The value is -1 if not known.)
INSTS_PER_ARGBYTE	DOUBLE	Estimated number of instructions per input argument byte. (The value is -1 if not known.)
PERCENT_ARGBYTES	SMALLINT	Estimated average percent of input argument bytes that the function will actually read. (The value is -1 if not known.)
INITIAL_IOS	DOUBLE	Estimated number of I/Os performed the first/last time the function is invoked. (The value is -1 if not known.)
INITIAL_INSTS	DOUBLE	Estimated number of instructions executed the first/last time the function is invoked. (The value is -1 if not known.)
CARDINALITY	BIGINT	The predicted cardinality of the function if it is a table function. (The value is -1 if not known or if the function is not a table function.)
IMPLEMENTED	CHAR(1)	Indicates whether or not the function or method has been implemented: Y = Function has been implemented. M = Method has been implemented and does not have function access. H = Method has been implemented and has function access. N = Method specification exists, but method has not been implemented.

(continued)

Table A-23   SYSCAT.FUNCTIONS System Catalog View *(continued)*

Column Name	Data Type	Description
SELECTIVITY	DOUBLE	The number of user-defined predicates used by the function or method. (The value is -1 if there are no user-defined predicates.)
OVERRIDEN_FUNCID	INTEGER	Reserved for future use.
SUBJECT_TYPESCHEMA	VARCHAR(128)	The subject type schema for the user-defined method.
SUBJECT_TYPENAME	VARCHAR(18)	The subject type name for the user-defined method.
FUNC_PATH	VARCHAR(254)	The value of the CURRENT PATH special register variable at the time the function was defined.
BODY	CLOB(1M)	When language is SQL, the text of the CREATE FUNCTION or CREATE METHOD statement.
REMARKS	VARCHAR(254)	A user-supplied comment.

SYSCAT.HIERARCHIES

This view contains one row for each relationship that exists between a subtype and its immediate supertype; a subtable and its immediate supertable; and a subview and its immediate superview. (Only immediate hierarchical relationships are included in this view.)

Table A-24   SYSCAT.HIERARCHIES System Catalog View

Column Name	Data Type	Description
METATYPE	CHAR(1)	Identifies the type of hierarchical relationship that exists: R = A relationship exists between structured data types. U = A relationship exists between Typed tables. W = A relationship exists between Typed views.
SUB_SCHEMA	VARCHAR(128)	The qualified name of the subtype, subtable, or subview in the relationship.
SUB_NAME	VARCHAR(128)	
SUPER_SCHEMA	VARCHAR(128)	The qualified name of the supertype, supertable, or superview in the relationship.
SUPER_NAME	VARCHAR(128)	
ROOT_SCHEMA	VARCHAR(128)	The qualified name of the structured data type, Typed table, or Typed view that is at the root of the hierarchy.
ROOT_NAME	VARCHAR(128)	

SYSCAT.INDEXAUTH

This view contains one row for each user or group that has been granted an index-level privilege.

Table A-25   SYSCAT.INDEXAUTH System Catalog View

Column Name	Data Type	Description
GRANTOR	VARCHAR(128)	The authorization ID of the user who granted the privilege. (Otherwise, the value is SYSIBM.)
GRANTEE	VARCHAR(128)	The authorization ID of the user or group that holds the privilege.
GRANTEETYPE	CHAR(1)	Indicates whether the grantee is a user or a group: U = The grantee is an individual user. G = The grantee is a group.
INDSCHEMA	VARCHAR(128)	The qualified name of the index to which the privilege applies.
INDNAME	VARCHAR(18)	
CONTROLAUTH	CHAR(1)	Indicates whether or not the grantee holds the CONTROL privilege on the index: Y = The grantee holds the CONTROL privilege. N = The grantee does not hold the CONTROL privilege.

SYSCAT.INDEXCOLUSE

This view contains one row for each column that participates in an index.

Table A-26   SYSCAT.INDEXCOLUSE System Catalog View

Column Name	Data Type	Description
INDSCHEMA	VARCHAR(128)	The qualified name of the index that contains the column.
INDNAME	VARCHAR(18)	
COLNAME	VARCHAR(128)	The name of the column.
COLSEQ	SMALLINT	The numeric position (starting at 1) of the column in the index.
COLORDER	CHAR(1)	Indicates how values in this column of the index are ordered: A = Ascending D = Descending I = INCLUDE column (ordering ignored)

SYSCAT.INDEXDEP

This view contains one row for each dependency that exists between an index and any other object.

Table A-27   SYSCAT.INDEXDEP System Catalog View

Column Name	Data Type	Description
INDSCHEMA	VARCHAR(128)	The qualified name of the index that has dependencies on another object.
INDNAME	VARCHAR(18)	
BTYPE	CHAR(1)	Identifies the type of object the index is dependent upon: A = Alias F = Function or method instance O = Privilege dependency on all subtables or subviews in a table or view hierarchy R = Structured data type S = Summary table T = Table U = Typed table V = View W = Typed view X = Index extension
BSCHEMA	VARCHAR(128)	The qualified name of the object the index is dependent upon. (If BTYPE = F, this is the specific name of a function.)
BNAME	VARCHAR(128)	
TABAUTH	SMALLINT	If BTYPE = O, S, T, U, V, or W, the privileges (encoded) on the table or view that are required by the index. (Otherwise, the value is null.)

SYSCAT.INDEXES

This view contains one row for each index (including inherited indexes, where applicable) that has been defined for a table.

Table A-28   SYSCAT.INDEXES System Catalog View

Column Name	Data Type	Description
INDSCHEMA	VARCHAR(128)	The qualified name of the index.
INDNAME	VARCHAR(18)	
DEFINER	VARCHAR(128)	The authorization ID under which the index was created.
TABSCHEMA	VARCHAR(128)	The qualified name of the table or nickname on which the index is defined.
TABNAME	VARCHAR(128)	
COLNAMES	VARCHAR(640)	A list of column names, each preceded by $+$ or $-$ to indicate ascending or descending order, respectively, that are included in the index. Warning: This column will be removed in the future. (This information is also found in SYSCAT.INDEXCOLUSE.)
UNIQUERULE	CHAR(1)	Identifies the unique rule for the index: D = Duplicates are allowed. P = Primary index—no duplicates allowed. U = Unique index—no duplicates allowed.
MADE_UNIQUE	CHAR(1)	Indicates whether or not the index has been converted to unique since it was created: Y = Index was originally nonunique, but was converted to a unique index to support a unique or primary key constraint. If the constraint is dropped, the index will revert to nonunique. N = Index has not been changed since it was created.
COLCOUNT	SMALLINT	The number of columns in the index key plus the number of INCLUDE columns used by the index, if any.

(continued)

Table A-28 SYSCAT.INDEXES System Catalog View *(continued)*

Column Name	Data Type	Description
UNIQUE_COLCOUNT	SMALLINT	The number of columns required for a unique key. Always <=COLCOUNT. < COLCOUNT only if there are INCLUDE columns. Otherwise, the value is -1 if index has no unique key (permits duplicates).
INDEXTYPE	CHAR(4)	Indicates whether or not the index is a clustering index: CLUS = Index is a clustering index. REG = Index is a regular index.
ENTRYTYPE	CHAR(1)	Indicates whether or not the index is associated with a Typed table: H = The index is on a hierarchy table (H-table). L = The index is a logical index on a Typed table. Blank = The index is not associated with a Typed table.
PCTFREE	SMALLINT	The percentage of each index leaf page that will be reserved during the initial building of the index. (This space is available for future inserts after the index is built.)
IID	SMALLINT	A system-generated internal index identifier.
NLEAF	INTEGER	The number of leaf pages currently being used by the index. (The value is -1 if statistics have not been collected.)
NLEVELS	SMALLINT	The number of index levels used. (The value is -1 if statistics have not been collected.)
FIRSTKEYCARD	BIGINT	The number of distinct first key values found in the index. (The value is -1 if statistics have not been collected.)
FIRST2KEYCARD	BIGINT	The number of distinct keys found using the first two columns of the index. (The value is -1 if statistics have not been collected or if inapplicable.)
FIRST3KEYCARD	BIGINT	The number of distinct keys found using the first three columns of the index. (The value is -1 if statistics have not been collected or if inapplicable.)

Column Name	Data Type	Description
FIRST4KEYCARD	BIGINT	The number of distinct keys found using the first four columns of the index. (The value is -1 if statistics have not been collected or if inapplicable.)
FULLKEYCARD	BIGINT	The number of distinct full key values found. (This is -1 if statistics have not been collected.)
CLUSTERRATIO	SMALLINT	The degree of data clustering found for the index. (The value is -1 if statistics have not been collected or if detailed index statistics have been collected [in which case, CLUSTERFACTOR will be used instead].)
CLUSTERFACTOR	DOUBLE	A finer measurement of the degree of clustering found for the index. (The value is -1 if detailed index statistics have not been collected or if the index is defined on a nickname.)
SEQUENTIAL_PAGES	INTEGER	The number of leaf pages located on disk, in index key order, with few or no large gaps between them. (The value is -1 if statistics have not been collected.)
DENSITY	INTEGER	The ratio of SEQUENTIAL_PAGES to the number of pages in the range of pages occupied by the index, expressed as a percent (integer between 0 and 100). (The value is -1 if statistics have not been collected.)
USER_DEFINED	SMALLINT	Indicates whether the index is system- or user-defined: 1 = The index was defined by a user and has not been dropped. 0 = The index was defined by the system.
SYSTEM_REQUIRED	SMALLINT	Indicates whether or not the index is a required index: 0 = The index is not a required index. 1 = The index is required for primary key or unique key constraint, or if the index is the index on the OID column of a Typed table. 2 = The index is required for primary key or unique key constraint, and the index is the index on the OID column of a Typed table.
CREATE_TIME	TIMESTAMP	The date and time at which the index was created.

(continued)

Table A-28 SYSCAT.INDEXES System Catalog View *(continued)*

Column Name	Data Type	Description
STATS_TIME	TIMESTAMP	The last date and time at which any change was made to the statistics recorded statistics for the index. (The value is null if statistics have not been collected.)
PAGE_FETCH_PAIRS	VARCHAR(254)	A list of pairs of integers, represented in character form, that represent the number of pages in a hypothetical buffer and the number of page fetches required to scan the table with the index using that hypothetical buffer. (This has a zero-length string if this data is not available.)
MINPCTUSED	SMALLINT	The threshold minimum amount of used page space to allow on a page before performing an online reorganization (and merge of pages) of the index. (The value is 0 if online reorganization is not enabled.)
REVERSE_SCANS	CHAR(1)	Indicates whether or not the index supports reverse scans: Y = The index supports reverse scans. N = The index does not support reverse scans.
INTERNAL_FORMAT	SMALLINT	The encoded internal representation of the index.
REMARKS	VARCHAR(254)	A user-supplied comment.

SYSCAT.INDEXOPTIONS

This view contains one row for each index-specific option defined.

Table A-29 SYSCAT.INDEXOPTIONS System Catalog View

Column Name	Data Type	Description
INDSCHEMA	VARCHAR(128)	The schema name of the index.
INDNAME	VARCHAR(18)	The local name of the index.
OPTION	VARCHAR(128)	The name of the index option.
SETTING	VARCHAR(255)	The index option value.

SYSCAT.KEYCOLUSE

This view contains one row for each column that participates in a key (including inherited primary or unique keys) that has been defined by a unique, primary key, or foreign key constraint.

Table A-30   SYSCAT.KEYCOLUSE System Catalog View

Column Name	Data Type	Description
CONSTNAME	VARCHAR(18)	The name of the constraint that contains the column.
TABSCHEMA	VARCHAR(128)	The qualified name of the table that contains the column.
TABNAME	VARCHAR(128)	
COLNAME	VARCHAR(128)	The name of the column.
COLSEQ	SMALLINT	The numeric position (starting at 1) of the column in the key.

SYSCAT.NAMEMAPPINGS

This view contains one row for each mapping that exists between logical objects and the corresponding implementation objects that implement the logical objects.

Table A-31   SYSCAT.NAMEMAPPINGS System Catalog View

Column Name	Data Type	Description
TYPE	CHAR(1)	Identifies the type of object the name mapping is for: C = Column I = Index U = Typed table
LOGICAL_SCHEMA	VARCHAR(128)	The qualified name of the logical object.
LOGICAL_NAME	VARCHAR(128)	
LOGICAL_COLNAME	VARCHAR(128)	The name of the logical column if TYPE = C. (Otherwise, the value is null.)
IMPL_SCHEMA	VARCHAR(128)	The qualified name of the implementation object that implements the logical object.
IMPL_NAME	VARCHAR(128)	
IMPL_COLNAME	VARCHAR(128)	The name of the implementation column if TYPE = C. (Otherwise, the value is null.)

SYSCAT.NODEGROUPDEF

This view contains one row for each partition that is contained in a nodegroup.

Table A-32   SYSCAT.NODEGROUPDEF System Catalog View

Column Name	Data Type	Description
NGNAME	VARCHAR(18)	The name of the nodegroup that contains the partition (or node).
NODENUM	SMALLINT	The partition (or node) number of a partition contained in the nodegroup. A valid partition number is between 0 and 999 inclusive.
IN_USE	CHAR(1)	Indicates the status of the partition (or node): A = The newly added partition is not in the partitioning map, but the containers for the table spaces in the nodegroup have been created. The partition will be added to the partitioning map when a Redistribute Nodegroup operation is successfully completed. D = The partition will be dropped when a Redistribute Nodegroup operation is successfully completed. T = The newly added partition is not in the partitioning map, and it was added using the WITHOUT TABLESPACES clause. Containers must be specifically added to the table spaces for the nodegroup. Y = The partition is in the partitioning map.

SYSCAT.NODEGROUPS

This view contains one row for each nodegroup that has been defined.

Table A-33 SYSCAT.NODEGROUPS System Catalog View

Column Name	Data Type	Description
NGNAME	VARCHAR(18)	The name of the nodegroup.
DEFINER	VARCHAR(128)	The authorization ID under which the nodegroup was defined.
PMAP_ID	SMALLINT	The system-generated internal partitioning map identifier of the partitioning map stored in SYSCAT.PARTITIONMAPS.
REBALANCE_PMAP_ID	SMALLINT	The system-generated internal partitioning map identifier of the partitioning map currently being used for redistribution. (The value is -1 if redistribution is currently not in progress.)
CREATE_TIME	TIMESTAMP	The date and time at which the nodegroup was created.
REMARKS	VARCHAR(254)	A user-supplied comment.

SYSCAT.PACKAGEAUTH

This view contains one row for each user or group that has been granted a package-level privilege.

Table A-34   SYSCAT.PACKAGEAUTH System Catalog View

Column Name	Data Type	Description
GRANTOR	VARCHAR(128)	The authorization ID of the user who granted the privilege. (Otherwise, the value is SYSIBM.)
GRANTEE	VARCHAR(128)	The authorization ID of the user or group that holds the privilege.
GRANTEETYPE	CHAR(1)	Indicates whether the grantee is a user or a group: U = The grantee is an individual user. G = The grantee is a group.
PKGSCHEMA	VARCHAR(128)	The qualified name of the package to which the privilege applies.
PKGNAME	CHAR(8)	
CONTROLAUTH	CHAR(1)	Indicates whether or not the grantee holds the CONTROL privilege on the package: Y = The grantee holds the CONTROL privilege. N = The grantee does not hold the CONTROL privilege.
BINDAUTH	CHAR(1)	Indicates whether or not the grantee holds the BIND privilege on the package: Y = The grantee holds the BIND privilege. N = The grantee does not hold the BIND privilege.
EXECUTEAUTH	CHAR(1)	Indicates whether or not the grantee holds the EXECUTE privilege on the package: Y = The grantee holds the EXECUTE privilege. N = The grantee does not hold the EXECUTE privilege.

SYSCAT.PACKAGEDEP

This view contains one row for each dependency that exists between an index and any other object.

Table A-35 SYSCAT.PACKAGEDEP System Catalog View

Column Name	Data Type	Description
PKGSCHEMA	VARCHAR(128)	The qualified name of the package that has dependencies on another object.
PKGNAME	CHAR(8)	
BINDER	VARCHAR(128)	The authorization ID of the individual who bound the package to the database.
BTYPE	CHAR(1)	Identifies the type of object the package is dependent upon: A = Alias D = Server definition F = Function or method instance I = Index M = Function mapping N = Nickname O = Privilege dependency on all subtables or subviews in a table or view hierarchy P = Page size R = Structured data type S = Summary table T = Table U = Typed table V = View W = Typed view
BSCHEMA	VARCHAR(128)	The qualified name of the object the package is dependent upon. (If BTYPE = F, this is the specific name of a function.)
BNAME	VARCHAR(128)	
TABAUTH	SMALLINT	If BTYPE = O, S, T, U, V, or W, the privileges (encoded) on the table or view that are required by the package. (Otherwise, the value is null.)

SYSCAT.PACKAGES

This view contains one row for each package created by binding an application program to the database.

Table A-36   SYSCAT.PACKAGES System Catalog View

Column Name	Data Type	Description
PKGSCHEMA	VARCHAR(128)	The qualified name of the package.
PKGNAME	CHAR(8)	
BOUNDBY	VARCHAR(128)	Authorization ID of the binder of the package.
DEFINER	VARCHAR(128)	The authorization ID under which the package was bound.
DEFAULT_SCHEMA	VARCHAR(128)	The value of the CURRENT SCHEMA special register variable at the time the package was bound. (This is used to resolve any unqualified references in static SQL statements.)
VALID	CHAR(1)	Indicates the current state of the package: Y = The package is valid. N = The package is invalid. X = The package is inoperative because some function instance that it depends on has been dropped. (Explicit rebind is needed.)
UNIQUE_ID	CHAR(8)	Internal date and time information that indicates when the package was first created.
TOTAL_SECT	SMALLINT	The total number of sections in the package.
FORMAT	CHAR(1)	The date and time format associated with the package: 0 = Date and time format associated with country code of the database 1 = USA date and time format 2 = EUR date and time format 3 = ISO date and time format 4 = JIS date and time format 5 = LOCAL date and time format
ISOLATION	CHAR(2)	Identifies the isolation used by the package: RR = Repeatable read RS = Read stability CS = Cursor stability UR = Uncommitted read

Column Name	Data Type	Description
BLOCKING	CHAR(1)	Identifies the cursor blocking option used during binding: N = No blocking. U = Block unambiguous cursors. B = Block all cursors.
INSERT_BUF	CHAR(1)	Identifies the insert option used during binding: Y = Inserts should be buffered. N = Inserts should not be buffered.
LANG_LEVEL	CHAR(1)	The LANGLEVEL value used during binding: 0 = SAA1 1 = SQL92E or MIA
FUNC_PATH	VARCHAR(254)	The value of the CURRENT PATH special register variable at the time the last bind operation for the package was performed. (This is used for rebind operations.)
QUERYOPT	INTEGER	The optimization class under which the package was bound. The classes are 0, 1, 3, 5 and 9. (This is used for rebind operations.)
EXPLAIN_LEVEL	CHAR(1)	Indicates whether or not Explain was requested (using the EXPLAIN or EXPLSNAP bind option) during binding. P = Plan selection level only. Blank = Explain was not requested.
EXPLAIN_MODE	CHAR(1)	The value of the EXPLAIN bind option during binding: Y = Yes (static) N = No A = All (static and dynamic)
EXPLAIN_SNAPSHOT	CHAR(1)	The value of the EXPLSNAP bind option during binding: Y = Yes (static) N = No A = All (static and dynamic)
SQLWARN	CHAR(1)	Indicates whether or not positive SQLCODEs resulting from dynamic SQL statements are returned to the application: Y = Yes, positive values are returned. N = No, positive values are suppressed.

(continued)

Table A-36 SYSCAT.PACKAGES System Catalog View *(continued)*

Column Name	Data Type	Description
SQLMATHWARN	CHAR(1)	The value of the database configuration parameter DFT_SQLMATHWARN at the time the package was bound—this indicates whether or not arithmetic errors and retrieval conversion errors encountered in static SQL statements are handled as null values with warnings: Y = Yes, such errors are handled as warnings. N = No, such errors are suppressed.
EXPLICIT_BIND_TIME	TIMESTAMP	The date and time at which the package was last explicitly bound or rebound. When the package is implicitly rebound, no function instance will be selected that was created later than this time.
LAST_BIND_TIME	TIMESTAMP	The date and time at which the package was last bound or rebound (either explicitly or implicitly).
CODEPAGE	SMALLINT	The application code page used at the time the package was bound. (The value is -1 if not known.)
DEGREE	CHAR(5)	The limit on intrapartition parallelism that was specified during binding. 1 = No degree of intrapartition parallelism was specified. 2 to 32,767 = The degree of intrapartition parallelism specified. ANY = The degree of intrapartition parallelism was determined by the DB2 Database Manager.
MULTINODE_PLANS	CHAR(1)	Indicates whether the package was bound in a single- or multiple-partition environment: Y = The package was bound in a multiple-partition environment. N = The package was bound in a single-partition environment.
INTRA_PARALLEL	CHAR(1)	Indicates whether or not static SQL statements within the package use intrapartition parallelism: Y = One or more static SQL statements in the package uses intrapartition parallelism. N = No static SQL statements in the package uses intrapartition parallelism. F = One or more static SQL statements in the package can use intrapartition parallelism; this parallelism has been disabled for use on a system that is not configured for intrapartition parallelism.

Column Name	Data Type	Description
VALIDATE	CHAR(1)	Indicates whether or not all SQL statement checking is performed during binding: B = All checking must be performed during binding. R = Reserved.
DYNAMICRULES	CHAR(1)	Indicates how dynamic SQL statements are handled at package run time: B = Dynamic SQL statements are handled like static SQL statements at run time; the binder's authorization ID is used. R = Dynamic SQL statements are handled like dynamic SQL statements at run time; the executor's authorization ID is used.
SQLERROR	CHAR(1)	Identifies the SQLERROR option used on the most recent subcommand that bound or rebound the package: C = Reserved N = No package
REFRESHAGE	DECIMAL (20,6)	The maximum length of time between when a REFRESH TABLE statement is run for a summary table and when the summary table is used in place of a base table.
REMARKS	VARCHAR(254)	A user-supplied comment.

SYSCAT.PARTITIONMAPS

This view contains one row for each partitioning map that is used to distribute rows of data in a table across all partitions in a node group (based upon hashing the table's partitioning key).

Table A-37   SYSCAT.PARTITIONMAPS System Catalog View

Column Name	Data Type	Description
PMAP_ID	SMALLINT	A system-generated internal partitioning map identifier.
PARTITIONMAP	LONG VARCHAR FOR BIT DATA	The actual partitioning map, which is a vector of 4,096 two-byte integers for a multiple-node nodegroup. (For a single-node nodegroup, there is only one entry in the map; this entry identifies the partition [or node] number of the single node.)

SYSCAT.PASSTHRUAUTH

This view contains one row for each user or group that has been granted a server-level privilege.

Table A-38   SYSCAT.PASSTHRUAUTH System Catalog View

Column Name	Data Type	Description
GRANTOR	VARCHAR(128)	The authorization ID of the user who granted the privilege. (Otherwise, the value is SYSIBM.)
GRANTEE	VARCHAR(128)	The authorization ID of the user or group that holds the privilege.
GRANTEETYPE	CHAR(1)	Indicates whether the grantee is a user or a group: U = The grantee is an individual user. G = The grantee is a group.
SERVERNAME	VARCHAR(128)	The name of the data source that the user or group is being granted the PASSTHRU privilege to.

SYSCAT.PROCEDURES

This view contains one row for each stored procedure that has been created.

Table A-39   SYSCAT.PROCEDURES System Catalog View

Column Name	Data Type	Description
PROCSCHEMA	VARCHAR(128)	The qualified name of the stored procedure.
PROCNAME	VARCHAR(128)	
SPECIFICNAME	VARCHAR(18)	The specific name of the stored procedure instance.
PROCEDURE_ID	INTEGER	A system-generated internal stored procedure identifier.
DEFINER	VARCHAR(128)	The authorization ID under which the stored procedure was created.
PARM_COUNT	SMALLINT	The number of parameters used by the stored procedure.
PARM_SIGNATURE	VARCHAR(180) FOR BIT DATA	A concatenation of up to 90 parameter data types, in internal format. (This has zero length if the function takes no parameters.)
ORIGIN	CHAR(1)	Identifies the source of the stored procedure: E = User-defined, external.
CREATE_TIME	TIMESTAMP	The date and time at which the stored procedure was registered.
DETERMINISTIC	CHAR(1)	Indicates whether or not the results of the stored procedure are deterministic: Y = The results are deterministic. N = The results are not deterministic.
FENCED	CHAR(1)	Indicates whether or not the stored procedure is fenced: Y = The stored procedure is fenced. N = The stored procedure is not fenced.
NULLCALL	CHAR(1)	Indicates how the stored procedure responds if called with a null parameter value: Y = The stored procedure will be called if a null parameter value is specified.
LANGUAGE	CHAR(8)	Implementation language (C, JAVA, COBOL, or SQL) used to produce the body of the stored procedure.

Column Name	Data Type	Description
IMPLEMENTATION	VARCHAR(254)	Identifies the path/module/function (LANGUAGE = C or COBOL) or method (LANGUAGE = JAVA) that is used to implement the procedure.
CLASS	VARCHAR(128)	If LANGUAGE = JAVA, this identifies the class that implements the stored procedure. (Otherwise, the value is null.)
JAR_ID	VARCHAR(128)	If LANGUAGE = JAVA, this identifies the jar file that implements the stored procedure. (Otherwise, the value is null.)
PARM_STYLE	CHAR(8)	Identifies the parameter style declared for the stored procedure when it was registered: DB2DARI = Language is C. DB2GENRL = Language is Java. DB2SQL = Language is C or COBOL. JAVA = Language is Java or SQL. GENERAL = Language is C or COBOL. GNLRNULL = Language is C or COBOL.
CONTAINS_SQL	CHAR(1)	Indicates whether or not the stored procedure contains SQL statements: C = The stored procedure contains SQL; only SQL that does not read or modify SQL data is allowed. M = The stored procedure contains SQL; all SQL allowed in stored procedures is allowed. N = The stored procedure does not contain SQL; SQL is not allowed. R = The stored procedure contains SQL; only SQL that reads SQL data is allowed.
DBINFO	CHAR(1)	Indicates whether or not a DBINFO parameter is passed to the stored procedure: Y = DBINFO is passed. N = DBINFO is not passed.
PROGRAM_TYPE	CHAR(1)	Indicates how the stored procedure is invoked: M = The stored procedure is invoked as a main procedure. S = The stored procedure is invoked as a subroutine.
RESULT_SETS	SMALLINT	The estimated upper limit of result sets returned by the stored procedure.

(continued)

Table A-39 SYSCAT.PROCEDURES System Catalog View *(continued)*

Column Name	Data Type	Description
VALID	CHAR(1)	Indicates the current state of the stored procedure: Y = The stored procedure is valid. N = The stored procedure is invalid. X = The stored procedure is inoperative because some function instance that it depends on has been dropped. (The stored procedure must be explicitly dropped and recreated.) Blank = It is not a stored procedure.
TEXT_BODY_OFFSET	INTEGER	The offset to the start of the stored procedure body as was provided in full text for the CREATE PROCEDURE statement. (The value is 0 if the stored procedure is an external stored procedure.)
TEXT	CLOB (1M)	The full text of the CREATE PROCEDURE statement, exactly as typed. (The value is null if the stored procedure is an external stored procedure or if the full text is longer than 1M.)
REMARKS	VARCHAR(254)	A user-supplied comment.

SYSCAT.PROCOPTIONS

This view contains one row for each procedure-specific option defined.

Table A-40 SYSCAT.PROCOPTIONS System Catalog View

Column Name	Data Type	Description
PROCSCHEMA	VARCHAR(128)	The qualified procedure name or nickname of the stored procedure.
PROCNAME	VARCHAR(128)	
OPTION	VARCHAR(128)	The name of the stored procedure option.
SETTING	VARCHAR(255)	The stored procedure option value.

SYSCAT.PROCPARMOPTIONS

This view contains one row for each procedure parameter-specific option defined.

Table A-41   SYSCAT.PROCPARMOPTIONS System Catalog View

Column Name	Data Type	Description
PROCSCHEMA	VARCHAR(128)	The qualified procedure name or nickname of the stored procedure.
PROCNAME	VARCHAR(128)	
ORDINAL	SMALLINT	The numeric position (starting at 0) of the parameter in the stored procedure's function signature.
OPTION	VARCHAR(128)	The name of the stored procedure parameter option.
SETTING	VARCHAR(255)	The stored procedure parameter option value.

SYSCAT.PROCPARMS

This view contains one row for each parameter of a stored procedure that has been defined in the database.

Table A-42   SYSCAT.PROCPARMS System Catalog View

Column Name	Data Type	Description
PROCSCHEMA	VARCHAR(128)	The qualified name of the stored procedure.
PROCNAME	VARCHAR(128)	
SPECIFICNAME	VARCHAR(18)	The specific name of the stored procedure instance.
SERVERNAME	VARCHAR(128)	The name of the data source on which the stored procedure resides.
ORDINAL	SMALLINT	The numeric position (starting at 0) of the parameter in the stored procedure's function signature.
PARMNAME	VARCHAR(18)	The name of the parameter.
TYPESCHEMA	VARCHAR(128)	The qualified name of data type of the parameter.
TYPENAME	VARCHAR(18)	
TYPEID	SMALLINT	Internal type code of the parameter's data type.
SOURCETYPEID	SMALLINT	Internal data type ID of the source data type used for distinct data types. (Otherwise, the value is null.)
NULLS	CHAR(1)	Indicates whether or not the column accepts null values (is nullable): Y = Column is nullable. N = Column is not nullable.
LENGTH	INTEGER	Maximum data length allowed by the data type (always 0 for system predefined parameterized types such as DECIMAL and VARCHAR).
SCALE	SMALLINT	The number of digits allowed to the right of the decimal point for distinct data types or reference representation data types based on the system predefined DECIMAL type (always 0 for all other data types, including DECIMAL itself).

(continued)

Table A-42   SYSCAT.PROCPARMS System Catalog View *(continued)*

Column Name	Data Type	Description
PARM_MODE	VARCHAR(5)	Indicates whether the parameter is an input parameter, an output parameter, or both: IN = The parameter is an input parameter. OUT = The parameter is an output parameter. INOUT = The parameter is an input/output parameter.
CODEPAGE	SMALLINT	The code page of the parameter. (For character-string parameters not defined with the FOR BIT DATA attribute, the value is 0.)
DBCS_CODEPAGE	SMALLINT	The DBCS code page of the parameter. (The value is null for numeric parameters.)
AS_LOCATOR	CHAR(1)	Indicates whether the parameter or result is passed as a locator: N = The parameter is not passed in the form of a locator.
TARGET_TYPESCHEMA	VARCHAR(128)	The qualified name of the target data type, if the data type of the parameter or result is REFERENCE. (This contains a null value if the data type of the parameter or result is not REFERENCE.)
TARGET_TYPENAME	VARCHAR(18)	
SCOPE_TABSCHEMA	VARCHAR(128)	The qualified name of the scope (target table) if the data type of the parameter or result is REFERENCE. (This contains a null value if the data type of the parameter or result is not REFERENCE or if the scope is not defined.)
SCOPE_TABNAME	VARCHAR(128)	

SYSCAT.REFERENCES

This view contains one row for each check constraint that has been defined.

Table A-43 SYSCAT.REFERENCES System Catalog View

Column Name	Data Type	Description
CONSTNAME	VARCHAR(18)	The name of the referential constraint.
TABSCHEMA	VARCHAR(128)	The qualified name of the child table to which the constraint applies.
TABNAME	VARCHAR(128)	
DEFINER	VARCHAR(128)	The authorization ID under which the relational integrity constraint was defined.
REFKEYNAME	VARCHAR(18)	The name of parent key.
REFTABSCHEMA	VARCHAR(128)	The qualified name of the parent table to which the constraint applies.
REFTABNAME	VARCHAR(128)	
COLCOUNT	SMALLINT	The number of columns in the foreign key.
DELETERULE	CHAR(1)	Identifies the delete rule that is used by the constraint: A = NO ACTION C = CASCADE N = SET NULL R = RESTRICT
UPDATERULE	CHAR(1)	Identifies the update rule that is used by the constraint: A = NO ACTION R = RESTRICT
CREATE_TIME	TIMESTAMP	The date and time at which the referential constraint was defined.
FK_COLNAMES	VARCHAR (640)	A list of columns that make up the foreign key. Warning: This column will be removed in the future. (This information is also found in SYSCAT.KEYCOLUSE.)
PK_COLNAMES	VARCHAR (640)	A list of columns that make up the foreign key. Warning: This column will be removed in the future. (This information is also found in SYSCAT.KEYCOLUSE.)

SYSCAT.REVTYPEMAPPINGS

This view contains one row for each reverse data type mapping (mappings from data types defined locally to data source data types) that has been defined.

Table A-44   SYSCAT.REVTYPEMAPPINGS System Catalog View

Column Name	Data Type	Description
TYPE_MAPPING	VARCHAR(18)	The name of the reverse data type mapping.
TYPESCHEMA	VARCHAR(128)	The qualified name of the local data type in a reverse data type mapping.
TYPENAME	VARCHAR(18)	
TYPEID	SMALLINT	The system-generated internal data type identifier.
SOURCETYPEID	SMALLINT	The system-generated internal data type identifier of the source data type.
DEFINER	VARCHAR(128)	The authorization ID under which the reverse data type mapping was created.
LOWER_LEN	INTEGER	The lower bound of the maximum number of digits allowed by the local data type if it is a DECIMAL type or the maximum number of characters allowed by the local data type if it is a character type. (Otherwise, the value is null.)
UPPER_LEN	INTEGER	The upper bound of the maximum number of digits allowed by the local data type if it is a DECIMAL type or the maximum number of characters allowed by the local data type if it is a character type. (Otherwise, the value is null.)
LOWER_SCALE	SMALLINT	The lower bound of the scale allowed for the local data type if the data type is DECIMAL.
UPPER_SCALE	SMALLINT	The upper bound of the scale allowed for the local data type if the data type is DECIMAL.
S_OPR_P	CHAR(2)	The relationship between the local data type scale and the local data type precision ($<, >, =, <=, >=$). (Null indicates that no specific relationship exists.)

Column Name	Data Type	Description
BIT_DATA	CHAR(1)	Indicates whether or not the data type was defined as FOR BIT DATA: Y = The data type was defined as FOR BIT DATA. N = The data type was not defined as FOR BIT DATA. NULL = The data type is not a character data type or the system determined the bit data attribute.
WRAPNAME	VARCHAR(128)	The name of the wrapper that the reverse data type mapping has been applied to.
SERVERNAME	VARCHAR(128)	The name of the data source that the reverse data type mapping has been applied to.
SERVERTYPE	VARCHAR(30)	The type of data source that the reverse data type mapping has been applied to.
SERVERVERSION	VARCHAR(18)	The version of the data source server that the reverse data type mapping has been applied to.
REMOTE_TYPESCHEMA	VARCHAR(128)	The schema name of the remote data type.
REMOTE_TYPENAME	VARCHAR(128)	The name of the remote data type as defined on the data source(s).
REMOTE_META_TYPE	CHAR(1)	Identifies what kind of data type the remote data type is: S = Remote data type is a system built-in type. T = Remote data type is a distinct type.
REMOTE_LENGTH	INTEGER	The maximum number of digits allowed by the remote data type if it is a DECIMAL type or the maximum number of characters allowed by the remote data type if it is a character type. (Otherwise, the value is null.)
REMOTE_SCALE	SMALLINT	The maximum number of digits allowed to the right of the decimal point if the remote data type is a DECIMAL type. (Otherwise, the value is null.)

(continued)

Table A-44   SYSCAT.REVTYPEMAPPINGS System Catalog View *(continued)*

Column Name	Data Type	Description
REMOTE_BIT_DATA	CHAR(1)	Indicates whether or not the remote data type was defined as FOR BIT DATA: Y = The remote data type was defined as FOR BIT DATA. N = The remote data type was not defined as FOR BIT DATA. NULL = The remote data type is not a character data type or the system determined the bit data attribute.
USER_DEFINED	CHAR(1)	Indicates whether or not the remote data type is a user-defined data type.
CREATE_TIME	TIMESTAMP	The date and time at which the reverse data type mapping was created.
REMARKS	VARCHAR(254)	A user-supplied comment.

SYSCAT.SCHEMAAUTH

This view contains one row for each user or group that has been granted a schema-level privilege.

Table A-45   SYSCAT.SCHEMAAUTH System Catalog View

Column Name	Data Type	Description
GRANTOR	VARCHAR(128)	The authorization ID of the user who granted the privilege. (Otherwise, the value is SYSIBM.)
GRANTEE	VARCHAR(128)	The authorization ID of the user or group that holds the privilege.
GRANTEETYPE	CHAR(1)	Indicates whether the grantee is a user or a group: U = The grantee is an individual user. G = The grantee is a group.
SCHEMANAME	VARCHAR(128)	The name of the schema to which the privilege applies.
ALTERINAUTH	CHAR(1)	Indicates whether or not the grantee holds the ALTERIN privilege on the schema: Y = The grantee holds the ALTERIN privilege. G = The grantee holds the ALTERIN privilege and can grant it to others. N = The grantee does not hold the ALTERIN privilege.
CREATEINAUTH	CHAR(1)	Indicates whether or not the grantee holds the CREATEIN privilege on the schema: Y = The grantee holds the CREATEIN privilege. G = The grantee holds the CREATEIN privilege and can grant it to others. N = The grantee does not hold the CREATEIN privilege.
DROPINAUTH	CHAR(1)	Indicates whether or not the grantee holds the DROPIN privilege on the schema: Y = The grantee holds the DROPIN privilege. G = The grantee holds the DROPIN privilege and can grant it to others. N = The grantee does not hold the DROPIN privilege.

SYSCAT.SCHEMATA

This view contains one row for each schema that has been defined.

Table A-46   SYSCAT.SCHEMATA System Catalog View

Column Name	Data Type	Description
SCHEMANAME	VARCHAR(128)	The name of the schema.
OWNER	VARCHAR(128)	The authorization ID of the individual who owns the schema. (The value SYSIBM is used for implicitly created schemas.)
DEFINER	VARCHAR(128)	The authorization ID under which the schema was created.
CREATE_TIME	TIMESTAMP	The date and time at which the schema was created.
REMARKS	VARCHAR(254)	A user-supplied comment.

SYSCAT.SERVEROPTIONS

This view contains one row for each server-specific option defined.

Table A-47   SYSCAT.SERVEROPTIONS System Catalog View

Column Name	Data Type	Description
WRAPNAME	VARCHAR(128)	The name of the wrapper the server option has been applied to.
SERVERNAME	VARCHAR(128)	The name of the data source that the server option has been applied to.
SERVERTYPE	VARCHAR(30)	The type of data source that the server option has been applied to.
SERVERVERSION	VARCHAR(18)	The version of the data source server that the server option has been applied to.
CREATE_TIME	TIMESTAMP	The date and time at which the server option was created.
OPTION	VARCHAR(128)	The name of the server option.
SETTING	VARCHAR(2048)	The server option value.
SERVEROPTIONKEY	VARCHAR(18)	A system-generated internal server option identifier.
REMARKS	VARCHAR(254)	A user-supplied comment.

SYSCAT.SERVERS

This view contains one row for each data source that can be accessed in a federated system.

Table A-48   SYSCAT.SERVERS System Catalog View

Column Name	Data Type	Description
WRAPNAME	VARCHAR(128)	The name of the wrapper the server is associated with.
SERVERNAME	VARCHAR(128)	The name of a data source as it is known to the system.
SERVERTYPE	VARCHAR(30)	The type of data source as it is known to the system.
SERVERVERSION	VARCHAR(18)	The version of the data source server.
REMARKS	VARCHAR(254)	A user-supplied comment.

SYSCAT.STATEMENTS

This view contains one or more rows for each SQL statement used in each package in the database.

Table A-49   SYSCAT.STATEMENTS System Catalog View

Column Name	Data Type	Description
PKGSCHEMA	VARCHAR(128)	The qualified name of the package.
PKGNAME	CHAR(8)	
STMTNO	INTEGER	Line number in the source module of the application program that identifies where the SQL statement is located.
SECTNO	SMALLINT	The number of the package section that contains the SQL statement.
SEQNO	SMALLINT	The sequence number of the statement, which at this time is always 1.
TEXT	CLOB(64K)	The text of the SQL statement.

SYSCAT.TABAUTH

This view contains one row for each user or group that has been granted a table-level privilege.

Table A-50   SYSCAT.TABAUTH System Catalog View

Column Name	Data Type	Description
GRANTOR	VARCHAR(128)	The authorization ID of the user who granted the privilege. (Otherwise, the value is SYSIBM.)
GRANTEE	VARCHAR(128)	The authorization ID of the user or group that holds the privilege.
GRANTEETYPE	CHAR(1)	Indicates whether the grantee is a user or a group: U = The grantee is an individual user. G = The grantee is a group.
TABSCHEMA	VARCHAR(128)	The qualified name of the table or view to which the privilege applies.
TABNAME	VARCHAR(128)	
CONTROLAUTH	CHAR(1)	Indicates whether or not the grantee holds the CONTROL privilege on the table: Y = The grantee holds the CONTROL privilege. N = The grantee does not hold the CONTROL privilege.
ALTERAUTH	CHAR(1)	Indicates whether or not the grantee holds the ALTER privilege on the table: Y = The grantee holds the ALTER privilege. G = The grantee holds the ALTER privilege and can grant it to others. N = The grantee does not hold the ALTER privilege.
DELETEAUTH	CHAR(1)	Indicates whether or not the grantee holds the DELETE privilege on the table: Y = The grantee holds the DELETE privilege. G = The grantee holds the DELETE privilege and can grant it to others. N = The grantee does not hold the DELETE privilege.

Column Name	Data Type	Description
INDEXAUTH	CHAR(1)	Indicates whether or not the grantee holds the INDEX privilege on the table: Y = The grantee holds the INDEX privilege. G = The grantee holds the INDEX privilege and can grant it to others. N = The grantee does not hold the INDEX privilege.
INSERTAUTH	CHAR(1)	Indicates whether or not the grantee holds the INSERT privilege on the table: Y = The grantee holds the INSERT privilege. G = The grantee holds the INSERT privilege and can grant it to others. N = The grantee does not hold the INSERT privilege.
SELECTAUTH	CHAR(1)	Indicates whether or not the grantee holds the SELECT privilege on the table: Y = The grantee holds the SELECT privilege. G = The grantee holds the SELECT privilege and can grant it to others. N = The grantee does not hold the SELECT privilege.
REFAUTH	CHAR(1)	Indicates whether or not the grantee holds the REFERENCE privilege on the table: Y = The grantee holds the REFERENCE privilege. G = The grantee holds the REFERENCE privilege and can grant it to others. N = The grantee does not hold the REFERENCE privilege.
UPDATEAUTH	CHAR(1)	Indicates whether or not the grantee holds the UPDATE privilege on the table: Y = The grantee holds the UPDATE privilege. G = The grantee holds the UPDATE privilege and can grant it to others. N = The grantee does not hold the UPDATE privilege.

SYSCAT.TABCONST

This view contains one row for each table constraint (check, unique, primary key, or foreign key) that has been defined.

Table A-51   SYSCAT.TABCONST System Catalog View

Column Name	Data Type	Description
CONSTNAME	VARCHAR(18)	The name of the constraint.
TABSCHEMA	VARCHAR(128)	The qualified name of the table to which the constraint applies.
TABNAME	VARCHAR(128)	
DEFINER	VARCHAR(128)	The authorization ID under which the constraint was defined.
TYPE	CHAR(1)	Indicates the constraint type: F = Foreign key K = Check constraint P = Primary key U = Unique constraint
REMARKS	VARCHAR(254)	A user-supplied comment.

SYSCAT.TABLES

This view contains one row for each table, view, nickname, or alias that has been defined.

Table A-52 SYSCAT.TABLES System Catalog View

Column Name	Data Type	Description
TABSCHEMA	VARCHAR(128)	The qualified name of the table, view, nickname, or alias.
TABNAME	VARCHAR(128)	
DEFINER	VARCHAR(128)	The authorization ID under which the table, view, nickname, or alias was defined.
TYPE	CHAR(1)	Identifies the object type: A = Alias H = Hierarchy table N = Nickname S = Summary table T = Table U = Typed table V = View W = Typed view
STATUS	CHAR(1)	Identifies the current status of the object: N = The object is a normal table, view, alias, or nickname that is operative. C = The object is a table or nickname that is in "Check Pending" state. X = The object is a view or nickname that is inoperative.
BASE_TABSCHEMA	VARCHAR(128)	If the object is an alias (TYPE = A), the table, view, alias, or nickname that is referenced by the alias. (Otherwise, the value is null.)
BASE_TABNAME	VARCHAR(128)	
ROWTYPESCHEMA	VARCHAR(128)	Contains the qualified name of the row type of the table, where applicable. (Otherwise, the value is null.)
ROWTYPENAME	VARCHAR(18)	
CREATE_TIME	TIMESTAMP	The date and time at which the object was created.

(continued)

Table A-52   SYSCAT.TABLES System Catalog View *(continued)*

Column Name	Data Type	Description
STATS_TIME	TIMESTAMP	The last time changes were made to the recorded statistics for the table. (The value is null if statistics have not been collected.)
COLCOUNT	SMALLINT	The number of columns in table.
TABLEID	SMALLINT	A system-generated internal table identifier.
TBSPACEID	SMALLINT	The system-generated internal identifier of the primary table space for the table.
CARD	BIGINT	The total number of rows in the table. For tables in a table hierarchy, this is the number of rows at the given level of the hierarchy. (The value is -1 if statistics have not been collected or if the row describes a view or alias; the value is -2 for hierarchy tables.)
NPAGES	INTEGER	The total number of pages on which the rows of the table exist. (The value is -1 if statistics have not been collected or if the row describes a view or alias; the value is -2 for hierarchy tables.)
FPAGES	INTEGER	The total number of pages allocated for the table. (The value is -1 if statistics have not been collected or if the row describes a view or alias; the value is -2 for hierarchy tables.)
OVERFLOW	INTEGER	The total number of overflow records found in the table. (The value is -1 if statistics have not been collected or if the row describes a view or alias; the value is -2 for hierarchy tables.)
TBSPACE	VARCHAR(18)	The name of the primary table space for the table. If no other table space is specified, all parts of the table are stored in this table space. (The value is null for aliases and views.)
INDEX_TBSPACE	VARCHAR(18)	The name of the table space that holds all indexes created on the table. (The value is null for aliases and views, or if the INDEX IN clause was omitted or specified with the same value as the IN clause of the CREATE TABLE statement.)

Column Name	Data Type	Description
LONG_TBSPACE	VARCHAR(18)	The name of the table space that holds all long data (LONG or LOB column types) for the table. (The value is null for aliases and views, or if the LONG IN clause was omitted or specified with the same value as the IN clause of the CREATE TABLE statement.)
PARENTS	SMALLINT	The number of parent tables of the table (the number of referential constraints in which the table is a dependent).
CHILDREN	SMALLINT	The number of dependent tables of the table (the number of referential constraints in which the table is a parent).
SELFREFS	SMALLINT	The number of self-referencing referential constraints for the table (the number of referential constraints in which the table is both a parent and a dependent).
KEYCOLUMNS	SMALLINT	The number of columns in the primary key of the table.
KEYINDEXID	SMALLINT	The system-generated internal identifier of the primary index for the table. (The value is null or 0 if no primary key has been defined for the table.)
KEYUNIQUE	SMALLINT	The number of unique constraints (other than primary key constraints) that have been defined on the table.
CHECKCOUNT	SMALLINT	The number of check constraints that have been defined on the table.
DATACAPTURE	CHAR(1)	Indicates whether or not the table participates in data replication: Y = The table participates in data replication. N = The table does not participate in data replication. L = The table participates in data replication, including replication of LONG VARCHAR and LONG VARGRAPHIC columns.

(continued)

Table A-52   SYSCAT.TABLES System Catalog View *(continued)*

Column Name	Data Type	Description
CONST_CHECKED	CHAR(32)	Encoded information about check constraints: Byte 1 represents foreign key constraints. Byte 2 represents check constraints. Byte 5 represents a summary table. Byte 6 represents generated columns. Other bytes are reserved. Encoded values can be interpreted as follows: Y = It was checked by the system. U = It was checked by the user. N = It was not checked (pending). W = It was in a "U" state when the table was placed in "Check Pending" state (pending).
PMAP_ID	SMALLINT	The system-generated internal identifier of the partitioning map used by the table. (The value is null for aliases and views.)
PARTITION_MODE	CHAR(1)	Identifies the mode used for partitioning the table if it resides in a partitioned database: H = The table is hashed on the partitioning key. R = The table is replicated across database partitions. (This is blank for aliases, views, nicknames, and tables in single partition nodegroups with no partitioning key defined.)
LOG_ATTRIBUTE	CHAR(1)	Indicates whether or not the table is logged initially: 0 = Default logging is used. 1 = The table was created as NOT LOGGED INITIALLY.
PCTFREE	SMALLINT	The percentage of each page that will be reserved for future inserts operations.
APPEND_MODE	CHAR(1)	Indicates how rows are inserted on pages: N = New rows are inserted into existing spaces if available. Y = New rows are appended at end of existing data.
REFRESH	CHAR(1)	Indicates how the table is refreshed, if the table is a summary table: D = Deferred I = Immediate O = Once (This is blank if the table is not a summary table.)

Column Name	Data Type	Description
REFRESH_TIME	TIMESTAMP	The date and time the table was last refreshed if REFRESH = D or O. (Otherwise, the value is null.)
LOCKSIZE	CHAR(1)	Identifies the preferred lock granularity to use when the table is accessed by Data Manipulation Language (DML) statements: R = Use row row-level locking. T = Use table-level locking. (This is blank if not applicable.)
VOLATILE	CHAR(1)	Identifies the cardinality of the table: C = The cardinality of the table is volatile. (This is blank if not applicable.)
REMARKS	VARCHAR(254)	A user-supplied comment.

SYSCAT.TABLESPACES

This view contains one row for each table space that has been defined.

Table A-53   SYSCAT.TABLESPACES System Catalog View

Column Name	Data Type	Description
TBSPACE	VARCHAR(18)	The name of the table space.
DEFINER	VARCHAR(128)	The authorization ID under which the table space was created.
CREATE_TIME	TIMESTAMP	The date and time at which the table space was created.
TBSPACEID	INTEGER	A system-generated internal table space identifier.
TBSPACETYPE	CHAR(1)	Identifies how the table space is managed: S = System managed space D = Database managed space
DATATYPE	CHAR(1)	Identifies the type of data that can be stored in the table space: A = All types of permanent data can be stored. L = Only long data can be stored. T = Only system temporary tables can be stored. U = Only declared temporary tables can be stored.
EXTENTSIZE	INTEGER	The number of pages (of size PAGESIZE) that are written to one container in the table space before moving to another next container.
PREFETCHSIZE	INTEGER	The number of pages (of size PAGESIZE) that are to be read when a prefetch operation is performed.
OVERHEAD	DOUBLE	Controller overhead and disk seek and latency time (in milliseconds) of the container the table space is stored on.
TRANSFERRATE	DOUBLE	The time needed (in milliseconds) to read one page, of size PAGESIZE, into a buffer pool.

Column Name	Data Type	Description
PAGESIZE	INTEGER	The size (in bytes) of pages in the table space.
NGNAME	VARCHAR(18)	The name of the nodegroup that the table space has been defined for.
BUFFERPOOLID	INTEGER	The system-generated internal buffer pool identifier of the buffer pool that is used by the table space. (A value of 1 indicates that the default buffer pool is used.)
DROP_RECOVERY	CHAR(1)	Indicates whether or not tables in the table space can be recovered after a DROP TABLE statement is executed: N = Tables cannot be recovered after a DROP TABLE statement is executed. Y = Tables can be recovered after a DROP TABLE statement is executed.
REMARKS	VARCHAR(254)	A user-supplied comment.

SYSCAT.TABOPTIONS

This view contains one row for each table-specific option defined.

Table A-54 SYSCAT.TABOPTIONS System Catalog View

Column Name	Data Type	Description
TABSCHEMA	VARCHAR(128)	The qualified name of the table, view, alias, or nickname.
TABNAME	VARCHAR(128)	
OPTION	VARCHAR(128)	The name of the table, view, alias, or nickname option.
SETTING	VARCHAR(255)	The table, view, alias, or nickname option value.

SYSCAT.TBSPACEAUTH

This view contains one row for each user or group that has been granted a table space-level privilege.

Table A-55 SYSCAT.TBSPACEAUTH System Catalog View

Column Name	Data Type	Description
GRANTOR	CHAR(128)	The authorization ID of the user who granted the privilege. (Otherwise, the value is SYSIBM.)
GRANTEE	CHAR(128)	The authorization ID of the user or group that holds the privilege.
GRANTEETYPE	CHAR(1)	Indicates whether the grantee is a user or a group: U = The grantee is an individual user. G = The grantee is a group.
TBSPACE	VARCHAR(18)	The name of the table space to which the privilege applies.
USEAUTH	CHAR(1)	Indicates whether or not the grantee holds the USE privilege on the table: Y = The grantee holds the USE privilege. G = The grantee holds the USE privilege and can grant it to others. N = The grantee does not hold the USE privilege.

SYSCAT.TRIGDEP

This view contains one row for each dependency that exists between a trigger and any other object.

Table A-56   SYSCAT.TRIGDEP System Catalog View

Column Name	Data Type	Description
TRIGSCHEMA	VARCHAR(128)	The qualified name of the trigger that has dependencies on another object.
TRIGNAME	VARCHAR(18)	
BTYPE	CHAR(1)	Identifies the type of object the trigger is dependent upon: A = Alias F = Function or method instance N = Nickname O = Privilege dependency on all subtables or subviews in a table or view hierarchy R = Structured data type S = Summary table T = Table U = Typed table V = View W = Typed view X = Index extension
BSCHEMA	VARCHAR(128)	The qualified name of the object the trigger is dependent upon. (If BTYPE = F, this is the specific name of a function.)
BNAME	VARCHAR(128)	
TABAUTH	SMALLINT	If BTYPE = O, S, T, U, V, or W, the privileges (encoded) on the table or view that are required by the trigger. (Otherwise, the value is null.)

SYSCAT.TRIGGERS

This view contains one row for each trigger that has been defined.

Table A-57   SYSCAT.TRIGGERS System Catalog View

Column Name	Data Type	Description
TRIGSCHEMA	VARCHAR(128)	The qualified name of the trigger.
TRIGNAME	VARCHAR(18)	
DEFINER	VARCHAR(128)	The authorization ID under which the trigger was defined.
TABSCHEMA	VARCHAR(128)	The qualified name of the table to which the trigger applies.
TABNAME	VARCHAR(128)	
TRIGTIME	CHAR(1)	Identifies the time that triggered actions are applied to the base table, relative to the event that fired the trigger: A = Triggered actions are applied after the event takes place. B = Triggered actions are applied before the event takes place.
TRIGEVENT	CHAR(1)	Identifies the type of event that will cause the trigger to be fired: I = Insert operation U = Update operation D = Delete operation
GRANULARITY	CHAR(1)	Identifies how frequently the trigger is executed: S = The trigger is executed once per statement. R = The trigger is executed once per row.
VALID	CHAR(1)	Indicates the current state of the trigger: Y = The trigger is valid. X = The trigger is inoperative because some instance that it depends on has been dropped. (The trigger must be dropped and re-created.)
CREATE_TIME	TIMESTAMP	The date and time at which the trigger was created. (This is used in resolving functions and user-defined data types that are used in the trigger, if any. No functions or user-defined data types will be chosen that were created after the trigger was defined.)

(continued)

Table A-57   SYSCAT.TRIGGERS System Catalog View *(continued)*

Column Name	Data Type	Description
QUALIFIER	VARCHAR(128)	The value of the CURRENT SCHEMA special register variable at the time the trigger was defined. (This is used to resolve any unqualified references.)
FUNC_PATH	VARCHAR(254)	The value of the CURRENT PATH special register variable at the time the trigger was defined.
TEXT	CLOB(64K)	The full text of the CREATE TRIGGER statement, exactly as it was typed.
REMARKS	VARCHAR(254)	A user-supplied comment.

SYSCAT.TYPEMAPPINGS

This view contains one row for each user-defined mapping of a remote built-in data type to a local built-in data type.

Table A-58   SYSCAT.TYPEMAPPINGS System Catalog View

Column Name	Data Type	Description
TYPE_MAPPING	VARCHAR(18)	The name of the data type mapping.
TYPESCHEMA	VARCHAR(128)	The qualified name of the local data type in a data type mapping.
TYPENAME	VARCHAR(18)	
TYPEID	SMALLINT	The system-generated internal data type identifier.
SOURCETYPEID	SMALLINT	The system-generated internal data type identifier of the source data type.
DEFINER	VARCHAR(128)	The authorization ID under which the data type mapping was defined.
LENGTH	INTEGER	The maximum length allowed for data values (always 0 for distinct data types). The LENGTH column indicates precision for DECIMAL fields.
SCALE	SMALLINT	The number of digits allowed to the right of the decimal point if the data type of the attribute is DECIMAL. (This contains the value 0 if the data type of the is not DECIMAL.)
BIT_DATA	CHAR(1)	Indicates whether or not the data type was defined as FOR BIT DATA: Y = The data type was defined as FOR BIT DATA. N = The data type was not defined as FOR BIT DATA. NULL = The data type is not a character data type or the system determined the bit data attribute.
WRAPNAME	VARCHAR(128)	The name of the wrapper that the data type mapping has been applied to.
SERVERNAME	VARCHAR(128)	The name of the data source that the data type mapping has been applied to.

Table A-58 SYSCAT.TYPEMAPPINGS System Catalog View *(continued)*

Column Name	Data Type	Description
SERVERTYPE	VARCHAR(30)	The type of data source that the data type mapping has been applied to.
SERVERVERSION	VARCHAR(18)	The version of the data source server that the data type mapping has been applied to.
REMOTE_TYPESCHEMA	VARCHAR(128)	The schema name of the remote data type.
REMOTE_TYPENAME	VARCHAR(128)	The name of the remote data type as defined on the data source(s).
REMOTE_META_TYPE	CHAR(1)	Identifies what kind of data type the remote data type is: S = Remote data type is a system built-in type. T = Remote data type is a distinct type.
REMOTE_LOWER_LEN	INTEGER	The lower bound of the maximum number of digits allowed by the remote data type if it is a DECIMAL type or the maximum number of characters allowed by the remote data type if it is a character type. (Otherwise, the value is null.)
REMOTE_UPPER_LEN	INTEGER	The upper bound of the maximum number of digits allowed by the remote data type if it is a DECIMAL type or the maximum number of characters allowed by the remote data type if it is a character type. (Otherwise, the value is null.)
REMOTE_LOWER_SCALE	SMALLINT	The lower bound of the scale allowed for the remote data type if the data type is DECIMAL.
REMOTE_UPPER_SCALE	SMALLINT	The upper bound of the scale for allowed for the remote data type if the data type is DECIMAL.
REMOTE_S_OPR_P	CHAR(2)	The relationship between the remote data type scale and the remote data type precision ($<$, $>$, $=$, $<=$, $>=$). (Null indicates that no specific relationship exists.)

Column Name	Data Type	Description
REMOTE_BIT_DATA	CHAR(1)	Indicates whether or not the remote data type was defined as FOR BIT DATA: Y = The remote data type was defined as FOR BIT DATA. N = The remote data type was not defined as FOR BIT DATA. NULL = The remote data type is not a character data type or the system determined the bit data attribute.
USER_DEFINED	CHAR(1)	Indicates whether or not the remote data type is a user-defined data type.
CREATE_TIME	TIMESTAMP	The date and time at which the data type mapping was defined.
REMARKS	VARCHAR(254)	A user-supplied comment.

SYSCAT.USEROPTIONS

This view contains one row for each user-specific option defined.

Table A-59 SYSCAT.USEROPTIONS System Catalog View

Column Name	Data Type	Description
AUTHID	VARCHAR(128)	A local authorization ID for the user.
SERVERNAME	VARCHAR(128)	The name of the server for which the user is defined.
OPTION	VARCHAR(128)	The name of the user option.
SETTING	VARCHAR(255)	The user option value.

SYSCAT.VIEWDEP

This view contains one row for each dependency that exists between a view and any other object.

Table A-60   SYSCAT.VIEWDEP System Catalog View

Column Name	Data Type	Description
VIEWSCHEMA	VARCHAR(128)	The qualified name of the view or summary table that has dependencies on another object.
VIEWNAME	VARCHAR(128)	
DTYPE	CHAR(1)	Identifies the type of object that has the dependency: S = Summary table V = View (untyped) W = Typed view
DEFINER	VARCHAR(128)	The authorization ID under which the view was created.
BTYPE	CHAR(1)	Identifies the type of object the view or summary table is dependent upon: A = Alias F = Function or method instance N = Nickname O = Privilege dependency on all subtables or subviews in a table or view hierarchy I = Index (if recording a dependency on a base table) R = Structured data type S = Summary table T = Table U = Typed table V = View W = Typed view
BSCHEMA	VARCHAR(128)	The qualified name of the object the view or summary table is dependent upon. (If BTYPE = F, this is the specific name of a function.)
BNAME	VARCHAR(128)	
TABAUTH	SMALLINT	If BTYPE = O, S, T, U, V, or W, the privileges (encoded) on the table or view that are required by the view or summary table. (Otherwise, the value is null.)

SYSCAT.VIEWS

This view contains one row for each view or summary table that has been defined.

Table A-61 SYSCAT.VIEWS System Catalog View

Column Name	Data Type	Description
VIEWSCHEMA	VARCHAR(128)	The qualified name of the view or the name of the table used to define the summary table.
VIEWNAME	VARCHAR(128)	
DEFINER	VARCHAR(128)	The authorization ID under which the view or summary table was created.
SEQNO	SMALLINT	Reserved. Always 1.
VIEWCHECK	CHAR(1)	Indicates the view checking option specified when the view was created: N = No checking option was specified. L = The WITH LOCAL CHECK option was specified. C = The WITH CASCADE CHECK option was specified.
READONLY	CHAR(1)	Indicates whether the view is updateable or read-only: Y = The view is read-only because of its definition. N = The view is updateable.
VALID	CHAR(1)	Indicates the current state of the view: Y = The view or summary table is valid. X = The view or summary table is inoperative because some instance that it depends on has been dropped. (The view or summary table must be dropped and re-created.)
QUALIFIER	VARCHAR(128)	The value of the CURRENT SCHEMA special register variable at the time the view or summary table was defined. (This is used to resolve any unqualified references.)
FUNC_PATH	VARCHAR(254)	The value of the CURRENT PATH special register variable at the time the view or summary table was defined. When the view is used in DML statements, this path is used to resolve function calls made in the view.
TEXT	CLOB(64k)	The full text of the CREATE VIEW statement, exactly as it was typed.

SYSCAT.WRAPOPTIONS

This view contains one row for each wrapper-specific option defined.

Table A-62   SYSCAT.WRAPOPTIONS System Catalog View

Column Name	Data Type	Description
WRAPNAME	VARCHAR(128)	The name of the wrapper the option is for.
OPTION	VARCHAR(128)	The name of the wrapper option.
SETTING	VARCHAR(255)	The wrapper option value.

SYSCAT.WRAPPERS

This view contains one row for each wrapper that has been registered.

Table A-63   SYSCAT.WRAPPERS System Catalog View

Column Name	Data Type	Description
WRAPNAME	VARCHAR(128)	The name of the wrapper.
WRAPTYPE	CHAR(1)	Indicates what type of data source the wrapper is for: N = Nonrelational R = Relational
WRAPVERSION	INTEGER	The version of the wrapper.
LIBRARY	VARCHAR(255)	The name of the file that contains the code that is used to communicate with the data source associated with the wrapper.
REMARKS	VARCHAR(254)	A user-supplied comment.

SYSSTAT.COLDIST

This updatable view contains detailed column statistics that are used by the DB2 Optimizer. Each row describes the nth most frequent or the nth quantile value found for a column.

Table A-64   SYSSTAT.COLDIST System Catalog View

Column Name	Data Type	Description	Nullable/ Updatable
TABSCHEMA	VARCHAR(128)	The qualified name of the table that the entry applies to.	No/No
TABNAME	VARCHAR(128)		
COLNAME	VARCHAR(128)	The name of the column that the entry applies to.	No/No
TYPE	CHAR(1)	Indicates whether the record is for a frequency value or a quantile value: F = Frequency value Q = Quantile value	No/No
SEQNO	SMALLINT	The value for N: If TYPE = F, it identifies the n in the nth most -frequent value. If TYPE = Q, it identifies the n in the nth quantile value.	No/No
COLVALUE	VARCHAR(254)	The data value, converted to either a character literal value or null. This column can be updated with a valid representation of the value appropriate to the column that the statistic is associated with. If null is the required frequency value, the column should be set to NULL.	Yes/Yes

(continued)

Table A-64   SYSSTAT.COLDIST System Catalog View *(continued)*

Column Name	Data Type	Description	Nullable/ Updatable
VALCOUNT	BIGINT	The number of occurrences or rows found: If TYPE = F, it is the number of occurrences of COLVALUE in the column. If TYPE = Q, it is the number of rows with values less than or equal to COLVALUE. This column can be only updated with the values that are greater than or equal to 0.	No/Yes
DISTCOUNT	BIGINT	The number of distinct quantile values found: If TYPE = F, it is a null value. If TYPE = Q, it is the number of distinct values that are less than or equal to COLVALUE.	No/Yes

SYSSTAT.COLUMNS

This updatable view contains one row for each column for which statistics can be updated.

Table A-65   SYSSTAT.COLUMNS System Catalog View

Column Name	Data Type	Description	Nullable/ Updatable
TABSCHEMA	VARCHAR(128)	The qualified name of the table or view that contains the column.	No/No
TABNAME	VARCHAR(128)		
COLNAME	VARCHAR(128)	The name of the column.	No/No
COLCARD	BIGINT	Identifies the number of distinct values found in the column. (Otherwise, the value is -1 if statistics have not been collected or -2 if the column is an inherited column or a column of a hierarchy table.) For any column, COLCARD cannot have a value higher than the cardinality of the table containing that column. This column can only be updated with -1 or values that are greater than or equal to 0.	No/Yes
HIGH2KEY	VARCHAR(33)	Identifies the second highest value found in the column. (Otherwise, this is empty if statistics have not been collected or if the column is an inherited column or a column of a hierarchy table.) This column can be updated with a valid representation of the value appropriate to the column that the statistic is associated with. LOWKEY2 should not be greater than HIGH2KEY.	Yes/Yes

(continued)

Table A-65 SYSSTAT.COLUMNS System Catalog View *(continued)*

Column Name	Data Type	Description	Nullable/ Updatable
LOW2KEY	VARCHAR(33)	Identifies the second lowest value found in the column. (Otherwise, this is empty if statistics have not been collected or if the column is an inherited column or a column of a hierarchy table.) This column can be updated with a valid representation of the value appropriate to the column that the statistic is associated with.	Yes/Yes
AVGCOLLEN	INTEGER	The average length of data values in the column. (Otherwise, the value is -1 if the data type of the column is a long or LOB data type or if statistics have not been collected; the value is -2 if the column is an inherited column or a column of a hierarchy table.) This column can only be updated with -1 or values that are greater than or equal to 0.	No/Yes
NUMNULLS	BIGINT	The number of null values found in the column. (Otherwise, the value is -1 if statistics have not been collected.) This column can only be updated with -1 or values that are greater than or equal to 0.	No/Yes

SYSSTAT.FUNCTIONS

This updatable view contains one row for each UDF (scalar or aggregate) that has been created.

Table A-66   SYSSTAT.FUNCTIONS System Catalog View

Column Name	Data Type	Description	Nullable/ Updatable
FUNCSCHEMA	VARCHAR(128)	The qualified name of the function.	No/No
FUNCNAME	VARCHAR(18)		
SPECIFICNAME	VARCHAR(18)	The specific name of the function instance.	No/No
IOS_PER_INVOC	DOUBLE	Estimated number of I/Os required per invocation. (The value is -1 if not known.) This column can only be updated with -1 or values that are greater than or equal to 0.	No/Yes
INSTS_PER_INVOC	DOUBLE	Estimated number of instructions performed per invocation. (The value is -1 if not known.) This column can only be updated with -1 or values that are greater than or equal to 0.	No/Yes
IOS_PER_ARGBYTE	DOUBLE	Estimated number of I/Os required per input argument byte. (The value is -1 if not known.) This column can only be updated with -1 or values that are greater than or equal to 0.	No/Yes
INSTS_PER_ARGBYTE	DOUBLE	Estimated number of instructions per input argument byte. (The value is -1 if not known.) This column can only be updated with -1 or values that are greater than or equal to 0.	No/Yes

(continued)

Table A-66 SYSSTAT.FUNCTIONS System Catalog View *(continued)*

Column Name	Data Type	Description	Nullable/ Updatable
PERCENT_ARGBYTES	SMALLINT	Estimated average percent of input argument bytes that the function will actually read. (The value is -1 if not known.) This column can only be updated with -1 or values that are between 0 and 100.	No/Yes
INITIAL_IOS	DOUBLE	Estimated number of I/Os performed the first/last time the function is invoked. (The value is -1 if not known.) This column can only be updated with -1 or values that are greater than or equal to 0.	No/Yes
INITIAL_INSTS	DOUBLE	Estimated number of instructions executed the first/last time the function is invoked. (The value is -1 if not known.) This column can only be updated with -1 or values that are greater than or equal to 0.	No/Yes
CARDINALITY	BIGINT	The predicted cardinality of the function if it is a table function. (The value is -1 if not known or if the function is not a table function.)	No/Yes
SELECTIVITY	DOUBLE	The number of user-defined predicates used by the function or method. (The value is -1 if there are no user-defined predicates.)	No/No

SYSSTAT.INDEXES

This view contains one row for each attribute (including inherited attributes, where applicable) that has been defined for a user-defined structured data type.

Table A-67   SYSSTAT.INDEXES System Catalog View

Column Name	Data Type	Description	Nullable/ Updatable
INDSCHEMA	VARCHAR(128)	The qualified name of the index.	No/No
INDNAME	VARCHAR(18)		
TABSCHEMA	VARCHAR(128)	The qualified name of the table or nickname on which the index is defined.	No/No
TABNAME	VARCHAR(128)		
COLNAMES	CLOB(1M)	A list of column names, each preceded by + or − to indicate ascending or descending order respectively, that are included in the index.	No/No
NLEAF	INTEGER	The number of leaf pages currently being used by the index. (The value is -1 if statistics have not been collected.) This column can only be updated with -1 or values that are greater than or equal to 0.	No/Yes
NLEVELS	SMALLINT	The number of index levels used. (The value is -1 if statistics have not been collected.) This column can only be updated with -1 or values that are greater than or equal to 0.	No/Yes
FIRSTKEYCARD	BIGINT	The number of distinct first key values found in the index. (The value is -1 if statistics have not been collected.) This column can only be updated with -1 or values that are greater than or equal to 0.	No/Yes

(continued)

Table A-67   SYSSTAT.INDEXES System Catalog View *(continued)*

Column Name	Data Type	Description	Nullable/ Updatable
IFIRST2KEYCARD	BIGINT	The number of distinct keys found using the first two columns of the index. (The value is -1 if statistics have not been collected or if inapplicable.) This column can only be updated with -1 or values that are greater than or equal to 0.	No/Yes
FIRST3KEYCARD	BIGINT	The number of distinct keys found using the first three columns of the index. (The value is -1 if statistics have not been collected or if inapplicable.) This column can only be updated with -1 or values that are greater than or equal to 0.	No/Yes
FIRST4KEYCARD	BIGINT	The number of distinct keys found using the first four columns of the index (The value is -1 if statistics have not been collected or if inapplicable.) This column can only be updated with -1 or values that are greater than or equal to 0.	No/Yes
FULLKEYCARD	BIGINT	The number of distinct full key values found. (The value is -1 if statistics have not been collected.) This column can only be updated with -1 or values that are greater than or equal to 0.	No/Yes
CLUSTERRATIO	SMALLINT	The degree of data clustering found for the index. (The value is -1 if statistics have not been collected or if detailed index statistics have been collected [in which case, CLUSTERFACTOR will be used instead].) This column can only be updated with -1 or values that are between 0 and 100.	No/Yes

Column Name	Data Type	Description	Nullable/ Updatable
CLUSTERFACTOR	DOUBLE	A finer measurement of the degree of clustering found for the index. (The value is -1 if detailed index statistics have not been collected or if the index is defined on a nickname.) This column can only be updated with -1 or values that are greater than or equal to 0.	No/Yes
SEQUENTIAL_PAGES	INTEGER	The number of leaf pages located on disk, in index key order, with few or no large gaps between them. (The value is -1 if statistics have not been collected.) This column can only be updated with -1 or values that are greater than or equal to 0.	No/Yes
DENSITY	INTEGER	The ratio of SEQUENTIAL_PAGES to the number of pages in the range of pages occupied by the index, expressed as a percent (integer between 0 and 100). (The value is -1 if statistics have not been collected.) This column can only be updated with -1 or values that are between 0 and 100.	No/Yes

(continued)

Table A-67   SYSSTAT.INDEXES System Catalog View *(continued)*

Column Name	Data Type	Description	Nullable/ Updatable
PAGE_FETCH_PAIRS	VARCHAR(254)	A list of pairs of integers, represented in character form, that represent the number of pages in a hypothetical buffer, and the number of page fetches required to scan the table with the index using that hypothetical buffer. (This has a zero-length string if this data is not available.) This column can be updated with the following input values: • The pair delimiter and pair separator characters are the only nonnumeric characters accepted. • Blanks are the only characters recognized as a pair delimiter and pair separator. • Each number entry must have an accompanying partner number entry with the two being separated by the pair separator character. • Each pair must be separated from any other pairs by the pair delimiter character. • Each expected number entry must between 0 and 9 (only positive values).	No/Yes

SYSSTAT.TABLES

This updatable view contains one row for each base table that has been defined.

Table A-68   SYSSTAT.TABLES System Catalog View

Column Name	Data Type	Description	Nullable/ Updatable
TABSCHEMA	VARCHAR(128)	The qualified name of the base table.	No/No
TABNAME	VARCHAR(128)		
CARD	BIGINT	The total number of rows in the table. For tables in a table hierarchy, this is the number of rows at the given level of the hierarchy. (The value is -1 if statistics have not been collected.) Do not attempt to update CARD value for a table with a value that is less than the COLCARD value of any of the columns in that table. This column can only be updated with -1 or values that are greater than or equal to 0.	No/Yes
NPAGES	INTEGER	The total number of pages on which the rows of the table exist. (The value is -1 if statistics have not been collected or if the row describes a view or alias; the value is -2 for hierarchy tables.) This column can only be updated with -1 or values that are greater than or equal to 0.	No/Yes
FPAGES	INTEGER	The total number of pages allocated for the table. (The value is -1 if statistics have not been collected or if the row describes a view or alias; the value is -2 for hierarchy tables.) This column can only be updated with -1 or values that are greater than or equal to 0.	No/Yes

(continued)

Table A-68 SYSSTAT.TABLES System Catalog View *(continued)*

Column Name	Data Type	Description	Nullable/ Updatable
OVERFLOW	INTEGER	The total number of overflow records found in the table. (The value is -1 if statistics have not been collected or if the row describes a view or alias; the value is -2 for hierarchy tables.) This column can only be updated with -1 or values that are greater than or equal to 0.	No/Yes

Bibliography

Baklarz, George, and Bill Wong. *DB2 Universal Database V7.1 for UNIX, Linux, Windows, and OS/2 Database Administration Certification Guide*, 4th ed. Upper Saddle River, N.J.: Prentice Hall PTR, 2001.

Bergman, Robert, and Christopher Tsounis. *DB2 Universal Database Version 7 Features and Facilities*: IBM Data Management Solutions White Paper. IBM Corporation, 2000.

Chamberlin, Don. *A Complete Guide to DB2 Universal Database*. San Francisco: Morgan Kaufmann Publishers, Inc., 1998.

Cook, Jonathan, Robert Harbus, and Tetsuya Shirai. *DB2 Universal Database V6.1 for UNIX, Windows, and OS/2 Certification Guide*. 3rd ed. Upper Saddle River, N.J.: Prentice Hall PTR, 2000.

Date, C.J., and Hugh Darwen. *A Guide to the SQL Standard*. 3rd ed. Reading, Mass.: Addison-Wesley Publishing Company, 1993.

Davis, Judith R. *IBM's DB2 Spatial Extender: Managing Geo-Spatial Information within the DBMS*, 2000.

International Business Machines Corporation. *DB2 Warehouse Manager*. GC26-9309-02. IBM Corporation, 2000.

International Business Machines Corporation. *IBM DB2 OLAP Server*. GC26-9311-02. IBM Corporation, 2000.

International Business Machines Corporation. *IBM DB2 DataPropagator*. GC26-8463-02. IBM Corporation, 2000.

International Business Machines Corporation. *IBM DB2 Query Patroller V7.1*: IBM Data Management Solutions White Paper. IBM Corporation, 2000.

International Business Machines Corporation. *IBM DB2 XML Extender*. G325-5258-00. IBM Corporation, 2000.

International Business Machines Corporation. *Fast Path to DB2 UDB Advanced Administration for Experienced Relational DBAs Student Notebook.* IBM Corporation, 2000.

International Business Machines Corporation. *IBM DB2 Universal Database for Windows Quick Beginnings.* GC09-2971. IBM Corporation, 2000.

International Business Machines Corporation. *IBM DB2 Universal Database Administration Getting Started, Version 5.* S10J-8154-00. IBM Corporation, 1997.

International Business Machines Corporation. *IBM DB2 Universal Database Administration Guide: Implementation, Version 7.* SC09-2944. IBM Corporation, 2000.

International Business Machines Corporation. *IBM DB2 Universal Database Administration Guide: Performance, Version 7.* SC09-2945. IBM Corporation, 2000.

International Business Machines Corporation. *IBM DB2 Universal Database Administration Guide: Planning, Version 7.* SC09-2946. IBM Corporation, 2000.

International Business Machines Corporation. *IBM DB2 Universal Database Command Reference, Version 7.* SC09-2951. IBM Corporation, 2000.

International Business Machines Corporation. *IBM DB2 Universal Database SQL Getting Started: Version 7.* SC09-2973. IBM Corporation, 2000.

International Business Machines Corporation. *IBM DB2 Universal Database SQL Reference, Volume 1, Version 7.* SC09-2974. IBM Corporation, 2000.

International Business Machines Corporation. *IBM DB2 Universal Database SQL Reference, Volume 2, Version 7.* SC09-2975. IBM Corporation, 2000.

International Business Machines Corporation. *DATABASE 2 Text Extender Administration and Programming, Third Edition.* SH12-6194-02. IBM Corporation, 1996.

International Business Machines Corporation. *DB2 Universal Database Image, Audio, and Video Extenders Administration and Programming.* SC26-9107-00. IBM Corporation, 1997.

International Business Machines Corporation. *IBM DB2 Universal Database Spatial Extender Users Guide and Reference.* SC27-0701. IBM Corporation, 2000.

International Business Machines Corporation. *IBM DB2 Universal Database Connect Enterprise Edition for OS/2 and Windows Quick Beginnings.* GC09-2953. IBM Corporation, 2000.

International Business Machines Corporation. *IBM DB2 Universal Database Connect User's Guide.* SC09-2954. IBM Corporation, 2000.

International Business Machines Corporation. *IBM DB2 Universal Database Message Reference, Volume 1*. GC09-2978. IBM Corporation, 2000.

International Business Machines Corporation. *IBM DB2 Universal Database Message Reference, Volume 2*. GC09-2979. IBM Corporation, 2000.

International Business Machines Corporation. *IBM DB2 Universal Database System Monitor Guide and Reference, Volume 2*. SC09-2956. IBM Corporation, 2000.

International Business Machines Corporation. *IBM DB2 Universal Database Data Movement Utilities Guide and Reference, Volume 2*. SC09-2955. IBM Corporation, 2000.

Sanders, Roger E. *DB2 Universal Database SQL Developer's Guide*. New York: McGraw-Hill Companies, Inc., 2000.

Sanders, Roger E. *DB2 Universal Database API Developer's Guide*. New York: McGraw-Hill Companies, Inc., 2000.

Snow, Dwaine R. *LAB012: DB2 UDB V6.1 for UNIX, Windows and OS/2 Database Administration Certification Preparation*. Dwaine R. Snow/Professionals Leadership Technical Exchange, 2000.

INDEX

A

access controls for databases
    authentication, 74–75
    authorities, 77–82
    CLIENT authentication, 76
    database privileges, 83
    index privileges, 88
    instances, 71
    nickname privileges, 89
    object privileges, 84–86
    package privileges, 88
    security, 74
    server privileges, 89
    table privileges, 86–87
    view privileges, 87–88
access paths, lock states, 308
access plans, 528
    DB2 Optimizer, 482
    explain data, 488
    graphic views, 488–489
    quick explanations, 488
    SELECT statements, 484
    SQL statements, 308
    viewing, 482
access security, 338
    authentication, 338–339
    authorization, 341–343
    database privileges, 347–348

DBADM authority, 345
    groups, 341
    index privileges, 352
    LOAD authority, 346
    nickname privileges, 354
    object privileges, 348–349
    package privileges, 352
    schema privileges, 349
    server privileges, 353
    SYSADM authority, 343
    SYSCTRL authority, 344
    SYSMAINT authority, 344–345
    table privileges, 351
    table space privileges, 350
    trusted clients, 340–341
    untrusted clients, 340–341
    users, 341
    view privileges, 352
accessing data in tables, 308
ADD privilege, 83
adding data to base tables, 257–258
Administration Client, 37
administration tools, 49–50
    Alert Center, 57
    CCA, 61–62
    CLP, 58
    Command Center, 51
    Control Center, 50
    Journal, 57

INTERNATIONAL CONTACT INFORMATION

AUSTRALIA
McGraw-Hill Book Company Australia Pty. Ltd.
TEL +61-2-9417-9899
FAX +61-2-9417-5687
http://www.mcgraw-hill.com.au
books-it_sydney@mcgraw-hill.com

CANADA
McGraw-Hill Ryerson Ltd.
TEL +905-430-5000
FAX +905-430-5020
http://www.mcgrawhill.ca

**GREECE, MIDDLE EAST,
NORTHERN AFRICA**
McGraw-Hill Hellas
TEL +30-1-656-0990-3-4
FAX +30-1-654-5525

MEXICO (Also serving Latin America)
McGraw-Hill Interamericana Editores S.A. de C.V.
TEL +525-117-1583
FAX +525-117-1589
http://www.mcgraw-hill.com.mx
fernando_castellanos@mcgraw-hill.com

SINGAPORE (Serving Asia)
McGraw-Hill Book Company
TEL +65-863-1580
FAX +65-862-3354
http://www.mcgraw-hill.com.sg
mghasia@mcgraw-hill.com

SOUTH AFRICA
McGraw-Hill South Africa
TEL +27-11-622-7512
FAX +27-11-622-9045
robyn_swanepoel@mcgraw-hill.com

**UNITED KINGDOM & EUROPE
(Excluding Southern Europe)**
McGraw-Hill Education Europe
TEL +44-1-628-502500
FAX +44-1-628-770224
http://www.mcgraw-hill.co.uk
computing_neurope@mcgraw-hill.com

ALL OTHER INQUIRIES Contact:
Osborne/McGraw-Hill
TEL +1-510-549-6600
FAX +1-510-883-7600
http://www.osborne.com
omg_international@mcgraw-hill.com

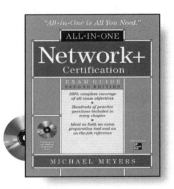